Deborah E. Combs

Programming for Embedded Systems

Programming for Embedded Systems

Cracking the Code™

Dreamtech Software Team

WILEY

Wiley Publishing, Inc.

Best-Selling Books • Digital Downloads • e-Books • Answer Networks •
e-Newsletters • Branded Web Sites • e-Learning

Programming for Embedded Systems: Cracking the Code™

Published by
Wiley Publishing, Inc.
909 Third Avenue
New York, NY 10022
www.wiley.com

ISBN: 0-7645-4954-5

Manufactured in the United States of America

10 9 8 7 6 5 4 3 2 1

1B/QW/QW/QS/IN

Published by Wiley Publishing, Inc., Indianapolis, Indiana
Published simultaneously in Canada

Credits

Executive Editor
Chris Webb

Project Editor
Eric Newman

Technical Editor
N R Parsa

Copy Editors
Luann Rouff
William A. Barton

Editorial Manager
Mary Beth Wakefield

Vice President and Executive Group Publisher
Richard Swadley

Vice President and Publisher
Joseph B. Wikert

Editorial Director
Mary Bednarek

Media Development Specialist
Megan Decraene

Permissions Editor
Laura Moss

Media Development Manager
Laura Carpenter VanWinkle

Project Coordinator
Nancee Reeves

Proofreader
Kim Cofer

Indexer
Johnna VanHoose Dinse

Cover Design
Michael Trent

About the Authors

Dr. K. V. K. K. Prasad is a renowned software engineer and professor with extensive experience in software engineering, wireless Internet, computer telephony integration, artificial intelligence, data communication, and telecommunication. He is a software consultant.

Vikas Gupta is co-founder and president of Dreamtech Software. Vikas holds a B.E. in electronics, with a postgraduate diploma in sales and marketing and in publishing and printing studies. Actively engaged in developing and designing new technologies in wireless applications, e-learning, and other cutting-edge areas, he is also the managing director of Wiley-Dreamtech India (P) Ltd.

Avnish Dass is co-founder and CEO of Dreamtech Software. Avnish is a talented and seasoned programmer who has 15 years of experience in systems and application/database programming. Avnish has developed security systems, antivirus programs, wireless and communication technologies, and ERP systems.

Ankur Verma, a senior software developer with Dreamtech Software, has expertise in technologies such as Windows Media, Direct X (Direct Show), Windows Shell Programming Services for Windows NT series, and IP-telephony. Ankur also provides commercial COM/DCOM solutions to Dreamtech Software India, Inc.

To our parents and family and beloved country, India, for providing an excellent environment for nurturing and creating world-class IT talent.

Preface

As you start your exciting journey into the world of embedded systems, take a minute to consider the number of embedded systems you are surrounded with in your daily life at the office and at home — printer, fax, mobile phone, personal digital assistant (PDA), microwave oven, television set, set top box, digital camera, air conditioner, and so on. Many of us are not even aware that all these devices contain a processor with a lot of software embedded. These embedded systems do highly focused and specific jobs. In contrast, desktop computers are general-purpose machines that can be programmed to do any general-purpose task.

With the advent of industrial automation, embedded systems have been around since the 1960s in all manufacturing organizations, including chemical plants, automobile manufacturing units, nuclear plants, energy generation units, and the like. Every industrial sector — telecommunications, banking, health care, avionics, automobile, food processing, semiconductor electronics, defense, etc. — uses embedded systems extensively for automation. It should not be surprising that nearly 90 percent of the microprocessors manufactured end up in embedded systems. Needless to say, embedded software development is a very lucrative business these days.

Recent Trends in Embedded Systems

Thanks to recent breathtaking developments in microelectronics, processor speeds are increasing tremendously and memory costs are dropping rapidly. As a result, we are now witnessing revolutionary changes in embedded systems. The most important development is in networked appliances. Now we can make embedded systems network-enabled and connect them to the Internet or corporate intranet. This feature enhances the utility of embedded systems multifold. For instance, you can embed a Web server into any appliance and connect it to the Internet, and the appliance can be monitored from a remote location through a browser running on a desktop. These networked information appliances can range from a simple Web camera to a complex system for monitoring a nuclear plant. You can even turn the door lock of your home into a networked appliance that you can control from a remote location.

Revolutionary developments are also taking place in the area of mobile devices. No longer is the mobile device used just for voice communication using the cellular mobile networks. The mobile device is now used for accessing data, voice, and video services using third-generation (3G) wireless networks. The mobile device, unlike in earlier days, is a very powerful unit with an embedded operating system and application software. Many mobile devices are capable of running a Java browser and can download Java applets and execute them locally. These devices are also capable of storing databases locally. In addition, these embedded systems have powerful computing and communication capabilities. Anywhere, anytime communication for data, voice, and video applications is now a reality, thanks to the power of embedded software in mobile devices.

Again, because of dramatic improvements in processor capabilities, many applications that previously ran only on desktop computers are now being run on embedded systems, which include protocol converters, routers and gateways for data communication equipment, Voice-Over-Internet Protocol (VOIP) terminals that provide low-cost voice communication over long distances using the Internet infrastructure, navigation systems in cars, etc.

Another interesting development is in *wearable computers*. A wearable computer, as the name implies, is an embedded system that one can wear — it can be tucked into a pocket or it can be a part of one's eyeglass frames. The wearable computer can act as a secretary, with capabilities to recognize faces, to remind the user about appointments, etc.

All these developments are leading to an era of invisible computing, or hidden computing, wherein the "computer" does the job we need but without a ubiquitous and/or physical presence. An ever-increasing number of appliances — from door locks to missiles — are embedded systems that can be monitored or controlled remotely.

The Changing Landscape of Embedded Software Development

These developments have led to a growing demand for embedded software development professionals. However, unlike in the olden days, when embedded software development was considered more like "rocket science," embedded software development today is much easier and faster.

In recent years, we have witnessed tremendous growth in the number of processors available for embedded systems. Today, you can find 8-bit, 16-bit, and 32-bit micro-controllers, microprocessors, and digital signal processors, each of which caters to various market segments. In addition, memory costs continue to fall, paving the way for embedding powerful operating systems. Many commercial real-time and embedded operating systems are available with a small memory requirement, making the software development much easier compared with earlier days when developers wrote their own operating system kernels.

Until relatively recently, embedded software development was done mostly in assembly languages. With the development of cross-compilers, C took over as the prominent language. Although C continues to be an important programming language for embedded software, object-oriented programming languages such as C++ are now extensively used. The main attraction of object-oriented programming languages — re-use — is exploited to reduce development time. During the past few years, Java has become a force to reckon with for embedded software development, with the availability of small-footprint Java Virtual Machines and powerful Application Programming Interfaces (APIs) for embedded programming. Java's main attraction, platform independence, makes it the most amenable to embedded software development because of the variety of processors and operating systems used in embedded systems.

With the availability of operating systems that occupy very small memory, coupled with Integrated Development Environments (IDEs), which facilitate fast development and easy debugging, embedded software development is no longer a daunting task. New development tools are making it increasingly easy for you to test your software before putting it on the embedded system. Moreover, these tools enable rapid development cycles and reduce the need for developers to have an in-depth knowledge of hardware.

Challenges for Embedded Software Programmers

These same factors — fast development cycles and the availability of a wide variety of processors, operating systems, development tools, and programming languages — present today's embedded software programmers with numerous challenges. Programmers need a good understanding of design alternatives — how to choose a processor, an operating system, a programming language, etc. so that one can develop cost-effective, reliable embedded software with minimal development time. In addition, the product should be delivered in the market just-in-time. This is a challenging task for budding embedded software programmers. Moreover, it is not enough to know the architecture of just one processor or just one programming language. As many of the embedded systems become network-enabled, a working knowledge of network programming is also important for programmers. Embedded software requirements span all application domains — consumer electronics, industrial automation, data communications, wired communications, wireless communications, avionics, automotive industries, and so on. Embedded software programmers need to be aware of the diversity of application areas and the specific requirements for each.

This book aims to equip you with enough ammunition to meet these challenges by providing comprehensive coverage of the various alternatives for writing embedded software, with an emphasis on the development of commercial-grade applications, rather than on theory.

What This Book Covers

This book is not meant for beginners. It teaches you the basics of specific technologies only. The "Cracking the Code" series is designed for software developers/programmers who wish to upgrade their skills and understand the secrets of writing professional-quality applications. This book starts where other tutorials books end. It enhances your skills by taking them to the next level as you learn a particular technology. This book is aimed at programmers who have a working knowledge of C, C++, and Java, with some exposure to application software development. If you want to take up embedded software development as a career, or if you have already done some programming for an embedded system and you want to expand your horizons by broadening your skill set, this book is for you. This book also serves as a handy reference for managers of embedded software projects, to assist you in making the right choice of development tools as well as to help you understand the process of embedded software development.

You can certainly find a good number of books on embedded software. However, many books explain embedded software development using one specific processor, and if you do not have access to the development system of that processor, you cannot do any experimentation. Some books explain the general concepts without providing any actual code, which limits your knowledge to only theoretical aspects of embedded software.

This book takes a totally different approach. Even if you do not have any access to a hardware development system, you can still "get your hands dirty" by working on the case studies presented in the book. All the applications have been carefully chosen so that you can run them on a desktop using emulators and other development tools. Certainly, having access to a hardware board is helpful, but even if you do not have one, you will get a good feel for embedded software development. A comprehensive review of available development environments is, of course, included for the inquisitive reader.

In the future, embedded software development will be done not just in C or C++, but in Java as well. Therefore, equal time is devoted to embedded software development using each of these languages.

Embedded software is being developed using a variety of embedded and real-time operating systems, such as Embedded NT, Windows CE, RTLinux, etc. In addition, a variety of development tools and IDEs for C, C++, and Java are available. You will learn application development in these various environments.

Embedded software is now required for a variety of applications — communications, databases, information appliances, mobile computing, etc. This book describes representative applications for these vertical market segments.

Each project, for which the full source code is presented, is an application of real practical importance, and a sound understanding of these applications will certainly make you a professional embedded software programmer with a broad set of skills. Despite the diversity in application domains, development environments, and tools, the embedded systems described in this book share numerous commonalities for software development. This book focuses on these commonalities so that you can broaden your skill set and stay ahead of the demands and challenges placed on you by a rapidly changing industry. Happy sailing in your voyage to develop state-of-the-art embedded systems.

How This Book Is Organized

Chapter 1 presents the basic concepts of embedded systems and reviews trends in embedded software development and the issues in developing embedded software.

Chapter 2 provides an overview of the applications of embedded software and systems. Typical applications in different industrial segments are presented so that the reader gets a good exposure to the variety of embedded systems and their architectures.

Chapter 3 presents an overview of the hardware architectures for embedded systems. Architectures of micro-controllers, microprocessors, and Digital Signal Processors (DSPs) are presented, along with their processing capabilities. A basic understanding of these architectures helps the programmer write better code for embedded systems, though the software engineer has to work hand-in-hand with the hardware engineers to make a final production-level embedded system.

Chapter 4 discusses the issues involved in embedded software development. The focus is on the process of embedded software development, comparing and contrasting the application software development with embedded software development. Issues such as code optimization, timing, and memory constraints are examined.

Chapter 5 presents an overview of the embedded software development environments. The details of various operating systems, programming languages, and development tools are presented here.

The first five chapters cover the fundamentals necessary to take up embedded software development. With a sound understanding of the material presented here, the reader can dive into the details of embedded software programming by running the applications presented in subsequent chapters.

Chapter 6 presents the first case study: serial communication programming. Serial communication programming provides insight into aspects of system-level programming. It is one of the most important modules for communication between embedded systems; and between an embedded system and a PC for data logging. It covers how to achieve serial communication between two PCs, and also between a PC and an 8051 micro-controller–based hardware board, to illustrate the intricacies of embedded programming and the process of embedding the software. Even if you do not have access to an 8051 board, you can still test the code between two PCs.

Chapter 7 develops a project for creating a navigation system. Using a Global Positioning System (GPS) receiver, the reader learns how to obtain the positional parameters and how to develop an embedded navigation system with graphics capability. Because location-based services will be a large revenue earner for the industry in the coming years, this case study helps you develop applications involving location parameters.

Chapter 8 describes embedded communication protocol development on an embedded NT platform using Microsoft eMbedded Visual Tools. Presented in this chapter are two projects: a protocol converter that converts Ethernet packets to serial communication packets, and an implementation of the voice-over-IP protocol stack. These projects provide insight into developing embedded communication software for data and voice processing.

Chapter 9 examines how to develop embedded mobile data applications using the Binary Runtime Environment for Wireless (BREW) development kit of Qualcomm. The software is developed in the VC++ environment, which can be converted into DLLs and ported onto embedded systems.

Chapter 10 presents real-time embedded systems case studies using Real Time Linux (RTLinux) as the development environment. The important issues and coding aspects of real-time programming are described in this chapter through examples.

Chapter 11 presents embedded database applications using Windows CE for a Pocket PC application. Pocket PC is likely to revolutionize the mobile data market, and this chapter describes how to create industry-grade database applications.

Chapter 12 provides case studies for developing networked information appliances using HP's Chai Appliance Platform. Embedding Web servers and accessing the data on the Internet and intranets through Java-enabled devices will be taken for granted in the near future, and this chapter offers a sound introduction to this exciting field.

Chapter 13 examines the development of Java appliances using Java 2 Micro Edition (J2ME) for mobile applications. This chapter also covers Jini connection technology for developing dynamic distributed applications.

Chapter 14 provides case studies for developing embedded systems using the Windows XP Embedded operating system. Presented in this chapter are details about application development for remote control of consumer electronics items, embedded databases, and electronic voting.

Chapter 15 presents an overview of future trends in embedded systems and embedded software development.

The contents of the CD-ROM that accompanies the book are described in Appendix A.

Internet resources for embedded software are presented in Appendix B.

Although readers can focus on embedded software development in either C/C++ or Java, it is advisable to work in both development environments, to broaden your skills and to appreciate the intricacies of embedded software development on both platforms.

Who Should Read This Book

This book is aimed at software professionals who have a good working knowledge of C, C++, and Java, and who would like to take up development work in embedded software. Although some knowledge of hardware helps, no prior experience in hardware design is assumed.

Currently, there is a great demand for embedded software development professionals, and embedded software can be developed using a variety of platforms and tools. Although an expertise in all of these is not necessary, a general understanding of the available options can help you make your decisions based on your application's requirements.

Acknowledgments

For their support in making this book possible, we acknowledge the contributions of V. K. Rajan and Priti, for their immense help in coordinating various activities throughout the project.

Contents

Programming for Embedded Systems

Chapter 1

An Overview of Embedded Software

In This Chapter

- Basic concepts of embedded systems and software
- Trends in embedded software development
- Embedded systems categorized
- Issues and challenges in embedded software development

Without our even being aware of it, we are surrounded by embedded systems. In our daily lives, we use a number of embedded systems — such as those found in TVs, VCRs, toasters, CD players, digital cameras, and mobile phones. Thanks to advances in semiconductor electronics, embedded systems have recently become increasingly powerful. And whereas writing software for these embedded systems used to be akin to "rocket science," this is no longer the case. However, the art and science of embedded software development is changing very rapidly.

What Is an Embedded System?

The desktop computers with which most of us are familiar, as well as workstations and mainframe computers, are "general purpose" computers in that we use them for performing a variety of everyday tasks such as playing games, word processing, accounting, scientific calculations,, and the like. In contrast, an embedded system performs a single well-defined task. An embedded system can be described as one consisting of a processor, associated peripherals, and software used for a specific purpose. For example, the VCR's very specific task is to record and play videocassettes. The hardware and the software of the VCR's embedded system are designed to carry out this specific task only.

Like any other computing system, an embedded system is a combination of hardware and software. However, the hardware of a general-purpose computer is typically pre-defined, consisting of a CPU, a monitor, a keyboard, a mouse, and secondary storage devices such as CD-ROM and/or 3.5" disk drives, and we procure it off the shelf. In the case of an embedded system, the hardware is generally custom-built for the system's specific purpose, mainly because the requirements of each system vary considerably. Consider the following two examples of typical embedded systems, illustrating the varying requirements of the hardware:

- In a manufacturing unit of a chemical plant, a number of temperatures have to be measured and based on the values, and certain operations need to be performed, such as opening a valve. The input to the system comes from various sensors that measure the temperatures, and the output is a signal that controls a valve. In other words, the input tells the device when it should do something, and the device does it. The hardware, obviously, must be based on this specific requirement if the device is to perform its function.
- The processor in a mobile phone needs to carry out a great deal of communication protocol processing to make telephone calls, and it also needs to perform voice processing to send and receive speech signals. The mobile phone is another example of an embedded system. However, unlike in the preceding example, the mobile phone has a mass market, and the hardware developers must keep in mind the specific requirements of the protocols used in the mobile networks. For instance, the mobile phones used in North America are different from those used in Europe because the network protocols are different. Hence the hardware is different. Differences in hardware can also arise because of the differing capabilities of the mobile phones.

Hence, depending on the quantity and functionality needed, the embedded system hardware needs to be developed with the cost kept in mind. Accordingly, the software that goes into the system also varies widely to meet the desired functionality.

Categories of Embedded Systems

Embedded systems can be broadly divided into the following categories. This categorization is based on whether the system has to work as an independent unit or it has to be networked, whether it has to perform real-time operations or not, and so on.

Stand-alone embedded systems

Stand-alone embedded systems work, as the name suggests, in a stand-alone mode (as opposed to a networked mode), taking input and producing output. The input can be electrical signals from sensors, or commands from a human being, such as the pressing of a button. The output can be electrical signals to drive another system, or an LED or LCD display for displaying information to users. Many embedded systems for process control in manufacturing units and automobiles fall into this category. In process control systems, the inputs come from transducers that convert a physical entity, such as temperature, into an electrical signal. The electrical signals become the output that can control devices such as valves. In some stand-alone systems, the deadlines to carry out a specific task may not be very strict; a few milliseconds this way or that way may not matter much. In other words, the response time is not crucial. For example, an air conditioning unit can be set to turn on when the temperature reaches a certain level. Other examples in this category are toys, CD players, and measuring instruments.

Real-time embedded systems

Some embedded systems are required to carry out specific tasks in a specified amount of time. Such systems are called *real-time embedded systems*. Consider, for example, a system that has to open a valve within 30 milliseconds when the humidity crosses a particular threshold. If the job is not carried out within that 30-millisecond period, a catastrophe may ensue. Such systems in which real-time constraints have to be strictly met are called *hard real-time embedded systems*. Real-time embedded systems are also extensively used in process control, when time-critical tasks have to be carried out. (Real-time "constraints" are often imposed in voice and video communication, but if these constraints are violated occasionally, nothing catastrophic will happen — for instance, a voice packet may be delayed, resulting in a short silence. Systems in which real-time constraints are present but not critical are called *soft real-time embedded systems*.)

Networked appliances

Some embedded systems are connected to a network — typically, one based on a TCP/IP (Transmission Control Protocol/Internet Protocol) protocol suite, such as the Internet or a company intranet. These systems are of a new brand that has emerged in recent years. They run the complete TCP/IP protocol stack and can communicate with other nodes on the network. Even a Web server running HTTP (HyperText Transfer Protocol) can be embedded into the system. The system can monitor some parameters (such as temperatures and pressures) and send the data over a network to a centralized system for online monitoring. A typical example is the monitoring of equipment in a manufacturing unit. The system sends the data over the TCP/IP network to a central management system, which can be a desktop computer running a Web browser. Another example is a network-enabled Web camera that can transmit its video output over the Internet. These are known as *Internet information appliances*.

Mobile devices

With the advent of wireless networks that can support very high speeds, mobile devices are capable of supporting high data rate services in addition to the voice services. Accessing Internet services such as e-mail, the World Wide Web, and so on can be done while a person is on the move. Such devices need to run a powerful mobile operating system and download information from Web sites. Many such devices are Java-enabled; hence, they can download Java applets and execute them. Field personnel can use devices such as handheld PCs and palmtops for data collection, and the data entered can be kept in local memory and later uploaded into the corporate databases. Hence, these mobile devices are capable of storing databases locally in their memory. The special requirements of these mobile devices are threefold: they should have powerful computing and communicating capabilities, they should be able to perform some real-time tasks in addition to non–real-time tasks, and they should be capable of handling multimedia applications. These requirements call for a powerful processor, a powerful operating system, and a lot of memory with minimal power consumption.

This book addresses software development for all four categories of embedded systems, using a variety of operating systems and development tools.

Requirements of Embedded Systems

Despite the varying types of embedded systems, they all have some common requirements. The following sections describe each of these fundamental characteristics.

Reliability

Embedded systems have to work without the need for the rebooting or resetting typical of many desktop systems. This calls for very reliable hardware and software. If, for example, the embedded system comes to a halt because of a hardware error, the system should reset itself without the need for human intervention. Certainly, reliability is critical in any system, but we are used to resetting our desktop systems once in a while, thanks to the unpredictability of operating systems and software. However, embedded software developers must make the reliability of the hardware, as well as that of the software, of paramount importance because the system is not readily accessible to human intervention.

Cost-effectiveness

If an embedded system is designed for a very special purpose, such as for a deep space probe or for use in a nuclear plant, cost may not be an issue. However, if the embedded system is for the mass market, such as those used in CD players, toys, and mobile devices, cost is a major consideration. Choosing the right processor, memory devices, and peripherals to meet the functionality and performance requirements while keeping the cost reasonable is of critical importance. In such cases, the designers will develop an Application Specific Integrated Circuit (ASIC) or an Application Specific Microprocessor to reduce the hardware components and hence the cost. Typically, a developer first creates a prototype by writing the software for a general-purpose processor, and subsequently develops an ASIC to reduce the cost.

Low power consumption

Many embedded systems are powered by batteries, rather than a main supply. In such cases, the power consumption should be minimized to avoid draining the batteries. Hardware designers must address this issue — for example, by reducing the number of hardware components, or by designing the processor to revert to low power or "sleep" mode when there is no operation to perform.

Efficient use of processing power

A wide variety of processors with varying processing powers are available to embedded systems. Developers must keep processing power, memory, and cost in mind when choosing the right processor. *Processor* is the term generally used to refer to a micro-controller, a microprocessor, or a Digital Signal Processor (DSP) used in embedded systems. The processing power requirement is specified in million instructions per second (MIPS). The MIPS requirement for the application has to be estimated first, and, given this estimate, the developer can choose the processor. With the availability of many processors with the same capabilities, choosing a processor has become a tough task nowadays. Considerations such as the cost of development tools, support provided by the vendor, and previous experience all play a role in the choice.

Efficient use of memory

Most embedded systems do not have secondary storage such as hard disk. The memory chips available on the embedded system are only Read-Only Memory (ROM), to hold the program; and Random Access Memory (RAM), to hold the data. Depending on the functionality, the developer may determine the program size and the data size based on which memory requirements are more important. The cost of memory is certainly going down, but even one dollar can make a big difference, particularly with regard to consumer items. As most embedded systems do not have secondary storage, *flash memory* is used to store the program, including the operating system. Micro-controllers and DSPs come with onboard memory (i.e., the same silicon contains the memory as well). Such processors are used for small embedded systems, as the cost generally is low and the execution generally is fast.

Appropriate execution time

In real-time embedded systems, certain tasks must be performed within a specified time. Consequently, analyzing the tasks to meet such performance constraints is of considerable importance. Normally, desktop PCs cannot achieve real-time performance. Therefore, special operating systems, known as real-time operating systems, run on these embedded systems. In hard real-time embedded systems, which are subject to very strict deadlines for performing specific tasks, the timing analysis is of great importance. In soft real-time systems, occasionally the task may not be performed in a timely manner. The software developer needs to ascertain whether the embedded system is a hard real-time system or a soft real-time system and perform the performance analysis accordingly. The performance requirement also calls for code optimization to the maximum possible extent. Though software is generally developed in a high-level language, some computation-intensive portions of the code may need to be written in assembly language in order for the desired real-time performance to be realized. In such cases, of course, you need to learn the assembly language of the target processor.

Challenges and Issues in Embedded Software Development

Developers of embedded systems have to deal with unique issues. These issues pose interesting challenges, which are discussed in the following sections.

Co-design

Because an embedded system consists of hardware and software, deciding which functions of the system should be implemented in hardware and which functions should be implemented in software is a major consideration. For example, consider the Cyclic Redundancy Check (CRC) that is used to check whether a bit stream has errors in it. Using a mathematical algorithm, CRC is calculated for a bit pattern, and the CRC is used to find errors in transmission. The algorithm can be implemented either in hardware or in software. Should you choose hardware implementation or software implementation? This is always a difficult question to answer. Hardware implementation has the advantage that the task execution is faster compared with that of software implementation. On the downside, a chip costs money, consumes valuable power, and occupies space. A software implementation is better if these are major concerns for a particular project. Moreover, software implementation offers flexibility — if the algorithm changes, it is easier to modify the software. This issue of choosing between hardware implementation and software implementation is known as a *co-design* issue. Co-design issues should be resolved between hardware engineers and software engineers, keeping in mind the foregoing considerations.

Another co-design example is the implementation of the TCP/IP stack. For decades, the stack has been implemented only through software, as it offers flexibility to change the protocols. The TCP/IP stack is bundled with the personal computer's operating system. This is acceptable because desktop computers have a lot of primary memory (RAM), as well as secondary storage. Now, however, a single-chip implementation of the TCP/IP stack is available, the use of which significantly accelerates the processing of the protocols. Another advantage of the TCP/IP chip solution is that it can be integrated into embedded system hardware, making the embedded system network-enabled. TCP/IP software implementation calls for huge amounts of memory (RAM), which is difficult to accommodate on embedded systems or expensive for a given application.

Embedding an operating system

It is possible to write embedded software without any operating system embedded into the system. Developers can implement services such as memory management, input/output management, and process management with a combination of assembly language and a high-level language such as C. It is also possible to build the software above the operating system. Which is the better choice? Writing your own routines necessary for a particular application results in compact and efficient code, thus saving on processing power and memory. Alternatively, a readily available operating system can be ported to the processor. In this case, the developer need not worry about mundane things like memory management, process management, and so on; he or she can focus on the application software development. Consequently, development should be faster and the code should be more reliable. The latter approach is being followed extensively nowadays. Embedded operating systems provide the necessary Application Programming Interfaces (APIs) to develop applications. However, note that when a commercial operating system is embedded into the system under development, the developer may have to pay a royalty for each copy of the operating system kernel that goes with the system.

Code optimization

Developers of typical desktop application software need not worry much about code optimization because the processor is powerful, plenty of memory is generally available, and a few seconds of difference in response time may not make an appreciable difference. Because memory and execution time are the important constraints in embedded systems, though, developers should optimize the code to the maximum possible extent. Though compilers perform code optimization, the programmer still has to optimize the code for faster execution and less memory occupation. Sometimes, to achieve the required response time, the programmer may have to write some portions of the code in assembly language. Of course, with the availability of sophisticated development tools, this is less of an issue in recent years.

Efficient input/output

In most embedded systems, the input interfaces have limited functionality. For instance, only a small keypad (with 8 or 12 function keys) may be available for inputting data. Similarly, the output interface may consist of a small number of LEDs, or a small LCD displaying only two lines and 8 to 12 characters per line. Writing embedded software is a different ball game compared with writing a user interface with a full-fledged keyboard, a mouse, and a large display! Some embedded systems have *no* input/output devices such as keyboard or display for user interaction — for example, many systems used in process control. These systems take electrical signals as input and produce an electrical signal as output. Developing, testing, and debugging such systems is much more challenging than doing the same with desktop systems. Special procedures have to be adopted for testing such systems.

Testing and debugging

Software for an embedded system cannot be tested on the target hardware during the development phase because debugging will be extremely difficult. A host system that has the development tools is used for the development and initial testing, and finally the software will be transferred to the target hardware for final testing. Testing and debugging the software on the host system by actual simulation of field conditions is very challenging. Nowadays, the job is made a bit simpler with the availability of *profilers* that tell you which lines of code are executed and which lines are not executed. Using the output of such profilers, you can locate the untested lines of code and ensure that they are also executed by providing the necessary input test data.

It is these challenges that made embedded software development a "black art" in earlier days, and many developers used to regard embedded software development as a tough nut to crack. This is no longer the case, however; recent trends in embedded software development are changing the scene completely, as you will learn in the following section.

Trends in Embedded Software Development

Because of the increased demand for applications of embedded systems, the marketplace is bubbling with major developments. The following sections provide an overview of these developments.

Processors

In an effort to cater to different applications, several semiconductor electronics vendors have released many processors. You can now find 8-bit, 16-bit, and 32-bit processors with different processing powers and memory addressing capability. Many sophisticated Digital Signal Processors are also available to cater to numerous application needs, including audio and video coding and image processing. The processor boards around which the embedded systems can be built come with the necessary RAM and ROM, as well as peripherals such as a serial port, a USB port, and Ethernet connectivity.

Memory

Both ROM and RAM memory devices are becoming increasingly cheaper, paving the way for devices that can store large numbers of programs and their data. Secondary storage devices such as hard disks are also being integrated into embedded systems such as mobile communication and computing devices. Devices that do not have secondary storage use flash memory, and the capacity of flash memory chips is also rising very rapidly, making it possible to incorporate "heavy" operating systems, such as an embedded version of Windows NT, into embedded systems.

Operating systems

As most everyone knows, Microsoft currently holds the lion's share of the market in operating systems that run desktop computers. However, a healthy competition exists in the arena of embedded operating systems. Now available are many operating systems that can be categorized as embedded operating systems, real-time operating systems, and mobile operating systems. These operating systems occupy much less memory (referred to as the footprint) than desktop operating systems, and they provide the APIs to develop applications above the operating system layer. This reduces the development time and effort considerably. It is also possible for the developer to write his or her own operating system kernel. But the trend is to use an off-the-shelf operating system. The operating system can be tailored to a specific need to reduce the memory requirement. The APIs for the operating systems are also being standardized; therefore, if you are familiar with programming for one operating system, switching to another is very easy.

Programming languages

The era of writing embedded software in assembly languages is now almost history, although programmers of embedded software do need to revert occasionally to assembly language programming. High-level languages are extensively used for embedded software development. Object-oriented programming languages such as C++ and ADA are also extensively used; they offer the advantages of data abstraction, polymorphism, inheritance, and, as a result, code re-use. Another important development is the use of Java. Because of Java's platform independence, it has become very popular for embedded software development. A main attraction of Java is that the byte code generated by the Java compiler can be ported to any platform as long as the platform has a Java Virtual Machine (JVM) running on it. If the JVM has a small footprint, using Java for embedded software is a great choice, and Java is one of the most popular languages for embedded software development.

Development tools

Many advances in development tools are accelerating embedded software development. These development tools include cross compilers, debuggers, and emulators. Using these tools, developers can write programs on host machines, test the software thoroughly, and port to the target hardware. The cycle time for development has been reduced considerably in recent years because of these development tools. Even better, many of them are available free of cost from major software vendors.

Because of these developments, creating embedded software is no longer a black art. Software developers without much knowledge of hardware can take up embedded software development and create industry-grade applications.

Summary

This chapter is a prelude to embedded software development. Unlike general-purpose mainframe computers, desktop computers, and workstations, embedded systems are designed to carry out well-defined, specific tasks. Embedded systems can be divided into four categories: stand-alone embedded systems; real-time embedded systems; networked appliances; and mobile devices. The requirements of embedded systems are high reliability, low cost, low power consumption, and the capability to meet the performance constraints imposed by the desired functionality. In addition, in order to meet these requirements, the right choice of processor and memory is important. The major challenges posed by embedded system development are co-design, choice of operating system, code optimization, limited input/output functionality, testing, and debugging. This chapter also covered trends in embedded software development, including processors, memory, operating systems, programming languages, and development tools. In the next chapter, you'll examine various applications of embedded systems.

Chapter 2
Applications of Embedded Systems

In This Chapter

- Market segments for embedded systems
- Typical applications in each market segment
- The basic architecture of representative embedded systems

Embedded systems are extensively used in control systems in the manufacturing industry, such as chemical plants, cement plants, semiconductor plants, food processing units, missile development units, nuclear plants, and so on. Most of the instruments we use for measurement are also embedded systems. In recent years, the applications for embedded systems have increased multifold with the advent of appliances that can be connected to networks, particularly the Internet. In this chapter, you will examine the various market segments for embedded systems and learn about typical applications in each. You will also examine the architecture of selected applications so you can appreciate the diversity and complexity involved in embedded systems development.

Application Market Segments

To understand the various applications of embedded systems, the applications are divided into the following market segments, each of which is covered in the following sections:

- Consumer electronics
- Control systems and industrial automation
- Biomedical systems
- Field instrumentation
- Handheld computers
- Data communication
- Networked information appliances
- Telecommunications
- Wireless communications

Consumer electronics

Consumer electronic items such as toys, air conditioners, refrigerators, microwave ovens, CD players, MP3 players, television sets, Web-enabled TV sets, and so on are embedded systems with varying processing power and memory requirements. However, each of these systems must be highly reliable and of low cost. Another important feature of these items is that each uses different processors; therefore, different software needs to be written for each type of item by each manufacturer. This was once a major problem, but in recent years, with the advent of Java, things are changing. The "Write once, run anywhere" slogan of Sun Microsystems will be applicable to these appliances once Java's use becomes widespread for embedded software development. Sun Microsystems' Jini technology enables faster embedded system development in the future. However, note that most reliable and efficient extant embedded systems existing as of now are not built using Java technologies. Some typical embedded systems in consumer electronics are described in the following sections.

Office automation products

Products such as laser printers, fax machines, scanners, copiers, and LCD projectors fall into the category of office automation products. Most of these systems used to be stand-alone embedded systems. They required an 8-bit processor with on-chip memory and simple buttons for user interaction. Now, however, these systems can be networked through a variety of technologies, such as Bluetooth, Universal Plug and Play (UPnP), and Jini. To make these products network-enabled, you need to implement the communication protocol stack on these embedded systems. This calls for higher power processor and larger memory.

Digital audio players

Pocket-sized MP3 players have recently become available and very popular. You can download MP3 music files from the Internet onto your desktop computer and then transfer these files to the flash memory of such an audio player by connecting the player to the desktop computer via the parallel port or, more typically, a USB port. A 64MB flash memory card can hold 4.5 hours of CD-quality music.

Digital cameras

Digital cameras are becoming increasingly sophisticated. The functional blocks of a digital camera are shown in Figure 2-1. The video signal from the transducer (which converts the real-world image into an analog signal) is converted into digital format using an Analog-to-Digital Converter (ADC). The signal processing is carried out through the microprocessor with the associated control circuitry and codecs. Other peripherals include a Charge-Coupled Device (CCD) and interface circuitry, to transfer the digital video to a desktop computer through the host interface.

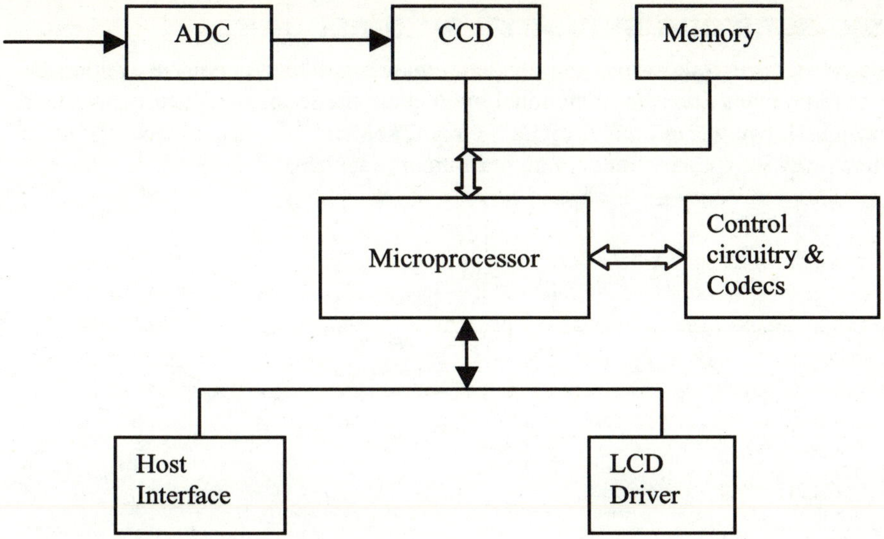

Figure 2-1: Digital camera functional blocks

Still and moving-picture digital cameras are very high-end embedded systems that now include features such as automatic adjustments of focus, exposure, flash on/off, and the like. Some of the cameras embed speech synthesizers, which instruct the user through voice commands, such as whether the lighting is insufficient or the shutter is closed.

Video game players

Video game players are also very high-end embedded systems, as they need to process video signals at a very fast rate. Both hardware and software requirements are very high for these systems. Unlike other consumer items, these systems use 64-bit processors. The software also needs to be very powerful in order to generate the necessary animation, and high-resolution graphic display is required. Writing embedded software for video games is one of the most challenging programming tasks.

Other consumer items

Many items currently available or in use — such as digital watches, television sets, VCRs, DVD players, and singing greeting cards — are embedded systems, and each has its own processing requirements. With the decreasing cost of silicon, these items typically offer a great deal of functionality. For instance, digital watches can show the longitude and latitude of your location by using an integrated GPS (Global Positioning System) receiver. Television sets have become Web-enabled and offer Internet browsing. The set top box can be used for applications such as Video on demand — wherein you can choose your own programs, rather than being at the mercy of cable TV suppliers.

Control systems and industrial automation

Using embedded systems in industrial control and automation has been pervasive ever since microprocessors came into vogue. The functional block diagram of an embedded system used in process control is shown in Figure 2-2. Process control applications vary widely, of course, and some of the blocks shown may not be required for some systems.

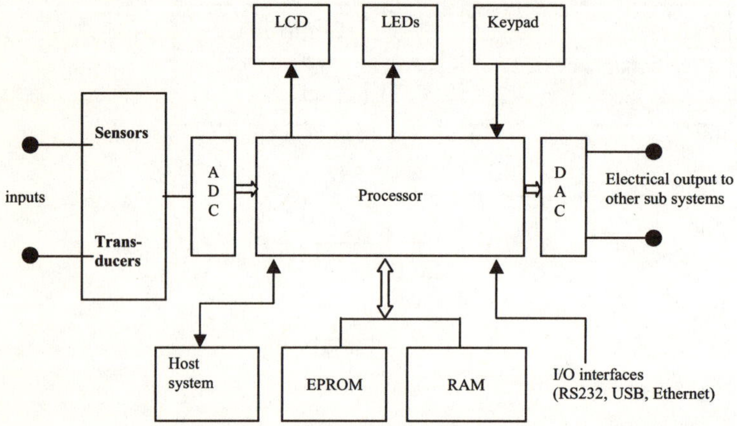

Figure 2-2: Block diagram of an embedded system for process control applications

The embedded system takes electrical signals as input. Generally, sensors or transducers are used to convert the physical entity into an electrical signal. For instance, a thermostat Integrated Circuit (IC) is used to sense the temperature and convert it into an electrical signal, the amplitude of the signal being proportional to the temperature. In applications such as those using voice or video, a transducer converts the voice or video signal into an equivalent electrical signal. An embedded security system that transmits video uses a video camera, which is the transducer that converts the image into an equivalent analog video signal. However, because the processor can process only digital signals, the ADC (Analog-to-Digital Converter) converts the analog signal into its equivalent digital signal, which is an electrical representation of a bit stream of 1s and 0s. The processor processes these signals using the software that resides on the memory chip (Read-Only Memory). RAM is used to store the volatile data. If the embedded system has to control another system or if it has to directly control another appliance, a DAC (Digital-to-Analog Converter) is used to convert the output digital signal to analog format. The processor board also includes input/output interfaces such as a serial interface, a USB port, and an Ethernet port for connectivity to external systems. For user interaction, LCD (Liquid Crystal Display), LEDs (Light Emitting Diodes), and a keypad are provided. These modules may or may not be required depending on the application. The LCD display size can also vary — some applications may require only a 2 × 8 display (2 lines with 8 characters on each line), whereas other applications may demand a 6.4-inch display. To display status information, LEDs of different colors may be used, such as red, green, and so on. A keypad can be a simple function-keypad of 12 keys, or it can be a full-fledged keyboard as used in some handheld organizers and palmtop computers. Another important interface to the embedded system is the host interface. Generally, the embedded software is developed on a host system (a desktop running the Windows or Unix operating system), and then the software is downloaded onto the memory. This is generally done through either a serial interface or a parallel interface.

Depending on the application, the designer chooses the necessary modules and carries out the design. While designing, reliability, performance, and cost need to be kept in mind. Some typical process control applications include detection and identification of characteristics of gas samples, controlling the appliances in nuclear plants, and telemetry and telecommand units in satellite communication systems. Automotive applications include fuel injection control, traction control, climate control, and antilock braking systems. Some embedded systems have to operate in very hostile environments — for instance, with very high temperatures or very low temperatures. Choice of components plays an important role for such systems. Most components work well in the temperature range of 0–50 degrees Celsius. If the system has to operate at lower temperatures, military-grade components need to be chosen. If an LCD display is to be used, note that it will not work beyond -5 degrees Celsius, as the liquid in the LCD becomes solid!

Biomedical systems

Much of the progress made in the health-care industry is due to developments in the electronics industry. Hospitals are full of embedded systems, including X-ray control units, EEG and ECG units, and other equipment used for diagnostic testing, such as colonoscopy and endoscopy. Nowadays, PC-based ECG and EEG equipment, which belong to a different type of embedded system, is becoming available. These systems use PC add-on cards, which take the ECG signals and process them; the PC monitor is used for the display, and the PC's secondary storage is used to store the ECG's records. The PC add-on cards include the processor and the associated circuitry for processing the signals. The card sits on the slots provided on the motherboard of the PC. The slot may be based on EISA or PCI architecture.

Biometric systems for fingerprint and face recognition are gaining wide use in agencies concerned with security. As you might guess, these are complex systems with high memory requirements. The input fingerprint must be processed and compared with the available database using pattern-recognition algorithms, which require intensive processing. The biometric systems use a Digital Signal Processor (DSP) for signal processing, such as filtering and edge enhancement of the image; and a general-purpose processor for implementing pattern-matching algorithms.

Field instrumentation

Testing and measuring instruments represent some of the oldest embedded systems. Instruments that measure parameters such as temperature, humidity, voltage, current, power, frequency, spectrum, and other signal characteristics need to perform a lot of processing. Response time is not always important for some instruments, whereas for others it is a critical factor. Instruments that monitor real-time signals must display their output with very little delay.

Instruments that measure signal parameters, such as for audio and video signals, use DSPs, whereas other instruments use general-purpose processors. The various protocol analyzers — such as for ISDN, frame relay, mobile networks, and so on — have to analyze and also simulate complex protocols; therefore, high-end processors are used for such embedded systems. Field personnel use these instruments to carry out testing and measurements in the field, and hence these systems have to be compact.

Virtual instruments are now becoming popular. Instead of having a stand-alone instrument, a PC add-on card can be used to carry out the measurements, and the PC resources are used for offline analysis and the display and storage of results. Instruments to measure speech signal parameters, video signal parameters, and the like fall under this category. The typical architecture of a virtual instrument is shown in Figure 2-3. National Instruments' LabView is one of the popular virtual instrumentation platforms.

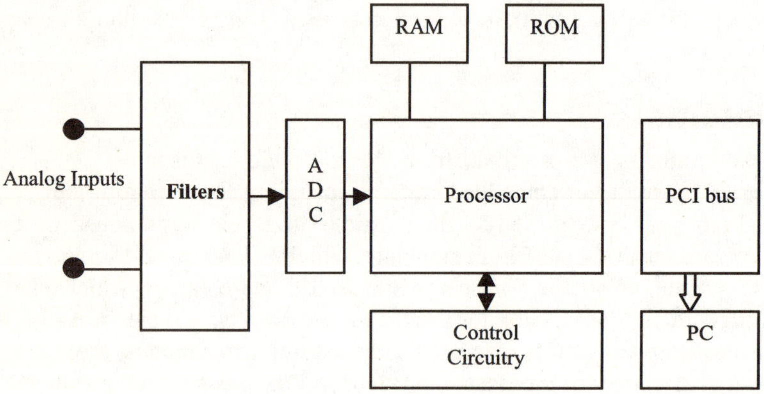

Figure 2-3: Virtual instrument

In spite of the popularity of virtual instruments, stand-alone embedded instrumentation continues to be important to field personnel. Handheld oscilloscopes, network analyzers, protocol analyzers, cable testing instruments, and so on are now available at a low cost because of the advances in embedded system hardware and software.

Figure 2-4 shows a simple instrument, a digital temperature measurement unit. Suppose the unit has to display two temperatures — a room's inside temperature and the outside temperature. You need a mechanism that integrates a sensor both outside the room and attached to the unit kept in the room. You can use a single IC, available as the digital thermostat (for instance, DS 1620 from Dallas Semiconductors). This is interfaced to the micro-controller. A switch provided for users enables them to select the display format (Celsius or Fahrenheit). If the thermostat gives the temperature in Celsius, the conversion is done by the micro-controller and displayed on the LCD, which is a two-line display. You don't need a separate memory module; the program and data memory available on the micro-controller itself can be used, as the application is a very small one.

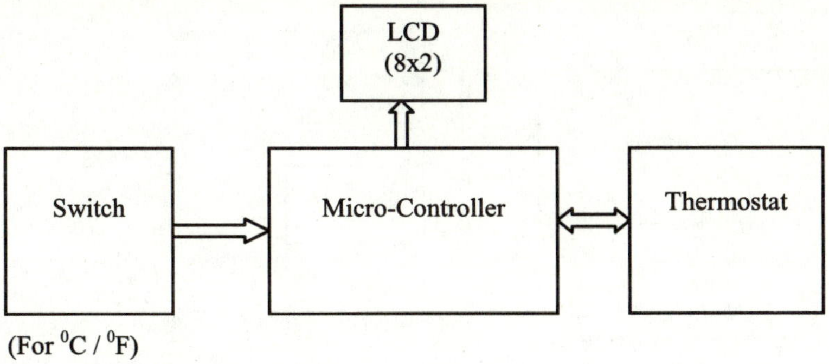

Figure 2-4: Digital thermometer

Handheld computers

Handheld computers are becoming increasingly powerful. The original Personal Digital Assistants (PDAs) were used mainly to store data. Now, with low-cost 32-bit processors, the computing power on the handheld has increased multifold. The typical architecture of the handheld computer is shown in Figure 2-5. Such a device runs a powerful operating system such as Windows CE, Palm OS, Symbian OS, and so on; and provides applications for numerous services, including e-mail, a calendar, and an address book. In addition to computing power, it offers a lot of communication power as well. Using interfaces such as USB, IrDA (Infra-red Data Association's standards-based communication using Infrared links), the RS 232 serial communication interface, or Ethernet, it can connect to the desktop PC or communicate through a built-in modem directly to the Internet Service Provider. The handheld computer can receive input via a full-fledged keyboard or via a form of handwriting recognition, such as that used on Palm OS devices. The output can be an LCD display, with touch screen. The memory, dynamic RAM and flash memory, capacities are also very high, although still not approaching as much as we have on desktops. To provide audio and video capability to the handheld computer, peripherals such as a microphone, a speaker, and a video camera are provided. The signal from the microphone or video camera is converted into digital format and vice versa using the *codec*, which is a combination of coder and decoder. The audio codec converts the audio signal into digital format to store it in the computer and also converts the stored digital speech data into audio format to be played through the speaker. Similarly, the video codec does coding and decoding of the video signal.

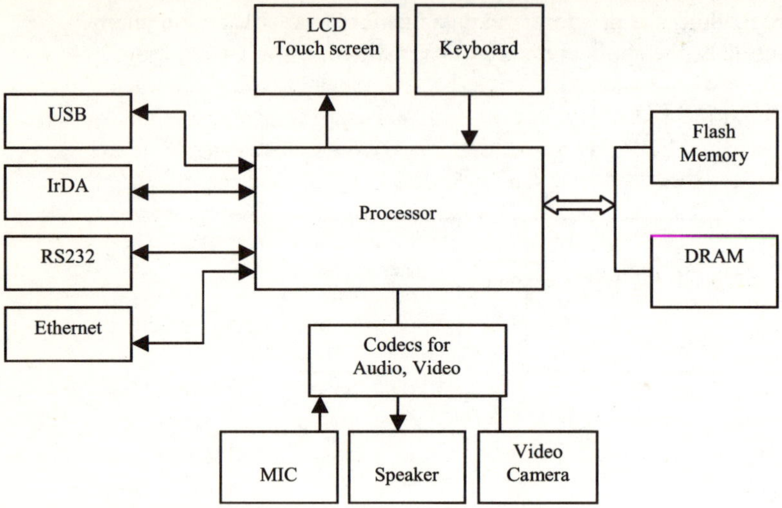

Figure 2-5: Handheld computer architecture

You've already seen how valuable handheld computers are to field personnel for data collection. These handheld computers also provide a software utility for data synchronization. Using this utility, you can download a database (for instance, in MS Access) onto your handheld, collect information from the field, and upload the updated database into the corporate database. For instance, Microsoft's ActiveSync facilitates synchronization of data between the desktop and the Pocket PC.

CROSS-REFERENCE See Chapter 11 for information about software development for field personnel using handheld computers.

Data communication

The Internet has acted as the catalyst for embedded systems. The modem that connects two computers — yours with one owned by your ISP — is an embedded system. With users demanding ever-increasing speeds to access the Internet, advanced modems providing speeds up to 8 Mbps are now becoming available.

Modems

The dial-up modems normally used to access the Internet are embedded systems with a DSP inside. Using the DSP and associated software, the modem establishes the connection using standard protocols. As line conditions vary, a modem can go into fallback mode — the speed of communication decreases as the line condition goes bad. As the digital signal is modulated, a lot of signal processing is involved; therefore, DSPs are used.

In recent years, Internet access speeds have increased multifold with advances in embedded systems. The *x*DSL (Digital Subscriber Line) family provides access speeds ranging from 64 Kbps to 8 Mbps. The HDSL (High Data Rate Digital Subscriber Line) provides access speeds up to 2 Mbps in both directions, and many corporate clients use HDSL modems to access the Internet. The ADSL (Asymmetric Digital Subscriber Line) modems are capable of download speeds up to 8 Mbps (from the ISP server to the subscriber), and upload speeds up to 1 Mbps (from the subscriber to the ISP server). ADSL modems are finding their way into many homes.

Data communication infrastructure

LAN cards, bridges, and routers are all embedded systems. The main feature of these systems is that each one needs to perform processing of data communication protocols. The LAN modules process the data link layer protocols, whereas routers process the Internet Protocol (IP) as well. The X.25, Frame Relay, and ATM-based networks also use a number of switches and gateways that do the protocol processing for the specific protocol architecture.

Multimedia over IP networks

Convergence is the mantra nowadays. For years, we used different networks for different services — the telephone network (Public Switched Telephone Network, or PSTN) for making voice calls and sending fax messages; the Internet for data services such as e-mail, file transfer, and Web services; and cellular mobile networks for making voice calls while on the move. In recent years, we have witnessed revolutionary changes — the Internet is used for voice, fax, and video communication as well. An IP (Internet Protocol)–based Wide Area Network (WAN) can be the backbone network supporting data, voice, and video communication services. The architecture for the multimedia communication over IP networks is shown in Figure 2-6. The various network elements shown in the figure are embedded systems of varying powers.

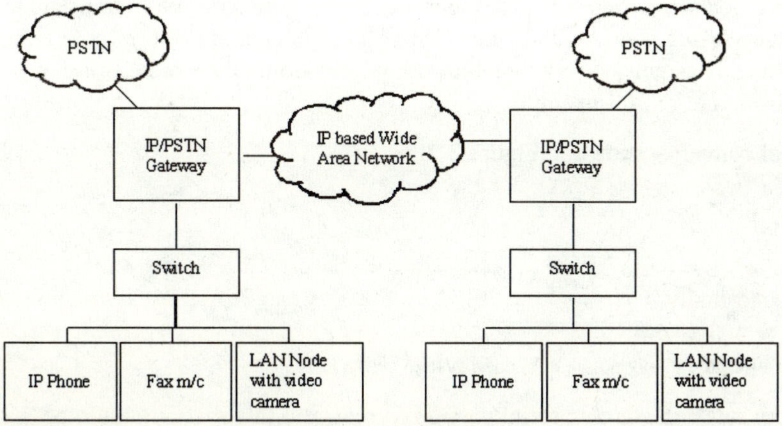

Figure 2-6: Multimedia communication over IP networks

The IP Phone is the terminal that will be at the subscriber's premises. Unlike the telephones we use today, IP Phone is a powerful embedded system. It will have an IP address of its own. It receives voice in the form of packets from the IP network and reassembles the packets to convert them into voice. It converts the voice into packet format and sends the packets over the IP network. Unlike the normal telephone, which transmits analog voice signals, the IP Phone sends the voice after performing voice compression; therefore, it needs a voice compression module to reduce the size of the data to be transmitted. In addition, it needs to do a lot of processing for call processing, as the protocols for call processing in IP networks are different from those of the normal telephone network. To take care of all the processing involved to carry out these operations, the IP Phone will have a 16-bit or 32-bit processor, a real-time operating system and TCP/IP protocol stack, and special protocols based on H.323 standards, in addition to the aforementioned functionality.

CROSS-REFERENCE Voice-over-IP implementation is discussed in Chapter 8.

The IP-PSTN gateway is another embedded system that performs the conversion of protocols between the IP cloud and the PSTN cloud. The important difference is that PSTN uses circuit switching — that is, a circuit is established between the calling party and the called party, and this circuit is disconnected only when the subscriber hangs up. This results in wasted bandwidth. On the other hand, in IP networks, the data is transmitted in packet format, and the same circuit can carry packets of voice from different subscribers. To take care of this difference, as well as other call processing protocols, a gateway is required. The gateway's functions are to translate the call processing protocols and to code the speech in the required format.

Protocol converters

The gateways or routers on the Internet are protocol converters, which convert the LAN protocols to WAN protocols and vice versa. These protocol converters normally translate the standard protocols such as X.25, ATM, and Frame Relay. Another set of protocol converters is required to handle special systems, such as satellite communication, or the monitoring of embedded systems from a LAN, for example.

Consider the protocol converter shown in Figure 2-7.

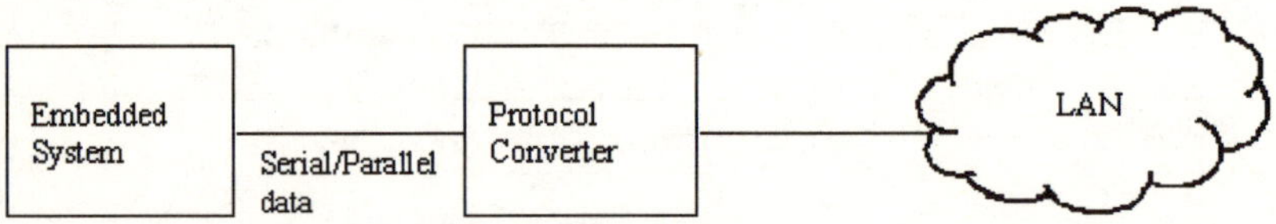

Figure 2-7: Protocol converter for monitoring an embedded system over a LAN

The embedded system sends the data in serial/parallel format, and this system should be monitored/controlled from any node on a LAN. The data received from the embedded system has a standard physical interface (such as RS 232 or RS 422), but uses a proprietary protocol for data transfer. The commands to be issued from the LAN node are specific to the application; therefore, you need to define your own protocols. In such a case, a protocol converter is required, which performs the translation between the serial packets and the Ethernet packets. The packets received from the embedded system are converted into Ethernet packets and broadcast over the LAN. Similarly, the packets sent by a LAN node and addressed to the embedded system are converted into serial format and sent to the embedded system. The protocol converter can be an embedded system with two interfaces — a serial interface to talk to the embedded system and an Ethernet interface to interact with the LAN.

Similar protocol converters are required in most telecommunication equipment. Consider the rudimentary satellite communication system shown in Figure 2-8.

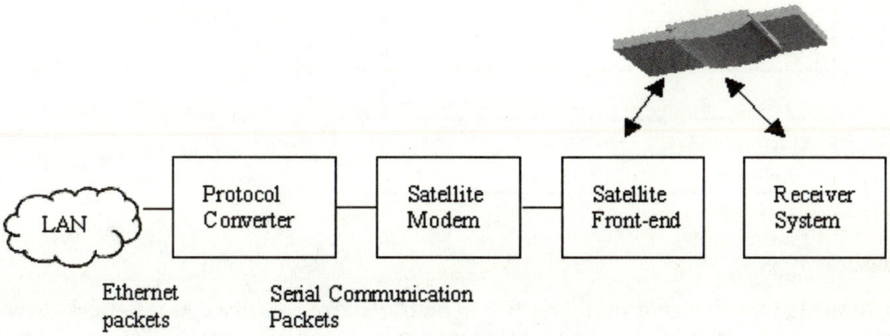

Figure 2-8: Protocol converter in satellite communication equipment

Suppose you would like to send data from a LAN node over the satellite communication network. The satellite modem may accept only serial communication data. In such a case, you need to use a protocol converter to convert the Ethernet packets into serial communication packets. Generally, the serial packets will be in a proprietary format; therefore, you cannot use any standard converters or gateways. You need to develop your own converter to meet the needs of the specific serial communication. As timing constraints are imposed on the conversion of the packets, you cannot use a desktop for protocol conversion. The embedded protocol converter needs to run a 32-bit processor with a real-time operating system.

Chapter 7 covers software development for a protocol converter that converts the Ethernet packets into serial communication packets. Developing software for all the aforementioned data communication equipment and protocol converters requires an understanding of the concept of *protocol encapsulation*. Figure 2-9 illustrates this concept.

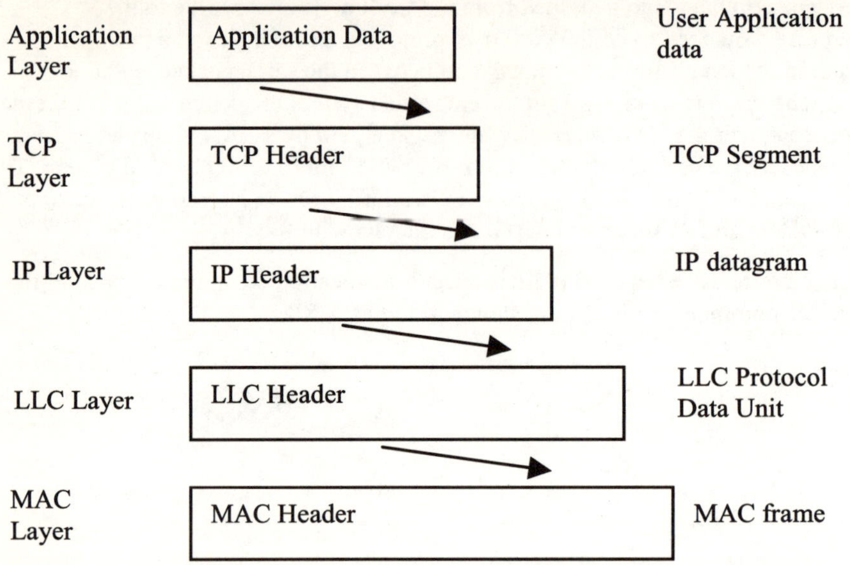

Figure 2-9: Protocol encapsulation

The application data (such as an e-mail or a file to be transferred) is divided into packets, and each packet is sent to the TCP (Transmission Control Protocol) layer. The TCP layer adds a header to the application data packet and a TCP segment is formed. The TCP segment is sent to the IP layer software. The IP layer adds its own header to the TCP segment and sends it to the LLC (Logical Link Control) layer of the LAN. This layer adds the LLC header, and the LLC Protocol Data Unit (PDU) is sent to the MAC (Media Access Control) layer. The MAC adds its own header and sends the MAC frame over the LAN. When the frame is received by another node, the software for each layer strips off the header and sends the rest of the packet to the upper layer. Finally, the application data reaches the application running on the receiving node.

Encryption devices

Every networked system is vulnerable to attacks. To secure the networks, servers, end-terminals, and the networked embedded systems, security devices are becoming available. The data is generally encrypted using encryption devices. These encryption devices take the data as input, modify the bit stream using an encryption key, and transmit over the communication medium. The length of the encryption key determines how secure the encryption mechanism is — 64-bit, 128-bit, and 256-bit encryption keys have been used until now, but we need still higher security algorithms. However, the longer the encryption key length, the higher the processing power required; 512-bit and 1,024-bit encryption key–based devices are now available as single chip solutions. These are embedded systems that can be integrated into a credit card–sized "smart" card. The smart card will have a processor as well as memory to hold the data.

Dynamic distributed systems

As the number of gadgets we use in our daily lives at the office and at home keeps increasing, we encounter a number of challenges. The major challenge is that we need to perform a lot of administrative work to keep these systems running and make the services available. Another challenge is synchronizing the data on various devices — the address book contents in the desktop and the mobile phone should be the same.

This has probably happened to you: You issue a print command from your office workstation and wait for a long time before realizing that the printer is out of order or has been taken out of the LAN. Ideally, if the networks and the services offered on the network are administration-free, we can be much more productive. Distributed systems that change dynamically (in terms of the topology and services offered) are called *dynamic distributed systems*. Sun Microsystems' Jini connection technology provides a platform for the development of administration-free dynamic distributed systems.

Consider the network shown in Figure 2-10. You can Jini-enable devices such as laptops, mobile phones, printers, and so on by running a piece of software on each of them. When you enter the office with your laptop, for example, it automatically discovers the presence of the printer and retrieves details about its service (such as printer type, paper size, and so on) using a special protocol called discovery protocol. Once the presence of the printer is discovered, you can issue a print command and get the printout. The physical connection between the printer and the laptop can be wired or wireless — with Jini, it does not matter. Small devices such as a door lock or a video camera will not have the capability to run the software for making them Jini-enabled because of lack of processing power. In such cases, another machine — such as the desktop — can act as a proxy and make the services available to others. Jini enables true plug-and-play of devices. Jini technology does, however, put some additional processing requirements on the embedded systems, such as office automation equipment and even consumer items such as air conditioners and microwave ovens.

CROSS-REFERENCE Development of dynamic distributed systems using Jini technology is discussed more in Chapter 13.

Networked information appliances

Devices that can be connected to a network and that can transmit information such as temperatures, pressure value, and the like over the network are known as *networked information appliances*. Typically, a network is a corporate intranet or the Internet running a TCP/IP protocol stack. One interesting personal application is a door lock (for your home, for example) with an embedded Web server. You can control the door lock from your office desktop. That is the power of networked appliances. Though these appliances were demonstrated in 1995, they have not become popular until recently.

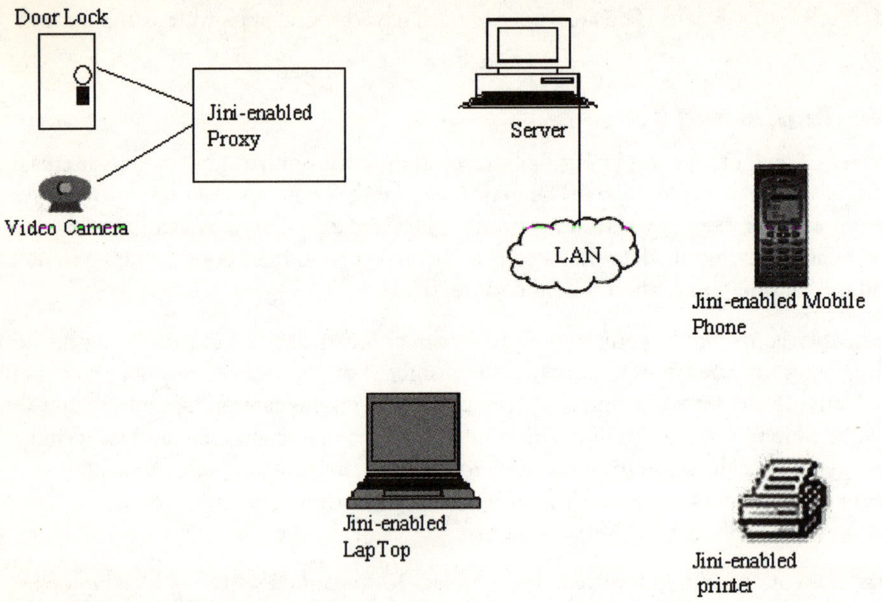

Figure 2-10: Dynamic distributed system

The requirements for such a system are threefold:

- It is an embedded system running an operating system.
- The TCP/IP protocol stack should be embedded in the software.
- The Web server (HTTP server) should be embedded in the system.

Figure 2-11 shows how the information appliances work in an Internet/intranet environment. A Web camera with an embedded Web server can be directly connected to the Internet. This Web camera can have a home page, and anyone on the Internet can access the Web page from a conventional desktop browser. For instance, a tourist spot can have a number of networked video cameras to show a real-time promotional video of its services. If an appliance does not have the necessary processing power, you can use a gateway (a desktop), which runs the Web server on behalf of the appliance. In homes, for example, you can network all the electronic appliances, which are then accessed through a gateway only. This system provides the necessary security features as well, as you probably don't want someone else to be able to control the appliances in your home!

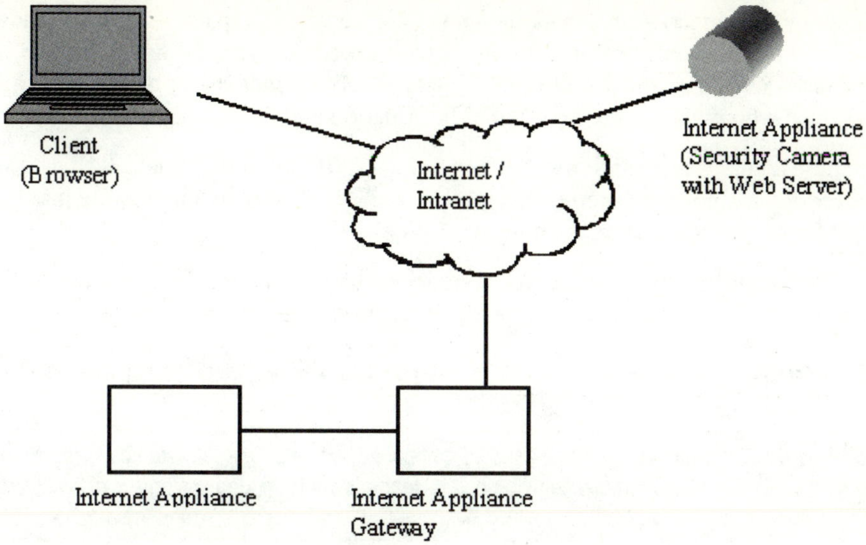

Figure 2-11: Networked information appliances

An embedded system that is networked and connected over the Internet can take some measurements through custom-built hardware or obtain the data from some other system, carry out the necessary computations, and generate the required information. This information can be stored in the home page of the appliance, and the home page can be accessed from anywhere on the 'Net. Depending on the format of the home page, it might be accessed from a normal desktop browser, a Wireless Application Protocol (WAP)–enabled phone, or a Java-enabled phone.

You can see the potential of networked appliances in the following four examples:

- The flow and storage of water in a city's water tanks can be monitored from a centralized place using a conventional Web browser. Each water tank will have an embedded system to monitor the flow and water levels. The information is sent over the TCP/IP network to the central location. The Web server needs to be integrated with an embedded system in each water tank.
- Security cameras can monitor activities at any number of strategic locations, such as highways, nuclear plants, the security gates of organizations, etc. These cameras are appliances that can be controlled from a central location for monitoring the activities. Traffic police already use such systems effectively.
- The diagnostic equipment in intensive care units can be information appliances, and the patient data that is generated can be monitored from a remote location — for example, from a doctor's office in another building (over the hospital intranet) or from a doctor's home (over the Internet).

- A weather monitoring system can use an embedded server, which automatically sends weather data (such as temperature, humidity, wind speed, etc.) in real time to any conventional desktop over the Internet. This embedded weather server obviates the need for personnel who must record the weather information and feed it to a Web server.

These information appliances need to run the complete TCP/IP protocol stack as well as a Web server. However, the memory requirement is not very high; Web servers that require just 10 to 300KB of RAM on target appliances are now available.

For monitoring or controlling the information appliances, you need not have a desktop — an embedded browser in a TV set or even a mobile phone will do the job.

CROSS-REFERENCE Implementation details of information appliances are discussed in Chapter 12.

NOTE Security is a major issue with network-enabled embedded systems. These systems are highly vulnerable to hacker attacks because building high-security features in embedded systems is difficult given their limited processing capabilities.

Telecommunications

Telecommunications infrastructure elements include networking components such as telephone switches, loop carriers, ISDN network terminations, terminal adapters, ATM switches, frame relays, and paging base stations. Mobile communications components include base stations, mobile switching centers, and satellite communication equipment such as earth station controllers, onboard processing elements, telemetry and telecommand systems, PBX control units, and cable TV infrastructure network elements. Some representative embedded systems for telecommunications are listed in the following sections.

Audio codecs

Normally, when voice is transmitted over the telephone network, the voice is coded at the rate of 64 Kbps using a technique known as *Pulse Code Modulation* (*PCM*). However, in radio systems (such as mobile communication systems, satellite communication systems, etc.), speech is compressed to save bandwidth. At the transmitting end, audio signals are compressed to achieve data rates in the range of 2.4–32 Kbps; and at the receiving end, the audio signal is expanded to retrieve the original signal. These *codecs* (*coder* + *decoder*) use DSPs extensively and embedded into cell phones, infrastructure equipment of mobile and fixed communication systems. An MP3 player is a good example; the music signals are encoded and transmitted from a music kiosk to be played on the MP3 device.

An important application of audio coding technique is the computer generation of speech. Talking computers, as depicted in science fiction, have been an active research area since the mid–twentieth century. Now systems are available that can synthesize speech. As shown in Figure 2-12, the vocal tract is modeled as a filter, and the filter is excited by a pulse generator or a noise generator. When the filter is excited by the pulse generator, voiced sounds such as vowels are produced. When the filter is excited by the noise generator, unvoiced sounds (consonants) are produced. By varying the filter characteristics, various speech sounds can be produced, and combining these sounds results in speech. This electrical model of speech generation is used for computer generation of speech. For example, talking toys and talking cameras use a small embedded system or an Application Specific Integrated Circuit (ASIC) to perform this function. Because audio signal processing is involved, these systems are based on DSPs.

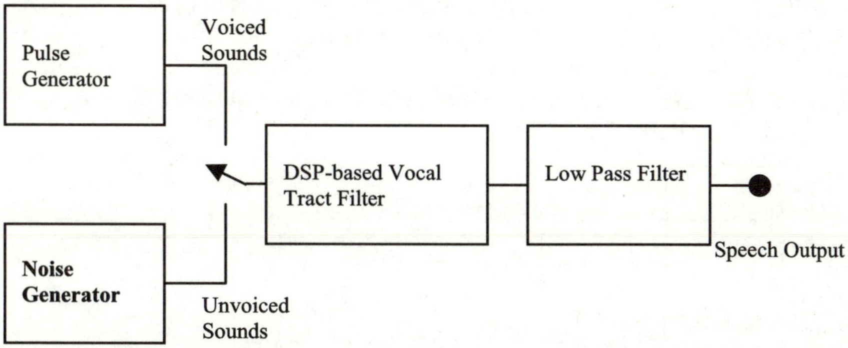

Figure 2-12: Automatic speech generation system

Interactive Voice Response (IVR) systems

Because of extensive automation during the latter part of the twentieth century, tremendous amounts of information are available on computer. Being able to access this information not just through computers but through telephones as well would be a great boon. Particularly in developing countries where computer penetration is still low, telephone access to computerized information would be of great value. Interactive Voice Response (IVR) systems facilitate this. For instance, in many countries, you can use any telephone to retrieve your bank account balance from the IVR system installed in your bank. A database in the bank stores this information in a computer, which can be accessed through a conventional telephone. An IVR system is an embedded system connected to the computer holding the bank database. The IVR system also has a telephone interface and is connected in parallel to a telephone line. After the bank assigns a specific number to the IVR system, any subscriber can call this number to get information about his or her bank account.

Using IVR, the bank can eliminate the expense of additional employees' doing the mundane work of checking the database and informing the account holders.

The block diagram of an IVR system is shown in Figure 2-13. You can implement it as a stand-alone system connected to the computer through a parallel port or USB port, or it can be implemented on a PC with an add-on card. The various blocks of the IVR system are the

PSTN interface, the ADC and DAC, S-to-P and P-to-S serial converters, FIFOs, DTMF decoders, and an interface circuitry to interface microphone and speaker. The PSTN interface receives the telephone calls and answers them. Filters limit the audio signal to the desired frequency band (up to 4 kHz). The ADC (Analog-to-Digital Converter) converts the input signal to digital format to send it for further processing. The DAC (Digital-to-Analog Converter) takes the speech files stored in the IVR system and converts them into analog signals for transmission over the telephone line. The ADC outputs the digitized voice data in serial format, which is converted into parallel format using the S-to-P (Serial-to-Parallel) converter. Similarly, the data in parallel format from the IVR system is converted into serial format using the P-to-S (Parallel-to-Serial) converter. FIFOs are buffers that temporarily hold the speech data. The digits entered by the subscriber (such as the account number) are in the form of DTMF (Dual Tone Multi Frequency) signals. An IC such as MT8880 is used to decode the digits from the DTMF signals.

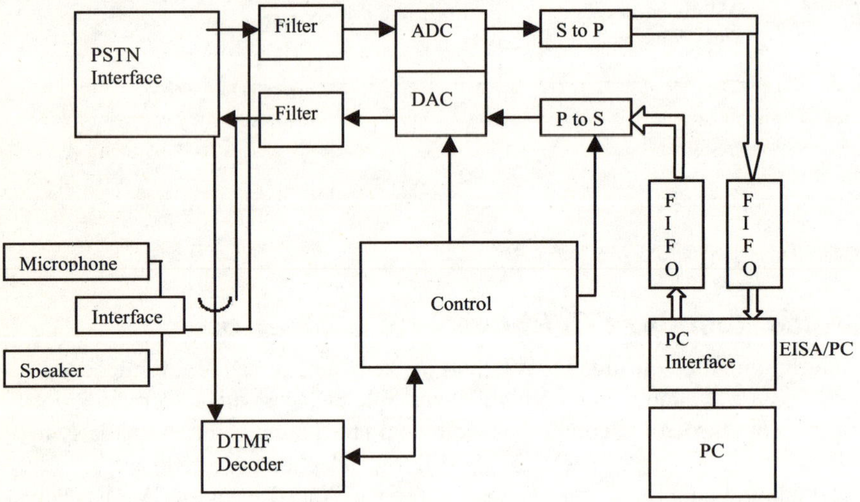

Figure 2-13: Interactive Voice Response system

Using this technology coupled with speech recognition and speech synthesis, you can now develop applications to browse the Web through voice commands. Speech recognition systems are becoming increasingly robust; some can recognize thousands of words with almost 99 percent accuracy. Unfamiliar words, such as proper nouns, can be added to the database, thus making these systems customizable.

Video codecs

Video conferencing has become very popular in recent years. Video occupies very large bandwidth, however, and to transmit video over the Internet, video signals must be compressed to reduce the data rate. Standards such as MPEG (Moving Picture Expert Group) and JPEG (Joint Photography Expert Group) are used to achieve video compression. To compress the video signal, a video coder is used and to bring it back to the original signal, a decoder is used. The functionality of coder and decoder is combined into a single unit known as *codec* (*coder* + *decoder*). These video codecs are available as add-on cards to PCs or as stand-alone systems. These embedded systems use DSP to implement video compression algorithms.

Global Positioning System (GPS) receivers

The Global Positioning System (GPS) is a gift from the U.S. Department of Defense (DOD) to humankind. Using a set of 24 NAVSTAR satellites, the DOD provides the GPS service for any moving or fixed object (e.g., a wristwatch or a car) anywhere on the earth, free of cost. Anyone with a GPS receiver receives the satellite signals and processes them to find the position parameters of the GPS receiver's location. The GPS receiver is a powerful embedded system that uses a DSP to process the satellite signals. From the data received from the satellites, the GPS receiver computes its longitude, latitude, altitude, velocity, and time. The block diagram of a GPS receiver is shown in Figure 2-14. The GPS receiver can simultaneously receive signals from up to six satellites. These signals are processed to obtain the position parameters. The GPS receiver has an RS 232 serial communication interface or a USB interface from which the position data is available. This data is processed by a processor-based system; and using mapping software, the location of the GPS receiver can be mapped onto a digital map. Many cars and taxis already use this navigation system, which helps lost drivers determine where they are.

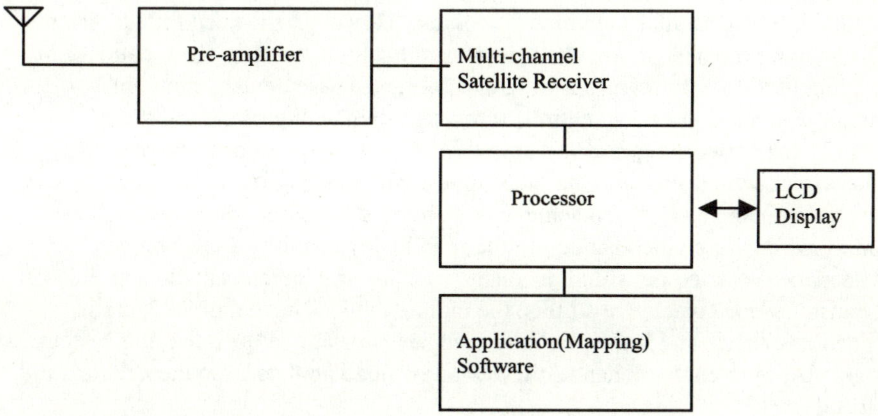

Figure 2-14: GPS receiver

To develop a navigation system, you need a GPS receiver with a serial or USB interface. You can develop your own embedded system consisting of a processor and navigation software to map the location data onto a map.

Because of their low cost, GPS receivers have been integrated into a number of devices, including wristwatches, pagers, mobile phones, PDAs, etc. GPS receivers are used extensively by emergency services. Common applications include locating accident spots for people in need of medical attention, and fire-fighting vehicles.

> **CROSS-REFERENCE** Developing a navigation system using a GPS receiver is discussed in Chapter 7.

Wireless communications

Wireless communication has been in use since the 1960s, but only since the last decade of the twentieth century has there been tremendous progress in digital wireless networks. The 2G (second-generation) wireless networks are capable of supporting voice services and data services only up to 14.4 Kbps. With the advent of 2.5G and 3G wireless networks, data rates in the range 64 Kbps to 2 Mbps are supported, paving the way for multimedia communication over the wireless networks. Wireless Internet access using these networks will be no different from wired Internet access in the coming years. The greatest challenge in this area lies in developing subscriber terminals that support high data rates, while at the same time keeping the cost, size, and power consumption low.

Mobile phones

Most of the mobile phones presently in use are used for voice communication. Generally, these systems have an 8-bit micro-controller to carry out the processing of voice call protocols, and a custom-built chip that handles the voice processing. However, the need for accessing data services is changing the design of mobile devices radically. Currently, 16-bit and 32-bit processors are being used to enhance processing capabilities. These devices run a micro-browser (a scaled-down version of conventional browsers such as Internet Explorer or Netscape) as well as the networking protocol software. With the advent of third-generation (3G) wireless networks, which support data rates up to 2 Mbps, using mobile devices we can carry out video conferencing as well. To achieve this, video streaming, which requires the implementation of low bit-rate video codecs on the mobile devices, is used. Moreover, multiple tasks need to be carried out simultaneously, such as simultaneous audio and video reception and transmission. To achieve all this, the mobile devices have mobile operating systems embedded into them, and the application software runs above the operating system. These devices are also Java-enabled; hence, they can download applets from the network and execute them locally.

Personal Digital Assistants

The limitations of a mobile phone are obvious to anyone who uses one: it has a very limited display area, and the keypad has very few keys. The newest generation of Personal Digital Assistants (PDAs) are extremely powerful and provide much better functionality. Pocket PCs and Palm OS devices belong to this category. These PDAs run an operating system such as

Windows CE, Palm OS, and Symbian OS; and they support the TCP/IP stack as well as application layer software such as POP3, SMTP, and HTTP. The present trend is to incorporate a Java Virtual Machine and a micro-browser to interpret the Java applets and HTML, XHTML, and WML content.

Bluetooth devices

Bluetooth is a low-cost radio technology designed to interconnect devices so that they can form a *personal area network* (*PAN*). A Bluetooth system consists of a small Bluetooth module (hardware) and Bluetooth software. A PC can be Bluetooth-enabled by attaching the hardware module to the PC's USB or serial port and running the software on the PC. A printer can be Bluetooth-enabled by embedding the software in the printer and attaching the hardware module to the printer. The PC and the printer can communicate with each other over the radio link, without the need for wires. Similarly, a number of devices used in the office, home, and even the car can be Bluetooth-enabled, including fax machines, modems, CD players, cellular phones, headsets, speakers, LCD projectors, overhead projectors, and air conditioners. The Bluetooth technology is an excellent example of an embedded system with mass-market appeal. Because of the high quantities of Bluetooth devices required, it has to be very small, consume little power, and be of low cost. Double-chip and single-chip solutions are now becoming available with the help of high integration and embedded software. The targeted price of hardware that makes another device Bluetooth-enabled is approximately U.S.$5 approximately.

Figure 2-15 shows a wireless personal area network. When all the devices shown here are Bluetooth-enabled, they can form a network instantaneously. For instance, when the cell phone enters the vicinity of the laptop (about 10 meters, which is the average range of Bluetooth devices), these two can form a network and exchange data without the need for wires to interconnect them. Similarly, the MP3 player can download music from the desktop.

Other technologies used for PANs include IEEE 802.11, Universal Plug and Play (UPnP), and Home RF. In each of these systems, you need to implement a complex protocol stack. An embedded system with a processor is a good choice, but to keep costs low, ASIC would be the better choice.

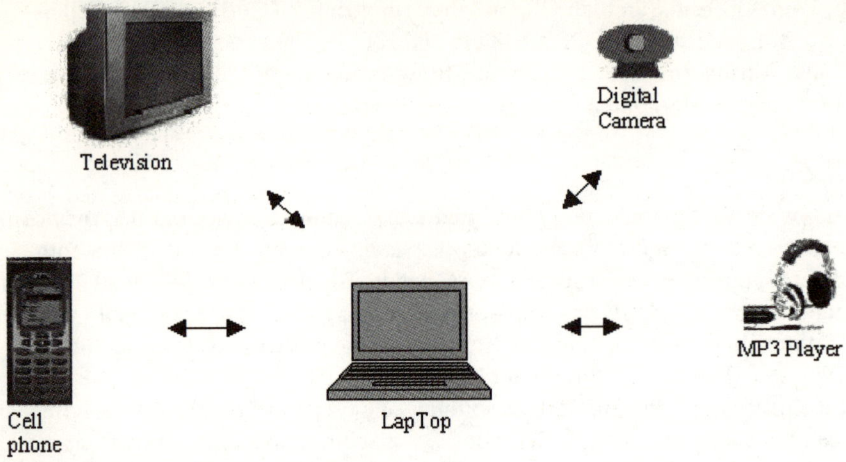

Figure 2-15: Wireless personal area networks

The Unity in Diversity

The diversity and varying complexity of embedded systems can be bewildering, or so it may seem if this is your first exposure to them. However, embedded systems — irrespective of their application domains — have many commonalities. In order to fully exploit the possibilities of embedded software development, you need to understand these commonalities so that you can embark on development work without worrying about lack of knowledge in one particular domain. Some important aspects are as follows:

- Embedded software developers need to understand bit-level details particularly, while implementing the interface software such as serial communication. Desktop application software developers do not worry about bits.
- Understanding implementation details for the TCP/IP protocol stack is now an added advantage, as the networking of embedded systems will be a common feature in the future.
- Understanding the intricacies of the operating system is also required in order to be able to program at the kernel level.
- The diversity of operating systems, programming languages, and development tools is to our advantage — the developer can choose the right platform for the right application provided that he or she has a working knowledge of the features and facilities each platform offers.

By exploiting the commonalities covered in this book, you can learn to develop embedded applications for a variety of application domains, using the variety of platforms currently available.

Summary

This chapter described the applications of embedded systems in various market segments. Embedded systems find use in every segment — industrial automation, consumer electronics, data communication, telecommunication, instrumentation, health care, and so on. In addition, a new breed of networked information appliances is now becoming widespread, for fixed as well as mobile applications. You examined the typical functional architecture of selected systems; and in subsequent chapters, you will learn how to implement these systems.

Chapter 3
Hardware Architectures for Embedded Systems

In This Chapter

- The general hardware architecture of an embedded system
- Circuit details of an embedded system based on a micro-controller
- Architecture of the Intel 8051 family of micro-controllers
- The architecture and functional blocks of systems based on general-purpose processors and digital signal processors
- Details of communication interfaces for embedded systems
- Hardware-software interactions required in embedded systems

Anyone who wants to program for embedded systems must have a fair understanding of the hardware needed to run such software. Although this chapter is not intended to make you a hardware designer, it does provide the necessary background understanding of the hardware architecture of an embedded system. It begins with a description of the general hardware architecture of an embedded system and offers additional details about a representative micro-controller. The chapter also focuses on the functional blocks of typical embedded systems using general-purpose processors and Digital Signal Processors. You are also given an overview of the communication interfaces to be provided for the embedded systems.

Hardware Architecture

An embedded system is built around a processor. The Central Processing Unit (CPU) does the necessary computations based on the input it receives from various external devices. The functionality of the CPU in an embedded system is same as the functionality of the CPU in a desktop, except that the CPU in an embedded system is less powerful. The processor has limited internal memory, and if this internal memory is not sufficient for a given application, external memory devices are used (e.g., the memory card often used with an MP3 player). The hardware also includes any components that facilitate the user-application interaction, such as display units, keypads, etc. Figure 3-1 shows various functional blocks of the hardware architecture of an embedded system. This is a general architecture applicable to both micro-controllers and microprocessors.

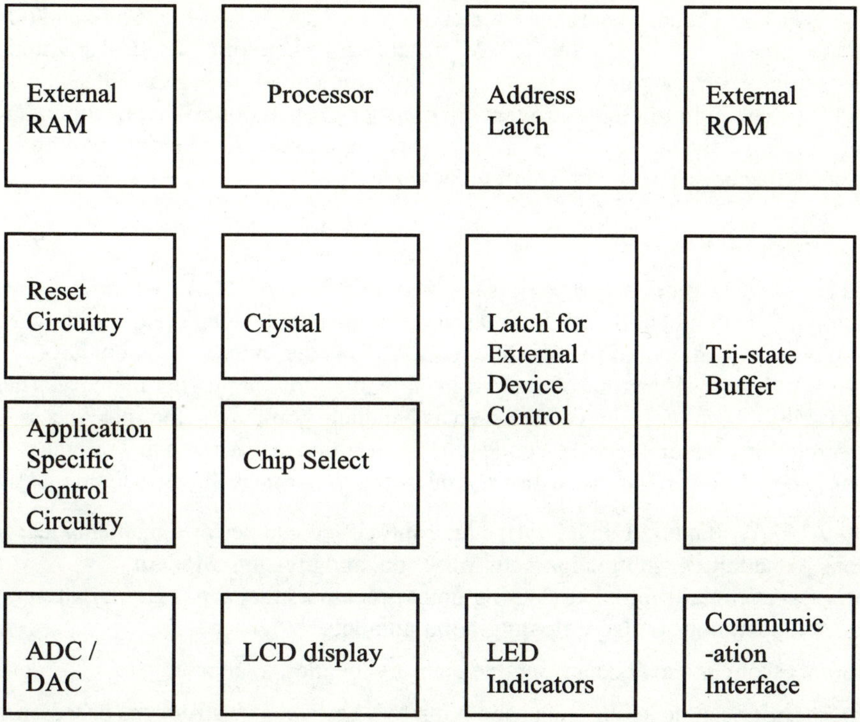

Figure 3-1: Functional blocks of the hardware architecture of an embedded system

Processor

The processor used in embedded systems can be of three types:

- Micro-controller
- Microprocessor
- Digital Signal Processor

Each of these processors is specified by clock speed (100 MHz, 200 MHz, etc.) and data word-length (8-bit, 16-bit, 32-bit, etc.). The higher the clock speed, the faster the processor. Similarly, bigger data word-length leads to higher precision. The word-length also indicates the processor's capability to address the memory. This addressing capability is specified by the number of bits used for addressing. For instance, an 8-bit processor can use 8 or 16 bits for addressing. The following sections describe each of the three processor types.

Micro-controller

Micro-controllers are mainly of Intel's 805x family, Motorola's 68HCxx, etc. A typical micro-controller contains a CPU, interrupts, timer/counter, memory (RAM, ROM, or both) and other peripherals in the same Integrated Circuit (IC). Micro-controllers are often an ideal solution for control applications because you can use them to build an embedded system with little additional circuitry. The 8-bit micro-controllers are used for process control applications, such as the ones found in toys and smart cards. If your processing power and memory requirements are high, you need to choose a 16-bit or 32-bit processor.

Microprocessor

A number of 16-bit and 32-bit microprocessors are available from ARM, Atmel, Intel, Motorola, National Semiconductors, etc. In order to develop an embedded system with these processors, you need a great deal of peripheral circuitry. However, microprocessors have higher clock speeds and word-length, so they are capable of addressing higher memory. These processors are used for high-end applications such as handheld computers, Internet Access Devices, etc. A microprocessor executes a collection of machine instructions that tell the processor what to do. Based on the instructions, a microprocessor does three basic things:

- Using its ALU (Arithmetic/Logic Unit), a microprocessor can perform mathematical operations like addition, subtraction, multiplication, and division. Modern microprocessors contain complete floating-point processors that can perform extremely sophisticated operations on large floating-point numbers.
- A microprocessor can move data from one memory location to another.
- A microprocessor can make decisions and jump to a new set of instructions based on those decisions.

Digital Signal Processor

The Digital Signal Processor (DSP) is a specially designed processor to handle signals, rather than data. Processing signals (whether audio or video) is much more complex than processing digital data signals. To process audio and video signals, the hardware/software needs to perform an operation called *filtering,* in which unwanted frequencies are removed. For example, a Low Pass Filter with a bandwidth of 4 kHz will remove unwanted frequencies above 4 kHz. A DSP facilitates easy implementation of filters. In signal processing, another important task is to convert the signals into frequency domain using Fourier Transforms, and analyze the spectrum of the signal in frequency domain. Analyzing a signal in frequency domain requires intensive mathematical computation, which general-purpose processors take a lot of time to carry out. However, the DSP carries out such mathematical computations quickly using a special module called the *Multiplier and Accumulator*. DSPs are available with various clock frequencies and word-lengths, with each catering to different market segments (such as speech processing, high-fidelity music processing, image compression, video processing, etc).

> **NOTE** When an application involves any type of signal processing — such as in communication, audio and video coding, etc. — a signal processor is a better choice than a general-purpose processor. You will learn more about these processors in more detail in the section "DSP Architecture."

Memory

The memory used in embedded systems can be either internal or external. The internal memory of a processor is very limited. For small applications, if this memory is sufficient, there is no need to use external memory. Otherwise, an external memory device has to be used.

Internal memory

Internal memory is found in the same silicon as the processor. It is accessible to the processor without any use of input and output. However, if the capacity of the internal memory is high, the cost is likely to be more. However, the advantage of larger memory internal to the chip is that there will be less program swapping, resulting in fast instruction and data access.

External memory

Instead of storing the program (instructions) and data in the internal memory, you can use memory devices (chips) external to the processor. Separate devices are used to store the program and temporary data. When the program and data are stored in external devices, data access takes more time than it would with internal memory. In addition, external devices require additional circuitry to be built around the processor, to generate the addresses for retrieving the memory contents.

Whether memory is external or internal to the processor, memory devices can be further divided into the following categories:

- Random Access Memory
- Read-Only Memory
- Hybrid Memory

Random Access Memory (RAM) is a type of memory that can be accessed randomly — that is, a memory location can be accessed without touching other locations. RAM is also called Read-Write Memory, as you can perform both read and write operations on this memory device. RAM is of two types: Static RAM (SRAM) and Dynamic RAM (DRAM). SRAM retains its contents as long as electrical power is being supplied to the device. For example, the desktop PC contains SRAM, which loses data when the power is switched off. Conversely, DRAM has a short data life cycle, typically one-fourth of a second, even if power is being supplied. A DRAM controller is used in conjunction with DRAM to refresh the memory periodically. A major advantage of DRAM is its lower cost. RAM contents can be modified by an embedded system. Handheld computers contain DRAM to store data. RAM is used to store temporary data. It is like a scratch pad for the processor, like the clipboard on a desktop PC. It can also be used to temporarily store the contents of the Read-Only Memory.

RAM can be internal to the processor, or external RAM can be interfaced with the processor. The interface signals for the processor are the address bus, the data bus, the chip select, and the read/write control signals.

An example of Read-Only Memory (ROM) is a memory device from which the processor can read data but to which it cannot write data, like the CD that comes with this book. The program (instructions to the processor) and the data that needs to be permanently stored are kept in the ROM devices. How, then, would you write the data for the first time? One option is to write the data in the factory, where the ROM is "fused" with the program. Another option is to use a special device to write the contents onto the chip. ROM is similar to CD-R.

ROM retains its contents even if power is switched off; therefore, it is used to store the program code and any permanent data required to initialize and operate an embedded system. The contents of the ROM cannot be updated by the embedded systems. A variety of ROM devices are available, each with different capabilities. Programmable ROM (PROM) is a ROM that can be programmed only once. Erasable PROM (EPROM) can be programmed many times. An EPROM programmer is required to program the EPROM chip. To erase the EPROM, an EPROM Eraser is required, which applies ultraviolet radiation to erase the contents of the device. EPROM is similar to CD-RW.

The compiled program is stored in the ROM in a special format called Hex format or S-record format. The format is specified by the processor vendor. The processor reads the code and executes it.

The ROM can be internal to the processor, or the external ROM can be interfaced with the processor. The control signals required are address bus, data bus, read signals, chip select, program enable, and, in some cases, latch devices.

The hybrid memory chips are of three types: Electrically Erasable Programmable ROM (EEPROM), Non-Volatile RAM (NVRAM), and flash memory. EEPROM is similar to EPROM, but it can be erased electrically by applying an electrical signal to one of the pins. NVRAM is SRAM with battery backup so that the contents are not erased even if power is switched off. Though NVRAM is very expensive, data access through it is fast. Flash memory is also non-volatile, fast EEPROM. The main attraction of flash is that it can be erased one block at a time, and programmed one bit at a time. Flash memory devices are high density, low cost, fast (to read but not to write), and electrically programmable. Typical sector sizes are in the range 256 bytes to 16 KB. Flash memory is now extensively used for embedded systems that contain the embedded OS and the application program such as handheld computers. The contents of the EEPROM and flash memory can be updated by the embedded system.

TIP Whenever data is transferred onto a memory device, irrespective of the type of device, it is necessary to ensure that the data is written correctly. Even when you switch on your desktop computer, it first checks the RAM — the processor writes some data into the RAM and checks both whether it is able to read the data and whether the read data is correct. This is accomplished with a small software routine that the processor executes on power-up.

Secondary storage devices

Hard disks, floppy disks, and CD-ROMs are secondary storage devices. High-end operating systems and application software require very large programs and virtual memory. Such requirements are driving the industry to introduce secondary storage on some embedded devices, such as industrial automation systems, mobile devices, etc. The secondary storage devices have very large memories compared to memory chips, but they need moving parts (motor and heads) in order for data to be written to them or read from them. Moreover, they consume more power as compared with primary memory devices. Now, with the availability of low-cost, high-capacity flash memory chips, flash is likely to be the choice for most embedded applications that require large non-volatile memory.

Figure 3-2(a) shows the memory model that is being used extensively. In this model, the processor writes the data to the RAM, and then the contents are transferred to the secondary storage device, such as the hard disk. The model shown in Figure 3-2(b) is likely to become more popular in the near future. In this model, the processor writes directly to the flash chip, making the data transfer much faster. Handheld computers and smart cards have already started using this new memory model.

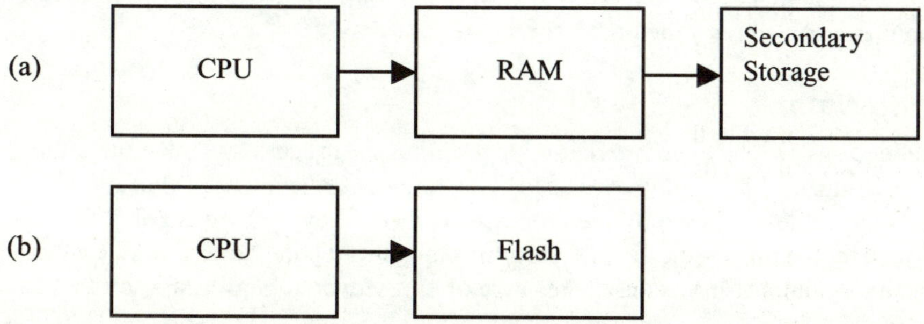

Figure 3-2: Present memory model (a); new memory model (b)

While writing the embedded software, the first job is to write a test routine to test the memory of the embedded system. The memory test routine will write test data into the memory chip and then read the contents to check whether the memory chip is functioning correctly. You will examine the code for testing the RAM using the Cyclic Redundancy Check (CRC) in the section "Hardware-Software Interaction" later in this chapter.

Latches and buffers

Processor-based systems need to drive external devices such as LED displays, relays, etc. The processor does not interact directly with these devices. Flip-flop logic chips are used to drive the external devices. These chips hold the processor output data to be sent to the external devices.

Similarly, the processor needs to obtain data from external devices such as keypads, switches, etc., although the processor does not handle these devices directly. You use Octal buffers to read data from the external devices onto the common data bus.

The flip-flops and buffers isolate the external devices from the common bus by using the tri-state feature of these chips.

Crystal

The CPU needs a clock source, and a crystal oscillator generates the clock. You need to choose the crystal based on the clock frequency of the processor. Many micro-controllers provide an on-chip oscillator, and you connect an external crystal or ceramic resonator. The clock generation circuitry determines the various states of the machine cycle.

Reset circuit

A reset circuit is generally built into the hardware to take care of any unforeseen problems. This circuit handles software hang-ups, power supply failures, etc. Periodically, the processor sends a status signal to this circuit. If this signal is not received, it is an indication that something is wrong with the processor, which is then reset by this circuit. Nowadays, single-chip solutions are available; these monitor software hang-ups, power supply problems, and voltage changes and also reset the processor.

Watchdog timer

Most embedded systems have no provision for resetting the processor. To facilitate the processor resetting, a *watchdog timer* is used. This timer is set to a large value and is counted down. When the value reaches zero, the processor is reset. If everything is going fine and there is no need to reset the processor, the processor resets the watchdog timer (by kicking the timer) to a large value again. This procedure takes care of undiscovered bugs in the software.

Chip-select logic circuit

In a processor-based system, many digital chips share the common bus. To carry out a transaction with a particular chip, the processor must be able to uniquely identify that chip. The processor performs this identification through a signal called the *chip-select signal*. The chip-select signal is available to all devices connected to the bus, and it is of either a high or low logic level. You can generate chip-select signals through a decoder/de-multiplexer chip.

ADC and DAC

Embedded systems receive their input from the external world in the form of analog signals. An analog signal's amplitude varies continuously with time. The processor, however, takes only a digital signal, a series of ones and zeros represented by voltage levels. Therefore, an analog signal has to be converted to a digital signal. The conversion of an analog signal to a digital signal is performed by an Analog-to-Digital Converter (ADC), and the reverse action — the conversion of a digital signal to an analog signal — is performed by a Digital-to-Analog Converter (DAC). To choose the right ADC and DAC chips, you must understand the concepts of *sampling* and *quantization.*

Every analog signal has a *bandwidth,* which specifies the highest significant frequency component of a signal. For instance, the voice signal has a bandwidth of 4 kHz, the music signal has a bandwidth of 20 kHz, and the video signal has a bandwidth of 5 MHz. If you want to convert the analog signal into digital format, the first step is to sample the signal. Nyquist's sampling theorem specifies how to sample the analog signal. According to this theorem, the minimum sampling rate required is twice the bandwidth. Therefore, to sample a voice signal, the minimum sampling rate is 8 kHz. In other words, you need to sample the voice signal 8,000 times per second. Then, the voice signal can be represented by 8,000 values of the amplitude of the signal. Take one second of the analog voice signal and determine the amplitude of the signal every 125 microseconds (1/8000 second), and that is the sampled signal for voice.

After sampling the signal, the second step is quantization. Suppose each sample value is to be represented by 8 bits, which corresponds to 256 quantization levels. In quantization, you take each sample value and map it to one of the quantization levels. In this way, you can represent each sample value not by its exact value but by one of the 256 values. Using this approach, you can represent each sample value by 8 bits. Therefore, for one second of speech, you need 8000*8 bits, i.e., 64,000 bits. In other words, storing one second of voice signal requires 64 Kbps.

If we use 16 bits instead of 8 bits, we can represent the signal more accurately, but doing so requires more storage. Representing a signal by a fewer number of bits results in a greater degree of error. Any error in sampled values due to quantization is known as *quantization error.* The number of bits needed for representing a sample value is known as the *resolution of the ADC.*

When you choose an ADC, you need to check the bandwidth of the signal it can handle (based on the sampling theorem) and the resolution. The same applies to the DAC as well. You can experiment with the ADC and DAC parameters using the sound card on your desktop system. It provides various sampling rates, such as 8 kHz and 20 kHz; and resolutions of 8 bits, 12 bits, 16 bits, etc.

Application-specific control circuitry

As you learned in Chapter 2, embedded systems are extremely diverse. You need circuitry specific to the application on hand. The various devices needed include sensors and transducers (to obtain real-world data from external sources), relays (to control external circuitry), and various input devices, such as keyboards, function keypads, etc. To control all these devices, you need special circuitry to interface to the processor board.

Display units

Some embedded systems — for instance, those in an unmanned spacecraft, or process control subsystems embedded in large machines — do not need any display units (as there is no one to display information to). Embedded systems that require user interaction must have display units, which can be either Liquid Crystal Display (LCD) displays or Light Emitting Diode (LED) indicators.

LCD displays

LCD displays come in various forms, such as two-line displays with eight characters per line, four-line displays with 12 characters per line, etc. The display on a typical mobile phone is an example. Another type of display is the touch screen like that on an automatic teller machine, which is more user-friendly. You need to write special software for displaying the data on the LCD unit. This software is called the LCD Driver.

> **NOTE** The LCD does not generally work for temperatures below -5 degrees Celsius, as the liquid inside becomes solid. If an embedded system has stringent environmental specifications — for example, to operate up to -20 degrees Celsius — you need an alternative, such as a plasma displays.

LED indicators

Some embedded systems use LED indicators to provide status information, such as power on, or whether or not a specific parameter being measured is within the prescribed limit. In addition, an audible cue may be required to bring any aberration to the user's attention. LEDs often use different colors to provide such status information (e.g., green if everything is OK, red if some parameter is aberrant, etc.).

Keypads

Each embedded system offers different capabilities for providing user input. Handheld computers are provided with either a full-fledged QWERTY keyboard or a form of handwriting recognition (such as Graffiti on Palm OS devices). Some embedded systems require only a function keypad to perform a limited number of operations. For example, function keypads with 20 keys (4 keys each in 5 rows) are available off-the-shelf to interface with the processor board.

Communication interfaces

In order for embedded systems to interact with external devices, they need communication interfaces. Most processors provide a serial interface to send and receive data in serial format. Networked embedded systems are provided with the Ethernet interface. Mobile phones and handheld computers are provided with a number of interfaces, including serial, parallel, infrared, Bluetooth, and Universal Serial Bus (USB). We'll explore the communication interfaces in detail later in this chapter.

Programmable logic devices

The design goals of an embedded system are to reduce size, cost, and power consumption and to increase performance and reliability. These manifold requirements are met using Programmable Logic Devices (PLDs). A PLD is a single chip in which a large amount of discrete logic and memory can be combined. Using design automation tools such as Verilog and VHDL, you can design a PLD, which has the functionality of a number of discrete components. This single chip can be Programmable Array Logic (PAL), Field Programmable Gate Array (FPGA), or Programmable Logic Device (PLD). The per-chip logic gate count of these devices is increasing daily. Major suppliers of these devices include Actel, Adaptive Silicon, Altera, Atmel, Cypress Semiconductors, QuickLogic, Triscend, and Xilinx.

Application Specific Integrated Circuit (ASIC) is another option for embedded hardware developers. The ASIC needs to be custom-built for a specific application, so it is costly. If the embedded system being designed is a consumer item and is likely to be sold in large quantities, then going the ASIC route is the best option, as it considerably reduces the cost of each unit. In addition, size and power consumption will also be reduced. As the chip count (the number of chips on the system) decreases, reliability increases.

Example: An 8031-Based Control System

Based on what you now know about the general hardware architecture of embedded systems, this section presents a practical hardware module, along with details about the specific Integrated Circuits (ICs). The circuit diagram shown in Figure 3-3 illustrates the complete interconnections of various ICs.

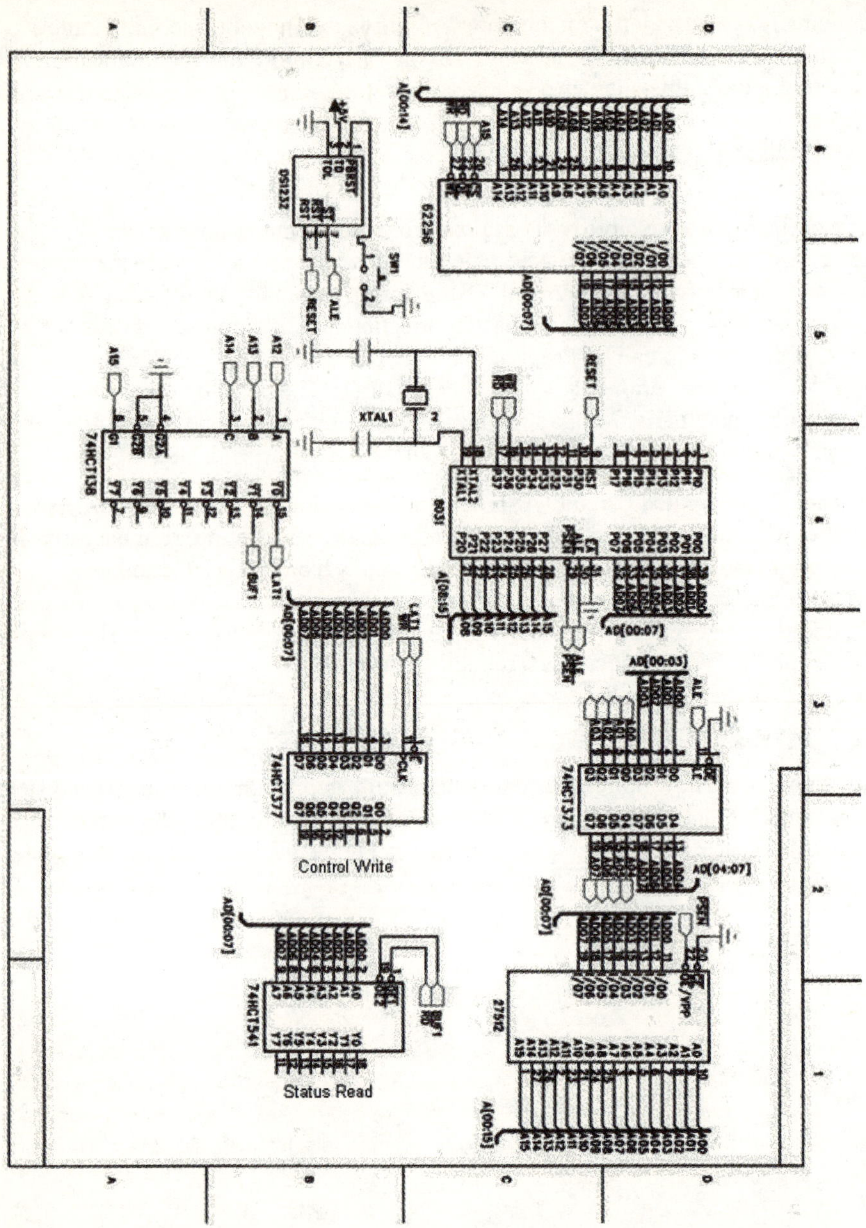

Figure 3-3: Circuit diagram of an 8031-based control system, with the necessary peripherals

This figure depicts how an embedded system can be built around an Intel 8031 controller. The system contains all of the components described in the preceding section. It includes each of the various peripherals, such as program memory, data memory, latches, buffers, reset circuit, clock circuit, and chip-select logic. The program memory is built around an EPROM 27C512, and a latch 74HC373 stores the executable code. When this code is read by the controller, the program is executed. An external data memory of 32K (IC 62256) is used to store temporary data and to do scratch-pad work. A reset circuit (IC 1232) is used to reset the controller in the event of a software hang or when power is switched on. The clock circuit is built with C1 and C2 (two capacitors), and the crystal is connected to pins 18 and 19 of the controller. Generally, many peripherals perform different functions. Therefore, you must identify the peripheral chip with a signal called a chip-select signal. Here, an IC 74HC138 (1 to 8 selector) is used to obtain chip-select signals to the peripherals, which work on the common bus. To write latched control signals to other peripherals, the IC 74HC377 latch device is used. To read status from other peripherals, the buffer IC 74HC541 is used. You can refer to the data sheets provided by the chip manufacturer of these ICs to understand the exact pin connections and the detailed functionality. If you have an inclination toward hardware, you can use this circuit as the basis to develop a small evaluation board and then try to port an operating system and application code on to the evaluation board to develop embedded systems. Most semiconductor vendors provide detailed application notes, which offer sample circuits. With these circuits, you can easily build an embedded system that fits your requirements. In terms of cost, you can build your own evaluation board around the Intel 8031 or 8051 micro-controller for less than $100.

Example: The Smart Card

Every embedded system has its own requirements. At this point, you should have a fair idea of the basic functional blocks required to develop an embedded system. Based on the requirements of your application, you choose a subset of these functional blocks. This section considers the smart card, which is one of the smallest embedded systems you will come across. For example, you can use a smart card as an electronic passbook to record your bank transactions and perform other banking-related tasks. It can also be used as a storage device — for example, to hold a patient's medical history and treatment information in a hospital database.

The functional blocks of a smart card are shown in Figure 3-4.

The smart card requires an 8-bit micro-controller. The memory requirements vary depending on the application. Typically, commercial smart cards use 128 to 512 bytes of RAM, 4 to 20KB of ROM, and 1 to 16KB of EEPROM. Generally, communication interfaces are not provided so as to make the smart card tamper-proof. The smart card requires special circuitry to keep its stored information confidential. The data, which is sent from the smart card to a smart card reader and then returned from the smart card reader to a server over a network, needs to be encrypted so that the information is kept confidential. The encryption hardware takes the data from the memory, changes the bit pattern using an encryption key, and then transmits the encrypted data. Similarly, the received data is decrypted by the hardware and then passed to the processor for interpretation.

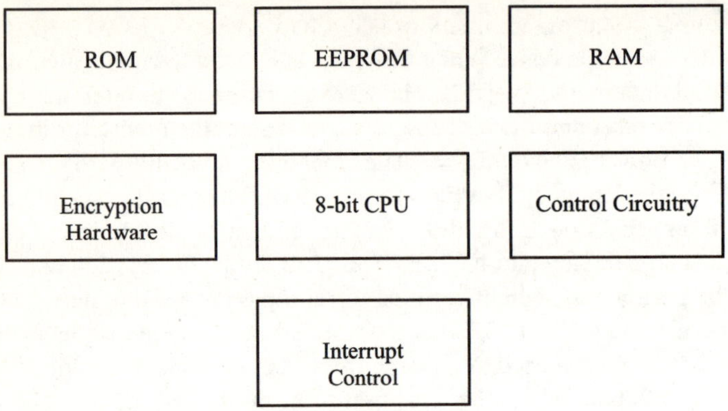

Figure 3-4: Functional blocks of a smart card

Putting all the components together

Once the hardware components are chosen and the hardware board is built as per your requirements, you need to write the software specific to your application. The software engineers and hardware engineers need to work in tandem during the design phase, determining which tasks are to be performed by the system, the priorities to be assigned to each task, etc. In embedded systems that require real-time performance, task scheduling is of paramount importance.

Embedded systems have to respond quickly to external events. They should be able to suspend an ongoing task and execute another code corresponding to another task. This capability is provided by Interrupt Service Routines (ISRs). The interrupt pin of the processor is *asserted* (made high or a voltage level corresponding to 1 is sent) to interrupt the processor, indicating that something more important is to be done. This arrangement enables the processor to execute the interrupt routine. Interrupt vectors store the addresses of the interrupt routines in an interrupt vector table. You can assign priority levels to the interrupts. The ISRs are usually written in assembly language for faster execution.

In the next section, you'll examine an Intel 805–based micro-controller system in more detail to understand the functionality of the hardware.

Case Study: A Micro-Controller Architecture

A micro-controller is a silicon chip with a CPU, memory, and input/output lines for control applications. A micro-controller contains on-chip program memory to store the program code, data memory to store temporary data, UART (Universal Asynchronous Receive/Transmit) for serial communication, timers to generate timely events and to obtain the required baud rate clocks for serial communication, and input/output lines to control external devices or to obtain status information about other devices.

Micro-controllers differ in terms of instruction set, bus width, and clock speed. Nowadays, advanced micro-controllers are available with built-in ADC and DAC to handle analog signals, high RAM and ROM and serial communication ports. The main advantage of the micro-controller is that it has all the peripherals and memory required for most control applications. Hence, it saves lot of space, consumes less power, and makes designing embedded systems relatively simple.

The following example uses a micro-controller from Intel's 8051 family. The equivalent IC from Atmel is numbered 8951. The functional blocks of the micro-controller are shown in Figure 3-5.

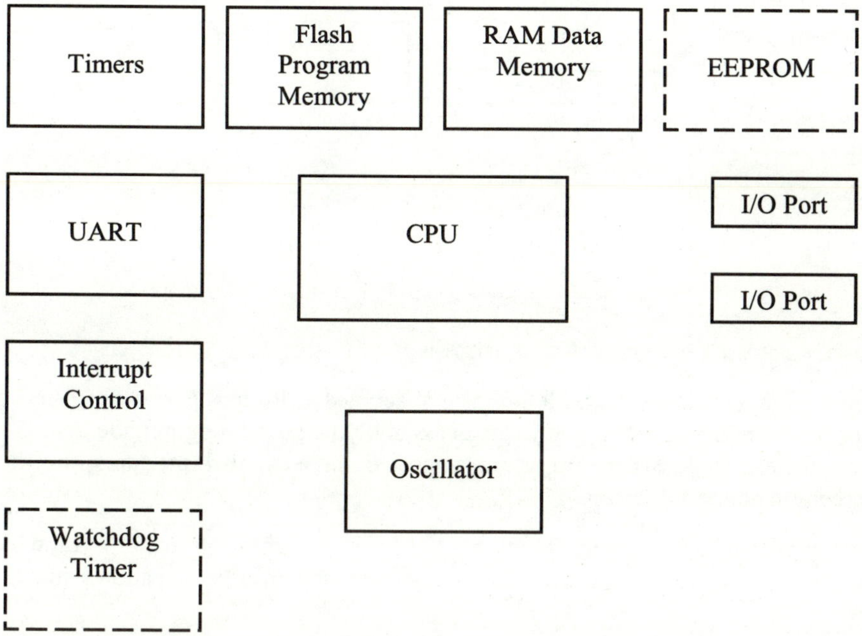

Figure 3-5: Functional blocks of a micro-controller from the 8051 family

In addition to an 8-bit CPU, the micro-controller contains (on the same silicon) program memory, data memory, timers, UART, a number of input/output ports, an oscillator, and interrupt control circuitry. The blocks shown in dotted lines (EEPROM and watchdog timer) are provided only in some micro-controllers. The capacities of the on-chip memory modules (ROM and RAM), as well as the number of timers, vary for different micro-controllers of the family.

Program memory size, data memory size, and the number of timers vary widely for different controllers. Based on your application, you need to assess your memory requirements, and then choose the appropriate processor. Memory size is a major factor affecting the processor's cost — as memory size increases, so does the cost of the micro-controller.

The 8051 Architecture

The block diagram of the 8051 family of flash micro-controller is shown in Figure 3-6.

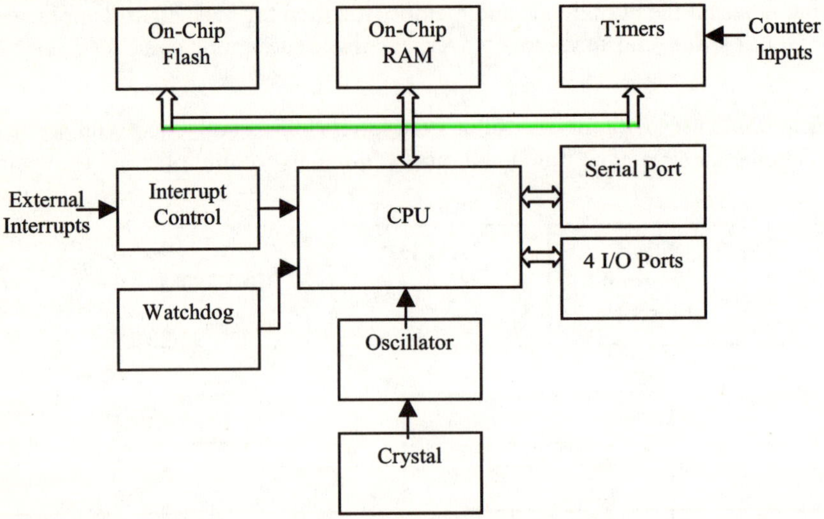

Figure 3-6: Architecture of flash's 8051 family of micro-controllers

The 8051 is an 8-bit micro-controller with 8 registers, denoted as R0 to R7. These registers can be accessed by a 3-bit address. When you write an assembly language program, the Accumulator is denoted by A. Six interrupts are supported: three external interrupts, two timer interrupts, and one serial port interrupt.

You have already examined the various functional blocks of this architecture. Now you will learn about the micro-controller's power modes, its memory organization and addressing, and its instruction set.

Reduced power modes

To conserve the power consumed by the embedded systems, every processor offers reduced power modes. In the 8051 family of micro-controllers, two reduced power modes are provided, which save power when the processor does not have much to do. These modes — called *Idle mode* and *Power Down mode* — are software-invoked. In Idle mode, the CPU is switched off, but the RAM and other on-chip peripherals continue to work. In Power Down mode, all the on-chip activities are suspended. Obviously, Power Down mode saves much more power than Idle mode.

Memory organization

A micro-controller has two types of memory: program memory and data memory. The micro-controller can only read the contents from the program memory, but it can write contents into the data memory.

Program memory

The maximum size of the micro-controller's program memory is 64KB. Of this, 4KB of memory may be on-chip memory, and the remaining 60KB can be external memory, as shown in Figure 3-7. Otherwise, 64KB of external memory can also be addressed by the controller. The program memory locations are addressed by a 16-bit address, even if the program memory size is less than 64KB. When the micro-controller is reset, it starts the execution of the code from the location 0000. Note that memory locations are always represented in hexadecimal notation. The data books of the micro-controller manufacturers refer to this location as 0000H.

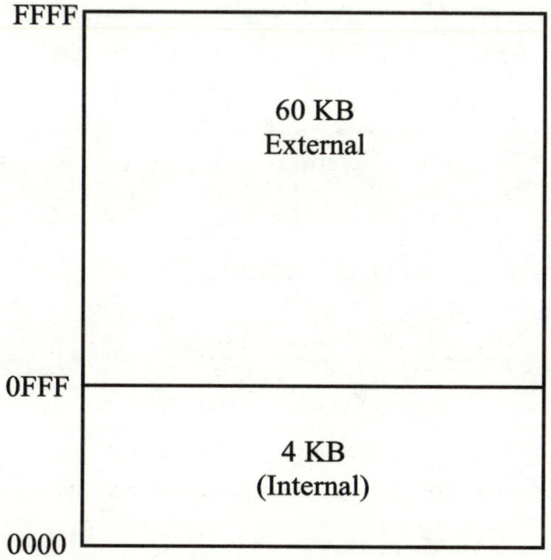

Figure 3-7: Program memory

In the program memory, each interrupt is assigned a memory location. When an interrupt is received, the CPU jumps to that location and executes the location-specific interrupt routine.

Data memory

Your application may use just the internal memory of the micro-controller, or you can have an external data memory device. The external data memory capacity is 64KB. The data memory organization for both internal and external memory, along with memory location addresses, is shown in Figure 3-8. Unlike the program memory, addressing the data memory is slightly complex.

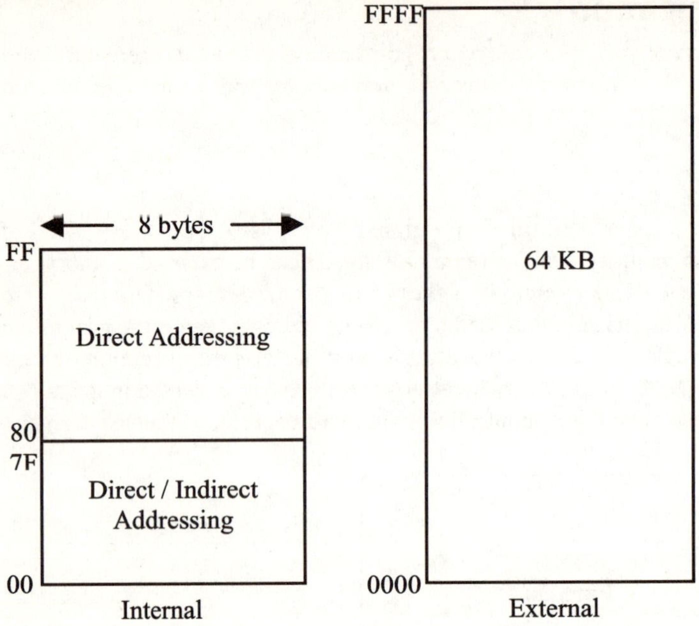

Figure 3-8: Data memory

For the data memory, the addressing can be done using either an 8-bit address or a 16-bit address. Because the internal data memory addresses have 8 bits, 256 bytes of internal data memory can be addressed.

There are two types of addressing modes: direct addressing and indirect addressing. When you want to add two numbers, you write an assembly language instruction such as the following:

```
ADD A, 6FH
```

The address of the operand is specified by an 8-bit address field (6F). This is known as direct addressing.

If you give an instruction such as

```
ADD A,@R0
```

the operand is a register that contains the address of the operand. This is known as indirect addressing.

The instruction set

The 8031 family of micro-controllers supports a large number of instructions with different addressing modes. However, for regular programming, you generally use a few instructions. The instructions can be classified into five groups based on their functionality:

- Arithmetic group
- Logical group
- Data transfer group
- Boolean group
- Jump group

The instructions in this group perform operations such as addition, subtraction, multiplication, and division. Each instruction takes two arguments and carries out the arithmetic operation.

Mnemonic	*Description*
ADD	Adds two byte variables
SUB	Substracts the source byte from the destination byte
MUL	Multiplies two unsigned 8-bit integer values
DIV	Divides an unsigned 8-bit integer value from another unsigned 8-bit integer value

The logical group instructions perform operations such as logical AND, logical OR, logical XOR (Exclusive OR), and NOT. These instructions perform Boolean operations on bytes on a bit-by-bit basis.

Mnemonic	*Description*
ANL	Logical AND for byte variables
ORL	Logical OR for byte variables
XRL	Logical Exclusive OR for byte variables

The instructions of this group are for data movement between internal/external RAM.

Mnemonic	*Description*
MOV	Moves the byte variable value from source byte to destination byte

The instructions in this group perform operations such as AND, OR, Clear, and the setting and testing of bit variables.

Mnemonic	*Description*
SETB bit	Sets the indicated bit to one
CLR bit	Clears the indicated bit to zero

This group of instructions carries out operations such as jumping to a particular address to call a subroutine and to return from a called routine.

Mnemonic	***Description***
LJMP address16	Unconditional branch to the indicated address
LCALL address16	Calls a subroutine located at the indicated address
RET	Return from subroutine

Note one special instruction as follows:

```
NOP
```

This indicates no operation. This instruction is used to insert additional clock cycles. If you want to generate a pulse that lasts for five machine cycles, you issue a CLR instruction followed by four NOP instructions.

16-Bit and 32-Bit Processors

Processors with data word-lengths of 16 bits and 32 bits have much higher processing power than the 8-bit micro-controllers just described. However, unlike the micro-controller, these processors do not include much built-in peripheral circuitry, which you need to build externally.

Addressing capability is another issue. If addressing is done using 16 bits, the maximum directly addressable memory capacity is only 64KB. The 16-bit and 32-bit processors provide much higher memory handling capability. For instance, if you use 32-bit addressing, you can directly address approximately 4GB of memory.

A variety of processors with data word-lengths of 16 bits and 32 bits are now available from semiconductor vendors such as ARM, Atmel, Intel, Motorola, National Semiconductors, and Siemens. It can be daunting to choose a 16-bit or 32-bit processor because most of them have almost the same capabilities in terms of clock frequency, processing power (expressed in MIPS), and memory addressing. The best approach is to obtain an evaluation board for the processor of your choice and then do your development on this board. A costly suggestion indeed! Many embedded systems developers choose a processor based on their experience and familiarity with a family of processors from a given vendor. Many people ask me for advice as to which DSP to choose — Analog Devices or Texas Instruments — and I can never give an answer! In addition to experience, one needs to consider the cost of development tools, support provided by the local distributor, design support, and so on. All of these considerations factor into a decision to regarding which particular processor to use.

If you want to experiment with an ARM processor, you can get an evaluation board. Along with the evaluation board hardware, you will also be supplied with a developer's toolkit containing the firmware and debug monitor. Using the evaluation board, you can work through the entire life cycle of embedded software development to ascertain its suitability for the applications to be developed for your organization. Every vendor offers a family of processors with different MIPS ratings. For instance, the ARM family of processors has wide-ranging capabilities — from 100 MIPS to 1000 MIPS.

The next example you will consider uses a high-end processor, rather than an 8-bit microcontroller. The following section describes the architecture of a handheld computer based on the 32-bit processor.

Example: 32-bit processor–based handheld computer

For smooth functioning, a handheld computer needs to run an operating system such as Palm OS, Windows CE, or Symbian OS; and it has to provide applications such as word processing, a calendar, an appointment diary, a calculator, etc. It should also have a provision for connecting to a desktop PC through some standard interface. In addition, it should be capable of being connected to a LAN through the Ethernet interface, as well as a capability to be connected to a Personal Area Network using Bluetooth. A handheld computer also needs to support audio capability through a microphone and speaker. Finally, for input/output operations, it should have an LCD display and a keypad, preferably a full-fledged keyboard.

After fulfilling each of these requirements, you end up with the block diagram shown in Figure 3-9. Obviously, you need a high-end, 32-bit processor. The memory is required for storing the operating system and application software packages and also the protocol stacks corresponding to Bluetooth, TCP/IP for network connectivity, etc. Based on these memory requirements, you can approximate the memory capability of ROM and RAM, as shown in the figure. The communication interfaces provided are RS 232 for serial communication; infrared communication for point-to-point communication with other devices, such as a mobile phone; the USB interface for connection to the desktop computer; Bluetooth for PAN; and Ethernet for LAN connectivity. The special circuitry codec (coder and decoder) is needed for voice-related functionality.

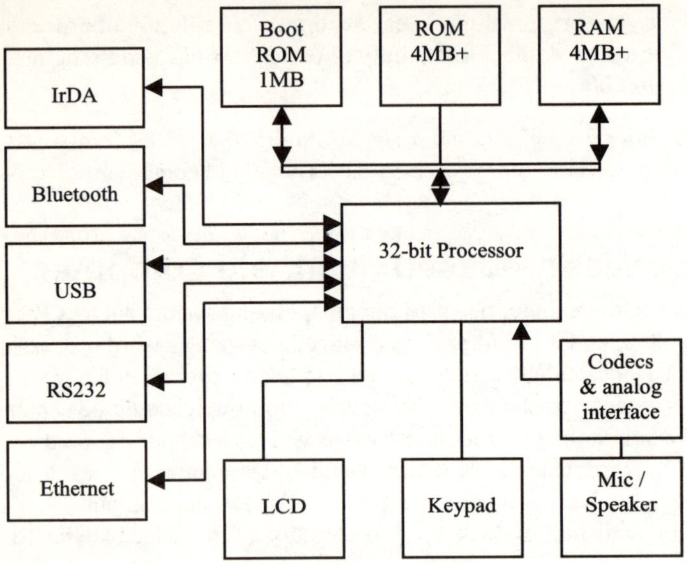

Figure 3-9: Handheld computer architecture

DSP Architecture

The rapid growth in the DSP market is driven by its multifaceted utility in the field of communications. Current applications include voice coding, video coding, modulation and demodulation, voice-over-IP protocols implementation, echo cancellation, filtering, cellular phones, infrastructure equipment for telecommunications, high-speed modems for accessing the Internet, etc.

A DSP is a microprocessor specially designed to handle mathematically intensive algorithm implementation. A typical audio processing application involves taking a speech signal in analog format, converting it into digital format using an ADC, and then processing it. The speech samples have to be processed by filtering them and calculating the filter coefficients based on the sample values, carrying out analysis in frequency domain. All of these operations involve intensive mathematical computations. To execute these operations, the DSP architecture has the following features not available in regular processors:

- A Multiply-and-Accumulate (MAC) module that can calculate sums very fast, whereas a general-purpose processor may take many cycles to compute one multiplication
- Support for bit manipulation through bit-shifting operations. A shifter is used for this operation.
- Separate address-generation units to generate the addresses for memory locations so that access to memory is faster

- Special hardware to implement loops. Through hardware, you can increment the loop counter, compare the counter value with the final target value, branch to the top of the loop after executing the loop, etc.

DSPs are classified as *fixed-point* DSPs and *floating-point* DSPs. Fixed-point DSPs can carry out mathematical operations only on fixed-point numbers, and floating-point DSPs can handle floating-point numbers only. Typically, 16-bit DSPs are used for fixed-point arithmetic, and 32-bit DSPs are used for floating-point arithmetic. Though the prices of DSPs are dropping, floating-point DSPs are much costlier than fixed-point DSPs.

Fixed-point DSPs are characterized by low precision, low power consumption, and low cost. Though floating-point DSPs are costly, their computation power is much higher. Therefore, these DSPs are the right choice for high-end applications such as video processing, image recognition systems, etc.

The leading DSP suppliers include Analog Devices, Lucent Technologies, Motorola, and Texas Instruments.

Figure 3-10 shows the architecture of a typical DSP, through a simplified version of the Analog Devices DSP ADSP 218x family. This architecture is called the *Harward Memory architecture*. The advantage of this architecture is that it has two buses (data bus and address bus) through which two separate memory blocks can be accessed. Like any other processor-based system, it has a program memory and data memory, Arithmetic and Logic Unit (ALU), serial ports for external interface, programmable input/output pins, and timer circuitry. As mentioned earlier, Multiply-and-Accumulate module, shifter and Data Address Generators are the special modules in DSP. DSPs also support power control modes to conserve power when the processor is not in a fully operational state.

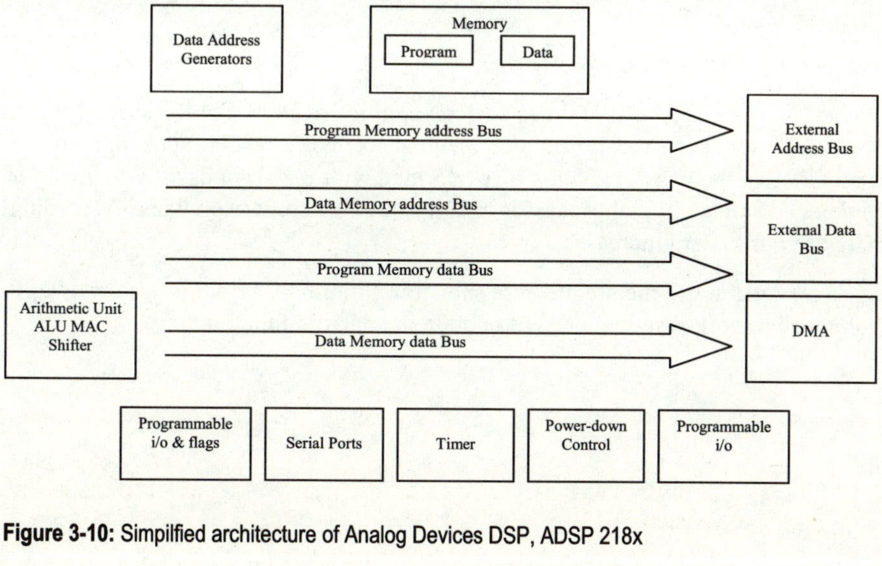

Figure 3-10: Simpilfied architecture of Analog Devices DSP, ADSP 218x

Example: Speech recognition system using DSP

You can better understand how a DSP works by examining a simple DSP application. Figure 3-11 shows how a speech recognition system can be built using a DSP. The desired functionality of this system is that it be able to recognize a 100-word vocabulary. You first need to speak these 100 words and store the corresponding data in ROM. This data is stored as templates. When you speak any of these 100 words, the system has to process the speech data corresponding to that word, compare this data with the templates, and recognize the particular word that closely matches the spoken word. Clearly, the entire procedure involves intensive processing of speech signals, so DSP is the right choice.

The functional blocks needed for the speech recognition system are a filter, ADC, DSP, and a comparator to compare the stored templates with the input word's parameters. The filter limits the speech signal to the desired bandwidth. The ADC converts the speech signal into digital format. The DSP analyzes the speech signal and obtains the speech parameters. Generally, parameters known as *Linear Prediction Coefficients* (*LPC parameters*) are obtained from the speech signal. The calculation of LPC parameters involves highly mathematical computations (in fact, solving simultaneous equations). Once the word's LPC parameters are computed, they need to be compared with the LPC parameters stored as templates for the 100 words. Figure 3-11 shows the process of the speech recognition system through its functional blocks.

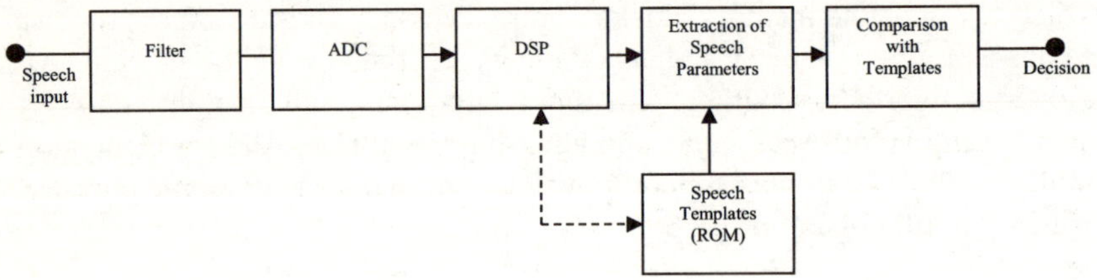

Figure 3-11: DSP-based speech recogntion system

Now we come to the working speed of the speech recognition system. For the system shown in Figure 3-11, a word may not be recognized until several seconds after it is spoken. However, if you want to require that the word-matching be performed within 2 seconds after the word is uttered, then you need an additional processor to carry out the comparison work. Accordingly, the complexity of your system increases.

In such a case, you need to use the architecture shown in Figure 3-12. In this system, a DSP and a micro-controller work simultaneously to obtain the desired functionality.

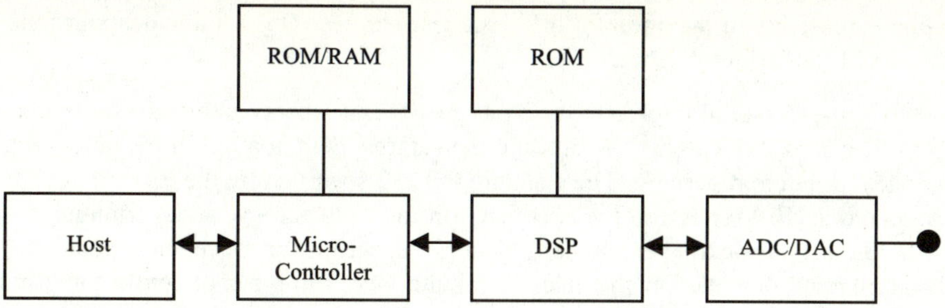

Figure 3-12: Combining DSP and a micro-controller

Choosing a DSP

As you have seen, using a DSP is a must when you do exhaustive signal processing for applications involving audio processing, video processing, image analysis, fingerprint analysis, etc. Such applications involve highly mathematical computations, analysis in frequency domain, etc.

Choosing the right DSP is an important task. A floating-point DSP generally has a 32-bit word-length and, therefore, a higher dynamic range and higher precision. Fixed-point DSPs are available with word-lengths of 16 bits, 20 bits, and 24 bits. Compared to fixed-point DSPs, they offer lower precision but are cheaper.

Another important aspect regarding selection of a DSP is programming. Programming a floating-point DSP is much easier, as you can use the floating-point variables and operations. If you choose a fixed-point DSP, the program needs to be converted to handle only fixed-point numbers. This is no easy task.

Applications such as high-fidelity audio and high-resolution video essentially require a 32-bit floating-point DSP. For speech processing applications and modem applications, for example, fixed-point DSPs are ideal and they will keep the cost of the system low.

Communication Interface Standards

To interface an embedded system with the external world, a number of interfaces are used, such as the serial interface, the Ethernet interface, USB, IEEE 1394, etc. All these interfaces provide different functionality and different data-transmission rates. Based on your requirements, you need to select the right interface. The following sections provide an overview of the commonly used interfaces.

Serial interface/UART

Almost every processor provides a serial interface for interfacing with the external device. You will study the programming aspects of the serial interface in Chapter 6, and also use serial communication extensively in the book for different case studies. This section describes the hardware aspects of the serial interface.

As the name suggests, the serial interface sends out the data and receives the data bit by bit in a serial format. The hardware catches the bits and then stores them in a buffer by converting the bits into bytes for later processing. The standard RS 232 specified by the Electronic Industries Association (EIA) specifies the necessary protocols to achieve serial communication accurately. RS 232 is a physical layer standard; hence, it specifies the mechanical and electrical interface requirements. For the mechanical interface, two types of connectors can be used: the 9-pin connector and the 25-pin connector, which we normally use on our desktops. For the electrical interface, the electrical signals carried by each of the 25 pins are specified. However, normally the following pins are used:

- Pin 1: Protective ground
- Pin 7: Signal common (connected to pin 1 for common ground)
- Pin 2: Transmit Data (TD)
- Pin 3: Receive Data (RD)
- Pin 4: Request To Send (RTS)
- Pin 5: Clear To Send (CTS)
- Pin 6: Data Set Ready (DSR)
- Pin 8: Data Carrier Detect (DCD)
- Pin 20: Data Terminal Ready (DTR)
- Pin 22: Ring Indicator

The preceding pins are commonly used when you connect your modem to the computer. You can connect two PCs directly without any modem using what is called a *null modem*. To connect two PCs, you need to connect the Pin 2 of one system to the Pin 3 of the other system and vice versa.

For transmission of 1s and 0s, the voltage levels are defined in the standard. The voltage levels differ for data signals and control signals, as shown in the following table:

Signal	***Voltage Levels***
Data input	+3volts and above for 0 -3 volts and below for 1
Data output	+5 volts and above 0 -5 volts and below 1
Control input	+3 volts and above for 1 (ON) -3 volts and below for 0 (OFF)

Control output	+5 volts and above for 1 (ON) - 5 volts and below for 0 (OFF)

As you can see in the table, an important feature is that the input and output signal levels are different. Also note that the voltage levels used are different from the voltages available on computers and the voltages used in embedded systems (mostly 5 volts and below, as most chips use these voltages only). To overcome this problem, the hardware used for the RS 232 interface is a bit different, as shown in Figure 3-13.

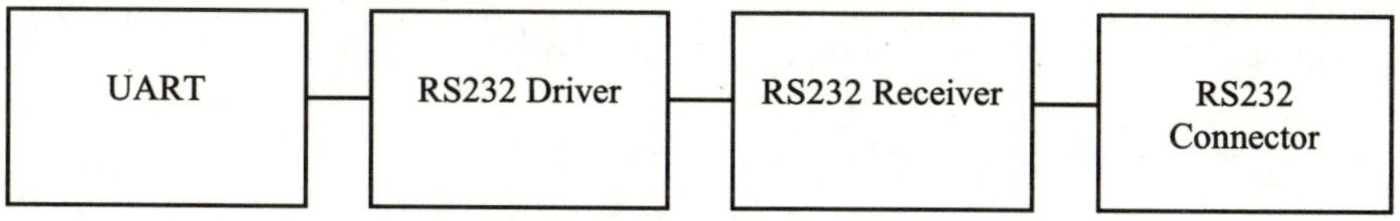

Figure 3-13: Hardware for the RS232 interface

Here, a UART (Universal Asynchronous Receive Transmit) chip is used, which operates off 5 volts. RS 232 driver chips and RS 232 receiver chips do the necessary level conversions as per the preceding table, and the signals are passed on to the RS 232 connector.

The RS 232 standard specifies a maximum distance of 19.2 meters, though in practice you can achieve up to 100 meters. The data transmission rates supported by the serial interface mainly depend on the UART chip. Most of the chips currently used in computers can support data rates up to 115 Kbps. Embedded systems typically use data rates of 4,800 bps, 9,600 bps, etc.

For serial communication between two devices, you specify the following parameters: data bits, parity and stop bits. The number of bits that form a character is specified by data bits; it can be 5, 6, 7, or 8. The parity detects any errors in transmission. Parity can be even, odd, or none. If even parity is set, an additional parity bit is added to the data bits to make the total number of 1s even. Similarly, for odd parity, a parity bit is added to make the total number of 1s odd. Parity of none indicates that no parity is set. Stop bits are added to indicate when the data bits stop. If the data bits are 5 or 6, 2 stop bits are added. Because no clock is transmitted, it is called *asynchronous communication*.

IEEE 1394

Apple Computers initiated the development of a mechanism to interconnect consumer devices using a serial bus, known as *Firewire*. Firewire led to the development of a standard known as IEEE 1394. This is a high-speed serial bus standard to connect PCs and consumer items such as printers, digital TVs, digital VCRs, CD players, digital cameras, etc. How the various consumer items can be connected using the IEEE 1394 bus is depicted in Figure 3-14(a). A restriction for this type of connection is that devices cannot be connected in loops. In addition, the cable length between nodes cannot exceed 4.5 meters.

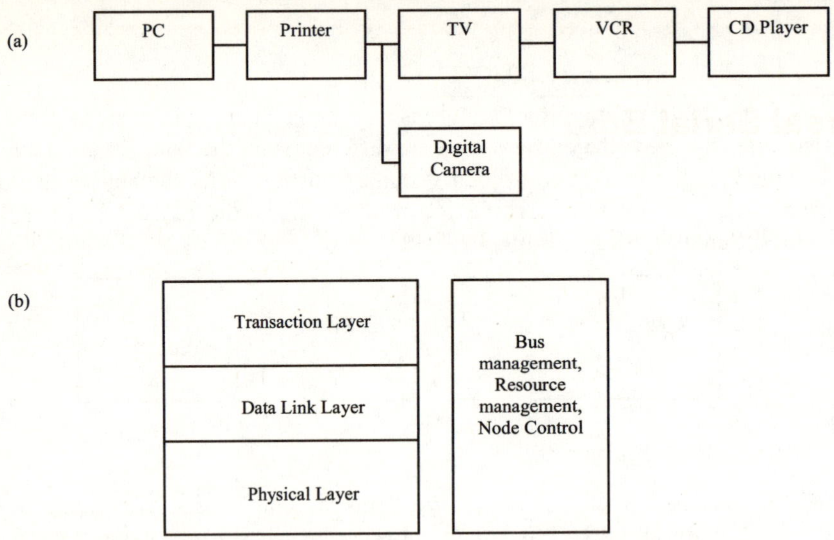

Figure 3-14: IEEE 1394 (a) Connecting devices through IEEE 1394 bus (b) Protocol architecture

The IEEE 1394 bus provides plug-and-play capability to the consumer devices. *Hot insertion* is also supported, i.e., you can insert or remove devices when the bus is active. The bus supports peer-to-peer communication; hence, you can connect any two devices even if a PC is not present.

Each node or device on the bus is given a 6-bit ID, and a maximum of 63 devices can be connected on a single bus. Using bridges, you can connect multiple buses. Each bus is given a 10-bit ID, and you can interconnect up to 1,023 buses to create a large network of devices. The standard supports data rates of 100, 200, and 400 Mbps, which is being extended to support 800, 1,600, and 3,200 Mbps. The transmission medium to interconnect the devices can be copper or optical fiber.

Because the devices share a bus, you need full-fledged layered protocols for communication between the devices. The protocol architecture is shown in Figure 3-14(b), and its components are described in the following list:

- **Physical layer:** This layer specifies the electrical and mechanical connections. Bus initialization and arbitration are the functions of this layer, ensuring that only one node is sending the data at a time.
- **Data Link layer:** The functions of this layer are data packet delivery, acknowledgements, and addressing of the devices on the bus.
- **Transaction layer:** This layer handles writing and reading of the data from the devices.
- **Bus management protocols:** These protocols are used to manage the bus, and they run on each of the connected devices.

In other words, the IEEE 1394 interface to a consumer item is itself an embedded system. Many future consumer items will have this interface.

Universal Serial Bus

The Universal Serial Bus (`www.usb.org`) standard specifies the interconnection between a host such as a PC and peripheral devices such as the keyboard, the mouse, printers, audio/video equipment, etc. USB has gained popularity in recent years. Most desktop motherboard manufacturers provide the USB interface to connect devices with the desktop.

The USB 1.1 standard supports data rates up to 12 Mbps, and the latest version, USB 2.0, supports 480-Mbps data rates. This is a hot-pluggable plug-and-play standard, i.e., you can connect the devices to the USB port without switching off the PC, and automatically the device will be recognized.

USB devices are controlled by a host, such as a PC. USB is based on the master/slave protocol; hence, two devices cannot talk to each other directly, but only through the host. A maximum of 127 devices can be connected in a hierarchical fashion, as shown in Figure 3-15.

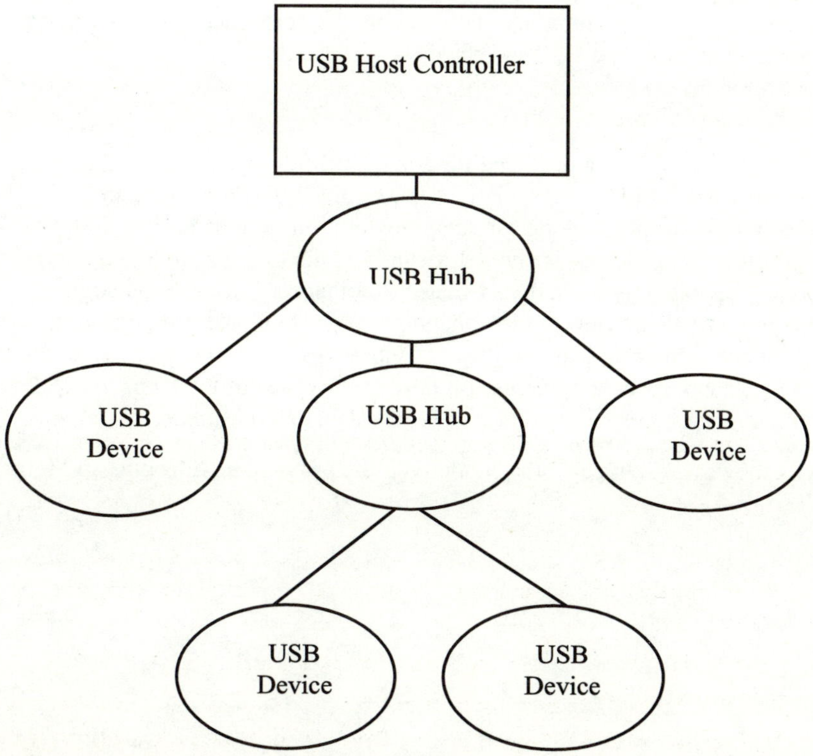

Figure 3-15: USB devices connected as a hierarchy

On the host system is a host controller, a combination of hardware and software that controls all of the USB devices. The host controller is integrated into most of the motherboard chips, and the driver software is provided either with the operating system or as a separate software package. You can connect devices to the host either directly or through *hubs*. A hub is also a USB device that extends the number of ports — from 2 to 8 — to connect other USB devices. These devices can be self-powered, powered by the bus, or both. USB can supply 500 milliAmperes current to the devices. Two types of USB devices are available: low-speed devices (such as the keyboard and the mouse) that support data rates up to 1.5 Mbps; and full-speed devices (such as audio and video systems) that support data rates up to 12 Mbps.

Each USB device is given a unique device number (1 to 127) and a device descriptor that provides information about the device class and its properties. The various device classes defined are display, communication, audio, mass storage, and human interface (such as keyboards, front panel knobs, control panels in VCRs, data gloves, etc.).

USB device drivers and USB host controller drivers are required for the USB operation. Windows XP supports USB 2.0. Office automation equipment, handheld PCs, laptops, etc., are now using the USB interface. In addition, USB-enabled video cameras, voice-over-IP telephones, and printers are now becoming available. Soon, the embedded systems will be connected to the peripherals using the USB interface.

IrDA

Nowadays, the IrDA interface is being provided for a number of devices, such as PCs, mobile phones, PDAs, etc. The Infra Red Data Association (IrDA) developed this interface to interconnect devices in point-to-point mode for data transfer with support for bi-directional communication. The range of IR device is about 1 meter; i.e., the devices communicating using IR should not be separated by more than 1 meter. Another restriction is the angle between the two devices known as view angle—the view angle should be + or -15 degrees. The data transmission rate supported is in the range of 9,600 bps to 4 Mbps. Infra Red Physical Layer Link (IrPHY) 1.0 supports data transmission rates in the range of 9.6 Kbps to 115.2 Kbps, and IrPHY 1.1 supports rates in the range of 115.2 Kbps to 4.0 Mbps.

The IrDA module is shown in Figure 3-16(a), along with the protocol architecture, in Figure 3-16(b).

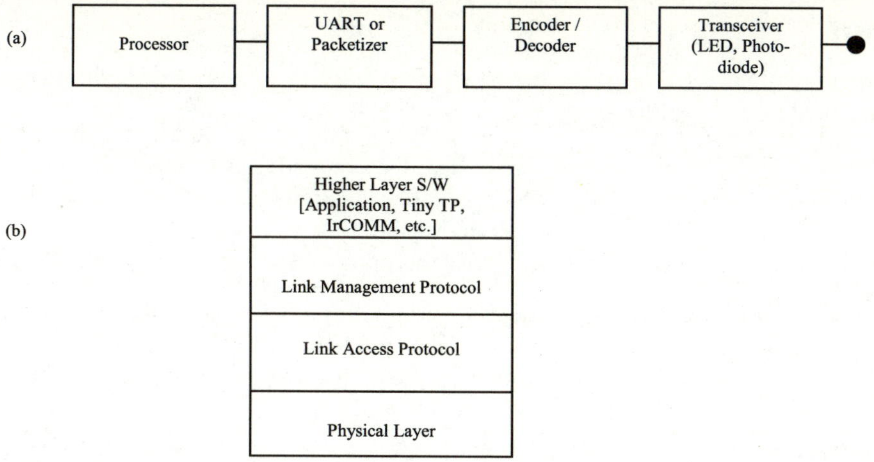

Figure 3-16: (a) IrDA module (b) Protocol layers

As shown in Figure 3-16(a), a transceiver transmits and receives infrared waves. The transceiver consists of a single LED and a photodiode to transmit/receive infrared rays. This transceiver is a very low-cost item; hence, at a little additional cost, an infrared interface can be provided for the devices. The transmission can be performed either in the serial format using UART or through the packet format. For error detection, 16-bit CRC is provided.

The protocol architecture for infrared communication is shown in Figure 3-16(b). The physical layer gives the specification for electrical signal characteristics. The Link Access Protocol (LAP) is based on HDLC (High-Level Data Link Control) protocols to ensure the reliable transfer of data. The Link Management Protocol (LMP) provides multiplexing of the data and the mechanism to discover what services are offered by another peer device with which it has to communicate. Above the LMP, other protocols are implemented, such as Tiny TP, a lightweight Transport Protocol that handles flow control, segmentation, and the re-assembly of packets; IrCOMM, to emulate serial or parallel communication; and other application layer software.

Although the infrared interface provides a low-cost method to transfer data between two devices (for example, to transfer e-mails from a desktop to a mobile phone), its major drawback is that it is only for point-to-point communication; i.e., a device can communicate with only one device at a time and data cannot be broadcast to multiple devices. Nonetheless, it is useful in process control embedded systems in which the data from an embedded system has to be transferred to a handheld PC when there are no obstructions such as walls between the PC and the embedded system.

Ethernet

Ethernet, based on the IEEE 802.3 standard, is the most popular interface for computer networking. With the availability of low-cost Ethernet chips, you can have an Ethernet-enabled embedded system that provides data transmission rates up to 100 Mbps. Ethernet chips can be integrated into high-end processor-based systems such as handheld computers, communicators, etc. Over the Ethernet (which specifies the protocols for the physical and data link layers), the complete TCP/IP stack is run to provide connectivity to a corporate intranet or the Internet. Networked embedded appliances use this approach to become network-enabled.

Another LAN standard, IEEE 802.11, is the standard for wireless LANs. With wireless LAN chips available at low cost, this is another communication alternative for embedded systems, particularly mobile devices. This standard supports data transmission rates up to 11 Mbps.

Bluetooth

A low-cost radio technology, Bluetooth is gaining popularity. Numerous devices can be Bluetooth-enabled, including PCs, mobile phones, handheld PCs, cameras, LCD projectors, headsets, air conditioners, etc. Bluetooth enables mobile phones to control appliances such as air-conditioners, VCRs, or TVs. The Bluetooth module is a single-chip or two-chip solution, and it can be integrated into any consumer item with little additional cost. It is popular because it works in the 2.4 GHz ISM (Industrial, Scientific and Medical) band, which does not require any approvals from government authorities.

A Bluetooth-enabled device can discover another Bluetooth-enabled device automatically when the two devices come in the vicinity of each other. The maximum distance between the two devices is 10 meters, although with high-power radio, it can be increased to 100 meters. The data rate supported is 1 Mbps. Bluetooth supports both point-to-point and point-to-multipoint communication. It has support for both data and voice services. Bluetooth is the ideal choice for forming Personal Area Networks (PANs) in the office, in the home, or even in a car. This technology is equally suited for networking a set of embedded systems, which can share data.

The Bluetooth hardware module configuration is shown in Figure 3-17. The hardware module consists of a radio, a baseband controller, and link management software — all integrated into a single chip or two chips. The Host Control Interface provides the interface to the host (the device to which the Bluetooth module is connected, such as a mobile phone). On the host (the mobile phone), the higher-layer software will be running, and the interaction takes place between the hardware module and the software. The higher layer software stack is available from a number of vendors. If you want to integrate Bluetooth into your embedded system, you need to port the protocol software onto your embedded system's platform and connect the Bluetooth hardware module to your hardware.

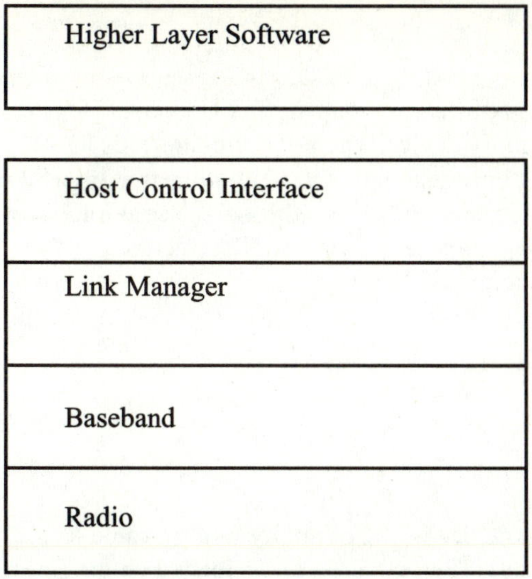

Figure 3-17: Bluetooth hardware module

PCI bus

If you are developing an embedded system that has to sit in a PC motherboard, the PCI (Peripheral Component Interface) bus interface is required. As discussed in Chapter 2, for applications such as virtual instrumentation, this architecture is required. Earlier, PCs had support for ISA (Industry Standard Architecture) and Extended ISA (EISA) architecture-based input/output slots on the motherboards. Though the industrial computers still provide EISA slots, PCI bus is now the standard bus available on the desktop motherboards. It has almost replaced the ISA, which supports data transfer rates of 5 Mbps.

PCI specifies mechanical and electrical requirements as well as the control and transfer protocols for the input/output cards that are placed in the motherboards. As compared to ISA and EISA, the data rates supported by PCI are very high. The standard specifies data rates of 132 Mbps at 33 MHz clock for 32-bit data path, and of 524 Mbps at 66 MHz clock for 64-bit data path. Many interactive voice response system cards, virtual instrumentation cards, software radio cards, etc., now use the PCI interface.

Development Tools

After you develop the embedded software on the host system, you need to transfer the program onto a memory chip on the target processor board. For this you need a few development tools. The following sections provide an overview of these tools.

EPROM programmer

To transfer data into the memory devices (such as EPROM, EPLD, FPGA, micro-controllers, flash, EEPROM, etc.), you need a programmer. Nowadays, you can find Universal Device Programmers that can program any type of memory device. The programmer needs RAM, a keyboard, and a display mechanism. One type of programmer is a stand-alone unit on which you place the memory device; the data is transferred to the device through a serial interface connected to the PC. Other types of programmers provide a serial/parallel interface to the computer and use the RAM and display of the computer.

The programming process involves three steps:

1. Blank checking
2. Program loading
3. Verification

In blank checking, it is determined whether the device is OK or not by writing some data (FFFF) into the memory device and reading it out. Then the program is loaded on the device and verification is done. Verification can be done by calculating the CRC.

While selecting a programmer, you need to check the following specifications:

- Types of devices that can be programmed
- Capacities of the devices to be programmed (e.g., flash, 8 Mbits; EPROM, 16 Mbits)
- The interface to the computer from which data has to be transferred
- The number of pins for supporting the memory devices
- Whether the programmer supports both 3V and 5V devices
- The time taken for a given (say, 8 Mbits) memory chip (typical values are given in parentheses)
  - Time for blank checking (15 seconds for 8 Mbit)
  - Time for program loading (45 seconds for 8 Mbits)
  - Time for verification (30 seconds for 8 Mbits)

EPROM Eraser

To erase the contents of an EPROM chip, you need a special device called the *EPROM Eraser*. You have to keep the EPROM device in an IC holder, and the Eraser applies ultraviolet radiation to the chip to erase the contents. Low-end Erasers erase only one EPROM chip at a time. High-end Erasers, in micro-controller-based embedded systems, can erase numerous chips simultaneously. Note that EPROM chips come with different pins — 28-pin and 40-pin chips are the most common. Some EPROM programmers are capable of erasing chips with different pin configurations. While selecting the EPROM Eraser, the following specifications need to be checked:

- The number of pins supported for the EPROM device
- How many devices can be simultaneously erased
- The erase time (this can range from 10 seconds to 3 minutes)
- The support for 3V and 5V devices

Signature validators

When you load a program onto a memory device, you would like to check the validity of the data, which you can do by calculating the CRC of the data. Devices are available that can compute the CRC using standard CRC algorithms, and then they store that signature on the chip. These devices are called *signature validators*.

The embedded system designers develop the software on a host system and then transfer the data onto the memory devices using the development tools discussed above. Before writing the application software, the embedded software developers need to write software to check whether the hardware is functioning properly. This hardware-software interaction is discussed in the next section.

Hardware-Software Interaction

Once your target hardware is ready and the software is loaded onto the memory, your embedded system is ready. However, if nothing happened after the software were loaded, what would you do? You need to do some low-level programming to find out the health of the hardware modules. In many embedded system projects, the appearance of errors leads to frequent fights between the hardware and software engineers. The hardware engineers say that the software is not working, and you can guess what the software engineers say. You can always put some debugging software within the program to find out to what extent the software is OK, but what if the software does not even start running? You need to incorporate simple test routines.

Self-testing

Just as your desktop does a self-test on power-up, your embedded system also needs to do a self-test. This includes the testing of memory, peripherals, etc. Cyclic Redundancy Check (CRC) is the standard method to test the memory. CRC is extensively used to test stored or transmitted data. This is because storing data is also a form of transmission — transmission from one unit to another. When you transmit some data, you calculate the CRC (in a 16-bit or 32-bit pattern) by dividing the bit stream with a polynomial. The result of this division is the CRC. When you transmit the data, you append the CRC bits to the original data and send the bit stream. At the receiving end, you recalculate the CRC and compare the received CRC with the calculated CRC. If they match, the data received is correct; otherwise, some error occurred in the transmission. The mathematical algorithm is used in both communication systems and memory testing.

The software presented in Listing 3-1 provides a program for calculating the CRC. It should give you some insight into system-level programming — how to manipulate the bits of the data stream.

To calculate the CRC, three standard algorithms are available: CCITT, CRC 16, and CRC 32. The data is divided by a polynomial, and the checksum is calculated. The polynomial is different for three standards. The checksum obtained by the division is the CRC, which is 16 bits for CCITT and CRC 16, and 32 bits for CRC 32. Table 3-1 summarizes the three standards.

Table 3-1: CRC Standards

Parameter	***CCITT***	***CRC 16***	***CRC 32***
Checksum (width of CRC)	16	16	32
Generator polynomial	$x^{16}+x^{12}+x^5+1$	$x^{16}+x^{15}+x^2+1$	$x^{32}+x^{26}+x^{23}+x^{22}+x^{16}+x^{12}+x^{11}+x^{10}+x^8+x^7+x^5+x^4+x^2+x+1$
Divisor (hexadecimal value)	0x1021	0x8005	0x04C11DB7

The program for CRC calculation takes a string and calculates the checksum. In addition to checking memory, this program is used extensively in communication systems for checking whether the data transmitted was received correctly. As it illustrates how to manipulate bits, rather than bytes, it provides an interesting case study of system-level programming. We use the bit manipulation operators of the C language to write the following program.

Source code listing for CRC32.cpp

Listing 3-1 describes the method for calculating the CRC for the message "Hello World" using the CRC32 polynomial.

Listing 3-1: Source code for CRC32.cpp

```
#include <iostream.h>
#include <cassert>
#include <string.h>

unsigned long CRC32 = 0x00000000L;
const unsigned long GenPolynomial = 0x04c11db7L; // Divisor for CRC32 Polynomial

void bitByBit(bool bit);

void main()
{
unsigned int MsgLength,OrgLength,Shift;
std::string SampleMsg ("Hello World");
```

```
OrgLength = SampleMsg.length();
std::cout<<"Actual Message : "<<SampleMsg<<std::endl<<std::endl;
SampleMsg.resize(OrgLength + 4); // Appending 32(8*4) 0 bits to the Message
MsgLength = SampleMsg.length();
std::cout<<"Message After Appending 32 '0' bits : ";
for(int i = 0;i<MsgLength;++i)
{
  unsigned char ch = SampleMsg[i];
  unsigned char mask = 0x80;
  for (int j = 0; j < 8; ++j)
  {
    bitByBit(ch & mask);
    mask >>= 1;
  }
    std::cout<<" ";
}
std::cout<<std::endl<<std::endl<<"Calculated CRC :0x"<<std::hex<<CRC32;
std::cout<<std::endl<<std::endl<<std::endl;


std::cout<<"+++++++++++++++++++++++++++++++++++++++++++++++++++++++++++++++++++++++++"<<std::endl<<std::endl;

Shift = 32;
for (int k = 0; k < 4; ++k)
{
 Shift -= 8;
 SampleMsg[OrgLength + k] = static_cast<unsigned char> (CRC32 >> Shift);
}
CRC32 = 0;
MsgLength = SampleMsg.length();
std::cout<<"Message To be Transmited (Actual Message + CRC) : ";
for(int l = 0;l<MsgLength;++l)
{
 unsigned char ch = SampleMsg[l];
 unsigned char mask = 0x80;
 for (int m = 0; m < 8; ++m)
 {
   bitByBit(ch & mask);
   mask >>= 1;
 }
 std::cout<<" ";
}
std::cout<<std::endl<<std::endl<<"ReCalculated CRC :0x"<<std::hex<<CRC32;
std::cout<<std::endl<<std::endl<<std::endl;
```

```
55. }
56:
57. void bitByBit(bool bit)
58. {
59.  std::cout<<bit;
60. bool firstBit = (CRC32 & 0x80000000L);
61.  CRC32 = CRC32 << 1;
62.  CRC32 = CRC32^bit;
63.  if (firstBit)
64. {
65.   CRC32 = CRC32 ^ GenPolynomial;
66.  }
67. }
```

Following is the line-by-line explanation of the source code.

- **Lines 1–3:** Header file declaration.
- **Lines 4–5:** Constants declaration. `0x04c11db7L` is constant for CRC-32 polynomial.
- **Line 6:** Prototype declaration of `bitByBit` function.
- **Lines 8–55:** Definition of the `Main` function.
  - **Line 11:** Assigning the message to be transmitted "Hello World" to `SampleMsg`.
  - **Line 13:** Printing the `SampleMsg`.
  - **Line 14:** Appending thirty-two 0 bits to the `SampleMsg`.
  - **Lines 17–27:** Reading each character of the `SampleMsg` and sending it to the `bitByBit` function one bit at a time.
  - **Lines 21–25:** Reading each bit of the character `ch` by masking and sending it to the `bitByBit` function for calculating CRC.
  - **Line 28:** Printing the calculated CRC.
  - **Lines 34-38:** Appending CRC to the actual message for transmitting.
  - **Lines 42-52:** Recalculating the CRC, which has to be calculated at the other end. The recalcuated CRC should be `0x00`. Otherwise, there is some error in the received message.
  - **Line 53:** Printing the recalculated CRC.
- **Lines 57-67:** Definition of method `bitByBit`, for calculating CRC bit by bit.

Executing the CRC calculation program

To test this CRC calculation program, you can initially execute the program on the desktop. Build the project in the Visual Studio environment. To calculate the CRC for various messages, change the message given in line 11 of Listing 3-1. The output screen looks like the one shown in Figure 3-18.

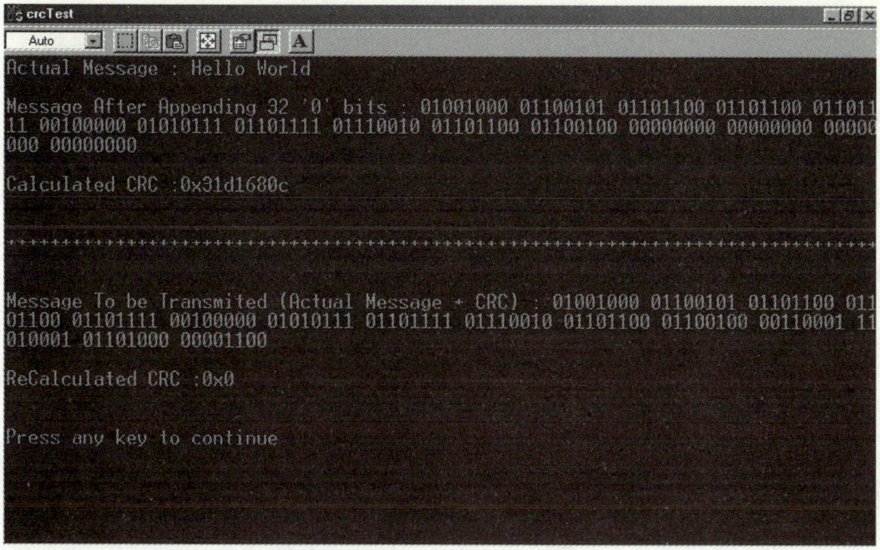

Figure 3-18: Output screen for CRC calculation

The source code for calculating CRC using CRC-16 and CCITT polynomials is similar to the code given in Listing 3-1, with the following modifications:

- For CRC16:
  - Line 5: `GenPolynomial = 0x8005;`
  - Line 14: SampleMsg.resize(OrgLength + 2);
  - Line 33: Shift = 16;
  - Line 60: bool firstBit = (CRC32 & 0x8000L);
- For CCITT:
  - Line 5: `GenPolynomial = 0x1021;`
  - Line 14: SampleMsg.resize(OrgLength + 2);
  - Line 33: Shift = 16;
  - Line 60: bool firstBit = (CRC32 & 0x8000L);

You can use a cross-compiler to convert this program into machine code for the target processor and use it for memory testing.

Summary

This chapter presented an overview of the hardware architectures for embedded systems. You examined the functional blocks of the general architecture of embedded hardware, along with 8031-based circuits and chip details. You also studied a typical application using a 32-bit processor and DSPs. You learned details about processors, memory modules, and associated circuitry. You also examined the details of various communication interfaces for embedded systems, and the development tools required. Finally, you learned how to develop memory-testing software using CRC. This chapter presents a basic introduction to the hardware embedded systems. The next two chapters describe the software of embedded systems.

Chapter 4
Developing for Embedded Systems

In This Chapter

- The software development process for embedded systems
- The steps in developing for embedded systems
- Issues involved in choosing the appropriate development platforms and tools

Writing software for embedded systems is certainly different from writing software for applications running on general-purpose desktops and mainframes. While writing software for embedded systems, you need to be cognizant of the constraints imposed by the embedded systems — namely, the limited processing power, limited memory, and limited input/output. This chapter describes the process of embedded software development, focusing on the discrete steps involved and the choices of development platforms and tools. Unlike in the 1970s and 1980s when the options for embedded software programmers were very limited, now developers have numerous options in terms of operating systems, processors, programming languages, and development tools. Understanding the process of embedded systems development and the options available will help you choose the right development environment for your projects.

Embedded System Development Process

In developing for embedded systems, you carry out the following steps:

1. Determine the requirements of the embedded system.
2. Design the system architecture.
3. Select the operating system.
4. Choose the processor and associated peripherals.
5. Choose the development platform.
6. Code the application and optimize the code according to code optimization guidelines.
7. Verify the software on the host system.
8. Verify the software on the target system.

Each of these steps is explained in the following sections.

Determine the requirements

The requirements of embedded systems can be broadly divided into functional requirements and nonfunctional requirements. The functional requirements are determined by the application's use. As discussed in Chapter 2, based on the application domain and the specifics of the application on hand, the functionality is obtained.

Based on functionality, embedded systems can be divided into one of the following two classes:

- **Multi-function systems:** These systems are capable of executing multiple applications simultaneously, such as capturing video signals and processing audio signals while Web browsing.
- **Multi-mode systems:** These systems offer users more than one mode of operation. Take, for example, a mobile device capable of handling voice calls from a terrestrial mobile network such as GSM (Global System for Mobile Communications) or from a satellite network such as International Maritime Satellite (INMARSAT). The mobile device processes only one set of protocols at a time and should be able to switch from one mode to another based on signal availability, without user input.

The computing and communication requirements for the two classes of embedded systems are different. In the case of multi-function systems, the computing requirements are much higher. In the case of multi-mode systems, two or more separate modules are required to cater to the different modes of operation.

The functional requirements dictate the hardware components, such as input/output peripheral components, and computing and communication components. These requirements provide the basis for the design of the hardware modules, which include the following:

- Application-specific hardware to process the input and output signals
- External interfaces such as serial interface, parallel interface, network interface (such as Ethernet), radio interface, etc.
- User input devices (e.g., function keypad, keyboard, buttons for carrying out specific operations)
- User output devices (e.g., LED display, LCD display)

After you determine the system's functional requirements, you need to determine the nonfunctional requirements as well. The most important nonfunctional requirements of embedded systems include size, cost, and power consumption. For highly specialized systems such as the ones used in nuclear power plants or process control systems, cost may not be a significant factor. However, for mass-market (consumer) products, cost is a critical consideration; therefore, hardware engineers must reduce the hardware components to the maximum possible extent. At this juncture, the hardware designers may want to consider using PLDs (Programmable Logic Devices) or FPGAs (Field Programmable Gate Arrays) to combine the hardware logic into a single-chip solution. Combining the discrete logic chips such as gates, flip-flops, and shift registers into a single chip reduces both cost and power consumption.

Design the system architecture

Knowing the system's functional and nonfunctional requirements is essential in planning the system architecture. The system architecture depends on the following factors:

- **Whether the system is a hard real-time system or a soft real-time system:** In the case of hard real-time systems, timing deadlines are very strict; therefore, timing analysis needs to be carried out in detail. In the case of soft real-time systems, timing deadlines are less stringent and can be missed occasionally without adversely affecting the performance of the system.
- **Whether an operating system needs to be embedded or not:** If the application involves very simple input/output operations, has only one or very few tasks to be handled, and only soft real-time performance is required, an operating system may not be necessary. You can build the necessary services by writing a small kernel. Otherwise, it is better to use an off-the-shelf operating system such as VxWorks or pSOS, thus accelerating the development process.
- **Whether cost, size of the physical system, and power consumption are critical for the success of the product:** If you are developing an embedded system for one customer for a specific application, some of these factors are not critical. However, if the system is for a mass market — as in the case of consumer electronic items — these factors are critical. Here, you need to consider the co-design issues in detail. In co-design, you need to determine if hardware or software implementation is the better choice. If the algorithms and computations to be used in the embedded system are likely to change, software implementation is the ideal choice. Hardware implementation of the modules requires more space, higher component cost, and greater power consumption. The production cost of hardware modules is higher than the production cost of the software (which is just the cost of copying the software to a memory chip). However, software implementation decreases the execution speed and calls for higher capacity memory chips, which are costly. The performance-intensive tasks that need to be carried out with critical time constraints must be implemented in hardware. Programmable algorithms can be implemented in software, particularly when flexibility and future enhancements are required. The hardware and software designers need to resolve these issues together. For mass-market embedded systems, initially a prototype is developed using readily available components, and once the design is proven, an Application Specific Integrated Circuit (ASIC) can be developed.
- **Choice of processor and related hardware:** The processor can be a micro-controller, a microprocessor, or a digital signal processor. Micro-controllers typically include the CPU, memory (RAM, ROM, or both), and other peripherals such as the serial communication controller. Intel 8051 family processors and Motorola 68HCxx series

processors fall into this category. For small applications, this will suffice; otherwise, a microprocessor is required. If the application involves signal processing such as audio or video processing, a DSP needs to be selected. In multi-function systems, the embedded system can contain a micro-controller or a microprocessor and a DSP, to cater to the different functionalities. Once the desired functionality is clearly identified, you must select the required peripherals, such as serial interface, parallel interface, Ethernet interface, audio in/out, video in/out, etc. You need to incorporate a host port interface, such as a serial interface if an external control is required. If you will need to access data from an external memory, DMA (Dynamic Memory Access) control circuitry is needed.

Based on these factors, you need to arrive at the basic system architecture, and then carry out detailed hardware and software design. The following sections describe the software aspects in detail.

Choose the operating system

For writing the embedded software, you have two options:

- Write the kernel yourself
- Use an off-the-shelf operating system (OS)

If the embedded software has to do a very small job, such as in toys, air conditioners, etc., there is no need for a full-fledged OS. For mass-market devices such as mobile phones, writing your own kernel avoids royalty issues. The functionality required can be achieved by writing your own code for processes such as input/output operations, memory management, and process management. However, if all the aforementioned services of the OS have to be provided, it is better to use an off-the-shelf OS. These operating systems provide the necessary APIs for task scheduling, interrupt handling, input/output management, memory management, and file management. Advantages of an operating system include the following:

- The APIs can be used to obtain the necessary operating system services, making the development faster.
- The code will be easy to maintain, as the application software will be written in a high-level language.
- There is no need to know the intricacies of the hardware; nor does the programmer need to learn the assembly language of the target processor, as the operating system services need to be implemented in an assembly language.

However, note that the OS used in embedded software is designed to have a small footprint; therefore, it does have some limitations:

- There will be no graphical user interface (although, while developing on the host system, the IDEs may provide the GUI).

- The OS caters to only one "user"; therefore, the functionality differs from, for example, that of Unix, which provides multi-user functionality. Obviously, multi-user security features are not provided.
- Generally, there is no file system in the embedded device as there is no secondary storage; however, users can build their own file systems in the memory of the device.

Therefore, it is very easy to arrive at the first decision: If the OS services needed are minimal for the given application, write your own kernel to provide the services. Otherwise, use an off-the-shelf embedded OS.

If you do determine that an off-the-shelf OS is appropriate for your system, you need to consider whether the operating system has to perform real-time tasks or not. A number of real-time operating systems, such as Wind River Systems' VxWorks and pSOS, Microware's OS/9, Microtec's VRTX, QNX Software Systems' QNX, Kodak's AMX, Red Hat's eCOS, and RTLinux, are available. If the system does not need real-time functionality, operating systems such as Windows CE, embedded Windows XP, embedded Windows NT, or embedded Linux can be chosen. For mobile applications, available operating systems include Palm's Palm OS, Symbian's EPOC, Windows CE, embedded Windows XP, and Microware's OS/9. Use the following guidelines when choosing the operating system:

- **Timing requirements:** If real-time performance is required, a real-time operating system is necessary. The operating system vendor provides the minumum, average, and maximum number of clock cycles required by each system call. Based on these values, you can determine whether the OS meets the desired real-time requirements for your particular application.
- **Processor support for the operating system:** The commercial operating systems support only some processors. For instance, embedded NT supports only the x86 family of processors, and Windows CE works on x86 as well as other processors, such as Hitachi Super-H and Motorola Power PC.
- **The footprint of the operating system:** Memory requirements — in terms of RAM and flash memory — are dependent on the footprint of the operating system. For example, embedded NT requires 9MB of memory and 8MB of persistent storage when the minimal configuration of embedded NT is used. If networking components and device drivers are included with the operating system, the requirement is 13MB of memory and 16MB of persistent storage. eCOS has a memory footprint starting at 2MB. Keep in mind that many operating systems will offer more functionality than you may require for the given application, and this unneeded functionality can be stripped off to reduce the footprint. For instance, if network connectivity is not required, all the software related to TCP/IP can be eliminated.
- **Support for Java:** If the operating system vendor provides a Java Virtual Machine (JVM) with a small footprint, you can develop your application in Java as well. However, depending on performance considerations, you need to determine whether Java, C, or C++ is your best option.

- **Cost of the operating system:** Obviously, cost is an important factor. You need to procure the development system, which consists of the OS (maybe even the source code) and the development tools containing the APIs, along with documentation, and debuggers. This is a one-time procurement cost for the development system. In addition, when the embedded application is built, it has to be integrated with the operating system and ported onto the memory chip; and for each copy, a royalty needs to be paid to the OS vendor. You should consider the royalty fee while selecting the operating system. Some operating system vendors offer royalty-free licensing, which is the best bet. Open-source embedded operating systems based on Linux and BSD Unix are becoming popular, and they present an attractive option.

Choose the processor

Based on the desired functionality, processing speed, and memory addressing capability, you need to select the right processor. However, with the availability of a large number of processors from different vendors with similar performance, choosing a processor is now a complicated task. The following guidelines can be helpful when selecting a processor:

- If the application involves minimal processing and a small number of input/output functions, you can use an 8-bit micro-controller. Digital watches, air conditioners, refrigerators, VCRs, etc., use a micro-controller. Because the micro-controller comes with on-chip memory and serial interface, the cost of the hardware will be minimal. For example, a digital watch can be implemented using an 8-bit micro-controller with on-chip ROM; the input may consist of a set of buttons and the output an LCD display.
- If the application calls for an embedded operating system because of the computation and communication requirements, you need a 16-bit or 32-bit processor. Components such as telecommunication switches, routers, and protocol converters are implemented using this type of processor. Most process control systems fall into this category.
- If the application involves signal processing and mathematical computation, such as in audio coding, video signal processing, or image processing, you need to select a Digital Signal Processor (DSP). Computation-intensive systems, such as those that involve video encoding or image analysis, may need a floating-point DSP. Applications such as audio coding, modems, etc., can be developed using fixed-point DSPs.
- If the application is highly graphics-oriented with fast response-time requirements, you probably need to use a 64-bit processor, such as those used on desktop computers (64-bit processors are used extensively in graphics accelerators and video game players). Industrial computers and Single Board Computers (SBCs) used in industrial automation also use 64-bit processors.

In each of the categories (8-bit micro-controllers; 16-, 32-, and 64-bit microprocessors; and DSPs), you have a number of vendors to choose from, including AMD, Analog Devices, Atmel, ARM, Hitachi, Lucent Technologies, Motorola, National Semiconductors, NEC, Siemens, and Texas Instruments. In order to choose among these vendors, you will need to consider more than just price and performance, as most of them are comparable. Additional factors to consider include customer support, training, design support, and cost of development tools.

Once the processor is identified, the peripheral devices need to be identified. These include static RAM, EPROM, flash memory, serial and parallel communication interfaces, the network interface, programmable timers/counters, status LEDs, and application-specific hardware circuitry.

Memory in embedded systems can be either internal memory or external memory. Internal memory is found in the same silicon as the processor. For small applications involving micro-controllers and DSPs, this memory may suffice. Otherwise, external memory needs to be used. If memory is internal to the device, there will be less program swapping, and access to data and instructions will be very fast. External memory is external to the processor as a separate chip. This causes more program swapping and less speedy execution.

Exactly calculating your memory requirements is extremely difficult at this stage. Generally, you develop the embedded software on a host system, and based on the memory occupied by the application and the operating system, you can calculate the memory required.

Once the hardware design is completed, the hardware engineers write the hardware initialization code in the assembly language of the processor. This code is for testing the memory chips and the peripherals.

Choose the development platform

The development platform consists of the following:

- The hardware platform
- The operating system
- The programming language
- The development tools

Once the processor is decided upon, the vendor provides the required development tools, which include the cross-compiler, linker, loader, and debugger. All these tools have to be loaded onto the desktop system, running Windows or the Unix operating system, after which development can be carried out.

The embedded operating system vendor also provides necessary development tools, such as the APIs for writing the application code above the operating system, debuggers, etc. These development tools are also loaded onto a desktop system for development, and the code can be later ported onto the embedded system.

In addition to the preceding development tools, the following may also be required:

- EPROM programmer

- ROM emulator
- In-circuit emulator
- Instruction set simulator, which simulates the processor and memory of the target system
- Test instruments, such as an oscilloscope, a logic analyzer, and a multimeter, to debug the hardware

Choice of programming language

Historically, major embedded software development projects involved writing code in C, but this is slowly changing. With the availability of Microsoft's Embedded Visual Tools, you can use your knowledge of developing in the Visual Studio environment to take up embedded software development. If you are writing applications for Windows CE or embedded NT, you can develop the programs in the VC++ or VB environment and then embed the software in processor boards without much effort.

If the embedded operating system you chose provides a JVM, you can write the application in Java as well. Of course, you need to consider performance issues before deciding on Java. If you want to develop the embedded software for a variety of hardware and operating system environments, then certainly Java is a good choice. If the embedded appliance is to be network-enabled, again Java is the best choice. This book demonstrates embedded software development using both C/C++ and Java. The following sections briefly outline the guidelines for writing C and Java programs for embedded software.

Coding issues

The process of embedded software development is shown in Figure 4-1. The software written in a high-level language such as C or C++ is converted into object code using a cross-compiler. The assembly-language code written in the target processor's assembly language is also converted into object code using the cross assembler. The linker/loader combines the various object files and converts into a single binary executable file. This executable file is ported to the target platform's memory.

As you can see in the figure, embedded software development requires two systems: the host system and the target system.

You use the host system to develop the software. The host system includes all the necessary development tools, such as compilers, assemblers, debuggers, etc., so that most of the development can be done on the host system itself and then loaded onto the target system.

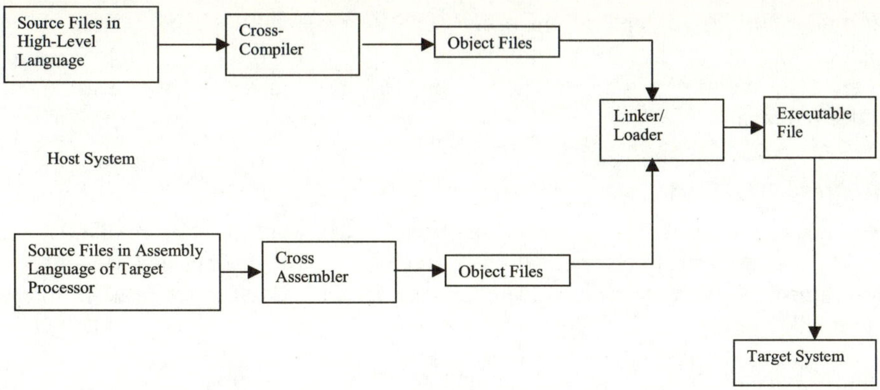

Figure 4-1: Embedded software development process

Code optimization

Code optimization is a trade-off between code size and speed of execution. Depending on your application, you need to decide which is of higher priority. If the embedded system has memory constraints but speed is not a primary concern, code size is important. If real-time constraints are to be met, speed of execution is more important than code size. Use the following checklist for code optimization:

- Eliminate dead code in the program — that is, any code that will not be executed at all. Experienced programmers will ensure that their programs contain no dead code, but many novice programmers include some dead code, such as that which initializes variables, that will not be used at all.
- Remove the code that has been introduced for debugging.
- Avoid large library routines.
- Avoid recursion routines, as they require a large stack. For example, you can write a program to calculate the factorial of a number with or without using recursion. Desktop application programmers use recursion; embedded software programmers avoid it.
- Avoid floating-point operations. If they are necessary, they must be converted into fixed-point operations.
- Reduce the computational requirement by using a very simple trick — multiplication can be done by left-shift operation.
- Declare the most frequently accessed variables as register variables or auto variables.
- Use unsigned data types wherever possible.
- If a particular function or routine consumes a great deal of computation time, use assembly-language programming to code that particular function or routine.

- The compiler provided along with the processor's development tools has a code optimizer. The compiler has code optimization levels — generally, levels 0 to 3. Level 3 offers the highest optimization. While compiling the program, set the optimization level to the desired level.

Programming in Java

Sun Microsystems has released the Connected, Limited Device Configuration (CLDC) specifications for writing embedded applications in Java for mobile devices that are highly memory-constrained. While writing embedded software for these devices, keep the following limitations in mind:

- No support is available for floating-point operations.
- They offer no finalization of class instances.
- Limited error classes are available because error handling in embedded systems is specific to the device.
- They do not support the Java Native Interface (JNI).
- No user-defined class loaders are allowed. The built-in class loader has to be used, which cannot be overridden by you. This was introduced for improving security.

Verify the software on the host system

You can convert the source code into executable binary code by performing the following three steps:

1. Compile and assemble the source code into object files. Compilers and assemblers are used to convert the source code into object files. A cross-compiler runs on one platform (such as a desktop) but produces the object code for another processor (the target embedded processor). The input to a cross-compiler is source code, and the output is object code.
2. Link all the object files to a single object file, which is known as the *relocatable object code*. A linker that runs on the host machine is used to achieve this. The input to the linker are the object files obtained in the previous step, and the output of the linker is a single object file containing the code and data of the program.
3. Relocate the single object file in which physical memory addresses are assigned. The code and data sections of the program are assigned physical addresses by the loader. The result of this step is an executable binary image of the program, which can be loaded into the target ROM of the embedded system. The locator also runs on the host system.

The compiler, assembler, and linker and loader are specific to the target embedded system and need to be procured from the vendor.

Verify the software on the embedded system

Once the software is tested on the host system, it can be ported onto the target board, where complete testing can be carried out for functionality and performance requirements. Certainly at this stage, the hardware engineers and software engineers have to work together to ensure that the software is working as per the original requirements. If performance objectives are not met, code optimization becomes essential at this stage. However, with the availability of good emulators, verification of the software can largely be done on the host system itself.

Summary

This chapter described the process of embedded system development. Based on the requirements of the embedded system under development, you have to prepare the system architecture, choose the embedded operating system, choose the processor and associated peripheral circuitry, and then carry out the implementation using the development tools chosen. During the coding, code optimization criteria have to be kept in mind. The process of embedding the software involves compilation, linking, and loading. The compilers, linkers, and loaders used to achieve these operations run on the host system. You examined the factors that influence the choice of operating system, processor, and programming language. In the next chapter, you will examine the software development environments in detail.

Chapter 5
Embedded Software Development Environments

In This Chapter

- Operating systems used in embedded systems
- Programming languages used in embedded software development
- Development tools for writing embedded software
- Tools for device driver development

In recent years, the landscape of embedded software development has changed drastically. With the availability of operating systems specifically targeted for embedded systems, development has become faster and code has become more reliable. Using object-oriented programming languages is paving the way for code re-use, resulting in faster development. With the advent of Java, platform independence can be achieved easily. In this chapter, we briefly review the operating systems, programming languages, and related development tools for embedded software.

Operating Systems

The embedded software has to interact with the hardware to achieve the desired functionality. This interaction consists of efficiently managing the input/output operations, the memory, the various tasks to be carried out, and the resources to do the specific tasks needed to obtain the desired response time. Generally, all of these functions are achieved through an operating system. However, in the good old days, embedded software developers wrote their own routines (called the *kernel*) in assembly languages, to achieve these functions. The advantage of using this approach is that the developer can write only the functionality required for the application; therefore, the processing power and memory requirements can be reduced to the bare minimum. On the downside, code debugging, testing, and maintenance are difficult, as most of the code is in assembly language. Porting the application to other processor-based hardware is a Herculean task because most of the code needs to be rewritten for the new processor. Therefore, using an operating system is certainly a better choice — particularly now, when fast processors are available and memory costs are dropping.

A number of commercial operating systems are now available to address the embedded systems market. Many of these operating systems use the design concepts of the Unix operating system. In fact, Unix can be considered the father of all operating systems, and many embedded/real-time operating systems are derived from Unix.

> **TIP** Inquisitive readers can investigate Unix operating system design issues in the excellent book *Advanced Topics in UNIX: Processes, Files, and Systems* by Ronald J. Leach (Wiley, 1994).

The following section briefly describes the architecture of a typical operating system kernel. This architecture is applicable to both desktops and embedded systems.

Kernel architecture

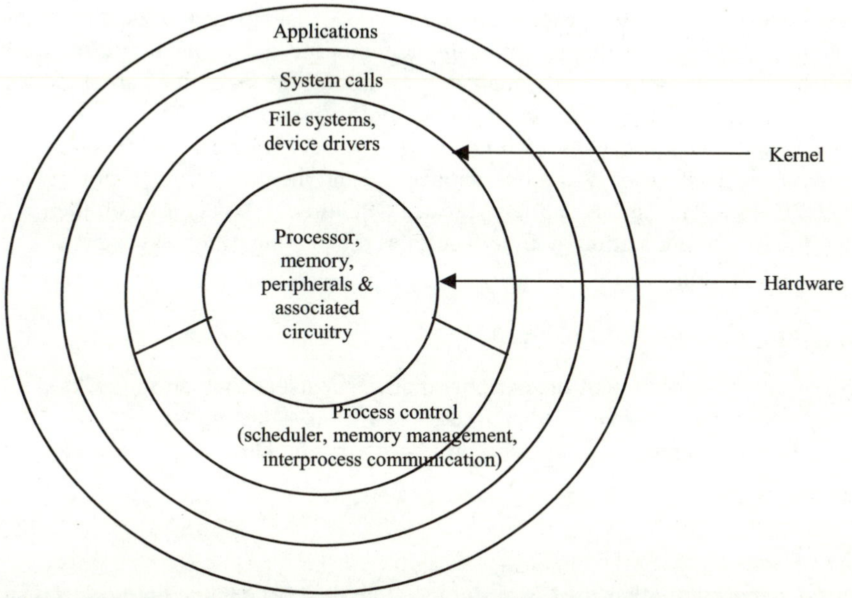

The architecture of an operating system kernel is shown in Figure 5-1.

Figure 5-1: Operating system kernel architecture

Hardware

The hardware is built around a processor. It consists of other peripherals — input/output devices, such as keyboard and LCD display, memory devices, timers, and other circuitry specific to the embedded system. Hardware control circuitry handles the various tasks to be carried out by the processor. The memory can be on the same silicon as the processor or it can be external to the processor chip.

The processor can be a micro-controller, a microprocessor, or a DSP. If the processor has enough on-chip RAM and ROM, the program executes fast, as the program need not be swapped onto the external memory device.

The processor may have to do many jobs, such as reading the data from a serial port, doing some computations, powering an LED to provide status information, sending warning messages onto the LCD unit, etc. Each of these jobs is referred to as a *task*. Multiple tasks have to be executed by the processor. However, some tasks may have a higher priority, in which case the task can interrupt the processor. A special utility in the kernel handles these interrupts; it is called the *Interrupt Service Routine*. The processor executes multiple tasks in a disciplined manner using the task/process control subsystem.

Task/process control subsystem

The task/process control subsystem is responsible for memory management, task scheduling, and inter-task communication. The memory management module is responsible for managing the memory. If the system does not have enough memory for all the tasks, the kernel moves the tasks from the primary memory to secondary memory in a process known as *swapping*. The swapping process is also known as *task scheduling*. The developer can assign high priority to a task so that tasks of lower priority can be swapped out and the task of higher priority can be assigned the CPU time. The task scheduler allocates CPU time to tasks based on their priority. The inter-task communication module facilitates the passing of messages between tasks.

Device drivers

Device drivers control the operation of the peripheral devices, just as they do for desktop computers. Every device should have a driver associated with it — such as serial communication driver, disk driver, LCD driver, printer driver, etc. Device drivers are kernel modules.

File subsystem

The secondary storage generally has the file system to store the user data and programs. If the hard disk is the secondary storage device, the data transfer between the kernel and the disk is done through *buffers*. The hard disk is called a block device because the data transfer takes place in units called *blocks,* typically consisting of 1,024 bytes each. A cache buffer regulates the data transfer between the kernel and the hard disk. In embedded systems, there may not be a hard disk. In such cases, flash memory is used in the place of hard disk. Flash can be considered as "Disk on chip." If the application demands it, you can have a file system on the flash itself. This virtual file system can follow the hierarchical file structure used in Unix or Windows operating systems — that is, you can have a root directory with subdirectories under it, and sub-subdirectories under those, and so on. However, you need to limit filenames to a few characters.

In addition to the block devices, you can have character devices such as the tape drive and other devices connected to the serial interface.

System calls

Developers of desktop applications generally do not access the operating system to write the applications. However, in embedded systems, the programmer needs to access the kernel and the hardware devices. System calls facilitate accessing the various operations of the kernel. In embedded operating systems, system calls are provided to manage the memory, to control the task scheduler, and to carry out inter-process communication. The vendors of embedded operating systems provide the system calls needed to facilitate this access to the kernel. However, porting the applications was a problem, as every operating system vendor had its own set of system calls. Since the development of the Portable Operating System Interface (POSIX), however, you can easily port your application from one operating system to another if the OS interface follows this standard.

C was the first high-level programming language to provide system calls to access the operating system. Not surprisingly, this facility provided the impetus to use C for embedded software development, and even today, the majority of embedded software developers are C programmers only.

Embedded operating systems

Now, many major vendors offer off-the-shelf operating systems that are specifically targeted toward embedded systems. These operating systems have a very small footprint and provide the necessary Application Programming Interfaces (APIs) to facilitate application development, without the need for writing any software to carry out the operating system services. The advantages of using an off-the-shelf operating system are as follows:

- The code can be written in a high-level language, making development faster.
- The code can be maintained easily.
- The programmer can focus on the application code, rather than the basic services, such as memory management, I/O management, etc.

However, these operating systems are designed to work on hardware with limited processing power and memory, and hence they have some limitations:

- There is no file system, as secondary storage devices, such as hard disks, are not used in the embedded systems. If the need arises, you can use flash memory for developing a small file system.
- There is no graphical user interface (GUI). A GUI consumes a lot of memory, and many embedded systems do not need a GUI for operation. However, this is changing with the advent of Java. Mobile devices need a GUI; hence, Java Abstract Window Toolkit

(AWT) with a minimal footprint is provided to develop applications that require a good GUI.

- The operating system works in a single-user mode, unlike Unix, which is a multi-user operating system. This is not a constraint, but for networked embedded systems, in which the system will eventually need to be accessed by multiple users, this will surely be a limitation.
- Security-related issues are not addressed by the developers of these operating systems. Security will be a major issue to be addressed in the future, particularly when embedded systems are accessible over the public network (the Internet).

Task scheduling in embedded systems

Embedded systems have to perform a number of tasks. Because the processor has to handle multiple tasks, a task context is maintained to determine how much of the processing has been completed. The task context consists of a task ID, a context, a task state, and the priority of the task. The task scheduler determines which task the processor has to run next.

A task can be in one of three states:

- Running
- Ready
- Waiting

Figure 5-2 illustrates the three possible states of a given task.

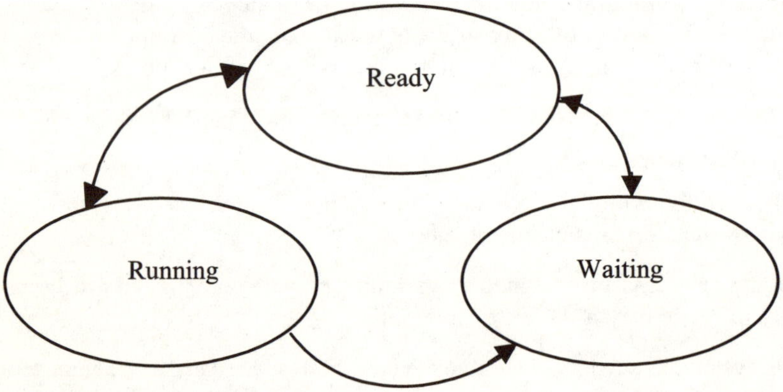

Figure 5-2: States of a task

- **Running state:** When the task is being executed by the processor, it is said to be in the running state. In an embedded system running a preemptive operating system, one task may not be allowed to run continuously (i.e., without interruption). Therefore, it has to be transferred to another state.

- **Ready state:** A task is said to be in ready state if it is waiting in a queue for the processor to execute it.
- **Waiting state:** If a task is waiting for an external event to occur, it is said to be in waiting state. In this state, it is not waiting in the queue. Even if the processor is free to do a job, this task is not ready. Only when the external event takes place will it move to the ready state.

Task scheduler

The task scheduler keeps track of the state of each task and decides which task to run, based on the priority assigned to the tasks. Depending on how the task scheduler works, operating systems are divided into two categories:

- Preemptive operating systems
- Non-preemptive operating systems

In a preemptive operating system, a low-priority task is stopped and a high-priority task is executed when the requirement arises. In a non-preemptive operating system, a low-priority task continues to run even if a high-priority task is ready.

Each task is assigned a task ID, a context, a task state, and a priority. The task scheduler decides which task to run based on this information. The four algorithms available to schedule the tasks are:

- First In First Out (FIFO)
- Shortest job first
- Round-robin
- Priority-based scheduling

First In First Out

FIFO is the simplest scheduling algorithm. When a number of tasks are to be executed, they are kept in a queue, and after the first task is executed, the processor takes on the next task in the queue. This algorithm is very simple to implement, but if one task takes too much time, other tasks have to wait for an unknown amount of time. It is difficult to write embedded software using this algorithm, as these applications often involve timing deadlines that need to be met.

DOS is an example of an OS that uses the FIFO algorithm; each task is completed in sequential order by the CPU.

Shortest job first

If the time required for each task can be estimated, then based on the number of tasks waiting in a queue, the shortest job can be executed by the processor first, followed by the next shortest job, and so on. Most mainframe computers use this algorithm. Like the FIFO algorithm, this algorithm may not be suitable for all embedded applications, particularly if deadlines are to be met for specific tasks.

Round-robin

In the round-robin algorithm, the processor allots a certain amount of execution time for each task and then moves on to the next in the queue. If three tasks are to be serviced, the tasks are executed 1, 2, 3; 1, 2, 3; and so on. If the software has to obtain data from three input devices, software will check each input device and service the task that needs the service. Embedded systems in which the round-robin algorithm can be implemented include a multimeter that measures voltage and current values and a microwave oven. These systems do not involve time-critical operations, so the algorithm works well.

The round-robin algorithm can be slightly complicated by introducing priority to the tasks. A high-priority task can interrupt the processor, temporarily halting the task presently running to execute the higher-priority task. A bar code scanner can be developed using the round-robin algorithm with priority interrupt. When the scanner has to do the scanning operation, it is a high-priority task, and the present task of displaying an item can be suspended until the scanning operation can be carried out.

Round-robin algorithms can be implemented in embedded systems in soft real-time operating systems.

Priority-based scheduling

An attractive scheduling algorithm for embedded systems is priority-based scheduling. The task scheduler uses a data structure called a *ready list* to track the tasks in ready state. The ready list is implemented as an ordered linked list containing the task ID, the state, the priority, and `pnext` (a pointer to the next task). An idle task is executed when the processor has nothing to do. The idle task is an infinite loop that does nothing. This idle task is kept at the end of the linked list.

Context switch

In the embedded system, the states of the tasks change continually. The running task is moved to ready state or waiting state, the waiting task is moved to ready state, and so on. The process of changing from one state to another is carried out by the *context switch,* which is implemented in the assembly language.

Task synchronization

Various tasks in an embedded system need to communicate with one another and share data, a process known as *task synchronization*. A number of mechanisms are used to carry out synchronization, most notable among them being mutexes and semaphores.

Mutex

It is important to ensure that some portions of the code are executed by only one process at a time. Mutual exclusion achieves this. *Mutex* is the short form of *mut*ual *ex*clusion, ensuring that different tasks do not execute the same portion of the code at the same time. Embedded operating systems provide the system calls for mutex operations.

Semaphore

In operating systems, the various tasks have to use the resources in a disciplined manner. An application may demand that only one task write to the memory at a time. Another application may demand that a set of tasks be executed in a specified sequence based on certain conditions. In such cases, *semaphores* are used. A simple implementation of a semaphore is as follows: When a task is executing in the kernel, it sets a "flag," and until this flag is cleared, other tasks have to wait, and this task cannot be interrupted. This flag is called a *semaphore;* it is a locking mechanism which informs other tasks that a particular resource is locked. A task can "take" a semaphore and "release" that semaphore. Only when a task releases the semaphore can other tasks take that semaphore.

Dijkstra's algorithm is extensively used in both Unix and real-time operating systems to implement semaphores. According to this algorithm, a semaphore is an integer-valued object. Two operations are defined on the semaphore, P and V. The P operation decrements the semaphore value if it is greater than 0. A V operation increments the semaphore's value. When a P or V operation is being performed by the kernel, no other task can modify the semaphore values. Hence, these operations are called *atomic operations.* Based on the values of the semaphore, the kernel decides which task has to run and which tasks have to sleep. Operating systems provide a number of system calls to initialize a semaphore to a non-negative integer to increment and decrement the semaphore (by 1 or a larger number), thereby locking the tasks for processing.

Timers

To provide real-time capability to the operating system, the developer should include various timing functions, such as locking a task in the memory for a specific duration, swapping out a task to enable another task to execute, etc. To control the timing, a clock interrupt handler is provided, whose functions include the following:

- Keeping track of the system time
- Controlling the task scheduling
- Restarting the various clocks
- Sending signals to the tasks based on timing considerations
- Providing statistical information, such as time taken for different tasks

- Providing execution profiles, which indicate the amount of time taken by the task and the individual function calls within a program (the `gprof` command in Linux or the `prof` command in Unix)

In embedded operating systems, clocks keep track of various times, such as when to poll a device to obtain the data, when to interrupt a task, etc. A number of system calls are provided to implement these functionalities. Real-time operating systems provide various system calls to implement mutexes and semaphores. These mechanisms provide the real-time capability. If a task has to complete in a specified amount of time, using these mechanisms can enable it to run in the kernel without being disturbed.

Depending on what functionalities are provided in the embedded operating systems, these operating systems are divided into *soft* real-time operating systems and *hard* real-time operating systems. If you use a simple round-robin algorithm, you cannot implement soft real-time functionality. If you implement priority with semaphores, you can implement hard real-time systems.

Types of embedded operating systems

Embedded operating systems can be broadly categorized into three types:

- **Non-real-time embedded operating systems:** These operating systems do not provide hard real-time functionality. In other words, if strict deadlines are to be met, these operating systems are not suitable. System calls are provided for process management, memory management, and I/O management for tasks that do not require real-time response.
- **Real-time operating systems:** These operating systems provide the necessary system calls to achieve real-time deadlines.
- **Mobile/handheld operating systems:** Operating systems that are fine-tuned to work in mobile environments are known as mobile/handheld operating systems. However, note that many real-time operating systems can be used as mobile/handheld operating systems as well.

Embedded versions of the major desktop operating systems are now becoming available; these include Microsoft's operating systems and Unix/Linux-based operating systems. The following sections provide a brief overview of such embedded operating systems.

Embedded Windows NT

Microsoft's Embedded NT is based on Windows NT 4.0. Embedded NT works on x86 and Pentium processors only. When you want to develop embedded applications using Embedded NT, you have to install the development system, which has the following hardware and software requirements:

- Windows NT 4.0

- Service Pack 4.0 or later
- Internet Explorer 5.0 or later
- Visual Studio 6.0 development environment
- Windows NT 4.0 Service Resource Kit

IIS 3.0 is included in Embedded NT. You can develop the applications in the Visual Studio environment (VB or VC++), and the application can be ported to the target system. The minimum requirements for the target system are as follows:

- 100 MHz 486 processor
- Minimum 16MB RAM

The exact requirement for the memory of the target system depends on the application. If the application is a single Win32 application with networking capability, then the minimum requirement is about 16MB. The footprint of Embedded NT is about 9MB of memory and 8MB of persistent storage (flash, for example) for minimal OS functionality without any network support. With networking components and device drivers, the requirement is 13MB of memory and 16MB of persistent storage.

Embedded NT provides development tools called the *Component Designer* and the *Target Designer*. The Component Designer facilitates defining and adding components to the Target Designer. The Target Designer is used to create a bootable NT target system. It generates a target image, which consists of a number of directories. All these directories and files need to be copied onto the target machine's file system. You can create a target system in the following ways:

- **Create a headless system.** In this case, the embedded system does not have the monitor, keyboard, mouse, etc. To create a headless system, the following components need to be added:
  - Null VGA
  - Null Keyboard Drive
  - Null Mouse

  In a headless embedded system, how do you check whether everything is OK? The *Console Administration Component* is provided, with which you can monitor the embedded system through a serial interface.

- **Create a target system that boots from the read-only storage medium, such as a CD-ROM.** In this case, you need to transfer the target image generated by the Target Designer onto a CD-ROM. The embedded system can be booted from this disk.
- **Create a bootable partition in the hard disk.** In this case, you can create a partition in the hard disk, from which a Windows NT embedded target image can boot.

- **Create the target image on an empty hard disk.** Take an empty hard disk, transfer the target image onto it, and connect this hard disk to the target embedded system. This approach is the best while testing the embedded software in the lab enviroment. We have used this approach in the applications described in later chapters.

Windows XP Embedded

The Windows XP Embedded (abbreviated embedded XP in the following discussion) operating system is the successor to Embedded NT 4.0. It is a pre-emptive multitasking operating system. It also uses Win32 applications and drivers; therefore, the existing Win32 applications can be directly ported into embedded XP without any major changes. Applications built using Visual Studio can be embedded without any modifications. This is the most attractive feature of the Windows embedded operating systems.

To install embedded XP on a development system, you need a system with the following configuration:

- A system with a 500 MHz processor, 256MB RAM, a CD-ROM drive, and a 1,024 × 768 VGA monitor
- Windows 2000 Service Pack 2 or later, or Windows XP Professional
- Internet Explorer 5.5 or later
- SQL Server 2000, if you want to develop database applications
- Visual Studio 6.0

You can install embedded XP onto a system with the preceding hardware and software configuration. The Embedded Studio provides a number of utilities to develop embedded applications. The most important tools are as follows:

- Target Designer, which is used to create the bootable runtime image of the application you have developed. You can transfer the runtime image to the target system, and the system will boot with embedded XP and the application will run from this image.
- Component Designer, which is used to create components required for the embedded application.
- Deployment tools, which are used to prepare the target device for the runtime image.

The bootable image you create from the Target Designer can be transferred to a CD-ROM, or a Disk-on-chip flash.

Embedded XP provides numerous features required to develop applications for information appliances, set top boxes, point-of-sale terminals, etc., by providing the necessary support for security features, Telephony APIs (TAPIs), IP version 6, IrDA compliance, 801.11 wireless LAN, Universal Plug and Play (PnP), etc. It also has support for NetMeeting to provide multimedia applications.

Open-source embedded OSs

Open-source embedded operating systems based on Linux and BSD Unix are now becoming popular. The main attraction of these operating systems is their royalty-free licensing. Another feature is the standard open APIs, which makes applications easy to port.

The Linux kernel, including the embedded Linux kernel software, is covered by the GNU General Public License (GPL). GPL permits redistribution of the source code even if it is modified as per the requirements of your application. However, the modified code must be made available in source form, usually for a nominal cost that is not more than the cost of reproducing the software.

> **NOTE** When you use the kernel source code for a particular application, you may also use other third-party software (which may or may not be free). When using software for commercial applications, you need to check the licensing agreement very carefully. The reader is advised to study the *Terms of Free Software Foundation* and other open-source license agreements to obtain a full understanding of the open source and its implications. You can study the GNU General Public License (GPL) at `www.gnu.org/copyleft/gpl.html`.

Embedded Linux (`www.embedded-linux.org`) is available freely and openly in source code form and is gaining popularity. It is being used for a wide spectrum of applications — from IP phones to telecommunication switches, in addition to mobile devices such as phones and PDAs. Compared with proprietary operating systems, this open-source operating system provides many advantages, as developers can modify the code as per their needs and a large pool of expertise is available for support services. A number of vendors offer embedded Linux for both real-time and non-real-time applications, including Coventive, FSM Laboratories, Lineo, LynuxWorks, Mizi, MontaVista, PalmPalm, Red Hat, RidgeRun, TimeSys, and so on.

NetBSD, based on the BSD (Berkeley Standard Distribution) of Unix, is another popular open source embedded OS. It requires 400KB to 1.5MB of flash memory and 2 to 16MB of RAM. NetBSD-based embedded systems include routers, telecommunication switches, Internet appliances, and the like.

Real-time operating sytems

Conventional desktop operating systems are not real-time operating systems. The most important requirement of a real-time OS is that it be deterministic. An OS is termed deterministic if the worst-case execution time of each system call can be calculated. OS vendors provide a minimum, average, and maximum number of clock cycles required by each system call. For a given application, based on the number of tasks, you can calculate the timing requirements and determine whether the real-time performance can be achieved. Of course, choosing the right processor speed and internal/external memory also plays an important role in achieving the desired real-time performance. Following are some popular real-time operating systems:

- Wind River Systems' VxWorks

- Integrated Systems' pSOS
- QNX Systems' QNX
- FSM Labs' Real Time Linux (RTLinux)
- Kodak's AMX
- Microtec's VRTX
- Microware's OS/9
- Accelerated Technology's Nucleus

The following section briefly reviews RTLinux.

RTLinux

RTLinux is a hard real-time OS. It runs on x86, Pentium, Power PC, and Alpha processors. You can also use it for soft real-time applications (such as audio/video applications). Note that the desktop version of Linux cannot be used for real-time operations for the following reasons:

- The kernel is not preemptive; therefore, a high-priority task has to wait.
- The scheduling algorithm depends on the load on the processor.
- The time resolution is coarse (10 milliseconds). If a task must wait at least 10 milliseconds to be serviced, it may not be acceptable.
- Linux uses virtual memory, wherein the task is swapped to virtual memory when it is not being executed.

RTLinux is based on the Portable Operating System Interface standard POSIX 1003.1b, which provides a portable interface for meeting the real-time requirements of the operating system. This standard calls for the following features:

- Preemptive priority scheduling for scheduling tasks
- Locking of virtual pages in memory
- Real-time signals — a signal can be sent to a task that is presently running
- Improved timers to increase the time resolution
- Improved interprocess communication

RTLinux supports all these features. It runs underneath the Linux operating system. The Linux OS becomes an idle task for RTLinux. To achieve real-time performance, interrupts from the Linux have to be disabled — this is accomplished with a layer of emulation software between the Linux kernel and the interrupt controller hardware. A footprint of 4MB is required for RTLinux.

To achieve real-time performance, tasks should be written as threads or signal handlers (interrupt handlers). The tasks, which do not have any timing constraints, will run in the Linux kernel only. Worst-case time is 15 microseconds between giving an interrupt signal and starting of the real-time handler. Soft real-time capabilities are provided by the underlying Linux system. In this real-time OS, the hard real-time software runs in the real-time kernel and makes use of services and programs running in the non-real-time thread. The real-time software is not delayed by the non-real-time software.

> **CROSS-REFERENCE** The various system calls provided in RTLinux to achieve real-time performance using mutexes, semaphores, timers, etc., are discussed in Chapter 10, which presents some real-world examples using RTLinux.

MiniRTL, a tiny implementation of RTLinux, runs on i486 machines. This implementation is suitable for devices that are highly constrained for memory.

eCOS

Red Hat's eCOS operating system is another open-source, real-time non–Linux-based operating system. It has a footprint of 2MB and above. It is used in such devices as laser printers and audio players.

Mobile/handheld operating systems

Handheld computers are used not only for local data entry operations but also as Internet Access Devices (IADs). Many of these handheld computers are now used not only for computing, but for voice and video communication as well. The requirements of mobile/handheld operating systems in terms of computing and communications are enormous. They need to process streaming audio and video in soft real-time mode, and also provide communication support using such technologies as Bluetooth, IrDA, UppnP, etc., in addition to TCP/IP support.

The layered architecture of a mobile/handheld system is shown in Figure 5-3.

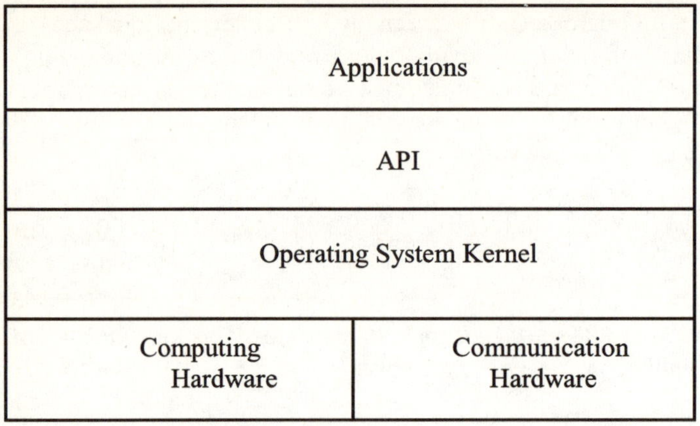

Figure 5-3: Mobile/handheld operating system

The handheld devices should be capable of accessing both the data and voice and video services. These devices need an operating system on which the applications can be run. The hardware consists of computing and communication hardware modules, which a mobile operating system runs. The important requirement for a mobile operating system is that it have a small footprint so that the memory requirement can be minimized. A footprint of 64 Kbytes to 2 Mbytes for the OS would be attractive. Two to 4MB of ROM and 2 to 16MB of flash RAM will keep the cost of the mobile device low. At the same time, to provide the desired functionality, the complete TCP/IP stack — along with the application layer software, such as SMTP, POP3, HTTP, etc. — should be running on the handheld device. In contrast, the desktop OS has a footprint of 4 to 16MB, 16 to 64MB of ROM, and several GB of persistent storage.

Mobile operating systems also require real-time performance for voice applications, and they should be able to handle the communication protocols to connect to the voice network. The operating system provides the APIs to develop applications. Although a number of operating systems have appeared in the marketplace for mobile devices, the real-time operating systems can also be used. These mobile operating systems are also referred to as *handheld operating systems*.

Following are three mobile/handheld operating systems:

- Microsoft's Windows CE, with a footprint of 2MB
- Palm's Palm OS, with a footprint of 1MB
- Symbian's EPOC, with a footprint of 1MB

In addition, any of the real-time operating systems such as RTLinux and Microware's OS-9 (a very small and powerful real-time operating system with a footprint of 68 to 308KB) can be used in the mobile devices.

Windows CE

Microsoft's Windows CE is targeted toward devices such as handheld computers, set top boxes, etc. It works on both the x86 family of processors as well as on non-x86 processors, such as Alpha, NEC, Toshiba, Motorola Power PC, and Hitachi's Super H. The handheld computers of Casio, HP, NEC, Phillips, Sharp, etc., run this OS. Windows CE 2.0 needs 2MB of ROM. Pocket PC is the hardware that can be used in conjunction with Windows CE. The main attraction of this OS is that it uses a subset of Win32 APIs to develop the applications; therefore, the large pool of software developers with knowledge of VB, VC++, and Java can develop programs for this environment. Previously developed applications in these languages can be ported onto the Windows CE platform without much effort. "Pocket" versions of Microsoft Office applications (Outlook, Excel, Word, etc.) are also available, obviating the need for users to learn a new user interface for these application software programs. ActiveSync software is used to synchronize the data between the desktop and the handheld computer.

Palm OS

Palm OS (`www.palmos.com`) is present on Palm's own line of handhelds, as well as those of other vendors (e.g., Sony and Handspring) that have licensed it, which have a processor of 16 MHz to 33 MHz, 512K to 8MB of ROM, and a heap memory of 32K to 256K. Software development is done using the Palm OS SDK, and applications can be developed in C or C++. It provides HotSync to synchronize data between a desktop and the handheld. The Palm Conduit Development Kit (CDK) is used to develop conduits (plug-ins to HotSync) in VC++ or VB or Java. The Palm OS also provides a virtual file system API to develop a file system. The OS is also Bluetooth-enabled, making it easy to integrate Bluetooth software. An emulator is available that runs on Windows, Unix/Linux, and Mac operating systems, so testing the software is easy. With a large pool of developers and applications for the Palm OS, it is one of the most popular and successful operating systems.

Symbian OS

Symbian OS (`www.symbian.com`) is targeted to mobile devices such as phones and PDAs for wireless data and telephony services. Ericsson's R380 smart phone and Nokia's 9210 communicator are based on this OS. Licensees of Symbian OS include major mobile phone suppliers, including Kenwood, Motorola, Panasonic, Psion, Sanyo, Siemens, and Sony. The OS architecture enables both voice services and packet switched data services on 2G and 2.5G wireless networks, with support for TCP/IP, Bluetooth, IrDA, and serial communication. The Software Development Kit enables programmers to develop their applications in either C++ or Java. The OS version 6.*x* has a POSIX-compliant interface and a Java Virtual Machine (JVM) for developing value-added services. Data synchronization is obtained with Symbian Connect.

Programming Languages

Embedded systems use different processors depending on performance requirements and cost. Each processor has its own instruction set; therefore, writing the software for the target processor requires your learning the corresponding assembly language instruction set. However, with the advances in software development tools, now you can do the programming in high-level languages as well. The following sections describe the various options available for writing embedded software, and the pros and cons of each.

Assembly languages

In assembly languages, each statement represents one machine instruction, and programmers have to deal with low-level details, such as register allocation and procedure-calling sequences. Therefore, hardware knowledge is required to do programming in assembly language. Moreover, the assembly language is dependent on the processor used. For example, the assembly language for Intel processors is different from the assembly language of Motorola processors or DSP. It is very difficult to write and maintain large programs written in assembly language, as they are very lengthy. The main attraction of the assembly language is that the resultant programs are highly efficient and execute fast.

To convert an assembly language program into machine code, an assembler is required. A program written in a high-level language such as C can be converted into the machine code of a target processor using a cross-compiler.

High-level languages

System programming languages, also called high-level languages, are easy to learn and the resultant software is easy to maintain. System programming languages can be divided into *procedural languages* and *object-oriented languages*. A system programming language (procedural or object oriented) can be classified as strongly typed or loosely typed. In a strongly typed language, every variable has to be declared. This makes the programmer disciplined and helps in easy debugging. FORTRAN and BASIC are loosely typed languages, whereas C, C++, and Java are strongly typed languages.

System programming languages increase the productivity of the programmer, but the programs run slower compared with assembly language programs. A compiler is needed to convert a program written in system programming language to its equivalent machine code. The system programming languages have the advantage of modular development through functions and constructs for control flow. With the availability of cross-compilers, you can write the code in C language and convert the code into the object code of the target processor. Hence, these languages are extensively used nowadays for embedded programming, particularly the C language.

C is a high-level language with a lot of functionality for low-level programming to directly access the hardware through pointers, and the OS can be accessed through function calls.

Compilers are available for every processor, and these compilers produce compact and efficient code. In addition, a large pool of C programmers are available. For these reasons, C is the most widely used language for embedded software development.

Presently, object-oriented programming languages, particularly C++ and Java, are also extensively used for embedded software development. However, C++ does not produce the compact, efficient code that C does. However, the main attraction of object-oriented languages is their reusability.

eMbedded Visual Tools

Microsoft's eMbedded Visual Tools can be used to develop embedded applications very fast, using your knowledge of application development for desktops in Visual Basic and Visual C++. eMbedded Visual Tools provides the IDE to develop applications for a Windows CE operating system that runs on handheld computers, such as Handheld PC Pro (H/PC Pro), Pocket PC, and PC 1.2. Windows CE is based on the Win32 API set. With minimal modifications, desktop applications written in VB or VC++ can be ported to the Windows CE platform. Note the following differences:

- The hardware for the handhelds is different from desktop hardware, particularly the input/output devices. Therefore, developing the user interface for the handhelds is quite a different game. You need to make numerous changes to the user interface portion of the application. In handheld computers, the display size is limited and it may not support a large number of colors (many displays support only 24 colors). In addition, input is not necessarily through a standard keyboard — it can be through a stylus, a touch screen, or a software-based form of handwriting recognition.
- Only a subset of Win32 APIs is supported.
- Windows CE is based on the Unicode environment.

BREW

Qualcomm's Binary Runtime Environment for Wireless (BREW) SDK facilitates the development of mobile data applications for wireless networks based on Code Division Multiple Access (CDMA) technology. You can develop mobile applications using the SDK in C or C++ using Visual Studio, test the applications using the emulators that run on the desktop, and then port the applications to an embedded system built around an ARM processor.

CROSS-REFERENCE Development of mobile data applications using BREW is covered in Chapter 9.

Structure of a C compiler

Because embedded software development is done extensively in C, this section examines the structure of a compiler to understand how the compiled code gets into memory and how the C program is organized in the memory.

The structure of a compiler is shown in Figure 5-4.

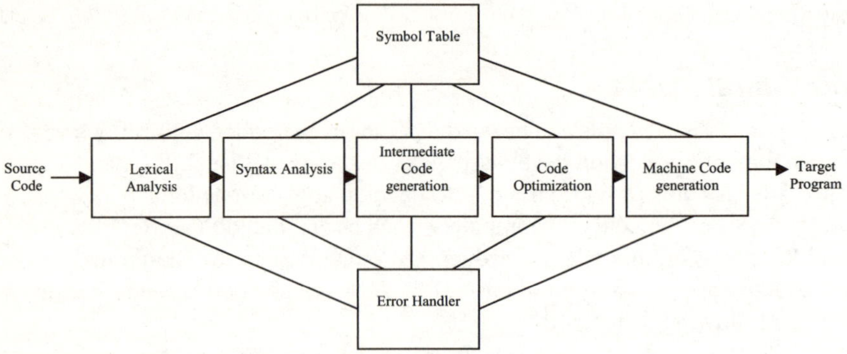

Figure 5-4: Structure of a compiler

Although you issue only one command to compile a program and generate the machine code, the compiler does a lot of things behind the scenes, as shown in Figure 5-4. It has a lexical analyzer, a syntax analyzer (also known as a parser), an intermediate code generator, a code optimizer, and a machine code generator. In addition, it has a symbol table and an error handler.

The following sections describe these components.

Lexical analyzer

The lexical analyzer takes the source code as input and separates the input characters into tokens. The output is a stream of tokens. Each token consists of a token type and token value. For instance, the operator > has a token type "operator" and a token value ">" (represented by a number). The lexical analyzer takes the statement's characters one by one, such as in the statement `int a,b;`. Because `int` is a valid keyword, `int` is declared as a token and is assigned a value and put in the symbol table. Similarly, `a` and `b` are valid variables, so they are also assigned numbers and kept in the symbol table. If an invalid token is encountered, such as an integer, then the lexical analyzer informs the error handler, which throws a compiler error message. In a nutshell, the lexical analyzer identifies the various constructs of the programming language, such as keywords, punctuation marks, operators, etc.

Syntax analyzer/parser

The stream of tokens sent by the lexical analyzer is parsed by the syntax analyzer, which checks whether each statement contains the correct grammar. If a semicolon is missing, or if the necessary arguments are not given for a particular statement, the syntax analyzer complains via the error handler. The parser groups the tokens into *syntactic structures*. The parser generates a tree-like structure called a *parse tree*.

Intermediate code generator

The intermediate code generator takes the syntactic structure as the input and generates a stream of simple instructions, similar to an assembly language program. Each statement will be in the following format:

```
T = Y op X
```

Consider the following statement:

```
x = a/b + c /d
```

The intermediate code for the preceding statement is as follows:

```
T1 = a/b
T2 = c/d
T3= T1 + T2
```

`T1`, `T2`, and `T3` are temporary variables.

Code optimization

The intermediate code that is generated as explained in the preceding section is optimized to make the program efficient. The objective is to minimize both the memory requirement and the time needed for execution.

Here, we need to differentiate between algorithm optimization and code optimization. Optimizing the algorithm is the programmer's job. For instance, if you want to implement a search or sort algorithm, which algorithm to choose depends on the timing and memory requirements of the various algorithms available for searching and sorting.

Code optimization is done by the compiler for a given algorithm implementation. This is an optional phase. By providing a compiler option, the user can bypass the code optimizer.

Consider the example of a program to determine the roots of a quadratic equation. If ($ax^2 + bx + c = 0$) is the quadratic equation, you could calculate the roots using the following formulas:

```
 Root1 = (-b + sqrt(b**2 - 4 * a * c)/(2*a)
Root2 = (-b - sqrt(b**2 - 4 * a * c)/(2*a)
```

However, a better option would be to calculate the value of the `sqrt`, assign it to the variable `d`, and then calculate the roots as follows:

```
 Root1 = (-b + d)/(2*a)
Root2 = (-b -d)/(2*a)
```

This is known as *local optimization*. The optimizer carries out the local optimization.

Another type of optimization done by the optimizer is called *loop optimization*. Consider the following code segment:

```
for (i=0, i < 10, ++i) {
x = 2.0 * a + 3.1 * b;
/* some other statements */
}
```

The statement to calculate the value of `x` within the `for` loop is called a *loop invariant*, because the value of `x` does not depend on the value of `i`. Therefore, it is unnecessary to keep that statement within the loop. A casual programmer may leave it in, but the optimizer, to produce efficient code, will place the statement above the loop.

Sometimes, the programmer may intentionally introduce loop invariants to produce a delay in the computation, as in the case of process control systems where a process has to wait for some time before measuring the temperature value. The code optimizer doesn't know that. Therefore, embedded programmers can use the code optimizer, but they need to later read through the assembler code generated to check for any discrepancies.

Code generator

The code generator produces the object code and determines the memory locations for the data registers. Embedded software developers need to focus on this aspect because the machine code depends on the target processor and the operating system used. The number of registers and the way the data is handled by these registers varies from processor to processor. The processor's supplier provides the development system, which has to be used to generate the code specific to that processor.

Symbol table

The symbol table keeps track of all variables and their data types. The data structure used to perform table management is called a *symbol table*.

Error handler

The error handler is invoked whenever an error occurs. This is a logical structure that can be built into each of the modules. Note that errors can occur in the lexical analysis stage, in the parsing stage, during intermediate code generation, or in the symbol table (when the same variable is declared twice). The compiler generates the errors through the error handler.

Runtime storage administration

When a C program is converted into machine code and executed, runtime administration of the storage is very important. In the C language, the storage needs to be allocated dynamically at runtime; you cannot specify a fixed size of memory for the program. When you use recursion, the function calls itself many times; therefore, the storage requirement increases as the function is called repeatedly. A stack is used to allocate memory dynamically at runtime, as shown in Figure 5-5.

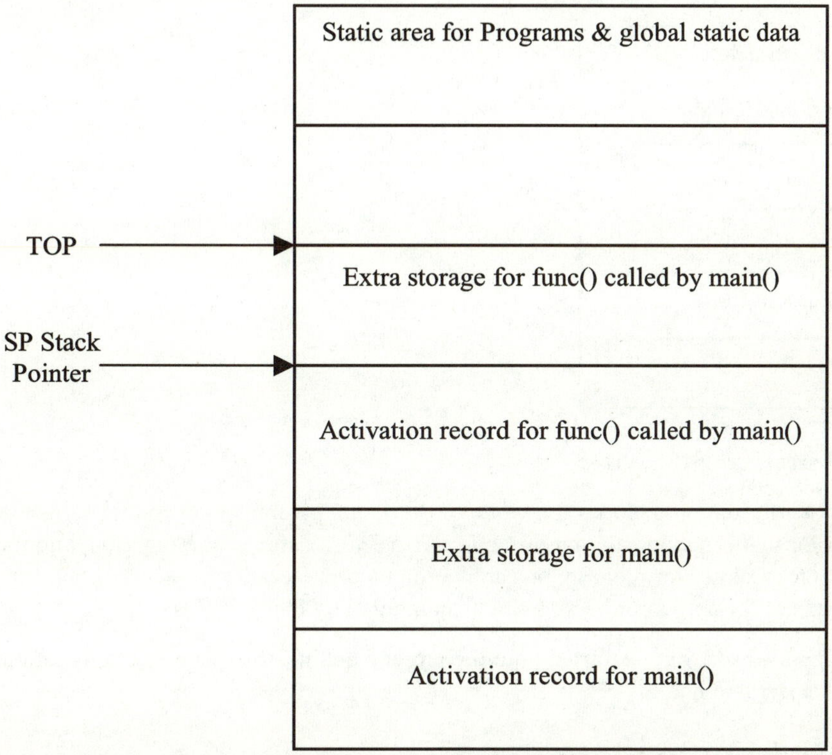

Figure 5-5: Memory organization for a C program

Consider a C program in which a `main()` function calls another function, `func()`. Memory allocation is required for the program and global data as well as for individual functions. On the top of the stack (the low-numbered memory locations), the code for the program is stored, along with the static global variables data. Starting from the highest numbered memory locations (the bottom of the stack), the activation records for the functions starting from `main()` are stored, and space is allocated for that function. Each function has an activation record on the stack, in which the values of the local variables are kept. Therefore, at the bottom of the stack, the activation record for the `main()` function is stored above which memory space is allocated for the `main()` function. Above this, the activation record for `func()` will be stored, and space for `func()` will be allocated.

There will be two pointers to this stack, which are registers permanently allocated for this purpose. One pointer is called the *Stack Pointer* (*SP*), which points to the currently active function. The second pointer is called *TOP,* which points to the top of the stack.

Each activation record corresponding to a function contains information about the local variables, as well as some additional information, as shown in Figure 5-6.

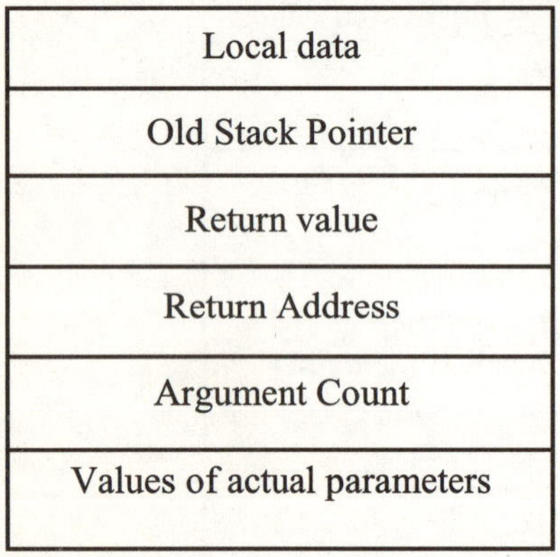

Figure 5-6: Activation record in C

This additional information includes the value of the actual parameters, a count of the number of arguments for that function call, a return address, a return value of the function, and the value of the Stack Pointer for the previous activation record. Because the size of the local data is fixed, the size of the activation record can be computed by the compiler.

When the embedded software is ported onto the target machine, the memory organization will be handled as described here.

Java programming language

The main attraction of Java is its platform independence. In fact, the Java programming language was developed to address the needs of programmers developing software applications for consumer appliances, to avoid rewriting the software for different processors. With the availability of Java Virtual Machines (JVMs), which occupy very little memory, Java is now being used extensively for embedded software development as well. The attractive features of encapsulation, inheritance, and message passing by invoking methods, rather than calling functions, are exploited for embedded programming in Java.

However, Java does not provide certain low-level services needed in embedded programming. Following are Java's limitations:

- Java does not support pointers; therefore, you cannot access memory locations and devices directly.
- Java does not support I/O port access.
- Java does not support a shared memory interface to non-Java tasks.

To overcome these limitations, the following options are available:

- Based on the target platform, the native code can be written in another language — C, for example — and then interfaced to the Java program using JNI. However, the JNI methods are not portable. Another problem is that while the native method is executed, garbage collection is turned off. If you have a hardware device, you can create a DLL in another language, such as C, and use it in your Java program. This approach defeats the purpose of using Java for platform independence, however.
- The second alternative is to write standard Java libraries to abstract the interface to low-level hardware. Using this approach, you can read or write to I/O ports, write interrupt handlers in Java, access memory devices, etc. A number of such commercial tools are available.

Java programs written for desktops can be ported to embedded systems if JVM and AWT are ported onto it. The standard AWT size of desktops is prohibitive for such applications. Lightweight graphic toolkits are available for embedded systems (for example, from `www.newmonics.com`).

Java 2 Micro Edition

Sun Microsystems has released three editions of Java to cater to different market segments:

- Java 2 Enterprise Edition (J2EE) for the server market
- Java 2 Standard Edition (J2SE) for the desktop market
- Java 2 Micro Edition (J2ME) for the consumer and embedded markets

J2ME addresses two types of devices. The first are Connected Device Configurations (CDCs), such as set top boxes, communicators, and Internet TVs, each of which can be connected to high-bandwidth networks, run a TCP/IP protocol stack, and have memory capacity in the range of 2 to 16MB. The second type of devices are Connected, Limited Device Configurations (CLDCs), such as mobile phones, pagers, and PDAs. These devices are connected to low-bandwidth networks such as wireless networks that support low data rates (even 9600 bps). They may not run the TCP/IP protocol stack, and they have a small memory capacity on the order of 128KB to 512KB. Java programming for CDCs is not much different from programming for desktops, but running Java applications on the CLDC devices is a challenging task because of the memory constraints. The CLDC devices contain a Kilobytes Virtual Machine (KVM), which is a compact virtual machine for running Java applications.

To run the Java applications, memory is required to hold the virtual machine, the Java class libraries, and the Java application. Because the total memory of CLDC devices is limited, the KVM was designed to occupy much less memory. The KVM is a compact virtual machine that requires just 40 to 80KB of memory. To run small Java applications, the minimum requirement is about 128KB for the KVM, the class libraries, and the application. For a larger application, you need 258KB, out of which 40 to 80KB are for the KVM and the rest are for class libraries and the application. CLDC applications run above the KVM.

The CLDC devices have a 16-bit or 32-bit processor and 160 to 512KB of memory. They require 128KB of nonvolatile memory for the KVM and CLDC libraries, and 32KB of volatile memory for runtime and object memory. CLDC is defined as a J2ME configuration. A Mobile Information Device Profile (MIDP) is defined for CLDC-type appliances to develop interoperable applications. The various components of the Java-enabled mobile device are shown in Figure 5-7 as a layered architecture.

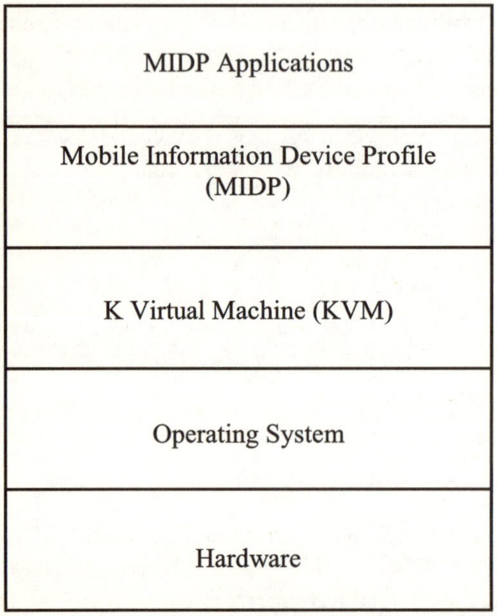

Figure 5-7: Layered architecture for Java-enabled mobile devices

When writing CLDC applications, the following restrictions apply:

- There is no floating-point support, as the hardware does not generally support floating-point operations. Hence, you cannot use floating-point literals, types, values, and operations.
- The `Object.finalize()` method is not available for the finalization of class instances.

- There is limited error handling capability: CLDC libraries support exception handling, but their capability is restricted because errors are handled in a hardware-dependent manner. Only `java.lang.Error`, `java.lang.VirtualMachineError`, and `java.lang.OutOfMemoryError` classes are supported.
- The following are removed:
  - Java Native Interface
  - **User-defined class loaders:** Available only as a built-in class loader, which cannot be overridden.
  - **Reflection:** Java programs cannot inspect the contents of classes, objects, methods, fields, threads, the execution stack, and the runtime status inside the virtual machine.
  - **Thread groups**: Multithreading is supported, but starting and stopping of threads is applied only to individual threads.

The process for developing MIDlets (applications for Mobile Information Devices) is shown in Figure 5-8. The Java source files are compiled into `.class` files, which are pre-verified and converted into packages to form MIDlet suites. The MIDlet suite is run on the emulator to test its functionality, and is subsequently ported to the actual mobile device.

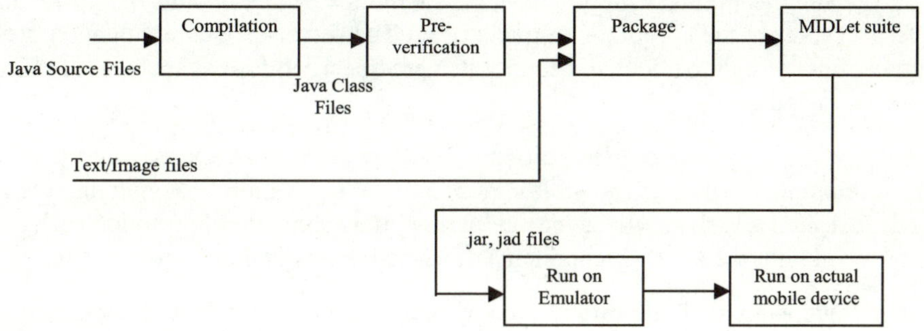

Figure 5-8: MIDlet development process

When mobile devices access applications on the Internet, security is an issue. To incorporate security for MIDP in the J2ME environment, the architecture shown in Figure 5-9 is used. A set of K Security classes and KSSL (K Secure Socket Layer) classes are available for KVM, with which the developer can develop secure applications. The Secure Socket Layer (SSL) runs above the TCP layer in the TCP/IP networks to provide authentication and encryption services.

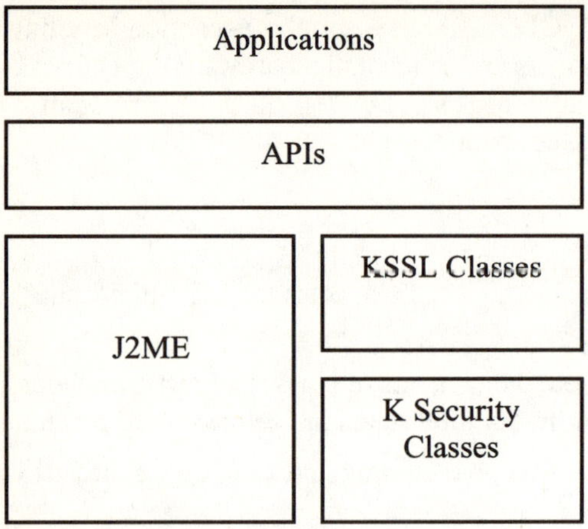

Figure 5-9: Securing applications for MIDP in J2ME

Server-side programming

When you develop applications for mobile devices, the mobile device obtains the information from the Internet server or the corporate intranet server. The server-side components retrieve the information required by the client and send it in a pre-specified format such as HTML or XHTML code, Java applets.

The architecture of the Java 2 Enterprise Edition (J2EE) provides a distributed multi-tier applications development, which is shown in Figure 5-10. When a mobile device running a browser needs to access a Web service over the Internet, the application to provide such a service is developed with the server components described in this architecture.

The application logic is divided into different components. Each component performs a specific function and can be installed on a different machine if desired:

- **Client tier** components run on the client machine, such as a desktop or a mobile device.
- **Web tier** components run on the J2EE server. The Web tier consists of components written in JSP (Java Server Pages) or Servlets.
- **Business tier** components also run on the J2EE server and consist of Enterprise JavaBeans.
- **EIS tier** components run on the EIS server. This tier can contain the legacy databases.

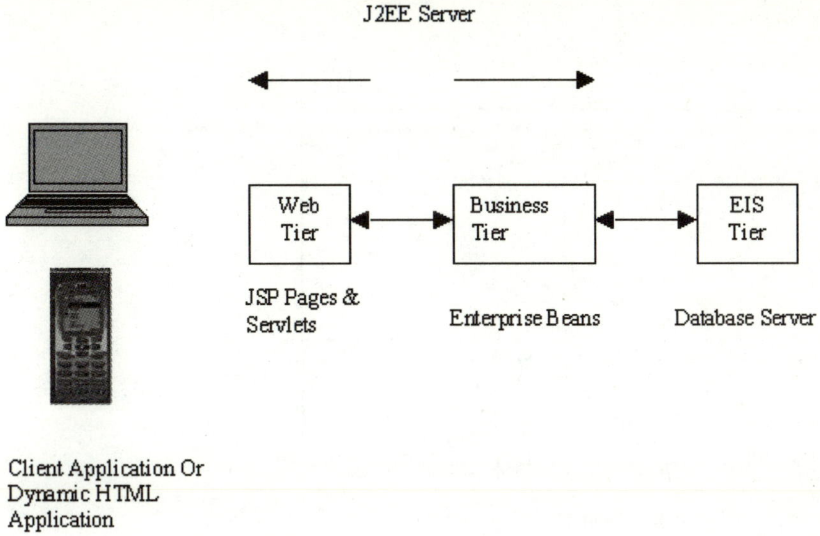

Figure 5-10: Java 2 Enterprise Edition multi-tier architecture

This division into tiers enables a modular design of the enterprise applications. Depending on your requirements, you can also have a three-tier architecture — client, J2EE server, and legacy database machine.

Information appliances

Networked information appliances are embedded systems with networking capability. An embedded system running the TCP/IP protocol stack and the application layer protocols such as HTTP, SMTP, etc., can be considered an information appliance. The architecture of information appliances is shown in Figure 5-11. Above the hardware, the operating system and the TCP/IP protocol stack are running, making the embedded system network-enabled. Above the operating system, the information appliance suite is running; it consists of mail, browser, and telephony application layer protocols, depending on the application. In addition, the virtual machine and class libraries are running, making the information appliance Java-enabled. APIs are provided for application development.

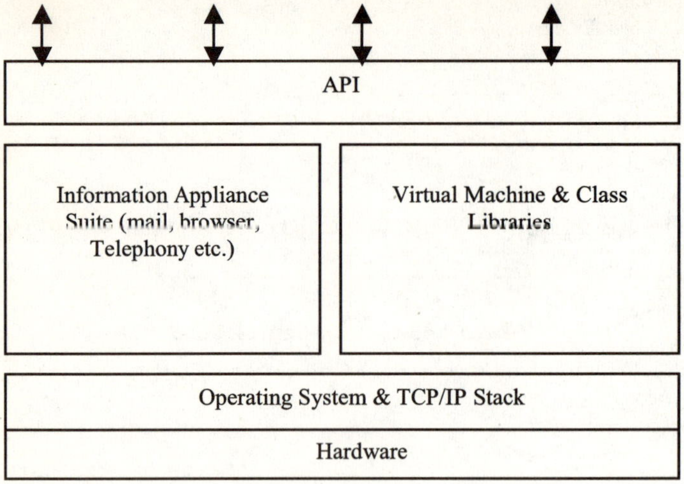

Figure 5-11: Information appliance architecture

HP's Chai Appliance Platform

Hewlett-Packard's platform to develop networked information appliances is called the Chai

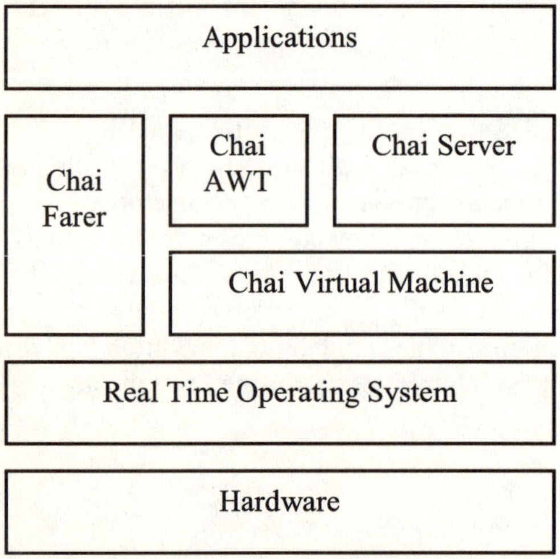

Appliance Platform. A simplified architecture of this platform is shown in Figure 5-12.

Figure 5-12: A simplified version of HP's Chai Appliance Platform

The various components of this platform are as follows:

- **Chai VM:** Provides a virtual machine for the information appliances.
- **Chai AWT:** A GUI for the information appliances.
- **Chai Server:** A Web server on which the applications are written for access by the mobile device or desktop browser.
- **ChaiFarer:** A Web browser for embedded devices.

In addition to these components, the platform provides components such as Micro Chai VM, which is a virtual machine for very small devices, and Oracle 8i Lite, which is a mobile extension for Oracle 8i for database applications. Using these components, you can develop very sophisticated networked information appliances.

An embedded system can run a Chai Server. It includes a home page, in which data generated by the appliance is kept — which can be static or can dynamically change. This home page can be accessed by a conventional desktop Web browser or a mobile device running ChaiFarer. Both the Chai Server and ChaiFarer have very small memory requirements, so developing networked information appliances with them is a very attractive proposition.

CROSS-REFERENCE Developing applications using HP's Chai Appliance Server is covered in Chapter 12.

Dynamic distributed systems

We've all encountered problems while using the LAN in our office: For example, you issue a command for a printout and realize after some time that the printer is down or has been taken offline. The administrator of a network needs to inform users whenever there is a change in the network topology or whenever new services are made available or existing services are taken out (such as a print service). These systems are called *dynamic distributed systems,* as the topology of services available keeps changing dynamically. Most networked systems (or distributed systems) are prone to failure as network topologies change and services are added and removed. According to Peter Deitsch, we make seven assumptions about networks, all of which are false — that (1) the network is reliable, (2) the latency is zero, (3) bandwidth is infinite, (4) the network is secure, (5) the topology does not change, (6) there is one administrator, and (7) the transport cost is zero.

All distributed systems are dynamic, and dynamic distributed systems have the following attributes:

- They need to be scaled up through periodic upgrading (i.e., by adding new nodes).
- The software, such as drivers, must be easy to install on the systems.
- The software must be able to run for a long time without the need for maintenance or administration.
- The network must be robust and reliable.
- The network must be able to evolve for new topologies.

Today, every LAN installation needs a system administrator, whose expertise is tapped when the topology changes, when new software or hardware is installed, or when the network is upgraded. In addition, when new services are provided (for example, the ability to fax from the desktop is added), numerous manual procedures are involved — such as informing users about the service's availability and configuring the network to make the service available. When a service becomes unavailable temporarily, users lose valuable time if they are not made aware of the unavailability. Dynamic distributed systems take care of all these issues. They provide "dynamism" to the distributed systems by making the software infrastructure on the devices robust, by making the devices support a true plug-and-play capability, by obviating the need to configure the networks, and by making the devices form "spontaneous communities." In short, the computers can be made administration-free, or almost free. Sun Microsystems' Jini connection technology provides the means of developing dynamic distributed systems.

Jini

Sun Microsystems introduced Jini in January 1999, to facilitate the development of dynamic distributed systems with the aim of providing plug-and-play capability to devices. The devices can form a network spontaneously. Jini is built on Java and uses the Remote Method Invocation (RMI) feature to create maintenance-free networks. When services are added to or removed from a network dynamically, Jini provides the mechanism to find the available services and make use of these services. For this, a set of devices forms a *spontaneous community* and the devices are made "Jini-enabled" by running a piece of software in them. Many instruments can be Jini-enabled, including computers, peripherals (such as printers, scanners, and digital cameras), and mobile devices such as phones and PDAs. A Jini device must be able to connect to a TCP/IP network, it must have an IP address, and it must be able to send and receive multicast addresses. Jini software can be run on a PC with a JVM, on devices with an embedded JVM (using personal Java or Embedded Java), or on devices without a JVM. For the last of these, however, another computer must act as a proxy for such a device to make it Jini-enabled. Conceptually, Jini-enabled devices work like this: When a device such as a desktop computer wants a print service, it checks the availability of the print service in the network. The desktop will then "lease" the print service for a fixed duration, use the service, and then free it. It is not necessary for the service to be a "hardware" service; it can be a software service, such as a program that converts PDFs into Microsoft Word files.

Jini architecture, shown in Figure 5-13, is based on five key concepts:

- **Lookup:** The lookup service is a directory service. A number of Jini-enabled devices together are called a Jini community. Within a Jini community, the lookup service provides the facility for finding and searching services. The lookup service resides on the server. It is like a market for Jini services — others can lease a service, use it, and leave it.
- **Discovery:** In a Jini community, when a new service is to be made available, that service first uses the discovery protocol to find a lookup service. Then it uses the Join protocol to register with the lookup service to become available to the clients. Discovery is the

process of finding communities on the network and joining with them. This process of discovery gives the devices access to the spontaneous community-building properties of the system.

To discover the services available on or provided by the network, various discovery protocols are defined in the Jini framework. Multicast Request Protocol is used when a service becomes active and it has to find nearby lookup services that may be active. Multicast Announcement Protocol is used by the lookup service to announce its presence to the community of devices. Unicast Discovery Protocol is used when a service knows about a specific lookup service with which it communicates. Unicast Lookup Protocol is used to create a static connection between the services.

- **Leasing:** A service can be leased by a client — for example, a print service can be leased by a client to create a printout. The client (service consumer) leases a service for a fixed amount of time. By default, a service is leased for a duration of 300 seconds (five minutes). Service leases can be renewed or canceled early. In addition, through appropriate protocols, a lease period can be negotiated. Third-party leasing is also possible. Leasing a service is actually similar to leasing a house or any other commodity.
- **Remote events:** The remote events enable services to notify the service directory of changes in their state.
- **Transactions:** Transactions are mechanisms that ensure data integrity and consistency. The transactions ensure that a process is fully completed, or it is not completed at all. Consider the example of a bank transaction in which money has to be withdrawn from one account and deposited to another account (a money transfer transaction). Clearly, both parts of the transaction must be completed; it is not acceptable if only the withdrawal portion of the transaction is completed (the bank may like it, but not the account holder). Known as *Two-Phase Commit (2PC)*, this process ensures that an entire transaction is completed. If there is a problem (of either the network or the end system), both transactions are canceled.

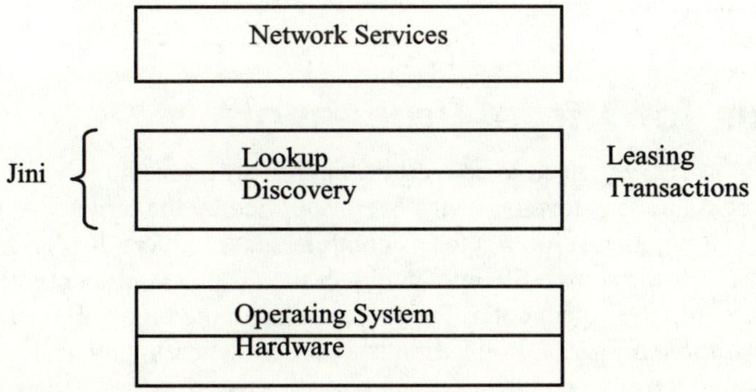

Figure 5-13: Jini architecture

Jini's use on a general-purpose computer is shown in Figure 5-14. The service provider can be a PC to which a printer is connected. On behalf of the printer, the PC can register itself with the lookup service and make its service available over the network. The service consumer, another PC, will look up the print service and then, over the network, connect to the other PC and use the print service. If for some reason the print service is not available, the lookup service is notified so that the service consumer can look for another available printer on the network.

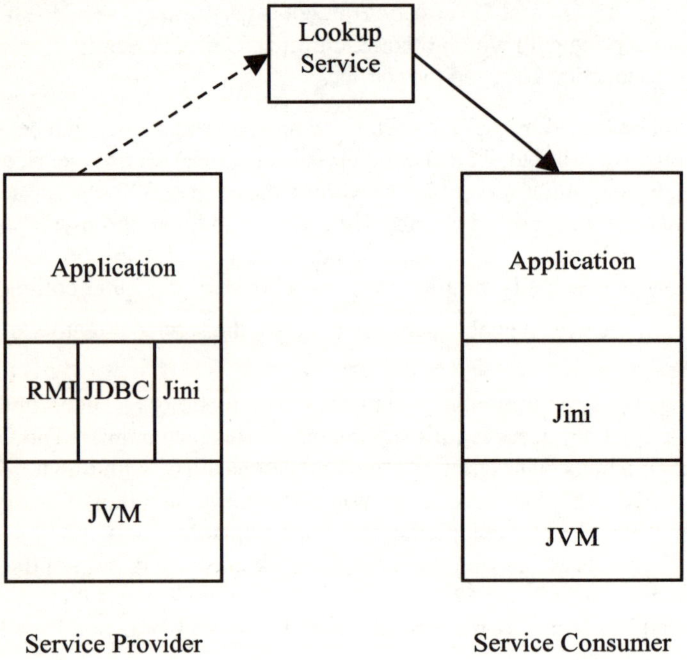

Figure 5-14: Using Jini

Development Tools for Target Processors

For embedded software development, you need to convert the source programs into the machine code of the target processor. The development system supplied by the target processor's vendor will contain a number of tools, such as compilers, assemblers, loaders, locators, etc. The compiler converts the source file into an object file. The assembler converts the assembly language program into the object code. The linker links all the object files into a single object file called a *relocatable program*. Relocation is a process wherein physical memory addresses are assigned to the code and data segments, as discussed in the chapter on the compiler's structure. The output of relocation is the executable binary image that can be run on the target platform. A cross-compiler runs on one platform and produces the code for another processor.

While developing the embedded software, you run all of these tools on a host system and then transfer the binary image to the target board.

Emulators

Before transferring the binary image to the target board, you need to check the software on the host machine itself. A number of emulators are available which emulate the hardware on the host itself. For instance, if you want to check how the output will look on a mobile device, you can invoke the emulator and run the software to see the output on the emulated mobile device. Subsequent chapters use a number of emulators — such as the Pocket PC emulator, mobile phone emulators, etc. — to present the case studies.

Device driver development

In any system — desktop or embedded — drivers are required to access the hardware peripherals, such as the serial port, the LCD display, the network card, etc. On desktops, the device driver is an extension of the operating system for accessing hardware resources, such as memory, interrupts, and input and output devices. Writing device drivers is a very challenging task because it requires an in-depth knowledge of the hardware, the operating system, the OS APIs, and bus protocols (such as USB, PCI, EISA, PCMCIA, and IEEE 1394). You can start by learning how to write a driver for an LCD module for the 8051 family of micro-controllers.

LCD driver for the 8051 family of micro-controllers

Generally, LCDs of size 2*16 (2 lines with 16 characters per line), 4*20 (4 lines with 20 characters per line), etc., with a data interface of either 4 bits or 8 bits can be easily controlled using the 8051 family of micro-controllers. LCDs use three control signals and a data bus of 4-bit or 8-bit width. You can use port P1 of the 8051 as the data bus, and some I/Os of port P3 can be used as LCD control signals (RS, R/W, and Enable).

Normally, LCD modules contain a few bytes of built-in data RAM in which you can write the ASCII value of the character to be displayed, along with the control signals. The LCD module automatically displays the character on the screen.

The LCD driver software does the following things: First, the LCD has to be initialized after power-up with a sequence of statements, which are generally defined by the LCD module vendor. After initialization, the LCD has to be programmed to work as per your requirements, such as left/right entry, blinking/nonblinking, etc. You have to write control and data words into the LCD and read the status word. The following assembly code demonstrates how the LCD can be controlled with the 8051 family micro-controller.

Source code listing for lcd.ASM

Listing 5-1 provides the LCD routine for the 8051 family of micro-controllers. The LCD module is controlled in 4-bit data mode. LCD control signals RS0, RW, and LCDEN are connected to port 1.0, port 1.1, and port 1.2, respectively. These routines display "Hello World" on the 1*16 character LCD module.

Listing 5-1: Source code for lcd.ASM

```
    RSO        BIT       P1.0
    RW         BIT       P1.1
    LCDEN      BIT       P1.2
    CLR_DISP             EQU       01H
    RT_HM                EQU       02H
    EM_SET               EQU       06H
    DISP_ON              EQU       0CH
    DISP_OFF             EQU       08H
    CURS_ON              EQU       0EH
    CURS_OFF             EQU       0CH
    DISP_LFST             EQU      18H
    DISP_RTST             EQU      1CH
    CURS_LFST             EQU      10H
    CURS_RTST             EQU      14H
    FUN_SET      EQU       28H
    DISP_WD      EQU        20H
    LEN          BIT        01H

MAIN:
    LCALL LCD_SETUP
    LCALL DISP_HEL_WORLD

WAIT:
    NOP
    SJMP WAIT

LCD_SETUP:
    MOV DISP_WD,#30H
    ACALL DDATC_WR
    ACALL DELAY_5MSEC
    MOV DISP_WD,#30H
    ACALL DDATC_WR
    ACALL DELAY_5MSEC
    ACALL DELAY_150MCSEC
    MOV DISP_WD,#30H
    ACALL DDATC_WR
    ACALL DELAY_5MSEC
    ACALL DELAY_150MCSEC
    MOV DISP_WD,#20H
    ACALL DDATC_WR
```

```
    ACALL DELAY_5MSEC
    ACALL DELAY_150MCSEC
    MOV DISP_WD,#FUN_SET
    ACALL DDATC_WR
    ACALL DELAY_150MCSEC
    MOV DISP_WD,#DISP_RTST
    ACALL DDATC_WR
    ACALL DELAY_150MCSEC
    MOV DISP_WD,#RT_HM
    ACALL DDATC_WR
    ACALL DELAY_150MCSEC
    MOV DISP_WD,#DISP_ON
        ACALL DDATC_WR
        ACALL DELAY_150MCSEC
        MOV DISP_WD,#EM_SET
        ACALL DDATC_WR
        ACALL DELAY_150MCSEC
        RET

DDATC_WR:
        MOV P1,#00H
        CLR LCDEN
        NOP
        CLR RS0
        NOP
        CLR RW
        NOP
        ANL P1,#0FH
        NOP
        NOP
        NOP
        NOP
        SETB LCDEN
        NOP
        NOP
        NOP
        NOP
        NOP
        NOP
        MOV A,DISP_WD
        ANL A,#0F0H
        ORL P1,A
        ACALL DELAY_400MCSEC
        NOP
        NOP
        NOP
        NOP
        NOP
        NOP
```

```
        CLR LCDEN
        ACALL DELAY_400MCSEC
        CLR RSO
        NOP
        CLR RW
        NOP
        CLR LCDEN
        JB LEN,DDATC_OUT
        ANL P1,#0FH
        NOP
        NOP
        NOP
        NOP
        NOP
        SETB LCDEN
        NOP
        NOP
        NOP
        NOP
        NOP
        MOV A,DISP_WD
        ANL A,#0FH
        SWAP A
        ORL P1,A
        ACALL DELAY_400MCSEC
        NOP
        NOP
        NOP
        NOP
        NOP
        NOP
        CLR LCDEN
        NOP

DDATC_OUT:
        RET

DDATD_WR:
        MOV P1,#00H
        CLR LCDEN
        NOP
        CLR RSO
        NOP
        CLR RW
        NOP
        SETB RSO
        NOP
        ANL P1,#0FH
        NOP
```

```
        NOP
        NOP
        NOP
        NOP
        SETB LCDEN
        NOP
        NOP
        NOP
        NOP
        MOV A,DISP_WD
        ANL A,#0F0H
        ORL P1,A
        LCALL DELAY_400MCSEC
        NOP
        NOP
        NOP
        NOP
        NOP
        NOP
        CLR LCDEN
        NOP
        NOP
        NOP
        NOP
        NOP
        CLR RSO
        LCALL DELAY_400MCSEC
        NOP
        CLR RW
        NOP
        CLR LCDEN
        NOP
        SETB RSO
        NOP
        ANL P1,#0FH
        NOP
        NOP
        NOP
        NOP
        NOP
        SETB LCDEN
        NOP
        NOP
        NOP
        NOP
        NOP
        MOV A,DISP_WD
        ANL A,#0FH
        SWAP A
```

```
        ORL P1,A
        LCALL DELAY_400MCSEC
        NOP
        NOP
        NOP
        NOP
        CLR LCDEN
        NOP
        NOP
        NOP
        NOP
        NOP
        CLR RSO
        RET

DISP_HEL_WORLD:
        MOV DISP_WD,#CLR_DISP
        LCALL DDATC_WR
        LCALL DELAY_5MSEC

        MOV DISP_WD,#RT_HM
        LCALL DDATC_WR
        LCALL DELAY_5MSEC

        MOV DISP_WD,#DISP_ON
        LCALL DDATC_WR
        LCALL DELAY_150MCSEC

        MOV DISP_WD,#CURS_OFF
        LCALL DDATC_WR
        LCALL DELAY_150MCSEC

        MOV DISP_WD,#80H
        LCALL DDATC_WR
        LCALL DELAY_150MCSEC

        MOV DISP_WD,#48H      ;H
        LCALL DDATD_WR
        LCALL DELAY_150MCSEC

        MOV DISP_WD,#45H      ;E
        LCALL DDATD_WR
        LCALL DELAY_150MCSEC

        MOV DISP_WD,#4CH      ;L
        LCALL DDATD_WR
        LCALL DELAY_150MCSEC

        MOV DISP_WD,#4CH      ;L
```

```
        LCALL DDATD_WR
        LCALL DELAY_150MCSEC

        MOV DISP_WD,#4FH      ;O
        LCALL DDATD_WR
        LCALL DELAY_150MCSEC
        LCALL BLANK

        MOV DISP_WD,#C0H
        LCALL DDATC_WR
        LCALL DELAY_150MCSEC

        MOV DISP_WD,#57H      ;W
        LCALL DDATD_WR
        LCALL DELAY_150MCSEC

        MOV DISP_WD,#4FH     ;O
        LCALL DDATD_WR
        LCALL DELAY_150MCSEC

        MOV DISP_WD,#52H     ;R
        LCALL DDATD_WR
        LCALL DELAY_150MCSEC

        MOV DISP_WD,#4CH     ;L
        LCALL DDATD_WR
        LCALL DELAY_150MCSEC

        MOV DISP_WD,#44H     ;D
        LCALL DDATD_WR
        LCALL DELAY_150MCSEC

        LCALL BLANK
        LCALL BLANK
        LCALL BLANK
        RET

BLANK:
        MOV DISP_WD,#20H
        LCALL DDATD_WR
        LCALL DELAY_150MCSEC
        RET

DELAY_150MCSEC:
        MOV R0,#4BH
        DJNZ R0,$
        RET
DELAY_5MSEC:
        MOV R2,#22H
```

```
261. DLY:
262.        LCALL DELAY_150MCSEC
263.        DJNZ R2,DLY
264.        RET
265. DELAY_60MCSEC:
266.        MOV R0,#1FH
267.        DJNZ R0,$
268.        RET
269. DELAY_400MCSEC:
270.        MOV R6,#07H
271. DLY400:
272.        LCALL DELAY_60MCSEC
273.        DJNZ R6,DLY400
274.        RET
       END;
```

Following is the line-by-line explanation of the source code:

- **Lines 1–17:** Variable declaration.
- **Lines 18–20:** Main routine.
- **Lines 21–23:** Wait routine.
- **Lines 24–55:** Initializes the LCD for Left-Entry, No_cursor, and 4-bit mode.
- **Lines 56–120:** Routine for commands to the LCD. These commands indicate whether or not the text should be blinking, whether the first character should appear on the left side or right side of the LCD, and the delay to be introduced between successive character display.
- **Lines 121–195:** Routine to write the data corresponding to the characters “Hello World” into the LCD.
- **Lines 196–249:** Routine for displaying the characters “Hello World.”
- **Lines 250–254:** Routine for displaying a blank character (i.e., a space).
- **Lines 255–274:** Delay routines.

Executing the program

By passing the preceding `.ASM` file to the assembler, we get the `.HEX` file (the executable for Intel’s micro-controller family). This `.HEX` file can be downloaded into an EPROM or on-chip memory of the micro-controller using a Universal Device Programmer. We can directly use this programmed device in a target board. The message “Hello World” will be displayed on the LCD unit.

Tools for embedded drivers

The previous section showed you how you can write your own code in the event that your embedded system does not have an OS. If your embedded system has an OS, you need not write the code in assembly language. GUI-based tools are now available, making the development of device drivers very easy and fast. Earlier, in the days of DOS, your application software could access the hardware devices, but now most of the operating systems are protected, and accessing the hardware is a problem. Most of the operating system vendors provide development kits for writing the device drivers. Such kits consist of the necessary header files, library routines, and sample code with which you can write the driver for your specific requirement. These device driver kits are available for different operating systems, which provide the necessary OS APIs, such as DDK for Windows NT, DDI/DKI for Solaris, and ETK/ETI for Linux. However, note the following points:

- Drivers are not compatible between operating systems; for every OS on which you want your hardware to work, you need to write the driver.
- You need to know the system calls of each OS in order to write the drivers.
- You need to understand the hardware.
- You need to understand the bus protocols for the interacation between your hardware and the host system.
- Device driver wizards are becoming available, with which you can easily build the driver software. Following are some of these tools:
  - QNX's DDK for graphics, input, printer, networking cards, and USB is available from `http://qdn.qnx.com/ddks`. The QNX real-time platform is available for noncommercial purposes from `http://get.qnx.com`.
  - Bsquare's WinDK provides the drivers for Windows 98/ME/CE 2000/NT, Linux, Solaris, VXWorks, and OS/2.
  - Jungo's WinDriver provides a 30-day trial version for driver development; it can be downloaded from `www.jungo.com/dnload.html`.

These device driver tools provide a wizard with which you can connect your hardware to the host system using a standard port and write the code based on the skeleton provided by the wizard.

Nowadays, many embedded systems are developed as PC add-on cards, and you need to write a device driver for this hardware, which interacts with the PC through either the EISA or PCI bus. The following section shows you how to write a device driver using the Windows NT DDK.

Device driver development

If you want to write the device driver for a PC add-on card, which sits on the motherboard at port address 0x300, you need not to start from scratch. You can take the already existing device driver sample code and modify it to suit your requirements. Take the example Genport file provided in the folder `DDK/SRC/GENERAL/PORTIO` for creating a driver for reading and writing from port address 0x300. Use the following step-by-step procedure to create and register the driver:

1. Edit the `Genport.h` file by changing the value for BASE_PORT to 0x300, and the value for NUMBER_PORTS to 0xa:

```
        #define     BASE_PORT          0x300
    #define     NUMBER_PORTS       0xa
```

2. At the DOS prompt, go to the `\Genport` directory.
3. Create the subdirectory for the BUILD product. For example:

```
MKDIR I386
MKDIR I386\CHECKED or MKDIR I386\FREE
```

4. Use the BUILD utility to create the driver:

```
BUILD -cef    (for the first build)
BUILD -Ze     (for later builds)
```

5. Copy the `Genport.SYS` file to the `%SystemRoot%\System32\Drivers` directory.
6. Use REGEDT32 to set up the following keys and values in the Registry:

```
HKEY_LOCAL_MACHINE
    |
    +-System
       |
       +-CurrentControlSet
           |
           +-Services
              |
              +-Genport
                  | ErrorControl REG_DWORD 0x1
                  | Start        REG_DWORD 0x3
                  | Type         REG_DWORD 0x1
                  |
                  +-Parameters
                      |      Port REG_DWORD 0x300
                      |      Span REG_DWORD 0xa
```

7. In order to see EventLog error messages, register Genport as a system event–logging component. Use REGEDT32 to add the following keys to the Registry:

```
HKEY_LOCAL_MACHINE
    |
    +-System
       |
       +-CurrentControlSet
           |
```

```
+-Services
  |
  +-EventLog
     |
     +-System
        |
        +-Genport
```

To the Genport EventLog key, add the following values:

```
EventMessageFile REG_EXPAND_SZ      %SystemRoot%\System32\IOLOGMSG.DLL
TypesSupported   REG_DWORD   0x7
```

8. If the Genport key (added in Step 6) was not previously in the Registry, reboot the system. Rebooting will make the Service Control Manager aware of the new driver. If the system has already been rebooted with this key in the Registry, the Service Control Manager knows about it and there is no need to reboot.
9. Use the Devices applet in the Windows Control Panel to start the driver. If the driver fails to load, the Event Log utility will indicate the cause of the problem.

Implementing Embedded Systems: Approach Followed in the Book

In the following chapters, you will examine in detail the implementation of embedded systems using case studies. You will develop applications for a variety of domains — process control applications, mobile applications, embedded database applications, application that control consumer appliances through wireless devices, and so on. You will do so using a variety of operating systems and programming languages, an overview of which is provided in this chapter. If you have access to a target board such as an 8051 micro-controller or an ARM processor or a mobile device, you can experiment with porting these applications using the development tools provided with the target board. Even if you do not have access to a target board, you can develop the complete code on your desktop and use the emulators to see the output. All the applications have been chosen so that you can do the development and then test the software using this approach.

Summary

This chapter presented an overview of the various software development tools for embedded software development. The operating systems, programming languages, and development tools have been discussed. From the next chapter onward, you explore the programming aspects of embedded systems using case studies for the development of embedded software using the tools and techniques discussed in the first five chapters.

Chapter 6
Serial Communication Programming

In This Chapter

- Serial communication programming between two PCs
- Serial communication between a PC and a 8051 micro-controller board
- Converting the C program into assembly language code

Serial communication is a fundamental building block of embedded software. It is used for communication between a host computer and the target embedded system. In many data logging applications, the data from the embedded system is transferred to a computer through serial communication. Almost every embedded controller board provides a serial communication interface to the external world. This chapter describes the intricacies of serial communication. After examining the code for achieving serial communication between two PCs, you will learn how serial communication is achieved between a PC and an 8051 micro-controller board.

Development Environment

You can test the code in this chapter by running the software on two PCs that share a serial communication link. The software is developed using VC++ in the Windows 9*x* environment. However, the code segment for achieving serial communication is written in C language so that you can port it to any other platform. To test the software, you need the following:

- Two PCs running the Windows 9*x* operating system.
- A null modem to connect the two PCs.
- Visual Studio 6.0 or later to convert the source code into a project file.

Serial Communication

In serial communication, the bits are transmitted serially. Most PCs have two serial ports designated as COM1 and COM2. You can use either of these two ports to achieve the communication. You need to connect the COM1 ports of the two PCs using a null modem.

You learn how to make a null modem in the section "Null Modem Cable Connections" later in this chapter.

In serial communication, one system sends the data and the other system receives the data through a designated pin. The communication is full duplex; that is, the data transfer can take place in both directions. To achieve this, two separate lines are used — one for transmitting and one for receiving. The serial communication is achieved using a standard developed by the Electronics Industries Association (EIA); the standard is defined in RS 232. This standard specifies the physical, electrical, mechanical, and functional characteristics of the interface for the communication.

Communication parameters

To achieve serial communication, you need to set the communication parameters. These parameters are set through the software running on the two systems. You cannot achieve data transfer unless the parameters are identical. You can use either the COM1 or the COM2 port to establish the communication.

To set the two serial ports to transmit data using serial communication, use the following communication parameters:

- **Baud rate:** Baud rate is the rate at which the data is transmitted between two serial ports — that is, the number of bits transmitted per second (bps). Generally, user baud rates are 4,800, 9,600, and 19,200 bps.
- **Data bits:** This is the number of bits to be transmitted in each word. Generally, the values used for data bits are 5, 6, 7, and 8.
- **Stop bits:** This is a bit appended to the end of the data bits that are going to be transmitted, to identify the end of character. This bit is known as a stop bit. Generally when the data bits are 7 or 8, one stop is appended; and for 5 or 6 data bits, two stop bits are appended.
- **Parity:** A parity bit is often appended to the character to be transmitted for error checking. A parity bit is used to enforce a rule that all characters should have either an odd (or even) number of `1` bits. If a `1` is added as the parity bit and the number of `1`s is even, it is called even parity. The parity bit can be set to `EVEN` or `ODD` or `NONE`.

Null Modem Cable Connections

You need to connect the two systems through a null modem cable. The null modem connections are shown in Figure 6-1. As you can see, the transmitting pin of the first system has to be connected to the receiving pin of the second system, and vice versa.

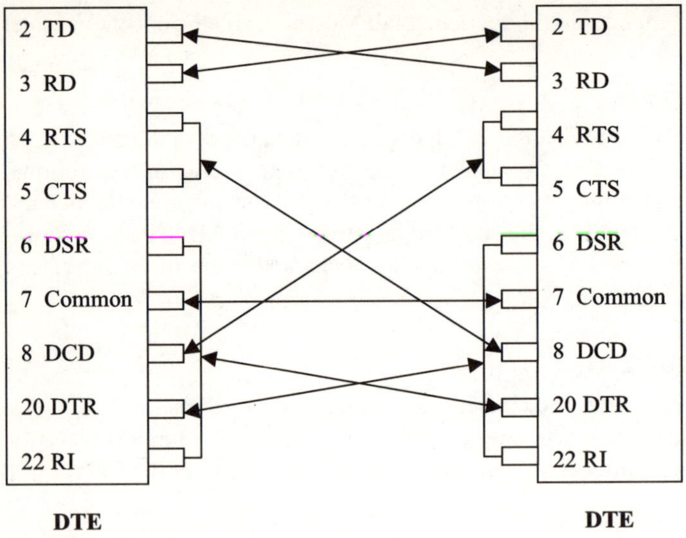

Figure 6-1: Null modem cable connections

Note that each RS 232 connector has 25 pins, but only the pins shown in Figure 6-1 are made use of. If your PC has a male RS 232 connector, you need to get a matching connector (a female connector) for the other PC, and the two "mating" connectors have to be connected as shown. This cable is called a null modem cable. The null modem cable is used to directly connect the two PCs. The DTE stands for Data Terminal Equipment. MODEM stands for MOdulator and DEModulator. A modem is used for communication between two PCs through a telephone line. If you use a modem, you also need to connect the PC and the modem through a serial interface. However, in such a case, the modem is called DCE or Data Circuit Terminating Equipment. Here, we are connecting the two PCs without a modem, hence the name null modem.

Project: PC-to-PC Communication

In this project, we will achieve serial communication between two systems to demonstrate a chat application between them. The two systems are connected through a null modem and the software is run on both the systems. The window shown in Figure 6-2 facilitates the selection of communication parameters. This window also has the necessary buttons and message boxes to send and receive chat messages.

Source code listing for CserialCommDlg.h

Listing 6-1 gives the source code for `CserialCommDlg.h`, which contains the declaration of the `CSerialCommDlg` class.

> **ON THE CD-ROM** This file is available on the CD-ROM that accompanies this book.

Listing 6-1: Source code for CSerialCommDlg.h

```
#if !defined(AFX_SERIALCOMMDLG_H__6859D5A7_F61D_11D5_A907_0080C805926D__INCLUDED_)
#define AFX_SERIALCOMMDLG_H__6859D5A7_F61D_11D5_A907_0080C805926D__INCLUDED_
#if _MSC_VER > 1000
#pragma once
#endif // _MSC_VER > 1000
class CSerialCommDlg : public CDialog
{
public:
CSerialCommDlg(CWnd* pParent = NULL); // standard constructor
//{{AFX_DATA(CSerialCommDlg)
enum { IDD = IDD_SERIALCOMM_DIALOG };
CEdit   m_recEdit;
CComboBox       m_stopbits;
CButton m_setbutton;
CEdit   m_send;
CButton m_sendbutton;
CComboBox       m_port;
CComboBox       m_parity;
CComboBox       m_databits;
CComboBox       m_baudrate;
//}}AFX_DATA
// ClassWizard generated virtual function overrides
//{{AFX_VIRTUAL(CSerialCommDlg)
protected:
virtual void DoDataExchange(CDataExchange* pDX);   // DDX/DDV support
//}}AFX_VIRTUAL
protected:
HICON m_hIcon;
//{{AFX_MSG(CSerialCommDlg)
virtual BOOL OnInitDialog();
afx_msg void OnSysCommand(UINT nID, LPARAM lParam);
afx_msg void OnPaint();
afx_msg HCURSOR OnQueryDragIcon();
afx_msg void OnSetButton();
afx_msg void OnSendButton();
//}}AFX_MSG
DECLARE_MESSAGE_MAP()
};
//{{AFX_INSERT_LOCATION}}
#endif // !defined(AFX_SERIALCOMMDLG_H__6859D5A7_F61D_11D5_A907_0080C805926D__INCLUDED_)
```

Listing 6-2 provides the source code for `CserialCommDlg.c` that contains the definition of the `CserialCommDlg` class, and various methods for setting the serial communication parameters, as well as for reading the data from and writing the data to the communication port.

Listing 6-2: Source code for CserialCommDlg.c

```
#include "stdafx.h"
#include "SerialComm.h"
#include "SerialCommDlg.h"
#include "stdio.h"
#include "conio.h"
#ifdef _DEBUG
#define new DEBUG_NEW
#undef THIS_FILE
static char THIS_FILE[] = __FILE;
#endif
unsigned int baseAdd;
int Receiver(void);
HANDLE hThread;
DWORD tid;
class CAboutDlg : public CDialog
{
public:
CAboutDlg();
// Dialog Data
//{{AFX_DATA(CAboutDlg)
enum { IDD = IDD_ABOUTBOX };
//}}AFX_DATA
//{{AFX_VIRTUAL(CAboutDlg)
protected:
virtual void DoDataExchange(CDataExchange* pDX);     // DDX/DDV support
//}}AFX_VIRTUAL
// Implementation
protected:
//{{AFX_MSG(CAboutDlg)
//}}AFX_MSG
DECLARE_MESSAGE_MAP()
};
CAboutDlg::CAboutDlg() : CDialog(CAboutDlg::IDD)
{
//{{AFX_DATA_INIT(CAboutDlg)
//}}AFX_DATA_INIT
}
void CAboutDlg::DoDataExchange(CDataExchange* pDX)
{
CDialog::DoDataExchange(pDX);
//{{AFX_DATA_MAP(CAboutDlg)
```

```
//}}AFX_DATA_MAP
}
BEGIN_MESSAGE_MAP(CAboutDlg, CDialog)
//{{AFX_MSG_MAP(CAboutDlg)
//}}AFX_MSG_MAP
END_MESSAGE_MAP()
CSerialCommDlg::CSerialCommDlg(CWnd* pParent /*=NULL*/)
        : CDialog(CSerialCommDlg::IDD, pParent)
{
//{{AFX_DATA_INIT(CSerialCommDlg)
//}}AFX_DATA_INIT
// Note that LoadIcon does not require a subsequent DestroyIcon in Win32
m_hIcon = AfxGetApp()->LoadIcon(IDR_MAINFRAME);
}
void CSerialCommDlg::DoDataExchange(CDataExchange* pDX)
{
CDialog::DoDataExchange(pDX);
//{{AFX_DATA_MAP(CSerialCommDlg)
DDX_Control(pDX, IDC_RECEIVE_EDIT, m_recEdit);
DDX_Control(pDX, IDC_STOPBITS_COMBO, m_stopbits);
DDX_Control(pDX, IDC_SET_BUTTON, m_setbutton);
DDX_Control(pDX, IDC_SEND_EDIT, m_send);
DDX_Control(pDX, IDC_SEND_BUTTON, m_sendbutton);
DDX_Control(pDX, IDC_PORT_COMBO, m_port);
DDX_Control(pDX, IDC_PARITY_COMBO, m_parity);
DDX_Control(pDX, IDC_DATABITS_COMBO, m_databits);
DDX_Control(pDX, IDC_BAUDRATE_COMBO, m_baudrate);
//}}AFX_DATA_MAP
}
BEGIN_MESSAGE_MAP(CSerialCommDlg, CDialog)
//{{AFX_MSG_MAP(CSerialCommDlg)
ON_WM_SYSCOMMAND()
ON_WM_PAINT()
ON_WM_QUERYDRAGICON()
ON_BN_CLICKED(IDC_SET_BUTTON, OnSetButton)
ON_BN_CLICKED(IDC_SEND_BUTTON, OnSendButton)
//}}AFX_MSG_MAP
END_MESSAGE_MAP()
BOOL CSerialCommDlg::OnInitDialog()
{
CDialog::OnInitDialog();
ASSERT((IDM_ABOUTBOX & 0xFFF0) == IDM_ABOUTBOX);
ASSERT(IDM_ABOUTBOX < 0xF000);
CMenu* pSysMenu = GetSystemMenu(FALSE);
if (pSysMenu != NULL)
{
CString strAboutMenu;
strAboutMenu.LoadString(IDS_ABOUTBOX);
```

```
if (!strAboutMenu.IsEmpty())
{
pSysMenu->AppendMenu(MF_SEPARATOR);
pSysMenu->AppendMenu(MF_STRING, IDM_ABOUTBOX,
                    strAboutMenu);
}
}
SetIcon(m_hIcon, TRUE);                         // Set big icon
SetIcon(m_hIcon, FALSE);                   // Set small icon
return TRUE;  // return TRUE  unless you set the focus to a control
}
void CSerialCommDlg::OnSysCommand(UINT nID, LPARAM lParam)
{
if ((nID & 0xFFF0) == IDM_ABOUTBOX)
{
CAboutDlg dlgAbout;
dlgAbout.DoModal();
}
else
{
CDialog::OnSysCommand(nID, lParam);
}
}
void CSerialCommDlg::OnPaint()
{
if (IsIconic())
{
CPaintDC dc(this); // device context for painting
SendMessage(WM_ICONERASEBKGND, (WPARAM) dc.GetSafeHdc(), 0);
int cxIcon = GetSystemMetrics(SM_CXICON);
int cyIcon = GetSystemMetrics(SM_CYICON);
CRect rect;
GetClientRect(&rect);
int x = (rect.Width() - cxIcon + 1) / 2;
int y = (rect.Height() - cyIcon + 1) / 2;
dc.DrawIcon(x, y, m_hIcon);
}
else
{
CDialog::OnPaint();
}
}
HCURSOR CSerialCommDlg::OnQueryDragIcon()
{
return (HCURSOR) m_hIcon;
}
void CSerialCommDlg::OnSetButton() // for setting comm port
parameters
{
```

```
CString stopBits,port,parity,dataBits,baudRate;
unsigned int LSB,MSB,dataFormat,temp;
m_stopbits.GetWindowText(stopBits);
m_port.GetWindowText(port);
m_parity.GetWindowText(parity);
m_databits.GetWindowText(dataBits);
m_baudrate.GetWindowText(baudRate);
if((stopBits == "")||(port == "")||(parity == "")||(dataBits ==
                        "")||(baudRate==""))
{
AfxMessageBox("All the 5 Parameters are Necessary");
return;
}
if(port == "1")
{
baseAdd = 0x3f8; // default address for comm. Port 1
}
else
{
baseAdd = 0x2f8; // default address for comm. Port 2
}
if(baudRate == "4800")
{
LSB     = 0x18;
MSB = 0x00;
}
else if(baudRate == "9600")
{
LSB = 0x0c;
MSB = 0x00;
}
else if(baudRate == "19200")
{
LSB = 0x06;
MSB = 0x00;
}
if((dataBits == "8")&&(stopBits == "1")&&(parity == "NONE"))
dataFormat = 0x03;
else if((dataBits == "8")&&(stopBits == "1")&&(parity == "EVEN"))
dataFormat = 0x1b;
else if((dataBits == "8")&&(stopBits == "1")&&(parity == "ODD"))
dataFormat = 0x0b;
else if((dataBits == "8")&&(stopBits == "2")&&(parity == "NONE"))
dataFormat = 0x07;
else if((dataBits == "8")&&(stopBits == "2")&&(parity == "EVEN"))
dataFormat = 0x1f;
else if((dataBits == "8")&&(stopBits == "2")&&(parity == "ODD"))
dataFormat = 0x0f;
else if((dataBits == "7")&&(stopBits == "1")&&(parity == "NONE"))
```

```
dataFormat = 0x02;
else if((dataBits == "7")&&(stopBits == "1")&&(parity == "EVEN"))
dataFormat = 0x1a;
else if((dataBits == "7")&&(stopBits == "1")&&(parity == "ODD"))
dataFormat = 0x0a;
else if((dataBits == "7")&&(stopBits == "2")&&(parity == "NONE"))
dataFormat = 0x06;
else if((dataBits == "7")&&(stopBits == "2")&&(parity == "EVEN"))
dataFormat = 0x1e;
else if((dataBits == "7")&&(stopBits == "2")&&(parity == "ODD"))
dataFormat = 0x0e;
_outp(baseAdd+3,dataFormat); // setting dataformat register
temp = _inp(baseAdd+3);
temp = temp | 0x10;
_outp(baseAdd+3,temp); //setting DLAb bit to 1
_outp(baseAdd,LSB);     // setting Baud Rate
_outp(baseAdd+1,MSB);
temp = _inp(baseAdd+3);
temp = temp & 0x7f;
_outp(baseAdd+3,temp); //Resetting DLAb bit to 1
m_stopbits.EnableWindow(FALSE);
m_port.EnableWindow(FALSE);
m_parity.EnableWindow(FALSE);
m_databits.EnableWindow(FALSE);
m_baudrate.EnableWindow(FALSE);
m_setbutton.EnableWindow(FALSE);
m_send.EnableWindow(TRUE);
m_sendbutton.EnableWindow(TRUE);
m_recEdit.EnableWindow(TRUE);
AfxBeginThread((AFX_THREADPROC)Receiver,NULL);
}
void CSerialCommDlg::OnSendButton()
{
CString sendMsg;
int i = 0;
unsigned int temp;
m_send.GetWindowText(sendMsg);
for(i=0;i<sendMsg.GetLength();i++)
{
while(!( (_inp(baseAdd+5)&0x40) && (_inp(baseAdd+5)&0x20)) );
                // waiting until output buffer to become empty
_outp(baseAdd,sendMsg[i]);
}
m_send.SetWindowText("");
}
int Receiver()
{
CEdit *recEdit = (CEdit*)AfxGetMainWnd()-
                  >GetDlgItem(IDC_RECEIVE_EDIT);
```

```
231. char ch;
232. CString str,str1;
233. while(1)
234. {
235. while(!(_inp(baseAdd+5)&0x01));  // waiting for data
236. ch = _inp(baseAdd);
237. str.Format("%c",ch);
238. recEdit->GetWindowText(str1);
239. str = str1 + str;
240. recEdit->SetWindowText("");
241. recEdit->SetWindowText(str);
242. }
243. return 0;
244. }
```

Following is the line-by-line explanation of the source code:

- **Lines 1–5:** Inclusion of header files. The file `SerialComm.h` will be created automatically when you create a project with the name SerialComm in the VC++ environment. If you compile the program without creating the project, you will get a compilation error.
- **Lines 6–10:** Code added by the VC++ editor to avoid re-definition of the file `CserialCommDlg.cpp`.
- **Lines 11–14:** Declaration of global variables.
- **Lines 15–32:** Class definition of `CAboutDlg` generated by the VC++ editor.
- **Lines 33–37:** Constructor definition for the `CAboutDlg` class generated by the VC++ editor.
- **Lines 38–43:** The `DoDataExchange` member function gets the data to an external form from the member data in the class. The `pDX` parameter is the context for doing this data exchange.
- **Lines 44–47:** Message map definition for handling events generated by the `CAboutDlg` dialog box.
- **Lines 48–54:** Constructor definition for the `CSerialCommDlg` class generated by the VC++ editor.
- **Lines 55–69:** Definition of the `DoDataExchange` method for handling data on `CSerialCommDlg` dialog generated by VC++.
- **Lines 70–78:** Message map definition for handling events generated on `CSerialCommDlg` dialog generated by VC++ editor.
- **Lines 79–98:** Definition of the `OnInitDialog` method generated by VC++ editor.
- **Lines 99–110:** Definition of the `OnSysCommand` method generated by VC++ editor.
- **Lines 111–129:** Definition of the `OnPaint` method generated by VC++ editor.

- **Lines 130–133:** Definition of the `OnQueryDragIcon` method generated by VC++ editor.
- **Lines 134–214:** Definition of the `OnSetButton` function, for setting communication port parameters depending on the values selected on the dialog box.
  - **Lines 136–137:** Local variable declaration.
  - **Lines 138–142:** Getting the values selected on the dialog box.
  - **Lines 143–147:** Checking whether any value is not selected.
  - **Lines 148–155:** Selecting the base address depending on the communication port selected. If the communication port selected is COM1, its default base address is 0x3f8. If the communication port selected is COM2, its default base address is 0x2f8.
  - **Lines 156–170:** Describes the selection of the hexadecimal baud rate divisor, which depends on the baud rate selected.
  - **Lines 171–194:** Describes the selection of the value to be set in the Data Format register, which depends on the data bits, parity, and stop bits selected.
  - **Line 195:** Setting the Data Format register with the value selected in the preceding condition.
  - **Lines 196–198:** Setting the DLAB bit of the Data Format register to 1 for setting the baud rate in the first two registers.
  - **Lines 199–200:** Setting the baud rate in the first two registers.
  - **Lines 201–203:** Resetting the `DLAB` bit to `0` for using the base register (first register) for `Tx` (Transmit) and `Rx` (Receive).
  - **Lines 204-212:** Code to enable and disable various controls present on the dialog box.
  - **Line 213:** Creating a thread to the `Receiver` function for receiving data from remote.
- **Lines 215–227:** Definition of `OnSendButton`, for sending data to remote.
  - **Line 223:** Waiting until the Transmitter Empty (`TXE`) bit and Transmitter Buffer Empty (`TBE`) bit of the Line Status register becomes 1.
  - **Line 224:** Writing a character of the sending message to output buffer.
- **Lines 225–244:** Definition of the `Receiver` function, for receiving data from remote continuously.
  - **Line 230:** Getting handle to receiver edit box.
  - **Line 235:** Waiting until the Data Ready (RxRDY) bit of the Line Status register becomes 1.
  - **Line 236:** Reading a character from input buffer.

Running the program

When you build the project and run the program on the two systems, you get a screen like the one shown in Figure 6-2. You can select the port (COM1 or COM2), data bits, baud rate, stop bits, and parity, and click the SET button. Once the parameters are set, you can use the application for chatting between the two PCs.

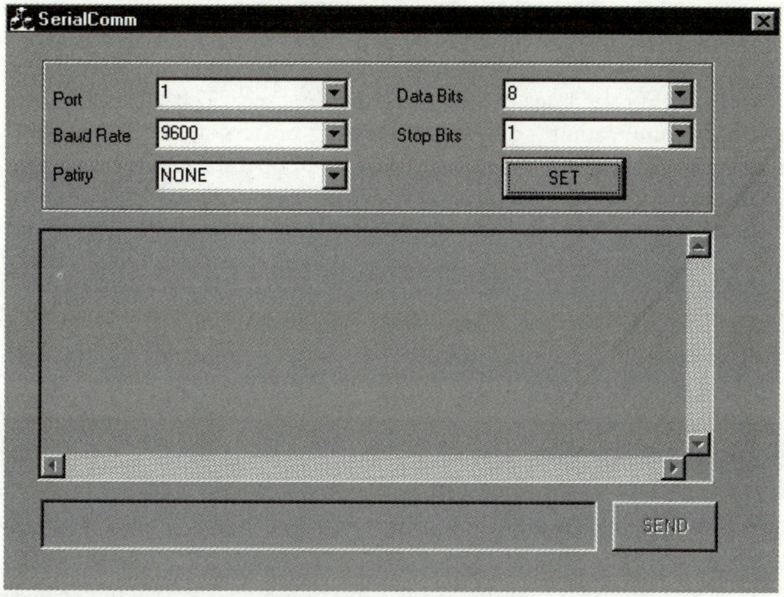

Figure 6-2: Window for setting communication parameters and for chatting

Select all the communication port parameters from the combo boxes and click the SET button. This enables the bottom three controls, which regulate the chatting application. Type the message to be sent in the edit box and click the SEND button. The message will appear on the remote computer. The messages coming from the remote computer (in this case, the second computer) will be displayed in the list box, demonstrating the full duplex communication capability. You can change the communication parameters and experiment.

Project: Serial Communication with the 8051 Family of Micro-controllers

This project demonstrates how to establish serial communication between an 8051 series micro-controller board and a PC. Through the serial link, the PC will send a series of characters, and when the character `'Y'` is sent, an LED on the 8051 controller board will blink at a fast rate. You can experiment with this code if you have access to an 8051 micro-controller. Even if you do not have access to one, you can analyze the code — this code is fundamental to serial communication with any embedded system. You can port this code to any other micro-controller board, or DSP, or microprocessor, by making any necessary changes as outlined in the data sheets. However, note that in the micro-controller board, additional circuitry is required to generate the serial data, as explained next.

The 8051 family of micro-controllers has integrated serial port hardware, with which you can establish full duplex serial communication. Two I/Os of port P3 can be programmed to perform serial transmit and serial receive operations. Other control signals, such as RTS and CTS, can also be implemented with I/O pins. The baud rate clock required for a serial port can be generated internal to the 8051 with integrated timer hardware; therefore, no external clock is required. You can set different baud rates by programming the timer. The serial port also supports interrupt-driven communication (i.e., Serial Tx and Rx buffers status via interrupt signals). You can set the serial port to work in different modes of operation — such as shift register with constant baud rate, 8-bit UART (Universal Asynchronous Receive/Transmit) with variable baud rate, and 9-bit UART with variable baud rate — by programming the serial port control register of the micro-controller. The transmit and receive sections of the serial port are associated with two registers, which can be accessed via a special function register. By writing a value into the special register, data is loaded into the transmit register and reading the special register will give data in the receive register. The serial data is transmitted/received serially with LSB (Least Significant Bit) first.

Source code listing for Serial.c

The source code for `Serial.c` is given in Listing 6-3. This file contains a group of functions that implement serial input/output in a polling mode. The code has been compiled using the Keil C51 compiler. To check that the communication is established, an LED with a register is connected between supply and P1.7 pins. Normally, the LED blinks at 1-second rate, and as soon as the character `'Y'` is received from the host, blinking rate changes to 0.25 sec.

Listing 6-3: Source code for Serial.c

```
#include <reg51.h>
#define    FLOW_TH0     0X0EA      //for 11.059MHz crystal
#define    FLOW_TL0     0X0CE
#define SOH 0X01
sbit LED = P1^7;
unsigned char c;
unsigned char k;
unsigned char MSec;
bit Led_Cont =0;
bit Speed =0;
timer0 () interrupt 1 using 1 {
TR0=0;
TH0=FLOW_TH0;
TL0=FLOW_TL0;
TR0=1;
MSec++;
if(MSec == 0x96 && Led_Cont == 0 && Speed ==0){
```

```
LED = 1;
Led_Cont=1;
MSec = 0;
}else if(MSec == 0x96 && Led_Cont == 1 && Speed ==0){
LED = 0;
Led_Cont=0;
MSec = 0;
}else if(MSec == 0x32 && Led_Cont == 0 && Speed == 1){
LED = 1;
Led_Cont=1;
MSec = 0;
}else if (MSec == 0x32 && Led_Cont == 1 && Speed == 1){
LED = 0;
Led_Cont=0;
MSec = 0;
}
}
void Start_Up(void)
{
CY=0;
ACC=0;
TH0=FLOW_TH0;
TL0=FLOW_TL0;
TMOD=0X01;
k=0;
RXD=1;
TXD=1;
}
void Sport_Init()
{
SCON=0X50;
TMOD |=0X20;
TH1=0XFD;
}
void Ena_Int()
{
TR0=1;
TR1=1;
ET0=1;
EA=1;
TI=1;
}
void main(void)
{
EA=0;
Start_Up();
Sport_Init();
Ena_Int();
while(1)  /* Infinite loop */
```

```
67. {
68.     for(;(k<=4 && TI);k++)
69.     {
70.         TI=0;
71.         SBUF=SOH;
72.     }
73.     if(RI)
74.     {
75.         c=SBUF;
76.         RI=0;
77.         if(c == 'Y')
78.         {
79.             Speed=1;
80.         }
81.     }
82. }
83. }
```

Following is the line-by-line explanation of the source code:

- **Line 1:** Inclusion of header file.
- **Lines 2– 4:** Definition of constants for timer initialization.
- **Lines 5–10:** Definition of variables.
- **Lines 11–34:** Definition of timer interrupt service routine.
- **Lines 35–45:** Definition of the `Start_Up` function for initializing micro-controller.
- **Lines 46–51:** Definition of `Sport_Init` function for setting serial port at 9,600 baud rate with 11.059 MHz crystal. The format is 1 start bit, 8 data bits, and 1 stop bit.
- **Lines 52–59:** Definition of `Ena_Int` function, for starting and enabling timer interrupt.
- **Lines 60–65:** Beginning of main function block followed by function calls for start up, starting and enabling of timer interrupt, and initializing the serial port.
- **Lines 66–83:** An infinite loop is used to collect the data from the serial port. Note that these types of infinite loops are common in embedded software, whereas you generally avoid infinite loops in normal desktop application development.
  - **Lines 68–72:** Sends 5 bytes of 0x01 to the remote terminal.
  - **Line 77:** If the character `'Y'` is received from the host, the LED connected to the P1.7 pin will blink fast.

Execution of the program

You can compile the preceding program using a cross-compiler, which generates the object code and creates a file with the name `Serial.obj`. The assembly language code generated by the cross-compiler is given in Listing 6-4.

Listing 6-4: Assembly language code generated by the cross-compiler

```
            ;FUNCTION timer0 (BEGIN)
0000 C0E0               PUSH    ACC
0002 C0D0               PUSH    PSW
0004 C28C               CLR     TR0
0006 758CEA             MOV     TH0,#0EAH
0009 758ACE             MOV     TL0,#0CEH
000C D28C               SETB    TR0
000E 0500      R        INC     MSec
     0010 E500     R       MOV      A,MSec
0012 B4960F             CJNE    A,#096H,?C0001
0015 20000C    R        JB      Led_Cont,?C0001
0018 200009    R        JB      Speed,?C0001
001B D297               SETB    LED
001D D200      R        SETB    Led_Cont
001F 750000    R        MOV     MSec,#00H
0022 803A               SJMP    ?C0008
0024     ?C0001:
0024 E500      R        MOV     A,MSec
0026 B4960F             CJNE    A,#096H,?C0003
0029 30000C    R        JNB     Led_Cont,?C0003
002C 200009    R        JB      Speed,?C0003
002F C297               CLR     LED
0031 C200      R        CLR     Led_Cont
0033 750000    R        MOV     MSec,#00H
0036 8026               SJMP    ?C0008
    0038          ?C0003:
0038 E500      R        MOV     A,MSec
003A B4320F             CJNE    A,#032H,?C0005
003D 20000C    R        JB      Led_Cont,?C0005
0040 300009    R        JNB     Speed,?C0005
0043 D297               SETB    LED
0045 D200      R        SETB    Led_Cont
0047 750000    R        MOV     MSec,#00H
004A 8012               SJMP    ?C0008
004C        ?C0005:
004C E500      R        MOV     A,MSec
004E B4320D             CJNE    A,#032H,?C0008
0051 30000A    R        JNB     Led_Cont,?C0008
0054 300007    R        JNB     Speed,?C0008
0057 C297               CLR     LED
0059 C200      R        CLR     Led_Cont
005B 750000    R        MOV     MSec,#00H
005E        ?C0008:
005E D0D0               POP     PSW
0060 D0E0               POP     ACC
0062 32                 RETI
```

```
        ; FUNCTION timer0 (END)

        ; FUNCTION Start_Up (BEGIN)
     0000 C2D7            CLR      CY
     0002 E4              CLR      A
     0003 758CEA          MOV      TH0,#0EAH
     0006 758ACE          MOV      TL0,#0CEH
     0009 758901          MOV      TMOD,#01H
     000C F500     R      MOV      k,A
     000E D2B0            SETB     RXD
     0010 D2B1            SETB     TXD
     0012 22              RET
       ; FUNCTION Start_Up (END)

                ; FUNCTION Sport_Init (BEGIN)
     0000 759850          MOV      SCON,#050H
     0003 438920          ORL      TMOD,#020H
     0006 758DFD          MOV      TH1,#0FDH
     0009 22              RET

                ; FUNCTION Sport_Init (END)

                ; FUNCTION Ena_Int (BEGIN)
     0000 D28C            SETB     TR0
     0002 D28E            SETB     TR1
     0004 D2A9            SETB     ET0
     0006 D2AF            SETB     EA
     0008 D299            SETB     TI
     000A 22              RET

               ; FUNCTION Ena_Int (END)

               ; FUNCTION main (BEGIN)

     0000 C2AF            CLR      EA
     0002 120000   R      LCALL    Start_Up
     0005 120000   R      LCALL    Sport_Init
     0008 120000   R      LCALL    Ena_Int
     000B          ?C0014:
     000B E500     R      MOV      A,k
     000D D3              SETB     C
     000E 9404            SUBB     A,#04H
     0010 500C            JNC      ?C0015
     0012 309909          JNB      TI,?C0015
     0015 C299            CLR      TI
     0017 759901          MOV      SBUF,#01H
     001A 0500     R      INC      k
     001C 80ED            SJMP     ?C0014
     001E          ?C0015:
```

```
80.     001E 3098EA          JNB     RI,?C0014
81.     0021 859900   R      MOV     c,SBUF
82.     0024 C298            CLR     RI
83.     0026 E500     R      MOV     A,c
84.     0028 B459E0          CJNE    A,#059H,?C0014
85.     002B D200     R      SETB    Speed
86.     002D 80DC            SJMP    ?C0014
87.     002F 22              RET
     ; FUNCTION main (END)
```

As you can see, the listing contains the assembly language instructions specific to the 8051 family of micro-controllers.

By passing this `.OBJ` file to the Linker/Locator, we get a `.HEX` file (an executable for the Intel micro-controller family). You can download this `.HEX` file into the EPROM/on-chip memory of the micro-controller using a Universal Device Programmer. We can directly use this programmed device in the target board for serial communication.

Summary

This chapter provided you with the detailed programming aspects of serial communication. Good understanding of the code is a must if one is to understand serial communication. You learned how to create a chat application between two PCs using serial communication. You also examined serial communication programming for a micro-controller board. Even if you do not have access to the hardware boards of these systems, going through the code will give you insight into the serial communication programming aspects of embedded systems. Serial communication is so fundamental to embedded software that many professionals specialize in serial communication alone. In the next chapter, you will learn how to build a navigation system that uses serial communication extensively.

Chapter 7
Development of a Navigation System

In This Chapter

- Using software to obtain location parameters from a GPS sensor
- Using navigation software to map location parameters onto a digitized map
- Studying the source code in detail

Market analysts estimate that location-based services will be a multibillion-dollar industry in the years to come. To obtain location parameters, a Global Positioning System (GPS) sensor is used, which retrieves the longitude, latitude, and altitude of the sensor's location. The longitude and latitude information can be mapped onto a digital map to display the position of a vehicle or a device, such as a PDA, in which the GPS sensor is embedded. Nowadays, because GPS sensors are relatively inexpensive, they are being integrated into even mass-market items such as wristwatches. In this chapter, we will develop software that demonstrates an embedded navigation system.

Development Environment

You need the following tools to develop the navigation system described in this chapter:

- A GPS sensor with a serial interface from Conexant Systems, Inc. (`www.conexant.com`).
- An embedded NT operating system loaded in a Windows NT desktop system.
- Microsoft Visual Studio 6.0 or later.
- A digitized map (scanned output of a map will do).

The GPS sensor is connected to the serial (RS 232) port of the system in which embedded NT is installed. The software obtains the positional parameters, and the position is mapped onto a digital map stored in the system.

Project Overview

The project consists of five files:

- `Serial.h` is a header file containing the declaration of the `CSerial` class.
- `Serial.cpp` is a file containing the definition of the `CSerial` class; the methods to open and close the serial port; and methods to read the data from the serial port.
- `GPSDlg.h` is a header file containing the declaration of the `CGPSDlg` class.
- `CGPSDlg.cpp` is a file containing the definition of the `CGPSDlg` class, and the methods to read the location parameters from the GPS sensor and map the location onto a digital map.
- `CityMap.bmp` is a scanned image of a city map. This file is added as a bitmap to the dialog box. You can scan a city map and store it as a `.BMP` file on your hard disk to test this application.

Source code listing for Serial.h

The file `Serial.h` contains the source code of the `CSerial` class declaration. The variables and methods used are described in the code explanation for the corresponding `.CPP` file; namely, `Serial.cpp`. The source code for `Serial.h` is provided in Listing 7-1, and the source code for `Serial.cpp` is provided in Listing 7-2.

ON THE CD-ROM These listings are available on the CD-ROM that accompanies this book.

Listing 7-1: Source code for Serial.h

```
#if
!defined(AFX_SERIAL_H__981F1CE1_F69E_11D5_AC16_0080C80496C8__INCLUDED_)
#define AFX_SERIAL_H__981F1CE1_F69E_11D5_AC16_0080C80496C8__INCLUDED_
#if _MSC_VER > 1000
#pragma once
#endif // _MSC_VER > 1000
// Serial.h : header file
// CSerial dialog
#define FC_DTRDSR       0x01
#define FC_RTSCTS       0x02
#define FC_XONXOFF      0x04
#define ASCII_BEL       0x07
#define ASCII_BS        0x08
#define ASCII_LF        0x0A
#define ASCII_CR        0x0D
#define ASCII_XON       0x11
#define ASCII_XOFF      0x13
class CSerial : public CDialog
{
    // Construction
    public:
    CSerial(CWnd* pParent = NULL);   // standard constructor
    // Dialog Data
```

```
    //{{AFX_DATA(CSerial)
    //enum { IDD = _UNKNOWN_RESOURCE_ID_ };
    enum { IDD = IDD_GPS_DIALOG};
    // NOTE: the ClassWizard will add data members here
    //}}AFX_DATA
    // Overrides
    // ClassWizard generated virtual function overrides
    //{{AFX_VIRTUAL(CSerial)
    protected:
    virtual void DoDataExchange(CDataExchange* pDX);     // DDX/DDV support
    //}}AFX_VIRTUAL
    // Implementation
    protected:
    // Generated message map functions
    //{{AFX_MSG(CSerial)
    // NOTE: the ClassWizard will add member functions here
    //}}AFX_MSG
    DECLARE_MESSAGE_MAP()
    public:
     BOOL Open (int,int,char,int,int);
     BOOL Close( void );
     int ReadData(void *,int);
     BOOL IsOpened(void);
  };
     //{{AFX_INSERT_LOCATION}}
#endif//!defined(AFX_SERIAL_H_981F1CE1_F69E_11D5_AC16_0080C80496C8__INCLUDED_)
```

Source code listing for Serial.cpp

This code obtains the location data from the GPS sensor through the serial communication port.

Listing 7-2: Source code for Serial.cpp

```
// Serial.cpp : implementation file
#include "stdafx.h"
#include "GPS.h"
#include "Serial.h"
#ifdef _DEBUG
#define new DEBUG_NEW
#undef THIS_FILE
static char THIS_FILE[] = __FILE__;
#endif
BOOL m_bOpened;
HANDLE m_hIDComDev;
OVERLAPPED m_OverlappedRead, m_OverlappedWrite;

// CSerial dialog
```

```
CSerial::CSerial(CWnd* pParent /*=NULL*/)
: CDialog(CSerial::IDD, pParent)
{
    //{{AFX_DATA_INIT(CSerial)
    // NOTE: the ClassWizard will add member initialization here
    //}}AFX_DATA_INIT
}

void CSerial::DoDataExchange(CDataExchange* pDX)
{
    CDialog::DoDataExchange(pDX);
    //{{AFX_DATA_MAP(CSerial)
    // NOTE: the ClassWizard will add DDX and DDV calls here
    //}}AFX_DATA_MAP
}

BEGIN_MESSAGE_MAP(CSerial, CDialog)
//{{AFX_MSG_MAP(CSerial)
// NOTE: the ClassWizard will add message map macros here
//}}AFX_MSG_MAP
END_MESSAGE_MAP()

BOOL CSerial::Open( int nPort, int nBaud ,char nParity,int
nDatabits,int nStopbits)
{
    char szPort[15];
    char szComParams[50];
    DCB dcb;
    unsigned char ucSet;
    COMMTIMEOUTS CommTimeOuts;
    if( m_bOpened ) return( TRUE );
    wsprintf( szPort, "COM%d", nPort );
    m_hIDComDev = CreateFile( szPort, GENERIC_READ | GENERIC_WRITE,
0, NULL, OPEN_EXISTING,          FILE_ATTRIBUTE_NORMAL |
FILE_FLAG_OVERLAPPED, NULL );
    if( m_hIDComDev == NULL ) return( FALSE );
    memset( &m_OverlappedRead, 0, sizeof( OVERLAPPED ) );
    memset( &m_OverlappedWrite, 0, sizeof( OVERLAPPED ) );
    CommTimeOuts.ReadIntervalTimeout = 0xFFFFFFFF;
    CommTimeOuts.ReadTotalTimeoutMultiplier = 0;
    CommTimeOuts.ReadTotalTimeoutConstant = 0;
    CommTimeOuts.WriteTotalTimeoutMultiplier = 0;
    CommTimeOuts.WriteTotalTimeoutConstant = 5000;
    SetCommTimeouts( m_hIDComDev, &CommTimeOuts );
    m_OverlappedRead.hEvent = CreateEvent( NULL, TRUE, FALSE, NULL );
    m_OverlappedWrite.hEvent = CreateEvent( NULL, TRUE, FALSE, NULL
);
    dcb.DCBlength = sizeof( DCB );
    GetCommState( m_hIDComDev, &dcb );
```

```
    dcb.BaudRate = nBaud;
    dcb.ByteSize = nDatabits;
    dcb.Parity = nParity;
    dcb.StopBits = nStopbits;
    ucSet = (unsigned char) ( ( FC_RTSCTS & FC_DTRDSR ) != 0 );
    ucSet = (unsigned char) ( ( FC_RTSCTS & FC_RTSCTS ) != 0 );
    ucSet = (unsigned char) ( ( FC_RTSCTS & FC_XONXOFF ) != 0 );
    if( !SetCommState( m_hIDComDev, &dcb ) ||
    !SetupComm( m_hIDComDev, 10000, 10000 ) ||
    m_OverlappedRead.hEvent == NULL ||
    m_OverlappedWrite.hEvent == NULL ){
      DWORD dwError = GetLastError();
    if( m_OverlappedRead.hEvent != NULL )CloseHandle(
m_OverlappedRead.hEvent );
    if( m_OverlappedWrite.hEvent !=
NULL)CloseHandle(m_OverlappedWrite.hEvent );
    CloseHandle( m_hIDComDev );
    return( FALSE );
}
  m_bOpened = TRUE;
  return( m_bOpened );
}

BOOL CSerial::Close( void )
{
    if( !m_bOpened || m_hIDComDev == NULL ) return( TRUE );
 if( m_OverlappedRead.hEvent != NULL ) CloseHandle( m_OverlappedRead.hEvent
);
    if( m_OverlappedWrite.hEvent != NULL ) CloseHandle(
m_OverlappedWrite.hEvent );
    CloseHandle( m_hIDComDev );
    m_bOpened = FALSE;
    m_hIDComDev = NULL;
    return( TRUE );
}

int CSerial::ReadData( void *buffer, int limit )
{
    BOOL bReadStatus;
    DWORD dwBytesRead, dwErrorFlags;
    COMSTAT ComStat;
    if( !m_bOpened || m_hIDComDev == NULL ) return( 0 );
    ClearCommError( m_hIDComDev, &dwErrorFlags, &ComStat );
    if( !ComStat.cbInQue ) return( 0 );
    dwBytesRead = (DWORD) ComStat.cbInQue;
    if( limit < (int) dwBytesRead ) dwBytesRead = (DWORD) limit;
    bReadStatus = ReadFile( m_hIDComDev, buffer, dwBytesRead,
&dwBytesRead, &m_OverlappedRead );
      if( !bReadStatus ){
```

```
97.         if( GetLastError() == ERROR_IO_PENDING ){
98.             WaitForSingleObject( m_OverlappedRead.hEvent, 2000 );
99.             return( (int) dwBytesRead );
100.        }
101.      return( 0 );
102.      }
103.    return( (int) dwBytesRead );
104.  }
```

Following is the line-by-line explanation of the source code:

- **Lines 2–4:** Inclusion of header files. Note that the header file `GPS.h` is the application header file automatically generated by the VC++ class wizard when you create the project GPS in the VC++ environment with the project name GPS. `Serial.h` is the header file provided in Listing 7-1.
- **Lines 5–9:** Preprocessor directives.
- **Lines 10–12:** Declaration of global variables.
- **Lines 14–20:** Definition of constructor for `CSerial` class, generated by the VC++ editor.
- **Lines 21–27:** Definition of `DoDataExchange` method, generated by the VC++ editor.
- **Lines 28–32:** Message map definition, generated by the VC++ editor.
- **Lines 33–75:** Definition of `Open` function for opening serial port and for setting the communication parameters: baud rate, parity, stop bits, and data bits.
  - **Line 42:** Creating and initializing a file to the `Tx` (Transmit) and `Rx` (Receive) buffers of the commmunication port.
  - **Lines 46–51:** Setting timeouts for read and write operations.
  - **Lines 55–59:** Setting baud rate, number of data bits, parity, and stop bits.
- Lines **76–84:** Definition of `Close` function for closing the serial port.
- Lines **85–104:** Definition of `ReadData` function for reading the data from the serial port.
  - **Line 90:** Checking whether the communication port is open or not.
  - **Line 92:** Checking whether the input buffer is empty or not (for reading the data).
  - **Line 95:** Reading data from the file.

Source code listing for GPSDlg.h

Listing 7-3 gives the source code for `GPSDlg.h`, a header file containing the declaration of the `CGPSDlg` class.

Listing 7-3: Source code for GPSDlg.h

```
#if !defined(AFX_GPSDLG_H__981F1CD7_F69E_11D5_AC16_0080C80496C8__INCLUDED_)
#define AFX_GPSDLG_H__981F1CD7_F69E_11D5_AC16_0080C80496C8__INCLUDED_
#if _MSC_VER > 1000
#pragma once
#endif // _MSC_VER > 1000
// CGPSDlg dialog
class CGPSDlg : public CDialog
{
   // Construction
   public:
   CGPSDlg(CWnd* pParent = NULL);     // standard constructor
   // Dialog Data
   //{{AFX_DATA(CGPSDlg)
   enum { IDD = IDD_GPS_DIALOG };
   CStatic       m_location;
   CStatic       m_lon;
   CStatic       m_lat;
   CStatic       m_alt;
   //}}AFX_DATA
   // ClassWizard generated virtual function overrides
   //{{AFX_VIRTUAL(CGPSDlg)
   protected:
    virtual void DoDataExchange(CDataExchange* pDX);       // DDX/DDV support
    //}}AFX_VIRTUAL
    // Implementation
   protected:
    HICON m_hIcon;
    // Generated message map functions
    //{{AFX_MSG(CGPSDlg)
    virtual BOOL OnInitDialog();
    afx_msg void OnSysCommand(UINT nID, LPARAM lParam);
    afx_msg void OnPaint();
    afx_msg HCURSOR OnQueryDragIcon();
    //}}AFX_MSG
    DECLARE_MESSAGE_MAP()
   public:
    void GpsReceiver(void);
};
//{{AFX_INSERT_LOCATION}}
// Microsoft Visual C++ will insert additional declarations immediately before the previous line.
#endif //!defined(AFX_GPSDLG_H__981F1CD7_F69E_11D5_AC16_0080C80496C8__INCLUDED_)
```

Source code listing for GPSDlg.cpp

The file `GPSDlg.cpp` contains the class definition and the methods for displaying the location information on a digitized map.

Listing 7-4: Source code for GPSDlg.cpp

```
// GPSDlg.cpp
#include "stdafx.h"
#include "GPS.h"
#include "GPSDlg.h"
#include "stdio.h"
#include "serial.h"
#ifdef _DEBUG
#define new DEBUG_NEW
#undef THIS_FILE
static char THIS_FILE[] = __FILE__;
#endif
// CAboutDlg dialog used for App About
class CAboutDlg : public CDialog
{
   public:
   CAboutDlg();
   // Dialog Data
   //{{AFX_DATA(CAboutDlg)
   enum { IDD = IDD_ABOUTBOX };
//}}AFX_DATA
// ClassWizard generated virtual function overrides
//{{AFX_VIRTUAL(CAboutDlg)
protected:
  virtual void DoDataExchange(CDataExchange* pDX);    // DDX/DDV
support
  //}}AFX_VIRTUAL
  // Implementation
protected:
  //{{AFX_MSG(CAboutDlg)
  //}}AFX_MSG
  DECLARE_MESSAGE_MAP()
};
CAboutDlg::CAboutDlg() : CDialog(CAboutDlg::IDD)
{
   //{{AFX_DATA_INIT(CAboutDlg)
   //}}AFX_DATA_INIT
}
void CAboutDlg::DoDataExchange(CDataExchange* pDX)
{
   CDialog::DoDataExchange(pDX);
   //{{AFX_DATA_MAP(CAboutDlg)
   //}}AFX_DATA_MAP
```

```
}
BEGIN_MESSAGE_MAP(CAboutDlg, CDialog)
//{{AFX_MSG_MAP(CAboutDlg)
// No message handlers
//}}AFX_MSG_MAP
END_MESSAGE_MAP()
CGPSDlg::CGPSDlg(CWnd* pParent /*=NULL*/)
: CDialog(CGPSDlg::IDD, pParent)
{
    //{{AFX_DATA_INIT(CGPSDlg)
    // NOTE: the ClassWizard will add member initialization here
    //}}AFX_DATA_INIT
    // Note that LoadIcon does not require a subsequent DestroyIcon in Win32
    m_hIcon = AfxGetApp()->LoadIcon(IDR_MAINFRAME);
}
void CGPSDlg::DoDataExchange(CDataExchange* pDX)
{
    CDialog::DoDataExchange(pDX);
    //{{AFX_DATA_MAP(CGPSDlg)
    DDX_Control(pDX, IDC_LOCATION, m_location);
    DDX_Control(pDX, IDC_LON, m_lon);
    DDX_Control(pDX, IDC_LAT, m_lat);
    DDX_Control(pDX, IDC_ALT, m_alt);
    //}}AFX_DATA_MAP
}
BEGIN_MESSAGE_MAP(CGPSDlg, CDialog)
//{{AFX_MSG_MAP(CGPSDlg)
ON_WM_SYSCOMMAND()
ON_WM_PAINT()
ON_WM_QUERYDRAGICON()
//}}AFX_MSG_MAP
END_MESSAGE_MAP()
BOOL CGPSDlg::OnInitDialog()
{
    CDialog::OnInitDialog();
    // Add "About..." menu item to system menu.
    // IDM_ABOUTBOX must be in the system command range.
    ASSERT((IDM_ABOUTBOX & 0xFFF0) == IDM_ABOUTBOX);
    ASSERT(IDM_ABOUTBOX < 0xF000);
    CMenu* pSysMenu = GetSystemMenu(FALSE);
    if (pSysMenu != NULL)
    {
        CString strAboutMenu;
        strAboutMenu.LoadString(IDS_ABOUTBOX);
        if (!strAboutMenu.IsEmpty())
        {
            pSysMenu->AppendMenu(MF_SEPARATOR);
```

```
            pSysMenu->AppendMenu(MF_STRING, IDM_ABOUTBOX, strAboutMenu);
        }
    }
// Set the icon for this dialog.  The framework does this automatically
//  when the application's main window is not a dialog
SetIcon(m_hIcon, TRUE);                       // Set big icon
SetIcon(m_hIcon, FALSE);                 // Set small icon
// call GpsReceiver method
GpsReceiver();
return TRUE;  // return TRUE  unless you set the focus to a control
}
void CGPSDlg::OnSysCommand(UINT nID, LPARAM lParam)
{
    if ((nID & 0xFFF0) == IDM_ABOUTBOX)
    {
    CAboutDlg dlgAbout;
    dlgAbout.DoModal();
    }
    else
    {
        CDialog::OnSysCommand(nID, lParam);
    }
}
void CGPSDlg::OnPaint()
{
    if (IsIconic())
    {
        CPaintDC dc(this); // device context for painting
        SendMessage(WM_ICONERASEBKGND, (WPARAM) dc.GetSafeHdc(), 0);
        // Center icon in client rectangle
        int cxIcon = GetSystemMetrics(SM_CXICON);
        int cyIcon = GetSystemMetrics(SM_CYICON);
        CRect rect;
        GetClientRect(&rect);
        int x = (rect.Width() - cxIcon + 1) / 2;
        int y = (rect.Height() - cyIcon + 1) / 2;
        // Draw the icon
        dc.DrawIcon(x, y, m_hIcon);
     }
     else
     {
        CDialog::OnPaint();
     }
}
HCURSOR CGPSDlg::OnQueryDragIcon()
{
    return (HCURSOR) m_hIcon;
```

```
}
void CGPSDlg::GpsReceiver()
{
    CString temp;
    CPoint point;
    int iLat,iLon;
    unsigned char ch[1],Lat[12],Lon[13],Alt[11],string[60];
    unsigned int i;
    CSerial serObj;

    if(!serObj.Open(1,9600,'n',8,1))
    {
        AfxMessageBox("failed to open Comm Port 1");
        return;
    }

while(1)
{
      if(serObj.ReadData(ch,1) > 0)
      {
        if((ch[0] == 'g') || (ch[0] == 'G'))
        {
          serObj.ReadData(ch,1);
          if((ch[0] == 'p') || (ch[0] == 'P'))
          {
                 serObj.ReadData(ch,1);
              if((ch[0] == 'g') || (ch[0] == 'G'))
              {
                   serObj.ReadData(ch,1);
                   if((ch[0] == 'g') || (ch[0] == 'G'))
                   {
                       serObj.ReadData(ch,1);
                       if((ch[0] == 'a') || (ch[0] == 'A'))
                       {
                         serObj.ReadData(ch,1);  // ','
                         if(ch[0] != ',')
                            continue;
                         serObj.ReadData(ch,1); //first char of time of','
                         if(ch[0] == ',')
                            continue;
                         serObj.ReadData(string,55);//remaining chars of time
                         string[55] = '\0';
/*
   A sample message packet that starts with GPGGA is as follows:
   $GPGGA,222435,3339.7334,N,11751.7598,W,2,06,1.33,27.0,M,-34.4,M,7,0000*41
   The contents of the above message are :
```

```
        Field Description                              Field Type
Example

        Start of sentence and address field
$GPGGA
        Time                                 hhmmss         222435
        Latitude                                  1111.1111
3333.7334
        Latitude Direction                        a              N
        Longitude                                 yyyyy.yy
11751.7598
        Longitude Direction                       a              W

        GPS Quality Indicator                     x              2
        Number of Satelites in use                xx             06
        Horizontal Dilution  of Precision         x.x            1.33
        Altitude                                  x.x            27.0
        Units of Altitude                         M              M
        Geodetic Separation                       x.x            -
34.4
        Units of Geodetic Separation              M              M
        Age of Differential GPS Data              x.x            7
        Differiential reference Station ID        xxxx
0000
        Checksum                                  *hh            *41
*/

                        Lat[0]  = string[6];
                        Lat[1]  = string[7];
                        Lat[2]  = string[8];
                        Lat[3]  = string[9];
                        Lat[4]  = string[10];
                        Lat[5]  = string[11];
                        Lat[6]  = string[12];
                        Lat[7]  = string[13];
                        Lat[8]  = string[14];
                        Lat[9]  = ' ';
                        Lat[10]  = string[16];
                        Lat[11]  = '\0';

                        Lon[0]  = string[18];
                        Lon[1]  = string[19];
                        Lon[2]  = string[20];
                        Lon[3]  = string[21];
                        Lon[4]  = string[22];
                        Lon[5]  = string[23];
                        Lon[6]  = string[24];
                        Lon[7]  = string[25];
```

```
                        Lon[8] = string[26];
                        Lon[9] = string[27];
                        Lon[10] = ' ';
                        Lon[11] = string[29];
                        Lon[12] = '\0';

                        for(i=0;i<10;i++)
                        {
                          Alt[i] = string[41+i];//obtain units of
longitude (meter or kilometer)
                          if(string[41+i] == 'M')
                          {
                             Alt[41+i-1] = ' ';
                             Alt[41+i+1] = '\0';
                             break;
                          }
                        }

                        temp.Format("Lat : %s",Lat);
                        m_lat.SetWindowText(temp);
                        temp.Format("Lon : %s",Lon);
                        m_lon.SetWindowText(temp);
                        temp.Format("Alt : %s",Alt);
                        m_alt.SetWindowText(temp);

                        Lat[4] = '\0';
                        Lon[5] = '\0';
                        temp.Format("%s",Lat);
                        iLat = atoi(temp);
                        temp.Format("%s",Lon);
                        iLon = atoi(temp);

                        point.x = iLon;
                        point.y = iLat;

m_location.SetWindowPos(NULL,point.x,point.y
                                    ,0,0,SWP_NOSIZE);
                        continue;
                   }
               }
            }
          }
     }
       }
     }
}
```

Following is the line-by-line explanation of the source code:

- **Lines 2–6:** Including the header files.
- **Lines 7–11:** Preprocessor directives.
- **Lines 12–31:** Definition of `CAboutDlg` class. This code is generated by the VC++ editor.
- **Lines 32–36:** Definition of constructor for `CAboutDlg` class, generated by the VC++ editor.
- **Lines 37–42:** Definition of `DoDataExchange` method for `CAboutDlg` dialog, generated by the VC++ editor.
- **Lines 43–47:** Message map definition for handling events generated on `CAboutDlg` dialog by the VC++ editor.
- **Lines 48–56:** Definition of constructor for `CGPSDlg` class, generated by the VC++ editor.
- **Lines 57–66:** Definition of `DoDataExchange` method for `CGPSDlg` dialog, generated by the VC++ editor.
- **Lines 67–73:** Message map definition for handling events generated on `CGPSDlg` dialog by the VC++ editor.
- **Lines 74–99:** Definition of `OnInitDialog` method, generated by the VC++ editor.
- **Line 97:** The method `GpsReceiver` is called. This method is for reading packets from the GPS sensor through serial interface.
- **Lines 100–111:** Definition of `OnSysCommand` method, generated by the VC++ editor.
- **Lines 112–132:** Definition of `OnPaint` method, generated by the VC++ editor.
- **Lines 133–136:** Definition of `OnQueryDragIcon` method, generated by the VC++ editor.
- **Lines 137–234:** Definition of `GPSReceiver` method for reading packets from the GPS receiver and extracting values for latitude, longitude, and altitude.
  - **Lines 139–144:** Declaration of local variables.
  - **Lines 145–149:** Opening of COM1 port with baud rate 9,600, parity NONE, data bits 8, and stop bits 1. These are the default communication parameters for the GPS sensor. If the opening of the port is not successful, the message box “failed to open comm. Port 1” is generated.
  - **Lines 150–166:** From the input buffer of COM1 port, each character is read and a check is carried out to match the string `GPGGA`. Beginning with `GPGGA`, the location parameters will be available on the serial port data.
  - **Lines 168–173:** Checking whether data is available in the `GPGGA` packet.
  - **Line 174:** Reading data from input buffer.

- **Line 176:** A comment explaining a sample message packet that starts with GPGGA is as follows:

```
    $GPGGA,222435,3339.7334,N,11751.7598,W,2,06,1.33,27.0,M,-
34.4,M,7,0000*41
```

The contents of the preceding packet are:

Field Description	*Field Type*	*Example*
Start of sentence and address field		$GPGGA
Time	hhmmss	222435
Latitude	llll.llll	3333.7334
Latitude Direction	A	N
Longitude	yyyyy.yy	11751.7598
Longitude Direction	A	W
GPS Quality Indicator	X	2
Number of satellites in use	Xx	06
Horizontal Dilution of Precision	x.x	1.33
Altitude	x.x	27.0
Units of Altitude	M	M
Geodetic Separation	x.x	-34.4
Units of Geodetic Separation	M	M
Age of Differential GPS Data	x.x	7
Differential reference Station ID	xxxx	0000
Checksum	*hh	*41

- **Lines 177–188:** The latitude value is obtained from the data string.
- **Lines 189–201:** The longitude value is obtained from the data string.
- **Lines 202–211:** The value of altitude is obtained from the data string.
- **Lines 212–217:** Latitude, longitude, and altitude values are displayed on the output window.
- **Lines 224–225:** Sets the location coordinates for display.
- **Line 226:** Sets the window position on the map.

Executing the program

To test the program, you can initially execute the program on the desktop. Build the project in the Visual Studio environment and run the project. The output will be displayed showing the map and a "star," which indicates the current location, as shown in Figure 7-1.

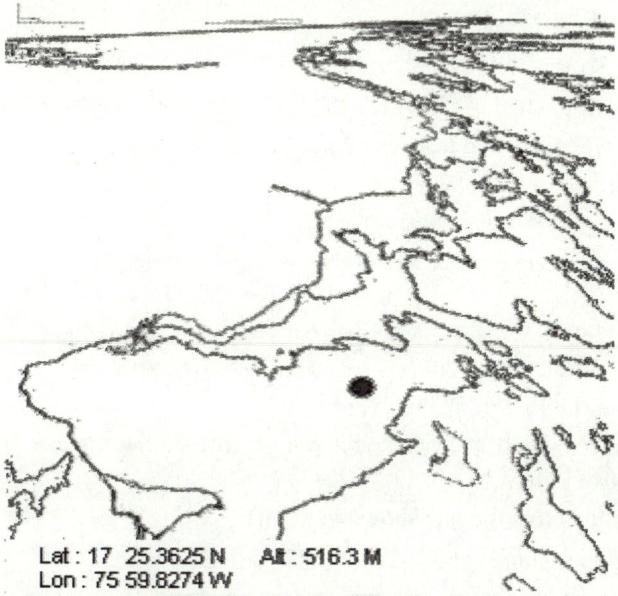

Figure 7-1: Digitized map indicating the current location

Porting the software to the embedded NT platform

To port the software to embedded NT, use the following steps:

1. Collect all the files required to run the application at the target. In this case, the following files are required:
   - `GPS.EXE` (application file)
   - `MFC42D.DLL`
   - `MFCO42D.DLL`
   - `MSVCRTD.DLL`

   The three DLLs are required to run an MFC application on the target platform.

2. Create a component using Component Designer. The following steps illustrate how to create a custom component:
   - Open Component Designer (from the Windows taskbar, select Start ⇨ Programs ⇨ Windows NT Embedded 4.0 ⇨ Component Designer).

- Save the component as `GPSSample.kdf` (`.KDF` is the file extension for a component file).
- In the navigation pane, right-click Component1, and then click Properties.
- In the Component Name text box, type **GPS Sample**.
- In the Vendor text box, type **Generic**.
- In the Description text box, type **Global Positioning System** and then click OK.
- In the navigation pane, right-click the GPS Sample, and then click Add Component.
- In the component text box, type **GPS** and leave the remaining fields empty.
- Verify that the hierarchy path is set as follows: `%ROOT%\Applications\Utilities`, and click OK.
- In the navigation pane, under the Generic SCSI Driver component, right-click Files, and then click AddFile.
- In the File Name text box, click Browse. Browse for `GPS.EXE` (the application file that is collected in Step 1). Set the target path as `\Winnt\GPS`. (The application `GPS.EXE` will be stored in this directory at the target.)
- Add the remaining three DLLs, which are collected in Step 1, in a similar manner. The target path for these three files should be `\Winnt\System32`.
- Finally, the window should look like the one shown in Figure 7-2.
- Save the component definition file and exit.

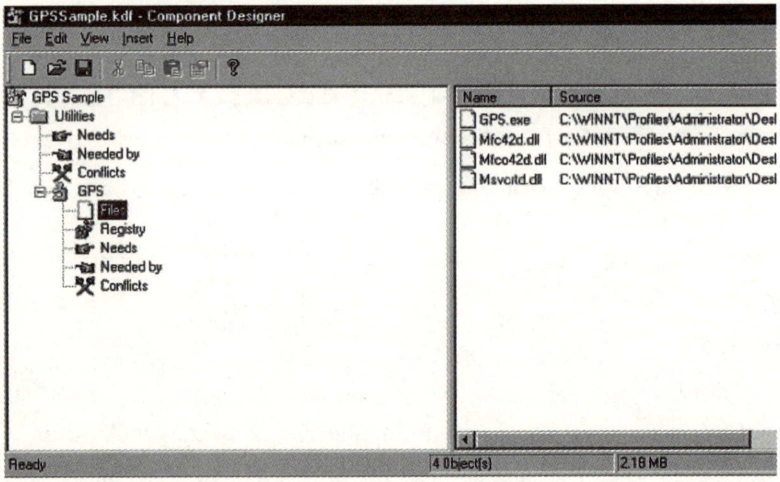

Figure 7-2: Component Designer

3. Create the target image using Target Designer.

- Open Target Designer (from the Windows taskbar, select Start ⇨ Programs ⇨ Windows NT Embedded 4.0 ⇨ Target Designer).
- In the All Nodes pane, expand the Target Designer system database (TDSD). Expand the Examples collection.
- Copy the Standard No Network configuration. Right-click on User Configuration and then click Paste.
- Right-click the Standard No Network configuration that was pasted under the User configurations collection, and then click Rename. Type **GPS**.
- Expand the tree structure under GPS. Right-click on Serial Mouse under `\GPS\System\Devices\Mouse` and click Add.
- Similarly, add COM1 and COM2, which are under `\GPS\System\Devices\Serial Ports`.
- To add the GPS Sample component created in Step 2, select Files ⇨ Tools ⇨ Component Management and then click Add. Browse for `GPSSample.kdf` and click OK.
- A node named GPS will be added to the tree structure under `\GPS\Applications\Utilities`. Right-click on GPS and click Add.
- In the All Nodes pane, verify that the GPS, which is under User Configuration, is selected. At this stage, the window looks as shown in Figure 7-3.
- On the Image menu, click Settings. Verify that the Source Repository Path for WinNT is CD1, which is in the Windows Embedded NT 4.0 CD-ROM; and that the Target path is set to *D*:`\GPSAppWithEmbeddedNT` (the final target image is stored in this directory; *D* represents the letter of your hard disk drive). Note that your Windows Embedded NT 4.0 is in CD-ROM and you are creating the target on a hard disk. The dialog box shown in Figure 7-4 appears.
- Now select Image ⇨ Build and Install ⇨ Start.
- When a message states that you have not entered a product identification (PID) number and asks if you want to build a time-limited test embedded runtime image, click Yes.
- When the "Install Complete" message appears, click OK. This will take a few minutes.
- Now go to the `\GPSAppWithEmbeddedNT` directory, which is in your local hard disk where the target image is created, and copy all the subdirectories and files into the target's hard disk.

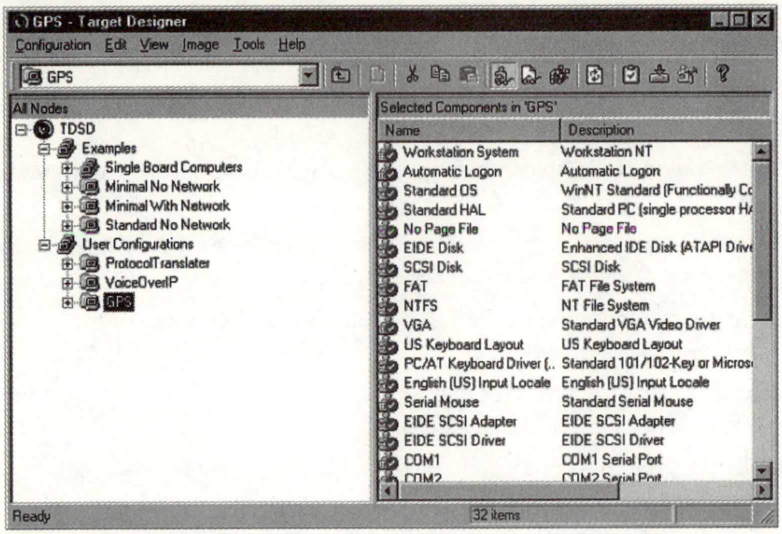

Figure 7-3: Target Designer

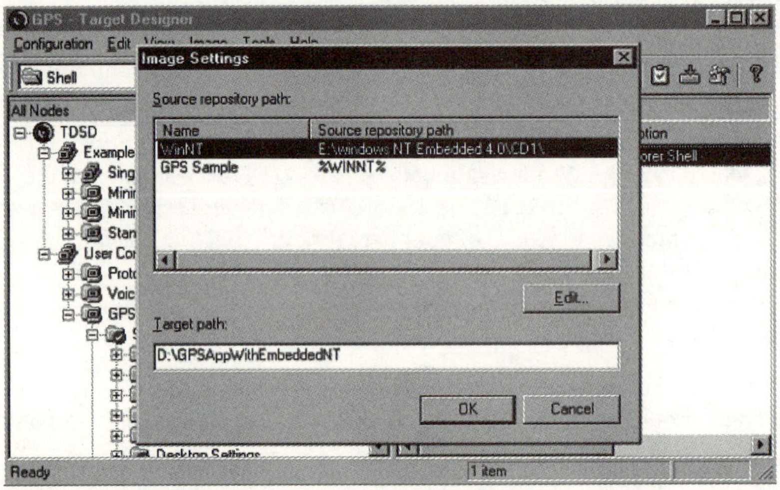

Figure 7-4: Image settings

The application and the required DLLs occupy approximately 2.17MB of memory. The target image that has to be embedded in the embedded system occupies approximately 78.5MB if you do not strip off any drivers. However, in our application, we need only a serial interface driver; therefore, you can remove all other drivers from the embedded NT, including the mouse driver, the second serial port driver, etc. After removing the components, you will need about 18MB of memory. Hence, embedding the application does not consume much memory. You also have the option of booting from the CD-ROM instead of the hard disk.

Summary

This chapter demonstrated the development of a navigation system using a GPS sensor. The source code for obtaining the location parameters from the GPS sensor through a serial interface is presented. The navigation software takes this positional data (i.e., longitude, latitude, and altitude) and maps it onto a digitized map to display the current location of the vehicle or device on which the GPS sensor is mounted. The application presented here can be easily extended to provide location-based services. For example, if a map contains information about restaurants, hospitals, and hotels, based on the current location, a user can find the nearest service needed. Alternatively, the service location data can be stored in a database and retrieved by the user based on the current location.

Chapter 8
Embedded Communication Systems

In This Chapter

- Implementing a protocol converter system
- Implementing an IP phone

The convergence of data communication and telecommunication is paving the way for a number of new systems using embedded software. One set of applications calls for converting the protocols in one format to another. This chapter examines the development of a protocol converter that translates Ethernet packets to serial communication. Another set of applications involves the transmission of Voice-Over-Internet Protocol (VOIP) networks, for which IP phones are now becoming available. An IP phone is an embedded system that processes voice calls and transmits and receives voice packets. You will also study the development of an IP phone in this chapter. In order to develop these systems, you should have a good understanding of TCP/IP protocol stack implementation in embedded systems, and voice-over-IP protocols. This chapter presents two case studies that will help you gain insight into the development of embedded communication systems.

Development Environment

To develop the projects described in this chapter, you need the following environment:

- A Windows NT system with embedded NT and Visual Studio 6.0 installed
- The following files from Microsoft's Windows NT DDK (Device Drivers Kit), which can be downloaded from `www.microsoft.com/downloads`:
  - `Devioctl.h`
  - `Ntdndis.h`
  - `Ntddpack.h`
  - `Packet32.h`
  - `Packon.h`

- `Packoff.h`
- `Packet32.sys` (packet driver)

To run the voice-over-IP application, you need to install sound card drivers in the target machine, as there is no default component in the Target Designer to include the sound card functionality.

Project: Protocol Converter

In this project, you will develop the software to convert Ethernet packets into serial communication packets. This type of protocol converter (or protocol translator) is required in applications such those that interconnect a LAN (Local Area Network) to a WAN (Wide Area Network). The WAN can be a terrestrial network or a satellite-based network. It takes the data packets in serial format and sends them on the communication medium, which can be cable or satellite. This project demonstrates how to catch Ethernet packets, analyze them, and translate them into the serial format. You can modify the application to develop a variety of tools. For instance, you can develop a firewall that will analyze the Ethernet packets and filter them with a specific IP address. You can also develop a *LAN analyzer,* which analyzes the packets on the Ethernet LAN and provides performance statistics.

The Ethernet packet can have a maximum size of 1,526 bytes. The protocol converter application captures the Ethernet packets, divides them into smaller packets of 100 bytes or less, converts the fragmented packets into serial communication packets, and transmits them through the serial port. The serial communication packet can actually contain 100 bytes of data plus 4 bytes of packet information. The packet structure is shown in the following table:

STX	***Length***	***Data***	***CRC***	***ETX***
0x02	—	—	—	0x03
(1Byte)	(1Byte)	(Max.100Bytes)	(1Byte)	(1Byte)

In this format, STX is Start of Text, ETX is End of Text, and CRC is the Cyclic Redundancy Check for checking the data for errors. Length denotes the length of the packet, and Data is the actual user data contained in the Ethernet packet.

The project consists of the following files:

- `Test.h`, which contains declarations of methods for accessing the packet driver
- `Test.c`, which contains the methods for capturing Ethernet packets, dividing them into small packets of 100 bytes or less and converting them into serial packets and transmitting them over the serial link
- `GlobalVar.h`, which contains declarations of methods to add and delete packets to buffers

- `Buffers.c`, which contains methods for adding and deleting packets from/to intermediate buffers
- `PTFunction.c`, which contains definitions of methods to convert fragmented Ethernet packets to serial communication packets and add them to the buffers

The source code and the explanation are given in the following sections.

> **ON THE CD-ROM** All these files are available on the CD-ROM that accompanies this book.

Source code listing for Test.h

This file (shown in Listing 8-1) contains declarations of various methods for accessing the packet driver.

Listing 8-1: Source code for Test.h

```
1.#ifndef __PACKET32
2.#define __PACKET32
3.#define        MAX_LINK_NAME_LENGTH   64
4.#include "packon.h"
5.#include "packoff.h"
6.typedef struct _ADAPTER {
7.HANDLE     hFile;
8.TCHAR      SymbolicLink[MAX_LINK_NAME_LENGTH];
9.} ADAPTER, *LPADAPTER;
10. typedef struct _PACKET {
11. HANDLE       hEvent;
12. OVERLAPPED   OverLapped;
13. PVOID        Buffer;
14. UINT         Length;
15. } PACKET, *LPPACKET;
16. PVOID          PacketOpenAdapter(LPTSTR AdapterName);
17. BOOLEAN PacketSendPacket(LPADAPTER lpAdapter,
           LPPACKET  lpPacket, BOOLEAN   Sync);
18. PVOID          PacketAllocatePacket(VOID);
19. VOID           PacketInitPacket(LPPACKET lpPacket,
             PVOID    Buffer,UINT     Length);
20. VOID           PacketFreePacket(LPPACKET lpPacket);
21. ULONG          PacketGetAddress(LPADAPTER lpAdapter, PUCHAR
addressBuffer);
22. BOOLEAN PacketReceivePacket(LPADAPTER lpAdapter,LPPACKET lpPacket,
                              BOOLEAN Sync,PULONG BytesReceived);
23. VOID           PacketCloseAdapter(LPADAPTER lpAdapter);
24. BOOLEAN PacketSetFilter(LPADAPTER lpAdapter, ULONG     Filter);
25. ULONG          PacketGetAdapterNames(PTSTR   pStr, PULONG
BufferSize);
26. #define NDIS_PACKET_TYPE_DIRECTED                 0x0001
27. #define NDIS_PACKET_TYPE_MULTICAST                0x0002
```

```
28. #define NDIS_PACKET_TYPE_ALL_MULTICAST          0x0004
29. #define NDIS_PACKET_TYPE_BROADCAST              0x0008
30. #define NDIS_PACKET_TYPE_SOURCE_ROUTING        0x0010
31. #define NDIS_PACKET_TYPE_PROMISCUOUS            0x0020
32. #define NDIS_PACKET_TYPE_SMT                    0x0040
33. #define NDIS_PACKET_TYPE_ALL_LOCAL              0x0080
34. #define NDIS_PACKET_TYPE_MAC_FRAME              0x8000
35. #define NDIS_PACKET_TYPE_FUNCTIONAL             0x4000
36. #define NDIS_PACKET_TYPE_ALL_FUNCTIONAL         0x2000
37. #define NDIS_PACKET_TYPE_GROUP                  0x1000
38. #endif
```

Following is the line-by-line explanation of the source code:

- **Lines 1–5:** Preprocessor directives and inclusion of header files.
- **Lines 6–9:** Structure `ADAPTER` declaration for storing the adapter name.
- **Lines 10–15:** Structure `PACKET` declaration for storing packet information.
- **Lines 16–25:** Declaration for various functions, including opening the adapter, closing the adapter, receving a packet, dropping a packet, and setting the filter.
- **Lines 26–38:** Declaration for constants for various filters.

Source code listing for Test.c

This file (shown in Listing 8-2) contains methods for opening the adapter, catching Ethernet packets, dividing Ethernet packets into small packets of 100 bytes or less, converting Ethernet packets into serial packets, and transmitting the packets through the serial port.

Listing 8-2: Source code for Test.c

```
#include <windows.h>
#include <stdio.h>
#include <string.h>
#include <conio.h>
#include <malloc.h>
#include <crtdbg.h>
#include "test.h"
#include "GlobalVar.h"
#include "serial.h"
int Receiver();
int E2SProtocolTx();
int SendSerial();
ULONG       Filters[6] = {0, NDIS_PACKET_TYPE_DIRECTED,
                          NDIS_PACKET_TYPE_MULTICAST,
                          NDIS_PACKET_TYPE_BROADCAST,
                          NDIS_PACKET_TYPE_ALL_MULTICAST,
                          NDIS_PACKET_TYPE_PROMISCUOUS};
TCHAR       szbuff[40];
```

```
LPADAPTER   lpAdapter;
LPPACKET    lpPacket,lpPacket1,lpPacket2;
ULONG       Filter = 0;
DWORD   tid1,tid2,tid3;
HANDLE  hThread1,hThread2,hThread3;
int         PacketCount = 0;
unsigned char *data=NULL;
unsigned int packetTx=1,packetRx=1;
int xt1,xt2,xt3,xt4,xt5,xt6;
UCHAR   Address[6];
int main(int nargs, char **args)
{
TCHAR   buf[256];
TCHAR   *Name;
ULONG   NameLength = 256;
UINT    i;
if (nargs != 2) {
printf("Usage: test [Adapter 0..3]\n");
return 0;
}
if ((atoi(args[1])) > 3) {
printf("Usage: test [Adapter 0..3]\n");
return 0;
}
Name = buf;
PacketGetAdapterNames(Name, &NameLength);
switch (atoi(args[1])) {
case 3: Name = &Name[strlen(Name)+1];
if (!strlen(Name))
break;
case 2: Name = (char *) &Name[strlen(Name)+1];
if (!strlen(Name))
break;
case 1: Name = (char *) &Name[strlen(Name)+1];
if (!strlen(Name))
break;
case 0: break;
}
if (strlen(Name) != 0)
{
  printf("Adapter Name: %s\n", Name);
}
else
{
  printf("Adapter  not present\n");
return 0;
}
lpAdapter = PacketOpenAdapter(Name);
Filter = Filters[5];
```

```
PacketSetFilter(lpAdapter, Filter);
PacketGetAddress(lpAdapter, Address);
printf("Adapter Addr: [");
for (i=0; i<5; i++)
printf("%02x:", Address[i]);
printf("%02x]\n\n", Address[i]);
if(Open(2,9600,'n',8,1))
{
   printf("port Opened");
}
else
{
   printf("failed to open\n");
}
hThread1 = CreateThread(0, 0, (LPTHREAD_START_ROUTINE) Receiver, 0,
                  0, &tid1);
hThread2 = CreateThread(0, 0,(LPTHREAD_START_ROUTINE)E2SProtocolTx
                  ,0,0,&tid2);
SuspendThread(hThread2);
hThread3 = CreateThread(0, 0, (LPTHREAD_START_ROUTINE) SendSerial,
0,
                  0, &tid3);
printf("Hit to terminate...\n\n");
getchar();
xt1=1;
xt2=1;
xt3=1;
PacketCloseAdapter(lpAdapter);
Close();
return 0;
}
int Receiver()
{
unsigned char buf1[1518];
ULONG  Length;
int i;
while (TRUE)
{
   memset(buf1,(char)NULL,sizeof(buf1));
   lpPacket = PacketAllocatePacket();
   PacketInitPacket(lpPacket, buf1, 1518);
   PacketReceivePacket(lpAdapter, lpPacket, TRUE, &Length);
   printf("\nReceived Data\n");
   for(i=0;i<Length;i++)
   printf("%02x ",buf1[i]);
   addE2PBuffer(buf1,Length);
   PacketFreePacket(lpPacket);
   E2PPacketcount++;
   ResumeThread(hThread2);
```

```
    if(xt1==1)
    {
      printf("exit1\n");ExitThread(0);
    }
} // while (true)
} // receive()
int E2SProtocolTx()
{
struct Delstruct s;
unsigned int i,j,pkcount,tempcount,spoint,pak[21][100],remote_id,cont;
while (TRUE)
{
   s = delE2PBuffer();
   E2PPacketcount--;
   pkcount=0;
   tempcount=0;
   remote_id = 1;
   if(s.Dellength > 100)
   {
    tempcount = s.Dellength / 100;
    if(s.Dellength % 100 == 0)
       pkcount = tempcount;
    else
       pkcount = tempcount + 1;
    spoint=0;
    for(i=1;i<pkcount;i++)
    {
       for(j=0;j<100;j++)
       pak[i][j] = s.Deldata[j+spoint];
       spoint +=100;
    } // for(i=1;i<pkcount;i++)
    for(j=0;j<s.Dellength-spoint;j++)
        pak[pkcount][j] = s.Deldata[spoint+j];
   } // if(s.Dellength > 100)
   else if(s.Dellength <= 100)
   {
     pkcount = 1;
     for(i=0;i<s.Dellength;i++)
     pak[1][i] = s.Deldata[i];
   }  // else if(s.Dellength <= 100)
  _sleep(100);
   if(s.Dellength > 100)
   {
     for(i=1;i<pkcount;i++)
     {
      convertEp2Sp(&pak[i][0],100,remote_id);
     _sleep(100);
     }
```

```
157.    _ sleep(100);
158.      convertEp2Sp(&pak[pkcount][0],s.Dellength-spoint,remote_id);
159.    }
160.    else if(s.Dellength <= 100)
161.    {
162.     _sleep(100);
163.      convertEp2Sp(&pak[1][0],s.Dellength,remote_id);
164.    }
165.   _sleep(100);
166.    if(E2PPacketcount <= 0)
167.    {
168.       SuspendThread(hThread2);
169.    }
170.    if(xt2==1){printf("exit2\n");ExitThread(0);}
171.   } // while(true)
172. }//void E2SProtocolTx()
173. int SendSerial()
174. {
175.    struct Delstruct p;
176.    unsigned int j;
177. while (TRUE)
178. {
179.    if( P2SPacketcount >0)
180.    {
181.     forNack = p = delP2SBuffer();
182.     P2SPacketcount--;
183.     SendData(p.Deldata,p.Dellength);
184.     printf("\nSend Data:\n");
185.     for(j=0;j<p.Dellength;j++)
186.         printf("%02x  ",p.Deldata[j]);
187.    }  // if( P2SPacketcount >1)
188.    if(xt3 == 1){ ExitThread(0);}
189. }// while(1)
190. }//int SendSerial()
```

Following is the line-by-line explanation of the source code:

- **Lines 1–9:** Header file declaration.
- **Lines 10–12:** Function prototypes.
- **Lines 13–24:** Global variable declaration.
- **Lines 25–90:** Definition of `main` function.
  - **Lines 27–30:** Local variable declaration.
  - **Lines 31–34:** Checking whether the command-line argument is passed along with the filename. The adapter number (0 to 3) should be passed as an argument.
  - **Lines 41–52:** Getting the adapter name, depending on the argument passed.

- **Lines 53–61:** Printing the adapter name. Note the `printf` statement in line 55. Generally `printf` cannot be used to print the data as it generates interrupts, thereby reducing the performance of the system. However, `printf` may be used for debug purposes, and removed (or disabled) in the final product. For this reason, it is a good practice to write your own routines for data I/O to and from the console.
- **Line 62:** Opening the adapter.
- **Lines 63–64:** Setting the adapter filter to `PROMISCUOUS` mode.
- **Lines 65–69:** Getting and printing the adapter address.
- **Lines 70–77:** Opening serial port 2 with baud rate 9,600, data bits 8, and stop bits 1.
- **Line 78:** Creating a thread for the `Receiver` method, to capture Ethernet packets from the LAN.
- **Line 79:** Creating a thread to the `E2SprotocolTx` method for converting the Ethernet packets to the serial packets.
- **Line 81:** Creating a thread for the `SendSerial` method, to transmit serial communication packets through the serial port.
- **Lines 91–114:** Definition of the `Receiver` method, for catching Ethernet packets from the LAN and storing them in the buffers.
  - **Line 100:** Initializing a buffer to store the captured Ethernet packet.
  - **Line 101:** Receiving packet from the LAN.
  - **Lines 103–104:** Displaying the received packet.
  - **Line 105:** Adding the received packet to the intermediate buffers.
  - **Line 108:** Resuming the `E2SprotocolTx` method for converting the received Ethernet packet to the serial packet.
- **Lines 115–172:** Definition of the `E2SprotocolTx` method for fragmenting the Ethernet packets into small packets of 100 bytes or less and converting them to serial communication packets.
  - **Lines 126–142:** If the Ethernet packet size is greater than 100 bytes, it is divided into small packets of 100 bytes or less.
  - **Lines 150–164:** Converting the fragmented packets into serial communication packets.
- **Lines 173–190:** Definition of the `SendSerial` method for transmitting the serial communication packets through the serial port.
  - **Line 181:** Reading a serial communication packet from the intermediate buffers.
  - **Line 183:** Sending the serial communication packet through the serial port.
  - **Lines 184–187:** Printing the transmitted packet.

Source code listing for GlobalVar.h

This file (shown in Listing 8-3) contains the declaration for the intermediate buffers, and the declaration of methods for adding packets to — and deleting packets from — buffers.

Listing 8-3: Source code for GlobalVar.h

```
1.#define size 1518
2.unsigned int E2PPacketcount;
3.unsigned int P2SPacketcount;
4.unsigned int sendrequest; // 1 for true and 0 for false
5.unsigned char strcuta[96];
6.struct Delstruct
7.{
8.unsigned char Deldata[size];
9.unsigned int Dellength;
10. };
/********** For Adding packets to the buffers ***********/
11. void addE2PBuffer(unsigned char *,unsigned int);
12. void addP2SBuffer(unsigned char *,unsigned int);
/******** For Deleting packets From the buffers *********/
13. struct Delstruct delE2PBuffer();
14. struct Delstruct delP2SBuffer();
/******** Buffer Between Ethernet Module ---> Protocol Tx Module ******/
15. struct E2PBuffer
16. {
17. unsigned char E2Pdata[size];
18. unsigned int E2Plength;
19. struct E2PBuffer *E2Plink;
20. };
21. struct E2PBuffer *E2Pfront,*E2Prear;
/******** Buffer Between Protocol Tx Module ---> SerialComm Module
******/
22. struct P2SBuffer
23. {
24. unsigned char P2Sdata[size];
25. unsigned int P2Slength;
26. struct P2SBuffer *P2Slink;
27. };
28. struct P2SBuffer *P2Sfront,*P2Srear;
29. void convertEp2Sp(unsigned int*,unsigned int ,unsigned int);
```

Following is the line-by-line explanation of the source code:

- **Lines 1–5:** Preprocessor directives and variable declaration.
- **Lines 6–10:** Declaration of structure `Delstruct`, for storing the packet that is deleted from the intermediate buffers.
- **Lines 11–12:** Declaration of functions for adding packets to the intermediate buffers.

- **Lines 13–14:** Declaration of functions for deleting packets from the intermediate buffers.
- **Lines 15–28:** Declaration of structures (intermediate buffers) for storing packets.
- **Line 29:** Declaration of function for converting Ethernet packets to serial communication packets.

Source code listing for Buffers.c

This file (shown in Listing 8-4) contains methods for adding and deleting packets to/from intermediate buffers.

Listing 8-4: Source code for Buffers.c

```
#include<stdlib.h>
#include "GlobalVar.h"
/******** For Adding Packets to E2PBuffer ******/
void addE2PBuffer(unsigned char *tempdata,unsigned int length)
{
struct E2PBuffer *q;
unsigned int ib1;
q=malloc(sizeof(struct E2PBuffer));
q->E2Plink=NULL;
q->E2Plength=length;
for( ib1=0;ib1<length;ib1++)
q->E2Pdata[ib1]=tempdata[ib1];
if(E2Pfront==NULL)
E2Pfront=q;
else
E2Prear->E2Plink=q;
E2Prear=q;
}
/******** For Adding Packets to P2SBuffer ******/
void addP2SBuffer(unsigned char *tempdata,unsigned int length)
{
struct P2SBuffer *q;
unsigned int ib2;
q=malloc(sizeof(struct P2SBuffer));
q->P2Slink=NULL;
q->P2Slength=length;
for(ib2=0;ib2<length;ib2++)
q->P2Sdata[ib2]=tempdata[ib2];
if(P2Sfront==NULL)
P2Sfront=q;
else
P2Srear->P2Slink=q;
P2Srear=q;
}
/******** For Deleting Packets From E2PBuffer ******/
```

```
33. struct Delstruct delE2PBuffer(){
34. struct E2PBuffer *q;
35. struct Delstruct s1;
36. unsigned int ib5;
37. if(E2Pfront != NULL)
38. {
39. q=E2Pfront;
40. for(ib5=0;ib5<q->E2Plength;ib5++)
41. {
42. s1.Deldata[ib5]=q->E2Pdata[ib5];
43. }
44. s1.Dellength=q->E2Plength;
45. E2Pfront=q->E2Plink;
46. free(q);
47. if(E2Pfront==NULL)
48. E2Prear=NULL;
49. }
50. return(s1);
51. }
/******** For Deleting Packets From P2SBuffer ******/
52. struct Delstruct delP2SBuffer(){
53. struct P2SBuffer *q;
54. struct Delstruct s2;
55. unsigned int ib6;
56. if(P2Sfront != NULL)
57. {
58. q=P2Sfront;
59. for(ib6=0;ib6<q->P2Slength;ib6++)
60. {
61. s2.Deldata[ib6]=q->P2Sdata[ib6];
62. }
63. s2.Dellength=q->P2Slength;
64. P2Sfront=q->P2Slink;
65. free(q);
66. if(P2Sfront==NULL)
67. P2Srear=NULL;
68. }
69. return(s2);
70. }
```

Following is the line-by-line explanation of the source code:

- **Lines 1–2:** Preprocessor directive for including header files.
- **Lines 3–17:** Definition of function `addE2Pbuffer` for adding Ethernet packets to the buffers.
- **Lines 18–32:** Definition of function `addP2Sbuffer` for adding the converted packets to the buffers.

- **Lines 33–51:** Definition of function `delE2Pbuffer` to delete the Ethernet packet from the buffer.
- **Lines 52–70:** Definition of function `delP2Sbuffer` to delete the serial communication packet from the buffer.

Source code listing for PTFunction.c

This file (shown in Listing 8-5) contains a method for converting fragmented Ethernet packets to serial communication packets and adding them to the buffers.

Listing 8-5: Source code for PTFunction.c

```
#include "GlobalVar.h"
#include <stdlib.h>
/*****function for converting ethernet packet to serial comm packet.

The Serial Comm. packet contains 100 bytes data plus 4 bytes packet
information.The packet structure is

      STX        Length          Data           CRC         ETX
      0x02         --             --             --         0x03
     (1Byte)     (1BYte)     (Max.100Bytes)    (1Byte)     (1Byte)

 ******/
void convertEp2Sp(unsigned int *data,unsigned int pksize )
{
unsigned char arr[104],LRC=0x00;
unsigned int l=0,temp=0,j;

arr[0] = 0x02;
arr[1] = pksize + 4;
temp = pksize + 4;
for(j=2;j<(pksize)+2;j++)
{
 arr[j]=*data;
     data++;
}
l=(pksize)+2;
for(j=1;j<l;j++)
{
     LRC = LRC ^arr[j];
}
arr[l] = LRC;
arr[l+1] = 0x03;
addP2SBuffer(arr,temp);
P2SPacketcount = P2SPacketcount +1;
}
```

Following is the line-by-line explanation of the source code:

- **Lines 1–2:** Preprocessor directives to include header files.
- **Lines 3–24:** Definition of function `convertEp2Sp`, for converting Ethernet packets to serial communication packets. Line 22 is for adding the converted serial communication packets to the intermediate buffers for transmission through the serial port.

Other files required for this application, including `Devioctl.h`, `ntddndis.h`, `ntddpack.h`, `packet32.h`, `packon.h`, and `packoff.h`, are taken from Microsoft's Windows NT DDK.

Executing the program

To test the program, initially execute it on the desktop. Build the project in the Visual Studio environment. On the Windows taskbar, select Start ⇨ Run... and browse for `ProtocolTx.EXE`. Enter **0** as an argument, along with the filename. The Run screen should look like the one shown in Figure 8-1.

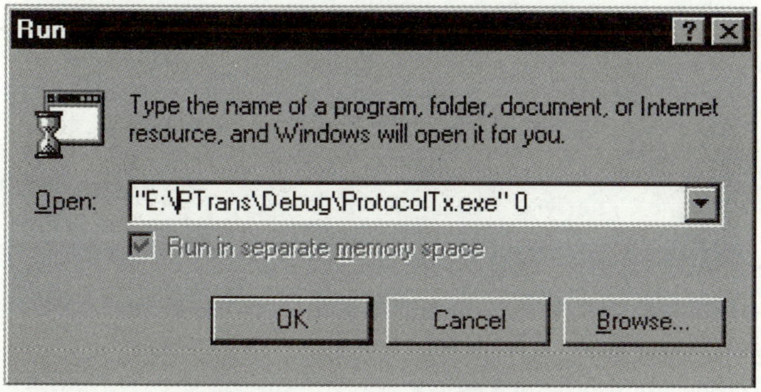

Figure 8-1: Run screen for the protocol converter application

If the application fails to run with argument 0, try it with numbers 1 to 3. If your computer has more than one network card installed, you need to check for each card's installed packet driver. You can check this by trial and error by modifying the argument value (0 to 3). Ultimately, the output screen should look like the one shown in Figure 8-2.

Embedding the software

You can port this application to a target system running embedded NT using the following steps:

1. Collect all the files required to run the application at the target. In this case, the file required is `ProtocolTx.EXE` (the application file).
2. Create a component using Component Designer. Use the following steps to create a custom component:

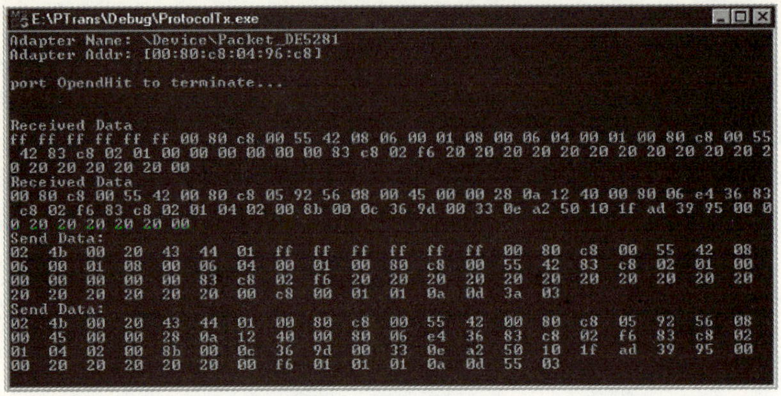

Figure 8-2: Output screen for protocol converter application

- Open Component Designer (on the Windows taskbar, select Start ⇨ Programs ⇨ Windows NT Embedded 4.0 ⇨ Component Designer).
- Save the component as `PTSample.kdf`.
- In the navigation pane, right-click Component1, and then click Properties.
- In the Component Name text box, type **PTx Sample**.
- In the Vendor text box, type **Generic**.
- In the Description text box, type **Protocol Translator** and then click OK.
- In the navigation pane, right-click PTx Sample, and then click Add Component.
- In the Component text box, type **PTx**; leave the remaining fields empty.
- Verify that the hierarchy path is set as follows: `%ROOT%\Applications\Utilities` and click OK.
- In the navigation pane, right-click Files, and then click Add File.
- In the File Name text box, click Browse. Browse for `ProtocolTx.EXE` (the application file collected in Step 1). Set the target path as `\Winnt\ProtocolTranslator`. (The application `ProtocolTx.EXE` will be stored in this directory at the target.)

The resulting window will look like the one shown in Figure 8-3. Save the component definition file and exit.

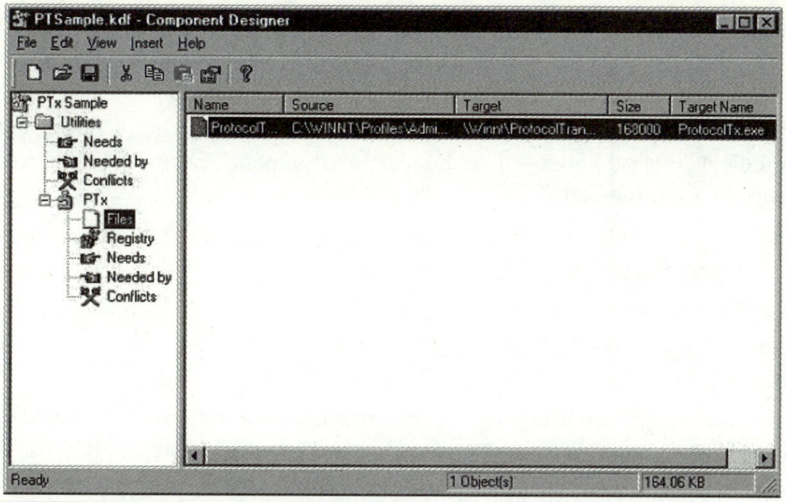

Figure 8-3: Use the Component Designer to create your own custom component.

3. Create the target image using Target Designer.

   - Open Target Designer (on the Windows taskbar, select Start ⇨ Programs ⇨ Windows NT Embedded ⇨ Target Designer).
   - In the All Nodes pane, expand the Target Designer system database (TDSD). Expand the Examples collection.
   - Copy the Minimal With Network configuration. Right-click on User Configuration and click Paste.
   - Right-click the Standard No Network configuration that was pasted under the User Configurations collection, and then click Rename. In the text box, type **ProtocolTranslator**.
   - Expand the tree structure under ProtocolTranslator. Right-click on Standard OS under `ProtocolTranslator\System\Platform\Core OS` and click Add.
   - Repeat the preceding steps to add the following components:

     Serial Mouse, under `System\Devices\Mouse`

     COM1 and COM2, under `System\Devices\Serial Ports`

     NetBEUI and IPX/SPX under `System\Network\Network Protocols`

     NetBios, RPC, and Computer Browser, under `System\Network\Network Services`

     TCP/IP Utilities, under `System\Network\Network Applications`

     MS Sans Serif Font, under `System\Desktop Settings\Fonts`

- Depending on the network card installed in the target machine, add components under `System\Network\Network Drivers` and `System\Network\Network Adapters`.
- To add the PTSample component that was created in Step 2, click Component Management (File ⇨ Tools ⇨ Component Management), click Add and browse for `PTSample.kdf`, then click OK.
- Now identify PTx, which is under `ProtocolTranslator\Applications \Utilities`, right-click on it, and click Add.
- In the All Nodes pane, verify that Protocol Translator, which is under User Configuration, is selected. At this stage, the window looks like the one shown in Figure 8-4.
- On the Image menu, click Settings. Verify that the Source Repository Path for WinNT is CD1, which is in the Windows Embedded NT 4.0 CD-ROM; and that the target path is set to `D:\PtxWithEmbeddedNT` (the final target image will be stored in this directory; *D* represents the hard disk drive in which the target image is stored).
- Now click Build and Install, which is under the Image menu, and click Start.
- When a message appears stating that you have not entered a product identification (PID) number and asks if you want to build a runtime image that works for a limited time, click Yes.
- When the Target Designer Network Settings dialog box appears, click OK.
- When the "Install Complete" message appears, click OK.
- Now go to the `\PTxWithEmbeddedNT` directory, which is under the drive letter representing your hard disk in which the target image is stored, and copy all the subdirectories and files onto the target's hard disk.

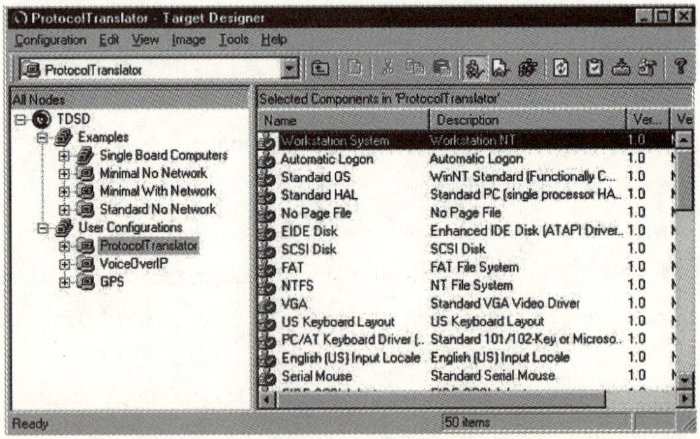

Figure 8-4: Target Designer is used to create the target image for the application.

This application occupies 164KB of memory, and the target image occupies 80.6MB of memory. Therefore, the target must have a minimum of 81MB of memory available in order to run the image. The protocol translator (or converter) generally will be a Single Board Computer (SBC) that has secondary storage onto which embedded NT can be ported. The booting can be performed through either the hard disk or a CD-ROM.

Project: Voice-over-IP

This project develops a voice-over-Internet Protocol (VOIP) system. Nowadays, the Internet and intranets are extensively used for voice communication. To achieve voice communication, you need not have a desktop. You can acquire an embedded system, called an IP phone, that runs the voice-over-IP software needed to establish communication and transfer voice packets over an intranet or the Internet. However, to achieve the communication between two IP phones, you need a server. This server is similar to the PBX control unit with which the PBX operator carries out operations such as transferring a call to an extension, putting the caller on hold, and so on. It validates the users connected over the network and provides the directory service. It is also possible to embed the server software. This application develops the software, which can be tested either on the desktops or on embedded systems.

The software consists of the following files:

- `serverDlg.h`, which contains the declaration of the `CserverDlg` class.
- `serverDlg.cpp`, which contains the class definition of `CserverDlg` and methods to initiate server sockets and client sockets and establishes the connection between clients for transmitting and receiving voice messages.
- `clientDlg.h`, which contains the declaration of the `CclientDlg` class.
- `clientDlg.cpp`, which contains the definition of the `CclientDlg` class.

Source code listing for serverDlg.h

Listing 8-6 contains the source code for `serverDlg.h`, which has the declaration of the `CServerDlg` class.

Listing 8-6: Source code for serverDlg.h

```
#if !defined(
AFX_SERVERDLG_H__A051048C_5FA9_45D9_81CE_D9ED862E1D59__INCLUDED_)
#define
AFX_SERVERDLG_H__A051048C_5FA9_45D9_81CE_D9ED862E1D59__INCLUDED_
#if _MSC_VER > 1000
#pragma once
#endif // _MSC_VER > 1000
#include "vtWave.h"
// CServerDlg dialog
class CServerDlg : public CDialog
```

```
{
// Construction
public:
CServerDlg(CWnd* pParent = NULL);    // standard constructor
~CServerDlg();
// Dialog Data
//{{AFX_DATA(CServerDlg)
enum { IDD = IDD_TALKSERVER_DIALOG };
CListBoxm_ClientList;                // List of available clients
CListBoxm_ProtList;                  // List of compatible protocols
//}}AFX_DATA
// ClassWizard generated virtual function overrides
//{{AFX_VIRTUAL(CServerDlg)
public:
protected:
virtual void DoDataExchange(CDataExchange* pDX);   // DDX/DDV support
//}}AFX_VIRTUAL
// Implementation
protected:
HICON m_hIcon;
// Generated message map functions
//{{AFX_MSG(CServerDlg)
virtual BOOL OnInitDialog();
afx_msg void OnSysCommand(UINT nID, LPARAM lParam);
afx_msg void OnPaint();
afx_msg HCURSOR OnQueryDragIcon();
afx_msg void OnTimer(UINT nIDEvent);
afx_msg LONG OnVTConnected(WPARAM wparam, LPARAM lparam);
afx_msg LONG OnVTDataReady(WPARAM wparam, LPARAM lparam);
//}}AFX_MSG
DECLARE_MESSAGE_MAP()
private:
LPVTMSG         m_vtMsgBuf;          // Buffer of communication message
VTSAPPACK       m_vtSAPData;         // SAP packet data
LPVTSOCKET      m_lpServSocks;       // Server sockets to listen
LPVTSOCKET      m_lpClientSocks;   // The sockets to connect
                                // with the clients
HANDLE      m_hConnectHeap;  // Handle of the heap for client sockets
LPPROTOCOL_INFO  m_lpProtBuf;        // Buffer for protocol information
SOCKET           m_SAPSocket;        // SAP socket
SOCKADDR_IPX     m_SAPSockAddr;      // SAP socket address
SOCKADDR_IPX  m_SAPDestSockAddr;     // SAP destination socket address
int     m_iNextFree;             // Available buffers for client sockets
int     m_iMaxConnects;          // The maximum connections of clients
int     m_iWorkProt;             // The compatible protocol numbers
protected:
BOOL    InitServSocks(void);
BOOL    InitClientSocks(void);
void    DeRegisterClient(char* sClientName);
```

```
void   UpdateProtList(int index);
void   UpdateClientList(char* name, int status, char* peername);
};
//{{AFX_INSERT_LOCATION}}
// Microsoft Visual C++ will insert additional declarations immediately before the previous line.
#endif // !defined( AFX_TALKSERVERDLG_H__A051048C_5FA9_45D9_81CE_D9ED862E1D59__INCLUDED_)
```

Source code listing for serverDlg.cpp

This file (shown in Listing 8-7) contains the definition of the `CserverDlg` class, and definitions of various methods for initializing server sockets and client sockets, for establishing connections with clients and for transmitting voice messages from one client to another.

Listing 8-7: Source code for serverDlg.cpp

```
#include "stdafx.h"
#include "server.h"
#include "serverDlg.h"
#ifdef _DEBUG
#define new DEBUG_NEW
#undef THIS_FILE
static char THIS_FILE[] = __FILE__;
#endif
class CAboutDlg : public CDialog
{
public:
CAboutDlg();
// Dialog Data
//{{AFX_DATA(CAboutDlg)
enum { IDD = IDD_ABOUTBOX };
//}}AFX_DATA
// ClassWizard generated virtual function overrides
//{{AFX_VIRTUAL(CAboutDlg)
protected:
virtual void DoDataExchange(CDataExchange* pDX);     // DDX/DDV support
//}}AFX_VIRTUAL
// Implementation
protected:
//{{AFX_MSG(CAboutDlg)
//}}AFX_MSG
DECLARE_MESSAGE_MAP()
};
CAboutDlg::CAboutDlg() : CDialog(CAboutDlg::IDD)
{
//{{AFX_DATA_INIT(CAboutDlg)
```

```
//}}AFX_DATA_INIT
}
void CAboutDlg::DoDataExchange(CDataExchange* pDX)
{
CDialog::DoDataExchange(pDX);
//{{AFX_DATA_MAP(CAboutDlg)
//}}AFX_DATA_MAP
}
BEGIN_MESSAGE_MAP(CAboutDlg, CDialog)
//{{AFX_MSG_MAP(CAboutDlg)
// No message handlers
//}}AFX_MSG_MAP
END_MESSAGE_MAP()
CServerDlg::CServerDlg(CWnd* pParent /*=NULL*/)
: CDialog(CServerDlg::IDD, pParent)
{
//{{AFX_DATA_INIT(CServerDlg)
// NOTE: the ClassWizard will add member initialization here
//}}AFX_DATA_INIT
// Note that LoadIcon does not require a subsequent DestroyIcon in Win32
m_hIcon = AfxGetApp()->LoadIcon(IDR_MAINFRAME);
m_iNextFree = 0;
m_iMaxConnects = 5;
m_iWorkProt = 0;
m_vtMsgBuf = new VTMSG;
memset((void*)m_vtMsgBuf, 0, sizeof(SIZEVTMSG));
}
CServerDlg::~CServerDlg()
{
}
void CServerDlg::DoDataExchange(CDataExchange* pDX)
{
CDialog::DoDataExchange(pDX);
//{{AFX_DATA_MAP(CServerDlg)
DDX_Control(pDX, IDC_CLIENT, m_ClientList);
DDX_Control(pDX, IDC_PROTOCOL, m_ProtList);
//}}AFX_DATA_MAP
}
BEGIN_MESSAGE_MAP(CServerDlg, CDialog)
//{{AFX_MSG_MAP(CServerDlg)
ON_WM_SYSCOMMAND()
ON_WM_PAINT()
ON_WM_QUERYDRAGICON()
ON_WM_TIMER()
ON_MESSAGE(VTM_CONNECTED, OnVTConnected)
ON_MESSAGE(VTM_DATAREADY, OnVTDataReady)
//}}AFX_MSG_MAP
END_MESSAGE_MAP()
```

```
BOOL CServerDlg::OnInitDialog()
{
CDialog::OnInitDialog();
// IDM_ABOUTBOX must be in the system command range.
ASSERT((IDM_ABOUTBOX & 0xFFF0) == IDM_ABOUTBOX);
ASSERT(IDM_ABOUTBOX < 0xF000);
CMenu* pSysMenu = GetSystemMenu(FALSE);
if (pSysMenu != NULL)
{
CString strAboutMenu;
strAboutMenu.LoadString(IDS_ABOUTBOX);
if (!strAboutMenu.IsEmpty())
{
pSysMenu->AppendMenu(MF_SEPARATOR);
pSysMenu->AppendMenu(MF_STRING, IDM_ABOUTBOX, strAboutMenu);
}
}
// Set the icon for this dialog.  The framework does this automatically
//  when the application's main window is not a dialog
SetIcon(m_hIcon, TRUE);                       // Set big icon
SetIcon(m_hIcon, FALSE);              // Set small icon
// TODO: Add extra initialization here
if(!InitClientSocks())
{
AfxMessageBox("Can't build connection sockets!");
return FALSE;
}
if(!InitServSocks())
{
AfxMessageBox("Can't build server sockets!");
return FALSE;
}
char strProt[128];
for(int iLoop = 0; iLoop < m_iWorkProt; iLoop++)
{
   wsprintf(strProt, "%s:  %d",
m_lpServSocks[iLoop].m_lpProtocolName,
                m_lpServSocks[iLoop].m_iConnects);
       m_ProtList.AddString(strProt);
}
return TRUE;  // return TRUE  unless you set the focus to a control
}
void CServerDlg::OnSysCommand(UINT nID, LPARAM lParam)
{
if ((nID & 0xFFF0) == IDM_ABOUTBOX)
{
CAboutDlg dlgAbout;
dlgAbout.DoModal();
```

```
}
else
{
CDialog::OnSysCommand(nID, lParam);
}
}
void CServerDlg::OnPaint()
{
if (IsIconic())
{
CPaintDC dc(this); // device context for painting
SendMessage(WM_ICONERASEBKGND, (WPARAM) dc.GetSafeHdc(), 0);
// Center icon in client rectangle
int cxIcon = GetSystemMetrics(SM_CXICON);
int cyIcon = GetSystemMetrics(SM_CYICON);
CRect rect;
GetClientRect(&rect);
int x = (rect.Width() - cxIcon + 1) / 2;
int y = (rect.Height() - cyIcon + 1) / 2;
// Draw the icon
dc.DrawIcon(x, y, m_hIcon);
}
else
{
CDialog::OnPaint();
}
}
HCURSOR CServerDlg::OnQueryDragIcon()
{
return (HCURSOR) m_hIcon;
}
BOOL CServerDlg::InitServSocks(void)
{
unsigned long  sizeProtBuf = 0;
int            cNumProt;
int            iLoop1;
int            iLoop2;
int            iAddrLen;
WORD           wVersionRequested;
WSADATA        wsaData;
BOOL           bCastStat;
wVersionRequested = MAKEWORD(1, 1);
if(WSAStartup(wVersionRequested, &wsaData) != 0)
{
  return FALSE;
}
if(EnumProtocols(NULL, NULL, &sizeProtBuf) != SOCKET_ERROR)
{
  return FALSE;
```

```
}
// Allocate buffer of appropriate size
if((m_lpProtBuf = (LPPROTOCOL_INFO)VirtualAlloc(NULL, sizeProtBuf,
                 MEM_COMMIT, PAGE_READWRITE)) == NULL)
{
return FALSE;
}
// Enumerate numbers of protocols
if((cNumProt = EnumProtocols(NULL, m_lpProtBuf, &sizeProtBuf)) ==
             SOCKET_ERROR)
{
return FALSE;
}
// Allocate the buffer for server sockets
if((m_lpServSocks = (LPVTSOCKET)VirtualAlloc(NULL,
cNumProt * sizeof(VTSOCKET), MEM_COMMIT,PAGE_READWRITE)) == NULL)
{
return FALSE;
}
for(iLoop1 = 0, iLoop2 = 0; iLoop1 < cNumProt; iLoop1++)
{
if((m_lpProtBuf[iLoop1].dwServiceFlags & XP_CONNECTIONLESS) == 0)
{
if(BuildServer(this->GetSafeHwnd(), &m_lpServSocks[iLoop2],
            &m_lpProtBuf[iLoop1]))
{
 iLoop2++;
}
}
}
m_iWorkProt =  iLoop2;
if((m_SAPSocket = socket(AF_IPX, SOCK_DGRAM, NSPROTO_IPX + 4)) !=
 INVALID_SOCKET)
{
  for(iLoop1 = 0; iLoop1 < m_iWorkProt; iLoop1++)
  {
     if(m_lpServSocks[iLoop1].m_iProtocol == NSPROTO_SPXII)
     {
       m_vtSAPData.m_iOperation = 0x200;
       m_vtSAPData.m_iService = VT_NETID;
       strcpy(m_vtSAPData.m_sServName, "VOICE TALK");
       memcpy((void *)m_vtSAPData.m_sNetID,
           (void *)(m_lpServSocks[iLoop1].m_sockAddr.sa_data),12);
       vtSAPData.m_iHops = 0;
       m_SAPSockAddr.sa_family = AF_IPX;
      Ascii2Hex("0452", (char *)&m_SAPSockAddr.sa_socket, 2);
      if(bind(m_SAPSocket,
(PSOCKADDR)&m_SAPSockAddr,sizeof(SOCKADDR_IPX))
      == SOCKET_ERROR)
```

```
          {
           return FALSE;
          }
        else
        {
          m_SAPDestSockAddr.sa_family = AF_IPX;
          Ascii2Hex("00000000",m_SAPDestSockAddr.sa_netnum, 4);
          Ascii2Hex("FFFFFFFFFFFF", m_SAPDestSockAddr.sa_nodenum, 6);
          Ascii2Hex("0452", (char *)&m_SAPDestSockAddr.sa_socket, 2);
          bCastStat = TRUE;
          iAddrLen = sizeof(bCastStat);
          setsockopt(m_SAPSocket, SOL_SOCKET, SO_BROADCAST,
                 (char *)&bCastStat, sizeof(bCastStat));
          sendto(m_SAPSocket, (char *)&m_vtSAPData,
sizeof(m_vtSAPData),
             MSG_DONTROUTE, (struct sockaddr *)&m_SAPDestSockAddr,
             sizeof(m_SAPDestSockAddr));
                SetTimer(1, 60000, NULL);
          }
         break;
     }
 }
 }
 return TRUE;
 }
 BOOL CServerDlg::InitClientSocks(void)
 {
 if((m_hConnectHeap = HeapCreate(0, sizeof(VTSOCKET) * 5,
sizeof(VTSOCKET)
    * 100)) == NULL)
 {
 return FALSE;
 }
 if((m_lpClientSocks = (LPVTSOCKET)HeapAlloc(m_hConnectHeap, 0,
    sizeof(VTSOCKET) * 5)) == NULL)
 {
 return FALSE;
 }
 return TRUE;
 }
 void CServerDlg::DeRegisterClient(char* sClientName)
 {
 int iLoop;
 m_vtMsgBuf->m_ucIdentity = VT_IDENTITY;
 m_vtMsgBuf->m_ucMsgType = VT_TEXT;
 m_vtMsgBuf->m_lLength = REALLEN(sClientName) + SIZEVTMSGHDR;
 m_vtMsgBuf->m_ucCmd = VTCMD_DEREGNAME;
 memcpy((void*)m_vtMsgBuf->m_pData, (void*)sClientName,
       REALLEN(sClientName));
```

```
for(iLoop = 0; iLoop < m_iNextFree; iLoop++)
{
    if(m_lpClientSocks[iLoop].m_iStatus== VTSOCKET_AVAILABLE)
   {
      SendVTMessage(m_lpClientSocks[iLoop].m_hSock, m_vtMsgBuf);
   }
}
}
void CServerDlg::UpdateProtList(int index)
{
int iReVal;
char strProt[128];
iReVal = m_ProtList.FindString(-
1,m_lpServSocks[index].m_lpProtocolName);
if(iReVal == LB_ERR)
   return;
m_ProtList.DeleteString(iReVal);
wsprintf(strProt, "%s:  %d", m_lpServSocks[index].m_lpProtocolName,
        m_lpServSocks[index].m_iConnects);
m_ProtList.InsertString(iReVal, strProt);
}
void CServerDlg::UpdateClientList(char* name,int status, char*
peername)
{
int index;
char strClient[128];
index = m_ClientList.FindString(-1, name);
if(index != LB_ERR)
{
m_ClientList.DeleteString(index);
}
switch(status)
{
 case VTSOCKET_CLOSED:
 return;
case VTSOCKET_AVAILABLE:
   wsprintf(strClient, "%s  AVAILABLE", name);
   break;
case VTSOCKET_REQSESSION:
   wsprintf(strClient, "%s  SESSION SETUP  %s",name, peername);
   break;
case VTSOCKET_INSESSION:
   wsprintf(strClient, "%s  in SESSION", name);
   break;
}
m_ClientList.InsertString(index, strClient);
}
void CServerDlg::OnTimer(UINT nIDEvent)
{
```

```
// Add message handler code
// Send out SAP package
sendto(m_SAPSocket, (char *)&m_vtSAPData, sizeof(m_vtSAPData),
       MSG_DONTROUTE, (struct sockaddr *)&m_SAPDestSockAddr,
       sizeof(m_SAPDestSockAddr));
CDialog::OnTimer(nIDEvent);
}
LONG CServerDlg::OnVTConnected(WPARAM wparam, LPARAM lparam)
{
int index, addrlen;
if(m_iNextFree >= m_iMaxConnects)
{
  if(HeapAlloc(m_hConnectHeap, 0, sizeof(VTSOCKET) * 5) == NULL)
  {
    return 0L;
  }
  m_iMaxConnects += 5;
}
index = 0;
while(m_lpServSocks[index].m_hSock != wparam)
index++;
m_lpServSocks[index].m_iStatus = VTSOCKET_ACCEPTING;
addrlen = sizeof(m_lpClientSocks[m_iNextFree].m_sockAddr) +
         sizeof(m_lpClientSocks[m_iNextFree].m_Reserved);
if ((m_lpClientSocks[m_iNextFree].m_hSock =
    accept(m_lpServSocks[index].m_hSock,
    &m_lpClientSocks[m_iNextFree].m_sockAddr,&addrlen)) ==
INVALID_SOCKET)
{
    AfxMessageBox("Cannot accept the client socket");
    return 0L;
}
if(WSAAsyncSelect(m_lpClientSocks[m_iNextFree].m_hSock,
  this->GetSafeHwnd(), VTM_DATAREADY, FD_READ | FD_CLOSE)==
SOCKET_ERROR)
{
  closesocket(m_lpClientSocks[m_iNextFree].m_hSock);
  AfxMessageBox("Cannot select the client socket");
  return 0L;
}
m_lpClientSocks[m_iNextFree].m_iProtocol =
                                m_lpServSocks[index].m_iProtocol;
m_lpClientSocks[m_iNextFree].m_iSockType =
                                m_lpServSocks[index].m_iSockType;
m_lpClientSocks[m_iNextFree].m_iServSockIndex = index;
m_lpClientSocks[m_iNextFree++].m_iStatus = VTSOCKET_CONNECTED;
m_lpServSocks[index].m_iConnects ++;
m_lpServSocks[index].m_iStatus = VTSOCKET_LISTENING;
UpdateProtList(index);
```

```
return 1L;
}
LONG CServerDlg::OnVTDataReady(WPARAM wparam, LPARAM lparam)
{
int iIndex1;
int iIndex2;
int iIndex3;
int byteRead;
int iStrLen;
for(iIndex1 = 0; iIndex1 < m_iNextFree; iIndex1++)
{
   if((m_lpClientSocks[iIndex1].m_hSock == wparam) &&
   (m_lpClientSocks[iIndex1].m_iStatus != VTSOCKET_CLOSED))
          break;
}
if(LOWORD(lparam) == FD_CLOSE)
{
  closesocket(m_lpClientSocks[iIndex1].m_hSock);
UpdateClientList(m_lpClientSocks[iIndex1].m_sUserName,VTSOCKET_CLOSED,
                    NULL);
  if(m_lpClientSocks[iIndex1].m_iStatus == VTSOCKET_AVAILABLE)
  {
    DeRegisterClient(m_lpClientSocks[iIndex1].m_sUserName);
  }
// First, find peer
for(iIndex2 = 0; iIndex2 < m_iNextFree; iIndex2++)
 {
if((m_lpClientSocks[iIndex2].m_hSock==lpClientSocks[iIndex1].m_hPeerSock
)
   &&(m_lpClientSocks[iIndex2].m_iStatus == VTSOCKET_INSESSION))
 {
    break;
 }
}
if(iIndex2 < m_iNextFree)
{
   m_vtMsgBuf->m_ucIdentity = VT_IDENTITY;
   m_vtMsgBuf->m_ucMsgType = VT_TEXT;
   m_vtMsgBuf->m_lLength = byteRead = SIZEVTMSGHDR;
   m_vtMsgBuf->m_ucCmd = VTCMD_SESSIONCLOSE;
  SendVTMessage(m_lpClientSocks[iIndex2].m_hSock, m_vtMsgBuf);
  // Update client's displayed status
  m_lpClientSocks[iIndex2].m_iStatus = VTSOCKET_AVAILABLE;
  UpdateClientList(m_lpClientSocks[iIndex2].m_sUserName,
                VTSOCKET_AVAILABLE, NULL);
  for(iIndex3 = 0; iIndex3 < m_iNextFree; iIndex3++)
  {
```

```
    if ((iIndex3 != iIndex2) &&
   (m_lpClientSocks[iIndex3].m_iStatus == VTSOCKET_AVAILABLE))
    {
       m_vtMsgBuf->m_ucCmd = VTCMD_REGNAME;
       memcpy((void*)m_vtMsgBuf->m_pData,
           (void*)m_lpClientSocks[iIndex3].m_sUserName,

REALLEN(m_lpClientSocks[iIndex3].m_sUserName)*sizeof(char));
      m_vtMsgBuf->m_lLength = REALLEN
                 (m_lpClientSocks[iIndex3].m_sUserName) +
SIZEVTMSGHDR;
      SendVTMessage(m_lpClientSocks[iIndex2].m_hSock, m_vtMsgBuf);
      memcpy((void*)m_vtMsgBuf->m_pData,
          (void*)m_lpClientSocks[iIndex2].m_sUserName,

REALLEN(m_lpClientSocks[iIndex2].m_sUserName)*sizeof(char));
             m_vtMsgBuf->m_lLength =
         EALLEN(m_lpClientSocks[iIndex2].m_sUserName)+ SIZEVTMSGHDR;
             SendVTMessage(m_lpClientSocks[iIndex3].m_hSock,
m_vtMsgBuf);
    }
}
}
m_lpClientSocks[iIndex1].m_iStatus = VTSOCKET_CLOSED;
iIndex2 = m_lpClientSocks[iIndex1].m_iServSockIndex;
m_lpServSocks[iIndex2].m_iConnects --;
UpdateProtList(iIndex2);
return 1L;
}
if(!RecvVTMessage(&m_lpClientSocks[iIndex1], m_vtMsgBuf))
{
   return 0L;
}
switch(m_vtMsgBuf->m_ucCmd)
{
case VTCMD_REGNAME:
   if(m_lpClientSocks[iIndex1].m_iStatus != VTSOCKET_CONNECTED)
   {
     AfxMessageBox("The client not connected");
     return 0L;
   }
  iStrLen = m_vtMsgBuf->m_lLength - SIZEVTMSGHDR;
  memcpy((void*)m_lpClientSocks[iIndex1].m_sUserName,
     (void*)m_vtMsgBuf->m_pData, iStrLen+1);
   m_lpClientSocks[iIndex1].m_iStatus = VTSOCKET_AVAILABLE;
   UpdateClientList(m_lpClientSocks[iIndex1].m_sUserName,
               VTSOCKET_AVAILABLE, NULL);
  // Send notification to other "AVAILABLE" sockets that
  // a new peer is available
```

```
   for(iIndex2 = 0; iIndex2 < m_iNextFree; iIndex2++)
   {
     if ((iIndex2 != iIndex1) &&
(m_lpClientSocks[iIndex2].m_iStatus ==
          VTSOCKET_AVAILABLE))
     {
   SendVTMessage(m_lpClientSocks[iIndex2].m_hSock, m_vtMsgBuf);
     }
   }
  // Send notifications back to registering client of
  // all the currently available clients
  for(iIndex2 = 0; iIndex2 < m_iNextFree; iIndex2++)
  {
   if ((iIndex2 != iIndex1) && (m_lpClientSocks[iIndex2].m_iStatus
==
       VTSOCKET_AVAILABLE))
   {
     m_vtMsgBuf->m_ucCmd = VTCMD_REGNAME;
     m_vtMsgBuf->m_ucMsgType = VT_TEXT;
     m_vtMsgBuf->m_lLength =
REALLEN(m_lpClientSocks[iIndex2].m_sUserName)
                           + SIZEVTMSGHDR;
     memcpy((void*)m_vtMsgBuf->m_pData,
        (void*)m_lpClientSocks[iIndex2].m_sUserName,
        REALLEN(m_lpClientSocks[iIndex2].m_sUserName)*sizeof(char));
     SendVTMessage(m_lpClientSocks[iIndex1].m_hSock, m_vtMsgBuf);
   }
  }
  return 1L;
// For passing data between two in-session clients
case VTCMD_MSGDATA:
   if(m_lpClientSocks[iIndex1].m_iStatus != VTSOCKET_INSESSION)
   {
    return 0L;
   }
   SendVTMessage(m_lpClientSocks[iIndex1].m_hPeerSock, m_vtMsgBuf);
   return 1L;
  // Client is asking another client for a chat
case VTCMD_REQSESSION:
    if(m_lpClientSocks[iIndex1].m_iStatus != VTSOCKET_AVAILABLE)
    {
      AfxMessageBox("Client not available!");
     return 0L;
    }
    m_lpClientSocks[iIndex1].m_iStatus = VTSOCKET_REQSESSION;
    UpdateClientList(m_lpClientSocks[iIndex1].m_sUserName,
              VTSOCKET_REQSESSION, (char*)m_vtMsgBuf->m_pData);
    for(iIndex2 = 0; iIndex2 < m_iNextFree; iIndex2++)
    {
```

```
        iStrLen = m_vtMsgBuf->m_lLength - SIZEVTMSGHDR;
        if(memcmp((void*)m_lpClientSocks[iIndex2].m_sUserName,
         (void*)m_vtMsgBuf->m_pData, iStrLen) == 0)
        {
         if(m_lpClientSocks[iIndex2].m_iStatus ==
VTSOCKET_AVAILABLE)
          {
             break;
          }
        }
      }
      if(iIndex2 == m_iNextFree)
      {
    AfxMessageBox("Not found in VTCMD_REQSESSION");
        return 0L;
   }
   m_vtMsgBuf->m_lLength =
REALLEN(m_lpClientSocks[iIndex1].m_sUserName)
                                  + SIZEVTMSGHDR;
   memcpy((void*)m_vtMsgBuf->m_pData,
          (void*)m_lpClientSocks[iIndex1].m_sUserName,

REALLEN(m_lpClientSocks[iIndex1].m_sUserName)*sizeof(char));
   SendVTMessage(m_lpClientSocks[iIndex2].m_hSock, m_vtMsgBuf);
   m_lpClientSocks[iIndex2].m_iStatus = VTSOCKET_REQSESSION;
   UpdateClientList(m_lpClientSocks[iIndex2].m_sUserName,
          VTSOCKET_REQSESSION, m_lpClientSocks[iIndex1].m_sUserName);
   m_lpClientSocks[iIndex2].m_hPeerSock =
m_lpClientSocks[iIndex1].m_hSock;
   m_lpClientSocks[iIndex1].m_hPeerSock =
m_lpClientSocks[iIndex2].m_hSock;
   return 1L;
 case VTCMD_SESSIONREQRESP:
   if(m_lpClientSocks[iIndex1].m_iStatus != VTSOCKET_REQSESSION)
    {
      return 0L;
    }
   for(iIndex2 = 0; iIndex2 < m_iNextFree; iIndex2++)
   {
     if ((m_lpClientSocks[iIndex2].m_hSock ==
      m_lpClientSocks[iIndex1].m_hPeerSock) &&
      m_lpClientSocks[iIndex2].m_iStatus == VTSOCKET_REQSESSION))
     {
        break;
     }
   }
   if(iIndex2 == m_iNextFree)
   {
     return 0;
```

```
    }
    SendVTMessage(m_lpClientSocks[iIndex1].m_hPeerSock, m_vtMsgBuf);
    if(m_vtMsgBuf->m_pData[0] == 1)
    {
      m_lpClientSocks[iIndex1].m_iStatus = VTSOCKET_INSESSION;
      m_lpClientSocks[iIndex2].m_iStatus = VTSOCKET_INSESSION;
      UpdateClientList(m_lpClientSocks[iIndex1].m_sUserName,
              VTSOCKET_INSESSION,
m_lpClientSocks[iIndex2].m_sUserName);
      UpdateClientList(m_lpClientSocks[iIndex2].m_sUserName,
              VTSOCKET_INSESSION,
m_lpClientSocks[iIndex1].m_sUserName);
      DeRegisterClient(m_lpClientSocks[iIndex1].m_sUserName);
      DeRegisterClient(m_lpClientSocks[iIndex2].m_sUserName);
    }
    else
    {
      m_lpClientSocks[iIndex1].m_iStatus = VTSOCKET_AVAILABLE;
      m_lpClientSocks[iIndex2].m_iStatus = VTSOCKET_AVAILABLE;
      UpdateClientList(m_lpClientSocks[iIndex1].m_sUserName,
                  VTSOCKET_AVAILABLE, NULL);
      UpdateClientList(m_lpClientSocks[iIndex2].m_sUserName,
                  VTSOCKET_AVAILABLE, NULL);
    }
    return 1L;
  case VTCMD_SESSIONCLOSE:
    if (m_lpClientSocks[iIndex1].m_iStatus != VTSOCKET_INSESSION)
     {
       return 0L;
     }
     for(iIndex2 = 0; iIndex2 < m_iNextFree; iIndex2++)
     {
       if ((m_lpClientSocks[iIndex2].m_hSock ==
        m_lpClientSocks[iIndex1].m_hPeerSock) &&
       (m_lpClientSocks[iIndex2].m_iStatus == VTSOCKET_INSESSION))
       {
         break;
       }
     }
     if(iIndex2 == m_iNextFree)
     {
       return 0;
     }
     SendVTMessage(m_lpClientSocks[iIndex1].m_hPeerSock,
m_vtMsgBuf);
     m_lpClientSocks[iIndex1].m_iStatus = VTSOCKET_AVAILABLE;
     m_lpClientSocks[iIndex2].m_iStatus = VTSOCKET_AVAILABLE;
     UpdateClientList(m_lpClientSocks[iIndex1].m_sUserName,
                 VTSOCKET_AVAILABLE, NULL);
```

```
    UpdateClientList(m_lpClientSocks[iIndex2].m_sUserName,
                VTSOCKET_AVAILABLE, NULL);
    for(iIndex3 = 0; iIndex3 < m_iNextFree; iIndex3++)
    {
      if(m_lpClientSocks[iIndex3].m_iStatus == VTSOCKET_AVAILABLE)
      {
       if(iIndex3 != iIndex1)
       {
         m_vtMsgBuf->m_ucIdentity = VT_IDENTITY;
         m_vtMsgBuf->m_ucMsgType = VT_TEXT;
         m_vtMsgBuf->m_ucCmd = VTCMD_REGNAME;
         m_vtMsgBuf->m_lLength =
           REALLEN(m_lpClientSocks[iIndex1].m_sUserName)
           + SIZEVTMSGHDR;
         memcpy((void*)m_vtMsgBuf->m_pData,
          (void*)m_lpClientSocks[iIndex1].m_sUserName,

REALLEN(m_lpClientSocks[iIndex1].m_sUserName)*sizeof(char));
         SendVTMessage(m_lpClientSocks[iIndex3].m_hSock,
m_vtMsgBuf);
         if (iIndex3 != iIndex2)
         {
           m_vtMsgBuf->m_lLength =
                 EALLEN(m_lpClientSocks[iIndex3].m_sUserName)
                 + SIZEVTMSGHDR;
           memcpy((void*)m_vtMsgBuf->m_pData,
          (void*)m_lpClientSocks[iIndex3].m_sUserName,

REALLEN(m_lpClientSocks[iIndex3].m_sUserName)*sizeof(char));
           SendVTMessage(m_lpClientSocks[iIndex1].m_hSock,
m_vtMsgBuf);
         }
       }
       if(iIndex3 != iIndex2)
        {
          m_vtMsgBuf->m_ucIdentity = VT_IDENTITY;
          m_vtMsgBuf->m_ucMsgType = VT_TEXT;
          m_vtMsgBuf->m_ucCmd = VTCMD_REGNAME;
          m_vtMsgBuf->m_lLength =
            EALLEN(m_lpClientSocks[iIndex2].m_sUserName)
            + SIZEVTMSGHDR;
          memcpy((void*)m_vtMsgBuf->m_pData,
           (void*)m_lpClientSocks[iIndex2].m_sUserName,

REALLEN(m_lpClientSocks[iIndex2].m_sUserName)*sizeof(char));
          SendVTMessage(m_lpClientSocks[iIndex3].m_hSock,
m_vtMsgBuf);
          if(iIndex3 != iIndex1)
          {
```

```
557.                m_vtMsgBuf->m_lLength =

EALLEN(m_lpClientSocks[iIndex3].m_sUserName)
558.                                + SIZEVTMSGHDR;
559.                memcpy((void*)m_vtMsgBuf->m_pData,
              (void*)m_lpClientSocks[iIndex3].m_sUserName,

REALLEN(m_lpClientSocks[iIndex3].m_sUserName)*sizeof(char));
560.                SendVTMessage(m_lpClientSocks[iIndex2].m_hSock,
m_vtMsgBuf);
561.              }
562.           }
563.        }
564.     }
565.     return 1L;
566.     default:
567.      AfxMessageBox("NOTHING");
568.    }
569.    return 1L;
570. }
```

Following is the line-by-line explanation of the source code:

- **Lines 1–3:** Header file declaration.
- **Lines 9–22:** Definition of class `CAboutDlg`, generated by the VC++ editor.
- **Lines 28–32:** Definition of the constructor for the `CAboutDlg` class, generated by the VC++ editor.
- **Lines 33–38:** Definition of the `DoDataExchange` method for the `CAboutDlg` dialog, generated by the VC++ editor.
- **Lines 39–43:** Message map definition for handling events generated on the `CAoutDlg` dialog.
- **Lines 44–57:** Definition of the constructor for the `CServerDlg` class, generated by the VC++ editor.
- **Lines 58–60:** Definition of the destructor for the `CServerDlg` class, generated by the VC++ editor.
- **Lines 61–68:** Definition of the `DoDataExchange` method, generated by the VC++ editor.
- **Lines 69–78:** Message map definition for handling events generated on the `CServerDlg` dialog.
- **Lines 79–118:** Definition of the `OnInitDialog` method for the `CServerDlg`.
  - **Line 102:** Initializing server sockets.
  - **Line 108:** Initializing client sockets.

- **Lines 111–118:** Finding all the protocols available on the server and adding them to the list box.
- **Lines 119–130:** Definition of the `OnSysCommand` method, generated by the VC++ editor.
- **Lines 131–151:** Definition of the `OnPaint` method, generated by the VC++ editor.
- **Lines 152–155:** Definition of the `OnQueryDragIcon` method, generated by the VC++ editor.
- **Lines 156–235:** Definition of the `InitServerSocks` method for finding all the available protocols available on server, allocating buffers of the appropriate size to server sockets, and displaying all the protocols in the list box.
- **Lines 236–247:** Definition of the `InitClientSocks` method for creating and allocating memory to client sockets.
- **Lines 248–263:** Definition of the `DeRegisterClient` method. When a client unregisters from the server, this method sends a message to all the other available clients.
- **Lines 264–274:** Definition of the `UpdateProtList` method for updating the available protocols in the protocol list box.
- **Lines 275–299:** Definition of the `UpdateClientList` method for updating the clients available in the client list box.
- **Lines 300–306:** Definition of the `OnTimer` method, generated by the VC++ editor.
- **Lines 307–342:** Definition of the `OnVTConnected` method. When a connection request comes from a client socket, the server registers that client and allocates buffers to it.
- **Lines 343–570:** Definition of the `OnVTDataReady` method. When data comes from a client socket, the server analyzes the data. The data is for establishing a connection, and this method registers that client. If it is a request to another client for a voice chat, it establishes a session between those two clients. If it is a request for closing the session, it breaks the connection between the two clients.
  - **Lines 350–354:** Checking for the particular client from which the data is coming.
  - **Lines 355–370:** If the client is disconnected, the client's socket is closed, the client list is updated, and the client's information is unregistered.
  - **Lines 373–377:** Sending the session close message to the other client.
  - **Line 380:** Updating the client's list.
  - **Lines 395–398:** Cleaning the client socket array.
  - **Line 401:** Reading the incoming message data.
  - **Lines 407–434:** If the data is a request from a client to connect with the server, these lines allocate memory for that client, update the client's list, and send a message to all other available clients.

- **Lines 436–441:** If the data is for another client that is in session, the data is sent to that client.
- **Lines 442–472:** If the data is a request for a session with another client, it checks whether the client is available or not, updates the client's list, and sends a message to that client.
- **Lines 473–505:** If the data is a session request response, these lines send a message to the requested client and update the client's list.
- **Line 507–560:** If the data is a session close message, it sends that message to the other client, updates the client's list, and changes the client's status at the server.

Source code listing for clientDlg.h

Listing 8-8 gives the source code for `clientDlg.h`, which contains the declaration of `CClientDlg` class.

Listing 8-8: Source code for clientDlg.h

```
#if !defined(AFX_CLIENTDLG_H__8068D458_3CAB_11D4_8ECB_00805FBDCBE4__INCLUDED_)
#define AFX_CLIENTDLG_H__8068D458_3CAB_11D4_8ECB_00805FBDCBE4__INCLUDED_
#if _MSC_VER >= 1000
#pragma once
#endif // _MSC_VER >= 1000
// CClientDlg dialog
#include "vtWave.h"
class CClientDlg : public CDialog
{
// Construction
public:
CClientDlg(CWnd* pParent = NULL);    // standard constructor
// Dialog Data
//{{AFX_DATA(CClientDlg)
enum { IDD = IDD_TALKCLIENT_DIALOG };
CButton m_btnConnect;                        // "Connect" Button
CButton m_chkVoice;                          // "Voice" Radio Button
CEdit   m_editUserName;       // "User name" edit box
CEdit   m_editServer;         // " Server" edit box
CComboBox      m_ComBoProts; // The ComboBox for the network protocols
CComboBox      m_ComBoTalker;// The ComboBox for the users name list
CprogressCtrl m_progctrlSend;// Indicator of incoming voice message
CprogressCtrl m_progctrlRecv;// Indicator of outgoing voice message
//}}AFX_DATA
// ClassWizard generated virtual function overrides
//{{AFX_VIRTUAL(CClientDlg)
```

```
protected:
virtual void DoDataExchange(CDataExchange* pDX);   // DDX/DDV support
//}}AFX_VIRTUAL
// Implementation
protected:
HICON m_hIcon;
// Generated message map functions
//{{AFX_MSG(CClientDlg)
virtual BOOL OnInitDialog();
afx_msg void OnSysCommand(UINT nID, LPARAM lParam);
afx_msg void OnPaint();
afx_msg HCURSOR OnQueryDragIcon();
afx_msg LONG OnVTDataReady(WPARAM wparam, LPARAM lparam);
afx_msg LONG OnVTReadyForWrite(WPARAM wparam, LPARAM lparam);
afx_msg LONG OnRecordEvent(WPARAM wparam, LPARAM lparam);
afx_msg LONG OnPlayEvent(WPARAM wparam, LPARAM lparam);
afx_msg void OnChangeEditname();
afx_msg void OnChangeEditserver();
afx_msg void OnSelchangeCombprot();
afx_msg void OnSelchangeCombchatter();
afx_msg void OnBtnconnect();
afx_msg void OnBtndisconnect();
afx_msg void OnChkvoice();
afx_msg void OnClose();
afx_msg void OnTimer(UINT nIDEvent);
//}}AFX_MSG
DECLARE_MESSAGE_MAP()
protected:
BOOL InitProtocols(void);
BOOL InitSockets(int iProtIndex);
void DoConnection(BOOL bTrue);
void EnableTalking(BOOL bTrue);
void ParseMsgData(void);
private:
VTSOCKET      m_MySock;      // The socket in client side
SOCKADDR_IPX  m_IPXAddr;     // The socket address for IPX
char   m_szSendBuf[VT_MAX];      // The buffer for sending message
char   m_szRecvBuf[VT_MAX];      // The buffer for receiving message
char   m_lpPeerName[16];         // The peer taker name
CSADDR_INFO  m_CSABuf[20];              // Socket address information
DWORD  m_dwCSABufsize;     // Size of Socket address buffer structure
int    m_iWorkProts[30]; // Information of workable network protocol
int    m_iNumWorkProts;  // Number of workable network protocol
LPPROTOCOL_INFO  m_lpProtBuf;  // Buffer for protocol information
VTMSG  m_vtRecvMsgBuf;           // Message structure for sending out
VTMSG  m_vtSendMsgBuf;           // Message structure for receiving
BOOL   m_bConnect;               // Flag to check connection
BOOL   m_bTalking;               // Flag to check communcation
```

```
BOOL      m_bVoiceMsg;     // Flag to check message type, text or voice
VTPlayWave m_vtPlay;  // Device to play receiving voice message
VTRecordWave m_vtRecord;//Device to record voice message to send out
char m_pWaveData[VT_MAX]; // Buffer to store receiving voice message
unsigned int m_uiBufLen; // Buffer length of voice message
int m_iWaveFormat;// Wave I/O device type, see definition in vtDef.h
Cstring  m_strUserName;            // The user name
CString  m_strServer;              // The server name
BOOL m_bVoiceTalk;    // Flag to check in voice talk or not
};
//{{AFX_INSERT_LOCATION}}
// Microsoft Developer Studio will insert additional declarations immediately before the previous line.
#endif // !defined(AFX_TALKCLIENTDLG_H__8068D458_3CAB_11D4_8ECB_00805FBDCBE4__INCLUDED_)
```

Source code listing for clientDlg.cpp

This file (shown in Listing 8-9) contains the definition of the `CClientDlg` class and the creation of the GUI.

Listing 8-9: Source code for clientDlg.cpp

```
#include "stdafx.h"
#include "talkclient.h"
#include "talkclientDlg.h"
#ifdef _DEBUG
#define new DEBUG_NEW
#undef THIS_FILE
static char THIS_FILE[] = __FILE__;
#endif
class CAboutDlg : public CDialog
{
public:
CAboutDlg();
// Dialog Data
//{{AFX_DATA(CAboutDlg)
enum { IDD = IDD_ABOUTBOX };
//}}AFX_DATA
// ClassWizard generated virtual function overrides
//{{AFX_VIRTUAL(CAboutDlg)
protected:
virtual void DoDataExchange(CDataExchange* pDX);     // DDX/DDV support
//}}AFX_VIRTUAL
// Implementation
protected:
```

```
//{{AFX_MSG(CAboutDlg)
//}}AFX_MSG
DECLARE_MESSAGE_MAP()
};
CAboutDlg::CAboutDlg() : CDialog(CAboutDlg::IDD)
{
//{{AFX_DATA_INIT(CAboutDlg)
//}}AFX_DATA_INIT
}
void CAboutDlg::DoDataExchange(CDataExchange* pDX)
{
CDialog::DoDataExchange(pDX);
//{{AFX_DATA_MAP(CAboutDlg)
//}}AFX_DATA_MAP
}
BEGIN_MESSAGE_MAP(CAboutDlg, CDialog)
//{{AFX_MSG_MAP(CAboutDlg)
// No message handlers
//}}AFX_MSG_MAP
END_MESSAGE_MAP()
CClientDlg::CClientDlg(CWnd* pParent /*=NULL*/)
: CDialog(CClientDlg::IDD, pParent)
{
//{{AFX_DATA_INIT(CClientDlg)
//}}AFX_DATA_INIT
// Note that LoadIcon does not require a subsequent DestroyIcon in Win32
m_strUserName = _T("");
m_strServer = _T("");
m_bVoiceTalk = FALSE;
m_hIcon = AfxGetApp()->LoadIcon(IDR_MAINFRAME);
m_bConnect = FALSE;
m_bTalking = FALSE;
memset(m_lpPeerName, 0, 16);
m_bVoiceMsg = FALSE;
m_uiBufLen = VT_MAX;
m_iWaveFormat = VT_WAVE1M08;
}
void CClientDlg::DoDataExchange(CDataExchange* pDX)
{
CDialog::DoDataExchange(pDX);
//{{AFX_DATA_MAP(CClientDlg)
DDX_Control(pDX, IDC_BTNCONNECT, m_btnConnect);
DDX_Control(pDX, IDC_CHKVOICE, m_chkVoice);
DDX_Control(pDX, IDC_EDITNAME, m_editUserName);
DDX_Control(pDX, IDC_EDITSERVER, m_editServer);
DDX_Control(pDX, IDC_COMBPROT, m_ComBoProts);
DDX_Control(pDX, IDC_COMBCHATTER, m_ComBoTalker);
DDX_Control(pDX, IDC_SENDMETER, m_progctrlSend);
```

```
DDX_Control(pDX, IDC_RECVMETER, m_progctrlRecv);
//}}AFX_DATA_MAP
}
BEGIN_MESSAGE_MAP(CClientDlg, CDialog)
//{{AFX_MSG_MAP(CClientDlg)
ON_WM_SYSCOMMAND()
ON_WM_PAINT()
ON_WM_QUERYDRAGICON()
ON_MESSAGE(VTM_DATAREADY, OnVTDataReady)
ON_MESSAGE(VTM_READYFORWRITE, OnVTReadyForWrite)
ON_MESSAGE(MM_WIM_DATA, OnRecordEvent)
ON_MESSAGE(MM_WOM_DONE, OnPlayEvent)
ON_EN_CHANGE(IDC_EDITNAME, OnChangeEditname)
ON_EN_CHANGE(IDC_EDITSERVER, OnChangeEditserver)
ON_CBN_SELCHANGE(IDC_COMBPROT, OnSelchangeCombprot)
ON_CBN_SELCHANGE(IDC_COMBCHATTER, OnSelchangeCombchatter)
ON_BN_CLICKED(IDC_BTNCONNECT, OnBtnconnect)
ON_BN_CLICKED(IDC_BTNDISCONNECT, OnBtndisconnect)
ON_BN_CLICKED(IDC_CHKVOICE, OnChkvoice)
ON_WM_CLOSE()
ON_WM_TIMER()
//}}AFX_MSG_MAP
END_MESSAGE_MAP()
BOOL CClientDlg::OnInitDialog()
{
CDialog::OnInitDialog();
// IDM_ABOUTBOX must be in the system command range.
ASSERT((IDM_ABOUTBOX & 0xFFF0) == IDM_ABOUTBOX);
ASSERT(IDM_ABOUTBOX < 0xF000);
CMenu* pSysMenu = GetSystemMenu(FALSE);
if (pSysMenu != NULL)
{
CString strAboutMenu;
strAboutMenu.LoadString(IDS_ABOUTBOX);
if (!strAboutMenu.IsEmpty())
{
pSysMenu->AppendMenu(MF_SEPARATOR);
pSysMenu->AppendMenu(MF_STRING, IDM_ABOUTBOX, strAboutMenu);
}
}
// Set the icon for this dialog.  The framework does this
automatically
//  when the application's main window is not a dialog
SetIcon(m_hIcon, TRUE);                    // Set big icon
SetIcon(m_hIcon, FALSE);            // Set small icon
// Add extra initialization here
m_editUserName.SetWindowText("");
m_editServer.SetWindowText("131.200.2.246"); // Server IP address
m_ComBoTalker.ResetContent();
```

```
m_ComBoProts.ResetContent();
m_editUserName.LimitText(15);
m_progctrlSend.SetRange(0, 1);
m_progctrlRecv.SetRange(0, 1);
m_progctrlSend.SetPos(0);
m_progctrlRecv.SetPos(0);
WORD        wVersionRequested;
WSADATA     wsaData;
char        outtext[128];
int         iLoop;
wVersionRequested = MAKEWORD(1,1);
if (WSAStartup(wVersionRequested, &wsaData) != 0)
{
   return FALSE;
}
// Check compatible network protocols
if(!InitProtocols())
return FALSE;
// Add compatible protocol to protocol combo-box
for(iLoop = 0; iLoop < m_iNumWorkProts; iLoop++)
{
 wsprintf(outtext, "%2d: %s", iLoop,
     m_lpProtBuf[m_iWorkProts[iLoop]].lpProtocol);
 m_ComBoProts.InsertString(-1, outtext);
}
// Set the controls status
DoConnection(FALSE);
m_bVoiceMsg = FALSE;
m_vtPlay.SetHwnd(GetSafeHwnd());
m_vtPlay.SetVTWaveFormat(m_iWaveFormat);
m_vtPlay.AllocMemory();
m_vtRecord.SetHwnd(GetSafeHwnd());
m_vtRecord.SetVTWaveFormat(m_iWaveFormat);
m_vtRecord.AllocMemory();
m_ComBoProts.SetCurSel(0);
// return TRUE  unless you set the focus to a control
SetTimer(1, 3000, NULL);
return TRUE;
}
void CClientDlg::OnClose()
{
// Add your message handler code here and/or call default
// Clean the combo-boxes
m_ComBoTalker.ResetContent();
m_ComBoProts.ResetContent();
// Close the socket
closesocket(m_MySock.m_hSock);
WSACleanup();
// Close the wave I/O device and
```

```
if(m_bVoiceMsg)
    m_vtPlay.StopPlay();
if(m_bVoiceTalk)
m_vtRecord.StopRecord();
m_vtPlay.CleanMemory();
m_vtRecord.CleanMemory();
CDialog::OnClose();
}
void CClientDlg::OnSysCommand(UINT nID, LPARAM lParam)
{
if ((nID & 0xFFF0) == IDM_ABOUTBOX)
{
CAboutDlg dlgAbout;
dlgAbout.DoModal();
}
else
{
CDialog::OnSysCommand(nID, lParam);
}
}
void CClientDlg::OnPaint()
{
if (IsIconic())
{
CPaintDC dc(this); // device context for painting
SendMessage(WM_ICONERASEBKGND, (WPARAM) dc.GetSafeHdc(), 0);
// Center icon in client rectangle
int cxIcon = GetSystemMetrics(SM_CXICON);
int cyIcon = GetSystemMetrics(SM_CYICON);
CRect rect;
GetClientRect(&rect);
int x = (rect.Width() - cxIcon + 1) / 2;
int y = (rect.Height() - cyIcon + 1) / 2;
// Draw the icon
dc.DrawIcon(x, y, m_hIcon);
}
else
{
CDialog::OnPaint();
}
}
HCURSOR CClientDlg::OnQueryDragIcon()
{
return (HCURSOR) m_hIcon;
}
BOOL CClientDlg::InitProtocols(void)
{
int       numStrucs;
int       index;
```

```
unsigned long  iProtBufSize = 0;
EnumProtocols(NULL, NULL, &iProtBufSize);
if((m_lpProtBuf = (LPPROTOCOL_INFO)VirtualAlloc(NULL,
                                                iProtBufSize,
                                                MEM_COMMIT,
                                                PAGE_READWRITE)) ==
NULL)
 {
     AfxMessageBox("Failed to allocate memory for m_lpProtBuf!");
     return FALSE;
 }
if((numStrucs = EnumProtocols(NULL, m_lpProtBuf, &iProtBufSize)) ==
          SOCKET_ERROR)
 {
   AfxMessageBox("Failed to numerate protocol!");
   return FALSE;
}
m_iNumWorkProts = 0;
for(index = 0; index < numStrucs; index++)
{
  if((m_lpProtBuf[index].dwServiceFlags & XP_CONNECTIONLESS) == 0)
  {
     m_iWorkProts[m_iNumWorkProts++] = index;
  }
}
return TRUE;
}
BOOL CClientDlg::InitSockets(int iProtIndex)
{
int numStrucs;
GUID guidNW = SVCID_NETWARE(VT_NETID);     // Generate GUID for
Novel prot
GUID guidDNS = SVCID_TCP(VT_DNSID);        // Generate GUID for DNS
char strServName[128];
char outtext[128];
// Check the protocol type
switch(m_lpProtBuf[iProtIndex].iAddressFamily)
{
case AF_IPX:
     //  SAP/Bindery Name Space
    m_dwCSABufsize = sizeof(m_CSABuf);
    numStrucs = GetAddressByName(0, &guidNW,
"VOICE_TALK_SERVER_IPX",
                               NULL, RES_FIND_MULTIPLE, NULL,
m_CSABuf,
                               &m_dwCSABufsize, NULL, NULL);
    if((numStrucs == SOCKET_ERROR) || (numStrucs == 0))
    {
```

```
      AfxMessageBox("Server not found.  Try a different
protocol");
      return FALSE;
    }
  break;
default:
  return FALSE;
}
m_MySock.m_iSockType = m_lpProtBuf[iProtIndex].iSocketType;
m_MySock.m_iProtocol = m_lpProtBuf[iProtIndex].iProtocol;
if((m_MySock.m_hSock =
  socket(m_lpProtBuf[iProtIndex].iAddressFamily,
  m_lpProtBuf[iProtIndex].iSocketType,
  m_lpProtBuf[iProtIndex].iProtocol)) == INVALID_SOCKET)
{
   wsprintf(outtext, "Failure: socket() returned %u",
WSAGetLastError());
   AfxMessageBox(outtext);
   return FALSE;
}
if(connect(m_MySock.m_hSock,m_CSABuf[0].RemoteAddr.lpSockaddr,
      m_CSABuf[0].RemoteAddr.iSockaddrLength) == SOCKET_ERROR)
{
  wsprintf(outtext, "Failure: connect() returned %u",
WSAGetLastError());
  AfxMessageBox(outtext);
  return FALSE;
}
if(WSAAsyncSelect(m_MySock.m_hSock, GetSafeHwnd(),
VTM_READYFORWRITE,
                  FD_WRITE) == SOCKET_ERROR)
{
  wsprintf(outtext, "Failure: WSAAsyncSelect() returned %u",
       SAGetLastError());
  AfxMessageBox(outtext);
  return FALSE;
}
return TRUE;
}
void CClientDlg::DoConnection(BOOL bTrue)
{
  m_bConnect = bTrue;
  if(bTrue)
  {
    m_ComBoTalker.ResetContent();
    m_ComBoTalker.InsertString(0, "No one to talk");
    if(WSAAsyncSelect(m_MySock.m_hSock,
GetSafeHwnd(),VTM_DATAREADY,
                       FD_READ | FD_CLOSE) == SOCKET_ERROR)
```

```
        {
         AfxMessageBox("Failure: WSAAsyncSelect() to get online users!");
         return;
        }
    }
    else
    {
     closesocket(m_MySock.m_hSock);
     m_ComBoTalker.ResetContent();
     m_ComBoTalker.InsertString(0, "No one to talk");
     m_chkVoice.SetCheck(0);
     m_bVoiceMsg = FALSE;
     m_progctrlSend.SetPos(0);
     m_progctrlRecv.SetPos(0);
    }
    m_btnConnect.EnableWindow(!bTrue);
    m_editUserName.EnableWindow(!bTrue);
    m_editServer.EnableWindow(!bTrue);
    m_ComBoProts.EnableWindow(!bTrue);
    if(!bTrue)
    {
     EnableTalking(FALSE);
  // Close wave I/O devices
     if(m_bVoiceMsg)
     m_vtPlay.StopPlay();
     if(m_bVoiceTalk)
       m_vtRecord.StopRecord();
    }
    }
    void CClientDlg::EnableTalking(BOOL bTrue)
    {
    char sShowText[128];
    int  iIndex;
     m_bTalking = bTrue;
     m_chkVoice.EnableWindow(bTrue);
     m_progctrlSend.EnableWindow(bTrue);
     m_progctrlRecv.EnableWindow(bTrue);
     if(bTrue)
     {
       wsprintf(sShowText, "%s: in talking with %s", m_MySock.m_sUserName, \
               m_lpPeerName);
       iIndex = m_ComBoTalker.FindString(0, m_lpPeerName);
       m_ComBoTalker.SetCurSel(iIndex);
    }
    else
    {
     if(lstrlen(m_MySock.m_sUserName) > 0)
```

```
        wsprintf(sShowText, "%s: free", m_MySock.m_sUserName);
  else
        wsprintf(sShowText, "Voice Talk Client");
}
SetWindowText(sShowText);
}
void CClientDlg::ParseMsgData(void)
{
 CString            strRecv;
switch(m_vtRecvMsgBuf.m_ucMsgType)
{
case VT_WAVE1M08:    // Voice message
case VT_WAVE1S08:
case VT_WAVE1M16:
case VT_WAVE1S16:
case VT_WAVE2M08:
case VT_WAVE2S08:
case VT_WAVE2M16:
case VT_WAVE2S16:
case VT_WAVE4M08:
case VT_WAVE4S08:
case VT_WAVE4M16:
case VT_WAVE4S16:
      m_progctrlRecv.SetPos(1);
// Get wave data buffer size
m_uiBufLen = m_vtRecvMsgBuf.m_lLength - SIZEVTMSGHDR;
// Copy wave data buffer
memcpy((void*)m_pWaveData,
(void*)m_vtRecvMsgBuf.m_pData,m_uiBufLen);
if(!m_bVoiceMsg)
{
   m_bVoiceMsg = TRUE;
       m_vtPlay.SetPlayData(m_pWaveData, m_uiBufLen);
      _vtPlay.StartPlay();
}
return;
}
}
LONG CClientDlg::OnVTDataReady(WPARAM wparam, LPARAM lparam)
{
// If the server connection was closed Clean the temporary buffers
char sPeerName[16];
char sShowText[128];
int  iIndex;
int  iCount;
memset((void*)sPeerName, 0, 16);
memset((void*)sShowText, 0, 128);
 if(LOWORD(lparam) == FD_CLOSE)
{
```

```
    AfxMessageBox("Server Connection Dropped!");
    DoConnection(FALSE);
    return 1L;
}
memset((void*)&m_vtRecvMsgBuf, 0, SIZEVTMSG);
// Read the incoming message data
if(!RecvVTMessage(&m_MySock, &m_vtRecvMsgBuf))
{
 return 0L;
}
switch(m_vtRecvMsgBuf.m_ucCmd)
{
case VTCMD_REGNAME:
// Add the Clients name to "Talk With" combobox
memcpy((void*)sPeerName, (void*)m_vtRecvMsgBuf.m_pData,
16*sizeof(char));
iCount = m_ComBoTalker.GetCount();
m_ComBoTalker.InsertString(iCount, sPeerName);
break;
case VTCMD_DEREGNAME:
// Remove name from list box
memcpy((void*)sPeerName,
(void*)m_vtRecvMsgBuf.m_pData,16*sizeof(char));
iIndex = m_ComBoTalker.FindString(-1, sPeerName);
if(iIndex != LB_ERR)
{
 m_ComBoTalker.DeleteString(iIndex);
}
break;
case VTCMD_REQSESSION:
// Someone is asking for a chat session
lstrcpy(sShowText, (char*)m_vtRecvMsgBuf.m_pData);
lstrcat(sShowText, " requests to talk.");
if(AfxMessageBox(sShowText, MB_OKCANCEL) == IDOK)
{
 lstrcpy(m_lpPeerName, (char*)m_vtRecvMsgBuf.m_pData);
 memset(&m_vtSendMsgBuf, 0, SIZEVTMSG);
 m_vtSendMsgBuf.m_ucIdentity = VT_IDENTITY;
 m_vtSendMsgBuf.m_ucCmd = VTCMD_SESSIONREQRESP;
 m_vtSendMsgBuf.m_ucMsgType = VT_TEXT;
 m_vtSendMsgBuf.m_lLength = SIZEVTMSGHDR + 2;
 m_vtSendMsgBuf.m_pData[0] = 1;
 if(SendVTMessage(m_MySock.m_hSock, &m_vtSendMsgBuf))
    EnableTalking(TRUE);
 else
    AfxMessageBox("Can't send message to server");
 return 1L;
}
else
```

```
{
 // Rejected the session request,// send the denial message
 memset(&m_vtSendMsgBuf, 0, SIZEVTMSG);
 m_vtSendMsgBuf.m_ucIdentity = VT_IDENTITY;
 m_vtSendMsgBuf.m_ucCmd = VTCMD_SESSIONREQRESP;
 m_vtSendMsgBuf.m_ucMsgType = VT_TEXT;
 m_vtSendMsgBuf.m_lLength = SIZEVTMSGHDR + 2;
 m_vtSendMsgBuf.m_pData[0] = 0;
 if(SendVTMessage(m_MySock.m_hSock, &m_vtSendMsgBuf))
    EnableTalking(FALSE);
}
break;
// Response to request
case VTCMD_SESSIONREQRESP:
if(m_MySock.m_iStatus != VTSOCKET_REQSESSION)
{
  return 0L;
}
if(*m_vtRecvMsgBuf.m_pData == 1)
{
 EnableTalking(TRUE);
}
else
{
  EnableTalking(FALSE);
}
break;
case VTCMD_SESSIONCLOSE:
 EnableTalking(FALSE);
 m_MySock.m_iStatus = VTSOCKET_AVAILABLE;
 wsprintf(sShowText, "%s: available for talking",
m_MySock.m_sUserName);
 SetWindowText(sShowText);
 if(m_bVoiceMsg)
   m_vtPlay.StopPlay();
 if(m_bVoiceTalk)
   m_vtRecord.StopRecord();
 return FALSE;
case VTCMD_MSGDATA:
   // Parse the message and display it
   ParseMsgData();
   break;
default:
  return 0L;
}
return 1L;
}
LONG CClientDlg::OnVTReadyForWrite(WPARAM wparam, LPARAM lparam)
{
```

```
 memset((void*)m_MySock.m_sUserName, 0, 16*sizeof(char));
 strncpy(m_MySock.m_sUserName,m_strUserName,
m_strUserName.GetLength()+1);
 memset(&m_vtSendMsgBuf, 0, SIZEVTMSG);
 m_vtSendMsgBuf.m_ucIdentity = VT_IDENTITY;
 m_vtSendMsgBuf.m_ucCmd = VTCMD_REGNAME;
 m_vtSendMsgBuf.m_ucMsgType = VT_TEXT;
 m_vtSendMsgBuf.m_lLength = SIZEVTMSGHDR +
REALLEN(m_MySock.m_sUserName);
 memcpy((void*)m_vtSendMsgBuf.m_pData, (void*)m_MySock.m_sUserName,
     REALLEN(m_MySock.m_sUserName));
if(SendVTMessage(m_MySock.m_hSock, &m_vtSendMsgBuf))
{
 DoConnection(TRUE);
}
return 1L;
}
LONG CClientDlg::OnRecordEvent(WPARAM wparam, LPARAM lparam)
{
 if(!m_bVoiceTalk)
  return 1L;
 m_progctrlSend.SetPos(1);
 WAVEHDR* lpwhdr = (WAVEHDR*)lparam;
// Reset the voice message packet
 memset(&m_vtSendMsgBuf, 0, SIZEVTMSG);
 m_vtSendMsgBuf.m_ucIdentity = VT_IDENTITY;
 m_vtSendMsgBuf.m_ucCmd = VTCMD_MSGDATA;
 m_vtSendMsgBuf.m_ucMsgType = m_iWaveFormat;
 m_vtSendMsgBuf.m_lLength = SIZEVTMSGHDR + lpwhdr->dwBufferLength;
 memcpy((void*)m_vtSendMsgBuf.m_pData, (void*)lpwhdr->lpData,
      lpwhdr->dwBufferLength);
 m_vtRecord.ResetRecord();
// Send the voice message packet
SendVTMessage(m_MySock.m_hSock, &m_vtSendMsgBuf);
 m_progctrlSend.SetPos(0);
return 1L;
}
LONG CClientDlg::OnPlayEvent(WPARAM wparam, LPARAM lparam)
{
 if(!m_bVoiceMsg)
  return 0L;
  m_progctrlRecv.SetPos(0);
  m_vtPlay.ResetPlay();
  m_vtPlay.SetPlayData(m_pWaveData, m_uiBufLen);
  m_vtPlay.RestartPlay();
return 1L;
}
void CClientDlg::OnChangeEditname()
{
```

```
 m_editUserName.GetWindowText(m_strUserName);
}
void CClientDlg::OnChangeEditserver()
{
   m_editServer.GetWindowText(m_strServer);
}
void CClientDlg::OnSelchangeCombprot()
{
 int iIndex;
 iIndex = m_ComBoProts.GetCurSel();
 if(iIndex == LB_ERR)
 {
  AfxMessageBox("An error ocurred in selecting protocols!");
  return;
 }
switch(m_lpProtBuf[m_iWorkProts[iIndex]].iAddressFamily)
{
case AF_INET:
  m_editServer.EnableWindow(TRUE);
  break;
default: // Nothing
  m_editServer.SetWindowText("");
  m_editServer.EnableWindow(FALSE);
  break;
}
}
void CClientDlg::OnSelchangeCombchatter()
{
// Add control notification handler code here
int     iIndex;
int     iRev;
char    sNewPeer[16];
memset(sNewPeer, 0, 16);
iIndex = m_ComBoTalker.GetCurSel();
if(iIndex == LB_ERR)
{
AfxMessageBox("An error occurred in selecting peer talker");
return;
}
if(iIndex == 0)
{
if(m_bTalking)
{
  memset(&m_vtSendMsgBuf, 0, SIZEVTMSG);
  m_vtSendMsgBuf.m_ucIdentity = VT_IDENTITY;
  m_vtSendMsgBuf.m_ucCmd = VTCMD_SESSIONCLOSE;
  m_vtSendMsgBuf.m_ucMsgType = VT_TEXT;
  m_vtSendMsgBuf.m_lLength = SIZEVTMSGHDR;
  if(SendVTMessage(m_MySock.m_hSock, &m_vtSendMsgBuf))
```

```
  {
   if(WSAAsyncSelect(m_MySock.m_hSock, GetSafeHwnd(), 0, !=
SOCKET_ERROR)
   {
    EnableTalking(FALSE);
    return;
   }
  }
}
return;
}
else
{
  iRev = m_ComBoTalker.GetLBText(iIndex, sNewPeer);
  if(iRev == CB_ERR)
  {
   AfxMessageBox("An error occurred in getting new talker's name");
   return;
  }
if(lstrcmp(sNewPeer, m_lpPeerName) == 0)
{
  return;
}
lstrcpy(m_lpPeerName, sNewPeer);
m_MySock.m_iStatus = VTSOCKET_REQSESSION;
memset(&m_vtSendMsgBuf, 0, SIZEVTMSG);
m_vtSendMsgBuf.m_ucIdentity = VT_IDENTITY;
m_vtSendMsgBuf.m_ucCmd = VTCMD_REQSESSION;
m_vtSendMsgBuf.m_ucMsgType = VT_TEXT;
m_vtSendMsgBuf.m_lLength = SIZEVTMSGHDR + REALLEN(sNewPeer);
memcpy((void*)m_vtSendMsgBuf.m_pData, (void*)sNewPeer,
REALLEN(sNewPeer));
if(SendVTMessage(m_MySock.m_hSock, &m_vtSendMsgBuf))
{
 if(WSAAsyncSelect(m_MySock.m_hSock, GetSafeHwnd(), VTM_DATAREADY,
FD_READ
                FD_CLOSE) != SOCKET_ERROR)
 {
    EnableTalking(TRUE);
    return;
}
}
}
}
void CClientDlg::OnBtnconnect()
{
int iIndex;
iIndex = m_ComBoProts.GetCurSel();
if(iIndex == LB_ERR)
```

```
{
AfxMessageBox("Did not select a protocol!");
return;
}
if(m_strUserName.IsEmpty())
{
AfxMessageBox("Did not input a user name");
return;
}
if(m_lpProtBuf[m_iWorkProts[iIndex]].iAddressFamily
== AF_INET && m_strServer.IsEmpty())
{
AfxMessageBox("Did not input a server name");
return;
}
if(!InitSockets(m_iWorkProts[iIndex]))
{
AfxMessageBox("Can't build connection with server!");
}
}
void CClientDlg::OnBtndisconnect()
{
if(m_bConnect)
DoConnection(FALSE);
}
void CClientDlg::OnChkvoice()
{
if(!m_bConnect)
return;
if(!m_bVoiceTalk)
{
 m_bVoiceTalk = TRUE;
 m_chkVoice.SetCheck(1);
 m_vtRecord.StartRecord();
}
else // If checked previously
{
 m_bVoiceTalk = FALSE;
 m_chkVoice.SetCheck(0);
 m_vtRecord.StopRecord();
}
}
void CClientDlg::OnTimer(UINT nIDEvent)
{
  CDialog::OnTimer(nIDEvent);
}
```

Following is the line-by-line explanation of the source code:

- **Lines 1–3:** Header file declaration.
- **Lines 9–27:** Definition of the `CAboutDlg` class, generated by the VC++ editor.
- **Lines 28–32:** Definition of the constructor for the `CAboutDlg` class, generated by the VC++ editor.
- **Lines 33–38:** Definition of the `DoDataExchange` method of `CAboutDlg` dialog, generated by the VC++ editor.
- **Lines 39–43:** Message map definition for handling events generated on `CAboutDlg` dialog, generated by the VC++ editor.
- **Lines 44–60:** Definition of the constructor for the `CClientDlg` class, generated by the VC++ editor.
- **Lines 61–74:** Definition of the `DoDataExchange` method for `CClientDlg` dialog, generated by the VC++ editor.
- **Lines 75–94:** Message map definition for handling events generated on `CClientDlg` dialog, generated by the VC++ editor.
- **Lines 95–156:** Definition of the `OnInitDialog` method.
  - **Line 117:** Setting the server's IP address in the text entry box.
  - **Line 135:** Collecting all the network protocols available at the client.
  - **Lines 138–142:** Adding all the available protocols to the protocol list box.
  - **Lines 145–153:** Initializing the wave I/O device.
- **Lines 157–174:** Definition of the `OnClose` method, which closes the client socket and frees the wave device buffers.
- **Lines 175–186:** Definition of the `OnSysCommand` method, generated by the VC++ editor.
- **Lines 187–207:** Definition of the `OnPaint` method, generated by the VC++ editor.
- **Lines 208–211:** Definition of the `OnQueryDragIcon` method, generated by the VC++ editor.
- **Lines 212–237:** Definition of the `InitProtocols` method, which finds and allocates buffers to all the available protocols.
- **Lines 238–280:** Definition of the `InitSockets` method, which creates an asynchronous socket and gets the client's system name.
- **Lines 281–316:** Definition of the `DoConnection` method; if the parameter `bTrue` is `TRUE`, this method opens a client socket. Otherwise, it closes the client socket and wave I/O devices.
- **Lines 317–340:** Definition of the `EnableTalking` method; if the client is talking with another peer, this method displays "Client1 is Talking With Client2." Otherwise, it displays "Client1 is free."

- **Lines 341–369:** Definition of the `ParseMsgData` method, which parses the incoming data. If it is voice data, it starts playing the incoming data.
- **Lines 370–467:** Definition of the `OnVTDataReady` method. When a message comes from the server, it analyzes the message and if it is a new client connection request, it adds the client's name in the combo box. If it is a request for voice chat, it establishes a session through the server for voice chat; if it is the server's disconnect message, it closes its client socket.
- **Lines 468–483:** Definition of the `OnVTReadyForWrite` method.
- **Lines 484–499:** Definition of the `OnRecordEvent` method, to start the recording of voice data by calling the `StartRecord` method.
- **Lines 500–509:** Definition of the `OnPlayEvent` method; when the play event is generated, it starts playing the incoming voice data.
- **Lines 510–513:** Definition of the `OnChangeEditName` method, which reads the username when it is changed in the edit box.
- **Lines 514–517:** Definition of the `OnChangeEditServer` method, which reads the server name when it is changed in the edit box.
- **Lines 518–537:** Definition of the `OnSelChangeCombPort` method, which reads the new protocol name.
- **Lines 538–601:** Definition of the `SelChangeCombchatter` method; when the user changes the remote client's name, it reestablishes the socket connection with the new client through the server.
- **Lines 602–626:** Definition of the `OnBtnconnect` method; when the Connect button is clicked, it checks whether all the input parameters are selected. If all are selected, it establishes a connection with the server.
- **Lines 627–631:** Definition of the `OnBtndisconnect` method; when the Disconnect button is clicked, it closes the client socket.
- **Lines 632–648:** Definition of the `OnChkvoice` method; when the voice chat checkbox is checked, it starts voice data playing and recording.
- **Lines 649–652:** Definition of the `OnTimer` method, generated by the VC++ editor.

In addition to the preceding files, based on the hardware you have (custom-built or sound card), you need to create your own classes for recording and replaying voice with the following functionality:

- Class Name: VTPlayWave, which contains the following methods:
  - `BOOL AllocMemory(void)`: to allocate memory for the header structure of wave output.
  - `void CleanMemory(void)`: to clean the memory of the header structure of wave output.

  - `BOOL Initialize (void)`: to initialize and open the wave output device.
  - `BOOL StartPlay(void)`: to play the sound.
  - `void StopPlay(void)`: to stop playing the sound.
  - `void ResetPlay(void)`: to reset the wave data buffer to read new sound data.
  - `BOOL RestartPlay(void)`: to play the sound after resetting the wave data buffer and reading new sound data.
  - `void SetPlayData(void* pWaveData, unsigned int BufSize)`: to set new sound data to the output header structure.
- Class Name: `VTRecordWave`, which contains the following methods:
  - `BOOL AllocMemory(void)`: to allocate memory for the header structure of wave input.
  - `void CleanMemory(void)`: to clean the memory of the header structure of wave input.
  - `BOOL Initialize(void)`: to initialize and open the wave input device.
  - `BOOL StartRecord(void)`: to record the sound.
  - `void StopRecord(void)`: to stop recording the sound.
  - `BOOL ResetRecord(void)`: to reset the input device to record new input sound data.

Executing the program

To test the program, initially execute the program on the desktop over a LAN. Build the project in the Visual Studio environment. First run the `Server.EXE` application. The screen should look like the one shown in Figure 8-5.

Run `Client.EXE` in two systems and connect to the server by providing the server's system name or IP address. To talk with a remote client, select that client's name from the Talk With combo box and enable the Voice Talk checkbox. The client's screen should look like the one shown in Figure 8-6.

To run this application successfully, you have to install sound card drivers explicitly in the target machine because there is no default component in the Target Designer to include the sound card functionality. In addition, note that the correct IP addresses need to be assigned to the server and the clients.

Figure 8-5: Server window for the voice-over-IP application

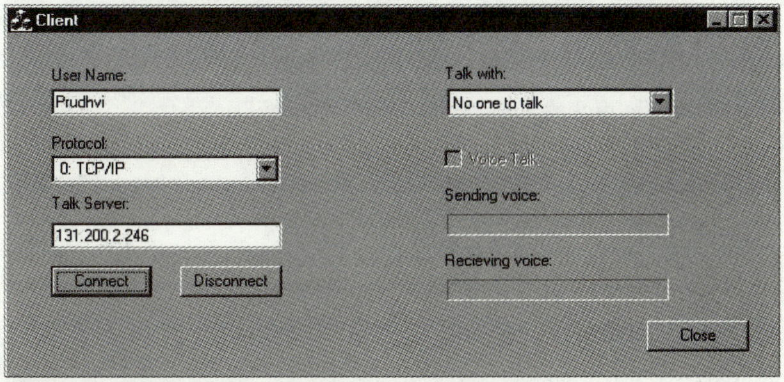

Figure 8-6: Client window for the voice-over-IP application

Embedding the software

The steps for embedding the software are similar to those in the preceding example. As the filenames will change, the step-by-step procedure is given below:

1. Collect all the files required to run the application at the target. In this case, the files required are as follows:
   - `Server.EXE` (Server application file)

- `Client.EXE` (Client application file)
- `MFC42D.DLL`
- `MFCO42D.DLL`
- `MSVCRTD.DLL`

The three DLLs are required to run an MFC application at the target.

2. Create a component using Component Designer. Use the following steps to create a custom component.
   - Open Component Designer (on the Windows taskbar, select Start ⇨ Programs ⇨ Windows NT Embedded 4.0 ⇨ Component Designer).
   - Save the component as `VOIPSample.kdf`.
   - In the navigation pane, right-click Component1, and then click Properties.
   - In the Component Name box, type **VOIP Sample**.
   - In the Vendor text box, type **Generic**.
   - In the Description text box, type **Voice Over IP** and then click OK.
   - In the navigation pane, right-click VOIP Sample, and then click Add Component.
   - In the Component text box, type **VOIP**; leave the remaining fields empty.
   - Verify that the hierarchy path is set as follows: `%ROOT%\Applications\Utilities`, and click OK.
   - In the navigation pane, right-click Files, and then click Add File.
   - In the File Name text box, click Browse. Browse for `Server.EXE` (the server application file collected in Step 1). Set the target path as `\Winnt\VOIP`. (The application `Server.EXE` will be stored in this directory at the target.)
   - Repeat the preceding steps to add all the other files, which are collected in Step 1. The resulting window should look like the one shown in Figure 8-7.
   - Save the component definition file and exit.
3. Create the target image using Target Designer.
   - Open Target Designer (on the Windows taskbar, select Start ⇨ Programs ⇨ Windows NT Embedded 4.0 ⇨ Target Designer).
   - In the All Nodes pane, expand the Target Designer system database (TDSD). Expand the Examples collection.
   - Copy the Minimal With Network configuration. Right-click on User Configuration and click Paste.

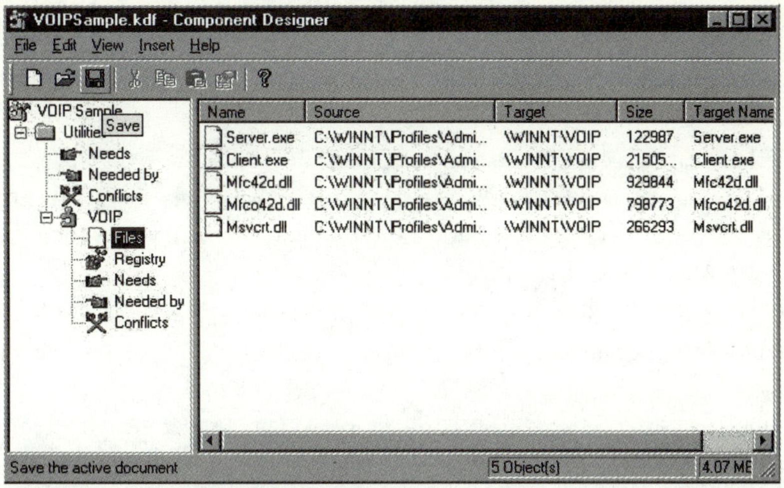

Figure 8-7: The VOIP Component Designer

- Right-click the Standard No Network configuration that was pasted under the User Configuration collection, and then click Rename. In the text box, type **VoiceOverIP**.
- Expand the tree structure under VoiceOverIP. Right-click on Standard OS under `\ProtocolTranslator\System\Platform\Core OS` and click Add.
- Repeat the preceding steps to add the following components:

  Serial Mouse, under `System\Devices\Mouse`

  COM 1 and COM 2, under `System\Devices\Serial Ports`

  NetBEUI and IPX/SPX, under `System\Network\Network Protocols`

  NetBios, RPC, and Computer Browser, under `System\Network\Network Services`

  TCP/IP Utilities, under `System\Network\Network Applications`

  MS Sans Serif Font, under `System\Desktop Settings\Fonts`
- Depending on the network card installed in the target machine, add components under `\System\Network\Network Drivers` and `\System\Network\Network Adapters`.
- To add the VOIPSample component created in Step 2, click Component Management, which is under Tools in the File Menu. Click Add, browse for `VOIPSample.kdf`, and click OK.
- Select VOIP, which is under `\VoiceOverIP\Applications\Utilities`, right-click on it, and click Add.
- In the All Nodes pane, verify that VoiceOverIP, which is under User Configuration, is selected. At this stage, the window should look like the one shown in Figure 8-8.

- On the Image menu, click Settings. Verify that the Source Repository Path for WinNT is CD1, which is in the Windows Embedded NT 4.0 CD-ROM; and that the target path is set to `D:\VOIPWithEmbeddedNT` (*D* represents the letter of your hard disk drive containing the target image).
- On the Image menu, click Build and Install, and then click Start.
- When a message states that you have not entered a product identification (PID) number, and asks if you want to build a run-time image which works for a limited time, click Yes.
- When the Target Designer Network Settings dialog box appears, click OK.
- When the "Install Complete" message appears, click OK. (This might take a few minutes.)
- Go to the `\VOIPWithEmbeddedNT` directory, which is under the letter representing your hard disk drive containing the target image, and copy all the subdirectories and files onto the target's hard disk.

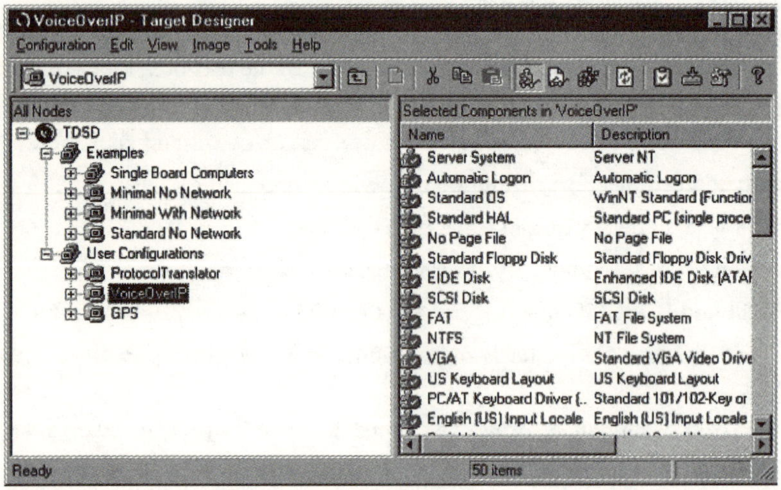

Figure 8-8: Target Designer for the VOIP application

This VOIP application occupies 4MB of memory. You can embed the client application in a target board, which can run a smaller operating system. If the target board has Ethernet connectivity, you can directly connect this IP phone on the LAN and use it for voice communication. Like any other node on the LAN, the IP phone also has an IP address assigned to it. You can build a small piece of software at the server, which maps the IP addresses of these phones to seven-digit or three-digit telephone numbers. In this type of application, you can develop an embedded server using Windows NT, which requires about 81MB of memory. The embedded server can be a Single Board Computer with either a hard disk or a CD-ROM, for secondary storage on which the operating system resides.

Summary

This chapter described embedded communication system development using two case studies: a protocol converter and a voice-over-IP server and client components. The first application, the protocol converter, converts Ethernet packets to serial communication packets. You can use parts of this application to develop a LAN analyzer or a firewall. The second application, an IP phone, can be embedded in a 32-bit processor-based system to achieve voice communication over IP networks. These projects provide some insight into application development over the TCP/IP protocol stack as well, knowledge that is very important to understanding the functioning of embedded networked appliances, which are becoming increasingly popular.

Chapter 9

Embedded Applications over Mobile Networks

In This Chapter

- Developing an embedded mobile music player application
- Developing a mobile database application
- Converting the applications into DLLs for porting to a mobile device

Mobile networks have been used for a long time for voice communication. With the advent of high-speed wireless networks and powerful mobile devices, we can now use mobile devices for a variety of applications, including downloading music and creating embedded database applications. Qualcomm, which pioneered CDMA (Code Division Multiple Access)–based wireless networks, released the Binary Runtime Environment for Wireless (BREW) SDK, with which you can develop mobile applications on the desktop and then port them to a mobile device. This chapter presents the source code for developing a music application and an embedded database application.

Development Environment

To develop the projects described in this chapter, you need the following environment:

- A Windows 2000 or Windows NT system
- Visual Studio 6.0 for writing the code in the VC++ environment
- BREW SDK version 1.0.0.21 (or later), which you can download from `http://www.qualcomm.com/brew/`

The BREW SDK facilitates the development of mobile data applications in the VC++ environment. After developing the required application in the VC++ environment, you can convert it into a DLL and port it to the embedded device. The BREW SDK provides a number of emulators that you can use to completely test the application's functionality, even if you do not have the target embedded system.

> **NOTE** You can deploy the applications developed in the BREW environment on the current wireless networks and on future third-generation (3G) networks.

> **TIP** Before developing the applications presented in this chapter, run the sample applications provided with the BREW SDK to familiarize yourself with the development process. The applications developed using BREW are called *applets;* in this book, the words *application* and *applet* are used interchangeably.

Project: MP3 Sound Player

With the popularity of MP3 (Moving Picture Expert Group Layer 3) music, a number of devices are now available on the market for playing MP3 music. These gadgets are actually embedded systems with processors and flash memory. You can store the music files in the flash memory and play them whenever you want. You can download the MP3 files from the Internet directly to the device, or you can transfer the files from the desktop. (Users with high-speed Internet connections often download files to the desktop. Subsequently, the file can be transferred onto the MP3 player.) Emerging now are 2.5G (two-and-a-half generation) and 3G (third-generation) wireless networks that support downloading speeds ranging from 144 Kbps to 2 Mbps. Using wireless networks and mobile devices that support high-speed data transfers and large memory, you can download MP3 files directly to any mobile phone enabled to play such files. You can use the BREW SDK to develop the necessary application on the mobile device, and the following project will achieve just that.

Source code listing for sound.c

Listing 9-1 provides the source code for `sound.c`, developed in the VC++ environment for the BREW SDK.

> **ON THE CD-ROM** This file is available on the CD-ROM that accompanies this book.

Listing 9-1: Source code for sound.c

```
#include "AEEModGen.h"
#include "AEEAppGen.h"
#include "AEEMenu.h"
#include "AEEStdLib.h"
#include "AEEUsageAppIDs.h"
#include "AEESound.h"
#include "AEESoundPlayer.h"
#include "AEEFile.h"
#include “sound.bid”
#define S_PLAY             103
#define S_STOP             104
#define S_REWIND           105
#define S_FASTFORWARD      106
#define S_PAUSE            107
```

```
#define S_RESUME                108
#define MIDI_MAX_FILES  10
#define TIME_INMILLISECONDS       5000  // 5000 ms
#define TEMPFACTOR                300
#ifndef DIRECTORY_CHAR
#ifdef AEE_SIMULATOR
#define DIRECTORY_CHAR  '\\'
#define DIRECTORY_STR   "\\"
#else
#define DIRECTORY_CHAR  '/'
#define DIRECTORY_STR   "/"
#endif
#endif
typedef struct _CISoundPlayerApp
{AEEApplet         a;
IMenuCtl     *  m_pIMenu;
ISoundPlayer *  m_pISoundPlayer;
char         *  m_szFileName;
boolean         m_bSPActive;
uint32          m_nPlayTime;
int             m_nLineHeight;
AEEDeviceInfo   m_deviceInfo;
}CISoundPlayerApp;
static boolean SoundPlayerApp_HandleEvent(IApplet * ap, AEEEvent ae,
uint16 i, uint32 d);
static boolean ISoundPlayer_InitAppData(IApplet* iap);
static void ISoundPlayer_FreeAppData(IApplet* iap);
static void ISoundPlayerUsage (CISoundPlayerApp * iap, uint16 i);
static void BuildPlayerMenu(CISoundPlayerApp *iap);
int AEEClsCreateInstance(AEECLSID ClsId,IShell * pIShell,IModule *
p,void ** obj){
*obj = NULL;
if(ClsId == AEECLSID_SOUNDPLAYER_APP){
if(AEEApplet_New(sizeof(CISoundPlayerApp), ClsId,
pIShell,p,(IApplet**)obj,
(AEEHANDLER)SoundPlayerApp_HandleEvent,(PFNFREEAPPDATA)ISoundPlayer_Free
AppData  ) == TRUE) {
if (ISoundPlayer_InitAppData((IApplet*)*obj) == TRUE){
return(AEE_SUCCESS);}}}
return (EFAILED);}
static boolean SoundPlayerApp_HandleEvent(IApplet * ap, AEEEvent ae,
uint16 i, uint32 d){
CISoundPlayerApp * iap = (CISoundPlayerApp*)ap;
if (iap == NULL || iap->a.m_pIShell == NULL || iap->a.m_pIDisplay ==
NULL)
return FALSE;
switch (ae) {
case EVT_APP_START:
```

```
if(ISHELL_CreateInstance(iap->a.m_pIShell, AEECLSID_MENUCTL, (void
**)&iap->m_pIMenu)  != SUCCESS){
return FALSE;}
BuildPlayerMenu (iap);
return(TRUE);
case EVT_APP_STOP:
return(TRUE);
case EVT_KEY:
if(iap->m_pIMenu != NULL && IMENUCTL_HandleEvent(iap->m_pIMenu,
EVT_KEY, i, 0))
return TRUE;
else
return FALSE;
case EVT_COMMAND:
switch(i){
case S_PLAY:
case S_STOP:
case S_REWIND:
case S_FASTFORWARD:
case S_PAUSE:
case S_RESUME:
ISoundPlayerUsage (iap, i);
return TRUE;
default:
return FALSE;}
default:
break;}
return FALSE;}
static boolean ISoundPlayer_InitAppData(IApplet* ap){
IFileMgr *  pIFileMgr = NULL;
FileInfo    fi;
int pnAscent = 0;
int pnDescent = 0;
char *   szStart;
CISoundPlayerApp * iap = (CISoundPlayerApp*)ap;
if (!iap)
return FALSE;
iap->m_pIMenu = NULL;
iap->m_pISoundPlayer = NULL;
iap->m_nPlayTime = 0;
iap->m_bSPActive = FALSE;
iap->m_szFileName = NULL;
iap->m_nLineHeight=IDISPLAY_GetFontMetrics(iap->a.m_pIDisplay,
AEE_FONT_NORMAL, &pnAscent, &pnDescent);
ISHELL_GetDeviceInfo(iap->a.m_pIShell,&iap->m_deviceInfo);
if(ISHELL_CreateInstance(iap->a.m_pIShell,EECLSID_FILEMGR, (void
**)&pIFileMgr))
return FALSE;
IFILEMGR_EnumInit(pIFileMgr, "Music", FALSE);
```

```
IFILEMGR_EnumNext(pIFileMgr, &fi);
szStart = fi.szName; // STRCHR(fi.szName, (int)DIRECTORY_CHAR) + 1;
if ( szStart ){
iap->m_szFileName = MALLOC(STRLEN(szStart) + 1);
STRCPY(iap->m_szFileName, szStart);}
IFILEMGR_Release(pIFileMgr);
return TRUE;}
static void ISoundPlayer_FreeAppData(IApplet* ap){
CISoundPlayerApp * iap = (CISoundPlayerApp*)ap;
if (iap->m_pIMenu != NULL){
IMENUCTL_Release (iap->m_pIMenu);
iap->m_pIMenu = NULL;}
if (iap->m_szFileName)
FREE (iap->m_szFileName);}
static void ISoundPlayerUsage (CISoundPlayerApp * iap, uint16 i){
AEEDeviceInfo *di = NULL;
if (iap == NULL || iap->a.m_pIShell == NULL || iap->a.m_pIDisplay == NULL)
return;
di = &iap->m_deviceInfo;
IDISPLAY_ClearScreen (iap->a.m_pIDisplay);
switch (i){
case S_PLAY:{
if (iap->m_pISoundPlayer == NULL){
ISHELL_CreateInstance(iap->a.m_pIShell, AEECLSID_SOUNDPLAYER, (void **)&iap->m_pISoundPlayer);      }
ISOUNDPLAYER_Set(iap->m_pISoundPlayer, SDT_FILE, iap->m_szFileName);
ISOUNDPLAYER_Play (iap->m_pISoundPlayer); }
return;
case S_STOP:{ {
ISOUNDPLAYER_Stop (iap->m_pISoundPlayer);}}
return;
case S_REWIND: {
uint32 dwTime; {
dwTime = TIME_INMILLISECONDS;    // in milliseconds
ISOUNDPLAYER_Rewind (iap->m_pISoundPlayer, dwTime); }}
return;
case S_FASTFORWARD:{
uint32 dwTime; {
dwTime = TIME_INMILLISECONDS;    // in milliseconds
ISOUNDPLAYER_FastForward (iap->m_pISoundPlayer, dwTime);}
return;
case S_PAUSE:   {{
ISOUNDPLAYER_Pause (iap->m_pISoundPlayer);}}
return;
case S_RESUME:{{
ISOUNDPLAYER_Resume (iap->m_pISoundPlayer);}}
return;
```

```
147. default:
148. return;  }
149. return;}
150. static void BuildPlayerMenu(CISoundPlayerApp *iap){
151. AEERect qrc;
152. AEEDeviceInfo di;
153. AECHAR szBuf[50];
154. int charHeight = 0;
155. int pnAscent = 0;
156. int pnDescent = 0;
157. if(iap == NULL || iap->m_pIMenu == NULL || iap->a.m_pIShell ==
NULL)
158. return;
159. ISHELL_GetDeviceInfo(iap->a.m_pIShell,&di);
160. SETAEERECT (&qrc, 0, 0, di.cxScreen, di.cyScreen);
161. IMENUCTL_SetRect(iap->m_pIMenu, &qrc);
162. STR_TO_WSTR("SoundPlayer Menu:", szBuf, sizeof(szBuf));
163. IMENUCTL_SetTitle(iap->m_pIMenu, NULL, 0, szBuf);
164. STR_TO_WSTR("Play", szBuf, sizeof(szBuf));
165. IMENUCTL_AddItem(iap->m_pIMenu, 0, 0, USAGE_PLAY, szBuf, 0);
166. STR_TO_WSTR("Stop", szBuf, sizeof(szBuf));
167. IMENUCTL_AddItem(iap->m_pIMenu, 0, 0, USAGE_STOP, szBuf, 0);
168. STR_TO_WSTR("Rewind (5 secs)", szBuf, sizeof(szBuf));
169. IMENUCTL_AddItem(iap->m_pIMenu, 0, 0, USAGE_REWIND, szBuf, 0);
170. STR_TO_WSTR("FastForward (5 secs)", szBuf, sizeof(szBuf));
171. IMENUCTL_AddItem(iap->m_pIMenu, 0, 0, USAGE_FASTFORWARD, szBuf, 0);
172. STR_TO_WSTR("Pause", szBuf, sizeof(szBuf));
173. IMENUCTL_AddItem(iap->m_pIMenu, 0, 0, USAGE_PAUSE, szBuf, 0);
174. STR_TO_WSTR("Resume", szBuf, sizeof(szBuf));
175. IMENUCTL_AddItem(iap->m_pIMenu, 0, 0, USAGE_RESUME, szBuf, 0);
176. IMENUCTL_SetActive(iap->m_pIMenu,TRUE);}
```

Following is the line-by-line explanation of the source code:

- **Line 1:** The `AEEModGen.h` header file contains the `AEEModule` declaration.
- **Line 2:** The `AEEAppGen.h` header file contains the `AEEApplet` declaration.
- **Lines 3–8:** Inclusion of the header files.
- **Line 9:** Inclusion of the `.BID` file, `sound.bid`.
- **Lines 10–18:** Defining the constants used in the application.
- **Lines 19–27:** Pre-processor directives.
- **Lines 28–37:** Definition of the `CIsoundPlayerApp` data structure. This structure holds the data members of the applet throughout the life of the applet. (When the applet is closed in the mobile device, its life ends.)
- **Line 38:** The `SoundPlayerApp_HandleEvent` function declaration.
- **Lines 39–42:** The application-specific functions.

- **Lines 43–49:** The `CreateInstance` method. This function is invoked while the applet is being loaded. The module must verify the `ClassID` and then invoke the `AEEApplet_New()` function that has been provided in `AEEAppGen.c`. After invoking `AEEApplet_New()`, this function can do applet-specific initialization. Note that every applet should have a unique `ClassID`.
- **Lines 50–81:** The `SoundPlayerApp_HandleEvent` method, which handles all the events of the application. The `app` parameter is a pointer to the `AEEApplet` structure. This structure contains information specific to this applet. It is initialized during the `AEEClsCreateInstance()` function, and `ae` specifies the event sent to this applet.
- **Lines 82–107:** The `InitAppData` method. This function initializes applet-specific data and allocates memory for the data.
- **Line 108–114:** The `FreeAppData` method. This method frees data contained in applet data and the memory for applet data itself.
- **Lines 115–149:** The `IsoundPlayerUsage` method. This function specifies the sound player's usage. The options for various functions of the music menu are called using the switch case. The music files have an `.MP3` extension (e.g., `apsample.mp3`). They are in the `\Music` folder, which is in the `\IsoundPlayer` application folder.
- **Lines 150–176:** The `BuildPlayerMenu` function. This function initially displays text on the screen.
  - **Line 163:** Displays the text as a title of the next screen.
  - **Lines 165, 167, 169, 171, 173,** and **175** display the optionssuch as Play, Stop, Rewind, Fast Forward, Pause, and Resume on the screen. When an option is selected, the corresponding functionality is performed.

Executing the program

To execute this application, follow these steps:

1. The first step to develop the BREW sound application is to create the `.BID` file. On the Windows taskbar, select Start ⇨ Programs ⇨ BREW ⇨ MIF Editor. The window shown in Figure 9-1 appears when the MIF Editor is invoked.

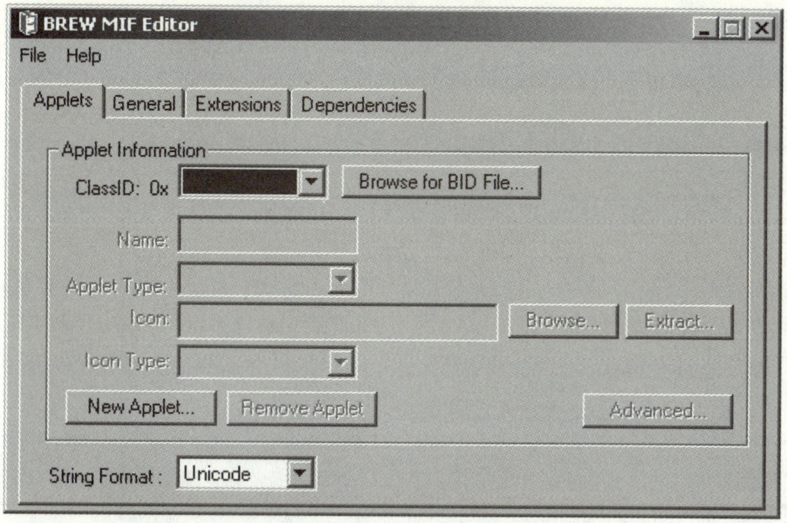

Figure 9-1: The BREW MIF editor window for generating the .BID file

This example is a new application. Therefore, click the New Applet button at the bottom of the window. The window shown in Figure 9-2 appears.

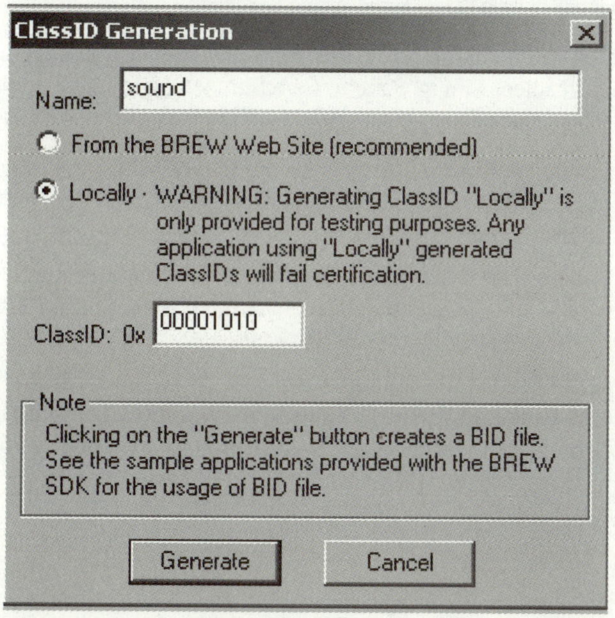

Figure 9-2: The new Applet ClassID generation window is used to assign ClassID to the applet.

Enter the name and Class ID of the applet. The Class ID should be unique. The Class ID name, `.BID` filename, and `.MIF` filename should be the same. Click the Generate button at the bottom of the window. Save the `.BID` file with an appropriate name in the application-specific folder or in the applet directory. The window shown in Figure 9-3 appears when you click the Generate button.

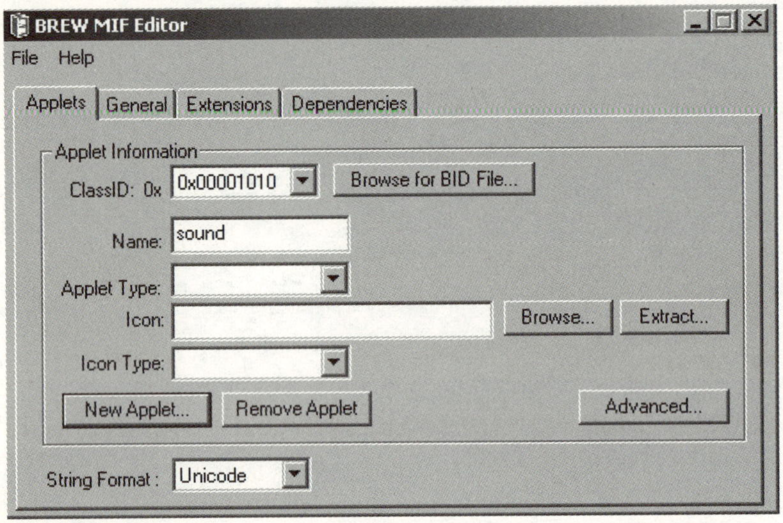

Figure 9-3: BREW MIF editor after entering the ClassID used to generate .MIF file

Enter the required information in the dialog box fields: Name, Applet Type, Icon, and Icon Type. From the menu bar, select File ⇨ Save to save the `.MIF` file in the applet directory or in a separate `\MIF` folder.

2. Copy the workspace of a sample application provided in the BREW SDK and write a new application. Open the workspace you copied and modify the C file in the workspace by writing the code provided in Listing 9-1.

3. Select Build ⇨ Rebuild All to convert the application into a DLL with the name `sound.dll`. The file size is 204KB. This size indicates the memory required for the application.

4. On the Windows taskbar, select Start ⇨ Programs ⇨ Brew ⇨ Brew Emulator. In the BREW emulator, set the paths of the `sound.dll` file and `sound.mif` file and then run the application. The screen shown in Figure 9-4 appears, displaying the options for playing the sound file.

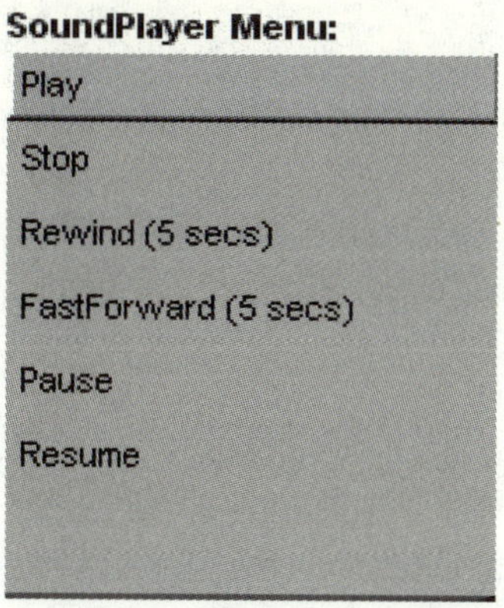

Figure 9-4: Display in the BREW emulator when the sound application is loaded

Listen to the music and try the different options provided in the menu. The BREW SDK provides a number of emulators with different memory capacities. Run the application with different emulators to ensure that the application runs successfully on all of them.

Project: Salary Survey

In this project, you develop a utility for creating an embedded database with a GUI for field personnel. The field personnel can carry out a salary survey by obtaining the data, such as designation, type of organization, annual salary, experience, etc. After developing the GUI, you can store the data in the internal database of the embedded system and later upload it onto a corporate database for analysis.

Source code listing for idbusage.c

The file `idbusage.c` provides the source code, given in Listing 9-2, for the salary survey application.

> **ON THE CD-ROM** This file is available on the CD-ROM that accompanies the book.

Listing 9-2: Source code for idbusage.c

```
#include "AEEModGen.h"
#include "AEEAppGen.h"
#include "AEEMenu.h"
#include "AEEDB.h"
#include "AEEText.h"
#include "AEEStdLib.h"
#include "AEEUsageAppIDs.h"
#include "idbusage_res.h"
#define APP_RES_FILE      "idbusage.bar"
#define ADDRECORD          102
#define CREATERECORD       104
```

```
#define GETNEXTRECORD      107
#define BORDER_WIDTH        5
typedef struct _CIDBApp
{
AEEApplet       a;
IMenuCtl *  m_pIMenu;
ITextCtl *  m_pIText1;
ITextCtl *  m_pIText2;
ITextCtl *  m_pIText3;
ITextCtl *  m_pIText4;
ITextCtl *  m_pIText5;
IMenuCtl * m_pSKMenu;
AEEDeviceInfo   di;
AEERect         rc;
int             lh;
}CIDBApp;
char szResFile[] = APP_RES_FILE;
AECHAR buf1[50] = {0};
AECHAR buf2[50] = {0};
AECHAR buf3[50] = {0};
AECHAR buf4[50] = {0};
AECHAR buf5[50] = {0};
char str1[50];
char str2[50];
char str3[50];
char str4[50];
char str5[50];
static boolean DBApp_HandleEvent(IApplet * ap, AEEEvent ae,
uint16 wp, uint32 dwp);
static boolean IDB_InitAppData(IApplet* iap);
static void IDB_FreeAppData(IApplet* iap);
static void BuildMainMenu(CIDBApp *iap);
static void IDBUsage (CIDBApp * iap, uint16 wp);
static void DisplayOutput(CIDBApp * iap, int nline, char *str);
int AEEClsCreateInstance(AEECLSID ClsId,IShell * pIShell,
IModule * po,void ** obj)
{
*obj = NULL;
if(ClsId == AEECLSID_DATABASE_APP)
{
if(AEEApplet_New(sizeof(CIDBApp), ClsId,pIShell,po,(IApplet**)obj,
(AEEHANDLER)DBApp_HandleEvent,(PFNFREEAPPDATA)IDB_FreeAppData)==
TRUE)
{
if (IDB_InitAppData((IApplet*)*obj) == TRUE)
{
return(AEE_SUCCESS);
}
}
```

```
}
return (EFAILED);
}
static boolean DBApp_HandleEvent(IApplet * ap, AEEEvent ae,
uint16 wp, uint32 dwp)
{
CIDBApp * iap = (CIDBApp*)ap;
AECHAR title[20], text[100];
switch (ae)
{
case EVT_APP_START:
if(ISHELL_CreateInstance(iap->a.m_pIShell, AEECLSID_MENUCTL,
(void **)&iap->m_pIMenu)
!= SUCCESS)
{
return FALSE;
}
BuildMainMenu(iap);
return(TRUE);
case EVT_APP_STOP:
return(TRUE);
case EVT_KEY:
if ((iap->m_pIText1 != NULL) &&
ITEXTCTL_HandleEvent(iap->m_pIText1, EVT_KEY, wp, 0))
return TRUE;
if ((iap->m_pIText2 != NULL) &&
ITEXTCTL_HandleEvent(iap->m_pIText2, EVT_KEY, wp, 0))
return TRUE;
if ((iap->m_pIText3 != NULL) &&
ITEXTCTL_HandleEvent(iap->m_pIText3, EVT_KEY, wp, 0))
return TRUE;
if ((iap->m_pIText4 != NULL) &&
ITEXTCTL_HandleEvent(iap->m_pIText4, EVT_KEY, wp, 0))
return TRUE;
if ((iap->m_pIText5 != NULL) &&
ITEXTCTL_HandleEvent(iap->m_pIText5, EVT_KEY, wp, 0))
return TRUE;
if (iap->m_pSKMenu != NULL && IMENUCTL_HandleEvent(iap->m_pSKMenu,
EVT_KEY, wp, 0))
return TRUE;
if(iap->m_pIMenu != NULL && IMENUCTL_HandleEvent(iap->m_pIMenu,
EVT_KEY, wp, 0))
return TRUE;
return FALSE;
case EVT_COMMAND:
switch(wp)
{
case IDS_RETURN_TO_MENU:
if (iap->m_pIText1 != NULL)
```

```
{
IMENUCTL_Release(iap->m_pIText1);
iap->m_pIText1 = NULL;
}
if (iap->m_pIText2 != NULL)
{
IMENUCTL_Release(iap->m_pIText2);
iap->m_pIText2 = NULL;
}
if (iap->m_pIText3 != NULL)
{
IMENUCTL_Release(iap->m_pIText3);
iap->m_pIText3 = NULL;
}
if (iap->m_pIText4 != NULL)
{
IMENUCTL_Release(iap->m_pIText4);
iap->m_pIText4 = NULL;
}
if (iap->m_pIText5 != NULL)
{
IMENUCTL_Release(iap->m_pIText5);
iap->m_pIText5 = NULL;
}
if (iap->m_pSKMenu != NULL)
{
IMENUCTL_Release(iap->m_pSKMenu);
iap->m_pSKMenu = NULL;
}
IMENUCTL_SetActive(iap->m_pIMenu, TRUE);
IMENUCTL_Redraw(iap->m_pIMenu);
return TRUE;
case IDS_ITEM_1:
case IDS_ITEM_2:
case IDS_ITEM_3:
case IDS_ITEM_4:
case ADDRECORD:
case CREATERECORD:
case GETNEXTRECORD:
IDBUsage(iap, wp);
return TRUE;
default:
return FALSE;
}
default:
break;
}
return FALSE;
}
```

```
static boolean IDB_InitAppData(IApplet* ap)
{
int pnAscent;
int pnDescent;
CIDBApp * iap = (CIDBApp*)ap;
iap->m_pIMenu = NULL;
iap->lh = IDISPLAY_GetFontMetrics (iap->a.m_pIDisplay,
AEE_FONT_NORMAL,
&pnAscent, &pnDescent);
ISHELL_GetDeviceInfo(iap->a.m_pIShell,&iap->di);
iap->rc.x = BORDER_WIDTH;
iap->rc.y = BORDER_WIDTH;
iap->rc.dx = iap->di.cxScreen - (2 * BORDER_WIDTH);
iap->rc.dy = iap->di.cyScreen - (2 * BORDER_WIDTH);
return TRUE;
}
static void IDB_FreeAppData(IApplet* ap)
{
CIDBApp * iap = (CIDBApp*)ap;
if (iap->m_pIMenu != NULL)
{
IMENUCTL_Release (iap->m_pIMenu);
iap->m_pIMenu = NULL;
}
}
static void IDBUsage (CIDBApp * iap, uint16 wp)
{
IShell *pIShell = iap->a.m_pIShell;
AEERect rect1,rect2,rect3;
AECHAR szBuf [50] = {0};
AECHAR szBuf1[50] = {0};
IDISPLAY_ClearScreen (iap->a.m_pIDisplay);
switch (wp)
{
case ADDRECORD:
{
ISHELL_CreateInstance(pIShell, AEECLSID_TEXTCTL,
(void **)&iap->m_pIText1);
STR_TO_WSTR("Designation :", szBuf1, sizeof(szBuf1));
ITEXTCTL_SetTitle(iap->m_pIText1, NULL, NULL, szBuf1);
ITEXTCTL_SetProperties(iap->m_pIText1, TP_FRAME | TP_MULTILINE );
SETAEERECT (&rect1, 10,50,120,40);
ITEXTCTL_SetRect(iap->m_pIText1, &rect1);
ITEXTCTL_SetActive (iap->m_pIText1, TRUE);
if(ISHELL_CreateInstance(iap->a.m_pIShell, AEECLSID_SOFTKEYCTL,
(void **)&iap->m_pSKMenu) != SUCCESS)
return TRUE;
STR_TO_WSTR("Next Field >>", szBuf, sizeof(szBuf));
IMENUCTL_AddItem(iap->m_pSKMenu, 0, 0, IDS_ITEM_1,szBuf , 0);
```

```
IMENUCTL_SetActive(iap->m_pSKMenu,TRUE);
}
break;
case IDS_ITEM_1:
{
ITEXTCTL_GetText (iap->m_pIText1, buf1, sizeof (buf1));
WSTR_TO_STR (buf1, str1, sizeof (str1));
if (iap->m_pIText1 != NULL)
{
ITEXTCTL_SetActive (iap->m_pIText1, FALSE);
}
IDISPLAY_ClearScreen (iap->a.m_pIDisplay);
ISHELL_CreateInstance(pIShell, AEECLSID_TEXTCTL,
(void **)&iap->m_pIText2);
STR_TO_WSTR("Type of ORG :", szBuf1, sizeof(szBuf1));
ITEXTCTL_SetTitle(iap->m_pIText2, NULL, NULL, szBuf1);
ITEXTCTL_SetProperties(iap->m_pIText2, TP_FRAME | TP_MULTILINE );
SETAEERECT (&rect2, 10,50,120,40);
ITEXTCTL_SetRect(iap->m_pIText2, &rect2);
ITEXTCTL_SetActive (iap->m_pIText2, TRUE);
if(ISHELL_CreateInstance(iap->a.m_pIShell, AEECLSID_SOFTKEYCTL,
(void **)&iap->m_pSKMenu) != SUCCESS)
return TRUE;
STR_TO_WSTR("Next Field >>", szBuf, sizeof(szBuf));
IMENUCTL_AddItem(iap->m_pSKMenu, 0, 0, IDS_ITEM_2,szBuf , 0);
IMENUCTL_SetActive(iap->m_pSKMenu,TRUE);
}
break;
case IDS_ITEM_2:
{
ITEXTCTL_GetText (iap->m_pIText2, buf2, sizeof (buf2));
WSTR_TO_STR (buf2, str2, sizeof (str2));
if (iap->m_pIText2 != NULL)
{
ITEXTCTL_SetActive (iap->m_pIText2, FALSE);
}
IDISPLAY_ClearScreen (iap->a.m_pIDisplay);
ISHELL_CreateInstance(pIShell, AEECLSID_TEXTCTL,
(void **)&iap->m_pIText3);
STR_TO_WSTR("Annual Salary :", szBuf1, sizeof(szBuf1));
ITEXTCTL_SetTitle(iap->m_pIText3, NULL, NULL, szBuf1);
ITEXTCTL_SetProperties(iap->m_pIText3, TP_FRAME | TP_MULTILINE );
SETAEERECT (&rect3, 10,50,120,40);
ITEXTCTL_SetRect(iap->m_pIText3, &rect3);
ITEXTCTL_SetActive (iap->m_pIText3, TRUE);
if(ISHELL_CreateInstance(iap->a.m_pIShell, AEECLSID_SOFTKEYCTL,
(void **)&iap->m_pSKMenu) != SUCCESS)
return TRUE;
STR_TO_WSTR("Next Field >>", szBuf, sizeof(szBuf));
```

```
IMENUCTL_AddItem(iap->m_pSKMenu, 0, 0, IDS_ITEM_3,szBuf , 0);
IMENUCTL_SetActive(iap->m_pSKMenu,TRUE);
}
break;
case IDS_ITEM_3:
{
ITEXTCTL_GetText (iap->m_pIText3, buf3, sizeof (buf3));
WSTR_TO_STR (buf3, str3, sizeof (str3));
if (iap->m_pIText3 != NULL)
{
ITEXTCTL_SetActive (iap->m_pIText3, FALSE);
}
IDISPLAY_ClearScreen (iap->a.m_pIDisplay);
ISHELL_CreateInstance(pIShell, AEECLSID_TEXTCTL,
(void **)&iap->m_pIText4);
STR_TO_WSTR("Service :", szBuf1, sizeof(szBuf1));
ITEXTCTL_SetTitle(iap->m_pIText4, NULL, NULL, szBuf1);
ITEXTCTL_SetProperties(iap->m_pIText4, TP_FRAME | TP_MULTILINE );
SETAEERECT (&rect1, 10,50,120,40);
ITEXTCTL_SetRect(iap->m_pIText4, &rect1);
ITEXTCTL_SetActive (iap->m_pIText4, TRUE);
if(ISHELL_CreateInstance(iap->a.m_pIShell, AEECLSID_SOFTKEYCTL,
(void **)&iap->m_pSKMenu) != SUCCESS)
return TRUE;
STR_TO_WSTR("Next Field >>", szBuf, sizeof(szBuf));
IMENUCTL_AddItem(iap->m_pSKMenu, 0, 0, IDS_ITEM_4,szBuf , 0);
IMENUCTL_SetActive(iap->m_pSKMenu,TRUE);
}
break;
case IDS_ITEM_4:
{
ITEXTCTL_GetText (iap->m_pIText4, buf4, sizeof (buf4));
WSTR_TO_STR (buf4, str4, sizeof (str4));
if (iap->m_pIText4 != NULL)
{
ITEXTCTL_SetActive (iap->m_pIText4, FALSE);
}
IDISPLAY_ClearScreen (iap->a.m_pIDisplay);
ISHELL_CreateInstance(pIShell, AEECLSID_TEXTCTL,
(void **)&iap->m_pIText5);
STR_TO_WSTR("Tot. Exp :", szBuf1, sizeof(szBuf1));
ITEXTCTL_SetTitle(iap->m_pIText5, NULL, NULL, szBuf1);
ITEXTCTL_SetProperties(iap->m_pIText5, TP_FRAME | TP_MULTILINE );
SETAEERECT (&rect1, 10,50,120,40);
ITEXTCTL_SetRect(iap->m_pIText5, &rect1);
ITEXTCTL_SetActive (iap->m_pIText5, TRUE);
if(ISHELL_CreateInstance(iap->a.m_pIShell, AEECLSID_SOFTKEYCTL,
(void **)&iap->m_pSKMenu) != SUCCESS)
return TRUE;
```

```
STR_TO_WSTR("Finish", szBuf, sizeof(szBuf));
IMENUCTL_AddItem(iap->m_pSKMenu, 0, 0, CREATERECORD,szBuf , 0);
STR_TO_WSTR("Return", szBuf, sizeof(szBuf));
IMENUCTL_AddItem(iap->m_pSKMenu, 0, 0, IDS_RETURN_TO_MENU,szBuf ,
0);
IMENUCTL_SetActive(iap->m_pSKMenu,TRUE);
}
break;
case CREATERECORD:
{
IDBMgr *dbm = NULL;
IDatabase * db = NULL;
IDBRecord *rec = NULL;
int num = 5;
AEEDBField field[5];
const char desg[50] ;
const char org [50];
const char sal[50];
const char serv[50] ;
const char exp[50] ;
boolean bCreate = FALSE;
ITEXTCTL_GetText (iap->m_pIText5, buf5, sizeof (buf5));
WSTR_TO_STR (buf5, str5, sizeof (str5));
if (iap->m_pIText5 != NULL)
{
ITEXTCTL_SetActive (iap->m_pIText5, FALSE);
}
IDISPLAY_ClearScreen (iap->a.m_pIDisplay);
strcpy(desg,str1);
strcpy(org,str2);
strcpy(sal,str3);
strcpy(serv,str4);
strcpy(exp,str5);
field[0].fName = AEEDBFIELD_FULLNAME;
field[0].fType = AEEDB_FT_STRING;
field[0].pBuffer = (void *)desg;
field[0].wDataLen = STRLEN (desg);
field[1].fName = AEEDBFIELD_ADDRESS;
field[1].fType = AEEDB_FT_STRING;
field[1].pBuffer = (void *)org;
field[1].wDataLen = STRLEN (org);
field[2].fName = AEEDBFIELD_TEXT;;
field[2].fType = AEEDB_FT_STRING;
field[2].pBuffer = (void *)sal;
field[2].wDataLen = STRLEN (sal);
field[3].fName = AEEDBFIELD_TEXT;;
field[3].fType = AEEDB_FT_STRING;
field[3].pBuffer = (void *)serv;
field[3].wDataLen = STRLEN (serv);
```

```
field[4].fName = AEEDBFIELD_TEXT;;
field[4].fType = AEEDB_FT_STRING;
field[4].pBuffer = (void *)exp;
field[4].wDataLen = STRLEN (exp);
ISHELL_CreateInstance(pIShell, AEECLSID_DBMGR, (void **)&dbm);
if (dbm == NULL)
return;
if ((db = IDBMGR_OpenDatabase (dbm, "db1", bCreate))
== NULL)
{
bCreate = TRUE;
if ((db = IDBMGR_OpenDatabase (dbm, "db1", bCreate))
!= NULL)
{
DisplayOutput (iap, 1, "Database open successful");
if ((rec = IDATABASE_CreateRecord (db, field,
num))
!= NULL)
{
DisplayOutput (iap, 2, "Create DB: successful");
IDBRECORD_Release (rec);
}
else
{
DisplayOutput (iap, -1, "Create DB: Failed");
}
IDATABASE_Release (db);
}
else
{
DisplayOutput (iap, -1, "Database open failed");
}
}
else
{
DisplayOutput (iap, 1, "Opened an already existing Database.");
if ((rec = IDATABASE_CreateRecord (db, field,
num))!= NULL)
{
DisplayOutput (iap, 2, "Create DB: successful");
IDBRECORD_Release (rec);
}
else
{
DisplayOutput (iap, -1, "Create DB: Failed");
}
IDATABASE_Release (db);
}
IDBMGR_Release (dbm);
```

```
}
break;
case GETNEXTRECORD:
{
IDBMgr    * dbm = NULL;
IDatabase * db = NULL;
IDBRecord * pIDBRec1 = NULL;
char szBuf[10] = {0};
char szBuf1[100] = {0};
AEEDBFieldType type;
AEEDBFieldName name;
uint16 len;
byte * data = NULL;
int i,j=1;
uint32 count=0;
ISHELL_CreateInstance(pIShell, AEECLSID_DBMGR, (void **)&dbm);
if (dbm == NULL)
return;
if ((db = IDBMGR_OpenDatabase (dbm, "db1", FALSE)) ==
NULL)
{
IDBMGR_Release (dbm);
return;
}
count=IDATABASE_GetRecordCount(db);
DisplayOutput (iap, 0,"Desg      Org   Sal   Serv   Exp" );
for(i=0;i<count;i++){
pIDBRec1 = IDATABASE_GetNextRecord (db);
if (pIDBRec1 != NULL)
{
type = IDBRECORD_NextField (pIDBRec1, &name, &len);
data = IDBRECORD_GetField (pIDBRec1, &name, &type,
&len);
if (data != NULL)
{
SPRINTF (szBuf, "%4s", (char *)data);
strcat(szBuf1,szBuf);
}
type = IDBRECORD_NextField (pIDBRec1, &name, &len);
data = IDBRECORD_GetField (pIDBRec1, &name, &type,
&len);
if (data != NULL)
{
SPRINTF (szBuf, " %10s", (char *)data);
strcat(szBuf1,szBuf);
}
type = IDBRECORD_NextField (pIDBRec1, &name, &len);
data = IDBRECORD_GetField (pIDBRec1, &name, &type,
&len);
```

```
if (data != NULL)
{
SPRINTF (szBuf, " %6s",(char *)data);
strcat(szBuf1,szBuf);
}
type = IDBRECORD_NextField (pIDBRec1, &name, &len);
data = IDBRECORD_GetField (pIDBRec1, &name, &type,
&len);
if (data != NULL)
{
SPRINTF (szBuf, " %3s",(char *)data);
strcat(szBuf1,szBuf);
}
type = IDBRECORD_NextField (pIDBRec1, &name, &len);
data = IDBRECORD_GetField (pIDBRec1, &name, &type,
&len);
if (data != NULL)
{
SPRINTF (szBuf, " %3s",(char *)data);
strcat(szBuf1,szBuf);
DisplayOutput (iap, ++j, szBuf1);
}
strcpy(szBuf1,"");
}
IDBRECORD_Release(pIDBRec1);
}
IDATABASE_Release (db);
IDBMGR_Release (dbm);
}
break;
default:
return;
}
return;
}
static void BuildMainMenu(CIDBApp *iap)
{
AEERect rc;
AECHAR szBuf[40];
if (iap->m_pIMenu == NULL || iap->a.m_pIShell == NULL)
return;
STR_TO_WSTR("IDB Functions:", szBuf, sizeof(szBuf));
IMENUCTL_SetTitle(iap->m_pIMenu, NULL, 0, szBuf);
SETAEERECT (&rc, 0, 0, iap->di.cxScreen,
iap->di.cyScreen);
IMENUCTL_SetRect(iap->m_pIMenu, &rc);
STR_TO_WSTR("1.  AddRecord", szBuf, sizeof(szBuf));
IMENUCTL_AddItem(iap->m_pIMenu, 0, 0, ADDRECORD, szBuf, 0);
STR_TO_WSTR("2.  RetrieveRecords", szBuf, sizeof(szBuf));
```

```
IMENUCTL_AddItem(iap->m_pIMenu, 0, 0, GETNEXTRECORD, szBuf, 0);
IMENUCTL_SetActive(iap->m_pIMenu,TRUE);
}
static void DisplayOutput(CIDBApp * iap, int nline, char *str)
{
AECHAR * pszBuf = NULL;
AECHAR * psz = NULL;
int width;
AEEFont font = AEE_FONT_NORMAL;
int fits = 0, dy;
int tch = 0;
if (iap == NULL)
return;
if ((pszBuf = (AECHAR *)MALLOC(200)) == NULL)
return;
STR_TO_WSTR ((char *)str, pszBuf, 200);
if (nline < 0) {
dy = iap->di.cyScreen*2/5;
}
else{
dy = nline * iap->lh;
}
psz = pszBuf;
tch = STRLEN ((char *)str);
while ((tch > 0) && (*psz != NULL))
{
width = IDISPLAY_MeasureTextEx(iap->a.m_pIDisplay,
font,
(AECHAR *) psz,
-1,
iap->di.cxScreen - 5,
&pnFits);
if (fits== 0)
{
FREE (pszBuf);
return;
}
IDISPLAY_DrawText(iap->a.m_pIDisplay, AEE_FONT_NORMAL, psz,
pnFits, 5 ,dy, 0 , 0);
psz += pnFits;
tch -= pnFits;
dy += iap->lh;
IDISPLAY_Update(iap->a.m_pIDisplay);
if (tch < pnFits)
fits= tch;
}
FREE (pszBuf);
return;
}
```

Following is the line-by-line explanation of the source code:

- **Lines 1–5:** Header files for the interface definition, applet interface definition, menu interface definition, database interface definition, and text control interface definition.
- **Lines 6–7:** Header files for variable definitions.
- **Line 8:** Resource header file.
- **Lines 9–13:** Code for defining macros and constants.
- **Lines 14–27:** Definition of the database applet structure. This is the main structure for this applet. This will hold all the data members that need to be remembered throughout the life of the applet. The first data member of this structure must be an `AEEApplet` object.
- **Lines 28–38:** Definition of necessary variables.
- **Lines 39–45:** Declarations of the function prototypes.
- **Lines 46–63:** `CreateInstance()` method. This function is invoked while the applet is being loaded. This section returns `AEE_SUCCESS` status upon loading the applet. `EFAILED` is returned when loading is not successful. Line 50 verifies the ClassID. If it is true, line 52 invokes the `AEEApplet_New()` function, and then `InitAppData()` is called to initialize AppletData.
- **Lines 64–158:** The `HandleEvent()` method. All events to the applet are handled in this function. It returns `TRUE` if the applet has processed the event; otherwise, it returns `FALSE`. If it receives `EVT_APP_START`, it creates the `Imenu` interface object and then invokes the `BuildMainMenu()` function. If the applet receives the `EVT_APP_STOP` event, it returns `TRUE`. When the user presses a key, the applet receives `EVT_KEY`, which invokes either the Text control or Menu control handle event. When the user selects a menu item, the applet receives `EVT_COMMAND`. If the user selects any of the menu items (the main menu items or any softkey menu items other than Return), the `IDBUsage()` method is invoked. If the user selects the Return menu item, it releases all the interface objects and redraws the main menu.
- **Lines 159–174:** `InitAppData()` method. This method initializes applet-specific data and allocates memory for AppletData.
- **Lines 175–183:** `IDB_FreeAppData()` method. It frees data contained in app data and memory for app data itself.
- **Lines 184–487:** `IDBUsage()` method. This method is called when the user clicks any of the menu items and the menu ID is passed to this function as a parameter.
  - **Lines 193–210:** If the ID is `ADDRECORD`, it creates a Text control and names it Designation; it also creates a softkey and names it Next Field.
  - **Lines 211–235:** If the ID is `IDS_ITEM_1`, it retrieves content from the Designation text field; it creates a Text control, names it Type of `ORG`, and creates a softkey named Next Field.

- **Lines 236–260:** If the ID is `IDS_ITEM_2`, it retrieves content from the Type of `ORG` text field and creates a Text control named Annual Salary (USD); it also creates a softkey named Next Field.
- **Lines 261–285:** If the ID is `IDS_ITEM_3`, it retrieves content from the Annual Salary text field and creates a Text control named Service in that ORG; it also creates a softkey named Next Field.
- **Lines 286–313:** If the ID is `IDS_ITEM_4`, it retrieves content from the Services text field and creates a Text control named Total Service. It also creates two softkeys named Next Field and Return.
- **Lines 314–405:** If the ID is `CREATERECORD`, it retrieves content from the Services text field and creates an `IDBRecord` object and an `AEEDBField` object. It then populates the fields with data retrieved from the text fields. It creates an `IDBmgr` object using the `ISHELL_CreateInstance()` function, creates an `IDatabase` object, opens the existing database (e.g., `db1`) or creates a new database using the `DBMGR_OpenDatabase()` method, and creates a record using the `DATABASE_CreateRecord()` method.
- **Lines 406–482:** If the ID is `GETNEXTRECORD`, it creates an `IDBRecord` object, an `AEEDBFieldType` object, and an `AEEDBFieldName` object. The `ISHELL_CreateInstance()` method is invoked to create an `IDBmgr` object. The `DBMGR_OpenDatabase()` method is invoked to open the existing database, `db1`, and then retrieves records sequentially using the following methods: `IDBRECORD_NextField()`, `IDBRECORD_GetField()`, and `IDATABASE_GetRecordCount()`.

- **Lines 488–499:** `BuildMainMenu()` method. This method builds the main menu when the applet is started. In line 495, `IMENUCTL_SetTitle()` is invoked to set the title to the menu. In line 498, the `IMENUCTL_SetRect()` method is invoked to set the menu's size.
- **Lines 500–503:** The `IMENUCTL_AddItem()` method is invoked to set the menu items.
- **Lines 505–524:** The `DisplayOutput()` method. This function displays an output string at a given line number on the screen. Line 515 allocates a buffer to hold the string. Line 517 converts the string into Unicode. In line 524, `psz` keeps track of the point from which to write from the string buffer in case the string does not fit in one line and needs to wrap to the next line.
- **Line 525:** Calculates the total string length to determine if wrapping is required.
- **Lines 526–547:** To display the output text in multiple lines. Lines are spaced 15 pixels apart.

Executing the program

To execute this program, follow these steps:

1. To create the `.BID` file, invoke the MIF editor (on the Windows taskbar, select Start ⇨ Programs ⇨ Brew ⇨ MIF Editor). The MIF Editor window is shown in Figure 9-5.

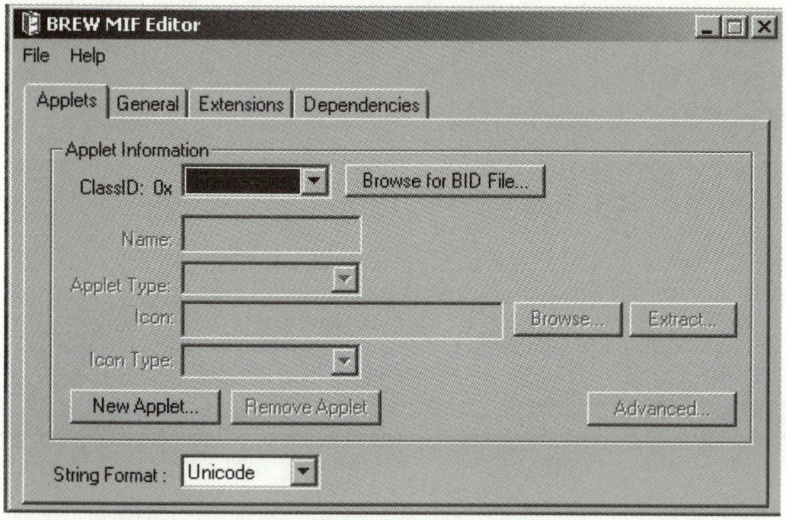

Figure 9-5: The BREW MIF editor window for generating the .BID file

This application is a new one. Therefore, click the New Applet button at the bottom of the window. The window shown in Figure 9-6 appears.

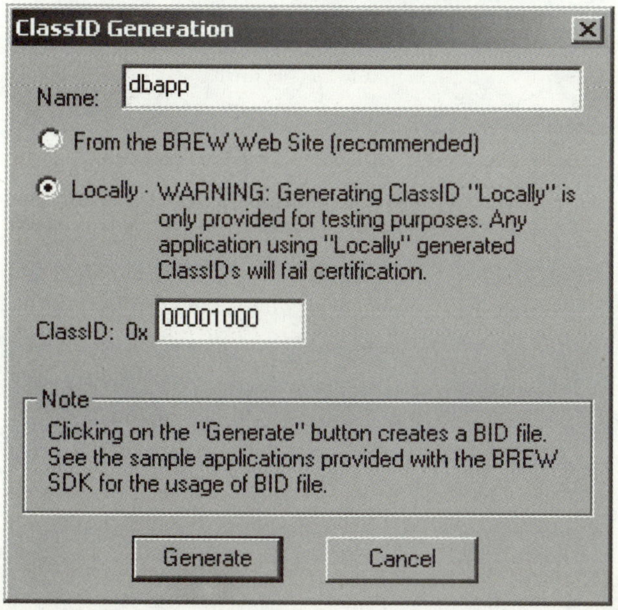

Figure 9-6: The new Applet Class ID generation window to assign unique ClassID

Enter the name and Class ID of the applet. The Class ID should be unique. The Class ID name, `.BID` filename, and `.MIF` filename should be the same. Click the Generate button at the bottom of the window. Save the `.BID` file in the application-specific folder or in the applet directory. The window shown in Figure 9-7 appears when you click the Generate button.

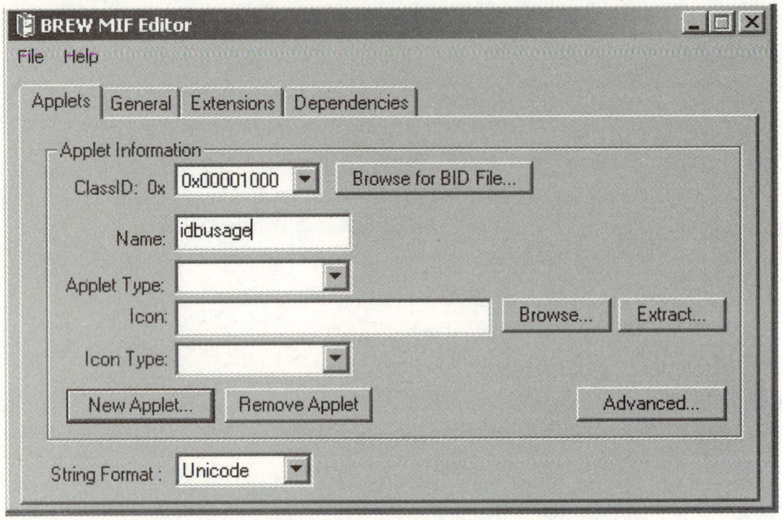

Figure 9-7: The BREW MIF Editor window after entering the ClassID

Populate the Name, Applet Type, Icon, and Icon Type fields. Select File ⇨ Save to save the `.MIF` file in the applet directory or in a separate `\MIF` folder.

2. Copy the workspace of a sample application and write a new application. The code provided in Listing 9-2 is the new code to be copied onto the workspace.
3. To build the `idbusage.dll` file, select Build ⇨ Rebuild All from the menu bar. The `idbusage.dll` file size is 212KB.
4. Open the BREW emulator (Start ⇨ Programs ⇨ BREW ⇨ BREW Emulator) and set the paths of the `idbusage.dll` file and the `dbapp.mif` file and then run the application.

Output

Figures 9-8 to 9-14 show the BREW emulator when the application is executed.

Figure 9-8: Display in the emulator when the salary survey application is loaded

Figure 9-9: Display in the emulator when the user has to enter data in the Designation field

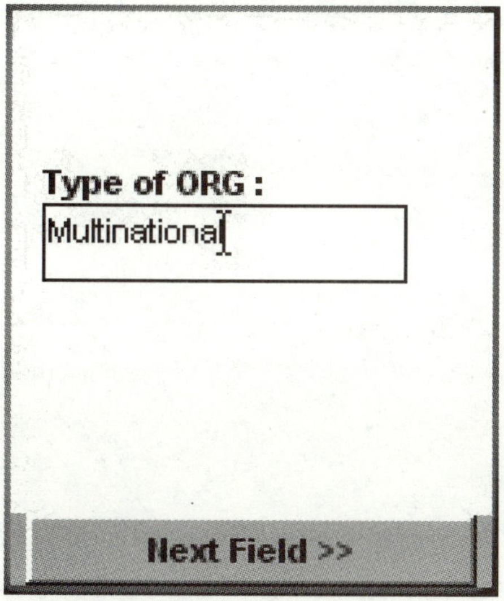

Figure 9-10: Display in the emulator when the user presses the Next Field button

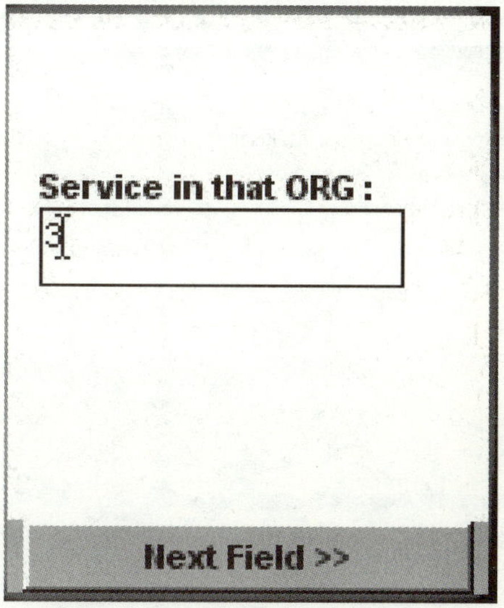

Figure 9-11: Display in the emulator when the user selects the Next Field button to enter data for the field "Service in that ORG"

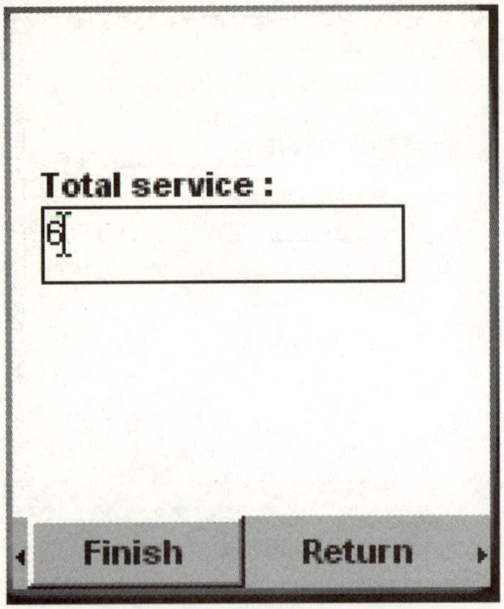

Figure 9-12: Display in the emulator when the user selects the Next Field button to enter data for the field "Total Service"

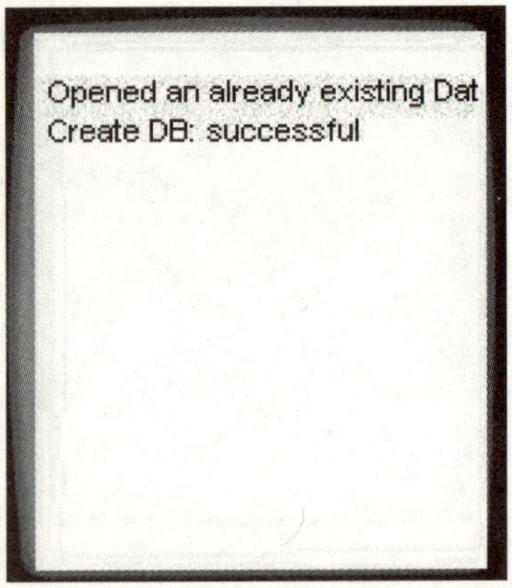

Figure 9-13: Display in the emulator when the user selects the Finish key

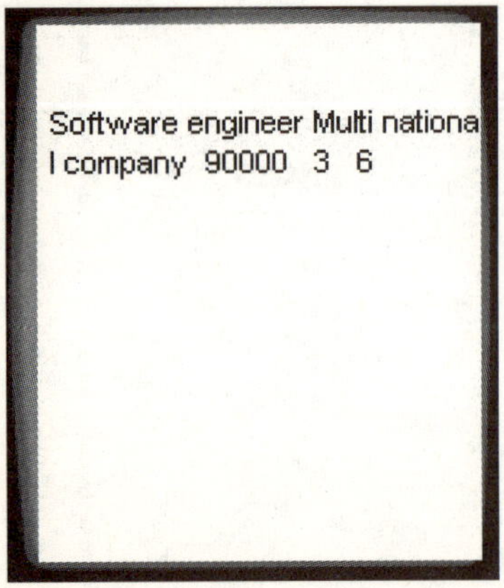

Figure 9-14: Display in the emulator when the user selects the Retrieve Record Menu Item

You can see details about the internally stored data by opening the VC ++ editor and selecting File ⇨ Open and then choosing `db1` file, which is in the `\idbusage` application folder. Then, click the Open button on the Open dialog box.

Embedding BREW Applications

You can embed the BREW applications in a target platform that has an ARM processor. The target board will have flash memory and a heap memory. For the ARM board, an ARM compiler is also available. Note that if you want to create commercial BREW applications, you need to have TRUE BREW compatibility testing performed and you need to have an official Class ID assigned to your application. This compatibility testing will ensure that your wireless applications can be deployed on wireless networks and work with mobile devices without any problem. The applications shown in this chapter merely illustrate application development using the BREW SDK.

Summary

In this chapter, you learned how to create embedded mobile applications using the BREW SDK. The first application is designed to download music and then play it on a mobile device. The second application is designed to develop an embedded database application, which can be used to conduct a field survey. The BREW SDK provides a powerful development environment for developing mobile data applications over wireless networks.

Chapter 10

Real-Time Embedded Software Development

In This Chapter

- System calls for real-time embedded software development in RTLinux
- Compilation and execution processes
- Case studies for real-time embedded software development

Developing embedded software to achieve real-time performance is a challenging task, mainly because meeting the various deadlines is always a complex undertaking. In many process control applications, as well as applications involving audio and video transmission, real-time performance is a must. Real-time operating systems provide the necessary APIs to achieve this functionality. In this chapter, using RTLinux, you examine case studies to develop real-time embedded software.

Development Environment

To test the applications presented in this chapter, you need the following:

- RTLinux installed on a Linux system
- A Windows 9*x* (or later) system to communicate with the RTLinux system
- A null modem cable to interconnect the RTLinux system with the Windows system

If you have already done some programming in the Unix/Linux environment, you'll find that picking up RTLinux programming quite easy. Otherwise, you may want to try out the basic commands (to copy, delete, edit, rename files and directories, etc.). Before you begin tackling the projects, this section briefly describes the challenges you may encounter while working on RTLinux.

Once in a while, your Linux system may crash. This is mainly because there is no protection against any bugs in the application source code written by you. As the real-time programs are executed in the kernel space, you may inadvertently create a situation in which the processor enters a state from which it cannot recover, leading to the crash. To minimize this risk, use the debugger provided with RTLinux before the final testing.

By default, the RTLinux tasks do not have access to the computer's floating-point unit. Hence, you need to explicitly set the permission for every RTLinux task that requires the floating-point unit.

As RTLinux is an embedded operating system, you cannot pass arguments from the command prompt, as you normally do in C programs.

RTLinux Modules

RTLinux programs are not created as stand-alone units; they are created as modules, which are loaded into the Linux kernel space. The C source files are compiled into object files using the `gcc` command with the argument `-c flag`. In the C file, the `main()` function gets replaced with the following:

```
int init_module();
void cleanup_module();
```

`int_module()` is called when the module is first loaded into the kernel. This function returns 0 if the module is successfully loaded; it returns a negative value in case of failure. When the module is to be unloaded, the `cleanup_module()` is called.

Compiling modules in RTLinux

In RTLinux, a program is viewed as a module. To compile the C modules in the RTLinux environment, the presence of a file with the name `rtl.mk` is a must. It is created during installation of RTLinux and contains the paths to `include` files and compiler options. This file should be in the directory `/user/include/rtlinux`.

You can compile a module using the following command:

```
make -f     rtl.mk     filename.o
```

Executing RTLinux modules

You can execute modules in three possible ways:

You can load (or start) and remove (or stop) user modules using the `rtlinux` command. Using this command, you can also obtain status information about RTLinux modules. The command syntax is as follows:

```
$rtlinux start my_program
$rtlinux stop my_program
$rtlinux status my_program
```

The first command starts the program; the second command stops the program, when it is running; and the third command finds the status of the running program. Note that the character `$` is the system prompt.

To determine the status at the beginning of an RTLinux session, type the following command:

```
$rtlinux status
```

The output will be as follows:

```
Scheme :( _ ) not  loaded  (+) loaded .
(-)mbuff
(-)rtl_fifo
(-)rt;
(-)rt_posixio
(-)rt_sched
(-)rtl_time
```

To determine the status after running an RTLinux program, type the command:

```
$rtlinux status
```

The output will be as follows:

```
Scheme :( _ ) not  loaded  (+) loaded .
(+)mbuff
(+)rtl_fifo
(+)rt;
(+)rt_posixio
(+)rt_sched
(+)rtl_time
```

The second method of compiling the modules uses `modprobe`. The syntax of this command is as follows:

```
$modprobe -a rtl rtl_time rtl_sched rtl_posixio rtl_fifo
```

If you use this command, the modules must be installed in `/lib/modules/kernel version`.

Use the `insmod` and `rmmod` commands if you have the object file `program.o`. If all the other modules corresponding to a project have already been loaded and only one particular module has to be loaded into the kernel, you can issue the following command:

```
insmod program.o
```

To stop the module, the command is as follows:

```
rmmod my_program
```

Creating RTLinux POSIX threads

A real-time program generally consists of a number of threads. Each thread is a lightweight process, and the threads share a common address space. The `pthread_create()` function is used to create a new real-time thread. It is called from the Linux kernel thread by using `init_module()`.

The corresponding header file is

```
# include <pthread.h>
```

To achieve real-time performance, the various POSIX-compliant APIs are used. These function calls are to create and to cancel threads, mutexes, and semaphores.

Mutex, which stands for mutual exclusion, allows only one task to be run at a time, to ensure data integrity. If multiple tasks use shared resources, such as writing data onto a memory unit, data corruption may result. To avoid this, mutex is used. To implement mutex, you have to include the header file `rtlmutex.h` in the C program.

A semaphore is another utility for task management in operating systems. A semaphore is an integer value (positive or negative) manipulated by the kernel.

RTLinux provides a number of system calls for handling mutexes and semaphores.

Thread-related system calls

The following system calls are related to threads that get or set attributes related to the threads:

```
pthread_attr_init()
pthread_attr - set schedparam()
pthread_attr -get schedparam()
pthread_attr --get cpu_np()
pthread_attr—set cpu_np()
```

To cancel a thread, the system call is `pthread_cancel (pthread thread)`.

To de-allocate the resources of a thread, join the thread in `cleanup_module` with `pthread_join()`.

Timing facilities

RTLinux provides a number of system calls for timing-related activities. A number of internal clocks are available to take care of timing issues.

To obtain the current clock reading, you can use the clock `gettime()` function. `Clock_id` provides the identification of the clock to be read, including its structure, which stores the value obtained.

A general timing module might look like the following:

```
# include <rtl_time.h>
int clock_get time (clockid_t click_id, struct time spec *ts);
hr time_t clock_get hrtime (clockid_t clock);
struct timespec {
 time_t          tr_sec;               /*seconds*/
 long     tr_nsec;             /*nano seconds*/
}
```

Scheduling enables the thread code to run at specific times. RTLinux uses a priority-driven scheduler. You will learn more about it as you work through the following examples.

Compiling and Executing a Sample Program

In order to execute our program, we must first do the following:

1. **Compile the source code and create a module.** You can normally compile the source code by using the `gcc` compiler directly from the command line. A simpler way is to create a `makefile`. This way, you need only to type **make** to compile the code.
2. **Locate and copy the `rtl.mk` file.** The `rtl.mk` file is an `include` file, which contains all the flags needed to compile your code. For simplicity, you can copy it from the RTLinux source tree and place it in your home directory along with your file `hello.c`.
3. **Insert the module into the running RTLinux kernel.** The object binary file obtained after compiling the source code has to be "plugged in" to the kernel, where it will be executed by RTLinux.

The following section examines these steps in some detail.

We begin by creating the `makefile` that will be used to compile our `hello.c` file. Type the following into a file called `makefile` and put it in the same directory as your `hello.c` file:

```
hello.o: hello.c
gcc $(CFLAGS) hello.c
```

Locate the file `rtl.mk` and copy it into the same directory as your `hello.c` and `makefile` files. The `rtl.mk` file can usually be found at `/usr/include/rtlinux/rtl.mk`. The command to do this operation is:

```
cp /usr/include/rtlinux/rtl.mk.
```

Now, type the following command:

```
make -f rtl.mk hello.o
```

This compiles the `hello.c` program and produces an object file named `hello.o`.

We now need to load the RTLinux module. There are several ways to do this. The easiest is to use the `rtlinux` command:

```
$rtlinux start hello
```

You can check the status of your module by typing the following command:

```
$rtlinux status hello
```

You should now be able to see your `hello.o` file printing its message twice per second. Depending on the configuration of your machine, you should be able to see it either directly in your console, or by typing the following command:

```
$dmesg
```

To stop the program, you need to remove it from the kernel with the following command:

```
$rtlinux stop hello
```

Note the following points regarding the locations of the various files:

- RTLinux will be installed in the directory `/usr/rtlinux-xxx`, where *xxx* is the version number.
- `/usr/rtlinux/include` contains all the `include` files necessary for development projects.
- `/usr/rtlinux/examples` contains the RTLinux example programs. They illustrate the use of most of the API calls.
- `/usr/doc/rtlinux/man` contains the manual pages for RTLinux.
- `/usr/rtlinux/modules` contains the core RTLinux modules.
- `/usr/rtlinux/bin` contains RTLinux scripts and utilities.

Core RTLinux API

For your reference, the following list describes the important RTLinux API calls.

- `clock_gethrtime`: To get high-resolution time using the specified clock
- `clock_gettime`: To get the system clock time
- `clock_settime`: To set the system clock time
- `gethrtime`: To get high-resolution time
- `nanosleep`: To get high-resolution sleep
- `pthread_attr_getcpu_np`: To examine and change the CPU `pthread` attribute
- `pthread_attr_getschedparam`: To access dynamic thread scheduling parameters
- `pthread_attr_getdetachstate`: To get `detachstate` attributes
- `pthread_attr_getstacksize`: To get the `stacksize` attribute
- `pthread_attr_init`: To initialize the thread's attribute object
- `pthread_attr_setcpu_np`: To examine and change the CPU `pthread` attribute
- `pthread_attr_setdetachstate`: To set `detachstate` attributes
- `pthread_attr_setfp_np`: To set and get the floating-point enable attribute
- `pthread_attr_setschedparam`: To access dynamic thread scheduling parameters
- `pthread_attr_setstacksize`: To set the `stacksize` attribute
- `pthread_cancel`: To stop or cancel a thread
- `pthread_create`: To create a thread

- `pthread_condattr_destroy`: To destroy an object with conditional variable attributes
- `pthread_condattr_getshared`: To get the process-shared condition variable attributes
- `pthread_condattr_init`: To initialize an object with conditional variable attributes
- `pthread_condattr_setpshared`: To set the process-shared condition variable attributes
- `pthread_cond_broadcast`: To broadcast a condition
- `pthread_cond_destroy`: To destroy a condition variable
- `pthread_cond_init`: To initialize a condition variable
- `pthread_cond_signal`: To signal a condition
- `pthread_cond_timedwait`: To wait on a conditional variable for a specified time
- `pthread_cond_wait`: To wait on a condition variable
- `pthread_delete_np`: To delete a real-time thread
- `pthread_exit`: To terminate a thread
- `pthread_join`: To terminate a thread and to deallocate the resources
- `pthread_kill`: To send a `kill` signal to a thread
- `pthread_linux`: To get the thread identifier of the Linux thread
- `pthread_make_periodic_np`: To mark a real-time thread as periodic
- `pthread_mutexattr_destroy`: To destroy a mutex attribute object
- `pthread_mutexattr_getprioceiling`: To get the priority ceiling attribute of a mutex attribute object
- `pthread_mutexattr_getpshared`: To obtain the process-shared setting of a mutex attribute object
- `pthread_mutexattr_gettype`: To get the mutex type
- `pthread_mutexattr_init`: To initialize a mutex attribute object
- `pthread_mutexattr_setprioceiling`: To set the priority ceiling attribute of a mutex attribute object
- `pthread_mutexattr_setpshared`: To set the process-shared attribute of a mutex attribute object
- `pthread_mutexattr_settype`: To set the mutex type
- `pthread_mutex_destroy`: To destroy a mutex
- `pthread_mutex_init`: To initialize a mutex with the attributes specified in the mutex attribute object

- `pthread_mutex_lock`: To lock an unlocked mutex. If you try to lock an already locked mutex, the calling thread gets blocked until the thread that currently holds the mutex releases it.
- `pthread_mutex_trylock`: To try to lock a mutex. If the mutex is already locked, the calling thread returns without waiting for the mutex to be freed.
- `pthread_mutex_unlock`: To unlock a mutex.
- `pthread_getschedparam`: To get the `schedparam` attribute
- `pthread_self`: To get the ID of the calling thread
- `pthread_setcancelstate`: To set the cancel state
- `pthread_setschedparam`: To set the `schedparam` attribute
- `pthread_setfp_np`: To enable the use of floating-point operations in a thread
- `pthread_suspend_np`: To suspend execution of a real-time thread
- `pthread_wait_np`: To suspend the current thread until the next period
- `pthread_wakeup_np`: To wake up a real-time thread
- `rt_com`: Serial port driver for RTLinux
- `rt_com_read`: To read data in real time from a serial port
- `rt_com_setup`: To dynamically change the parameters of each real-time serial port
- `rt_com_table`: An array of descriptions, one per serial port
- `rt_com_write`: To write data in real time to a serial port
- `rtf_create`: To create a real-time FIFO (First In First Out) buffer
- `rtf_create_hander`: To install a handler for real-time FIFO data
- `rtf_create_rt_handler`: To install a handler for real-time FIFO data
- `rtf_destroy`: To remove a real-time FIFO created with `rtf_create`
- `rtf_flush`: To empty a real-time FIFO
- `rtf_get`: To read data from a real-time FIFO
- `rtf_link_user_ioctl`: To install an `ioctl` (I/O control) handler for a real-time FIFO
- `rtf_put`: To write data to a real-time FIFO
- `rtf_make_user_pair`: To make a pair of receive-transmit FIFOs act like a bidirectional FIFO
- `rtf_allow_interrupts`: To control the CPU interrupt state
- `rtf_free_irq`: To install and remove real-time interrupt handlers
- `rtf_free_soft_irq`: To install and remove software interrupt handlers

- rtf_getcpuid: To get the current processor ID
- rtl_getschedclock: To get the current scheduler clock
- rtl_global_pend_irq: To schedule a Linux interrupt
- rtl_hard_disable_irq: To disable hardware interrupt control
- rtl_hard_enable_irq: To enable hardware interrupt control
- rtl_no_interrupts: To control the CPU interrupt state
- rtl_printf: For formatted print
- rtl_request_irq: To install and remove real-time interrupt handlers
- rtl_restore_interrupts: To control the CPU interrupt state
- rtl_setclockmode: To set the RTLinux clock mode
- rtl_stop_interrupts: To control the CPU interrupt state
- rtlinux_sigaction: To get RTLinux v3 user-level signal handling functions
- rtlinux_signal: To get list of available RTLinux user-level signals
- rtlinux_sigprocmask: To get RTLinux v3 user-level signal handling functions
- rtlinux_sigetops: To get RTLinux user-level signal set operations
- rt_task_delete: To delete a real-time task
- rt_task_init: To create a real-time task
- rt_task_make_periodic: To mark a real-time task for execution
- rt_task_suspend: To suspend a real-time task
- sched_get_priority_max: To get maximum priority limits for the scheduling policy
- sched_get_priority_min: To get minimum priority limits for the scheduling policy
- sem_init: To initialize POSIX semaphore
- sem_destroy: To destroy an unnamed POSIX semaphore
- sem_getvalue: To get the value of a semaphore
- sigaction: To get RTLinux POSIX signal handling functions
- sysconf: To get configurable system variables
- time: Clock and timer functions
- uname: To get name of the system
- usleep: To suspend execution for an interval

In the following sections, you'll examine the details of the source code for the projects. How to use these system calls is evident in the source code.

Project: To Print a Message Every 10 Seconds

This project demonstrates how to achieve real-time operations. Every 10 seconds, the program sends a message (as usual, it is "hello world") to the receive buffer. To display the message on the Linux terminal, you have to provide `dmesg` at the command prompt.

The following files are on an RTLinux system:

- `hello.c`: This file is used to display the "hello world" message every 10 seconds in the RTLinux system.
- `rtl.mk`: This file makes the object file.
- `hello.o`: This is the object file for `hello.c`.

Source code listing for hello.c

Listing 10-1 gives the source code for `hello.c`.

Listing 10-1: Source code for hello.c

```
1.#include <rtl.h>
2.#include <time.h>
3.#include <pthread.h>
4.pthread_t thread;
//The execution thread is in the hello function
5.void * hello()
6.{
7.struct sched_param p;
//assigning the thread with a scheduling priority 1
8.p . sched_priority = 1;
//this sets the scheduler behavior to be SCHED_FIFO for all subsequent
execution
9.pthread_setschedparam (pthread_self(), SCHED_FIFO, &p);
10. while (1) {
//it blocks all further execution of the thread until the scheduler
calls it again
11. for(i=1;i<=10;i++)
12. {
13. pthread_wait_np ();
14. }
15. rtl_printf("hello world");
16. }
17. return 0;
18. }
/* This module begins the entire process by creating an execution thread
with init_module */
19. int init_module(void) {
//it creates the thread
20. return pthread_create (&thread, NULL, hello, 0);
21. }
```

```
/* This module ends the entire process by clearing the  execution thread
with cleanup_module */
22. void cleanup_module(void) {
//it delete the real-time thread
23. pthread_delete_np (thread);
24. }
```

Following is the line-by-line explanation of the source code:

- **Lines 1–3:** Including header files for RTLinux, time, and the `pthread`.
- **Line 4:** Declaring a thread of type `pthread`.
- **Lines 5–9:** The `hello` function has three components. These components are initialization, runtime, and termination. The newly created thread gets a default priority of 1. The `pthread setschdedparam` sets the scheduler behavior to `sched_fifo`.
- **Lines 10–18:** The loop `while(1)` is an infinite loop; hence, the thread continues to execute forever. The way to stop the program is to remove it from the kernel with `rm_mod().pthread_wait_np` will make the thread wait for 10 seconds.
- **Lines 19–21:** The `init module()` starts the entire program by creating an execution thread, which exists in the hello function.
- **Lines 22–24:** The `cleanup_module` function cancels the thread process, and the CPU cycles that are allocated to the thread are freed.

There are three steps in executing any RTLinux program:

1. Compile the source code and create a module.
2. Locate and copy the `rtl.mk` file and the `hello.c` file.
3. Insert the module in the RTLinux kernel.

Compiling files on the RTLinux system

You first need to create the `makefile` that will be used to compile the `hello.c` program. Enter the following code into the file named `makefile` and store it in the same directory as that of your `hello.c` program:

```
hello.c:hello.c
gcc $(CFLAGS) hello.o
```

Locate the file `rtl.mk`, which is in the directory `/usr/include/rtlinux/rtl.mk`, and copy that file into the same directory in which `hello.c` exists:

```
cp  /usr/include/rtlinux/rtl.mk.
```

Note that it must end with a period.

Then enter the following command:

```
$ make -f  rtl.mk hello.o
```

This compiles the `hello.c` program, and the object file called `hello.o` is created.

Executing the module

To execute the module, you have to load the module in RTLinux. The easiest way to do this is as follows:

```
$rtlinux start hello
$rtlinux status hello
$rtlinux help
```

To observe the output on the RTLinux console, enter the following command:

```
$dmesg
```

To stop the program, you remove it from the kernel as follows:

```
$rtlinux stop hello
```

You will see the message "hello world" displayed every 10 seconds.

Project: Sending a Message over a Serial Link

This project demonstrates how to send a message over a serial link to a Windows 9*x* system. In many process control systems, after the data collected by the embedded system is processed, the result is sent over a serial link to a host system. In this case, we will use the Windows system as the host. A given message will be sent every 10 seconds from the RTLinux system.

The following files are on a Linux system:

- `blink.c`: This file is used for transmitting a message to another terminal.
- `rtl.mk`: This file makes the object file.
- `blink.o`: This is the object file for `blink.c`.
- `rt_com.c`: This file is used for establishing serial communication.
- `rt_com.h` and `rt_comp.h`: These are the header files corresponding to the serial communication.
- `rt_com.o`: This is the object file for `rt_com.c`.

Source code listing for blink.c

Listing 10-2 gives the source code for `blink.c`.

Listing 10-2: Source code for blink.c

```
#include <rtl.h>
#include <rtl_fifo.h>
```

```
#include <time.h>
#include <pthread.h>
#include <asm/io.h>
#include "rt_com.h"
#include "rt_comP.h"
int period=100000000;
int fifo_size=4000;
pthread_t thread;
int fd_fifo;
void *blink(void *t) {
//makes  a realtime thread as periodic
pthread_make_periodic_np (thread, gethrtime(), period);
do {
for(i=1;i<=10;i++)
{
//suspend the current thread until the next period
pthread_wait_np();
}
//writes 15 characters from buffer to the realtime serial port com
rt_com_write(0, "HAPPY NEW YEAR", 15);
} while (1);
return 0;
}
/* This module begins the entire process by creating an execution thread
with init_module */
int init_module(void)
{
pthread_attr_t attr;
struct sched_param sched_param;
int thread_status;
//it is used to dynamically change the parameters of each realtime
serial port
rt_com_setup(0, 9600, RT_COM_PARITY_NONE, 1, 8);
//to initialize threads attribute object
pthread_attr_init (&attr);
//to examine and change the CPU pthread attribute
pthread_attr_setcpu_np(&attr, 0);
sched_param.sched_priority = 1;
//dynamic thread scheduling parameters access
pthread_attr_setschedparam (&attr, &sched_param);
//creating the thread and maintaining its parameters status
thread_status = pthread_create (&thread,  &attr, blink, (void *)1);
return 0;
}
/* This module ends the entire process by clearing the  execution thread
with cleanup_module */
void cleanup_module(void)
{
//it deletes the realtime thread
```

```
38. pthread_delete_np (thread);
39. rt_com_setup(0, -1, 0, 0, 0);
40. }
```

Following is the line-by-line explanation of the source code:

- **Lines 1–7:** Inclusion of the various header files to support the RTLinux functionality, including FIFO creation, time management, thread handling, and input and output interactions.
- **Line 8:** It initializes the duration of the thread in nanoseconds.
- **Line 9:** To allocate the memory to the queue.
- **Line 13:** `pthread_make_periodic_np` makes the real-time thread process execute periodically. This function utilizes a structure called `itimerspec`. Its parameters are `it_interval` and `it_value`, which specify the timer period and its expiration, respectively. The `it_value` parameter also specifies the time of its first invocation, which is passed to the structure `itimerspec`.
- **Lines 14–22:** The `for` loop begins with a call to the function `pthread_wait_np`, which basically blocks all further execution of the thread for 10 cycles. Then, with `rt_com_write`, we can write 15 characters from the buffer to the real-time serial port `com1`. This is implemented in a `do while` loop so that it is an everlasting thread. In line 19, a fixed string is provided, which is the data sent over the serial communication link. In an embedded system, the values generated will be passed. Note that it is not possible to give the string a command-line argument.
- **Lines 23–35:** To set the following parameters of the serial port, such as `com1`: baud rate, parity type, stop bits, and word length. Then we initialize the thread with its attribute object. Next, we allocate the default CPU cycles for the thread by sending 0 to `pthread_attr_setcpu_np()`. We then allocate the scheduling priority for the thread as 1 and set the schedule with `pthread_attr_setschedparam()`. Finally, we create the thread with all the selected parameters using `pthread_create`. We will know its status from the variable `thread_status`.
- **Lines 36–40:** The `cleanup_module` function cancels the thread process on the `pthread` join and frees the CPU cycles, which are otherwise allocated to the thread.

Executing the program

Because this project involves communication between a Windows machine and an RTLinux machine, we have to execute programs on both the machines. To do this, a null modem connection is required between them.

Execution procedure on a Windows machine

We use HyperTerminal on the Windows machine. When we open HyperTerminal, the Connection Description dialog box shown in Figure 10-1 appears.

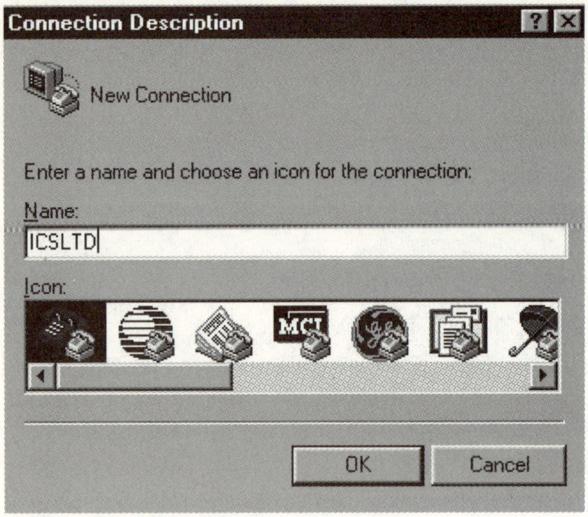

Figure 10-1: HyperTerminal connection window

Enter a name and click OK. The Connect To dialog box shown in Figure 10-2 appears.

Figure 10-2: Establishing the connection through a null modem over Com1

Select Direct to Com1 in the Connect Using field and then click OK. The dialog box shown in Figure 10-3 appears.

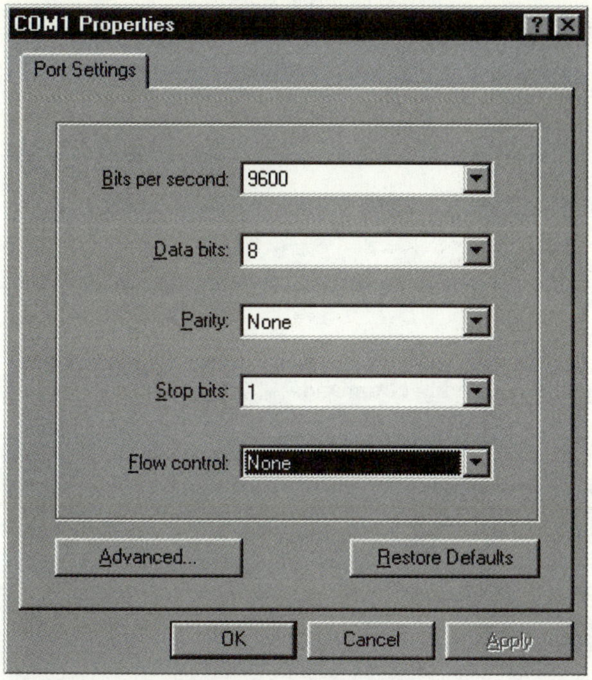

Figure 10-3: COM1 properties window

Leave the default values in each of the fields except for the number of bits per second, for which you can select 9600. Then click OK. The window shown in Figure 10-4 appears.

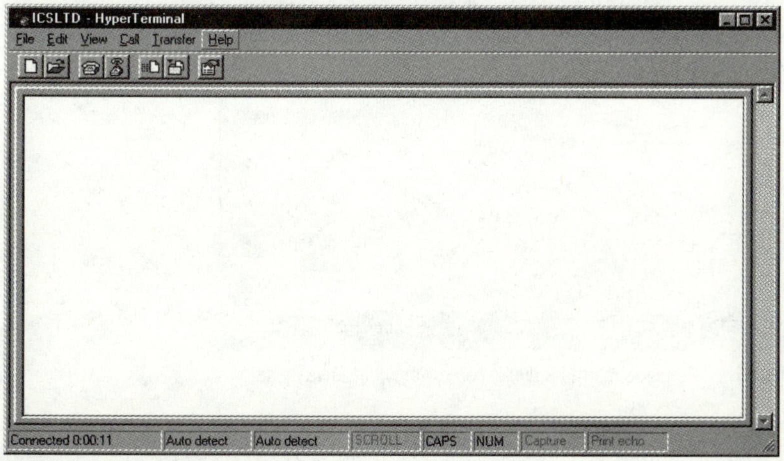

Figure 10-4: HyperTerminal screen

With this, the Windows machine waits to receive the data on the null modem cable from RTLinux machine.

This project consists of various files: `blink.c`, `rt_com.c`, `rt_com.h`, `rt_comp.h`, and `rtl_mk`. The `blink.c` program source code is provided in Listing 10-2. The files `rtl_mk`, `rtlinux.rt_com.c`, `rt_com.h`, and `rt_comp.h` can be freely downloaded from `www.rtlinux.org`, thanks to their open-source code policy for the development of RTLinux applications.

To compile RTLinux programs, issue the following commands at the system prompt:

```
$make -f  rtl.mk rt_com.o
$make -f rtl.mk blink.o
```

Execution steps on the RTLinux machine

To establish the serial connection, issue the following command:

```
$setserial /dev/ttyS0 uart none
```

To execute the project, type the following command:

```
$rtlinux start rt_com blink
```

Output

The output screen that appears on the Windows machine will look like the one shown in Figure 10-5.

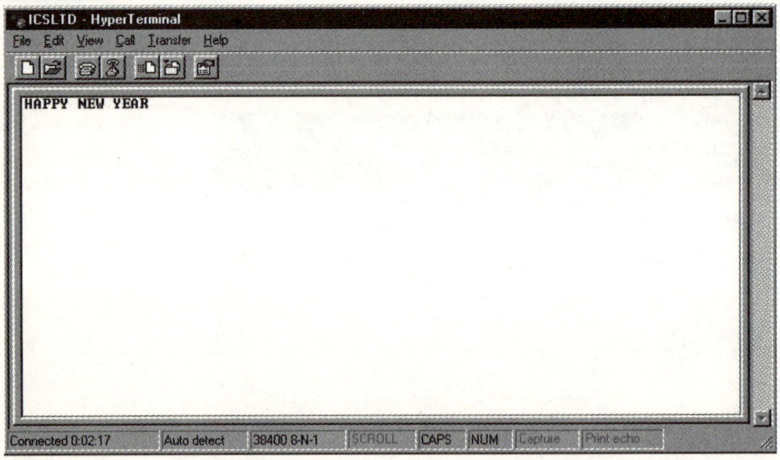

Figure 10-5: Message from the RTLinux system as displayed on the Windows system

To stop the communication, you have to type the following:

```
$rtlinux stop rt_com blink
```

Project: Simulation of a Process Control System

In process control industries, parameters such as the temperature of a chamber or a liquid must be collected by an embedded system at regular intervals. This information is transferred to the server, which checks for compliance with any constraints. Any instance of noncompliance will prompt an alarm or a control signal to the embedded system.

In this project, the RTLinux machine functions as a client to transmit data, and the Windows machine functions as the server, processing the data and generating the message to the client.

The following files are found on a Windows system:

- `SerialcommDlg.cpp`: This file is used for communication between the two systems.
- `Serialcomm.cpp`, `serialcomm.h`, `serialcommDlg.h`, and `resources.h`: These are default files created by the VC++ class wizard.

The following files are found on a Linux system:

- `temperature.c`: This file is used for transmitting and receiving temperatures to and from the Windows machine.
- `rtl.mk`: This file makes an object file.
- `temperature.o`: This is the object file for `temperature.c`.
- `rt_com.c`: This file is used for establishing serial communication.
- `rt_com.h`, `rt_comp.h`: These are the header files.
- `rt_com.o`: This is the object file for `rt_com.c`.

Source code listing for SerialCommDlg.cpp

Listing 10-3 gives the source code for `SerialCommDlg.cpp`, which runs on the Windows 9*x* system.

Listing 10-3: Source code for SerialCommDlg.cpp

```
/* serialcommDlg.cpp*/
#inlcude <stdio.h>
unsigned int baseAdd;
int Receiver(void);
HANDLE hThread;
DWORD tid;
void CSerialCommDlg::OnSetButton()
{
// TODO: Add your control notification handler code here
CString stopBits,port,parity,dataBits,baudRate;
unsigned int LSB,MSB,dataFormat,temp;
m_stopbits.GetWindowText(stopBits);
m_port.GetWindowText(port);
```

```
m_parity.GetWindowText(parity);
m_databits.GetWindowText(dataBits);
m_baudrate.GetWindowText(baudRate);
if((stopBits == "")||(port == "")||(parity == "")||(dataBits == "")||(baudRate==""))
{
AfxMessageBox("All the 5 Parameters are Necessary");
return;
}
if(port == "1")
{
baseAdd = 0x3f8;//comm 1 port setting
}
else
{
baseAdd = 0x2f8;//comm 2 port setting
}
if(baudRate == "4800")
{
LSB = 0x18;
MSB = 0x00;
}
else if(baudRate == "9600")
{
LSB = 0x0c;
MSB = 0x00;
}
else if(baudRate == "19200")
{
LSB = 0x06;
MSB = 0x00;
}
else if(baudRate == "38400")
{
LSB = 0x03;
MSB = 0x00;
}
if((dataBits == "8")&&(stopBits == "1")&&(parity == "NONE"))
dataFormat = 0x03;
else if((dataBits == "8")&&(stopBits == "1")&&(parity == "EVEN"))
dataFormat = 0x1b;
else if((dataBits == "8")&&(stopBits == "1")&&(parity == "ODD"))
dataFormat = 0x0b;
else if((dataBits == "8")&&(stopBits == "2")&&(parity == "NONE"))
dataFormat = 0x07;
else if((dataBits == "8")&&(stopBits == "2")&&(parity == "EVEN"))
dataFormat = 0x1f;
else if((dataBits == "8")&&(stopBits == "2")&&(parity == "ODD"))
dataFormat = 0x0f;
```

```
else if((dataBits == "7")&&(stopBits == "1")&&(parity == "NONE"))
dataFormat = 0x02;
else if((dataBits == "7")&&(stopBits == "1")&&(parity == "EVEN"))
dataFormat = 0x1a;
else if((dataBits == "7")&&(stopBits == "1")&&(parity == "ODD"))
dataFormat = 0x0a;
else if((dataBits == "7")&&(stopBits == "2")&&(parity == "NONE"))
dataFormat = 0x06;
else if((dataBits == "7")&&(stopBits == "2")&&(parity == "EVEN"))
dataFormat = 0x1e;
else if((dataBits == "7")&&(stopBits == "2")&&(parity == "ODD"))
dataFormat = 0x0e;
_outp(baseAdd+3,dataFormat); // setting dataformat register
temp = _inp(baseAdd+3);
temp = temp | 0x10;
_outp(baseAdd+3,temp); //setting DLAb bit to 1
_outp(baseAdd,LSB);     // setting Baud Rate
_outp(baseAdd+1,MSB);
temp = _inp(baseAdd+3);
temp = temp & 0x7f;
_outp(baseAdd+3,temp); //Resetting DLAb bit to 1
m_stopbits.EnableWindow(FALSE);
m_port.EnableWindow(FALSE);
m_parity.EnableWindow(FALSE);
m_databits.EnableWindow(FALSE);
m_baudrate.EnableWindow(FALSE);
m_setbutton.EnableWindow(FALSE);
m_send.EnableWindow(TRUE);
m_sendbutton.EnableWindow(TRUE);
m_recEdit.EnableWindow(TRUE);
AfxBeginThread((AFX_THREADPROC)Receiver,NULL);
}
void CSerialCommDlg::OnSendButton()
{
// TODO: Add your control notification handler code here
CString sendMsg;
int i = 0;
unsigned int temp;
m_send.GetWindowText(sendMsg);
for(i=0;i<sendMsg.GetLength();i++)
{
while(!( (_inp(baseAdd+5)&0x40) && (_inp(baseAdd+5)&0x20)) );
_outp(baseAdd,sendMsg[i]);
}
m_send.SetWindowText("");
}
// serial_com code for receiveing the characters from buffer
int Receiver()
{
```

```
107. CEdit *recEdit = (CEdit*)AfxGetMainWnd()-
>GetDlgItem(IDC_RECEIVE_EDIT);
108. char ch;
109. CString str,str1;
110. while(1)
111. {
112. while(!(_inp(baseAdd+5)&0x01));
113. ch = _inp(baseAdd);
114. if(ch != NULL)
115. {
116. str.Format("%d Degrees",ch);
117. recEdit->SetWindowText("");
118. recEdit->SetWindowText(str);
119. }
120. }
121. return 0;}
```

Following is the line-by-line explanation of the source code:

- **Lines 1–5:** Variables declaration.
- **Lines 8-9:** Variables corresponding to the serial communication parameters: stop bits, port, parity, data bits, baud rate, LSB, MSB, and Dataformat are declared as appropriate data types.
- **Lines 10–14:** To read all the values into the corresponding controls on the SerialComm dialog box.
- **Lines 20–27:** To set parameters for port 1 or 2 and provide the appropriate base address.
- **Lines 28–47:** To check the baud rate and set the values for LSB and MSB accordingly.
- **Lines 48–71:** To assign the data format field by taking the input values for data bits, stop bits, and parity type.
- **Lines 72–80:** To set the data format register DLAB bit and the baud rate.
- **Lines 81–89:** Enables and disables various control buttons.
- **Lines 90–91:** Implementation of a thread, which calls the `receiver` function.
- **Lines 92–104:** The body for Send button functionality. This function sends the message in the edit text to the RTLinux system through the null modem.
- **Lines 106–121:** Implementation of the `receiver` function. It continuously waits until the data is received in the buffer from the RTLinux system, and then reads it.

Source code listing for temperature.c

Listing 10-4 gives the source code for `temperature.c`. This file will be on the RTLinux machine.

Listing 10-4: Source code for temperature.c

```
#include <rtl.h>
#include <rtl_fifo.h>
#include <time.h>
#include <pthread.h>
#include <asm/io.h>
#include "rt_com.h"
#include "rt_comP.h"
#include <stdio.h>
pthread_t thread;
int fd_fifo;
int period=100000000;
int fifo_size=4000;
int a,temp;
void *temperature(void *t) {
//makes  a realtime thread as periodic
pthread_make_periodic_np (thread, gethrtime(), period);
temp=10;
do {
int n;
int i;
char b[210]={};
char a[1];
for(i=1;i<=10;i++)
{
//suspend the current thread until the next period
pthread_wait_np();
}
//attempts to read total characaters to buffer  from the realtime
serialport com
n = rt_com_read(0, b, sizeof(b));
if (n > 0) {
b[n] = 0;
rtl_printf("%s", b);
}
if(temp  != 50 ){a[0]=temp;
//writes 1 chraracter from buffer to the realtime serial port com
rt_com_write(0, a, 1);
temp = 10 + temp;
}
else{
temp = 10;
a[0]=temp;
//writes 1 character from buffer to the realtime serial port com
rt_com_write(0, a, 1);
}
} while (1);
return 0;
```

```
42. }
/* This module begins the entire process by creating an execution thread
with init_module */
43. int init_module(void)
44. {
45. pthread_attr_t attr;
46. struct sched_param sched_param;
47. int thread_status;
//it is used to dynamically change the parameters of each realtime
serial port
48. rt_com_setup(0, 9600, RT_COM_PARITY_NONE, 1, 8);
//to initialize threads attribute object
49. pthread_attr_init (&attr);
//to examine and change the CPU pthread attribute
50. pthread_attr_setcpu_np(&attr, 0);
51. sched_param.sched_priority = 1;
//dynamic thread scheduling parameters access
52. pthread_attr_setschedparam (&attr, &sched_param);
//creating the thread and maintaining its parameters status
53. thread_status = pthread_create (&thread,  &attr, temperature, (void
*)1);
54. return 0;
55. }
/* This module ends the entire process by clearing the  execution thread
with cleanup_module */
56. void cleanup_module(void)
57. {
//it deletes the realtime thread
58. pthread_delete_np (thread);
59. rt_com_setup(0, -1, 0, 0, 0);
60. }
```

Following is the line-by-line explanation of the source code:

- **Lines 1–8:** Including the necessary header files.
- **Lines 9–10:** Declaration of variables.
- **Line 11:** It initializes the duration of the thread in nanoseconds.
- **Line 12:** To allocate the memory to the FIFO.
- **Line 15:** `pthread_make_periodic_np` causes the real-time thread to execute periodically. This function utilizes a structure called `itimerspec`. Its parameters are `it_interval` and `it_value`, which specify the timer period and its expiration, respectively. The `it_value` parameter also specifies the time of its first invocation, which is passed to the structure `itimerspec`.
- **Line 16:** Initializing the temperature with a value — in this case, 10.
- **Lines 17–40:** An infinite do `while` loop has been implemented.

- **Lines 20–25:** The `for` loop begins with a call to the function `pthread_wait_np`, which basically blocks any further execution of the thread for 10 cycles.
- **Line 26:** The function `rt_com_read` attempts to read all characters into `array b[]` from the real-time serial port com1.
- **Lines 31–42:** The function `rt_com_write` writes temp value from buffer to serial port. The next step is to increment the value of temp by 10.

- **Lines 43–55:** Dynamically sets the following parameters of the serial port, such as com1: baud rate, parity type, stop bits, and word length. Then we initialize the thread with its attribute object. Next, we allocate the default CPU cycles for the thread by sending 0 to `pthread_attr_setcpu_np()`. We then allocate the scheduling priority for the thread as 1 and set the schedule with `pthread_attr_setschedparam()`. Finally, we create the thread with all the selected parameters using the function call `pthread_create`.
- **Lines 56–60:** The `cleanup_module` function cancels the thread process on the `pthread` join and frees the CPU cycles.

Executing the program

This project involves communication between the RTLinux machine and the Windows machine. We have to execute a set of steps on both sides. A null modem connection is required between them.

Execution steps on the RTLinux machine

This project consists of various files: `temperature.c`, `rt_com.c`, `rt_com.h`, `rt_comp.h`, and `rtl_mk`. The `temperature.c` program source code is provided in Listing 10-4. The file `rtl_mk` will be available with RTLinux. The `rt_com.c`, `rt_com.h`, and `rt_comp.h` files can be freely downloaded from `www.rtlinux.org`.

Compiling RTLinux programs

Issue the following commands at the system prompt:

```
$make -f  rtl.mk rt_com.o
$make -f rtl.mk Temperature.o
```

Execution steps on the RTLinux machine

To establish the serial connection, type the following command:

```
$setserial /dev/ttyS0 uart none
```

To execute the project, issue this command:

```
$rtlinux start rt_com temperature
```

When you want to observe the received message from the Windows system, you have to type:

```
$dmesg
```

Execution steps on the Windows machine

When you open a new file in Microsoft Visual C++, the dialog box shown in Figure 10-6 appears. Select `MFCAppWizard(exe)` and enter the project name and its location. Click OK.

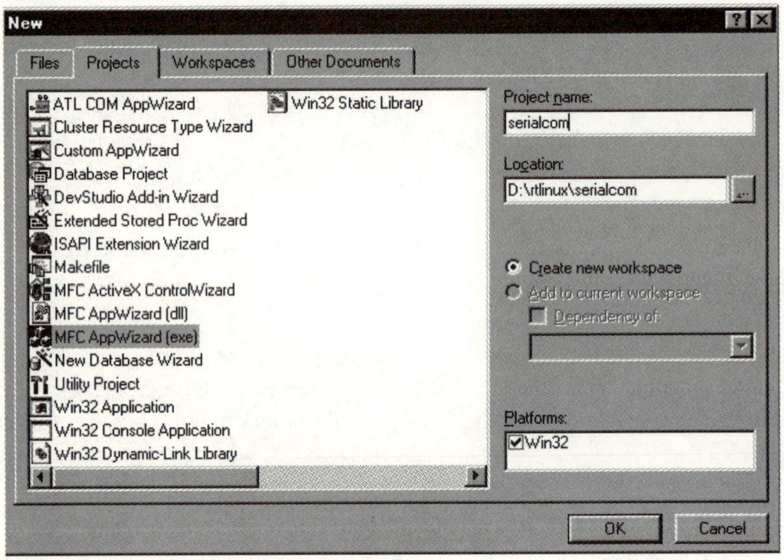

Figure 10-6: The Projects panel of the New dialog box

In the next dialog box you see (shown in Figure 10-7), select the dialog-based application and click Finish.

On the New Project info dialog window, just click OK.

The VC++ IDE will automatically create `serialcom.cpp`, `serialcomDlg.cpp`, `stdAfx.cpp`, and `serialcom.rc`; and the corresponding header files. On the SerialComm dialog box, all the controls will be placed as shown in Figure 10-8. You need to create member variables for the required controls. To activate these controls, you write the corresponding code in `serialcommDlg.cpp`, which is shown in Listing 10-3.

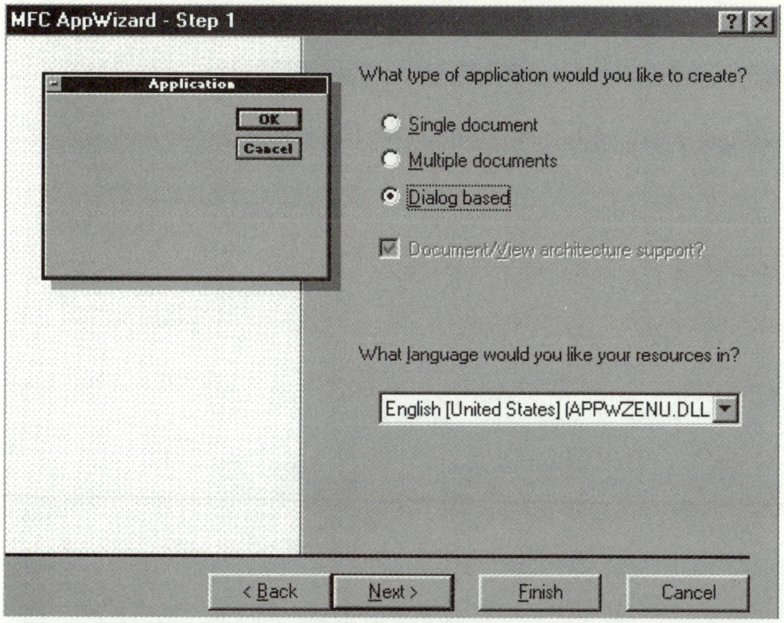

Figure 10-7: New Project applet wizard screen

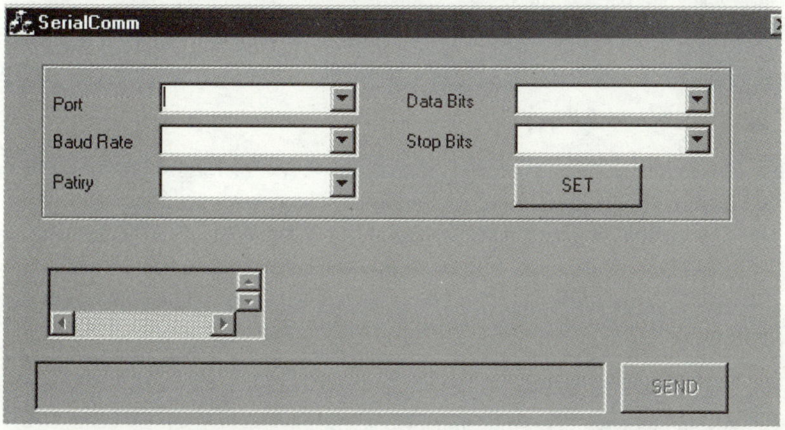

Figure 10-8: The SerialComm dialog box, for setting the serial communication parameters

Use this dialog box to set the serial communication parameters and then click Set.

When you want to send any message from the Windows system to the RTLinux system, you enter the message in the text box provided at the bottom of the dialog box and click SEND. The message will appear on the RTLinux terminal. At the same time, you can observe the temperature values in the corresponding text box on the Windows machine.

Any message the user inputs on the Windows machine will appear on the RTLinux terminal.

The output screen on the Windows system will look like the one shown in Figure 10-9.

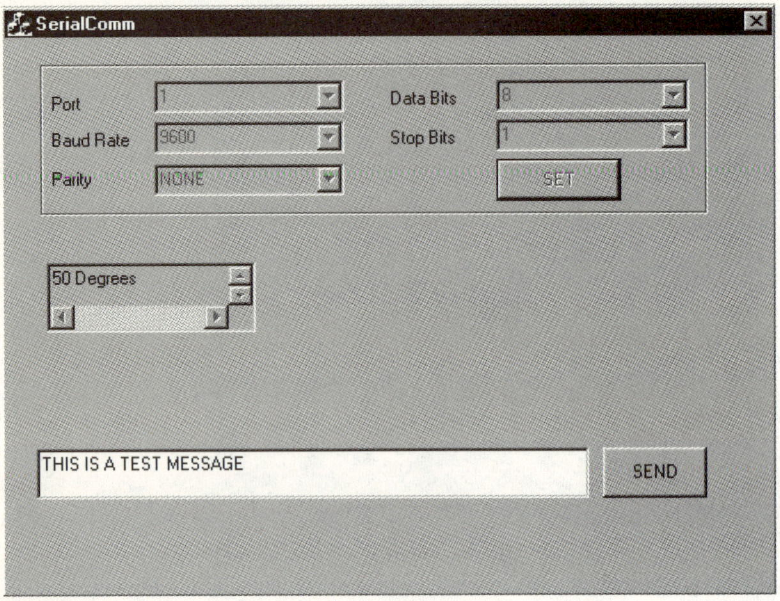

Figure 10-9: Output screen on the Windows machine

Project: Controlling an Appliance from the RTLinux System

This project develops a device to control the playing of a tape recorder remotely. An audio player program is controlled from an RTLinux machine by commands issued from the RTLinux terminal. You can control the audio player running on the Windows machine by using the Play, Stop, and Repeat commands. The tape recording controls on the Windows system are accessed remotely from the RTLinux application. To issue the commands for Play, Stop, and Repeat, you need to write separate modules in the RTLinux machine.

The following files are found on an RTLinux system:

- `rt_com.c`: This file is used for establishing the serial communication.
- `rt_com.h` and `rt_comp.h`: These are the header files.
- `play.c`: This file is used to send an instruction to the Windows machine to play the audio file.
- `stop.c`: This file is for sending an instruction to stop the audio play.
- `repeat.c`: This file is for sending an instruction to repeat the playing of the audio file.
- `rtl.mk`: This file makes an object file.

- rtl_com.o, play.o, stop.o, repeat.o: These are the object files.

The following files are found on a Windows system:

- AudioplayerDlg.cpp: This file is used to control the audio player and to establish serial communication.
- Audioplayer.cpp, stdafx.h, resource.h, audioplayer.h, and audioplayerdlg.h: These are the system-generated files. When you create project with the name Audioplayer in the VC++ environment, these files are automatically generated. Note that if you do not create the project and try to run the AudioplayerDlg.cpp file directly, you will get compilation errors.

Source code listing for play.c

Listing 10-5 gives the source code for play.c, which is on the RTLinux machine.

Listing 10-5: Source code for play.c

```
/*play.c*/
1.#include <rtl.h>
2.#include <rtl_fifo.h>
3.#include <time.h>
4.#include <pthread.h>
5.#include <asm/io.h>
6.#include "rt_com.h"
7.#include "rt_comP.h"
8.int fd_fifo;
9.char a[210]={};
10.pthread_t thread;
11.int fifo_size=4000;
12.int period=100000000;
13.void *play(void *t) {
//makes  a realtime thread as periodic
14.pthread_make_periodic_np (thread, gethrtime(), period);
15.a[0]='2';
//writes 1 character from buffer to the realtime serial port com
16.rt_com_write(0, a, 1);
17.return 0;
18.}
/* This module begins the entire process by creating an execution thread
with init_module */
19.int init_module(void)
20.{
21.pthread_attr_t attr;
22.struct sched_param sched_param;
23.int thread_status;
//it is used to dynamically change the parameters of each realtime
serial port
```

```
24. rt_com_setup(0, 9600, RT_COM_PARITY_NONE, 1, 8);
//to initialize threads attribute object
25. pthread_attr_init (&attr);
//to examine and change the CPU pthread attribute
26. pthread_attr_setcpu_np(&attr, 0);
//dynamic thread scheduling parameters access
27. sched_param.sched_priority = 1;
28. pthread_attr_setschedparam (&attr, &sched_param);
//creating the thread and maintaining its parameters status
29. thread_status = pthread_create (&thread,  &attr, play, (void *)1);
30. return 0;
31. }
/* This module ends the entire process by clearing the  execution thread
with cleanup_module */
32. void cleanup_module(void)
33. {
34. printk ("Removing module on CPU %d\n", rtl_getcpuid());
//it delete the realtime thread
35. pthread_delete_np (thread);
36. rt_com_setup(0, -1, 0, 0, 0);
37. }
```

Following is the line-by-line explanation of the source code:

- **Lines 1–7:** Inclusion of the various header files to support the RTLinux functionality, including FIFO creations, time management, thread handling, and input and output interactions.
- **Line 11:** Allocates the memory to the FIFO.
- **Line 12:** It initializes the duration of the thread in nanoseconds.
- **Line 14:** `pthread_make_periodic_np` call is to make the real-time thread execute periodically. This function utilizes a structure called `itimerspec`. Its parameters are `it_interval` and `it_value`, which specify the timer period and its expiration, respectively. The `it_value` parameter also specifies the time of its first invocation, which is passed to the structure `itimerspec`.
- **Line 16:** The function `rt_com_write` writes the character `2` from buffer pointer to real-time serial port. The character `2` represents the Play button.
- **Lines 19–31:** Dynamically sets the following parameters of the serial port, such as com1: baud rate, parity type, stop bits, and word length. We initialize the thread with its attribute object. Next, we allocate the default CPU cycles for the thread by sending 0 to `pthread_attr_setcpu_np()`. Next, we allocate the scheduling priority for the thread as 1 and set the schedule with `pthread_attr_setschedparam()`. Finally, we create the thread with all the selected parameters with `pthread_ create`; and obtain the status from the variable `thread_ status`.

- **Lines 32–37:** The `cleanup_module` function cancels the thread process on the `pthread` join and frees the CPU cycles.

Source code listing for stop.c

Listing 10-6 gives the source code for `stop.c`.

Listing 10-6: Source code for stop.c

```
/*stop.c*/
1.#include <rtl.h>
2.#include <rtl_fifo.h>
3.#include <time.h>
4.#include <pthread.h>
5.#include <asm/io.h>
6.#include "rt_com.h"
7.#include "rt_comP.h"
8.pthread_t thread;
9.int fifo_size=4000;
10. int period=100000000;
11. int fd_fifo;
12. char a[210]={};
13. void *stop(void *t) {
//makes  a realtime thread as periodic
14. pthread_make_periodic_np (thread, gethrtime(), period);
15. a[0]='3';
//writes 1 chraracter from buffer to the realtime serial port com
16. rt_com_write(0, a, 1);
17. return 0;
18. }
/* This module begins the entire process by creating an execution thread
with init_module */
19. int init_module(void)
20. {
21. pthread_attr_t attr;
22. struct sched_param sched_param;
23. int thread_status;
//it is used to dynamically changed the parameters of each realtime
serial port
24. rt_com_setup(0, 9600, RT_COM_PARITY_NONE, 1, 8);
//to initialize threads attribute object
25. pthread_attr_init (&attr);
//to examine and change the CPU pthread attribute
26. pthread_attr_setcpu_np(&attr, 0);
27. sched_param.sched_priority = 1;
//dynamic thread scheduling parameters access
28. pthread_attr_setschedparam (&attr, &sched_param);
//creating the thread and maintaining its parameters status
29. thread_status = pthread_create (&thread,  &attr, stop, (void *)1);
```

```
30. return 0;
31. }
/* This module ends the entire process by clearing the  execution thread
with cleanup_module */
32. void cleanup_module(void)
33. {
//it delete the realtime thread
34. pthread_delete_np (thread);
35. rt_com_setup(0, -1, 0, 0, 0);
36. }
```

The code in the preceding file is almost the same as that of `play.c`. One important difference is in line 16, where the function `rt_com_write` writes the character `3` from buffer pointer to serial port. The character `3` represents the Stop button.

Source code listing for repeat.c

Listing 10-7 gives the source code for `repeat.c`.

Listing 10-7: Source code for repeat.c

```
/* repeat.c*/
1.#include <rtl.h>
2.#include <rtl_fifo.h>
3.#include <time.h>
4.#include <pthread.h>
5.#include <asm/io.h>
6.#include "rt_com.h"
7.#include "rt_comP.h"
8.int period=100000000;
9.int fifo_size=4000;
10. pthread_t thread;
11. int fd_fifo;
12. char a[210]={};
13. void *autore13ind(void *t) {
//makes  a realtime thread as periodic
14. pthread_make_periodic_np (thread, gethrtime(), period);
15. do {
16. for(i=1;i<=20;i++)
17. {
//suspend the current thread until the next period
18. pthread_wait_np();
19. }
20. a[0]='4';
//writes 1 chraracter from buffer to the realtime serial port com
21. rt_com_write(0, a, 1);
22. } while (1);
23. return 0;
24. }
```

```
/* This module begins the entire process by creating an execution thread
with init_module */
25. int init_module(void)
26. {
27. pthread_attr_t attr;
28. struct sched_param sched_param;
29. int thread_status;
//it is used to dynamically change the parameters of each realtime
serial port
30. rt_com_setup(0, 9600, RT_COM_PARITY_NONE, 1, 8);
//to initialize threads attribute object
31. pthread_attr_init (&attr);
//to examine and change the CPU pthread attribute
32. pthread_attr_setcpu_np(&attr, 0);
33. sched_param.sched_priority = 1;
//dynamic thread scheduling parameters access
34. pthread_attr_setschedparam (&attr, &sched_param);
//creating the thread and maintaining its parameters status
35. thread_status = pthread_create (&thread,  &attr, autorewind, (void
*)1);
36. return 0
37. }
/* This module ends the entire process by clearing the  execution thread
with cleanup_module */
38. void cleanup_module(void)
39. {
//it deletes the realtime thread
40. pthread_delete_np (thread);
41. rt_com_setup(0, -1, 0, 0, 0);
42. }
```

The code in the preceding file is also self-explanatory. However, note the important change in line 21, where the function `rt_com_write` writes the character `4` from buffer pointer to the serial port. The character `4` represents the Repeat button.

Source code listing for AudioPlayerDlg.cpp

The source code for `AudioPlayerDlg.cpp` is given in Listing 10-8. This file has to be created in the VC++ environment on a Windows 9*x* machine.

Listing 10-8: Source code for AudioPlayerDlg.cpp

```
// AudioPlayerDlg.cpp : implementation file
1.#include <mmsystem.h>
2.#include "conio.h"
3.unsigned int baseAdd;
4.int Receiver(void);
5.CString stopBits,port,parity,dataBits,baudRate;
6.unsigned int LSB,MSB,dataFormat,temp;
```

```
UINT MYThread(LPVOID v)
{
sndPlaySound( "kitty.wav",0); //any .wav file and is placed in your
project folder
return (0);
}
BOOL CAudioPlayerDlg::OnInitDialog()
{
CDialog::OnInitDialog();
// TODO: Add extra initialization here
baseAdd = 0x3f8;
LSB = 0x03;
MSB = 0x00;
dataFormat = 0x03;
_outp(baseAdd+3,dataFormat); // setting dataformat register
temp = _inp(baseAdd+3);
temp = temp | 0x10;
_outp(baseAdd+3,temp); //setting DLAb bit to 1
_outp(baseAdd,LSB);     // setting Baud Rate
_outp(baseAdd+1,MSB);
temp = _inp(baseAdd+3);
temp = temp & 0x7f;
_outp(baseAdd+3,temp);
AfxBeginThread((AFX_THREADPROC)Receiver,NULL);
m_text1.SetWindowText("kitty.wav");
return TRUE;  // return TRUE  unless you set the focus to a control
}
void CAudioPlayerDlg::OnButtonPlay()
{
// TODO: Add your control notification handler code here
AfxBeginThread(MYThread,THREAD_PRIORITY_NORMAL);
}
void CAudioPlayerDlg::OnButtonStop()
{
// TODO: Add your control notification handler code here
PlaySound( NULL, NULL, NULL );
}
int Receiver()
{
char ch;
CAudioPlayerDlg *xx=(CAudioPlayerDlg*)AfxGetMainWnd()-
>GetDlgItem(IDD_AUDIOPLAYER_DIALOG);
while(1)
{
while(!(_inp(baseAdd+5)&0x01));
ch = _inp(baseAdd);
switch(ch)
{
case '2':
```

```
51. xx->OnButtonPlay();
52. break;
53. case '3':
54. xx->OnButtonStop();
55. break;
56. case '4':
57. xx->OnButtonPlay();
58. }
59. }
60. return 0;
61. }
62. void CAudioPlayerDlg::OnButtReplay()
63. {
// TODO: Add your control notification handler code here
64. AfxBeginThread(MYThread,THREAD_PRIORITY_NORMAL);
65. }
```

Following is the line-by-line explanation of the preceding source code:

- **Lines 1–11:** Inclusion of header files and variables declaration. In line 9, the file `kitty.wav` is provided, which is played. You can replace it with any `.WAV` file. You also need to change line 29 by providing the `.WAV` filename.
- **Lines 14–31:** `OnInitDialog` constructor, along with all variables and method declarations.
- **Lines 32–35:** The action to be carried out when the Play button is pressed. This is `onButtonPlay()`.
- **Lines 36–39:** Code corresponding to the Stop button. The method is `onButtonStop()`.
- **Lines 40–61:** Implementation of the receiver function. It continuously waits until the data is received in the buffer from the RTLinux system and reads it. If the value is 2, it activates the Play button. If the value is 3, it activates the Stop button. If the value is 4, the Rewind button is activated.
- **Lines 62–65:** Code corresponding to the Rewind button. The method is `onButtonReplay()`.

Execution steps

This project consists of various files: `play.c`, `stop.c`, `repeat.c`, `rt_com.c`, `rt_com.h`, `rt_comp.h`, and `rtl_mk`. The source code for `play.c`, `stop.c`, and `repeat.c` are given in Listings 10-5 to 10-7. The files `rtl_mk`, `rt_com.c`, `rt_com.h`, and `rt_comp.h` can be freely downloaded from `www.rtlinux.org`.

To compile RTLinux programs, type the following commands at the `$` prompt:

```
$make -f  rtl.mk rt_com.o
$make -f rtl.mk play.o
```

```
$make -f rtl.mk stop.o
$make -f rtl.mk repeat.o
```

Execution steps on the RTLinux machine

To establish the serial connection, type the following:

```
$setserial /dev/ttyS0 uart none
```

To execute the project, issue the following commands, based on the functionality you require. For example, to start the audio player, issue the command with the argument `start`:

```
$rtlinux start rt_com play
$rtlinux stop rt_com stop
$rtlinux start rt_com stop
$rtlinux stop rt_com stop
$rtlinux start rt_com repeat
$rtlinux stop rt_com repeat
```

Execution steps on the Windows machine

When a new file is opened in Microsoft Visual C++, the dialog box shown in Figure 10-10 appears. Select `MFCAppWizard(exe)`, enter the project name and its location, and click OK.

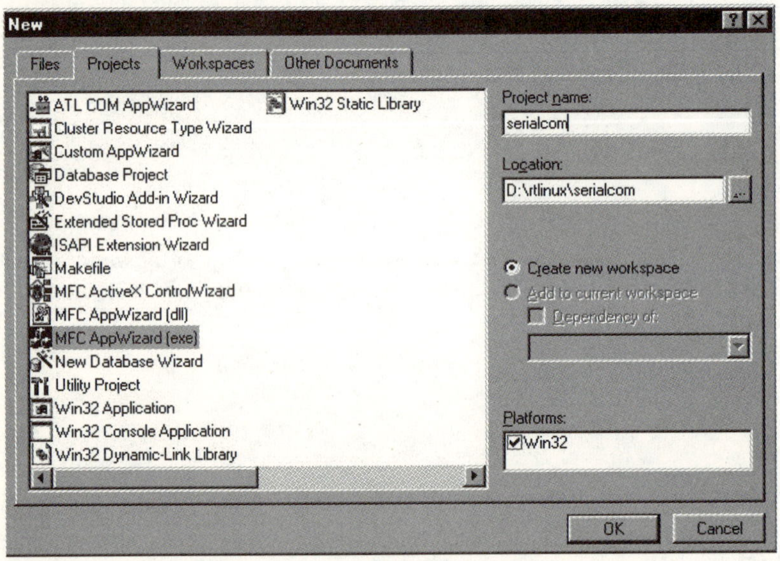

Figure 10-10: Enter the project's name and its location in the New dialog box.

In the next window (shown in Figure 10-11), select the dialog-based application option and click the Finish button.

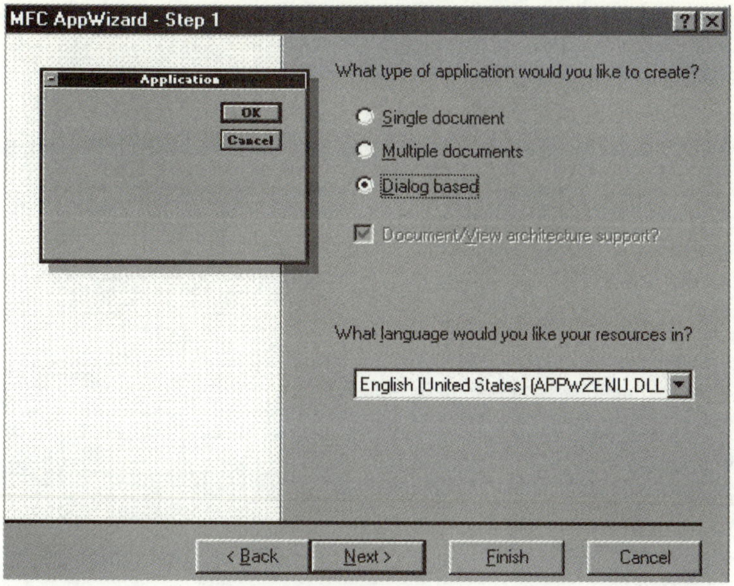

Figure 10-11: Step 1 of the MFC Applet wizard

On the New Project info dialog window, just click OK.

The VC++ IDE will automatically create `audioplayer.cpp`, `audioplayerDlg.cpp`, `stdAfx.cpp`, and `audioplayer.rc`; and the corresponding header files. On the AudioPlayer dialog box, all the controls will be placed as shown in Figure 10-12. You have to create member variables for the required controls. To activate these controls, write the corresponding code in `AudioplayerDlg.cpp`, which is shown in Listing 10-8. You're now ready to build the project.

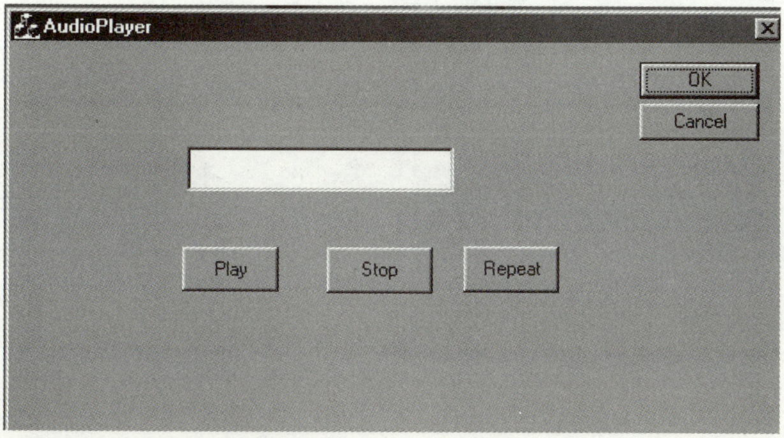

Figure 10-12: AudioPlayer dialog box

To activate the audio player required for this project, you need to specify the necessary project settings. On the VC ++ menu bar, select Project ⇨ Settings. In the Project Settings dialog box (shown in Figure 10-13), enter **winmm.lib** in the Object/Library Modules text box. This library module comes with Visual Studio 6.0 and will be available in the `Windows\Systems` directory. In this step, we are linking `winmm.lib` to the project to activate the player. Finally, click the OK button.

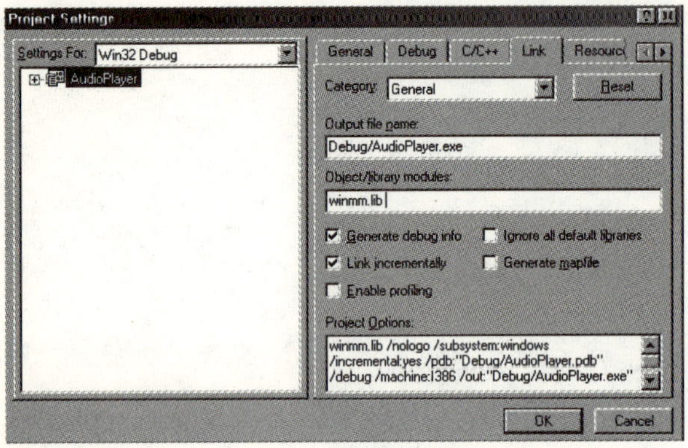

Figure 10-13: Project Settings dialog box for the audio player

Output

After the screen shown in Figure 10-14 appears, you can issue the desired commands from the RTLinux machine to play, stop, or repeat as per the syntax provided in the section "Execution steps on the RTLinux machine."

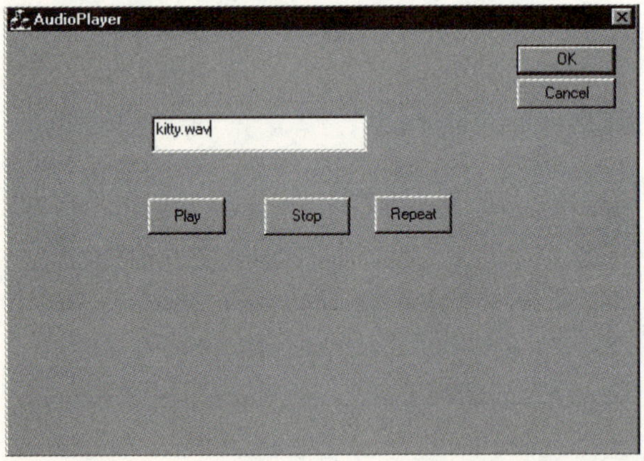

Figure 10-14: Output screen for the Audio Player control application

Summary

This chapter demonstrated software development in the RTLinux environment. You can develop both soft real-time and hard real-time applications using this operating system. You learned how an embedded system can communicate with a host system using a serial communication link for applications such as process control, controlling consumer appliances, etc. Because RTLinux is POSIX-compliant, you can easily write applications in any other POSIX-compliant real-time operating system based on the knowledge you gained in this chapter.

Chapter 11

Embedded Database Applications

In This Chapter

- Developing two embedded database applications, for a salary survey and an energy meter reading
- Source code for the two applications

With the availability of handheld computers, field personnel can use these devices to obtain field data, store the data directly in the handheld computer, and then upload the data to the corporate database. The challenge of developing an embedded database such as this lies in creating a user-friendly interface that enables the field personnel to enter the data without extensive training. With the advent of Pocket PC and Windows CE, you can use your knowledge of development in the Microsoft Visual Studio environment to create embedded database applications. Handheld computers are embedded systems, and to develop databases for these systems can be challenging. Using two applications — a salary survey and an energy meter reading — this chapter illustrates how you can accomplish this.

Development Environment

To work on the two projects presented in this chapter, you need the following development environment:

- eMbedded Visual Tools 3.0 (the project is developed in Embedded Visual Basic) installed on a Windows 2000/NT system
- Pocket PC hardware (if you do not have a Pocket PC, you can use the emulator provided with eMbedded Visual Tools to test the software)
- Database: Pocket Access

Project: Salary Survey

This project enables field personnel to visit different organizations and conduct a salary survey. The objective is to obtain the following information from different people: designation (programmer, systems analyst, project manager, etc.), organization type (small scale, medium scale, multinational), annual salary, service (experience) in the present organization, and total service (i.e., experience gained prior to the current position). The application will provide a GUI to the Pocket PC hardware so that the field personnel can enter the data, browse it, edit it, and save it. Subsequently, the field personnel can upload the database to the corporate database for final analysis. Table 11-1 gives the database definition for this application.

Table 11-1: SalarySurvey Table

Field Name	*Field Type*	*Field Size*	*Constraints*
ID	Int	3 (Default 3 only)	Primary Key, Indexed
Designation	Varchar	30	—
TypeOfOrg	Varchar	30	—
Salary	Varchar	10	—
ServiceOfOrg	Int	3	—
TotalService	Int	3	—

Database issues

The database used in eMbedded Visual Tools is Pocket Access. Using ActiveSync, you can transfer databases between a desktop PC and the Pocket (handheld) PC. However, to achieve this, the following guidelines must be met:

- ActiveSync has to be used to synchronize the data.
- The table name should not be longer than 31 characters.
- Field names should not be longer than 64 characters.
- Index name should not be longer than 64 characters.
- System tables cannot be copied or converted.
- If the system table `MySysTables` does not have an entry for your table, your table cannot be converted or copied.

Source code listing for SalarySurvey.ebf

Listing 11-1 provides the source code for the file `SalarySurvey.ebf`, which provides all the functionality for the database operations.

> **ON THE CD-ROM** This file is available on the CD-ROM that accompanies this book.

Listing 11-1: Source code for SalarySurvey.ebf

```
' Form Global Declarations
Dim RSSalary As ADOCE.Recordset
Dim RSSalaryModify As ADOCE.Recordset
Dim RSSalarySave As ADOCE.Recordset
Dim CNSalary As ADOCE.Connection
```

```
Dim MyQuery As String
Dim MyQueryModify As String
Dim MyButtonAction As String
Dim ModifyID As Integer
Dim MyFirstBookMark As Variant
Dim MyLastBookMark As Variant
Dim MyCurrentBookMark As Variant
' This control event is to enter data for new record.
Private Sub cmdADD_Click()
     EnableFields
     txtID.SetFocus
     MyButtonAction = "New"
     ClearAllFields
     cmdClose.Caption = "Cancel"
     DisablecmdButtons
End Sub
'This control event is to cancel the operation or close the application.
Private Sub cmdClose_Click()
      If cmdClose.Caption = "Exit" Then
             Form_OKClick
      Else
             EnablecmdButtons
             cmdClose.Caption = "Exit"
             MyButtonAction = ""
             ClearAllFields
             Display
             DisableFields
      End If
End Sub
  'This Control event is to delete a record.
Private Sub cmdDelete_Click()
       MyQuery = "Select * FROM SalarySurvey where ID='" & txtID.text & "'"
       Set RSSalaryModify = CreateObject("ADOCE.Recordset.3.0")
       RSSalaryModify.Open MyQuery, CNSalary, adOpenKeyset, adLockOptimistic
       If RSSalaryModify.RecordCount > 0 Then
           Dim MyVar
           MyVar = MsgBox("Do You Want to Delete ?", 65, "SalarySurvey")
           If MyVar = 1 Then
                RSSalaryModify.Delete
                RSSalaryModify.Close
                Set RSSalaryModify = Nothing
                RefreshDB
                RSSalary.MoveFirst
                EnableFields
                ClearAllFields
                Display
```

```
                DisableFields
            Else
                MsgBox "No Record Deleted"
                RSSalaryModify.Close
                Set RSSalaryModify = Nothing
            End If
        Else
            MsgBox "No Record to Delete"
            RSSalaryModify.Close
            Set RSSalaryModify = Nothing
        End If
End Sub
  ' This control event is to dispaly the first record
Private Sub cmdFirst_Click()
        cmdSave.Enabled = False
        ClearAllFields
        RSSalary.MoveFirst
        Display
End Sub
  ' This control event is to display the last record
Private Sub cmdLast_Click()
        cmdSave.Enabled = False
        ClearAllFields
        RSSalary.MoveLast
        Display
End Sub
  ' This control event is to get the record to be modified
Private Sub cmdModify_Click()
        EnableFields
        txtID.SetFocus
        MyQuery = "SELECT * FROM SalarySurvey where ID='" & txtID.text & "'"
        Set RSSalaryModify = CreateObject("ADOCE.Recordset.3.0")
        RSSalaryModify.Open MyQuery, CNSalary, adOpenKeyset, adLockOptimistic
        If RSSalaryModify.RecordCount > 0 Then
            ModifyID = RSSalaryModify.Fields("ID")
            DisablecmdButtons
            cmdClose.Caption = "Cancel"
            MyButtonAction = "Modify"
            RSSalaryModify.Close
            Set RSSalaryModify = Nothing
        Else
            MsgBox "NO Record"
            RSSalaryModify.Close
            Set RSSalaryModify = Nothing
        End If
End Sub
  'This control event is to display the next record
```

```
Private Sub cmdNext_Click()
       cmdSave.Enabled = False
       ClearAllFields
       If RSSalary.Bookmark = MyLastBookMark Then
           RSSalary.MoveLast
           MsgBox "Last Record"
       Else
           RSSalary.MoveNext
       End If
       Display
End Sub
  'This control event is to display the previous record
Private Sub cmdPrevious_Click()
       cmdSave.Enabled = False
       ClearAllFields
       If RSSalary.Bookmark = MyFirstBookMark Then
           RSSalary.MoveFirst
           MsgBox "First Record"
       Else
           RSSalary.MovePrevious
       End If
       Display
End Sub
 'This control event is to add new record or to update existing
record
Private Sub cmdSave_Click()
  If MyButtonAction = "New" Then
    MyQuery = "SELECT * FROM SalarySurvey where ID='" & txtID.text
& "'"
    Set RSSalarySave = CreateObject("ADOCE.Recordset.3.0")
    RSSalarySave.Open MyQuery, CNSalary, adOpenKeyset,
adLockOptimistic
    If RSSalarySave.RecordCount > 0 Then
      MsgBox "With This Id Record Already Exists"
      RSSalarySave.Close
      Set RSSalarySave = Nothing
    Else
      RSSalarySave.AddNew
      AddDataFromFieldsToDB
      RSSalarySave.Update
      RSSalarySave.Close
      Set RSSalarySave = Nothing
      EnablecmdButtons
      cmdClose.Caption = "Exit"
      MyButtonAction = ""
      RefreshDB
      RSSalary.MoveFirst
      ClearAllFields
      Display
```

```
      DisableFields
    End If
  ElseIf MyButtonAction = "Modify" Then
    MyQuery = "SELECT * FROM SalarySurvey where ID='" & txtID.text
& "'"
    Set RSSalaryModify = CreateObject("ADOCE.Recordset.3.0")
    RSSalaryModify.Open MyQuery, CNSalary, adOpenKeyset,
adLockOptimistic
    If RSSalaryModify.RecordCount > 0 Then
      If CInt(Trim(txtID.text)) = ModifyID Then
        MyQueryModify = "SELECT * FROM SalarySurvey where ID='" &
ModifyID
                           & "'"
        Set RSSalarySave = CreateObject("ADOCE.Recordset.3.0")
        RSSalarySave.Open MyQueryModify, CNSalary, adOpenKeyset,
                        adLockOptimistic
        If RSSalarySave.RecordCount > 0 Then
          AddDataFromFieldsToDB
          RSSalarySave.Update
          RSSalarySave.Close
          Set RSSalarySave = Nothing
          EnablecmdButtons
          cmdClose.Caption = "Exit"
          MyButtonAction = ""
          MyCurrentBookMark = RSSalary.Bookmark
          RefreshDB
          RSSalary.Bookmark = MyCurrentBookMark
          DisableFields
        End If
        RSSalaryModify.Close
        Set RSSalaryModify = Nothing
      Else
        MsgBox "With This Id Record Already Exists"
        RSSalaryModify.Close
        Set RSSalaryModify = Nothing
      End If
    Else
      MyQueryModify = "SELECT * FROM SalarySurvey where ID='" &
ModifyID &
                       "'"
      Set RSSalarySave = CreateObject("ADOCE.Recordset.3.0")
      RSSalarySave.Open MyQueryModify, CNSalary, adOpenKeyset,
                           adLockOptimistic
      If RSSalarySave.RecordCount > 0 Then
        AddDataFromFieldsToDB
        RSSalarySave.Update
        RSSalarySave.Close
        Set RSSalarySave = Nothing
        EnablecmdButtons
```

```
        cmdClose.Caption = "Exit"
        MyButtonAction = ""
        MyCurrentBookMark = RSSalary.Bookmark
        RefreshDB
        RSSalary.Bookmark = MyCurrentBookMark
        DisableFields
      End If
      RSSalaryModify.Close
      Set RSSalaryModify = Nothing
    End If
  End If
End Sub
'This form event is to display first record data while the application is    loading.
Private Sub Form_Load()
    'CreateDBandTable
    Set CNSalary = CreateObject("ADOCE.Connection.3.0")
    CNSalary.Open "\My Documents\Salary\SalaryDB.cdb"
    EnablecmdButtons
    ClearAllFields
    MyQuery = "SELECT * FROM SalarySurvey"
    Set RSSalary = CreateObject("ADOCE.Recordset.3.0")
    RSSalary.Open MyQuery, CNSalary, adOpenKeyset, adLockOptimistic
    If RSSalary.RecordCount > 0 Then
        RSSalary.MoveFirst
        MyFirstBookMark = RSSalary.Bookmark
        RSSalary.MoveLast
        MyLastBookMark = RSSalary.Bookmark
        RSSalary.MoveFirst
        Display
    Else
        MsgBox "No Records In the Database"
    End If
    DisableFields
End Sub
'this control event is to close the record set, connection and application
Private Sub Form_OKClick()
    RSSalary.Close
    Set RSSalary = Nothing
    CNSalary.Close
    Set CNSalary = Nothing
    App.End
End Sub
'This procedure is to clear all the text fields.
Private Sub ClearAllFields()
    txtID.text = ""
    txtDesignation.text = ""
    txtOrgType.text = ""
```

```
    txtAnnualSalary.text = ""
    txtServiceinOrg.text = ""
    txttotalService.text = ""
End Sub
'This procedure is to assign database fields data to text fields
Private Sub Display()
    txtID.text = RSSalary.Fields("ID")
    txtDesignation.text = RSSalary.Fields("Designation")
    txtOrgType.text = RSSalary.Fields("TypeOfOrg")
    txtAnnualSalary.text = RSSalary.Fields("Salary")
    txtServiceinOrg.text = RSSalary.Fields("ServiceOfOrg")
    txttotalService.text = RSSalary.Fields("TotalService")
End Sub
'This procedure is to create database and table
Private Sub CreateDBandTable()
    Dim SQl As String
    Set RSSalary = CreateObject("ADOCE.Recordset.3.0")
     ' create database
    RSSalary.Open "CREATE DATABASE '\My
Documents\Salary\SalaryDB.cdb'"
     ' create SalarySurvey Table
    SQl = "CREATE TABLE SalarySurvey ("
    SQl = SQl & "ID int ,"
    SQl = SQl & "Designation varchar(30) ,"
    SQl = SQl & "TypeOfOrg varchar(30) ,"
    SQl = SQl & "Salary varchar(10) ,"
    SQl = SQl & "ServiceOfOrg int ,"
    SQl = SQl & "TotalService int )"
    RSSalary.Open SQl, "\My Documents\Salary\SalaryDB.cdb"
     'Create Index for SalarySurvey Table
    RSSalary.Open "CREATE INDEX PrimaryKey ON SalarySurvey(ID)", _
                  "\My Documents\Salary\SalaryDB.cdb"
    Set RSSalary = Nothing
End Sub
'This procedure is to disable all text fields
Private Sub DisableFields()
    txtID.Enabled = False
    txtDesignation.Enabled = False
    txtOrgType.Enabled = False
    txtAnnualSalary.Enabled = False
    txtServiceinOrg.Enabled = False
    txttotalService.Enabled = False
End Sub
'This procedure is to enable all text fields
Private Sub EnableFields()
    txtID.Enabled = True
    txtDesignation.Enabled = True
    txtOrgType.Enabled = True
    txtAnnualSalary.Enabled = True
```

```
    txtServiceinOrg.Enabled = True
    txttotalService.Enabled = True
End Sub
 'This procedure is to enable the command buttons
Private Sub EnablecmdButtons()
    cmdSave.Enabled = False
    cmdADD.Enabled = True
    cmdModify.Enabled = True
    cmdDelete.Enabled = True
    cmdFirst.Enabled = True
    cmdLast.Enabled = True
    cmdNext.Enabled = True
    cmdPrevious.Enabled = True
End Sub
 'This procedure is to disable the command buttons
Private Sub DisablecmdButtons()
    cmdSave.Enabled = True
    cmdADD.Enabled = False
    cmdModify.Enabled = False
    cmdDelete.Enabled = False
    cmdFirst.Enabled = False
    cmdLast.Enabled = False
    cmdNext.Enabled = False
    cmdPrevious.Enabled = False
End Sub
 'This procedure is to assign text fields data to database fields
    Private Sub AddDataFromFieldsToDB()
    RSSalarySave.Fields("ID") = Trim(txtID.text)
    RSSalarySave.Fields("Designation") = Trim(txtDesignation.text)
    RSSalarySave.Fields("TypeOfOrg") = Trim(txtOrgType.text)
    RSSalarySave.Fields("Salary") = Trim(txtAnnualSalary.text)
    RSSalarySave.Fields("ServiceOfOrg") = Trim(txtServiceinOrg.text)
    RSSalarySave.Fields("TotalService") = Trim(txttotalService.text)
End Sub
 'This procedure is to refresh the database
Private Sub RefreshDB()
    RSSalary.Close
    Set RSSalary = Nothing
    MyQuery = "SELECT * FROM SalarySurvey"
    Set RSSalary = CreateObject("ADOCE.Recordset.3.0")
    RSSalary.Open MyQuery, CNSalary, adOpenKeyset, adLockOptimistic
    RSSalary.MoveFirst
    MyFirstBookMark = RSSalary.Bookmark
    RSSalary.MoveLast
    MyLastBookMark = RSSalary.Bookmark
End Sub
 ' This event is to validate for null.
```

```
Private Sub txtAnnualSalary_LostFocus()
    If txtAnnualSalary.text = "" Then
       MsgBox "This field is mandatory"
       txtAnnualSalary.SetFocus
    End If
End Sub
 ' This event is to validate for null.
Private Sub txtDesignation_LostFocus()
    If txtDesignation.text = "" Then
       MsgBox "This field is mandatory"
       txtDesignation.SetFocus
    End If
End Sub
 ' This event is to validate for null
Private Sub txtID_LostFocus()
    If txtID.text = "" Then
       MsgBox "This field is mandatory"
       txtID.SetFocus
    End If
End Sub
' This event is to validate for null
Private Sub txtTotalService_LostFocus()
    If txtTotalService.text = "" Then
       MsgBox "This field is mandatory"
       txtTotalService.SetFocus
    End If
End Sub
 ' This event is to validate for null.
Private Sub txtOrgType_LostFocus()
    If txtOrgType.text = "" Then
       MsgBox "This field is mandatory"
       txtOrgType.SetFocus
    End If
End Sub
 ' This event is to validate for null.
Private Sub txtServiceinOrg_LostFocus()
    If txtServiceinOrg.text = "" Then
       MsgBox "This field is mandatory"
       txtServiceinOrg.SetFocus
    End If
End Sub
' This event is to validate for numeric values
Private Sub txtID_KeyPress(ByVal KeyAscii As Integer)
    If KeyAscii = 8 Or KeyAscii >= 48 And KeyAscii <= 57 Then
    Else
        KeyAscii = 0
        MsgBox "Enter Numbers only"
    End If

```

```
345. End Sub
     ' This event is to validate for numeric values
346. Private Sub txtAnnualSalary_KeyPress(ByVal KeyAscii As Integer)
347.  If KeyAscii = 8 Or KeyAscii = 46 Or KeyAscii >= 48 And KeyAscii <=
57 Then
348.     Else
349.         KeyAscii = 0
350.         MsgBox "Enter Numbers only"
351.     End If
352.
353. End Sub
    ' This event is to validate for numeric values
354. Private Sub txtServiceinOrg_KeyPress(ByVal KeyAscii As Integer)
355.     If KeyAscii = 8 Or KeyAscii >= 48 And KeyAscii <= 57 Then
356.     Else
357.         KeyAscii = 0
358.         MsgBox "Enter Numbers only"
359.     End If
360. End Sub
     ' This event is to validate for numeric values
361. Private Sub txtTotalService_KeyPress(ByVal KeyAscii As Integer)
362.     If KeyAscii = 8 Or KeyAscii >= 48 And KeyAscii <= 57 Then
363.     Else
364.         KeyAscii = 0
365.         MsgBox "Enter Numbers only"
366.     End If
367. End Sub
```

Following is the line-by-line explanation of the source code:

- **Lines 1–11:** Declaration of variables.
- **Lines 12–19:** Definition of the `cmdADD_Click()` event, to enter data for a new record.
    - **Line 13:** Calling the procedure `EnableFields` to enable all text fields.
    - **Line 16:** Calling the procedure `ClearAllFields` to clear all the text boxes.
    - **Line 18:** Calling the procedure `DisablecmdButtons` to disable the command buttons.
- **Lines 20–31:** Definition of the `cmdClose_Click()` event, to cancel the operation or close the application.
    - **Line 22:** Calling the procedure `Form_OKClick` event, to close the application.
    - **Line 24:** Calling the procedure `EnablecmdButtons` to enable the command buttons.
    - **Line 28:** Calling the procedure `Display` to assign database field data to text fields.
    - **Line 29:** Calling the procedure `DisableFields` to disable all text fields.
- **Lines 32–59:** Definition of the `cmdDelete_Click()` event, to delete a record.

  - **Lines 33–36:** Creating a recordset and finding the current record in the database.
  - **Line 40:** Deleting a record from the database.
  - **Lines 41–42:** Closing the database.
  - **Line 43:** Calling the procedure `RefreshDB` to refresh the database.
- **Lines 60–65:** Definition of the `cmdFirst_Click()` event, to display the first record.
- **Lines 66–71:** Definition of the `cmdLast_Click()` event, to display the last record.
- **Lines 72–90:** Definition of the `cmdModify_Click()` event, to get the record to be modified.
- **Lines 91–101:** Definition of the `cmdNext_Click()` event, to display the next record.
  - **Line 94:** Checking for the last record.
- **Lines 102–112:** Definition of the `cmdPrevious_Click()` event, to display the previous record.
  - **Line 105:** Checking for the first record.
- **Lines 113–187:** Definition of the `cmdSave_Click()` event, to add a new record or to update the existing record.
  - **Line 118:** Checking for a duplicate record.
  - **Line 123:** Adding a new record to the database.
  - **Line 124:** Calling the procedure `AddDataFromFieldsToDB` to assign text field data to database fields.
  - **Line 141:** Checking for a duplicate record.
  - **Line 142:** Checking whether the ID is changed.
  - **Line 146:** Getting the record to be modified.
- **Lines 188–208:** Definition of the `Form_Load()` event, to display the first record's data while the application is loading. Line 189 is a call to the procedure `CreateDBandTable`. This procedure is given at lines 232–246. Before executing this program, you need to create a database table using this procedure.
- **Lines 209–215:** Definition of the `Form_OKClick()` event, to close the recordset, the connection, and the application.
- **Lines 216–223:** Definition of the `ClearAllFields()` procedure, to clear all the text fields.
- **Lines 224–231:** Definition of the `Display()` procedure, to assign database field data to text fields.
- **Lines 232–246:** Definition of the `CreateDBandTable()` procedure, to create a database and table.

- **Line 235:** Creating a database with `SalaryDB.cdb` and saving it in the specified location, `\My Documents\Salary\`.
- **Lines 236–242:** Creating a string named SQL. This string contains the table name and the field names. For each field, the type and size are also specified.
- **Line 243:** Executing the string that creates a table with the table name `SalarySurvey`, including `ID`, `Designation`, `TypeOfOrg`, `Salary`, `ServiceOfOrg`, and `TotalService` as fields.
- **Line 244:** Creating an index for the table on the field named ID.

- **Lines 247–254:** Definition of the `DisableFields()` procedure, to disable all text fields.
- **Lines 255–262:** Definition of the `EnableFields()` procedure, to enable all text fields.
- **Lines 263–272:** Definition of the `EnablecmdButtons()` procedure, to enable all command buttons.
- **Lines 273–282:** Definition of the `DisablecmdButtons()` procedure, to disable all command buttons.
- **Lines 283–290:** Definition of the `AddDataFromFieldsToDB()` procedure, to assign text field data to database fields.
- **Lines 291–301:** Definition of the `RefreshDB()` procedure, to refresh the database.
- **Lines 302–307:** Definition of the `txtAnnualSalary_LostFocus()` event, to validate a null value.
- **Lines 308–313:** Definition of the `txtDesignation_LostFocus()` event, to validate for a null value.
- **Lines 314–319:** Definition of the `txtID_LostFocus()` event, to validate for a null value.
- **Lines 320–325:** Definition of the `txtTotalService_LostFocus()` event, to validate for a null value.
- **Lines 326–331:** Definition of the `txtOrgType_LostFocus()` event, to validate for a null value.
- **Lines 332–337:** Definition of the `txtServiceinOrg_LostFocus()` event, to validate for a null value.
- **Lines 338–345:** Definition of the `txtID_KeyPress()` event, to validate for a numeric value.
- **Lines 346–353:** Definition of the `txtAnnualSalary_KeyPress()` event, to validate for a numeric value.
- **Lines 354–360:** Definition of the `txtServiceinOrg_KeyPress()` event, to validate for a numeric value.

- **Lines 361–367:** Definition of the `txtTotalService_KeyPress()` event, to validate for a numeric value.

Executing the program

Execute the program and test it with the Pocket PC emulator, using the following steps:

1. Invoke eMbedded Visual Tools 3.0 from the Start menu of your desktop. A window will open with tabs for Existing Projects, New Projects, and Recent Projects. Select the New Projects tab and choose Windows CE for the Pocket PC Project; the default form will be displayed.
2. In the Project menu, select Project Properties and set the project name as "SalarySurvey." Save the form as `SalarySurvey.ebf` and save the project as `SalarySurvey.ebp`. Note that `.EBF` is the extension for eMbedded Visual Basic Form. The extension for Embedded Visual Basis Project is `.EBP`.
3. Select the form and set the following form properties in the Properties window:
   - Name: `frmSalarySurvey`
   - Caption: SalarySurvey
   - Height: 4380
   - Width: 3780
4. Select the required controls from the Toolbox and set them as shown in Figure 11-1.

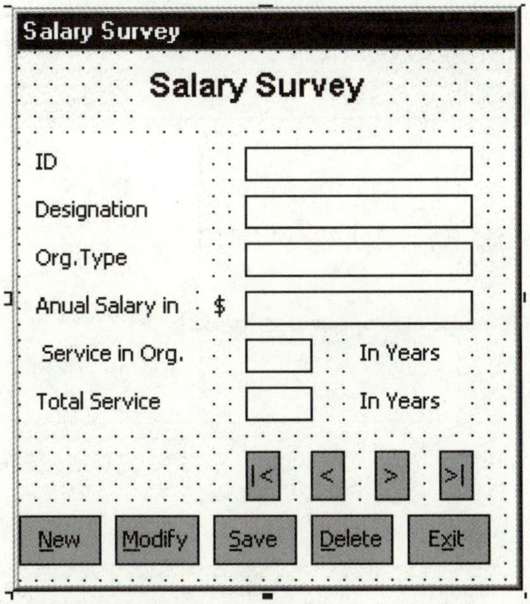

Figure 11-1: Salary Survey form

The Salary Survey title shown in bold at the top of the form is a Label control. Set the label properties as follows:

- Name: `lblTitle`
- Caption: `Salary Survey`
- Font: Arial, Bold.

ID is a Label control. Set the label properties as follows:

- Name: `lblID`
- Caption: `ID`

Designation is a Label control. Set the label properties as follows:

- Name: `lblDesignation`
- Caption: `Designation`

Org.Type is a Label control. The label properties are to be set as follows:

- Name: `lblOrganization`
- Caption: `Org.Type`

Annual Salary is a Label control. The label properties are to be set as follows:

- Name: `lblASalary`
- Caption: Annual Salary in

The character `$` is a Label control. Set the label properties as follows:

- Name: `lblDollar`
- Caption: $

Service in Org. is a Label control. The label properties are to be set as follows:

- Name: `lblNYService`
- Caption: `Service in Org.`

Total Service is a Label control. Set the label properties as follows:

- Name: `lblTotalService`
- Caption: Total Service

The In Years elements are Label controls. The label properties are to be set as follows:

- Name: `lblYears`
- Caption: In Years

The text box next to the ID label is a Text Box control. Set the text box properties as follows:

- Name: `txtID`
- MaxLength: 3

The text box next to the Designation label is a Text Box control. The text box properties are to be set as follows:

- Name: `txtDesignation`
- MaxLength: 30

The text box next to the Org.Type label is a Text Box control. Set the text box properties as follows:

- Name: `txtOrgType`
- MaxLength: 30

The text box next to the Annual Salary label is a Text Box control. The text box properties are to be set as follows:

- Name: `txtAnnualSalary`
- MaxLength: 10

The text box next to the Service in Org label is a Text Box control. Set the text box properties as follows:

- Name: `txtServiceinOrg`
- MaxLength: 3

The text box next to the Total Service label is a Text Box control. The text box properties are to be set as follows:

- Name: `txtTotalService`
- MaxLength: 3

The |< command button is a Command Button control. Set the command button properties as follows:

- Name: `cmdFirst`
- Caption: |<

Functionality: When clicked, this button displays the first record available in the database.

The < command button is a Command Button control. The command button properties are to be set as follows:

- Name: `cmdPrevious`
- Caption: <

Functionality: When clicked, this button displays the previous record available in the database.

The > command button shown is a Command Button control. Set the command button properties as follows:

- Name: `cmdNext`
- Caption: >

Functionality: When clicked, this button displays the next record available in the database.

The >| command button is a Command Button control. The command button properties are to be set as follows:

- Name: `cmdLast`
- Caption: >|

Functionality: When clicked, this button displays the last record available in the database.

The New command button is a Command Button control. Set the command button properties as follows:

- Name: `cmdADD`
- Caption: `&New`

Functionality: When clicked, this button clears all the text fields and enables the user to input data.

The Modify command button shown is a Command Button control. The command button properties are to be set as follows:

- Name: `cmdModify`
- Caption: `&Modify`

Functionality: When clicked, this button enables the user to modify the values of the currently displayed record.

The Save command button is a Command Button control. Set the command button properties as follows:

- Name: `cmdSave`
- Caption: `&Save`

Functionality: When clicked, this button saves the existing record; it may be either a new record or a modified record.

The Delete command button is a Command Button control. The command button properties are to be set as follows:

- Name: `cmdDelete`
- Caption: `&Delete`

Functionality: When clicked, this button deletes the existing record after asking for a confirmation.

The Exit command button is a Command Button control. Set the Command Button properties as follows:

- Name: `cmdClose`
- Caption: E&exit

Functionality: When clicked, this button unloads the application.

5. On the menu bar, select Project ⇨ References ⇨ Microsoft CE ADO Control 3.0. This reference is used for database connectivity.
6. In the Run menu, select Execute or click the Run button on the toolbar.

Output

When you execute the program, the screen shown in Figure 11-2 appears. The first record of the table will be displayed. Using the buttons provided, you can add, modify, and delete the records or navigate through them. Figure 11-3 shows the screen shot that appears when the Delete button is pressed. Note that the Save button is enabled only when you click the New or Modify button.

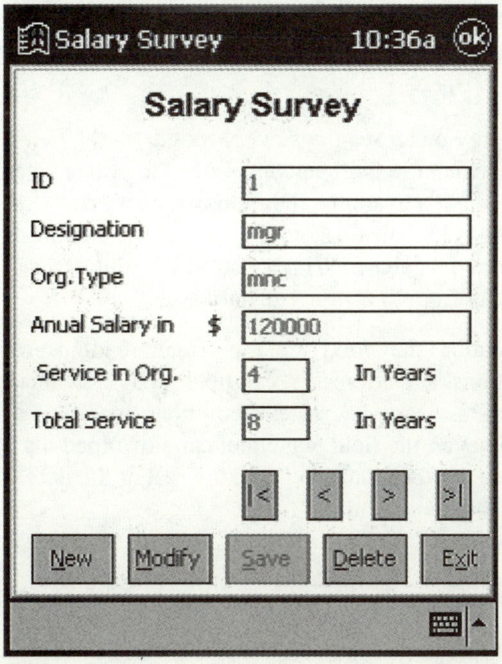

Figure 11-2: Output screen on a Pocket PC for the Salary Survey project

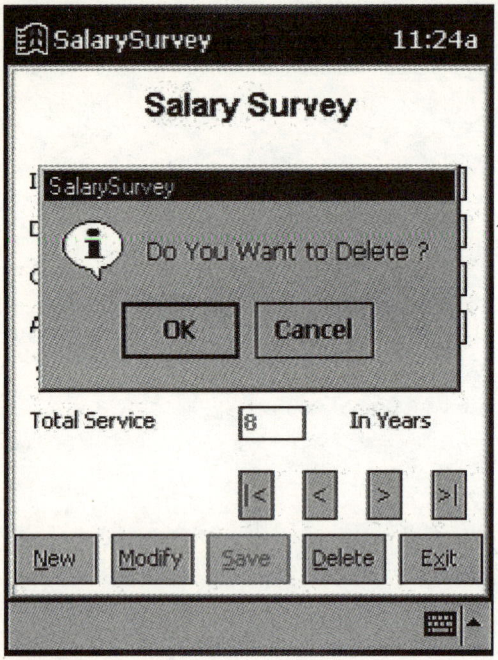

Figure 11-3: Output screen on a Pocket PC while deleting a record

Project: Energy Meter Reading

This database project is designed to obtain energy meter readings every month by the field personnel. Unlike the previous example — in which the field personnel need to obtain data and then upload it to the corporate database — in this example, the field personnel can download data available in the corporate database to their Pocket PCs, collect the data from the field, and then upload the data to the corporate database. With a Pocket PC, this can be achieved using ActiveSync to download the data from the corporate database.

The field personnel input two pieces of information: the month and the present reading. Any other data, such as meter numbers, initial readings, and addresses, can be directly downloaded from the database before the personnel begin. This example creates a complete application, which facilitates the entry of all the fields. However, the field personnel can download the information from the desktop computer and use the form only to fill in the rest of the data. The database definition for `EnergyMeter` Table is given in Table 11-2.

Table 11-2: EnergyMeter Table

Field Name	***Field Type***	***Field Size***	***Constraints***
SNo	Varchar	8	Primary Key, Indexed
Date	Varchar	10	—

MeterNo	Varchar	10	—
BilledMonth	Varchar	10	—
Address	Varchar	250	—
InitialReading	Varchar	10	—
presentReading	Varchar	10	—

Source code listing for EnergyConsumption.ebf

Listing 11-2 gives the source code for `EnergyConsumption.ebf`, which carries out all the database operations.

> **ON THE CD-ROM** This file is available on the CD-ROM that accompanies this book.

Listing 11-2: Source code for EnergyConsumption.ebf

```
' Form Global Declarations
Dim CNEnergyMeter As ADOCE.Connection
Dim RSEnergyMeter As ADOCE.Recordset
Dim RSEnergyMeterSave As ADOCE.Recordset
Dim RSEnergyMeterModify As ADOCE.Recordset
Dim RSEnergyMeterNew As ADOCE.Recordset
Dim MyQuery As String
Dim MyQueryNew As String
Dim MyQueryModify As String
Dim MyButtonAction As String
Dim MyFirstBookMark As Variant
Dim MyLastBookMark As Variant
Dim MyCurrentBookMark As Variant
Dim ModifySNo As String
Dim MyMonth As String
Dim MyMonthText As String
  ' This control event is to enter data for new record.
Private Sub cmdADD_Click()
    EnableFields
    txtSNo.SetFocus
    MyButtonAction = "New"
    ClearAllFields
    cmdClose.Caption = "Cancel"
    DisablecmdButtons
    cmdSave.Enabled = False
    txtDate.Enabled = False
    txtInitialReading.Enabled = False
    cboMonths.Enabled = False
    txtAddress.Enabled = False
    AddMonthsToComboBox
    BilledMonthToComboBox
    txtDate.Text = Date
```

```
End Sub
  'This control event is to cancel the operation or close the application.
Private Sub cmdClose_Click()
    If cmdClose.Caption = "Exit" Then
        Form_OKClick
    Else
        EnablecmdButtons
        cmdClose.Caption = "Exit"
        MyButtonAction = ""
        ClearAllFields
        Display
        DisableFields
    End If
End Sub
  'This control event is to delete a record.
Private Sub cmdDelete_Click()
    MyQuery = "Select * FROM EnergyMeter where SNo='" & txtSNo.Text & "'"
    Set RSEnergyMeterModify = CreateObject("ADOCE.Recordset.3.0")
    RSEnergyMeterModify.Open MyQuery, CNEnergyMeter, adOpenKeyset,
                                adLockOptimistic
    If RSEnergyMeterModify.RecordCount > 0 Then
        Dim MyVar
        MyVar = MsgBox("Do you want to Delete ?", 65, "EnergyMeter")
        If MyVar = 1 Then
            RSEnergyMeterModify.Delete
            RSEnergyMeterModify.Close
            Set RSEnergyMeterModify = Nothing
            RefreshDB
            RSEnergyMeter.MoveFirst
            EnableFields
            ClearAllFields
            Display
            DisableFields
        Else
            MsgBox "NO Record Deleted"
            RSEnergyMeterModify.Close
            Set RSEnergyMeterModify = Nothing
        End If
    Else
        MsgBox "NO Record to Delete"
        RSEnergyMeterModify.Close
        Set RSEnergyMeterModify = Nothing
    End If
End Sub
  ' This control event is to Display the first record
Private Sub cmdFirst_Click()
    cmdSave.Enabled = False
```

```
    ClearAllFields
    RSEnergyMeter.MoveFirst
    Display
End Sub
  ' This control event is to Display the last record
Private Sub cmdLast_Click()
    cmdSave.Enabled = False
    ClearAllFields
    RSEnergyMeter.MoveLast
    Display
End Sub
  ' This control event is to get the record to be modified
Private Sub cmdModify_Click()
    EnableFields
    txtSNo.SetFocus
    txtMeterNo.Enabled = False
    txtDate.Enabled = False
    cboMonths.Enabled = False
    txtInitialReading.Enabled = False
    txtAddress.Enabled = False
    MyQuery = "SELECT * FROM EnergyMeter where SNo='" & txtSNo.Text &
"'"
    Set RSEnergyMeterModify = CreateObject("ADOCE.Recordset.3.0")
    RSEnergyMeterModify.Open MyQuery, CNEnergyMeter, adOpenKeyset,
                              adLockOptimistic
    If RSEnergyMeterModify.RecordCount > 0 Then
        ModifySNo = RSEnergyMeterModify.Fields("SNo")
        DisablecmdButtons
        cmdClose.Caption = "Cancel"
        MyButtonAction = "Modify"
        RSEnergyMeterModify.Close
        Set RSEnergyMeterModify = Nothing
    Else
        MsgBox "NO Record"
        RSEnergyMeterModify.Close
        Set RSEnergyMeterModify = Nothing
    End If
End Sub
  'This control event is to display the next record
Private Sub cmdNext_Click()
    cmdSave.Enabled = False
    ClearAllFields
    If RSEnergyMeter.Bookmark = MyLastBookMark Then
        RSEnergyMeter.MoveLast
        MsgBox "Last Record"
    Else
        RSEnergyMeter.MoveNext
    End If
    Display
```

```
End Sub
    'This control event is to display the previous record
Private Sub cmdPrevious_Click()
  cmdSave.Enabled = False
  ClearAllFields
  If RSEnergyMeter.Bookmark = MyFirstBookMark Then
      RSEnergyMeter.MoveFirst
      MsgBox "First Record"
  Else
      RSEnergyMeter.MovePrevious
  End If
  Display
End Sub
    'This control event is to add new record or update existing record
Private Sub cmdSave_Click()
  If MyButtonAction = "New" Then
     MyQuery = "SELECT * FROM EnergyMeter where SNo='" &
txtSNo.Text & "'"
     Set RSEnergyMeterSave = CreateObject("ADOCE.Recordset.3.0")
     RSEnergyMeterSave.Open MyQuery, CNEnergyMeter, adOpenKeyset,
                    adLockOptimistic
     If RSEnergyMeterSave.RecordCount > 0 Then
          MsgBox "With This SNo Record Already Exists"
          RSEnergyMeterSave.Close
          Set RSEnergyMeterSave = Nothing
     Else
          RSEnergyMeterSave.AddNew
          AddDataFromFieldsToDB
          RSEnergyMeterSave.Update
          RSEnergyMeterSave.Close
          Set RSEnergyMeterSave = Nothing
          EnablecmdButtons
          cmdClose.Caption = "Exit"
          MyButtonAction = ""
          RefreshDB
          ClearAllFields
          Display
          DisableFields
     End If
  ElseIf MyButtonAction = "Modify" Then
     MyQuery = "SELECT * FROM EnergyMeter where SNo='" &
txtSNo.Text & "'"
     Set RSEnergyMeterModify = CreateObject("ADOCE.Recordset.3.0")
     RSEnergyMeterModify.Open MyQuery, CNEnergyMeter, adOpenKeyset,
                       adLockOptimistic
     If RSEnergyMeterModify.RecordCount > 0 Then
          If Trim(txtSNo.Text) = ModifySNo Then
              MyQueryModify = "SELECT * FROM EnergyMeter where
SNo='" &
```

```
                              ModifySNo & "'"
                    Set RSEnergyMeterSave =
CreateObject("ADOCE.Recordset.3.0")
                    RSEnergyMeterSave.Open MyQueryModify, CNEnergyMeter,
                                   adOpenKeyset, adLockOptimistic
                    If RSEnergyMeterSave.RecordCount > 0 Then
                          AddDataFromFieldsToDB
                          RSEnergyMeterSave.Update
                          RSEnergyMeterSave.Close
                          Set RSEnergyMeterSave = Nothing
                          EnablecmdButtons
                          cmdClose.Caption = "Exit"
                          MyButtonAction = ""
                          MyCurrentBookMark = RSEnergyMeter.Bookmark
                          RefreshDB
                          RSEnergyMeter.Bookmark = MyCurrentBookMark
                          DisableFields
                    End If
                    RSEnergyMeterModify.Close
                    Set RSEnergyMeterModify = Nothing
                Else
                    MsgBox "With this SNo Record Already Exists"
                    RSEnergyMeterModify.Close
                    Set RSEnergyMeterModify = Nothing
                End If
           Else
                MyQueryModify = "SELECT * FROM EnergyMeter where SNo='" &
                             ModifySNo & "'"
                Set RSEnergyMeterSave =
CreateObject("ADOCE.Recordset.3.0")
                RSEnergyMeterSave.Open MyQueryModify, CNEnergyMeter,
                   adOpenKeyset, adLockOptimistic
                If RSEnergyMeterSave.RecordCount > 0 Then
                      AddDataFromFieldsToDB
                      RSEnergyMeterSave.Update
                      RSEnergyMeterSave.Close
                      Set RSEnergyMeterSave = Nothing
                      EnablecmdButtons
                      cmdClose.Caption = "Exit"
                      MyButtonAction = ""
                      MyCurrentBookMark = RSEnergyMeter.Bookmark
                      RefreshDB
                      RSEnergyMeter.Bookmark = MyCurrentBookMark
                      DisableFields
                End If
                RSEnergyMeterModify.Close
                Set RSEnergyMeterModify = Nothing
           End If
        End If
```

```
End Sub
    'This form event is to display first record data while the
application is loading.
Private Sub Form_Load()
    Set CNEnergyMeter = CreateObject("ADOCE.Connection.3.0")
    CNEnergyMeter.Open "\My
Documents\EnergyMeter\EnergyMeterDB.cdb"
    'CreateDBandTable
    ClearAllFields
    EnablecmdButtons
    MyQuery = "SELECT * FROM EnergyMeter"
    Set RSEnergyMeter = CreateObject("ADOCE.Recordset.3.0")
    RSEnergyMeter.Open MyQuery, CNEnergyMeter, adOpenKeyset,
                adLockOptimistic
    If RSEnergyMeter.RecordCount > 0 Then
        RSEnergyMeter.MoveFirst
        MyFirstBookMark = RSEnergyMeter.Bookmark
        RSEnergyMeter.MoveLast
        MyLastBookMark = RSEnergyMeter.Bookmark
        RSEnergyMeter.MoveFirst
        Display
    Else
        MsgBox "No Records In the Database"
    End If
    DisableFields
End Sub
    'This control event is to close the record set, connection and
application
Private Sub Form_OKClick()
    RSEnergyMeter.Close
    Set RSEnergyMeter = Nothing
    CNEnergyMeter.Close
    Set CNEnergyMeter = Nothing
    App.End
End Sub
    'This procedure is to add months to combobox
Private Sub AddMonthsToComboBox()
    cboMonths.AddItem ("January")
    cboMonths.AddItem ("February")
    cboMonths.AddItem ("March")
    cboMonths.AddItem ("April")
    cboMonths.AddItem ("May")
    cboMonths.AddItem ("June")
    cboMonths.AddItem ("July")
    cboMonths.AddItem ("August")
    cboMonths.AddItem ("September")
    cboMonths.AddItem ("October")
    cboMonths.AddItem ("November")
    cboMonths.AddItem ("December")
```

```
End Sub
   'This procedure is to enable the command buttons
Private Sub EnablecmdButtons()
    cmdSave.Enabled = False
    cmdADD.Enabled = True
    cmdModify.Enabled = True
    cmdDelete.Enabled = True
    cmdFirst.Enabled = True
    cmdLast.Enabled = True
    cmdNext.Enabled = True
    cmdPrevious.Enabled = True
End Sub
   'This procedure is to disable the command buttons
Private Sub DisablecmdButtons()
    cmdSave.Enabled = True
    cmdADD.Enabled = False
    cmdModify.Enabled = False
    cmdDelete.Enabled = False
    cmdFirst.Enabled = False
    cmdLast.Enabled = False
    cmdNext.Enabled = False
    cmdPrevious.Enabled = False
End Sub
   'This procedure is to disable all text fields
Private Sub DisableFields()
    txtSNo.Enabled = False
    txtDate.Enabled = False
    txtMeterNo.Enabled = False
    cboMonths.Enabled = False
    txtAddress.Enabled = False
    txtInitialReading.Enabled = False
    txtPresentReading.Enabled = False
End Sub
   'This procedure is to enable all text fields
Private Sub EnableFields()
    txtSNo.Enabled = True
    txtDate.Enabled = True
    txtMeterNo.Enabled = True
    cboMonths.Enabled = True
    txtAddress.Enabled = True
    txtInitialReading.Enabled = True
    txtPresentReading.Enabled = True
End Sub
   'This procedure is to assign database fields data to text fields
Private Sub Display()
    txtSNo.Text = RSEnergyMeter.Fields("SNo")
    txtDate.Text = RSEnergyMeter.Fields("Date")
    txtMeterNo.Text = RSEnergyMeter.Fields("MeterNo")
    cboMonths.Clear
```

```
    cboMonths.AddItem RSEnergyMeter.Fields("BilledMonth")
    cboMonths.ListIndex = 0
    txtAddress.Text = RSEnergyMeter.Fields("Address")
    txtInitialReading.Text = RSEnergyMeter.Fields("InitialReading")
    txtPresentReading.Text = RSEnergyMeter.Fields("PresentReading")
End Sub
'This procedure is to clear all the text boxes
Private Sub ClearAllFields()
    txtSNo.Text = ""
    txtDate.Text = ""
    txtMeterNo.Text = ""
    cboMonths.Clear
    txtAddress.Text = ""
    txtInitialReading.Text = ""
    txtPresentReading.Text = ""
End Sub
'This procedure is to refresh the database
Private Sub RefreshDB()
    RSEnergyMeter.Close
    Set RSEnergyMeter = Nothing
    MyQuery = "SELECT * FROM EnergyMeter"
    Set RSEnergyMeter = CreateObject("ADOCE.Recordset.3.0")
    RSEnergyMeter.Open MyQuery, CNEnergyMeter, adOpenKeyset,
                   adLockOptimistic
    RSEnergyMeter.MoveFirst
    MyFirstBookMark = RSEnergyMeter.Bookmark
    RSEnergyMeter.MoveLast
    MyLastBookMark = RSEnergyMeter.Bookmark
End Sub
'This procedure is to assign text fields data to database fields
Private Sub AddDataFromFieldsToDB()
    RSEnergyMeterSave.Fields("SNo") = Trim(txtSNo.Text)
    RSEnergyMeterSave.Fields("Date") = Trim(txtDate.Text)
    RSEnergyMeterSave.Fields("MeterNo") = Trim(txtMeterNo.Text)
    RSEnergyMeterSave.Fields("BilledMonth") = Trim(cboMonths.Text)
    RSEnergyMeterSave.Fields("Address") = Trim(txtAddress.Text)
    RSEnergyMeterSave.Fields("InitialReading") =
                   Trim(txtInitialReading.Text)
    RSEnergyMeterSave.Fields("PresentReading") =
                   Trim(txtPresentReading.Text)
End Sub
'This procedure is to set current month in combobox
Private Sub BilledMonthToComboBox()
    MyMonth = Mid(Date, 1, 2)
    If MyMonth >= "10" And MyMonth <= "12" Then
        MyMonth = MyMonth
    Else
        MyMonth = Mid(MyMonth, 1, 1)
    End If
```

```
    If CInt(MyMonth) = 1 Then
          cboMonths.ListIndex = 0
    ElseIf CInt(MyMonth) = 2 Then
          cboMonths.ListIndex = 1
    ElseIf CInt(MyMonth) = 3 Then
          cboMonths.ListIndex = 2
    ElseIf CInt(MyMonth) = 4 Then
          cboMonths.ListIndex = 3
    ElseIf CInt(MyMonth) = 5 Then
          cboMonths.ListIndex = 4
    ElseIf CInt(MyMonth) = 6 Then
          cboMonths.ListIndex = 5
    ElseIf CInt(MyMonth) = 7 Then
          cboMonths.ListIndex = 6
    ElseIf CInt(MyMonth) = 8 Then
          cboMonths.ListIndex = 7
    ElseIf CInt(MyMonth) = 9 Then
          cboMonths.ListIndex = 8
    ElseIf CInt(MyMonth) = 10 Then
          cboMonths.ListIndex = 9
    ElseIf CInt(MyMonth) = 11 Then
          cboMonths.ListIndex = 10
    ElseIf CInt(MyMonth) = 12 Then
          cboMonths.ListIndex = 11
    End If
End Sub
'This procedure is to assign month numbers to text format
Private Sub MonthsInTextFormat()
     If CInt(MyMonth) = 1 Then
         MyMonthText = "January"
     ElseIf CInt(MyMonth) = 2 Then
         MyMonthText = "February"
     ElseIf CInt(MyMonth) = 3 Then
         MyMonthText = "March"
     ElseIf CInt(MyMonth) = 4 Then
         MyMonthText = "April"
     ElseIf CInt(MyMonth) = 5 Then
         MyMonthText = "May"
     ElseIf CInt(MyMonth) = 6 Then
         MyMonthText = "June"
     ElseIf CInt(MyMonth) = 7 Then
         MyMonthText = "July"
     ElseIf CInt(MyMonth) = 8 Then
         MyMonthText = "August"
     ElseIf CInt(MyMonth) = 9 Then
         MyMonthText = "September"
     ElseIf CInt(MyMonth) = 10 Then
         MyMonthText = "October"
     ElseIf CInt(MyMonth) = 11 Then
```

```
            MyMonthText = "November"
        ElseIf CInt(MyMonth) = 12 Then
            MyMonthText = "December"
        End If
End Sub
  'This procedure is to create database and tables
Private Sub CreateDBandTable()
        Dim RS As ADOCE.Recordset
        Dim SQl As String
        Set RS = CreateObject("ADOCE.Recordset.3.0")
         ' create database
        RS.Open "CREATE DATABASE '\My
               Documents\EnergyMeter\EnergyMeterDB.cdb'"
         ' create EnergyMeter Table
        SQl = "CREATE TABLE EnergyMeter ("
        SQl = SQl & "SNo varchar(8),"
        SQl = SQl & "Date varchar(10),"
        SQl = SQl & "MeterNo varchar(10) ,"
        SQl = SQl & "BilledMonth varchar(10) ,"
        SQl = SQl & "Address varchar(250) ,"
        SQl = SQl & "InitialReading varchar(10) ,"
        SQl = SQl & "PresentReading varchar(10))"
        RS.Open SQl, "\My Documents\EnergyMeter\EnergyMeterDB.cdb"
         'Create Index for EnergyMeter Table
        RS.Open "CREATE INDEX PrimaryKey ON EnergyMeter(SNo)", _
               "\My Documents\EnergyMeter\EnergyMeterDB.cdb"
        Set RS = Nothing
End Sub
 'This control event is for checking the current month for a given
meterno
     already Billed or not.
Private Sub txtMeterNo_LostFocus()
       MyQuery = "SELECT * FROM EnergyMeter where MeterNo='" &
               txtMeterNo.Text & "'"
       Set RSEnergyMeterNew = CreateObject("ADOCE.Recordset.3.0")
       RSEnergyMeterNew.Open MyQuery, CNEnergyMeter, adOpenKeyset,
                      adLockOptimistic
       If RSEnergyMeterNew.RecordCount > 0 Then
            MyMonth = MyMonth - 1
            If CInt(MyMonth) = 0 Then
                MyMonth = 12
            Else
                MyMonth = MyMonth
            End If
            MonthsInTextFormat
            MyQueryNew = "SELECT * FROM EnergyMeter where MeterNo='" &
        txtMeterNo.Text & "' and BilledMonth='" & cboMonths.Text & "'
"
```

```
414.            Set RSEnergyMeterModify =
CreateObject("ADOCE.Recordset.3.0")
415.            RSEnergyMeterModify.Open MyQueryNew, CNEnergyMeter,
adOpenKeyset,
                 AdLockOptimistic
416.            If RSEnergyMeterModify.RecordCount > 0 Then
417.                MsgBox "For this Meter Number For this month Record
already
                     Exits"
418.            Else
419.                Dim i As Integer
420.                For i = 1 To RSEnergyMeterNew.RecordCount
421.                 If RSEnergyMeterNew.Fields("BilledMonth") =
MyMonthText Then
422.                     txtAddress.Text =
RSEnergyMeterNew.Fields("Address")
423.                     txtInitialReading.Text =
                           RSEnergyMeterNew.Fields("PresentReading")
424.                 Else
425.                     RSEnergyMeterNew.MoveNext
426.                 End If
427.                Next
428.                RSEnergyMeterNew.Close
429.                Set RSEnergyMeterNew = Nothing
430.                cmdSave.Enabled = True
431.                txtPresentReading.SetFocus
432.            End If
433.            RSEnergyMeterModify.Close
434.            Set RSEnergyMeterModify = Nothing
435.       Else
436.            txtAddress.Enabled = True
437.            txtInitialReading.Enabled = True
438.            RSEnergyMeterNew.Close
439.            Set RSEnergyMeterNew = Nothing
440.            cmdSave.Enabled = True
441.       End If
442. End Sub
```

Following is the line-by-line explanation of the source code:

- **Lines 1–15:** Declaration of variables.
- **Lines 16–31:** Definition of the `cmdADD_Click()` event, to enter data for a new record.
  - **Line 17:** Calling the procedure `EnableFields`, to enable all text fields.
  - **Line 20:** Calling the procedure `ClearAllFields`, to clear all the text boxes.
  - **Line 22:** Calling the procedure `DisablecmdButtons`, to disable the command buttons.

  - **Line 28:** Calling the procedure `AddMonthsToComboBox`, to add months to the combo box.
  - **Line 29:** Calling the procedure `BilledMonthToComboBox`, to set the current month in the combo box.
- **Lines 32–43:** Definition of the `cmdClose_Click()` event, to cancel the operation or close the application.
  - **Line 34:** Calling the procedure `Form_OKClick` event, to close the application.
  - **Line 36:** Calling the procedure `EnablecmdButtons`,to enable the command buttons.
  - **Line 39:** Calling the procedure `ClearAllFields`, to clear all the text boxes.
  - **Line 40:** Calling the procedure `Display`, to assign database fields data to text fields.
  - **Line 41:** Calling the procedure `DisableFields`, to disable all text fields.
- **Lines 44–71:** Definition of the `cmdDelete_Click()` event, to delete a record.
  - **Lines 45–48:** Creating a recordset and finding the current record in the database.
  - **Line 52:** Deleting a record from the database.
  - **Lines 53–54:** Closing the recordset.
  - **Line 55:** Calling the procedure `RefreshDB`, to refresh the database.
- **Lines 72–77:** Definition of the `cmdFirst_Click()` event, to display the first record.
- **Lines 78–83:** Definition of the `cmdLast_Click()` event, to display the last record.
- **Lines 84–107:** Definition of the `cmdModify_Click()` event, to get the record to be modified.
- **Lines 108–118:** Definition of the `cmdNext_Click()` event, to display the next record.
  - **Line 111:** Checking for the last record.
- **Lines 119–129:** Definition of the `cmdPrevious_Click()` event, to display the previous record.
  - **Line 122:** Checking for the first record.
- **Lines 130–203:** Definition of the `cmdSave_Click()` event, to add a new record or update an existing record.
  - **Line 135:** Checking for a duplicate record.
  - **Line 140:** Adding a new record to database.
  - **Line 141:** Calling the procedure `AddDataFromFieldsToDB`, to assign text fields data to database fields.
  - **Line 157:** Checking for a duplicate record.
  - **Line 158:** Checking whether the ID changed.
  - **Line 162:** Getting the record to be modified.

- **Lines 204–224:** Definition of the `Form_Load()` event, to display the first record's data while the application is loading.
- **Lines 225–231:** Definition of the `Form_OKClick()` event, to close the record set, the connection, and the application.
- **Lines 232–245:** Definition of the `AddMonthsToComboBox()` procedure, to add months to the combo box.
- **Lines 246–255:** Definition of the `EnablecmdButtons()` procedure, to enable all command buttons.
- **Lines 256–265:** Definition of the `DisablecmdButtons()` procedure, to disable all command buttons.
- **Lines 266–274:** Definition of the `DisableFields()` procedure, to disable all text fields.
- **Lines 275–283:** Definition of the `EnableFields()` procedure, to enable all text fields.
- **Lines 284–294:** Definition of the `Display()` procedure, to assign database field data to text fields.
- **Lines 295–303:** Definition of the `ClearAllFields()` procedure, to clear all text fields.
- **Lines 304–314:** Definition of the `RefreshDB()` procedure, to refresh the database.
- **Lines 315–323:** Definition of the `AddDataFromFieldsToDB()` procedure, to assign text field data to database fields.
- **Lines 324–356:** Definition of the `BilledMonthToComboBox()` procedure, to set the current month in the combo box.
- **Lines 357–383:** Definition of the `MonthsInTextFormat()` procedure, to assign month numbers to the text format.
- **Lines 384–400:** Definition of the `CreateDBandTable()` procedure, to create the database and the table.
  - **Line 388:** Creating the database with `EnergyMeterDB.cdb` and saving it in the specified location provided: `\My Documents\EnergyMeter\`.
  - **Lines 389–396:** Creating a string SQL containing table name and the field names. The type and size of each field are also specified here.
  - **Line 397:** Executing the string that creates a table with table name `EnergyMeter`, including the fields `SNo`, `Date`, `MeterNo`, `BilledMonth`, `Address`, `InitialReading`, and `PresentReading`.
  - **Line 398:** Creating an index on `SNo`.
- **Lines 401–432:** Definition of the `txtMeterNo_LostFocus()` event, to check whether billing has been done for a given meter number for the current month.

Executing the program

Execute the program using the following steps:

1. Invoke eMbedded Visual Tools 3.0. A window will open showing tabs for Existing Projects, New Projects, and Recent Projects. Select the New projects tab and choose Windows CE for Pocket PC Project; the default form will be displayed.
2. On the menu bar, select Project ⇨ Project Properties. Set the project name as "EnergyConsumptionDetails," save the form as `EnergyConsumption.ebf`, and save the project as `EnergyConsumption.ebp`.
3. Select the form and set the following form properties in the Properties window:
   - Name: `frmEnergyMeter`
   - Caption: `Energy Meter Details`
   - Height: 4380
   - Width: 3780
4. Select the required controls from the Toolbox and set them as shown in Figure 11-4.

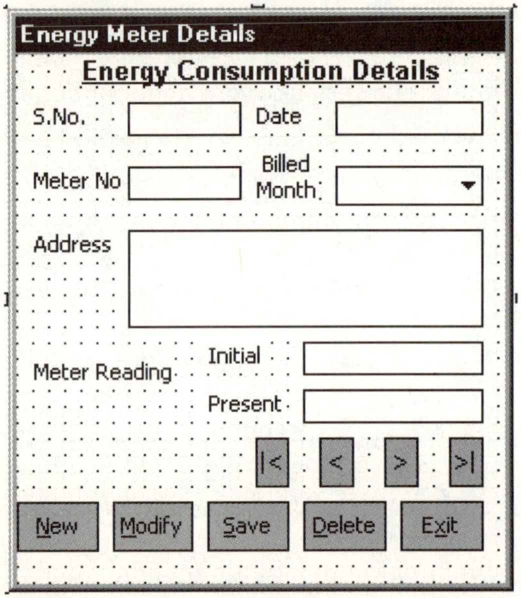

Figure 11-4: Form for the collection of energy meter readings

The Energy Consumption Details title shown in bold at the top of the form is a Label control. Set the label properties as follows:

- Name: `lblEnergyConsumptionDetails`
- Caption: `Energy Consumption Details`

- Font: Arial, Bold.

S.No. is a Label control. Set the label properties as follows:

- Name: `lblSNo`
- Caption: `S.No.`

Date is a Label control. The label properties are to be set as follows:

- Name: `lblDate`
- Caption: `Date`

Meter No. is a Label control. Set the label properties as follows:

- Name: `lblMeterNo`
- Caption: `Meter No`

Billed Month is a Label control. Set the label properties as follows:

- Name: `lblMonth`
- Caption: `Billed Month`

Address is a Label control. The label properties are to be set as follows:

- Name: `lblAddress`
- Caption: `Address`

Meter Reading is a Label control. Set the label properties as follows:

- Name: `lblMeterReading`
- Caption: `Meter Reading`

Initial is a Label control. Set the label properties as follows:

- Name: `lblInitial`
- Caption: `Initial`

Present is a Label control. The label properties are to be set as follows:

- Name: `lblPresent`
- Caption: `Present`

The text box next to the S.No. label is a Text Box control. The text box properties should be set as follows:

- Name: `txtSNo`
- MaxLength: `8`

The text box next to the Date label is a Text Box control. Set the text box properties as follows:

- Name: `txtDate`
- MaxLength: `10`

The text box next to the Meter No. label is a Text Box control. The text box properties should be set as follows:

- Name: `txtMeterNo`
- MaxLength: `10`

The combo box next to the Billed Month label is a Combo Box control. Set the combo box properties as follows:

- Name: `cboMonths`

The combo box contains all the months in a year.

The text box next to the Address label is a Text Box control. Set the text box properties as follows:

- Name: `txtAddress`
- MaxLength: `250`

The text box next to the Initial label is a Text Box control. The text box properties should be set as follows:

- Name: `txtInitialReading`
- MaxLength: `10`

The text box next to the Present label is a Text Box control. Set the Text Box properties as follows:

- Name: `txtPresentReading`
- MaxLength: `10`

The |< command button shown is a Command Button control. Set the command button properties as follows:

- Name: `cmdFirst`
- Caption: |<

Functionality: When clicked, this button displays the first record available in the database.

The < command button shown is the Command Button control. The command button properties should be set as follows:

- Name: `cmdPrevious`
- Caption: <

Functionality: When clicked, this button displays the previous record available in the database.

The > command button shown is a Command Button control. Set the command button properties as follows:

- Name: `cmdNext`
- Caption: >

Functionality: When clicked, this button displays the next record available in the database.

The >| command button shown is a Command Button control. The command button properties should be set as follows:

- Name: `cmdLast`
- Caption: >|

Functionality: When clicked, this button displays the last record available in the database.

The New command button shown is a Command Button control. The command button properties are to be set as follows:

- Name: `cmdADD`
- Caption: `&New`

Functionality: When clicked, this button clears all the text fields and enables the user to enter data.

The Modify command button shown is a Command Button control. Set the command button properties as follows:

- Name: `cmdModify`
- Caption: `&Modify`

Functionality: When clicked, this button enables user to modify the values of the currently displayed record.

The Save command button shown is a Command Button control. Set the command button properties as follows:

- Name: `cmdSave`
- Caption: `&Save`

Functionality: When clicked, this button saves the existing record, which may be either a new record or a modified record.

The Delete command button shown is a Command Button control. Set the command button properties as follows:

- Name: `cmdDelete`
- Caption: `&Delete`

Functionality: When clicked, this button deletes the existing record after asking for a confirmation.

The Exit command button shown is a Command Button control. The command button properties should be set as follows:

- Name: `cmdClose`
- Caption: E&xit

Functionality: When clicked, this button unloads the application.

5. On the menu bar, select Project ⇨ References ⇨ Microsoft CE ADO Control 3.0. This reference is used for database connectivity.
6. In the Run menu, select Execute or click the Run button on the toolbar.

Output

When you execute the program, the screen shown in Figure 11-5 is displayed. The first record in the database is displayed here. You can add, delete, or modify the records or navigate through the records in the database with the buttons provided.

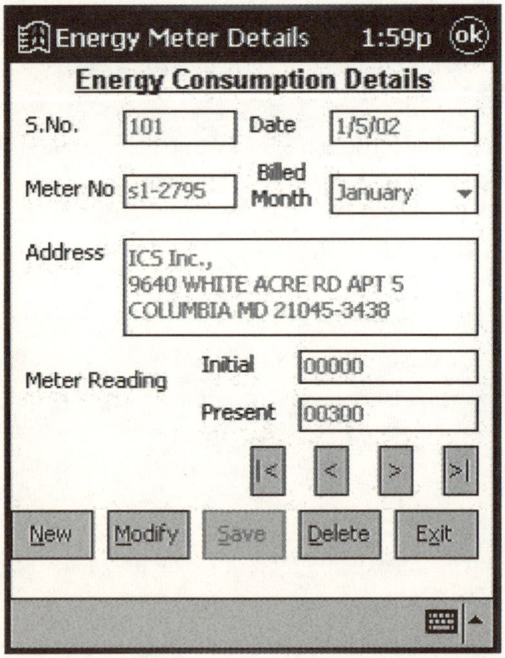

Figure 11-5: Ouptut screen on a Pocket PC for the energy meter reading

Synchronizing Data Between the Desktop and Pocket PC

The field personnel can synchronize the data in various application programs — such as Outlook Express and Access — between the desktop system and the Pocket PC using ActiveSync. ActiveSync 3.5 can be downloaded from the URL `http://www.microsoft.com/mobile/pocketpc/downloads/activesync35.asp`. The ActiveSync software has to be installed on a desktop running Windows 2000/NT. You can connect the Pocket PC to the desktop through a serial interface, USB, or Ethernet interface, or using Infrared; Ethernet offers the fastest speed. After connecting the desktop and the Pocket PC, run ActiveSync on the desktop, select the program for which data needs to be synchronized, and the data is automatically synchronized between the desktop and the Pocket PC.

Summary

This chapter demonstrated the development of embedded database applications using Pocket PC hardware. The two applications presented — a salary survey and an energy meter reading program — are useful for field personnel who obtain the data from a field survey and then upload the remote database to a corporate database for later processing. To achieve the data transfer between the databases on the desktop and the handheld computer, the constraints imposed for a Pocket Access database are described. The projects presented here can be easily extended for a variety of field applications.

Chapter 12

Networked Java-Enabled Information Appliances

In This Chapter

- Developing a Customer Relations Management (CRM) module for field personnel
- Developing location-based service software for access over the Internet
- Developing a network-enabled process control system for monitoring over the Internet

Networked Java-enabled information appliances have found relevant application in a variety of areas. Mobile devices can access information on the Internet or corporate intranet; the user merely needs to enter a URL. Any embedded system can be network-enabled, and the information on the appliance can be obtained over the Internet or corporate intranet by making the appliance Java-enabled. If a Web server is also embedded in the embedded system, it can contain a home page, which can be accessed through a normal desktop browser over the Internet. This chapter demonstrates how to develop information appliances using Hewlett-Packard's Chai Appliance Platform, which provides an excellent platform for developing mobile data applications and networked embedded appliances very easily and very fast.

Development Environment

To execute the projects described in this chapter, you need the following:

- A Windows NT system
- J2SDK 1.2 or later, which can be downloaded from `www.java.sun.com/downloads`
- HP's Chai Appliance Platform (Chai VM, Chai Server, and ChaiFarer), which can be downloaded from `www.hp.com/go/embedded`. The readme files for each of these modules explain the installation procedure and classpath settings.
- A database engine such as MS Access or MS SQL, running on the Windows NT system. The explanation here pertains to MS SQL.

You can install the Chai Appliance Platform on a desktop connected to a LAN, and the database can run on the server of the LAN. Alternatively, you can install the Chai Appliance Platform and the database on the desktop itself. This platform provides a Chai Server on which you can develop the server-side components. The ChaiFarer will be on the client side, and the client can be a mobile device such as a mobile phone or a PDA. By simply providing a URL corresponding to the service available in the Chai Server, the user can retrieve the information onto the mobile device.

Project: Customer Relations Management Software

Customer support engineers need timely information on a daily basis in order to respond to the questions, problems, and complaints they receive. A corporate Customer Relations Management (CRM) software package contains data based on the service calls received. Each customer support engineer can download the data corresponding to his or her service calls and then attend to the calls. This downloading of the information can be done from anywhere, through a Java-enabled mobile phone or a PDA over a wireless network. This project demonstrates this application.

The project involves the development of a database to hold information about customer complaints and the names of the customer support engineers who attend to the service calls. It also describes how to develop the server modules (customer module and service engineer module).

Project files

The project consists of three modules:

- A customer module with which a user can register a complaint and obtain a complaint ID.
- A service engineer module with which a service engineer can get the details of the customer calls he or she has to attend to on a particular date.
- A database that stores the complaints and details of service engineers. The database can be in MS Access or MS SQL. The description provided here pertains to MS SQL.

The customer module contains the following files:

- `ICustomer.java`: This file contains the declaration of the user-defined method `customerStore`.
- `CustomerImpl.java`: This file contains implementation of the user-defined method. The `homepage` method is called when the object's home page is requested. Every Chai Server object can have a home page that can be displayed by a Web browser. The `exportMethods` method is called to retrieve information about the operations an object supports, and that object will respond with a list of operations and the arguments that each operation requires.
- `CustomerStub.java`: After the ChaiService Engine has parsed all the information from the request of the mobile device, that is, the ChaiFarer, it builds the appropriate data structures and calls the ChaiService dispatcher, which is the starting point into the

ChaiService implementation. The ChaiService dispatcher provides a stub into the ChaiService implementation and uses the method name to determine which method to call (in our case, it is `customerStore`). The ChaiService dispatcher then passes the argument list and environment structures on to the method `customerStore` implementation in `CustomerImpl`.

- `Customer.pkg`: This file contains information about the classes to be installed in the Chai Server. Provided here is information about the Worker object, Worker status, home page lists, MIME types, and descriptions of the customer service, etc.

The service engineer module contains the following files:

- `ICSEngineer.java`: This file contains the user-defined method `CSEngineerRetrieve` declaration.
- `CSEngineerImpl.java`: This file contains the implementation of the user-defined method `CSEngineerRetrieve`, to retrieve information from the database, `homepage` method, and `exportMethods` method.
- `CSEngineerStub.java`: This file contains information for the dispatcher. The ChaiService dispatcher provides a stub in the ChaiService implementation and uses the method name to determine which method to call (in our case, it is `CSEngineerRetrieve`). The ChaiService dispatcher then passes the argument list and environment structures on to the method `CSEngineerRetrive` implementation in `CSEngineerImpl`.
- `CSEngineer.pkg`: This file contains information about the classes to be installed in the Chai Server. This file contains the description of the classes related to the customer service engineer module.

Database details

You need to create a database consisting of the following tables:

- A table to store the customer-support details. The table name is CSD.

Field Name	***Field Type***	***Description***
Tno	int	Ticket Number or Complaint ID
cdatetime	smalldatetime	Complaint Date and Time
cname	varchar(25)	Customer Name
address	varchar(60)	Customer Address
support	varchar(60)	Complaint Description/Support Details

- A service engineer timetable (note that when the complaint is registered, the data in the following table has to be populated) The table name is CSETT.

Field Name	***Field Type***	***Description***
Tno	int	Ticket Number or Complaint ID
adatetime	smalldatetime	Schedule Date and Time
Cseid	varchar(15)	Service Engineer ID

- A table of service engineer details. The table name is CSED.

Field Name	***Field Type***	***Description***
cseid	varchar(15)	Service Engineer ID
name	varchar(25)	Service Engineer Name
qualification	varchar(20)	Service Engineer Qualification

Source code listings

The source code for the customer module and support engineer module is provided in Listings 12-1 to 12-4 and 12-5 to 12-8, respectively. Each source code listing is immediately followed by an explanation of the code.

Customer module

Using this module, the customer can register a complaint. He or she enters a name and address, and a description of the problem. After the details have been filled out and the complaint is submitted with a click of the Submit button, the complaint is registered and a ticket number (complaint ID) is displayed.

Listing 12-1: Source code for ICustomer.java

```
1.import hp.chaiserver.*;
2.public interface ICustomer {
// customerStore is a User Defined Method
3.  public void customerStore(String format,ArgVector args, Environment
env);
4.  }
```

- **Line 1:** Imports the package needed for the various classes used to build this application.
- **Line 2:** Declaration of the public interface `ICustomer`.
- **Line 3:** This is a user-defined method, `customerStore`.

Listing 12-2: Source code for CustomerImpl.java

```
1.import java.net.*;
2.import java.util.*;
3.import java.io.*;
4.import hp.chaiserver.*;
5.import java.sql.*;
```

```
public class CustomerImpl implements ICustomer, IChaiServer {
  public void initWorkerArgs(String name, IDaemon daemon, ArgVector
args) {
     System.out.println("What is sysLogCommand\t" +
Utils.getSysLogCmd() + "\n");
  }
// customerStore is an implementation of the method defined in ICustomer
  public void customerStore(String retFormat, ArgVector args,
Environment   env) {
// The next two lines obtain utility objects from the environment
// retStat is used to return status information
// html is used to stream HTML data back to client

     HTMLStatus retStat = env.getErrResponder();
     HTMLHelper html = (HTMLHelper) env.getHTMLHelper();
// The following lines extract an argument from the ArgVector
// The CustomerString argument contains the String entered into the
// form.

     String cname = args.getArg("cname");
     String address = args.getArg("address");
     String support = args.getArg("support");

     if((cname == null) || (address == null) || (support == null)) {
        retStat.sendError(400, "Insufficient Information");
        return;
     }
// Customer name trimmed to 25 characters.
     if(cname.length() > 25){
       cname = cname.substring(0,24);
     }
// Customer address trimmed to 60 characters.
     if(address.length() > 60){
       address = address.substring(0,59);
     }
// Customer Support details trimmed to 60 characters.
     if(support.length() > 60){
       support = support.substring(0,59);
     }
// The following lines check the return format specified by
// client. This implementation supports HTML and Text.
// An error is sent to the client if return format is not supported
     try {
       if(retFormat.equalsIgnoreCase("html")) {
// startHTMLDoc sends the Header information to the client
         html.startHTMLDoc();
// send a <HR> Tag
         html.startTag("HR");
// send a <CENTER> Tag
```

```
         html.startTag("CENTER");
// send a </CENTER> Tag
         html.endTag("CENTER");
         int count=0;
         try {
           Class.forName("sun.jdbc.odbc.JdbcOdbcDriver");
           java.sql.Connection conn =
DriverManager.getConnection("jdbc:odbc:chaidsn");
           Statement st = conn.createStatement();
           ResultSet rs1= st.executeQuery("select count(*) from csd");

           Calendar calendar = Calendar.getInstance();
           String date = new String(calendar.get(Calendar.YEAR)+"-
"+(calendar.get(Calendar.MONTH)+1)+"-"+calendar.get(Calendar.DATE));
           String time = new
String(calendar.get(Calendar.HOUR)+":"+calendar.get(Calendar.MINUTE)+":"
+calendar.get(Calendar.SECOND));
           String datetime = new String(date+" "+ time);
           if(rs1.next()) {
              count = rs1.getInt(1) + 1;
           } else {
              count = 1;
             }
           rs1.close();
           html.startTag("CENTER");
           html.appendSimpleHTMLPara("Customer Support", "H2");
           html.endTag("CENTER");
           int rs = st.executeUpdate("insert into csd
values("+count+",'"+datetime+"','"+cname+"','"+address+"','"+support+"')
");
           st.close();
           conn.close();
         }catch(Exception e) { e.printStackTrace(); }
         html.startNewHTMLParagraph();
         html.appendSimpleHTMLPara("Your complaint is Registered",
"H2");
         html.appendSimpleHTMLPara("and your ticket no is :"+count,
"H2");
// send a <HR> Tag
         html.startTag("HR");
// send a sequence of tags to create a link to
// this server's homepage
         html.sendHomeLink();
// send the end of document tags
         html.endHTMLDoc();
       } else if(retFormat.equalsIgnoreCase("txt")) {
// send the MIME header for a text document and
// append the contents of CustomerString to the document
        html.sendText(cname);
```

```
      } else {
//retStat.send400("Return type " + retFormat + " not supported");
          retStat.sendError(400, "Return type" + retFormat + "not
supported");
          }
      }catch(IOException IO) {  }
     }
// homePage is an implementation of a method declared in
hp.chaiserver.IChaiServer
  public void homePage(OutputStream out, Environment env) {
// get HTMLHelper object from Environment. Used for streaming HTML
HTMLHelper html = (HTMLHelper) env.getHTMLHelper();
//System.out.println("What is sysLogComand\t" + Utils.getSysLogCmd() +
"\n");
  try {
// send HTML document header
    html.startHTMLDoc();
// send <CENTER> Tag
    html.startTag("CENTER");
// send Heading String
//html.appendSimpleHTMLPara("Customer Object", "H1");
    html.appendSimpleHTMLPara("Customer ChaiService", "H1");
// send </CENTER> Tag
    html.endTag("CENTER");
// send <HR> Tag
    html.startTag("HR");
// send Tag sequence to start a form
    html.startForm("GET", "/this.customer");
// send <P> Tag
    html.startNewHTMLParagraph();
// add Hidden field called customerStore
// Note this represents the Method name to be
// called when the form is submitted. See the
// customerStore method above.
    html.addHiddenField("customerStore", "html"); // Method and
return type
// add a Text field called CSEID
// Note this represents the argument CSEID
// accessed in the customerStore method above.
    html.appendSimpleHTMLPara("Customer Name: ", "H3");
    html.addTextField("cname", 30, null);
    html.startNewHTMLParagraph();
    html.appendSimpleHTMLPara("Address: ", "H3");
    html.addTextField("address", 60, null);
    html.appendSimpleHTMLPara("Support Required/Problem:", "H3");
    html.addTextField("support", 60, null);
// send <P> Tag
    html.startNewHTMLParagraph();
// add a Submit button and reset button
```

```
    html.addSubmitButton("Submit");
    html.addResetButton();
// send the </FORM> tag
    html.endForm();
// send <HR> Tag
    html.startTag("HR");
// send a sequence of Tags for a link to
// the home page of the local server
    html.sendHomeLink(); // send end of document Tags
    html.endHTMLDoc();
   }catch (IOException io) {  }
}
// Export is an implementation of a method declared in
hp.chaiserver.IChaiServer
  public void exportMethods(OutputStream out, String str,
Environment env) {
// get HTMLHelper object from Environment. Used for streaming HTML
    HTMLHelper html = (HTMLHelper) env.getHTMLHelper();
    if(str.equalsIgnoreCase("html")) {
      try {
// send HTML document header
          html.startHTMLDoc();
// send <CENTER> Tag
          html.startTag("CENTER");
// send Heading String
          html.appendSimpleHTMLPara("Customer ChaiService", "H1");
// send </CENTER> Tag
          html.endTag("CENTER");
// send <HR> Tag
          html.startTag("HR");
          html.appendSimpleHTMLPara("Method support: customerStore",
"H3");
          html.appendSimpleHTMLPara("Argument: CustomerString",
"H3");
          html.sendHomeLink(); // send end of document Tags
          html.endHTMLDoc();
        }catch(IOException io) {}
     } else if(str.equalsIgnoreCase("txt")) {
        try {
          html.sendText("Method: customerStore\nArgument:
CustomerString");
        } catch(IOException io) {  }
     } else {
        HTMLStatus retStat = env.getErrResponder();
        retStat.sendError(400);
     }
   }
}
```

- **Lines 1–5:** Importing the packages needed for the various classes used to build this application, such as those for communicating with the Internet, streaming facility, file I/O, database access, Chai services, text manipulations, etc.
- **Line 6:** Declaration of a public class, `CustomerImpl`.
- **Lines 7–9:** Implementation of the method `initWorkerArgs`, of the `IChaiServer` interface.
- **Lines 10–69:** Implementation of the user-defined method `customerStore`.
- **Line 10:** Declaration of the method `customerStore`.
- **Line 11:** Initializing the `HTMLStatus` object.
- **Line 12:** Initializing the `HTMLHelper` object for streaming HTML.
- **Lines 13–15:** Getting the information for customer name, address, and support details.
- **Lines 16–19:** Validation of customer name, address, and support details.
- **Lines 20–22:** Customer name trimmed to 25 characters.
- **Lines 23–25:** Customer address trimmed to 60 characters.
- **Lines 26–28:** Customer support details trimmed to 60 characters.
- **Line 30:** Checking the return format specified by the client.
- **Line 37:** Indicating the `Class` object to initialize the SQL driver.
- **Line 38:** Creating an object of `java.sql.Connection`.
- **Line 40:** Retrieving the number of rows in the CSD table.
- **Line 42:** Getting the date in the format "YYYY-MM-DD".
- **Line 43:** Getting the time in the format "HH:MM:SS".
- **Line 54:** Inserting a row in the CSD table with the retrieved values.
- **Lines 70–95:** Implementation of the method `homepage`. This method is called when the object's home page is requested. Every Chai Server object can have a home page, which can be displayed by a Web browser.
    - **Line 77:** This method is used to start an HTML form. The HTML content is sent across the network. The following HTML code is generated:

      ```
      <FORM ACTION="/this.customer" METHOD="GET">
      ```

    - **Line 79:** This method is used to add a hidden field to a form. The following HTML code is generated:

      ```
      <INPUT TYPE="hidden" NAME=" customerStore" VALUE="html">
      ```

    - **Lines 80–89:** User interface design.

- **Line 90:** Appending the end-of-form tag to the form. The following HTML code is generated:

```
</FORM>
```

- **Lines 96–118:** Implementation of the method `exportMethods`. This method is called to retrieve information about the operations that an object supports. The object should respond with a descriptive list of operations and the set of arguments that each operation requires.

Listing 12-3: Source code for CustomerStub.java

```
1. import hp.chaiserver.*;
2. import java.io.*;

3. public final class CustomerStub extends Worker implements IWorker {
4.    private final String DISCOVERPROPS = new
String("__DISCOVERPROPS");
5.    public final String WORKER_VERSION = "ChaiServer.3.0.0.0";
6.    private final static String CustomerStore = new
String("customerStore");

// Helper methods for worker
7.    protected Object createObject() {
8.      return (Object) new CustomerImpl();
9.    }

10.   protected String getObjectClassName() {
11.     return new String("CustomerImpl");
12.   }

13.   protected boolean invokeMethod(Object obj, String method, String
format)
14.  throws Exception {
15.    CustomerImpl cs_obj = (CustomerImpl) obj;

16.    if(method.equalsIgnoreCase(DISCOVERPROPS)) {
17.      webProtocol.sendToClient("HTTP/1.1 200 OK\r\n");
18.      webProtocol.sendToClient("MIME-Version: 1.0\r\n");
19.      webProtocol.sendToClient("Server: HP/ChaiServer 3.0\r\n");
20.      webProtocol.sendToClient("Content-type: text/plain\r\n\n");
21.      webProtocol.sendToClient("customerStore");
22.      return true;
23.    }
24.    if (method.equalsIgnoreCase(CustomerStore))
25.     cs_obj.customerStore(format, args, reqEnv);
26.    else
27.     return false;
28.    return true;
```

```
29.   }
30.   protected boolean isObjectInstance(Object obj) {
31.     return (obj instanceof CustomerImpl);
32.   }

// Methods callable outside of worker
33.   public String getVersion() {
34.      return WORKER_VERSION;
35.   }
36. }
```

- **Lines 1–2:** Importing the packages.
- **Line 3:** Declaration of the public class `CustomerStub`; its base class is `Worker` and it implements the `IWorker` interface.
- **Lines 7–35:** Implementation of the Helper methods for `Worker`.
  - **Lines 7–9:** Implementation of the `createObject` method. It returns an instance of the `CustomerImpl` class.
  - **Lines 10–12:** Implementation of the `getObjectClassName` method. It returns the class name `CustomerImpl`.
  - **Lines 13–29:** Implementation of the `invokeMethod` method.
  - **Lines 30–32:** Implementation of the `isObjectInstance` method.
  - **Lines 33–35:** Implementation of the `getVersion` method.

Listing 12-4: Source code for Customer.pkg

```
Worker
file:///g:\ChaiAP\Multi_Target\ChaiWeb\home\repository\Customer\Customer
Stub.class {
StartWorkers 2
MimeType hp/customer customer
DependsOn /repository/Customer/ICustomer.class
DependsOn /repository/Customer/CustomerImpl.class
Object {
Name Customer
LinkID this.customer
Description  ** CRM Appliction -- Customer **
CreateLink
}
}
```

The code given in this listing is self-explanatory — the file `Customer.pkg` contains information about the file corresponding to the class, the MIME type, and the dependency on the various class files and the name of the object.

To test this module, follow these steps:

1. Save the `ICustomer.java`, `CustomerImpl.java`, `CustomerStub.java`, and `Customer.pkg` files in the `\Multi_Platform\ChaiWeb\home\repository\Customer` folder.
2. To compile the Java programs, run MS-DOS, go to your `\Multi_Platform\ChaiWeb\home\repository\Customer` folder, and enter the following commands:

```
javac ICustomer.java
javac CustomerImpl.java
javac CustomerStub.java
```

3. Create a DSN with the name "chaidsn."
4. Start the Chai Server. Run MS-DOS, go to your Chai Server installation directory, and enter **ChaiServer**:

```
c:\ChaiServer: ChaiServer <return>
```

   To stop Chai Server, enter **s** or **stop** at the Chai Server prompt.

5. Open ChaiFarer (Start ⇨ Programs ⇨ ChaiFarer2.0 ⇨ ChaiFarer).
6. Load the customer package in Chai Server.
   - Click the Open button in ChaiFarer.

     Enter the following in the Address field: **http://<*hostname*>:4242/this.loader**, where *hostname* is the name of the host on which the Chai Server is running.

     The Chai Server Package Loader page will be displayed.

   - To install the customer package, enter the package URL:

```
http://<hostname>:4242/repository/customer/Customer.pkg
```

   - Select the Copy Class Files and Install Permanently checkboxes and Click the Install Package button (see Figure 12-1).

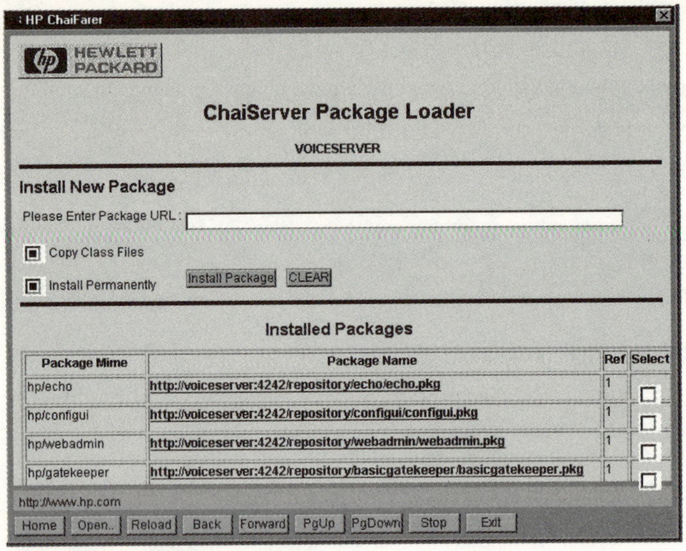

Figure 12-1: Installing a new package

7. Run the customer application.
   - Click the Open button in ChaiFarer (see Figure 12-2).
   - Enter the following in the Address field: **http://<*hostname*>:4242/this.customer**. The screen shown in Figure 12-2 will be displayed.

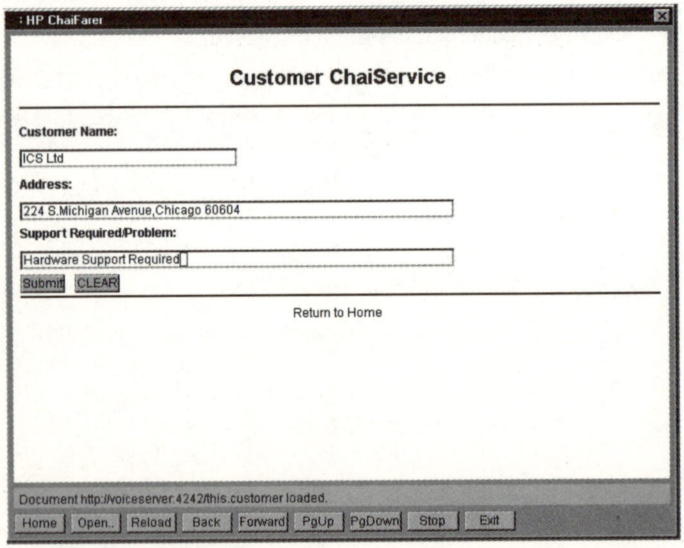

Figure 12-2: Use the ChaiFarer screen to register a customer complaint.

8. Fill in the fields and click the Submit button; this will display the complaint ID shown in Figure 12-3.

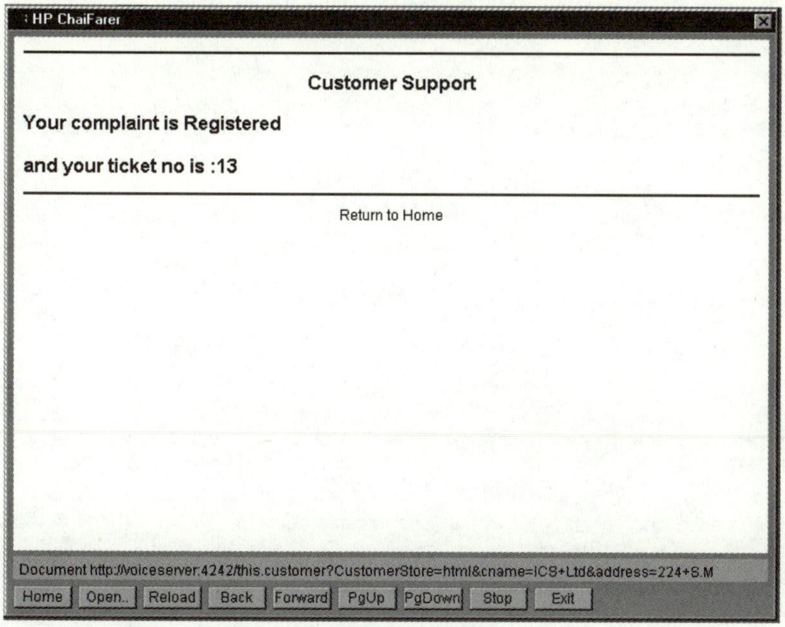

Figure 12-3: Display of the complaint ID on ChaiFarer

Service engineer module

In this module, if a service engineer wants to know the schedule, he or she enters the service engineer ID, selects the particular date, and clicks Submit. Then the schedule for that particular service engineer is displayed. Listing 12-5 gives the source code for `ICSEngineer.java`. Listing 12-6 gives the source code for `CSEngineerImpl.java`. Listing 12-7 gives the source code for `CSEngineerStub.java`, and Listing 12-8 gives the source code for `CSEngineer.pkg`.

Listing 12-5: Source code for ICSEngineer.java

```
1. import hp.chaiserver.*;
2. public interface ICSEngineer {
//CSEngineerRetrieve is an User Defined Method
3.   public void CSEngineerRetrieve(String format,ArgVector args,
Environment env);
4. }
```

- **Line 1:** Importing the package needed for the various classes used to build this application.
- **Line 2:** Declaration of a public interface, `ICSEngineer`.

- **Line 3:** Declaration of a user-defined method, `CSEngineerRetrieve`.

Listing 12-6: Source code for CSEngineerImpl.java

```
import java.net.*;
import java.util.*;
import java.io.*;
import hp.chaiserver.*;
import java.sql.*;

public class CSEngineerImpl implements ICSEngineer, IChaiServer {
  public void initWorkerArgs(String name, IDaemon daemon, ArgVector
args) {
    System.out.println("What is sysLogComand\t" +
Utils.getSysLogCmd() + "\n");
  }
// CSEngineerRetrieve is an implementation of the method defined in
ICSEngineer
  public void CSEngineerRetrieve(String retFormat, ArgVector args,
Environment env) {
// The next two lines obtain utility objects from the environment
// retStat is used to return status information
// html is used to stream HTML data back to client
    HTMLStatus retStat = env.getErrResponder();
    HTMLHelper html = (HTMLHelper) env.getHTMLHelper();
// The following lines extract an argument from the ArgVector
// The CSEngineerString argument contains the String entered into the
// form.
// If CSEngineerString is null then an error is sent to the client
    String cseid = args.getArg("CSEID");
    String dd = args.getArg("DD");
    String mm = args.getArg("MM");
    String yyyy = args.getArg("YYYY");
    if(cseid == null) {
//retStat.send400("Not enough arguments");
      retStat.sendError(400, "Not enough arguments");
      return;
     }
// The following lines check the return format specified by
// client. This implementation supports HTML and Text.
// An error is sent to the client if return format is not supported
    try {
      if(retFormat.equalsIgnoreCase("html")) {
// startHTMLDoc sends the Header information to the client
      html.startHTMLDoc();
// send a <HR> Tag
      html.startTag("HR");
// send a <CENTER> Tag
      html.startTag("CENTER");
```

```
// send contents of CSEngineerString formatted as H1 in a paragraph
//html.appendSimpleHTMLPara(CSEngineerString, "H1");
// send a </CENTER> Tag
        html.endTag("CENTER");
        try {
          Class.forName("sun.jdbc.odbc.JdbcOdbcDriver");
          java.sql.Connection conn =
DriverManager.getConnection("jdbc:odbc:chaidsn");
          Statement st = conn.createStatement();
          String name=null;
          try {
            ResultSet rs1= st.executeQuery("select name from cseid
where cseid like '"+cseid+"'");
          while(rs1.next())
          {
            name = rs1.getString(1);
          }
          rs1.close();
        }catch(Exception e)
         { html.appendSimpleHTMLPara(" No CS Engineer found with ID
"+cseid, "H3");
         }
        html.startTag("CENTER");
        html.appendSimpleHTMLPara(name+"'s Schedule on
"+dd+"/"+mm+"/"+yyyy, "H2");
        html.endTag("CENTER");
        ResultSet rs = st.executeQuery("select
adatetime,cname,address,support from csett,csd where csett.tno = csd.tno
and datepart(dd,adatetime)= '"+dd+"' and datepart(mm,adatetime)=
'"+mm+"' and datepart(yyyy,adatetime)= '"+yyyy+"' and csett.cseid like
'"+cseid+"'");
        while(rs.next())
        {
          String str1 = rs.getString(1);
          String str2 = rs.getString(2);
          String str3 = rs.getString(3);
          String str4 = rs.getString(4);
          html.appendSimpleHTMLPara(" "+str1.substring(11)+" "+str2+"
"+str3+" "+str4, "H3");
          System.out.print(str1.substring(11));
          System.out.print(str2);
          System.out.print(str3);
          System.out.println(str4);
        }
        rs.close();
        st.close();
        conn.close();
      }catch(Exception e) {
```

```
    html.appendSimpleHTMLPara(" No CS Engineer found with ID
"+cseid, "H3");
    }
// send a <HR> Tag
    html.startTag("HR");
// send a sequence of tags to create a link to
// this server's homepage
    html.sendHomeLink();
// send the end of document tags
   html.endHTMLDoc();
   } else if(retFormat.equalsIgnoreCase("txt")) {
// send the MIME header for a text document and
// append the contents of CSEngineerString to the document
     htm l.sendText(cseid);
   } else {
//retStat.send400("Return type " + retFormat + " not supported");
     retStat.sendError(400, "Return type" + retFormat + "not
supported");
    }
   }catch(IOException IO){}
  }
// homePage is an implementation of a method declared in
hp.chaiserver.IChaiServer
  public void homePage(OutputStream out, Environment env){
// get HTMLHelper object from Environment. Used for streaming HTML
    HTMLHelper html = (HTMLHelper) env.getHTMLHelper();
      try {
// send HTML document header
         html.startHTMLDoc();
// send <CENTER> Tag
         html.startTag("CENTER");
// send Heading String
//html.appendSimpleHTMLPara("CSEngineer Object", "H1");
         html.appendSimpleHTMLPara("CSEngineer ChaiService", "H1");
// send </CENTER> Tag
         html.endTag("CENTER");
// send <HR> Tag
         html.startTag("HR");
// send Tag sequence to start a form
         html.startForm("GET", "/this.csengineer");
// send <P> Tag
         html.startNewHTMLParagraph();
// add Hidden field called CSEngineerRetrieve
// Note this represents the Method name to be
// called when the form is submitted. See the
// CSEngineerRetrieve method above.
         html.addHiddenField("CSEngineerRetrieve", "html");
// Method and return type
// add a Text field called CSEID
```

```
// Note this represents the argument CSEID
// accessed in the CSEngineerRetrieve method above.
            html.appendSimpleHTMLPara("CSE ID: ", "H3");
            html.addTextField("CSEID", 30, null);
            html.startNewHTMLParagraph();
            html.appendSimpleHTMLPara("Date: ", "H3");
            html.addTextField("DD", 2, "DD");
            html.addTextField("MM", 2, "MM");
            html.addTextField("YYYY", 4, "YYYY");
// send <P> Tag
            html.startNewHTMLParagraph();
// add a Submit button and reset button
            html.addSubmitButton("Submit");
            html.addResetButton();
// send the </FORM> tag
            html.endForm();
// send <HR> Tag
            html.startTag("HR");
// send a sequence of Tags for a link to
// the home page of the local server
            html.sendHomeLink(); // send end of document Tags
            html.endHTMLDoc();
        }catch (IOException io){}
    }
// Export is an implementation of a method declared in
hp.chaiserver.IChaiServer
    public void exportMethods(OutputStream out, String str,
Environment env) {
// get HTMLHelper object from Environment. Used for streaming HTML
        HTMLHelper html = (HTMLHelper) env.getHTMLHelper();
        if(str.equalsIgnoreCase("html")) {
            try {
// send HTML document header
                html.startHTMLDoc();
// send <CENTER> Tag
                html.startTag("CENTER");
// send Heading String
                html.appendSimpleHTMLPara("CSEngineer ChaiService", "H1");
// send </CENTER> Tag
                html.endTag("CENTER");
// send <HR> Tag
                html.startTag("HR");
                html.appendSimpleHTMLPara("Method support:
CSEngineerRetrieve", "H3");
                html.appendSimpleHTMLPara("Argument: CSEngineerString",
"H3");
                html.sendHomeLink(); // send end of document Tags
                html.endHTMLDoc();
            }catch(IOException io) {}
```

```
115.       } else if(str.equalsIgnoreCase("txt")) {
116.         try {
117.           html.sendText("Method: CSEngineerRetrieve\nArgument:
CSEngineerString");
118.         } catch(IOException io) {}
119.       } else {
120.         HTMLStatus retStat = env.getErrResponder();
121.         retStat.sendError(400);
122.       }
123.    }
124. }
```

- **Lines 1–5:** The familiar code to import packages.
- **Line 6:** Declaration of a public class, `CSEngineerImpl`.
- **Lines 7–9:** Implementation of the method `initWorkerArgs` of `IChaiServer` interface.
- **Lines 10–69:** Implementation of the user-defined method `CSEngineerRetrieve`.
  - **Line 10:** Declares the method `CSEngineerRetrieve`.
  - **Line 11:** Initializes the `HTMLStatus` object.
  - **Line 12:** Initializes the `HTMLHelper` object for streaming HTML.
  - **Lines 13–15:** Gets the information for the following: service engineer ID, day, month, and year.
  - **Lines 16–20:** Validation of `cseid`.
  - **Line 22:** Checks the return format specified by the client.
  - **Line 28:** Indicates the `Class` object for initializing the SQL driver.
  - **Line 29:** Creates an object of `java.sql.Connection`.
  - **Line 30:** Creates an instance of `java.sql.Statement`.
  - **Line 33:** Retrieves the service engineer name from the CSED table along with the corresponding service engineer ID.
  - **Line 45:** Retrieves the schedule of service engineers for the corresponding date from the CSETT and CSD tables.
  - **Line 66:** Returns an error message if the format specified by the client is not supported.
- **Lines 70–96:** Implementation of the method `homepage`. This method is called when the object's home page is requested. Every Chai Server object can have a home page, which can be displayed by a Web browser.
  - **Line 78:** This method is used to start an HTML form. The HTML content is sent across the network. The following HTML code is generated:

```
<FORM ACTION="/this.csengineer " METHOD="GET">
```

- **Line 80:** This method is used to add a hidden field to a form. The following HTML code is generated:

```
<INPUT TYPE="hidden" NAME=" CSEngineerRetrieve " VALUE="html">
```

- **Lines 81–90:** This is a user interface design.
- **Line 91:** Appends the end-of-form tag to the form. The following HTML code is generated:

```
</FORM>
```

- **Lines 97–119:** Implementation of the method `exportMethods`. This method is called to retrieve information about what operations an object supports. The object should respond with a descriptive list of operations and the set of arguments that each operation requires.

Listing 12-7: Source code for CSEngineerStub.java

```
import hp.chaiserver.*;
import java.io.*;

public final class CSEngineerStub extends Worker implements IWorker {
  private final String DISCOVERPROPS = new String("__DISCOVERPROPS");
  public final String WORKER_VERSION = "ChaiServer.3.0.0.0";
  private final static String CSEngineerRetrieve    = new
String("CSEngineerRetrieve");
// Helper methods for worker
  protected Object createObject() {
    return (Object) new CSEngineerImpl();
  }
  protected String getObjectClassName() {
    return new String("CSEngineerImpl");
  }

  protected boolean invokeMethod(Object obj, String method, String
format)
throws Exception {
    CSEngineerImpl cs_obj = (CSEngineerImpl) obj;

    if(method.equalsIgnoreCase(DISCOVERPROPS)) {
      webProtocol.sendToClient("HTTP/1.1 200 OK\r\n");
      webProtocol.sendToClient("MIME-Version: 1.0\r\n");
      webProtocol.sendToClient("Server: HP/ChaiServer 3.0\r\n");
      webProtocol.sendToClient("Content-type: text/plain\r\n\n");
      webProtocol.sendToClient("CSEngineerRetrieve");
      return true;
    }
    if (method.equalsIgnoreCase(CSEngineerRetrieve))
      cs_obj.CSEngineerRetrieve(format, args, reqEnv);
    else
```

```
27.         return false;
28.       return true;
29.     }

30.     protected boolean isObjectInstance(Object obj) {
31.       return (obj instanceof CSEngineerImpl);
32.     }

// Methods callable outside of worker
33.     public String getVersion() {
34.       return WORKER_VERSION;
35.     }
36. }
```

- **Lines 1–2:** Importing the packages.
- **Line 3:** Declaration of a public class `CSEngineerStub`; its base class is `Worker` and it implements the `IWorker` interface.
- **Lines 7–35:** Implementation of Helper methods for `Worker`.
  - **Lines 7–9:** Implementation of the `createObject` method, which returns an instance of the `CSEngineerImplclass`.
  - **Lines 10–12:** Implementation of the `getObjectClassName` method, which returns the class name `CSEngineerImpl`.
  - **Lines 13–29:** Implementation of the `invokeMethod` method.
  - **Lines 30–32:** Implementation of the `isObjectInstance` method.
  - **Lines 33–35:** Implementation of the `getVersion` method.

Listing 12-8: Source code for CSEngineer.pkg

```
Worker
file:///g:\ChaiAP\Multi_Target\ChaiWeb\home\repository\CSEngineer\CSEngi
neerStub.class  {
StartWorkers 2
MimeType hp/csengineer csengineer
DependsOn /repository/CSEngineer/ICSEngineer.class
DependsOn /repository/CSEngineer/CSEngineerImpl.class
Object {
Name CSEngineer
LinkID this.csengineer
Description  ** CRM Appliction -- CSEngineer **
CreateLink
}
}
```

To test this module, follow these steps:

1. Save the `ICSEngineer.java`, `CSEngineerImpl.java`, `CSEngineerStub.java`, and `CSEngineer.pkg` files in your `\Multi_Platform\ChaiWeb\home\repository\CSEngineer` folder.
2. To compile the Java programs, run MS-DOS, go to your `\Multi_Platform\ChaiWeb\home\repository\CSEngineer` folder, and enter the following commands:

```
javac ICSEngineer.java
javac CSEngineerImpl.java
javac CSEngineerStub.java
```

3. Create a DSN with the name "chaidsn."
4. To start Chai Server, run MS-DOS, go to your Chai Server installation directory, and enter **ChaiServer**.

```
C:\ChaiServer: ChaiServer <return>
```

   To stop Chai Server, enter **s** or **stop** at the Chai Server prompt.

5. Open ChaiFarer (Start ⇨ Programs ⇨ ChaiFarer2.0 ⇨ ChaiFarer).
6. Load the customer package in Chai Server.
   - Click the Open button in ChaiFarer.
   - Enter the following in the Address field: **http://<*hostname*>:4242/this.loader**, where *hostname* is the name of the host where the Chai Server is running.

     The Chai Server Package Loader page will be displayed.
   - To install the customer package, enter the package URL:

```
        http://<hostname>:4242/repository/csengineer/CSEngineer.pkg
```

   - Select the Copy Class Files and Install Permanently checkboxes and click Install Package. Note that in line 1 of Listing 12-8, you need to replace `g:` with the appropriate drive on which your Chai Server is installed.
7. Run the Customer Service Engineer application:
   - Click the Open button in ChaiFarer.
   - Enter the following in the Address field: **http://<*hostname*>:4242/this.csengineer**. This will display the screen shown in Figure 12-4.

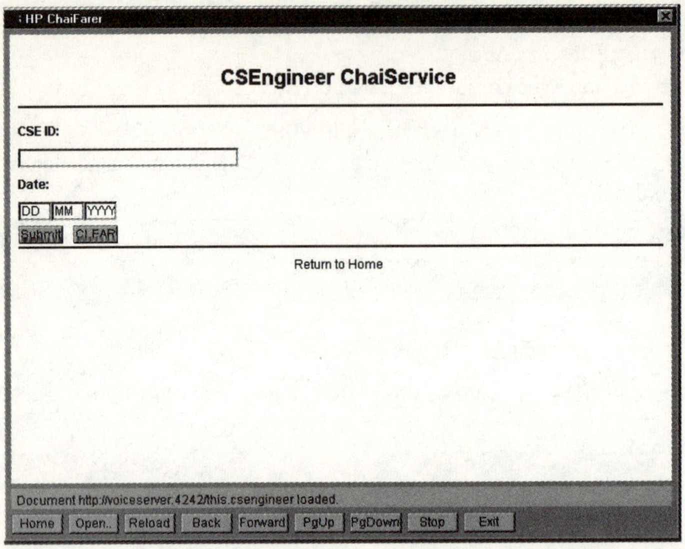

Figure 12-4: Inputting the customer support engineer details in ChaiFarer

8. Fill in the form and then click Submit. This will display the screen shown in Figure 12-5. The customer support engineer can use this form to get the details of his or her schedule for a particular date.

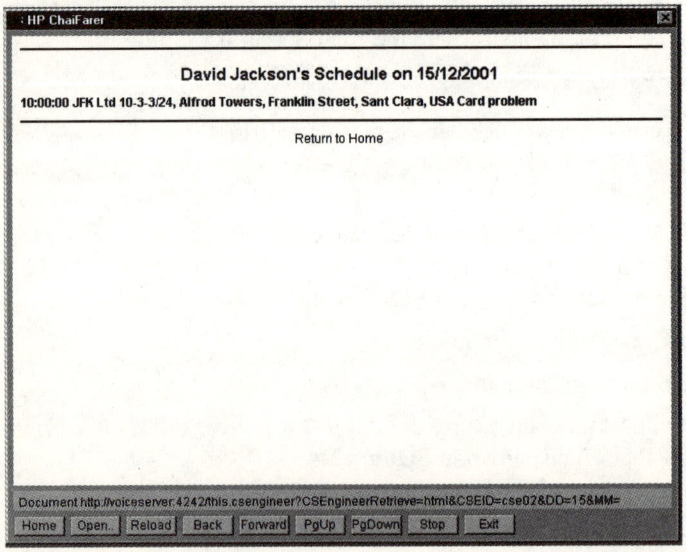

Figure 12-5: Output in ChaiFarer, showing details of service calls to be attended

Embedding the application

Embedding the application in a mobile device is essentially running ChaiFarer with support for HTML, HTTP, and optionally XML. ChaiFarer requires about 220KB for a complete user interface supporting XML, HTML, and HTTP. Our application on the Chai Server system takes about 15KB of memory. The Chai VM is one of the most compact Virtual Machines available, and the development environment facilitates very fast and easy development of network-enabled Java appliances. Note that you can access the same information from a desktop as well.

Project: Developing Location-based Services

This project demonstrates the development of location-based services. Visitors to a new city want information about the hotels and restaurants it offers. If they have a Java-enabled mobile device, which can automatically pass the location data to a server, the server will obtain the information corresponding to that location and provide the details on the mobile device. Of course, if the mobile device has no capability for location information, the user has to enter the longitude and latitude values.

Project files

This project consists of the following four files.

- `ILocation.java`: This file contains declaration of the user-defined method `locationRetrieve`.
- `LocationImpl.java`: This file contains the implementation of the user-defined method `locationRetrieve` for retrieving information from the database, `homepage` method, and `exportMethods` method.
- `LocationStub.java`: This file contains information for the dispatcher. The ChaiService dispatcher provides a stub into the ChaiService implementation and uses the method name to determine which method to call — in our case, `locationRetrieve`. The ChaiService dispatcher then passes the argument list and environment structures on to the method `locationRetrieve` in the `LocationImpl` class.
- `Location.pkg`: This file contains information about the classes to be installed in the Chai Server. This information is the location of the stub class and MIME types.

Database details

Latitude and Longitude Values. The table name is LALValues.

Field Name	*Field Type*	*Description*
Latitude	Float	Latitude Value
Longitude	Float	Longitude Value
City	varchar(20)	Name of the City

Hospitals Details. The table name is Hospitals.

Field Name	*Field Type*	*Description*
City	varchar(20)	Name of the City
Hname	varchar(30)	Hospital Name
Location	varchar(30)	Location of the Hospital

Restaurants Details. The table name is Restaurants.

Field Name	*Field Type*	*Description*
City	varchar(20)	Name of the City
Rname	varchar(30)	Restaurant Name
Location	varchar(30)	Location of the Restaurant

Source code listings

The source code listings for the four project files are given in Listings 12-9 to 12-12, along with explanations of the code.

Listing 12-9: Source code for Ilocation.java

```
1. import hp.chaiserver.*;
2. public interface ILocation {
3.   public void locationRetrieve(String format,ArgVector args,
Environment env);
4. }
```

- **Line 1:** Importing the package needed for the various classes used to build this application.
- **Line 2:** Declaration of the public interface `ILocation`.
- **Line 3:** Declaration of the user-defined method `locationRetrieve`.

Listing 12-10: Source code for LocationImpl.java

```
import java.net.*;
import java.util.*;
import java.io.*;
import hp.chaiserver.*;
import java.sql.*;
public class LocationImpl implements ILocation, IChaiServer {
```

```
public void initWorkerArgs(String name, IDaemon daemon, ArgVector args) {
    System.out.println("What is sysLogComand\t" + Utils.getSysLogCmd() + "\n");
}
// locationRetrieve is an implementation of the method defined in ILocation
public void locationRetrieve(String retFormat, ArgVector args, Environment env) {
// The next two lines obtain utility objects from the environment
// retStat is used to return status information
// html is used to stream HTML data back to client
    HTMLStatus retStat = env.getErrResponder();
    HTMLHelper html = (HTMLHelper) env.getHTMLHelper();
// The following lines extract an argument from the ArgVector
// The LocationString argument contains the String entered into the
// form.
// If LocationString is null then an error is sent to the client
    String latitude = args.getArg("latitude");
    String longitude = args.getArg("longitude");
    String service = args.getArg("service");
    System.out.println("Latitude: "+latitude);
    System.out.println("Longitude: "+longitude);
    System.out.println("Service: "+service);
    if((latitude == null) || (longitude == null) || (service == null)) {
      retStat.sendError(400, "Not enough arguments");
      return;
    }
// The following lines check the return format specified by
// client. This implementation supports HTML and Text.
// An error is sent to the client if return format is not supported
    try {
      if(retFormat.equalsIgnoreCase("html")) {
// startHTMLDoc sends the Header information to the client
      html.startHTMLDoc();
// send a <HR> Tag
      html.startTag("HR");
// send a <CENTER> Tag
      html.startTag("CENTER");
// send a </CENTER> Tag
      html.endTag("CENTER");
      try {
        Class.forName("sun.jdbc.odbc.JdbcOdbcDriver");
        java.sql.Connection conn = DriverManager.getConnection("jdbc:odbc:chaidsn");
        Statement st = conn.createStatement();
        ResultSet rs1= st.executeQuery("select city from lalvalues where latitude =
```

```
+latitude+" and longitude = "+longitude);
        String city=null;
        int flag = 0;
        while(rs1.next())
        {
          city = rs1.getString(1);
          flag = 1;
        }
        rs1.close();
        html.startTag("CENTER");
        html.appendSimpleHTMLPara("Location Services", "H2");
        html.endTag("CENTER");
        if(flag==0){
          html.appendSimpleHTMLPara("Unable to locate", "H2");
         }  else {
           ResultSet rs=null;
           html.appendSimpleHTMLPara("You are located  in "+ city,
"H2");
           if (service.equalsIgnoreCase("Hospital"))
           {
             rs=st.executeQuery("select * from hospitals where city
like '"+city+"'");
             html.appendSimpleHTMLPara("Nearest Hospitals: ", "H3");
           }
         else if (service.equals("Restaurant"))
         {
             rs=st.executeQuery("select * from restaurants where
city like '"+city+"'");
             html.appendSimpleHTMLPara("Nearest Restaurants: ",
"H3");
         }
         while(rs.next())
         {
           String sname = rs.getString(2);
           String location = rs.getString(3);
           html.appendSimpleHTMLPara(sname+" at "+location, "H3");
           html.startNewHTMLParagraph();
         }
       rs.close();
       st.close();
       conn.close();
     }
   }catch(Exception e) { e.printStackTrace(); }
// send a <HR> Tag
   html.startTag("HR");
// send a sequence of tags to create a link to
// this server's homepage
   html.sendHomeLink();
// send the end of document tags
```

```
    html.endHTMLDoc();
    } else if(retFormat.equalsIgnoreCase("txt")) {
// send the MIME header for a text document and
// append the contents of LocationString to the document
       html.sendText(service);
    } else {
//retStat.send400("Return type " + retFormat + " not supported");
       retStat.sendError(400, "Return type" + retFormat + "not
supported");
    }
  }catch(IOException IO){}
}
// homePage is an implementation of a method declared in
hp.chaiserver.IChaiServer
  public void homePage(OutputStream out, Environment env){
// get HTMLHelper object from Environment. Used for streaming HTML
    HTMLHelper html = (HTMLHelper) env.getHTMLHelper();
    try {
// send HTML document header
      html.startHTMLDoc();
// send <CENTER> Tag
      html.startTag("CENTER");
// send Heading String
//html.appendSimpleHTMLPara("Location Object", "H1");
      html.appendSimpleHTMLPara("Location Services", "H1");
// send </CENTER> Tag
      html.endTag("CENTER");
// send <HR> Tag
      html.startTag("HR");
// send Tag sequence to start a form
      html.startForm("GET", "/this.location");
// send <P> Tag
      html.startNewHTMLParagraph();
// add Hidden field called locationRetrieve
// Note this represents the Method name to be
// called when the form is submitted. See the
// locationRetrieve method above.
      html.addHiddenField("locationRetrieve", "html"); // Method and
return type
      html.appendSimpleHTMLPara("Latitude: ", "H3");
      html.addTextField("latitude", 8, null);
      html.startNewHTMLParagraph();
      html.appendSimpleHTMLPara("Longitude: ", "H3");
      html.addTextField("longitude", 8, null);
      html.startNewHTMLParagraph();
      html.appendSimpleHTMLPara("Recommend a ", "H3");
       html.startSelect("service",1,false);
       html.addSelectOption("Hospital","Hospital",true);
       html.addSelectOption("Restaurant","Restaurant",false);
```

```
        html.endSelect();
// send <P> Tag
        html.startNewHTMLParagraph();
// add a Submit button and reset button
        html.addSubmitButton("Submit");
        html.addResetButton();
// send the </FORM> tag
        html.endForm();
// send <HR> Tag
        html.startTag("HR");
// send a sequence of Tags for a link to
// the home page of the local server
        html.sendHomeLink(); // send end of document Tags
        html.endHTMLDoc();
      }catch (IOException io){}
   }
// Export is an implementation of a method declared in
hp.chaiserver.IChaiServer
   public void exportMethods(OutputStream out, String str,
Environment env) {
// get HTMLHelper object from Environment. Used for streaming HTML
     HTMLHelper html = (HTMLHelper) env.getHTMLHelper();
     if(str.equalsIgnoreCase("html")) {
       try {
// send HTML document header
          html.startHTMLDoc();
// send <CENTER> Tag
          html.startTag("CENTER");
// send Heading String
          html.appendSimpleHTMLPara("Location ChaiService", "H1");
// send </CENTER> Tag
          html.endTag("CENTER");
// send <HR> Tag
          html.startTag("HR");
          html.appendSimpleHTMLPara("Method support:
locationRetrieve", "H3");
          html.appendSimpleHTMLPara("Argument: LocationString",
"H3");
          html.sendHomeLink(); // send end of document Tags
html.endHTMLDoc();
       }catch(IOException io) {}
     } else if(str.equalsIgnoreCase("txt")) {
     try {
       html.sendText("Method: locationRetrieve\nArgument:
LocationString");
     } catch(IOException io) {}
    } else {
      HTMLStatus retStat = env.getErrResponder();
      retStat.sendError(400);
```

```
134.         }
135.     }
136. }
```

- **Lines 1–5:** The familiar code, importing the packages needed for the various classes used to build this application. This includes packages used for processes such as communicating with the Internet, streaming facility, file I/O, database access, Chai services, text manipulations, etc.
- **Line 6:** Declaration of the public class `LocationImpl`.
- **Lines 7–9:** Implementation of the method `initWorkerArgs` of the Chai Server interface.
- **Lines 10–78:** Implementation of the user-defined method `locationRetrieve`.
  - **Line 10:** Declaration of the method `locationRetrieve`.
  - **Line 11:** Initializing the `HTMLStatus` object.
  - **Line 12:** Initializing the `HTMLHelper` object for streaming HTML.
  - **Lines 13–15:** Getting the information for latitude, longitude, and service.
  - **Lines 16–19:** Validation of latitude, longitude, and service.
  - **Line 21:** Checking the return format specified by the client.
  - **Line 27:** Indicating the `Class` object for initializing the SQL driver.
  - **Line 28:** Creating an object of `java.sql.Connection`.
  - **Line 29:** Creating an instance of `java.sql.Statement`.
  - **Line 30:** Retrieving the name of the city from the `lalvalues` table for corresponding latitude and longitude.
  - **Line 49:** Retrieving the hospitals for the corresponding city from the hospitals table.
  - **Line 54:** Retrieving the restaurants for the corresponding city from the restaurants table.
  - **Line 66:** Returns an error message if the format specified by the client is not supported.
- **Lines 79–109:** Implementation of the method `homepage`. This method is called when the object's home page is requested.
  - **Line 87:** This method is used to start an HTML form. The HTML content is sent across the network. The following HTML code is generated:

    ```
    <FORM ACTION="/this.location" METHOD="GET">
    ```

  - **Line 89:** This method can be used to add a hidden field to a form. The following HTML code is generated:

    ```
    <INPUT TYPE="hidden" NAME=" locationRetrieve" VALUE="html">
    ```

- **Lines 90–103:** This is a user interface design.
- **Line 104:** Appends the end-of-form tag to the form. The following HTML code is generated:

```
</FORM>
```

- **Lines 113–135:** Implementation of the method `exportMethods`. This method is called to retrieve information about what operations an object supports. The object should respond with a descriptive list of operations and the set of arguments that each operation requires.

Listing 12-11: Source code for LocationStub.java

```
import hp.chaiserver.*;
import java.io.*;
public final class LocationStub extends Worker implements IWorker {
  private final String DISCOVERPROPS = new String("__DISCOVERPROPS");
  public final String WORKER_VERSION = "ChaiServer.3.0.0.0";
  private final static String locationRetrieve       = new
String("locationRetrieve");
// Helper methods for worker
  protected Object createObject() {
    return (Object) new LocationImpl();
  }
  protected String getObjectClassName() {
    return new String("LocationImpl");
  }
  protected boolean invokeMethod(Object obj, String method, String
format)
throws Exception {
    LocationImpl cs_obj = (LocationImpl) obj;
    if(method.equalsIgnoreCase(DISCOVERPROPS)) {
      webProtocol.sendToClient("HTTP/1.1 200 OK\r\n");
      webProtocol.sendToClient("MIME-Version: 1.0\r\n");
      webProtocol.sendToClient("Server: HP/ChaiServer 3.0\r\n");
      webProtocol.sendToClient("Content-type: text/plain\r\n\n");
      webProtocol.sendToClient("locationRetrieve");
      return true;
     }
    if (method.equalsIgnoreCase(locationRetrieve))
      cs_obj.locationRetrieve(format, args, reqEnv);
    else
      return false;
    return true;
  }

  protected boolean isObjectInstance(Object obj) {
    return (obj instanceof LocationImpl);
  }
```

```
// Methods callable outside of worker
33.   public String getVersion() {
34.     return WORKER_VERSION;
35.   }
36. }
```

- **Lines 1–2:** Importing the packages needed for the various classes used to build this application. This includes packages used for file I/O, Chai services, text manipulations, etc.
- **Line 3:** Declaration of the public class `LocationStub`; its base class is `Worker` and it implements the `IWorker` interface.
- **Lines 7–35:** Implementation of Helper methods for `Worker`.
  - **Lines 7–9:** Implementation of the `createObject` method, which returns an instance of `LocationImplclass`.
  - **Lines 10–12:** Implementation of the `getObjectClassName` method, which returns the class name `LocationImpl`.
  - **Lines 13–29:** Implementation of the `invokeMethod` method.
  - **Lines 30–32:** Implementation of the `isObjectInstance` method.
  - **Lines 33–35:** Implementation of the `getVersion` method.

Listing 12-12: Source code for Location.pkg

```
Worker
file:///g:\ChaiAP\Multi_Target\ChaiWeb\home\repository\Location\Location
Stub.class  {
StartWorkers 2
MimeType hp/location location
DependsOn /repository/Location/ILocation.class
DependsOn /repository/Location/LocationImpl.class
Object {
Name Location
LinkID this.location
Description  ** Location Services **
CreateLink
}
}
```

Testing the application

The procedure for testing the application is as follows:

1. Save the `ILocation.java`, `LocationImpl.java`, `LocationStub.java`, and `Location.pkg` files in your `\Multi_Platform\ChaiWeb\home\repository\Location` folder.

2. To compile the Java programs, run MS-DOS, go to your `\Multi_Platform\ChaiWeb\home\repository\Location` folder, and enter the following commands:

```
javac ILocation.java
javac LocationImpl.java
javac LocationStub.java
```

3. Create a DSN with the name "chaidsn."

4. To start the Chai Server, run MS-DOS, go to your Chai Server installation directory, and enter **ChaiServer**.

```
C:\ChaiServer: ChaiServer <return>
```

To stop Chai Server, enter **s** or **stop** at the Chai Server prompt.

5. Open ChaiFarer (Start ⇨ Programs ⇨ ChaiFarer2.0 ⇨ ChaiFarer).

6. Load the location services package in Chai Server.
   - Click the Open button in ChaiFarer.
   - Enter the following in the Address field: **http://<*hostname*>:4242/this.loader**, where *hostname* is the name of the host on which the Chai Server is running.

     The Chai Server Package Loader page will be displayed.
   - To install the location package, enter the package URL:

     ```
     http://<hostname>:4242/repository/location/Location.pkg
     ```
   - Select the Copy Class Files and Install Permanently checkboxes and click the Install Package button.

7. Run the location services application.
   - Click the Open button in ChaiFarer.
   - Enter the following in the Address field: **http://<*hostname*>:4242/this.location**. This will display the screen shown in Figure 12-6.

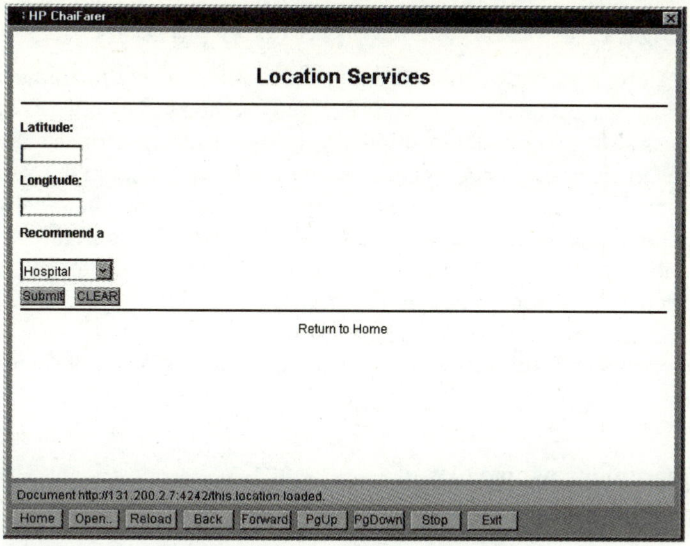

Figure 12-6: Form for inputting data for location services

8. Fill in the form and click the Submit button. This will display the location-based information, as shown in Figure 12-7.

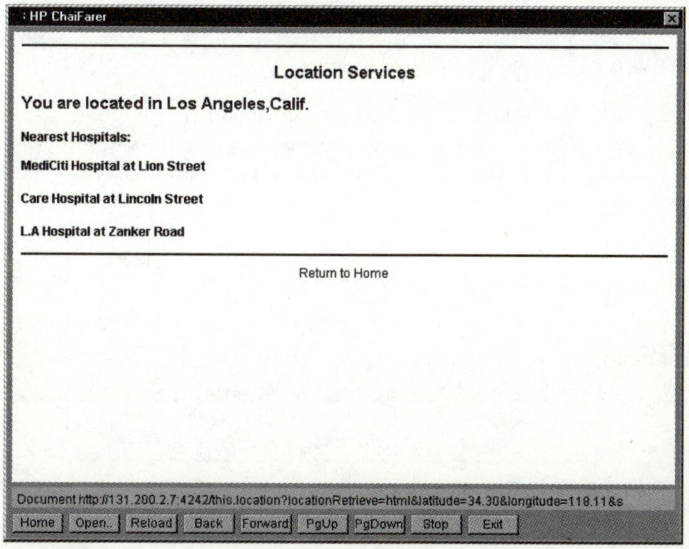

Figure 12-7: Location-based information displayed on the device running ChaiFarer

Project: Embedded Process Control System

An embedded system in a process control unit continuously monitors a set of parameters (such as temperatures). If the embedded system is network-enabled and an HTTP server is also embedded, it can be accessed from a remote location through a normal desktop using a standard browser, such as Internet Explorer. This capability is demonstrated in this project. Temperatures are generated automatically through a program that simulates the process control unit. The fluctuations in the temperatures can be monitored. You can also configure the Chai Server so that it automatically sends an alert (through e-mail) whenever a change in temperature has been detected. In our application, to simulate the boiler temperatures, we generate the temperatures through a Java program and store them in a database. Any security application can be developed using the concepts demonstrated in this application.

Project files

This project consists of the following five files:

- `TempMeasure.java`: This file inserts the four temperature values in the database.
- `ISecurity.java`: This file contains the declaration of the user-defined method `securityRun`.
- `SecurityImpl.java`: This file contains implementation of the user-defined method `securityRun`, `homepage` method, which retrieves the information from the database for every one hour and advises the user of any fluctuation in the temperature; and also the implementation of the `exportMethods` method.
- `SecurityStub.java`: This file contains information for the dispatcher. The ChaiService dispatcher provides a stub into the ChaiService implementation and uses the method name to determine which method to call; in our case, it is `securityRun`.
- `Security.pkg`: This file contains information about the classes to be installed in the Chai Server. Details of Worker object, Worker Status, home page lists, MIME types, and description of the Security service are mentioned in this file.

Database details

We have one table, named Security, in the database. It stores the four temperatures, as shown in the following table.

Field Name	***Field Type***	***Description***
slno	int	Serial Number
tempat	smalldatetime	Date and time when temperatures are recorded
temp1	numeric(6,2)	Temperature of boiler1
temp2	numeric(6,2)	Temperature of boiler2

temp3	numeric(6,2)	Temperature of boiler3
temp4	numeric(6,2)	Temperature of boiler4

Source code listings

The source code for the five project files is given in Listings 12-13 to 12-17, along with code explanations.

Listing 12-13: Source code for TempMeasure.java

```
import java.sql.*;
import java.util.*;
public class TempMeasure implements Runnable
{
  static Thread thread;
  public TempMeasure(){
  }
  public void run()
  {
     int i=1,rows;
     try {
     Class.forName("sun.jdbc.odbc.JdbcOdbcDriver");
     java.sql.Connection conn =
DriverManager.getConnection("jdbc:odbc:chaidsn");
     Statement st = conn.createStatement();
     while(true){
       Calendar calendar = Calendar.getInstance();
       String date = new String(calendar.get(Calendar.YEAR)+"-
"+(calendar.get(Calendar.MONTH)+1)+"-"+calendar.get(Calendar.DATE));
       String time = new
String(calendar.get(Calendar.HOUR)+":"+calendar.get(Calendar.MINUTE)+":"
+calendar.get(Calendar.SECOND));
       int t1 = getTemp(0);
       int t2 = getTemp(1);
       int t3 = getTemp(2);
       int t4 = getTemp(3);
       String datetime = new String(date+" "+ time);
       rows = st.executeUpdate("insert into security
values("+i+",'"+datetime+"',"+t1+","+t2+","+t3+","+t4+")");
       System.out.println("Thread: "+i);
       try{
         thread.sleep(1000*60*60);
        }catch(Exception e){ e.printStackTrace(); }
       i++;
      }
     }catch(Exception e) { e.printStackTrace(); }
   }
   public int getTemp(int i){
     int t[] ={100,105,100,100};
```

```
35.     return t[i];
36.   }
37.   public static void main(String args[]){
38.     TempMeasure tm = new TempMeasure();
39.     thread = new Thread(tm);
40.     thread.start();
41.   }
42.}
```

- **Lines 1–2:** Importing the packages needed for the various classes used to build this application. The packages are for database access, Calendar, threads, and text manipulations.
- **Line 3:** Declaration of a public class, `TempMeasure`.
- **Line 5:** Defines a `Thread` object named `thread`.
- **Lines 6–7:** Default constructor null implementation.
- **Lines 8–32:** Implementation of the `run` method.
  - **Line 12:** Indicating the `Class` object for initializing the SQL driver.
  - **Line 13:** Creating an object of `java.sql.Connection`.
  - **Line 14:** Creating an instance of `java.sql.Statement`.
  - **Line 16:** Getting an instance of the `Calendar` class.
  - **Lines 17–18:** Initializing the date and time in the format of YYYY-MM-DD and HH:MM:SS, respectively.
  - **Lines 19–22:** Getting the temperatures t1, t2, t3, and t4 using the method `getTemp`.
  - **Line 23:** Creating the date and time string.
  - **Line 27:** Putting the thread in sleep mode for one hour.
- **Lines 33–36:** Implementation of the `getTemp` method.
- **Lines 37–41:** Implementation of the `main` method.
- **Line 38:** Creating an instance of the `TempMeasure` class named `tm`.
- **Line 39:** Creating a thread for the `tm` object.
- **Line 40:** Invoking the `run` method.

Listing 12-14: Source code for Isecurity.java

```
import hp.chaiserver.*;
public interface ISecurity {
  public void securityRun(String format,ArgVector args, Environment env);
}
```

- **Line 1:** Importing the basic package needed for the various classes used to build this application.
- **Line 2:** Declaration of the public interface `ISecurity`.
- **Line 3:** Declaration of a user-defined method, `securityRun`.

Listing 12-15: Source code for SecurityImpl.java

```
1.import java.net.*;
2.import java.util.*;
3.import java.io.*;
4.import java.sql.*;
5.import hp.chaiserver.*;
6.public class SecurityImpl implements ISecurity,
hp.chaiserver.IChaiServer{
7.  Environment env1;
8.  public void initWorkerArgs(String name, IDaemon daemon, ArgVector
args) {
9.  }
10.  Thread thread;
// securityRun is an implementation of the method defined in ISecurity
11.  public void securityRun(String retFormat, ArgVector args,
Environment env) {
// The next two lines obtain utility objects from the environment
// retStat is used to return status information
// html is used to stream HTML data back to client
12.     HTMLStatus retStat = env.getErrResponder();
13.     HTMLHelperBase html = (HTMLHelperBase) env.getHTMLHelper();
14.     try {
// Replace the following three lines of code with your implementation
15.       html.sendDataHeader("ChaiServer Object", null);
16.       html.sendData("<P>securityRun called");
17.       html.sendDataFooter();
18.     } catch (Exception exe) {
19.       Daemon.out.println("Exception thrown by HtmlHelper" + exe);
20.     }
21.  }
// homePage is an implementation of a method declared in
//hp.chaiserver.IChaiServer
22.  public void homePage(OutputStream out, Environment env) {
// get HTMLHelperBase object from Environment. Used for streaming HTML
23.     HTMLHelper html = (HTMLHelper) env.getHTMLHelper();
24.     try {
//html.startHTMLDoc();
25.       html.startHTMLMetaDoc("content=\"360\"");
// send <CENTER> Tag
26.       html.startTag("CENTER");
//send Heading String
27.       html.appendSimpleHTMLPara("Security Application", "H1");
```

```
send </CENTER> Tag
      html.endTag("CENTER");
// send <HR> Tag
      html.startTag("HR");
      try {
        java.sql.Connection conn,conn1;
        Statement st,st1;
        ResultSet rs,rs1;
        String ctime1,ptime1;
        int ct1,ct2,ct3,ct4,pt1,pt2,pt3,pt4,dt1,dt2,dt3,dt4;
        pt1=pt2=pt3=pt4=0;
        ct1=ct2=ct3=ct4=0;
        dt1=dt2=dt3=dt4=0;
////******        ******/////
        Class.forName("sun.jdbc.odbc.JdbcOdbcDriver");
        conn = DriverManager.getConnection("jdbc:odbc:test2000");
        st = conn.createStatement();
        rs = st.executeQuery("select * from security where slno =
(select count(*) from security)");
        while(rs.next()){
          ctime1 = rs.getString(2);
          ct1 = rs.getInt(3);
          ct2 = rs.getInt(4);
          ct3 = rs.getInt(5);
          ct4 = rs.getInt(6);
          System.out.println("CTime "+ctime1+"CT1 "+ct1+"CT2
"+ct2+"CT3 "+ct3+"CT4 "+ct4);
          html.appendSimpleHTMLPara("Current values:","H2");
          html.appendSimpleHTMLPara("Time "+ctime1+" Temp1: "+ct1+"
Temp2: "+ct2+" Temp3: "+ct3+" Temp4: "+ct4, "H3");
        }
        conn1 = DriverManager.getConnection("jdbc:odbc:test2000");
        st1 = conn1.createStatement();
        rs1 = st1.executeQuery("select * from security where slno =
(select count(*)-1 from security)");
        while(rs1.next()){
          ptime1 = rs1.getString(2);
          pt1 = rs1.getInt(3);
          pt2 = rs1.getInt(4);
          pt3 = rs1.getInt(5);
          pt4 = rs1.getInt(6);
          System.out.println("PTime "+ptime1+"PT1 "+pt1+"PT2
"+pt2+"PT3 "+pt3+"PT4 "+pt4);
          html.appendSimpleHTMLPara("Previous values:","H2");
          html.appendSimpleHTMLPara("Time: "+ptime1+" Temp1: "+pt1+"
Temp2: "+pt2+" Temp3: "+pt3+" Temp4: "+pt4, "H3");
        }
        dt1 = ct1 - pt1;
        dt2 = ct2 - pt2;
```

```
        dt3 = ct3 - pt3;
        dt4 = ct4 - pt4;
        if(dt1 < 0){
          dt1 = -dt1;
        }
        if(dt2 < 0){
          dt2 = -dt2;
        }
        if(dt3 < 0){
          dt3 = -dt3;
        }
        if(dt4 < 0){
          dt4 = -dt4;
        }
        if(dt1 > 5){
          System.out.println("Fluctuation in Temperature1: "+dt1);
          html.appendSimpleHTMLPara("Fluctuation in Temperature1: "+dt1, "H3");
        }
        if(dt2 > 5){
          System.out.println("Fluctuation in Temperature2: "+dt2);
          html.appendSimpleHTMLPara("Fluctuation in Temperature2: "+dt2, "H3");
        }
        if(dt3 > 5){
          System.out.println("Fluctuation in Temperature3: "+dt3);
          html.appendSimpleHTMLPara("Fluctuation in Temperature3: "+dt3, "H3");
        }
        if(dt4 > 5){
          System.out.println("Fluctuation in Temperature4: "+dt4);
          html.appendSimpleHTMLPara("Fluctuation in Temperature4: "+dt4, "H3");
        }
        rs.close();
        rs1.close();
        st.close();
        st1.close();
        conn.close();
        conn1.close();
////******        *****/////
      }catch(Exception e) {   }
// send <P> Tag
      html.startNewHTMLParagraph();
// send <HR> Tag
      html.startTag("HR");
// send a sequence of Tags for a link to
// the home page of the local server
      html.sendHomeLink(); // send end of document Tags
```

```
108.        html.endHTMLDoc();
109.      }catch (IOException io){}
110.    }
// exportMethods is an implementation of a method declared in
hp.chaiserver.IChaiServer
111.    public void exportMethods(OutputStream out, String str,
Environment env) {
// If you don't want to implement this Method, use the next three lines
of code
// HTMLStatus retStat = env.getErrResponder();
// retStat.sendError(400,"The exportMethods Property is not supported");
// return;
// Otherwise at least return the name of all methods
112.      HTMLHelperBase html = (HTMLHelperBase) env.getHTMLHelper();
// send HTML document header
113.      try {
114.        html.sendDataHeader("ChaiServer Object", null);
115.        html.sendData("<P>ISecurity has the following methods:<P>");
116.        html.sendData("<P>securityRun");
117.        html.sendDataFooter();
118.      } catch (Exception exe) {
119.        Daemon.out.println("Exception thrown by HtmlHelperBase" +
exe);
120.      }
121.    }
122. }
```

- **Lines 1–5:** Importing the packages needed for the various classes used to build this application.
- **Line 6:** Declaration of a public class, `SecurityImpl`.
- **Lines 8–9:** Implementation of the method `initWorkerArgs` of `IChaiServer` interface.
- **Lines 11–21:** Implementation of the user-defined method `securityRun`.
  - **Line 11:** Declaration of the method `securityRun`.
  - **Line 12:** Initializing the `HTMLStatus` object.
  - **Line 13:** Initializing the `HTMLHelperBase` object for streaming HTML.
- **Lines 22–110:** Implementation of the method `homepage`.
  - **Line 23:** Initializing the `HTMLHelper` object for streaming HTML.
  - **Line 25:** Generating the HTML metatag with refresh every 3,600 seconds (every hour). The following HTML code is generated:

```
<HTML>
<HEAD>
<TITLE> ChaiServer Object </TITLE>
<META HTTP-EQUIV="REFRESH" content="360"></HEAD>
```

```
<BODY >
```

- **Lines 31–38:** Variables declaration.
- **Line 39:** Indicates the `Class` object associated with the class or interface with the string name `sun.jdbc.odbc.JdbcOdbcDriver` to initialize the SQL driver.
- **Line 40:** Creating an object of `java.sql.Connection`.
- **Line 41:** Creating an instance of `java.sql.Statement`.
- **Line 42:** Retrieving the current (latest) record values from the security table.
- **Line 53:** Creating an object of `java.sql.Connection`.
- **Line 54:** Creating an instance of `java.sql.Statement`.
- **Line 55:** Retrieving the previous (penultimate) record values from the security table.
- **Lines 66–81:** Determing the difference between previous and current values.
- **Lines 82–97:** Indicating to the user if the difference is more than 5° C.
- **Lines 98–103:** Closing resultsets, statements, and connections.

- **Lines 111–121:** Implementation of the method `exportMethods`. This method is called to retrieve information about the operations that an object supports. The object should respond with a descriptive list of operations and the set of arguments that each operation requires.

Listing 12-16: Source code for SecurityStub.java

```
import hp.chaiserver.*;
import hp.chaiserver.security.*;
import java.io.*;
public final class SecurityStub extends Worker implements IWorker {
  private final String DISCOVERPROPS = new String("__DISCOVERPROPS");
  static String realmName = null;
  private IGateKeeperAuth gateK = null;
  private final String AUTOSEC = new String("AUTOSEC");
  public final String WORKER_VERSION = "ChaiServer.3.0.0.0";
  private final static String SECURITYRUN   = new
String("securityRun");
// Helper methods for worker
  protected Object createObject() {
    return (Object) new SecurityImpl();
  }
  protected String getObjectClassName() {
    return new String("SecurityImpl");
  }
  public boolean checkSecurity() {
    gateK = (IGateKeeperAuth)pl.getObject("master", "gk");
    if (gateK != null) {
```

```
20.       if (realmName != null) {
21.         IRealmMgr rlmMgr = gateK.getRealmMgr();
22.         Realm     rlmObj = rlmMgr.getRealmObject(realmName);
23.         if (rlmObj == null)
24.            gateK.addRealm(realmName);
25.        }
26.     }
27.      if ((gateK != null) && (realmName != null)) {
28.      if(!gateK.authorize(args, reqEnv, realmName, true))
29.       return false;
30.     }
31.    return true;
32.   }
33.   protected boolean invokeMethod(Object obj, String method, String
format)
34. throws Exception {
35.     SecurityImpl cs_obj = (SecurityImpl) obj;
36.     if(method.equalsIgnoreCase(DISCOVERPROPS)) {
37.       webProtocol.sendToClient("HTTP/1.1 200 OK\r\n");
38.       webProtocol.sendToClient("MIME-Version: 1.0\r\n");
39.       webProtocol.sendToClient("Server: HP/ChaiServer 3.0\r\n");
40.       webProtocol.sendToClient("Content-type: text/plain\r\n\n");
41.       webProtocol.sendToClient("securityRun");
42.       return true;
43.     }
44.     if (method.equalsIgnoreCase(SECURITYRUN))
45.        cs_obj.securityRun(format, args, reqEnv);
46.     else
47.        return false;
48.     return true;
49.   }
50.   protected boolean isObjectInstance(Object obj) {
51.     return (obj instanceof SecurityImpl);
52.   }
// Methods callable outside of worker
53.   public void initArgs(ArgVector args) {
54.     super.initArgs(args);
55.     realmName=args.getArg(AUTOSEC);
56.   }
57.   public String getVersion() {
58.     return WORKER_VERSION;
59.   }
60. }
```

- **Lines 1–3:** Importing the packages needed for the various classes used to build this application, such as for file I/O, Chai services, text manipulations, etc.
- **Line 4:** Declaration of a public class `SecurityStub`; its base class is `Worker` and it implements the `IWorker` interface.

- **Lines 11–32:** Implementation of `Helper` methods for `Worker`.
  - **Lines 11–13:** Implementation of the `createObject` method, which returns an instance of the `SecurityImpl` class.
  - **Lines 14–16:** Implementation of the `getObjectClassName` method, which returns the class name `SecurityImpl`.
  - **Lines 17–32:** Implementation of the `checkSecurity` method, which checks username and password.
- **Lines 33–49:** Implementation of the `invokeMethod` method to set the MIME type, version of the application, version of the server, and user-defined method.
- **Lines 50–52:** Implementation of the `isObjectInstance` method, which checks whether the `SecurityImpl` object is created.
- **Lines 53–56:** Implementation of the `initArgs` method, which initializes the arguments.
- **Lines 57–59:** Implementation of the `getVersion` method, which returns the version of the application.

Listing 12-17: Source code for Security.pkg

```
Worker
file:///g:\ChaiAP\Multi_Target\ChaiWeb\home\repository\Security\Security
Stub.class  {
    StartWorkers 2
    MimeType hp/security security
    DependsOn /repository/Security/ISecurity.class
    DependsOn /repository/Security/SecurityImpl.class
    Object {
      Name Security
      LinkID this.security
      Description  **Security method**
       CreateLink
     }
}
```

Testing the application

To test the application, follow these steps:

1. Save the `TempMeasure.java`, `ISecurity.java`, `SecurityImpl.java`, `SecurityStub.java`, and `Security.pkg` files in your `\Multi_Platform\ChaiWeb\home\repository\Security` folder.
2. To compile the Java programs, run MS-DOS, go to your `\Multi_Platform\ChaiWeb\home\repository\Security` folder, and enter the following commands:

```
javac TempMeasure.java
javac ISecurity.java
javac SecurityImpl.java
javac SecurityStub.java
```

3. Create a DSN with the name "chaidsn."
4. To run `TempMeasure.java`, run MS-DOS and go to your `\java TempMeasure` folder.
5. Start Chai Server, run MS-DOS, go to your Chai Server installation directory, and enter **ChaiServer**.

   ```
   C:\ChaiServer: ChaiServer <return>
   ```

   To stop Chai Server, enter **s** or **stop** at the Chai Server prompt.
6. Open ChaiFarer (Start ⇨ Programs ⇨ ChaiFarer2.0 ⇨ ChaiFarer).
7. Load the security package in Chai Server.
   - Click the Open button in ChaiFarer.
   - Enter the following in the Address field: **http://<*hostname*>:4242/this.loader**, where *hostname* is the name of the host on which the Chai Server is running.

     The Chai Server Package Loader page will be displayed.
   - To install the security package, enter the package URL:

     ```
     http://<hostname>:4242/repository/security/Security.pkg
     ```
   - Select the Copy Class Files and Install Permanently checkboxes and Click the Install Package button.
8. To run the security application:
   - Invoke Internet Explorer.
   - Enter the following in the Address field: **http://<*hostname*>:4242/this.security**. The screen shown in Figure 12-8 will be displayed.

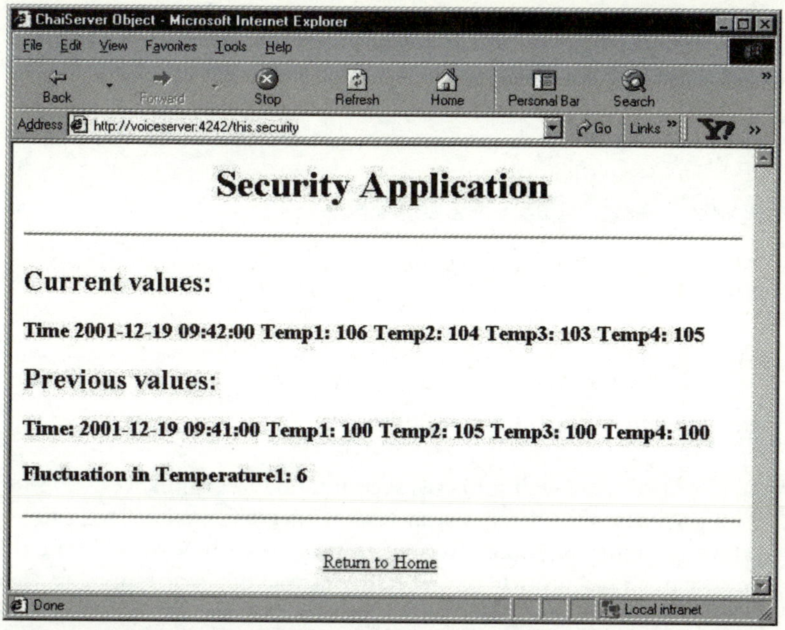

Figure 12-8: Monitoring the security application from a desktop browser

Summary

In this chapter, you learned how you can use Hewlett-Packard's Chai Appliance Server to create a variety of applications for both mobile and fixed applications. In the case of mobile devices, a small-footprint JVM running on the mobile device can access information on servers connected to the Internet or an intranet, as demonstrated in the first two applications — a Customer Relations Management module and location-based services. The HP platform can also be used to create applications in which an embedded system with a built-in HTTP server can continuously update its home page with information about its status. This home page can be accessed from the Internet through a conventional browser running on a desktop computer. The power of network-enabled embedded systems running an HTTP server is evident in the applications developed in this chapter — you can now visualize how your home door lock can be controlled from your office desktop.

Chapter 13

Mobile Java Appliances

In This Chapter

- Developing an electronic city guide project with Sun Microsystems' Wireless Toolkit
- Controlling appliances with Jini connection technology

Java has become a force to be reckoned with for networked information appliances. Java appliances can be used for a variety of applications, such as mobile data applications and dynamic distributed systems, and to control consumer items that use Java devices. This chapter describes application development in Java using Sun Microsystems' development tools. If you have a Java-enabled mobile phone, you can use it for two very different purposes: to access information available on the Internet, and to control the air conditioner in your office or home. The two software applications are developed using Sun's Wireless Toolkit and the Jini development kit.

Project: Electronic City Guide

This project teaches you how to develop an electronic city guide. This guide will help a visitor to a city obtain, on a Java-enabled device such as a mobile phone or a PDA, information about places of importance, including all related details. You will develop the application using J2ME, to understand the development of embedded applications for mobile devices, which have limited processing power and memory. A server contains a database of the cities and the places of interest, along with details about each place. A user can access this information through a GUI provided on the mobile device using the MIDP (Mobile Information Device Profile) APIs.

Development Environment

To develop the electronic city guide, you need a Windows 9*x*/NT/2000 system on which the following packages are installed:

- JDK 1.3 or later
- J2ME Wireless Toolkit Version 1.0.3 using MIDP, which can be downloaded from `http://java.sun.com/products/j2mewtoolkit/`

- Forte for Java, which can be downloaded from `http://www.sun.com/Forte/ffj/`

  If you prefer to use Forte with J2ME, you first have to install Forte and then the Wireless Toolkit with the Option for Integrating selected.
- A database engine: MS Access or MS SQL
- JavaWebServer 2.0 or later.

ON THE CD-ROM JDK, J2ME Wireless Toolkit, and Forte for Java are available on the CD-ROM that accompanies this book.

Database details

Create a database as per the details given in the following table. The table name is TourDetails.

Field Name	***Field Type***	***Description***	***Length***
Name	Text	Name of the place	50
Category	Text	Category of the place (e.g., museum, park, etc.)	50
Timings	Text	Hours of operation	150
EntryFee	Text	Entry fee	50
RecomDuration	Text	Recommended length of the visit	50
PublicMobility	Text	Public transport	50
PrivateMobility	Text	Private transport	50
Description	Memo	Description of the place	Up to 65,535 characters
City	Text	Name of the city	50

Source code listing for CityGuide.java

Listing 13-1 provides the source code for `CityGuide.java`, which creates the user interface and provides output to the user on the mobile device. Using an HTTP connection, the data on the server is retrieved and presented to the user.

Listing 13-1: Source code for CityGuide.java

```
/*
 * CityGuide.java
 * This application is for Tour Guide
 *i.e to visit the places of Visitor's
 *interest in a particular City and know
```

```
 *the details of that place.
 */
package TourGuide;
 import javax.microedition.midlet.*;
 import javax.microedition.lcdui.*;
 import javax.microedition.io.*;
 import java.io.*;
public class CityGuide extends MIDlet   implements CommandListener
 {
/* This HttpConnection object connects to the web server and Retreives
from the
Data base */
  HttpConnection hc = null;
/* Declaring variable for Display
   class.  */
  private Display display = null;
/* Declaration of Commands  */
 Command quit = null;
 Command ok = null;
 Command details=null;
 Command inform=null;
 Command back1 = null;
/* Declaration of Form  */
 Form frm = null;
 Ticker t =null;
/* Declaration of Lists */
 List menu = null;
 List menuc = null;
 List menud = null;
 List menui=null;
 String url, temp, str, item, tempp,
  tempm;
 StringItem cityname;
 StringItem st1 = null,st2 = null,
  st3= null,st4 = null,st5 = null,
  st6 = null;
// Initialize the Display and place system controls in the Constructor..
  public CityGuide()
{
/* This will get the Display Object  */
 display = Display.getDisplay(this);
 quit = new Command
          ("Quit",Command.SCREEN,1);
  ok = new Command
          ("OK",Command.OK,2);
  details = new Command
          ("SELECT",Command.SCREEN,2);
  inform = new Command
          ("CLICK",Command.SCREEN,2);
```

```
back1 = new Command
        ("BACK",Command.BACK,2);
t = new Ticker("Welcome To Electronic City Guide" );
}
/**
  This method is called when the application starts ..
*/
public void startApp()
{
  try {
   System.out.println("Started
                Application");
   cityDetails(str);
  }catch(IOException ie)
  {
   System.out.println("start App after cityDetails(str)"+ie);
  }
} // end of startApp()
  /**   This method is to retrieve Cities from Database using JSP  */
private void cityDetails(String str)
      throws IOException
{
StringBuffer sb=new StringBuffer();
/* This InputStream Object is used to read data from the InputStream
opened on a URL */
InputStream is = null;
 /* HttpConnection Object */
 HttpConnection hc = null;
try{
     long len = 0;
     int ch = 0;
     String name="";
/* Connecting to the given url.The url String contains a url pointing to
jsp which will retrieve from the database */
hc=(HttpConnection)Connector.open
  ("http://localhost:8080/Cities.jsp");
/* An inputstream is opened to read from that connection  */
is = hc.openInputStream();
 len = hc.getLength();
 if(len !=-1){
     for(int i=0;i<len;i++){
      if((ch = is.read()) !=-1)
     {
      sb.append((char)ch);
     }
    }
     }
   else{
    while(( ch = is.read()) !=-1){
```

```
        len = is.available() ;
        sb.append((char)ch);
         }
       }
     String str1 = sb.toString();
        str1.trim();
/* Initializing a List to select cities  from the List.*/
    menu = new List("Please Select a City",List.IMPLICIT);
    menu.setTicker(t);
    int index = str1.indexOf("#");
    while(index != -1)
    {
         index = str1.indexOf("#");
       if(index != -1)
       {
  String item = str1.substring(0,str1.indexOf("#"));
   str1 = str1.substring
            (str1.indexOf("#")+1);
 item=item.trim();
/* Append Item to a menu(List) */
    menu.append(item,null);
 }
 }
/* menu is registered for OK command */
menu.addCommand(ok);
menu.addCommand(quit);
/* Menu registered for receiving command*/
 menu.setCommandListener(this);
/* This will set the current display to List containing the items
ie,Cities */
 display.setCurrent(menu);
 }catch(Exception e)  {  System.out.println(e+"Exception In Menu");}
   finally{
     try{
          is.close();
          hc.close();
       }catch(Exception e)
     {  System.out.println(e+"Exception in Finally");
  }
 }
 }
     // end of cityDetails(String str)
/**This is a method to retrieve Details when a particular city is
Clicked */

private void cityClicked(){
   List down =
            (List)display.getCurrent();
 temp = down.getString
```

```
        (down.getSelectedIndex());
 if(temp.equals("Washington D.C.")){
categoryDetails(temp);
}
else if(temp.equals("Chicago"))
{
categoryDetails(temp);
}
}
     //end of cityClicked()
/**
  This is a method to retrieve Category Details of a paticular City from
Database using JSP */
private void categoryDetails
     (String temp)  {
StringBuffer sb1 = new StringBuffer();
InputStream is1 = null;
HttpConnection hcp = null;
  try{
       long lenp = 0;
       int ch = 0;
       String name=" ";
       temp = temp.replace('','_');
 String url= "http://localhost:8080/Categories.jsp?City="+temp;
hcp = (HttpConnection)Connector.open(url);
is1 = hcp.openInputStream();
lenp = hcp.getLength();
if(lenp !=-1){
for(int i=0;i<lenp;i++){
if((ch = is1.read()) !=-1)
{
sb1.append((char)ch);
}
}
}else{
while(( ch = is1.read()) !=-1){
lenp = is1.available() ;
sb1.append((char)ch);
}
}
String str1 = sb1.toString();
str1.trim();
cityname=new StringItem("Select Category ",temp);
menuc = new List("Please Select a Category",List.IMPLICIT);
int index = str1.indexOf("#");
while(index != -1)
{
index = str1.indexOf("#");
if(index != -1)
```

```
{
String item = str1.substring(0,str1.indexOf("#"));
str1 = str1.substring(str1.indexOf("#")+1);
item=item.trim();
menuc.append(item,null);
}
}
menuc.addCommand(details);
menuc.addCommand(back1);
menuc.setCommandListener(this);
display.setCurrent(menuc);
}catch(Exception e){System.out.println(e+"Exception In Menu city clicked");}
finally{
try{
is1.close();
 hcp.close();
 }catch(Exception e){ System.out.println(e+"Exception in Finally in city clicked");}
 }
 }  /* end of categoryDetails(String temp)*/
/**
This is a method for Action Performed i.e when a Command is Clicked
i.e. Event handling routine..
*/
 public void commandAction(Command c,Displayable d){
 if(c == quit) {
 destroyApp(true);
 } else if(c==ok) {
 cityClicked();
 } else if(c==details) {
 List down = (List)display.getCurrent();
 String cname=cityname.getText();
 tempp = down.getString(down.getSelectedIndex());
 informationDetails(cname,tempp);
 } else if(c==inform) {
 List down = (List)display.getCurrent();
 String cname=cityname.getText();
 tempm = down.getString(down.getSelectedIndex());
 informationCategory(cname,tempm);
 } else if(c==back1) {
 try{
 String cname=cityname.getText();
 cityDetails(cname);
 }catch(Exception p) {
 System.out.println("Exception in back "+p);
 }
 }
 }  //end of commandAction(Command c,Displayable d)
```

```
/**
This is a method to retrieve Information when a particular city and Name
of the Category is Clicked */
private void informationCategory(String cname,String tempm){
StringBuffer sbc = new StringBuffer();
InputStream isc = null;
HttpConnection hcc = null;
int count = 1;
try{
long lenc = 0;
int ch = 0;
String name=" ";
cname = cname.replace(' ','_');
tempm=tempm.replace(' ','_');
String param=cname+" & name="+tempm;
param = param.replace(' ','_');
String url ="http://localhost:8080/NameCategory.jsp?city="+param;
hcc = (HttpConnection)Connector.open(url);
isc = hcc.openInputStream();
lenc = hcc.getLength();
if(lenc !=-1){
for(int i=0;i<lenc;i++){
if((ch = isc.read()) !=-1)
{
sbc.append((char)ch);
}
}
}else{
while(( ch = isc.read()) !=-1){
lenc = isc.available() ;
sbc.append((char)ch);
}
}
String str1 = sbc.toString();
str1.trim();
menui = new List("Information ",List.IMPLICIT);
int index = str1.indexOf("#");
while(index != -1){
index = str1.indexOf("#");
if(index != -1){
String item = str1.substring(0,str1.indexOf("#"));
str1 = str1.substring(str1.indexOf("#")+1);
item=item.trim();
if(count == 1){
/*The str is passed as an argument to the Constructer of StringItem
which will
display the value in str  */
st1 = new StringItem("Description : ",item);
}
```

```
if(count == 2){
st2 = new StringItem("Timing : ",item);
}
if(count == 3){
st3 = new StringItem("Entry : ",item);
}
if(count == 4){
st4 = new StringItem("RecomTime : ",item);
}
if(count == 5){
st5 = new StringItem("PublicTransport : ",item);
}
if(count == 6){
st6 = new StringItem("PrivateTransport : ",item);
}
count++;
}
}
/* Initializing a Form */
frm =new Form("Details");
/* Append StringItem's to a Form */
frm.append(st1);
frm.append(st2);
frm.append(st3);
frm.append(st4);
frm.append(st5);
frm.append(st6);
/*form is registered for quit command*/
frm.addCommand(quit);
frm.addCommand(back1);
/*frm registered for receiving command*/
frm.setCommandListener(this);
display.setCurrent(frm);
}catch(Exception e)
{System.out.println(e+"Exception In Menu city clicked");
}
finally{
try{
isc.close();
hcc.close();
}catch(Exception e){
System.out.println(e+"Exception in Finally in city clicked");
}
}
System.out.println("information category"+tempm);
}
 /*end of informationCategory(String
     cname,String tempm)*/
/**
```

```
    This is a method to retrieve names
    of a particular Category
    when a particular City and Category is Clicked */
private void informationDetails(String cname,String tempp)
{
StringBuffer sbd = new StringBuffer();
InputStream isd = null;
HttpConnection hcd = null;
try{
long lend = 0;
int ch = 0;
String name=" ";
cname = cname.replace(' ','_');
tempp=tempp.replace(' ','_');
String param=cname+" & category="+tempp;
param = param.replace(' ','_');
String url ="http://localhost:8080/CityDetails.jsp?city="+param;
hcd = (HttpConnection)Connector.open(url);
isd = hcd.openInputStream();
lend = hcd.getLength();
if(lend !=-1){
for(int i=0;i<lend;i++){
if((ch = isd.read()) !=-1){
sbd.append((char)ch);
}
}
}else{
while(( ch = isd.read()) !=-1){
lend = isd.available() ;
sbd.append((char)ch);
}
}
String str1 = sbd.toString();
str1.trim();
cityname=new StringItem("Select",temp);
menud = new List("Please Select an Option",List.IMPLICIT);
int index = str1.indexOf("#");
while(index != -1){
index = str1.indexOf("#");
if(index != -1){
String item = str1.substring(0,str1.indexOf("#"));
str1 = str1.substring(str1.indexOf("#")+1);
item=item.trim();
menud.append(item,null);
}
}
menud.addCommand(inform);
menud.addCommand(back1);
menud.setCommandListener(this);
```

```
320. display.setCurrent(menud);
321. }catch(Exception e)
322. {
323. System.out.println(e+"Exception In Menu city clicked");
324. }
325. finally{
326. try{
327. isd.close();
328. hcd.close();
329. }catch(Exception e)
330. {
331. System.out.println(e+"Exception in Finally in city clicked");
332. }
333. }
334. }
 /* End of informationDetails(String cname,String tempp) */
/* This method is called when the application is paused*/
335. public void pauseApp(){
336. menu = null;
337. menuc = null;
338. menud = null;
339. }
 // end of pauseApp()
/* This method is called when the application is terminated. This is the
ideal method to free resources */
340. public void destroyApp(boolean unconditional){
341. menu = null;
342. menuc = null;
343. menud = null;
344. notifyDestroyed();
345. }
/* end of destroyApp(boolean unconditional) */
346. }
```

Following is the line-by-line explanation of the source code:

- **Lines 1–5:** Importing the various packages required for the program. These statements import various GUI components, such as `List` and `StringItem`; HTTP connection classes, such as `HttpConnection`; and the `Connector` class and the `InputStream` class, for communication.
- **Line 6:** Declaration of the class `CityGuide`.
- **Lines 7–23:** Declaration of objects for user-interface classes such as `List` and `Form`, and several `command` objects.
- **Lines 24–33:** Constructor for the class `CityGuide`. This code initializes different command objects. The commands are generated when the user presses any button on the device.

- **Lines 34–43:** Declaration of the `startApp()` method, which is called when the MIDlet starts. (MIDlet is an application that runs on the Mobile Information Device.)
- **Line 38:** Invoking the `cityDetails()` method within the `try..catch` block.
- **Lines 44–99:** Implementation of the `cityDetails` method.
- **Line 46:** Instantiating the `StringBuffer` object.
- **Lines 50–52:** Declaration and initialization of the variables.
- **Lines 54–69:** `InputStream` is opened to read from the connection, get the length, and process the data.
- **Line 71:** Removes white spaces from both ends of the string.
- **Line 74:** Returns the index within this string of the first occurrence of the specified substring (#).
- **Line 80:** City name is assigned to the string `item`.
- **Lines 100–110:** Implementation of the `cityClicked` method.
  - **Line 101:** Current displayable object of the MIDlet is assigned to the list.
  - **Line 102:** Selected string of the list is assigned to the string `temp`.
  - **Lines 103–109:** If the string is Washington D.C. or Chicago, invokes the method `categoryDetails`.
- **Lines 111–164:** Implementation of the `categoryDetails` method.
- **Line 112:** Instantiates the `StringBuffer` object.
- **Line 113:** Null will be assigned to the `InputStream` object.
- **Line 114:** Null will be assigned to the `HttpConnection` object.
- **Lines 116–118:** Declares and initializes the variables.
- **Line 119:** Replaces the spaces with underscores in the string `temp`, which contains the city name.
- **Line 120:** URL is assigned to the `url` string, which points to the JSP file.
- **Line 121:** Opens the connection.
- **Line 122:** An `InputStream` is opened to read from the connection.
- **Lines 123–136:** Gets the length and processes the data.
- **Line 139:** Instantiates the `StringItem` object.
- **Line 140:** Initializes the `List`.
- **Line 141:** Returns the index within this string of the first occurrence of the specified substring (#).
- **Line 147:** Categories will be assigned to the string `item`.
- **Line 150:** Appends `item` to the List (`menuc`).

- **Lines 153–154:** Adds the command buttons to the List.
- **Lines 165–188:** Definition of the `commandAction` method, which performs the action when the user presses a button.
- **Lines 166–167:** If the Quit button is clicked, the `destroyApp` method will be invoked.
- **Lines 168–169:** If the OK button is clicked, the `cityClicked` method will be invoked.
- **Lines 170–174:** If the Details button is clicked, the `informationDetails` method will be invoked.
- **Lines 175–179:** If the Inform button is clicked, the `informationCategory` method will be invoked.
- **Lines 180–183:** If the Back button is clicked, the `cityDetails` method will be invoked.
- **Lines 189–273:** Implementation of the `informationCategory` method.
  - **Line 198:** Replaces the spaces with an underscore in the `cname` string, which contains the city name.
  - **Line 199:** Replaces the spaces with underscore in the `tempm` string, which contains the category name.
  - **Line 200:** Concatenates the `cname` string and the `tempm` string and assigns it to another string `param`.
  - **Line 201:** Replace the spaces with underscore in the `param` string.
  - **Lines 223–249:** Within the `while` loop, a value will be assigned to the StringItem.
  - **Lines 229–248:** Instantiates the StringItem with string `item`.
  - **Lines 250–258:** Instantiates the `Form` object and appends the commands to the `Form`.
- **Lines 274–334:** This is an implementation of the `informationDetails` method. The code here is same as that in the other methods and is self-explanatory.
- **Lines 335–339:** This is an implementation of the `pauseApp` method. When the application is paused, this method is invoked.
- **Lines 340–345:** Implementation of the `destroyApp` method. When the application is terminated, this method is invoked to free the resources.

Source code listing for Cities.jsp

Listing 13-2 provides the source code for `Cities.jsp`. This program retrieves the names of the cities from the database.

Listing 13-2: Source code for Cities.jsp

```
<%-- This is a JSP File to retrieve Cities from the Database   --%>
<%@ page import="java.sql.*,java.util.*" %>
<%! Connection conn; %>
```

```
3. <%! Statement stmt; %>
4. <%! ResultSet rs; %>
5. <%! String str1; %>
6. <%
7. try{
/* Connecting to the Data Base */
8. Class.forName("sun.jdbc.odbc.JdbcOdbcDriver");
9. conn = DriverManager.getConnection("jdbc:odbc:ETour");
10. stmt = conn.createStatement();
/* Information of Cities from
    Database*/
11. rs = stmt.executeQuery("select Distinct(City) from TourDetails ");
12. str1 = "";
13. while(rs.next())
14. {
15. str1 += rs.getString(1) +"#";
16. }
17. out.println(str1);
18. System.out.println(str1);
19. rs.close();
20. stmt.close();
21. conn.close();
22. }catch(Exception e) {
23. System.out.print(e);
24. }
25. %>
```

Following is the line-by-line explanation of the source code:

- **Line 1:** Importing the packages.
- **Lines 2–5:** Declaration of the variables.
- **Line 8:** Indicates the `Class` object associated with the class or interface with the string name `sun.jdbc.odbc.JdbcOdbcDriver` to initialize the driver.
- **Line 9:** Creates an object of `Connection`. If your database has to be accessed through a username and a pasword, you need to change this line to the following:

```
conn=DriverManager.getConnection("jdbc:odbc:Etour","user_name","passwo
rd");
```

- **Line 10:** Creates an instance of `Statement`.
- **Line 11:** Retrieves the distinct cities from the table `TourDetails`.
- **Lines 13–16:** Selects the city and adds it to the string until the end of the `Resultset`.
- **Line 19:** Closes the `Resultset`.
- **Line 20:** Closes the `Statement`.
- **Line 21:** Closes the `Connection`.

- **Lines 22–24:** Catches any exceptions.

Source code listing for Categories.jsp

Listing 13-3 provides the source code for `Categories.jsp`. This program retrieves from the database the categories of places that can be visited in a particular city.

Listing 13-3: Source code for Categories.jsp

```
 <%-- This is a JSP File to retrieve Categories of a particular City
from the      Database   --%>
1.<%@ page import="java.sql.*,java.util.*" %>
2.<%! Connection conn; %>
3.<%! Statement stmt; %>
4.<%! ResultSet rs; %>
5.<%! String str1,cityname; %>
6.<%
7.try{
8.cityname=request.getQueryString();
9.cityname = cityname.substring(cityname.indexOf("=")+1);
10. cityname = cityname.replace('_',' ');
11. Class.forName("sun.jdbc.odbc.JdbcOdbcDriver");
12. conn = DriverManager.getConnection("jdbc:odbc:ETour");
13. stmt = conn.createStatement();
/* Information on Categories based on City from Database */
14. rs = stmt.executeQuery("select Distinct(Category) from TourDetails
where City='"+cityname+"'");
15. str1 = "";
16. while(rs.next())
17. {
18. str1 += rs.getString(1) +"#";
19. }
20. out.println(str1);
21. System.out.println(str1);
22. rs.close();
23. stmt.close();
24. conn.close();
25. }catch(Exception e) {
26. System.out.print(e);
27. }
28. %>
```

Following is the line-by-line explanation of the source code:

- **Line 1:** Importing the packages.
- **Lines 2–5:** Declaration of the variables.
- **Line 8:** `QueryString` is assigned to the string `cityname`.

- **Line 9:** Gets the substring of the string `cityname` to the specified index and assigns it to the string `cityname`.
- **Line 10:** Replaces the underscore with the space for the specified string `cityname`.
- **Line 11:** Indicates the Class object associated with the class or interface with the string `sun.jdbc.odbc.JdbcOdbcDriver` for initializing the driver.
- **Line 12:** Creates an object of `Connection`.
- **Line 13:** Creates an instance of `Statement`.
- **Line 14:** Retrieves the distinct categories from the table `TourDetails` for the corresponding city.
- **Lines 16–19:** Selects the category and adds it to the string until the end of the `Resultset`.
- **Line 22:** Closes the `Resultset`.
- **Line 23:** Closes the `Statement`.
- **Line 24:** Closes the `Connection`.
- **Lines 25–28:** Catches any exceptions.

Source code listing for CityDetails.jsp

Listing 13-4 provides the source code for `CityDetails.jsp`. This program retrieves information from the database based on the city and category selected.

Listing 13-4: Source code for CityDetails.jsp

```
  <%-- This is a JSP File to retrieve Names based on Category and City
from the Database --%>
<%@ page import="java.sql.*,java.util.*" %>
<%! Connection conn; %>
<%! Statement stmt; %>
<%! ResultSet rs; %>
<%! String str1,category,city,cityname;
String param; %>
<%
try{
city = request.getQueryString();
city = city.replace('_',' ');
cityname = city.substring(city.indexOf("=")+1,city.indexOf("&"));
category=city.substring(city.lastIndexOf("=")+1);
param="select Name from TourDetails where City='"+cityname+"' and
Category='"+category+"'";
/*Connecting to the Data Base */
Class.forName("sun.jdbc.odbc.JdbcOdbcDriver");
conn = DriverManager.getConnection("jdbc:odbc:ETour");
stmt = conn.createStatement();
```

```
17. System.out.println(param);
18. rs = stmt.executeQuery(param);
19. str1 = "";
20. while(rs.next())
21. {
22. str1 += rs.getString(1) +"#";
23. }
24. out.println(str1);
25. System.out.println(str1);
26. rs.close();
27. stmt.close();
28. conn.close();
29. }catch(Exception e) {
30. System.out.print(e);
31. }
32. %>
```

Following is the line-by-line explanation of the source code:

- **Line 1:** Importing the packages.
- **Lines 2–6:** Declaring the variables.
- **Line 9:** `QueryString` will be assigned to the string `city`.
- **Line 10:** Replaces the underscore with the space.
- **Line 11:** Gets the substring starting after equal to (=) and up to, but not including, the character `&` and assigns it to the string `cityname`.
- **Line 12:** Gets the substring of the string `city` to the specified index and assigns it to the string `Category`.
- **Line 14:** Indicates the Class object associated with the class or interface with the string `sun.jdbc.odbc.JdbcOdbcDriver` for initializing the driver.
- **Line 15:** Creates an object of `Connection`.
- **Line 16:** Creates an instance of `Statement`.
- **Line 18:** Retrieves the `Name` from the table `TourDetails` for the corresponding city and category.
- **Lines 20–23:** Selects the category and adds it to the string until the end of the `Resultset`.
- **Line 26:** Closes the `Resultset`.
- **Line 27:** Closes the `Statement`.
- **Line 28:** Closes the `Connection`.

Source code listing for NameCategory.jsp

Listing 13-5 provides the source code for `NameCategory.jsp`. This program retrieves information about a particular city for the selected category.

Listing 13-5: Source code for NameCategory.jsp.

```
<%-- This is a JSP File to retrieve Infromation of Particular Category
of a particular City from the Database  --%>
<%@ page import="java.sql.*,java.util.*" %>
<%! Connection conn; %>
<%! Statement stmt; %>
<%! ResultSet rs; %>
<%! String str1,category,city,cityname;
String param; %>
<%
try{
city = request.getQueryString();
city = city.replace('_',' ');
cityname = city.substring(city.indexOf("=")+1,city.indexOf("&"));
category=city.substring(city.lastIndexOf("=")+1);
param="select
Description,Timings,EntryFee,RecomDuration,PublicMobility,PrivateMobilit
y,City,Name from TourDetails where City='"+cityname+"' and
Name='"+category+"'";
/*Connecting to the Data Base */
Class.forName("sun.jdbc.odbc.JdbcOdbcDriver");
conn = DriverManager.getConnection("jdbc:odbc:ETour");
stmt = conn.createStatement();
System.out.println(param);
rs = stmt.executeQuery(param);
str1 = "";
while(rs.next())
{
str1 = rs.getString(1) +"#";
str1 += rs.getString(2) +"#";
str1 += rs.getString(3) +"#";
str1 += rs.getString(4) +"#";
str1 += rs.getString(5) +"#";
str1 += rs.getString(6) +"#";
str1 += rs.getString(7) +"#";
}
out.println(str1);
System.out.println(str1);
rs.close();
stmt.close();
conn.close();
}catch(Exception e) {
System.out.print(e);
```

```
37. }
38. %>
```

Following is the line-by-line explanation of the source code:

- **Line 1:** Importing the packages.
- **Lines 2–6:** Declaring the variables.
- **Line 9:** `QueryString` will be assigned to the string `city`.
- **Line 10:** Replaces the underscore with the space.
- **Line 11:** Gets the substring starting after equal to (=) and up to, but not including, the character `&` and assigns it to the string `cityname`.
- **Line 12:** Gets the substring of the string `city` to the specified index and assigns it to the string `Category`.
- **Line 14:** Indicates the Class object associated with the class or interface with the string `sun.jdbc.odbc.JdbcOdbcDriver` for initializing the driver.
- **Line 15:** Creates an object of `Connection`.
- **Line 16:** Creates an instance of `Statement`.
- **Line 18:** Retrieves the `Description`, `Timings`, `EntryFee`, `RecomDuration`, `PublicMobility`, `PrivateMobility`, `City`, and `Name` from the table `TourDetails` for the corresponding `city` and `category`.
- **Lines 20–29:** Selects the fields and adds them to the string until the end of the `Resultset`.
- **Line 32:** Closes the `Resultset`.
- **Line 33:** Closes the `Statement`.
- **Line 34:** Closes the `Connection`.
- **Lines 35–38:** Catches any exceptions.

Executing the program

To execute the program, follow these steps:

1. Copy all the JSP files in `c:\javawebserver2.0\public_html`.
2. Start the Java Web server using the command `c:\javawebserver2.0\bin\httpd.exe`.
3. After installing Forte, select Start ⇨ Programs ⇨ Forte for Java CE ⇨ Forte for Java CE as shown in Figure 13-1.
4. The File System Explorer will open. From the menu bar, select File ⇨ Explorer.
5. Select New Package, as shown in Figure 13-2.

6. Enter the Package name as **TourGuide** in the text box.
7. Right-click on the package TourGuide and select New ⇨ MIDP ⇨ MIDletClass, as shown in Figure 13-3.
8. The source code editor will be automatically displayed. In the editor, write the source code for `CityGuide.java`.
9. Right-click on the package TourGuide, select New ⇨ MIDP ⇨ MIDletSuite, and then enter the suite name as **CityGuide**.
10. In the CityGuide dialog box that appears, click the Content pane and add the MIDPClass (CityGuide), as shown in Figure 13-4.
11. Right-click on CityGuide and select Compile, as shown in Figure 13-5.
12. After compilation is finished, right-click on CityGuide again and select Execute.

The MIDlet running under the emulator appears as shown in Figures 13-6 and 13-7 (on the Default Color Phone) and in Figures 13-8 and 13-9 (on the RIMJavaHandheld).

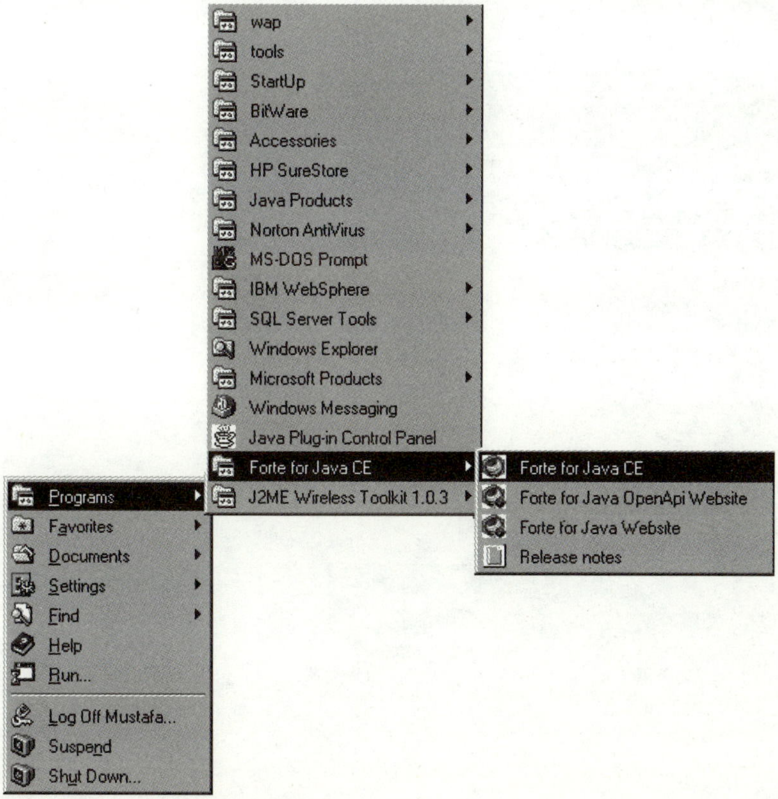

Figure 13-1: Invoking Forte for Java

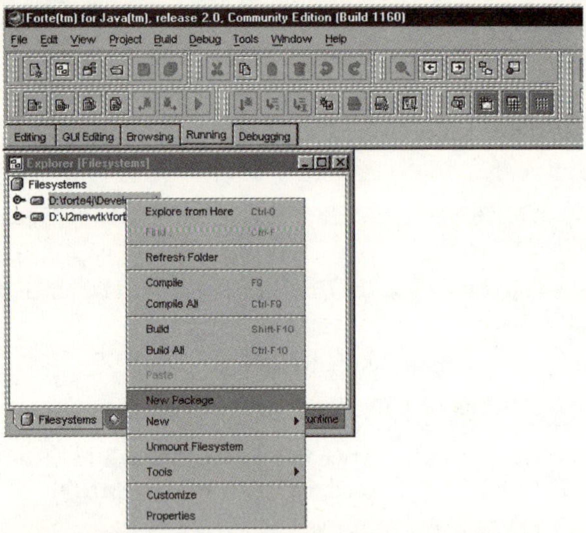

Figure 13-2: Selection of a new package

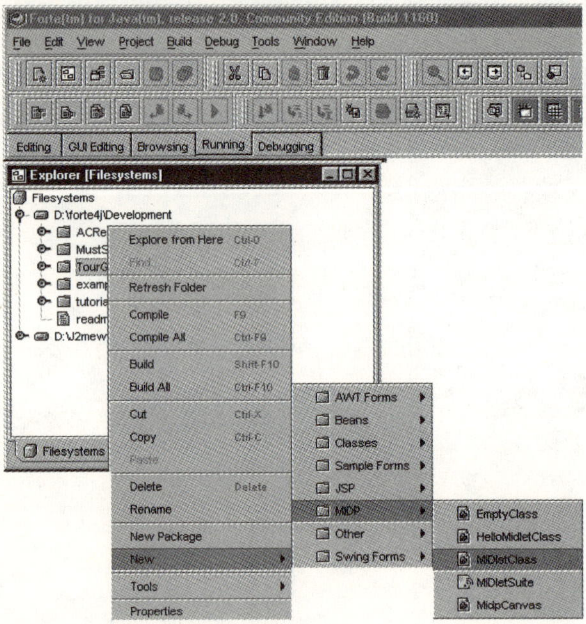

Figure 13-3: Selection of the MIDlet class

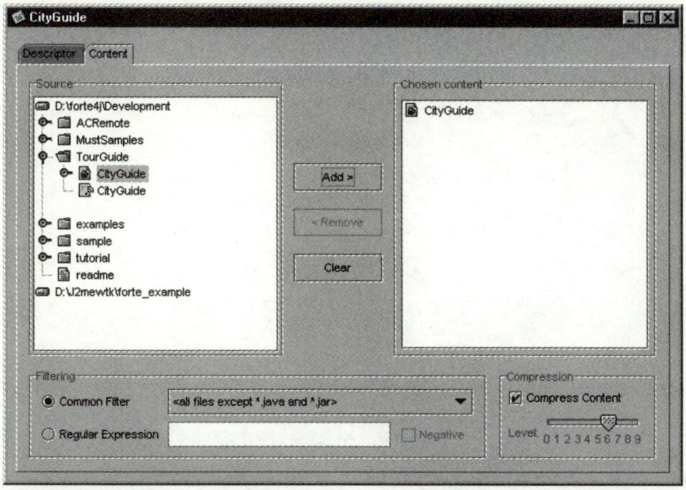

Figure 13-4: Adding the MIDP class

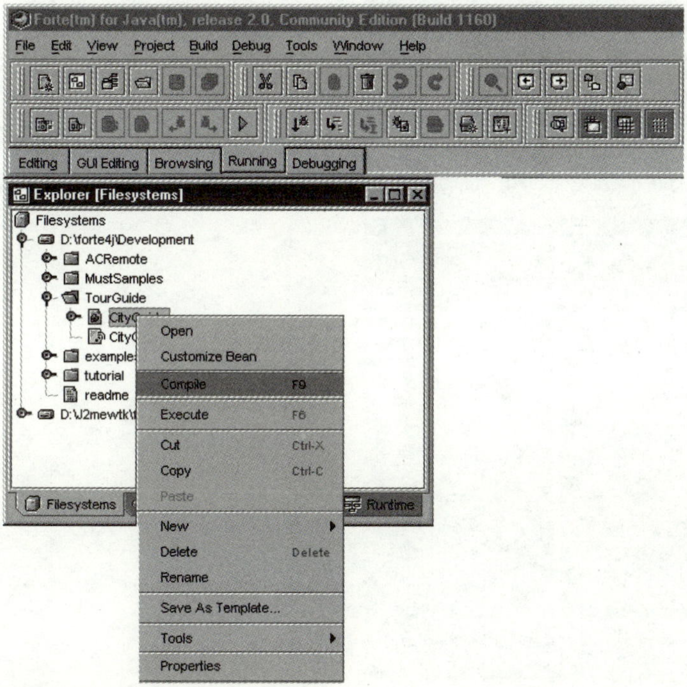

Figure 13-5: Compiling the program

Figure 13-6: Emulator display for the CityGuide application. The first screen displays the application name, and when you click the Launch button, the next screen is diplayed. The second screen displays the names of the cities.

Figure 13-7: Emulator display when a particular city is selected. The first screen shows the categories of the places to be visited. The second screen shows the places of the selected category. The third screen shows the details of the selected place.

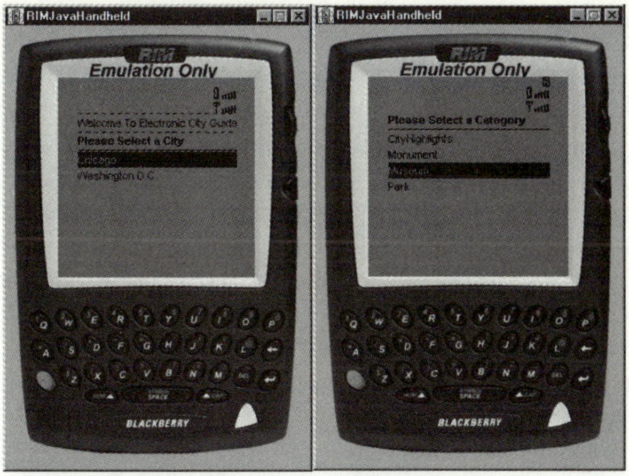

Figure 13-8: Output of the CityGuide application on the RIMJavaHandheld. The first screen shows the list of cities. The second screen shows the categories for the selected city.

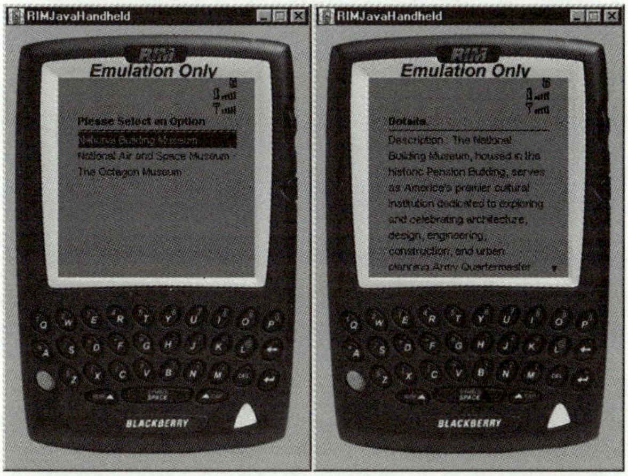

Figure 13-9: Output of the CityGuide application on the RIMJavaHandheld. The first screen shows the list of places for the selected category. The second screen shows the details of the selected place.

Project: Appliance Control Using Jini

Jini connection technology provides a mechanism for developing *dynamic distributed systems*. In a network of workstations and appliances, each device can tell all the other devices what services it can support and make those services available to the other devices. For example, a printer can inform all other nodes that it provides a laser printing service on A3 papers. Any other device can lease that service and use it. It is also possible to control a device from other devices. Jini provides the platform to develop such applications. However, many devices do not have the capability to inform other devices about their services. In such a case, another device (for example, a PC) can act as a proxy to that device. This proxy does all the work on behalf of a server.

Consider an air conditioner. If the air conditioner has good processing power, it can run a Jini service, and another Jini-enabled device can control its operation. If the air conditioner's embedded software is not powerful, a PC can act as a proxy to the air conditioner. If your mobile phone is Jini-enabled as well, you can control the air conditioner through a mobile device. This project uses Jini connection technology to transfer control of an air conditioner to a mobile device. Before you start working on this project, you need to install the Jini software on your system and start the Jini service. The following section explains how to install the Jini service.

Jini installation and class path setting

To install Jini, follow these steps:

1. Install the Java 2 SDK, if you don't have it already.
2. Make sure that the `\bin` directory of the Java 2 SDK is in your executable path:

```
path=%path%;<j2sdk_installation_directory>\jdk1.2\bin;
```

3. Set the class path of the Java 2 SDK:

```
set classpath=%classpath%;
<j2sdk_installation_directory>\jdk1.2\lib\tools.jar
```

4. The downloaded file `jini-1_2-src.zip` includes the binaries, source code, and support documentation, and by default extracts into the directory `\jini1_2`.

   For example, if this zip file is extracted into `D:\`, the class path setting will appear as follows:

```
set classpath=%classpath%; d:\jini1_2\lib\ jini-ext.jar;
d:\jini1_2\lib\sun-util.jar; d:\jini1_2\lib\tools.jar;
d:\jini1_2\lib\jini-core.jar
```

Starting the Jini service

Jini depends on the network infrastructure at runtime. As Jini uses Remote Method Invocation (RMI) and HTTP, you need to run these services on your network (e.g., your LAN). The services that Jini requires for our current application are as follows:

- Web server
- RMI daemon
- Jini's lookup service, Reggie

To start the Jini service, follow these steps:

1. **Start an HTTP server.** An HTTP server is needed for downloading classes that clients need in order to interact with services. A small and simple HTTP server is provided to make the JAR files available via the HTTP daemon (`httpd`). Of course, you can use any other Web server that can serve documents.
2. **Start the RMI activation daemon.** The RMI activation daemon is needed by the Jini lookup service implementation, Reggie. The activation daemon, `rmid`, can be found in the `\bin` directory of the Java 2 SDK, Standard Edition, Version 1.2.2. Ensure that this `\bin` directory is in your executable path.
3. **Start the Jini lookup service.** The Jini lookup service is used to locate services. In our application, the air conditioner control is a Jini service that will be accessed through another device.

To run these services through the GUI, the procedure is as follows:

1. Run a command prompt.
2. Issue the following command:

```
java -cp \jini_soft\jini1_2\lib\jini-ext.jar;
 \jini_soft\jini1_2\lib\jini-examples.jar
     com.sun.jini.example.launcher.StartService
```

   The screen shown in Figure 13-10 will be displayed.

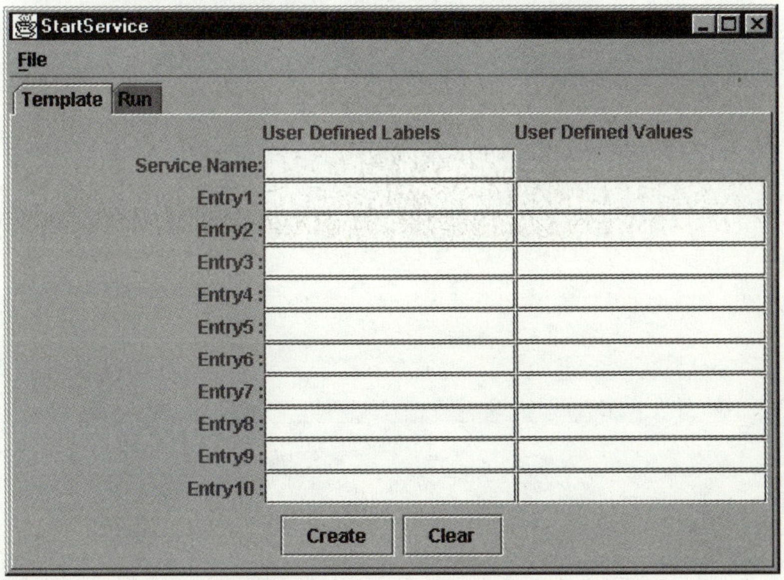

Figure 13-10: StartService GUI

3. On the menu bar, select File ⇨ Open Property File, as shown in Figure 13-11.

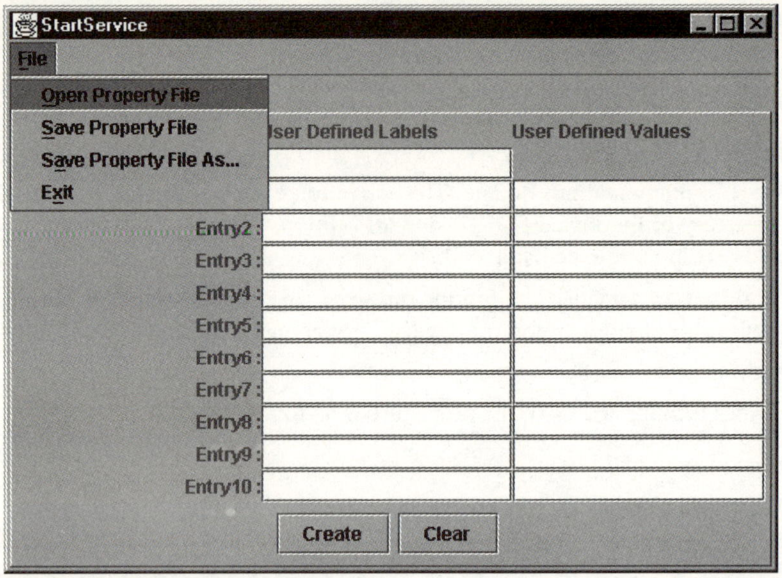

Figure 13-11: Starting the Jini service

4. The window shown in Figure 13-12 appears. Select the property file: `<jini_installed_directory>\jini1_2\example\launcher\jini12_win32.properties`.

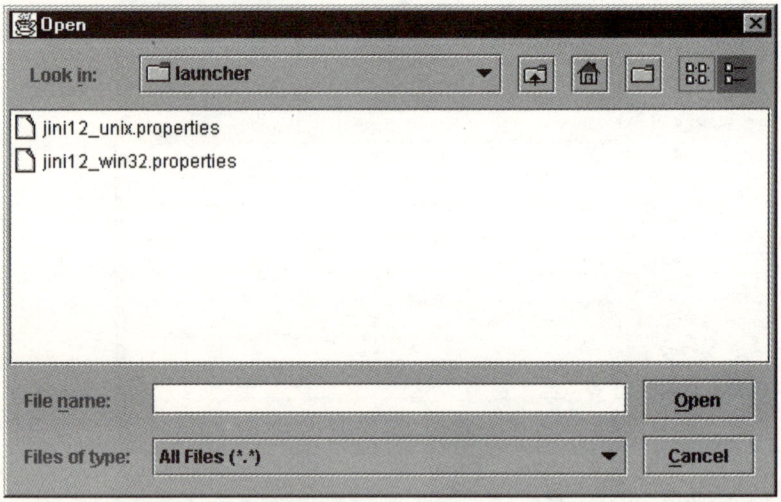

Figure 13-12: Selecting the property file

The screen shown in Figure 13-13 will be displayed. Using this GUI, you can start/stop various services such as RMID and WebServer.

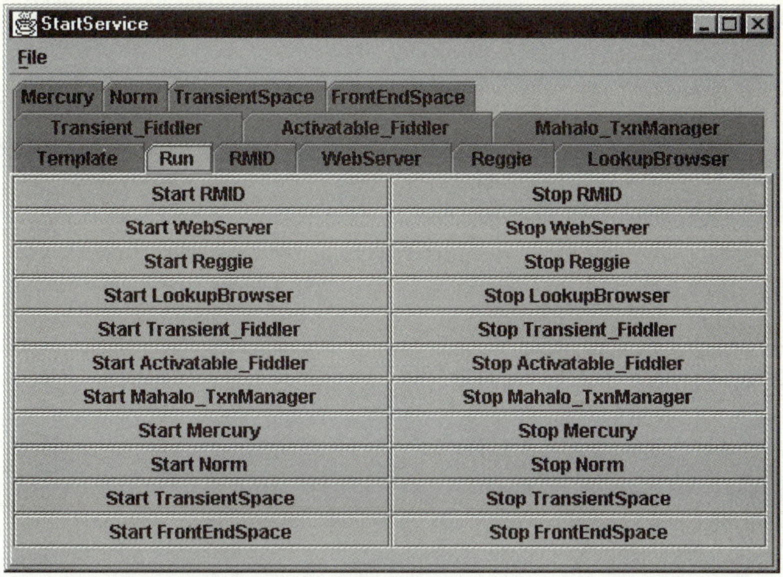

Figure 13-13: GUI to start/stop various services

5. Select the RMID tab. This panel, shown in Figure 13-14, enables you to specify any optional arguments to RMID prior to startup.

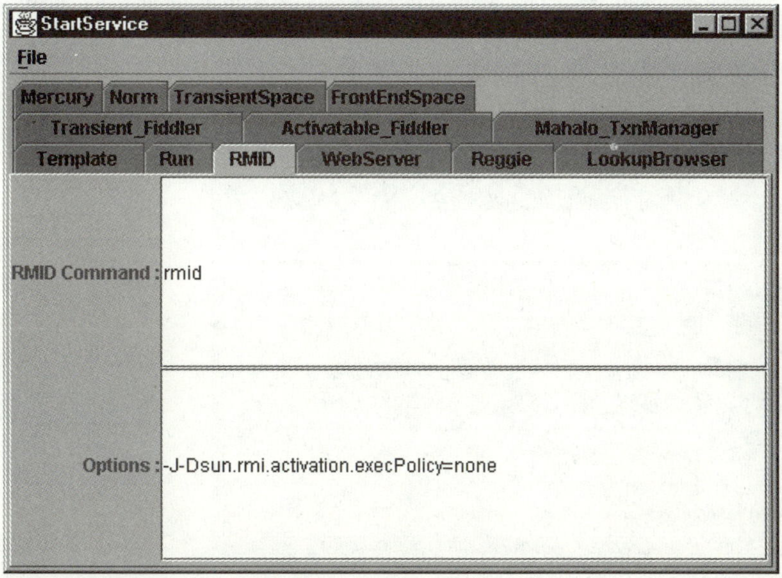

Figure 13-14: Setting the RMID service parameters

In the screen shown in Figure 13-14, we need to indicate the policy file in the Options field. For this example, the default value will suffice.

6. Select the Run tab, and then click the Start RMID button as shown in Figure 13-15.

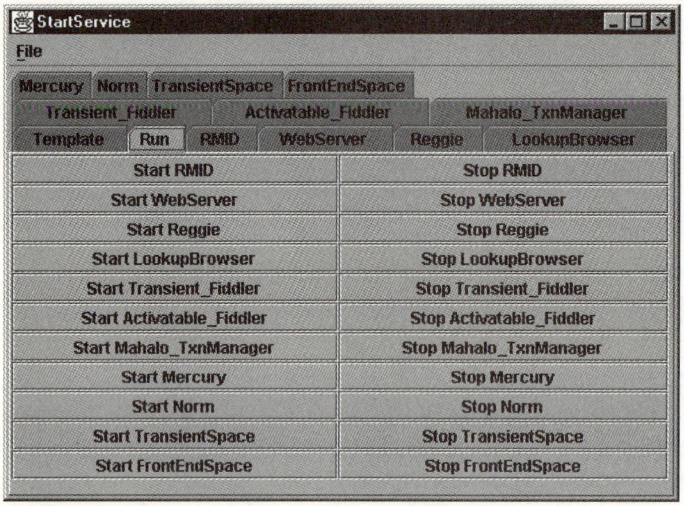

Figure 13-15: Starting the Jini runtime service, RMID

7. Select the WebServer tab. This tab, shown in Figure 13-16, enables you to configure a simple HTTP server on this host to be used for code downloading.

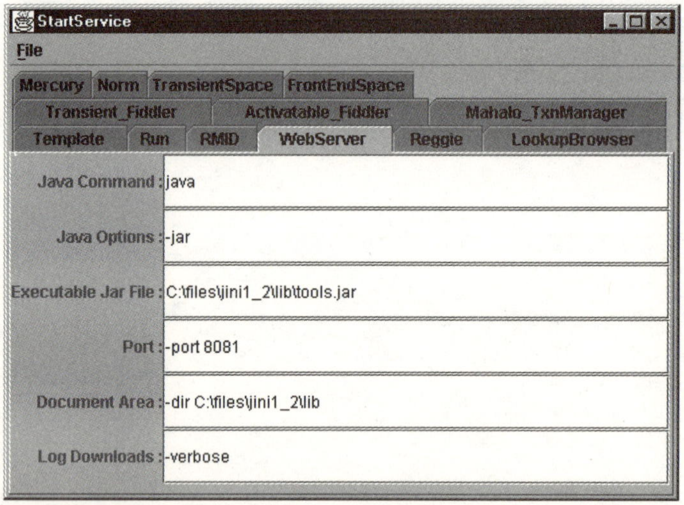

Figure 13-16: Setting the HTTP server parameters

8. Change the values of the Executable Jar File and Document Area fields to match the location of your Jini installation directory. Select the Run tab, shown in Figure 13-17, and then click the Start WebServer button.

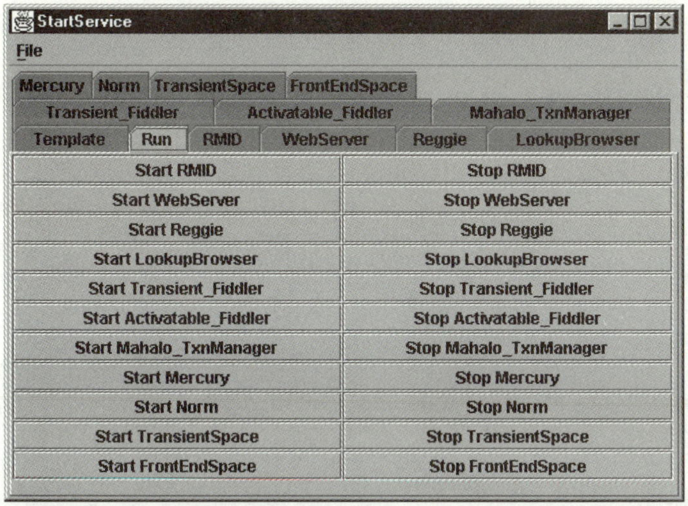

Figure 13-17: Start the Jini runtime service, WebServer

9. Select the Reggie tab. This panel, shown in Figure 13-18, enables you to configure the Jini lookup service implementation.

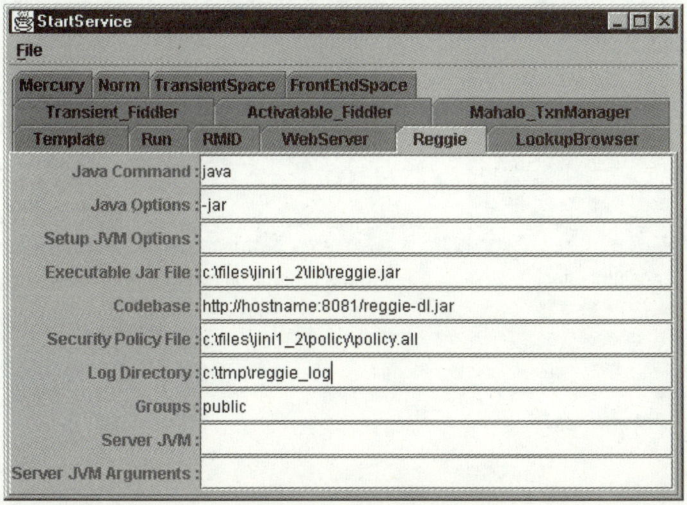

Figure 13-18: Set the lookup service (Reggie) parameters

10. Change the values of the Executable Jar File, Codebase, Security Policy File, and Log Directory fields. Executable Jar File and Security Policy File have to match the location

of your Jini installation directory. In the Codebase field, change the host name; and in the Log Directory field, enter your temporary directory name for creating log files. Select the Run tab (shown in Figure 13-19) and then click the Start Reggie button.

Now you can start executing the following Jini application, ACRemote.

ACRemote application

You can familiarize yourself with this application by examining the output screenshots. When you run the client program, the air conditioner control panel screen, shown in Figure 13-19, will be displayed with the default values: Off, temperature at 24, and timer at 0:00. Initially, the Temperature and Time list boxes are disabled. When the user selects the On/Off checkbox, the Temperature and Time list boxes are enabled, and the user can enter new values for the temperature and the timer (duration for keeping the air-conditioner on).

After selecting the On/Off checkbox, the user interface appears as shown in Figure 13-20.

Now you can set the temperature and timer values as shown in Figure 13-21.

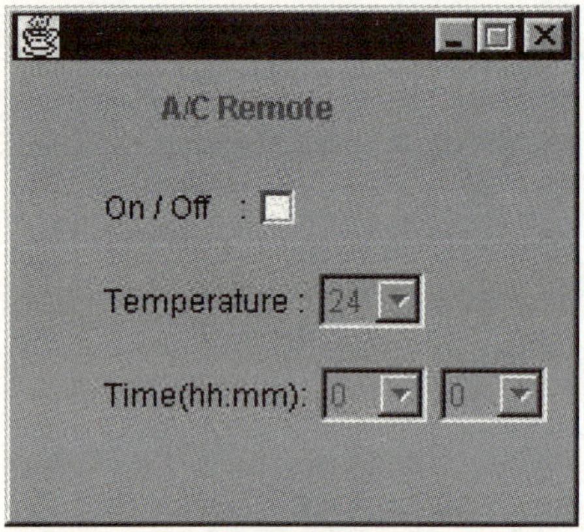

Figure 13-19: Air conditioner control panel

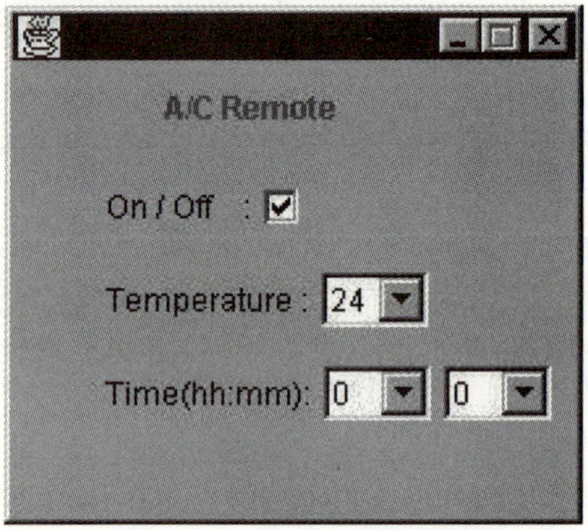

Figure 13-20: Control panel with enabled controls

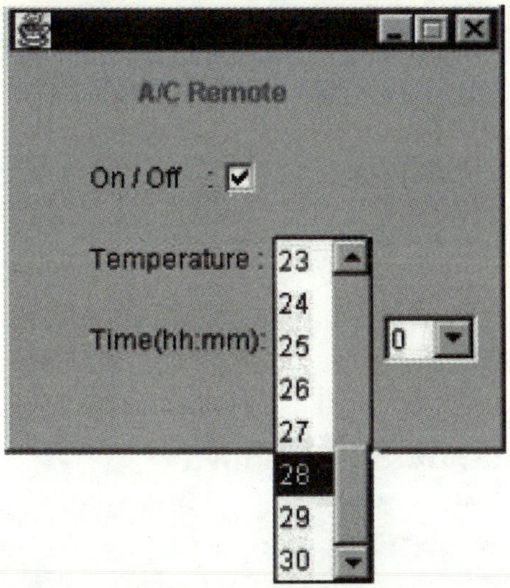

Figure 13-21: Setting the values on the control panel

Project files

The project consists of the following files:

- `ACRemoteServiceInterface.java`: This file contains the declarations of all the user-defined methods.
- `ACRemoteService.java`: This file contains a proxy class implementation, `ACRemoteServiceProxy`, and a service class implementation, `ACRemoteService`, which is the wrapper class that handles publishing the service item `AC remote service`.
- `ACRemoteClient.java`: This file contains the implementation of the client class `ACRemoteClient`. A search is done of the services already registered with the lookup service, and if the required service is found, an instance of that service is created.
- `ClientGUI.java`: This file contains the implementation of the user interface.

Source code listings

Listing 13-6 provides the source code for `ACRemoteServiceInterface.java`.

Listing 13-6: Source code for ACRemoteServiceInterface.java

```
// This is the interface that the service's proxy implements
package ACRemote;
public interface ACRemoteServiceInterface{
public void setOnOff(int state);
public void setTemp(int temp);
public void setTimer(int hh,int min);
```

```
6.public String getStatus();
7.}
```

Following is the line-by-line explanation of the source code:

- **Line 1:** Package declaration.
- **Line 2:** Declaration of the public interface `ACRemoteServiceInterface`.
- **Line 3:** Declaration of the method to change the state of the air conditioner (On/Off).
- **Line 4:** Declaration of the method to set the temperature.
- **Line 5:** Declaration of the method to set the timer.
- **Line 6:** Declaration of the method to retrieve the status of the air condtioner.

Listing 13-7: Source code for ACRemoteService.java

```
// This is AC Remote Service, a proxy that returns status of the AC
// machine and set to On/Off, temperature, timer.
package ACRemote;
import java.util.Hashtable;
import java.io.IOException;
import java.io.Serializable;
import java.rmi.RemoteException;
import java.rmi.RMISecurityManager;
import net.jini.discovery.DiscoveryListener;
import net.jini.discovery.DiscoveryEvent;
import net.jini.discovery.LookupDiscovery;
import net.jini.core.lookup.ServiceRegistrar;
import net.jini.core.lookup.ServiceItem;
import net.jini.core.lookup.ServiceRegistration;
// This is the proxy object that will be downloaded by clients. It's
// serilizable our interface ACRemoteServiceInterface.
class ACRemoteServiceProxy implements
Serializable,ACRemoteServiceInterface{
int state;
int temp;
int hh, mm;
public ACRemoteServiceProxy(){
this.state = 2;
this.temp=24;
this.hh=0;
this.mm=0;
}
public void setOnOff(int state){
this.state = state;
}
public void setTemp(int temp){
this.temp = temp;
}
```

```
public void setTimer(int hh,int mm){
this.hh = hh;
this.mm = mm;
}
public String getStatus(){
String str = new String(state+"#"+temp+"#"+hh+"#"+mm);
return str;
}
}
// ACRemoteService is the “wrapper” class that handles publishing the
// service item.
public class ACRemoteService implements Runnable{
protected final int LEASE_TIME = 10 * 60 * 1000;
protected Hashtable regs = new Hashtable();
protected ServiceItem item;
protected LookupDiscovery discovery;
// Inner Class to listen for Discovery Events.
class MyListener implements DiscoveryListener{
// This method is called when a new lookup service is found.
public void discovered(DiscoveryEvent de){
System.out.println("Discovered a lookup service!");
ServiceRegistrar newregs[] = de.getRegistrars();
for(int i=0;i<newregs.length;i++){
if(!regs.containsKey(newregs[i])){
registerWithLookup(newregs[i]);
}
}
}
// This method is called to discard a lookup service.
public void discarded(DiscoveryEvent de){
ServiceRegistrar deadregs[] = de.getRegistrars();
for(int i=0;i<deadregs.length;i++){
regs.remove(deadregs[i]);
}
}
}
public ACRemoteService() throws IOException{
item = new ServiceItem(null, createProxy(),null);
if(System.getSecurityManager() == null){
System.setSecurityManager(new RMISecurityManager());
}
String namedStr[] = {""};
discovery = new LookupDiscovery(namedStr);
discovery.addDiscoveryListener(new MyListener());
}
protected ACRemoteServiceInterface createProxy(){
return new ACRemoteServiceProxy();
}
// This method involves remote calls, and to register with the lookup
```

```
// service.
72. protected synchronized void registerWithLookup(ServiceRegistrar
registrar){
73. ServiceRegistration servicereg = null;
74. try{
75. servicereg = registrar.register(item,LEASE_TIME);
76. }catch(RemoteException e){
77. System.err.println("Unable to register: "+e.getMessage());
78. return;
79. }
80. regs.put(registrar,servicereg);
81. System.out.println("Service is Registered with Lookup Service.");
82. }
// This method is to keep in Sleep state for 1000000 msec.
83. public void run(){
84. while(true){
85. try{
86. Thread.sleep(1000000);
87. }catch(Exception e){
88. }
89. }
90. }
91. public static void main(String args[]){
92. try{
93. ACRemoteService remoteservice = new ACRemoteService();
94. new Thread(remoteservice).start();
95. }catch(IOException e){
96. System.err.println("Unable to create service: "+e.getMessage());
97. }
98. }
99. }
```

Following is the line-by-line explanation of the source code:

- **Line 1:** Package declaration.
- **Lines 2–12:** Importing the basic packages needed for the various classes used to build this application, such as for serializing, rmi security, discovering the Jini services available on the network, registering with the lookup service, text manipulations, etc.
- **Line 13:** Declaration of the class `ACRemoteServiceProxy`, which implements the interfaces `java.io.Serializable` and `ACRemoteServiceInterface`.
- **Lines 14–16:** Variables declaration.
- **Line 17:** Declaration of the default constructor.
- **Lines 18–21:** Initializing the variables with the default values.
- **Lines 23–25:** Implementation of the method `setOnOff`, to change the state of the air conditioner.

- **Lines 26–28:** Implementation of the method `setTemp`, to change the temperature.
- **Lines 29–32:** Implementation of the method `setTimer`, to change the timer.
- **Lines 33–36:** Implementation of the method `getStatus`, to retrieve information about the air conditioner's status — that is, whether the machine is on or off, and temperature and timer values.
- **Line 38:** Declaration of a class `ACRemoteService`, which implements the interface `Runnable`.
- **Line 39:** Declaration and initialization of the variable `LEASE_TIME` to 10 minutes.
- **Line 40:** Declaration of the variable `regs` for maintaining the services registration information.
- **Lines 41–42:** Variables decaration.
- **Lines 43–59:** This is an inner class implementation that implements `DiscoveryListener`.
  - **Line 44:** Declaration of the method discovered, which is called when one or more lookup service registrars have been discovered.
  - **Line 46:** Declaration and initialization of an array of registrars to which `DiscoveryEvent` applies.
  - **Lines 47–51:** Checks whether our service is registered with the lookup service.
  - **Line 53:** Declaration of the method discarded, which is called when one or more lookup service registrars have been discarded.
  - **Line 54:** Declaration and initialization of an array of registrars to which `DiscoveryEvent` applies.
- **Lines 55–57:** Removes registered services.
- **Line 60:** Declaration of the `ACRemoteService` constructor.
- **Line 61:** Initialization of the object`ServiceItem`. The attributes for this object are item service ID (null, if registering for the first time), service object, and attribute sets.
- **Lines 62–64:** Sets the security to our service.
- **Line 66:** Initialization of the `discovery` object to construct a new lookup discovery object, set to discover the `namedStr`.
- **Line 67:** To add `addDiscoveryListener` method to the `discovery` object with the reference of the `MyListener` class.
- **Lines 69–71:** Implementation of the `createProxy` method, which returns an instance of the `ACRemoteServiceProxy` object.
- **Lines 72–82:** Implementation of the `registerWithLookup` method.

- **Line 75:** Registers the service item with the `LEASE_TIME`; that is, for 10 minutes.
- **Line 80:** Puts the registered service information in the `regs` hash table.

- **Lines 83–90:** Implementation of the `run` method for keeping the available service on.
- **Lines 91–98:** Implementation of the `main` method.
  - **Line 93:** Creates an instance of the `ACRemoteService` class.
  - **Line 94:** Creates a new thread for the `ACRemoteService` object.

Listing 13-8: Source code for ACRemoteClient.java

```
// This is an AC Remote Client program
1. package ACRemote;
2. import java.util.Vector;
3. import java.io.IOException;
4. import java.rmi.RemoteException;
5. import java.rmi.RMISecurityManager;
6. import net.jini.discovery.DiscoveryListener;
7. import net.jini.discovery.DiscoveryEvent;
8. import net.jini.discovery.LookupDiscovery;
9. import net.jini.core.lookup.ServiceRegistrar;
10. import net.jini.core.lookup.ServiceTemplate;
11. public class ACRemoteClient implements Runnable{
12. protected ServiceTemplate template;
13. protected LookupDiscovery discovery;
14. static Object obj;
// This is an inner class to listen Discovery Events.
15. class MyListener implements DiscoveryListener{
16. public void discovered(DiscoveryEvent de){
17. ServiceRegistrar[] newregs = de.getRegistrars();
18. for(int i=0;i<newregs.length;i++){
19. lookForService(newregs[i]);
20. }
21. }
22. public void discarded(DiscoveryEvent de){
23. }
24. }
25. public ACRemoteClient() throws IOException{
26. Class types[] = { ACRemoteServiceInterface.class };
27. template = new ServiceTemplate(null, types, null);
28. if(System.getSecurityManager() == null){
29. System.setSecurityManager(new RMISecurityManager());
30. }
31. discovery = new LookupDiscovery(new String[] {""});
32. discovery.addDiscoveryListener(new MyListener());
33. }
34. protected Object lookForService(ServiceRegistrar lusvc){
35. Object o = null;
```

```
36. try{
37. o= lusvc.lookup(template);
38. }catch(RemoteException e) {
39. System.err.println("Error doing lookup : "+e.getMessage());
40. return null;
41. }
42. if(o == null){
43. System.out.println("\t \t No matching service found.");return null;
44. }
45. obj = o;
46. System.out.println("\t \t Found a matching service.");
47. return o;
48. }
49. public void run(){
50. while(true){
51. try{
52. Thread.sleep(1000000);
53. }catch(InterruptedException e){
54. System.err.println("Interrpted Exception occured: "+e.getMessage());
55. }
56. }
57. }
58. }
```

Following is the line-by-line explanation of the source code:

- **Line 1:** Package declaration.
- **Lines 2–10:** Includes the basic packages needed for the various classes used to build this application, such as packages for serializing, rmi security, discovering the Jini services available on the network, registering the lookup service, vector and hash tables of `java.util` packages, text manipulations, etc.
- **Line 12:** Declares a variable, `template`, which is an instance of `ServiceTemplate`.
- **Line 13:** Declares a variable, `discovery`, which is an instance of `LookupDiscovery`.
- **Line 14:** Declares a static object, `obj`, which is an instance of `Object`; this instance is used in the `ClientGUI` class.
- **Lines 15–24:** This is an inner class implementation, which implements `DiscoveryListener`.
  - **Lines 16–21:** Declares the method, `discovered`, which is called when one or more lookup service registrars have been discovered.
  - **Lines 17–20:** Checks whether our service is registered with the lookup service.
  - **Lines 22–23:** This is a null implementation of the method `discarded`.
- **Line 25:** Declares the `ACRemoteClient` constructor.

- **Line 27:** Initializes the `ServiceTemplate` variable, with the arguments service ID, service types, and attribute of the templates.
- **Lines 28–30:** Sets the security to our service.
- **Line 32:** To add `addDiscoveryListener` method to the `discovery` object with the reference of the `MyListener` class.
- **Lines 34–48:** This is an implementation of the `registerWithLookup` method.
  - **Line 37:** Searches for a service with the `ServiceTemplate` information.
- **Lines 49–57:** This is an implementation of the `run` method.

Listing 13-9: Source code for ClientGUI.java

```
// This class is for Client GUI.
1.package ACRemote;
2.import ACRemote.*;
3.import java.io.*;
4.import java.awt.*;
5.import java.util.*;
6.import javax.swing.*;
7.import java.awt.event.*;
8.import javax.swing.event.*;
9.import javax.swing.border.*;
10.public class ClientGUI extends JFrame implements ActionListener,
ItemListener{
11.JLabel label1,label2,label3,label4;
12.JPanel panelh =new JPanel(new FlowLayout(FlowLayout.CENTER));
13.JPanel panelm =new JPanel(new FlowLayout(FlowLayout.LEFT));
14.JPanel panel1 =new JPanel();
15.JPanel panel2 =new JPanel();
16.JPanel panel3 =new JPanel();
17.JCheckBox ch1;
18.JComboBox cb1,cb2,cb3;
19.String strserver,str;
20.String ON="On";
21.String OFF="Off";
22.int status,temp,hh,mm;
23.StringTokenizer stoken;
24.Color c=new Color(100,100,255);
25.Font f1=new Font("Arial",Font.BOLD,12);
26.public ClientGUI(){
27.getContentPane().setLayout(null);
28.setResizable(false);
29.setBackground(Color.lightGray);
30.addWindowListener(new WindowAdapter(){
31.public void windowClosing(WindowEvent we){
32.System.exit(0);}
```

```
});
panelh.setBounds(15,5,150,30);
panelm.setBounds(25,35,185,150);
panel1.setBounds(30,65,150,30);
panel2.setBounds(30,95,150,30);
panel3.setBounds(30,125,185,30);
label1=new JLabel("A/C Remote");
label1.setFont(f1);
label1.setForeground(c);
panelh.add(label1);
panelm.add(panel1);
panelm.add(panel2);
panelm.add(panel3);
panel1.add(label1=new JLabel("On / Off     :"));
panel1.add(ch1= new JCheckBox());
panel2.add(label2=new JLabel("Temperature :"));
panel2.add(cb1= new JComboBox());
panel3.add(label2=new JLabel("Time(hh:mm):"));
panel3.add(cb2= new JComboBox());
panel3.add(cb3= new JComboBox());
for(int i=10;i<=30;i++){
String s = new String(""+i);
cb1.addItem(s);
}
for(int j=0;j<=12;j++){
String s=new String(""+j);
cb2.addItem(s);
}
for(int j=0;j<=60;j+=5){
String s=new String(""+j);
cb3.addItem(s);
}
strserver =
((ACRemoteServiceInterface)ACRemoteClient.obj).getStatus();
Tokenize();
if(status == 1) {
ch1.setSelected(true);
} else {
ch1.setSelected(false);
cb1.setEnabled(false);
cb2.setEnabled(false);
cb3.setEnabled(false);
}
cb1.setSelectedItem(""+temp);
cb2.setSelectedItem(""+hh);
cb3.setSelectedItem(""+mm);
ch1.addItemListener(this);
cb1.addActionListener(this);
cb2.addActionListener(this);
```

```
cb3.addActionListener(this);
getContentPane().add(panelh);
getContentPane().add(panelm);
}
// This method is to listen Action Events.
public void actionPerformed(ActionEvent ae){
Object o = ae.getSource();
if(o.equals(cb1)){
temp=Integer.parseInt((String)cb1.getSelectedItem());
((ACRemoteServiceInterface)ACRemoteClient.obj).setTemp(temp);
}
if(o.equals(cb2)){
hh=Integer.parseInt((String)cb2.getSelectedItem());
((ACRemoteServiceInterface)ACRemoteClient.obj).setTimer(hh,mm);
}
if(o.equals(cb3)){
mm=Integer.parseInt((String)cb3.getSelectedItem());
((ACRemoteServiceInterface)ACRemoteClient.obj).setTimer(hh,mm);
}
strserver =
((ACRemoteServiceInterface)ACRemoteClient.obj).getStatus();
Tokenize();
}
// This method is to listen items state events.
public void itemStateChanged(ItemEvent ie){
status = (int)ie.getStateChange();
((ACRemoteServiceInterface)ACRemoteClient.obj).setOnOff(status);
strserver =
((ACRemoteServiceInterface)ACRemoteClient.obj).getStatus();
Tokenize();
if(status == 1){
cb1.setEnabled(true);
cb2.setEnabled(true);
cb3.setEnabled(true);
} else {
cb1.setEnabled(false);
cb2.setEnabled(false);
cb3.setEnabled(false);
}
}
// To parse the string strserver, which is accessed from the
ACRemoteProxy.
public void Tokenize(){
stoken = new StringTokenizer(strserver,"#");
status=Integer.parseInt(stoken.nextToken());
temp=Integer.parseInt(stoken.nextToken());
hh=Integer.parseInt(stoken.nextToken());
mm=Integer.parseInt(stoken.nextToken());
```

```
123. System.out.println("Status : "+((status == 1) ? ON : OFF)+" temp :
"+temp+" hh : "+hh+" mm : "+mm);
124. }
125. static ACRemoteClient acremote;
126. public static void main(String args[])
127. {
128. try{
129.
 UIManager.setLookAndFeel("com.sun.java.swing.plaf.windows.WindowsLookAn
dFeel");
130. }catch (Exception e){
131. }
132. System.out.println("\n Please wait.....");
133. try{
134. acremote = new ACRemoteClient();
135. new Thread(acremote).start();
136. }catch(Exception e) {
137. System.err.println("Unable to create client: "+e.getMessage());
138. }
139. try{
140. Thread.sleep(15*1000);
141. }catch(Exception e){
142. System.err.println("Interrpted Exception occured:
"+e.getMessage());
143. }
144. ClientGUI sac=new ClientGUI();
145. sac.setSize(220,200);
146. sac.setVisible(true);
147. }
148. }
```

Following is the line-by-line explanation of the source code:

- **Line 1:** Package declaration.
- **Lines 2–9:** Importing the basic packages needed for the various classes used to build this application, such as packages for the user interface design, events handling, text manipulations, etc.
- **Line 10:** Declaration of the public class `ClientGUI`.
- **Line 11:** Declaration of objects of `JLabel`.
- **Lines 12–16:** `JPanel` objects declarations.
- **Line 17:** Declaration of a `JCheckBox` variable.
- **Line 18:** Declaration of three `JComboBox` variables.
- **Lines 19–22:** Variable declaration for `String` and `int` data types.
- **Line 23:** Declares a `StringTokenizer` variable.

- **Line 24:** Creates a `Color` class instance with blue color.
- **Line 25:** Creates a `Font` class instance with the attribute's name, style, and size.
- **Line 26:** Declares the `ClientGUI` constructor.
- **Line 27:** Sets the null layout for the `JFrame`.
- **Line 28:** Sets the resize to false for the `JFrame`.
- **Line 29:** Sets the background color to light gray.
- **Lines 30–33:** This is a Window Adapter class for window closing (`Client GUI`).
- **Lines 34–38:** Sets the bounds to the `JPanels`.
- **Line 39:** Creates a `JLabel` object.
- **Line 40:** Sets the font of a `JLabel`.
- **Line 41:** Sets the foreground of a `JLabel`.
- **Line 42:** Adds the `JLabel` to the `JPanel`.
- **Lines 43–45:** Adds the `JPanels` to main `JPanel`, `panelm`.
- **Line 46:** Creates an object for `JLabel` (On/Off) and adds it to the `JPanel` (`Panel1`).
- **Line 47:** Creates an object for `JCheckBox` and adds it to the panel (`Panel1`).
- **Line 48:** Creates an object for `label` (Temperature) and adds it to the panel (`Panel2`).
- **Line 49:** Creates an object for `JComboBox` and adds it to the panel (`Panel2`).
- **Line 50:** Creates an object for label (Time(hh:mm)) and adds it to the panel (`Panel3`).
- **Lines 51–52:** Creates an object for `JComboBox` and adds it to the panel (`Panel3`).
- **Lines 53–56:** Adds an item to the item list of `JComboBox`.
- **Lines 57–60:** Adds an item to the item list of `JComboBox`.
- **Lines 61–64:** Adds an item to the item list of `JComboBox`.
- **Line 65:** Calls the `getStatus` method of `ACRemoteClient` and type casts it to `ACRemoteServiceInterface` and assigns it to the string.
- **Line 66:** Calls the method `Tokenize`.
- **Lines 67–70:** If the status is 1, `JCheckBox` is set to true; otherwise, `JCheckBox` is set to false.
- **Lines 71–73:** Disables the combo box.
- **Lines 75–77:** Sets the combo boxes to the selected items (temp,hh,mm). Status, temp, hh, and mm are the variables assigned in the `Tokenize` method.
- **Line 78:** Adds the `ItemListener` to the `JCheckBox`.
- **Lines 79–81:** Adds the ActionListener to the `JComboBox`.
- **Lines 82–83:** Adds the panels to the content pane.

- **Line 85:** This method performs an action when the user selects the `JComboBox`.
- **Line 86:** Gets the source of the event and assigns it to the object.
- **Lines 87–88:** If the object equals to `JComboBox` (`cb1`), parses the currently selected item of that `JComboBox` and assigns it to the integer (`temp`).
- **Line 89:** Calls the method `setTemp` of `ACRemoteClient` to set the selected temperature.
- **Lines 91–92:** If the object equals to `JComboBox` (`cb2`), parses the currently selected item of that `JComboBox` and assigns it to the integer (`hh`).
- **Line 93:** Calls the method `setTimer` of `ACRemoteClient` to set the selected hour.
- **Lines 95–96:** If the object equals to `JComboBox` (`cb3`), parses the currently selected item of that `JComboBox` and assigns it to the integer (mm).
- **Line 97:** Calls the method `setTimer` of `ACRemoteClient` to set the selected minute.
- **Line 99:** Calls the `getStatus` method of `ACRemoteClient`, type casts it to `ACRemoteServiceInterface`, and assigns it to the string.
- **Line 100:** Calls the method `Tokenize`.
- **Line 102:** This method is invoked when the item's state has been changed.
- **Line 103:** Gets the `JCheckBox` state change (`SELECTED` or `DESELECTED`), type casts it to the integer, and assigns it to the integer (status).
- **Line 104:** Calls the method `setOnOff` of `ACRemoteClient`.
- **Line 105:** Calls the `getStatus` method of `ACRemoteClient`, type casts it to `ACRemoteServiceInterface`, and assigns it to the string.
- **Line 106:** Calls the method `Tokenize`.
- **Lines 107–115:** If status is 1, enables the `JComboBox` so that items can be selected; otherwise, it disables the `JComboBox`.
- **Line 117:** This is a method to tokenize the String.
- **Line 118:** Constructs a string tokenizer for the specified string.
- **Line 119:** Returns the next token from the specified string tokenizer, parses it, and assigns it to the integer (`status`).
- **Line 120:** Returns the next token from the specified string tokenizer, parses it, and assigns it to the integer (`temp`).
- **Line 121:** Returns the next token from the specified string tokenizer, parses it, and assigns it to the integer (`hh`).
- **Line 122:** Returns the next token from the specified string tokenizer, parse its, and assigns it to the integer (mm).
- **Line 125:** Declares a static object for `ACRemoteClient`.

- **Line 126:** Implementation of the `main` method.
- **Line 129:** Sets the current default look and feel using a `LookAndFeel` object.
- **Line 134:** Creates an object for `ACRemoteClient`.
- **Line 135:** Creates a thread for `ACRemoteClient`.
- **Line 140:** Causes the thread to sleep for 15 seconds.
- **Line 144:** Creates an object for `ClientGUI`.
- **Line 145:** Sets the size for `ClientGUI`.
- **Line 146:** Calls the method `setVisible` to display the GUI.

Testing the application

To test the application, follow these steps:

1. Save the `ACRemoteServiceInterface.java`, `ACRemoteService.java`, `ACRemoteClient.java`, and `ClientGUI.java` files in the `\jini_app\ACRemote` folder.
2. Create four folders — `\service`, `\service-dl`, `\client`, and `\client-dl` — in the `\jini_app` folder:

```
cd jini_app
md service
md service-dl
md client
md client-dl
```

3. Compile the programs:

```
cd ACRemote
javac -classpath d:\jini1_2\lib\jini-core.jar;
                      d:\jini1_2\lib\jini-ext.jar;
                      d:\jini1_2\lib\sun-util.jar;
                      d:\jini_app\service
        -d d:\ jini_app\service
ACRemoteServiceInterface.java  ACRemoteService.java

        javac -classpath c:\jdk1.3\lib\tools.jar;
                       d:\jini1_2\lib\jini-core.jar;
                       d:\jini1_2\lib\jini-ext.jar;
                       d:\jini1_2\lib\sun-util.jar;
                       d:\jini_app\client
        -d d:\jini_app\client
        ACRemoteServiceInterface.java
        ACRemoteClient.java
        ClientGUI.java
```

4. Copy the `ACRemoteServiceProxy.class` file to the `\service-dl` folder:

```
copy d:\jini_app\service\ACRemoteServiceProxy.class
d:\jini_app\service-dl\ACRemoteServiceProxy.class
```

5. Create a security policy file with the following code:

```
grant {
        permission java.security.AllPermission;
};
```

Create a folder named `d:\policy\` and save this security policy file as “policy”.

6. Start an HTTP server for the service using the following command:

```
java -jar d:\jini1_2\lib\tools.jar -dir d:\jini_app\service-dl
-verbose -port 8085
```

The screen shown in Figure 13-22 will be displayed.

7. Start the `ACRemoteService`:

```
        java -cp d:\jini1_2\lib\jini-core.jar;
               d:\jini1_2\lib\jini-ext.jar;
               d:\jini1_2\lib\sun-util.jar;
               d:\jini_app\service
        -Djava.rmi.server.codebase=http://localhost:8085/
        -Djava.security.policy=d:\policy\policy
        ACRemote.ACRemoteService
```

The screen shown in Figure 13-23 will be displayed.

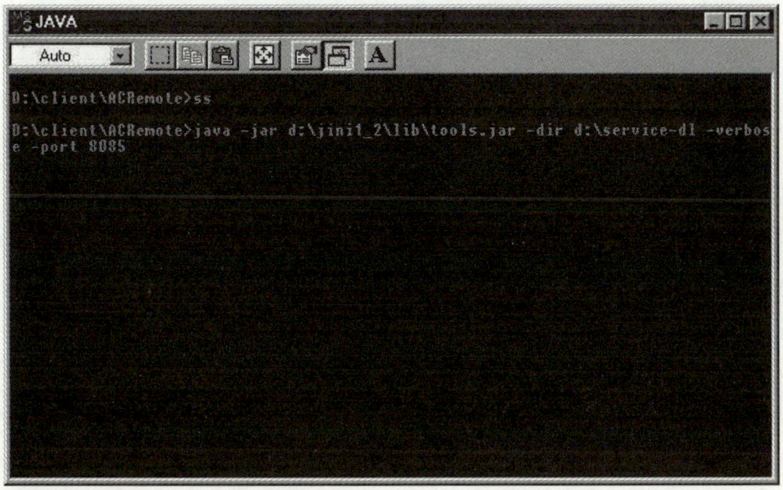

Figure 13-22: Starting the HTTP server

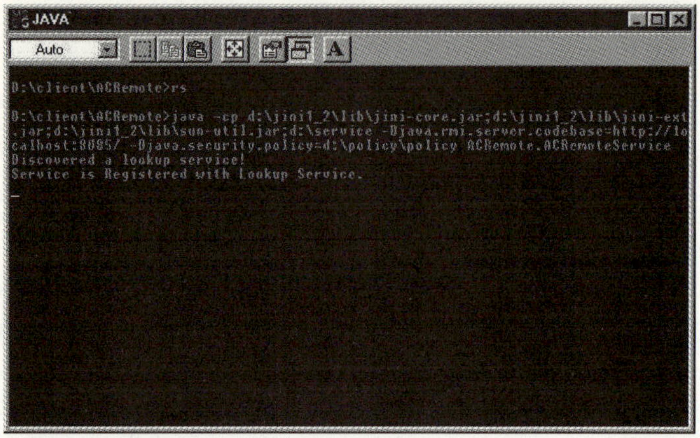

Figure 13-23: Starting the AC remote service

8. Run the client program:

```
java -cp c:\jdk1.3\lib\tools.jar;
        d:\jini1_2\lib\jini-core.jar;
d:\jini1_2\lib\jini-ext.jar;
        d:\jini1_2\lib\sun-util.jar;
        d:\jini_app\client
        -Djava.security.policy=d:\policy\policy
ACRemote.ClientGUI
```

The screen shown in Figure 13-24 will be displayed, followed by the one shown in Figure 13-25.

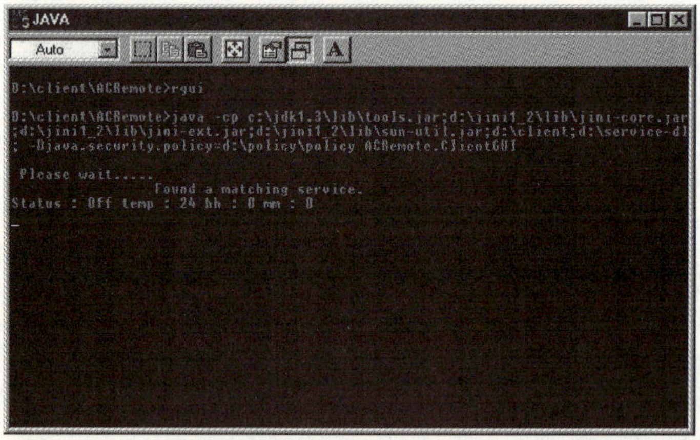

Figure 13-24: Running the client program

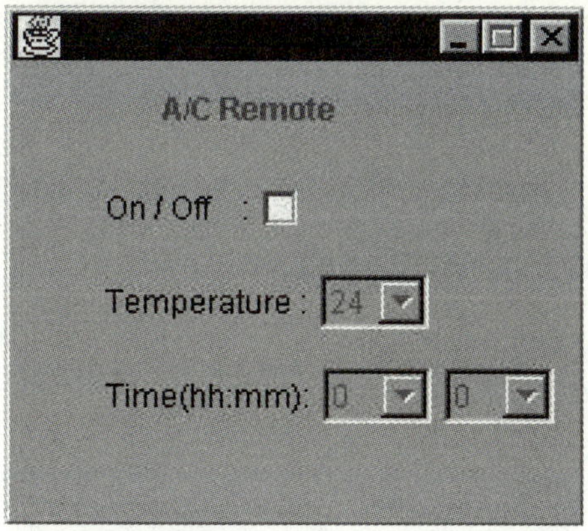

Figure 13-25: Air conditioner remote control panel

Summary

This chapter demonstrated the development of two applications using Sun Microsystems tools for creating Java-enabled devices using J2ME and Jini. The first application develops an electronic city guide using the J2ME platform with MIDP APIs. Java-enabled mobile devices can obtain information from the servers using the MIDlets. The second application demonstrated the use of Jini connection technology, which facilitates development of dynamic distributed systems. You learned how an air conditioner control can be a service in the Jini environment. If a mobile phone is both Java-enabled and Jini-enabled, the power of information appliances increases manifold. Normally, the mobile phone can access information available on the servers through the mobile network. Jini provides the capability to make a mobile device the node of another network dynamically. In the future, devices that are both Java- and Jini-enabled will be very powerful information appliances.

Chapter 14
Software Development in Windows XP Embedded

In This Chapter

- Controlling an air conditioner
- Controlling an audio player
- Testing typing speed
- Embedding a database for field personnel
- Implementing an electronic voting system

Microsoft's latest desktop operating system, Windows XP, is available as an embedded version called *Windows XP Embedded* (abbreviated as *Embedded XP* in the following discussion). This operating system is the successor to Embedded NT. The main attraction of using the embedded version of Microsoft's operating systems is that existing applications written using the Visual Studio environment (VB or VC++) can be directly ported onto the embedded system, if the embedded system has the necessary processing and memory capabilities. This chapter describes how to develop five projects using VC++, VB, and ASP and examines how these applications can be embedded into a target machine.

Development Environment

For testing the projects discussed in this chapter, you need the following:

- Embedded XP installed on a Windows 2000 or Windows XP system
- Visual Studio 6.0
- An MS Access database running on the system on which Embedded XP is installed
- A LAN with one of the nodes running IIS or Personal Web Server, for testing the electronic voting project
- A Windows 9*x* system, used for simulating the consumer items such as an air conditioner and an audio player

- A null modem cable to test the applications for controlling the air conditioner and audio player

Overview of the Projects

The embedded version of Windows XP provides a powerful environment for developing a variety of embedded applications. Diverse applications such as games, mobile data applications, point-of-sale devices, panel PCs, and the like are being developed using Embedded XP. This chapter demonstrates how you can develop five such applications. Two of the applications — for controlling an air conditioner from an embedded system (a mobile device running Embedded XP) and remote control of an audio player — are developed in the VC++ environment. Two other applications — a typing speed indicator and a database application for carrying out a field survey — are developed in the VB environment. The remaining application, an electronic voting system, is developed using ASP. In the browser running on the Embedded XP system, the user only has to provide a URL to access the electronic voting server. These applications were chosen because they demonstrate the advantages of using Embedded XP for embedded applications, which can be very easily ported to an embedded system when written in the Visual Studio environment.

To embed the operating system and the application program in the target system, you need to create the target image by specifying all the components required for the application. These include the components for display, a keyboard, a mouse, serial ports, a modem, a sound card, Internet Explorer 6.0, etc. If your embedded application does not require some of these components, you can delete them, which conserves the memory of the target system. If you keep each of the basic components previously listed, the target image will require memory in the range of 80MB to 120MB, including the application. The projects presented here include all the basic components needed, so testing the application is easy. You may want to modify the code to limit the display size, depending on the target system's display size.

Project: Remote Control of an Air Conditioner

You can use mobile devices such as a mobile phone or a PDA to control consumer items such as an air conditioner, a CD player, a digital TV, and the like. You need a communication medium between the two devices, using technologies such as infrared or Bluetooth. If the consumer item and the mobile device are equipped with one of these communication interfaces, the application software embedded in the mobile device can be used to control the appliance. This project demonstrates this capability. The air conditioner can be controlled through a user interface provided on the Embedded XP machine, and the commands are passed to a Windows 9*x* machine. Three controls are used: one for on and off settings, a timer setting, and a temperature setting. The two machines are connected through a null modem cable.

Project overview

This project contains two applications. ACRemote runs on the Embedded XP machine, and ACSimulator runs on the Windows 9*x* machine.

The ACRemote application contains four files:

- `Serial.h` is a header file containing the declaration of the `Cserial` class.
- `Serial.cpp` is a file containing the definition of the `Cserial` class and the methods to open and close the serial port, as well as methods to write data to the serial port.
- `ACRemoteDlg.h` is a header file containing the declaration of the `CACRemoteDlg` class.
- `ACRemoteDlg.cpp` is a file containing the definition of the `CACRemoteDlg` class and methods to send commands to switch the air conditioner on and off and to set temperature and timer values.

The ACSimulator application contains one file:

- `ACSimulator.cpp` is a file containing the definition of methods to read data from the serial port and to interpret the commands.

Source code listing for Serial.h

The file `Serial.h` contains the source code for the `CSerial` class declaration. The variables and methods used are described in the code explanation for the corresponding `.CPP` file (`Serial.cpp`). The source code for `Serial.h` is provided in Listing 14-1, and the source code for `Serial.cpp` is provided in Listing 14-2.

Listing 14-1: Source code for Serial.h

```
#if !defined(AFX_SERIAL_H__981F1CE1_F69E_11D5_AC16_0080C80496C8__INCLUDED_)
#define AFX_SERIAL_H__981F1CE1_F69E_11D5_AC16_0080C80496C8__INCLUDED_
#if _MSC_VER > 1000
#pragma once
#endif // _MSC_VER > 1000
#define FC_DTRDSR       0x01
#define FC_RTSCTS       0x02
#define FC_XONXOFF      0x04
#define ASCII_BEL       0x07
#define ASCII_BS        0x08
#define ASCII_LF        0x0A
#define ASCII_CR        0x0D
#define ASCII_XON       0x11
#define ASCII_XOFF      0x13
class CSerial : public CDialog
{
// Construction
```

```
public:
CSerial(CWnd* pParent = NULL);    // standard constructor
// Dialog Data
//{{AFX_DATA(CSerial)
//enum { IDD = _UNKNOWN_RESOURCE_ID_ };
enum { IDD = IDD_ACREMOTE_DIALOG};
// NOTE: the ClassWizard will add data members here
//}}AFX_DATA
// Overrides
// ClassWizard generated virtual function overrides
//{{AFX_VIRTUAL(CSerial)
protected:
virtual void DoDataExchange(CDataExchange* pDX);    // DDX/DDV
support
//}}AFX_VIRTUAL
// Implementation
protected:
// Generated message map functions
//{{AFX_MSG(CSerial)
// NOTE: the ClassWizard will add member functions here
//}}AFX_MSG
DECLARE_MESSAGE_MAP()
public:
BOOL Open (int,int,char,int,int);
BOOL Close( void );
BOOL IsOpened(void);
int SendData(const char*,int);
BOOL WriteCommByte(unsigned char );
};
//{{AFX_INSERT_LOCATION}}
// Microsoft Visual C++ will insert additional declarations
immediately before the previous line.
#endif //
!defined(AFX_SERIAL_H__981F1CE1_F69E_11D5_AC16_0080C80496C8__INCLUDED_)
```

Source code listing for Serial.cpp

Listing 14-2 provides the source code for `Serial.cpp`. This file contains methods for sending data through the serial communication port. This listing re-uses a number of lines from Listing 7-2, which describes navigation software development using the GPS receiver. The code explanation that follows Listing 14-2 indicates the changes made to Listing 7-2.

Listing 14-2: Source code for Serial.cpp

```
// Serial.cpp : implementation file
#include "stdafx.h"
#include "ACRemote.h"
#include "Serial.h"
#ifdef _DEBUG
```

```
#define new DEBUG_NEW
#undef THIS_FILE
static char THIS_FILE[] = __FILE__;
#endif
BOOL m_bOpened;
HANDLE m_hIDComDev;
OVERLAPPED m_OverlappedRead, m_OverlappedWrite;
CSerial::CSerial(CWnd* pParent /*=NULL*/)
    : CDialog(CSerial::IDD, pParent)
{
//{{AFX_DATA_INIT(CSerial)
// NOTE: the ClassWizard will add member initialization here
//}}AFX_DATA_INIT
}
void CSerial::DoDataExchange(CDataExchange* pDX)
{
CDialog::DoDataExchange(pDX);
//{{AFX_DATA_MAP(CSerial)
// NOTE: the ClassWizard will add DDX and DDV calls here
//}}AFX_DATA_MAP
}
BEGIN_MESSAGE_MAP(CSerial, CDialog)
//{{AFX_MSG_MAP(CSerial)
// NOTE: the ClassWizard will add message map macros here
//}}AFX_MSG_MAP
END_MESSAGE_MAP()
BOOL CSerial::Open( int nPort, int nBaud ,char nParity,int
nDatabits,int nStopbits)
{
char szPort[15];
char szComParams[50];
DCB dcb;
unsigned char ucSet;
COMMTIMEOUTS CommTimeOuts;
if( m_bOpened ) return( TRUE );
wsprintf( szPort, "COM%d", nPort );
m_hIDComDev = CreateFile( szPort, GENERIC_READ | GENERIC_WRITE, 0,
NULL, OPEN_EXISTING,          FILE_ATTRIBUTE_NORMAL |
FILE_FLAG_OVERLAPPED, NULL );
if( m_hIDComDev == NULL ) return( FALSE );
memset( &m_OverlappedRead, 0, sizeof( OVERLAPPED ) );
memset( &m_OverlappedWrite, 0, sizeof( OVERLAPPED ) );
CommTimeOuts.ReadIntervalTimeout = 0xFFFFFFFF;
CommTimeOuts.ReadTotalTimeoutMultiplier = 0;
CommTimeOuts.ReadTotalTimeoutConstant = 0;
CommTimeOuts.WriteTotalTimeoutMultiplier = 0;
CommTimeOuts.WriteTotalTimeoutConstant = 5000;
SetCommTimeouts( m_hIDComDev, &CommTimeOuts );
```

```
wsprintf( szComParams, "COM%d:%d,%c,%d,%d", nPort, nBaud
,nParity,nDatabits,nStopbits);
m_OverlappedRead.hEvent = CreateEvent( NULL, TRUE, FALSE, NULL );
m_OverlappedWrite.hEvent = CreateEvent( NULL, TRUE, FALSE, NULL );
dcb.DCBlength = sizeof( DCB );
GetCommState( m_hIDComDev, &dcb );
dcb.BaudRate = nBaud;
dcb.ByteSize = 8;
ucSet = (unsigned char) ( ( FC_RTSCTS & FC_DTRDSR ) != 0 );
ucSet = (unsigned char) ( ( FC_RTSCTS & FC_RTSCTS ) != 0 );
ucSet = (unsigned char) ( ( FC_RTSCTS & FC_XONXOFF ) != 0 );
if( !SetCommState( m_hIDComDev, &dcb ) ||
!SetupComm( m_hIDComDev, 10000, 10000 ) ||
m_OverlappedRead.hEvent == NULL ||
m_OverlappedWrite.hEvent == NULL ){
DWORD dwError = GetLastError();
if( m_OverlappedRead.hEvent != NULL )CloseHandle(
m_OverlappedRead.hEvent );
if( m_OverlappedWrite.hEvent!= NULL)CloseHandle(
m_OverlappedWrite.hEvent );
CloseHandle( m_hIDComDev );
return( FALSE );
}
m_bOpened = TRUE;
return( m_bOpened );
}
BOOL CSerial::Close( void )
{
if( !m_bOpened || m_hIDComDev == NULL ) return( TRUE );
if( m_OverlappedRead.hEvent != NULL )
CloseHandle(m_OverlappedRead.hEvent );
if( m_OverlappedWrite.hEvent!= NULL
)CloseHandle(m_OverlappedWrite.hEvent );
CloseHandle( m_hIDComDev );
m_bOpened = FALSE;
m_hIDComDev = NULL;
return( TRUE );
}
BOOL CSerial::WriteCommByte( unsigned char ucByte )
{
BOOL bWriteStat;
DWORD dwBytesWritten;
bWriteStat = WriteFile( m_hIDComDev, (LPSTR) &ucByte, 1,
&dwBytesWritten, &m_OverlappedWrite );
if( !bWriteStat && ( GetLastError() == ERROR_IO_PENDING ) ){
if(WaitForSingleObject(m_OverlappedWrite.hEvent,1000) )
dwBytesWritten = 0;
else{
```

```
91. GetOverlappedResult(m_hIDComDev,&m_OverlappedWrite,&dwBytesWritten,
FALSE );
92. m_OverlappedWrite.Offset += dwBytesWritten;
93. }
94. }
95. return( TRUE );
96. }
97. int CSerial::SendData( const char *buffer, int size )
98. {
99. DWORD dwBytesWritten = 0;
100. int i;
101. if( !m_bOpened || m_hIDComDev == NULL ) return( 0 );
102. for( i=0; i<size; i++ ){
103. WriteCommByte( buffer[i] );
104. dwBytesWritten++;
105. }
106. return( (int) dwBytesWritten );
107. }
```

Following is the line-by-line explanation of the source code:

- **Lines 1–82:** This code is explained in Listing 7-2.
- **Lines 83–97:** Definition of the method `WriteCommByte` for writing a character to the serial communication port.
  - **Line 88:** Writes the character into the file associated with the communication port buffer.
  - **Lines 89–94:** Checks whether any error has occurred while writing the data to the port.
- **Lines 98–107:** Definition of the `SendData` function.
  - **Line 101:** Checks whether the communication port is open.
  - **Lines 103–106:** Sends each character of the data to the `WriteCommByte` method.

Source code listing for ACRemoteDlg.h

Listing 14-3 provides the source code for `ACRemoteDlg.h`, a header file containing the declaration of the `CACRemoteDlg` class.

Listing 14-3: Source code for ACRemoteDlg.h

```
// ACRemoteDlg.h : header file
#if!defined(AFX_ACREMOTEDLG_H__4F8B62F7_0E2611D6_AC5C_0080C80496C8__INC
LUDED)
#define
AFX_ACREMOTEDLG_H__4F8B62F7_0E26_11D6_AC5C_0080C80496C8__INCLUDED_
#if _MSC_VER > 1000
```

```
#pragma once
#endif // _MSC_VER > 1000
class CACRemoteDlg : public CDialog
{
// Construction
public:
CACRemoteDlg(CWnd* pParent = NULL); // standard constructor
// Dialog Data
//{{AFX_DATA(CACRemoteDlg)
enum { IDD = IDD_ACREMOTE_DIALOG };
CComboBox       m_temp;
CComboBox       m_ss;
CComboBox       m_mm;
CComboBox       m_hh;
CButton m_on;
//}}AFX_DATA
//{{AFX_VIRTUAL(CACRemoteDlg)
protected:
virtual void DoDataExchange(CDataExchange* pDX);   // DDX/DDV support
//}}AFX_VIRTUAL
protected:
HICON m_hIcon;
//{{AFX_MSG(CACRemoteDlg)
virtual BOOL OnInitDialog();
afx_msg void OnSysCommand(UINT nID, LPARAM lParam);
afx_msg void OnPaint();
afx_msg HCURSOR OnQueryDragIcon();
afx_msg void OnOn();
afx_msg void OnSettimer();
afx_msg void OnSettemp();
//}}AFX_MSG
DECLARE_MESSAGE_MAP()
};
//{{AFX_INSERT_LOCATION}}
#endif // !defined(AFX_ACREMOTEDLG_H__4F8B62F7_0E26_11D6_AC5C_0080C80496C8__INCLUDED_)
```

Source code listing for ACRemoteDlg.cpp

The file `ACRemoteDlg.cpp` contains the class definition and methods for sending commands that switch the air conditioner on and off and change the temperature and timer values. The source code is provided in Listing 14-4.

Listing 14-4: Source code for ACRemoteDlg.cpp

```
#include "stdafx.h"
#include "ACRemote.h"
#include "ACRemoteDlg.h"
```

```
#include "Serial.h"
#ifdef _DEBUG
#define new DEBUG_NEW
#undef THIS_FILE
static char THIS_FILE[] = __FILE__;
#endif
CSerial serObj;
class CAboutDlg : public CDialog
{
public:
CAboutDlg();
// Dialog Data
//{{AFX_DATA(CAboutDlg)
enum { IDD = IDD_ABOUTBOX };
//}}AFX_DATA
// ClassWizard generated virtual function overrides
//{{AFX_VIRTUAL(CAboutDlg)
protected:
virtual void DoDataExchange(CDataExchange* pDX);    // DDX/DDV support
//}}AFX_VIRTUAL
// Implementation
protected:
//{{AFX_MSG(CAboutDlg)
//}}AFX_MSG
DECLARE_MESSAGE_MAP()
};
CAboutDlg::CAboutDlg() : CDialog(CAboutDlg::IDD)
{
//{{AFX_DATA_INIT(CAboutDlg)
//}}AFX_DATA_INIT
}
void CAboutDlg::DoDataExchange(CDataExchange* pDX)
{
CDialog::DoDataExchange(pDX);
//{{AFX_DATA_MAP(CAboutDlg)
//}}AFX_DATA_MAP
}
BEGIN_MESSAGE_MAP(CAboutDlg, CDialog)
//{{AFX_MSG_MAP(CAboutDlg)
// No message handlers
//}}AFX_MSG_MAP
END_MESSAGE_MAP()
CACRemoteDlg::CACRemoteDlg(CWnd* pParent /*=NULL*/): CDialog(CACRemoteDlg::IDD, pParent)
{
//{{AFX_DATA_INIT(CACRemoteDlg)
// NOTE: the ClassWizard will add member initialization here
//}}AFX_DATA_INIT
```

```
// Note that LoadIcon does not require a subsequent DestroyIcon in Win32
m_hIcon = AfxGetApp()->LoadIcon(IDR_MAINFRAME);
}
void CACRemoteDlg::DoDataExchange(CDataExchange* pDX)
{
CDialog::DoDataExchange(pDX);
//{{AFX_DATA_MAP(CACRemoteDlg)
DDX_Control(pDX, IDC_TEMP, m_temp);
DDX_Control(pDX, IDC_SS, m_ss);
DDX_Control(pDX, IDC_MM, m_mm);
DDX_Control(pDX, IDC_HH, m_hh);
DDX_Control(pDX, IDC_ON, m_on);
//}}AFX_DATA_MAP
}
BEGIN_MESSAGE_MAP(CACRemoteDlg, CDialog)
//{{AFX_MSG_MAP(CACRemoteDlg)
ON_WM_SYSCOMMAND()
ON_WM_PAINT()
ON_WM_QUERYDRAGICON()
ON_BN_CLICKED(IDC_ON, OnOn)
ON_BN_CLICKED(IDC_SETTIMER, OnSettimer)
ON_BN_CLICKED(IDC_SETTEMP, OnSettemp)
//}}AFX_MSG_MAP
END_MESSAGE_MAP()
BOOL CACRemoteDlg::OnInitDialog()
{
CDialog::OnInitDialog();
// Add "About..." menu item to system menu.
// IDM_ABOUTBOX must be in the system command range.
ASSERT((IDM_ABOUTBOX & 0xFFF0) == IDM_ABOUTBOX);
ASSERT(IDM_ABOUTBOX < 0xF000);
CMenu* pSysMenu = GetSystemMenu(FALSE);
if (pSysMenu != NULL)
{
CString strAboutMenu;
strAboutMenu.LoadString(IDS_ABOUTBOX);
if (!strAboutMenu.IsEmpty())
{
pSysMenu->AppendMenu(MF_SEPARATOR);
pSysMenu->AppendMenu(MF_STRING, IDM_ABOUTBOX, strAboutMenu);
}
}
// Set the icon for this dialog.  The framework does this automatically
//  when the application's main window is not a dialog
SetIcon(m_hIcon, TRUE);                     // Set big icon
SetIcon(m_hIcon, FALSE);            // Set small icon
// Add extra initialization here
```

```
if(!serObj.Open(2,9600,'n',8,1))
{
AfxMessageBox("failed to open Comm Port");
return FALSE;
}
return TRUE;  // return TRUE  unless you set the focus to a control
}
void CACRemoteDlg::OnSysCommand(UINT nID, LPARAM lParam)
{
if ((nID & 0xFFF0) == IDM_ABOUTBOX)
{
CAboutDlg dlgAbout;
dlgAbout.DoModal();
}
else
{
CDialog::OnSysCommand(nID, lParam);
}
}
void CACRemoteDlg::OnPaint()
{
if (IsIconic())
{
CPaintDC dc(this); // device context for painting
SendMessage(WM_ICONERASEBKGND, (WPARAM) dc.GetSafeHdc(), 0);
// Center icon in client rectangle
int cxIcon = GetSystemMetrics(SM_CXICON);
int cyIcon = GetSystemMetrics(SM_CYICON);
CRect rect;
GetClientRect(&rect);
int x = (rect.Width() - cxIcon + 1) / 2;
int y = (rect.Height() - cyIcon + 1) / 2;
// Draw the icon
dc.DrawIcon(x, y, m_hIcon);
}
else
{
CDialog::OnPaint();
}
}
HCURSOR CACRemoteDlg::OnQueryDragIcon()
{
return (HCURSOR) m_hIcon;
}
void CACRemoteDlg::OnOn()
{
// Add your control notification handler code here
CString str;
char buf[5];
```

```
m_on.GetWindowText(str);
buf[0] = 0x02;                  // STX
buf[1] = 0x05;                  // Length
if(str == "ON")
{
m_on.SetWindowText("OFF");
buf[2] = 'N';                   // ON
}
else
{
m_on.SetWindowText("ON");
buf[2] = 'F';                   // OFF
}
buf[3] = buf[1] ^ buf[2];       // CRC
buf[4] = 0x03;                  // ETX
serObj.SendData(buf,5);
}
void CACRemoteDlg::OnSettimer()
{
// Add your control notification handler code here
char buf[7];
CString hh,mm,ss;
int hour,min,sec;
m_hh.GetWindowText(hh);
m_mm.GetWindowText(mm);
m_ss.GetWindowText(ss);
hour = atoi(hh);
min = atoi(mm);
sec = atoi(ss);
buf[0] = 0x02;                 // STX
buf[1] = 0x07;                        // Length
buf[2] = hour;                 // Hours
buf[3] = min ;                 // Min
buf[4] = sec ;                 // Sec
buf[5] = buf[1] ^ buf[2]^ buf[3]^ buf[4];    // CRC
buf[6] = 0x03;                 // ETX
serObj.SendData(buf,7);
}
void CACRemoteDlg::OnSettemp()
{
// Add your control notification handler code here
char buf[5];
CString sTemp;
int temp;
m_temp.GetWindowText(sTemp);
temp = atoi(sTemp);
buf[0] = 0x02;                        // STX
buf[1] = 0x05;                        // Length
buf[2] = temp ;                       // Temperature
```

```
196. buf[3] = buf[1] ^ buf[2];            // CRC
197. buf[4] = 0x03;                        // ETX
198. serObj.SendData(buf,5);
199. }
```

Following is the line-by-line explanation of the source code:

- **Lines 1–4:** Includes the header files.
- **Lines 5–9:** Preprocessor declaration.
- **Line 10:** Declares an object of the `Cserial` class.
- **Lines 11–29:** Definition of the `CAboutDlg` class. This code is generated by the VC++ editor.
- **Lines 30–34:** Definition of the constructor for the `CAboutDlg` class, generated by the VC++ editor.
- **Lines 35–40:** Definition of the `DoDataExchange` method for `CAboutDlg` class, generated by the VC++ editor.
- **Lines 41–45:** Message map definition for handling events of the dialog box `CAboutDlg`, generated by the VC++ editor.
- **Lines 46–53:** Definition of the constructor for the `CACRemoteDlg` class, generated by the VC++ editor.
- **Lines 54–64:** Definition of the `DoDataExchange` method for the `CACRemoteDlg` dialog, generated by the VC++ editor.
- **Lines 65–74:** Message map definition for handling events generated on the `CACRemoteDlg` dialog, generated by the VC++ editor.
- **Lines 75–104:** Definition of the `OnInitDialog` method, generated by the VC++ editor.
  - **Lines 98–102:** Opens the serial communication port 2 with baud rate 9600, parity None, databits 8, and stop bit 1.
- **Lines 105–116:** Definition of the `OnSysCommand` method, generated by the VC++ editor.
- **Lines 117–137:** Definition of the `OnPaint` method, generated by the VC++ editor.
- **Lines 138–141:** Definition of the `OnQueryDragIcon` method, generated by the VC++ editor.
- **Lines 142–163:** Definition of the method `OnOn` for sending a command to switch the AC on or off. The command structure is as follows:

STX	*Length*	*Data*	*CRC*	*ETX*
(1 byte)	(1 Byte)	(variable)	(1 byte)	(1 byte)

STX	0x02
Length	Length of the packet
Data	'N' for switching **ON**, 'F' for switching **OFF**, or it may be Time or Temperature
CRC	CRC for length and data.
ETX	0x03

- **Line 153:** Sets `'N'` for switching on.
- **Line 158:** Sets `'F'` for switching off.
- **Line 162:** Sends data to the serial port.

- **Lines 164–184:** Definition of the `OnSettimer` method for sending a command to change the timer value.
  - **Line 178:** Sets hours.
  - **Line 179:** Sets minutes.
  - **Line 180:** Sets seconds.
  - **Line 181:** Calculates CRC.
  - **Line 183:** Sends data to the serial port.
- **Lines 185–199:** Definition of the `OnSettemp` method for sending a command to change the temperature value.
  - **Line 195:** Sets the temperature.
  - **Line 198:** Sends the data to the serial port.

Source code listing for ACSimulator.cpp

The file `ACSimulator.cpp` contains source code to read the command from the remote through the serial port and display the appropriate action. This program runs only on Windows 9*x*. The source code for the program is provided in Listing 14-5.

Listing 14-5: Source code for ACSimulator.cpp

```
#include "stdio.h"
#include "conio.h"
#include "windows.h"

int Receiver(void);
long baseAdd,LSB,MSB,dataFormat,temp;

main()
{
HANDLE hThread;
DWORD tid;
baseAdd = 0x2f8; // address for comm port 2
```

```
LSB = 0x0c; // for baudrate 9600
MSB = 0x00;
dataFormat = 0x03; // for 8,1,N
_outp(baseAdd+3,dataFormat); // setting dataformat register
temp = _inp(baseAdd+3);
temp = temp | 0x10;
_outp(baseAdd+3,temp); //setting DLAb bit to 1
_outp(baseAdd,LSB);     // setting Baud Rate
_outp(baseAdd+1,MSB);
temp = _inp(baseAdd+3);
temp = temp & 0x7f;
_outp(baseAdd+3,temp); //Resetting DLAb bit to 0
hThread = CreateThread(0, 0,(LPTHREAD_START_ROUTINE)
Receiver,0,0,&tid);
printf("Press Enter to terminate");
getch();
TerminateThread(hThread,0);
}
int Receiver(void)
{
char ch,data[4];
int length;
while(1)
{
while(!(_inp(baseAdd+5)&0x01));
ch = _inp(baseAdd);
if(ch==0x02) // STX
{
while(!(_inp(baseAdd+5)&0x01));
length = _inp(baseAdd);
for(int i=0;i<(length-2);i++)
{
while(!(_inp(baseAdd+5)&0x01));
data[i] = _inp(baseAdd);
}
data[i] = '\0';
if(length == 0x05)
{
switch(data[0])
{
case 'N':
    printf("\nCommand for Switching On");
    break;
case 'F':
    printf("\nCommand for Switching Off\n");
    break;
default:
    printf("\nCommand to set the Temperature to %d degrees",data[0]);
    break;
```

```
59. }
60. }
61. else
62. {
63. printf("\nCommand to set the timer to
%d:%d:%d",data[0],data[1],data[2]);
64. }
65. }
66. }
67. return 1;
68. }
```

Following is the line-by-line explanation of the source code:

- **Lines 1–3:** Includes the header files. These three headers files are provided in the VC++ compiler in the directory `C:\Program Files\Microsoft Visual Studio\VC98\include`, if Visual Studio 6.0 is installed in the C drive.
- **Line 4:** Prototype declaration of the methode `Receiver`.
- **Lines 6-27:** Definition of the `main` method.
  - **Line 10:** Initializes the `baseAdd` to 0x3f8 for comm. port 2. For comm. port 1, the `baseAdd` is 0x3f8.
  - **Lines 11–12:** Initializes the baud rate to 9600.
  - **Line13:** Initializes `dataFormat` to 8 data bits, 1 stop bit, and NONE parity.
  - **Line 14:** Sets the Data format register.
  - **Lines 15–17:** Sets the DLAB bit to 1.
  - **Lines 18–19:** Sets the baud rate in the first two registers.
  - **Lines 20–22:** Resets the DLAB bit to 0.
  - **Line 23:** Creates a thread to the `Receiver` method.
  - **Line 26:** Terminates the thread.
- **Lines 29–39:** Definition of the method `Receiver` for reading the characters from the serial port.
  - **Line 34:** Waiting for the data.
  - **Line 35:** Reads a character from the buffer.
  - **Line 36:** Checks whether the character is STX (0x02) or not.
  - **Line 39:** Reads the length of the packet.
- **Lines 40–44:** Reads the data, depending on the length of the packet.
- **Lines 46–66:** Distinguishes the command, depending on the data.

Executing the program

To test this project, connect two PCs (one running Embedded XP and one running Windows 9*x*) using a null modem cable. Port and run the ACRemote application in Embedded XP using the procedure explained in this section, and run the ACSimulator application in the Windows 9*x* system. Figure 14-1 shows the remote control panel on the Embedded XP system. Figure 14-2 displays the commands received from the AC remote control.

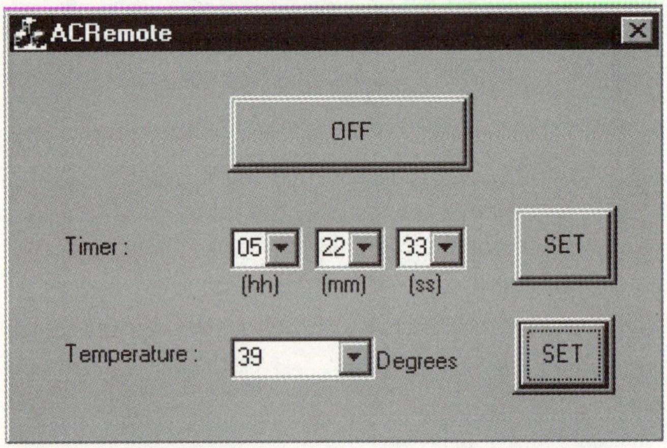

Figure 14-1: AC remote control panel on the Embedded XP system

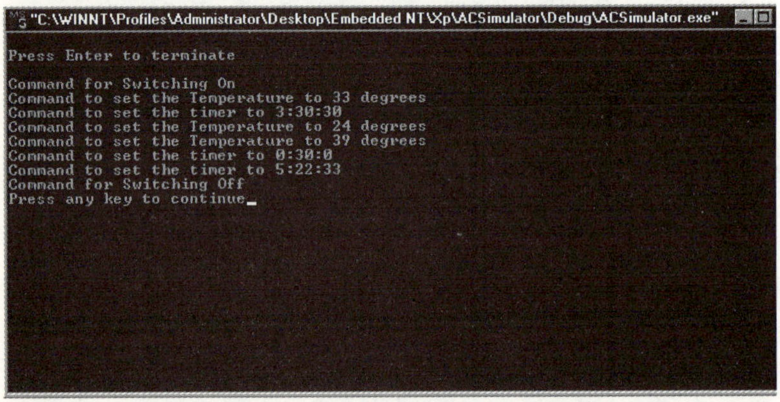

Figure 14-2: The commands received by the Windows 9*x* machine from the AC remote control

Porting the software onto the Embedded XP platform

To port the software onto Embedded XP, follow these steps:

1. Collect all the files required to run the application on the target. In this case, the files required are as follows:
   - `ACRemote.EXE` (application file)

- `MFC42D.DLL`
- `MFCO42D.DLL`
- `MSVCRTD.DLL`

The three DLLs are required to run an MFC application on the target platform.

2. Create a component using the Component Designer. The following steps indicate how to create a custom component:
   - Open the Component Designer (on the Windows taskbar, select Start ⇨ Programs ⇨ Microsoft Windows Embedded studio ⇨ Component Designer).
   - Save the component as ExampleComponent.
   - In the navigation pane, right-click Components, which is under Windows XP Embedded Client(x86), and then click Add Component.
   - In the Component Properties text box, enter the name **ACRemoteComponent**.
   - In the Navigation pane, right-click on Files, which is under Components/ACRemoteComponent, and click Add File. Enter the following information:

     Target Name: **ACRemote.EXE**

     Source Name: **ACRemote.EXE**

     Destination Path : **%24%\Documents and Settings\Administrator\Desktop\Examples**

   Now Click the Advanced… button. This brings up the Advanced Properties dialog box, shown in Figure 14-3.

   - Similarly add the remaining three files listed in Step 1. The resulting window should look like the one shown in Figure 14-4.
   - Save the component and exit.
3. Create the target image using the Target Designer.
   - Run the `tap.exe` file, which is provided with the Embedded XP software, at the DOS prompt of the target system. This file creates the `devices.pmq` file, which contains information about the target system's hardware.

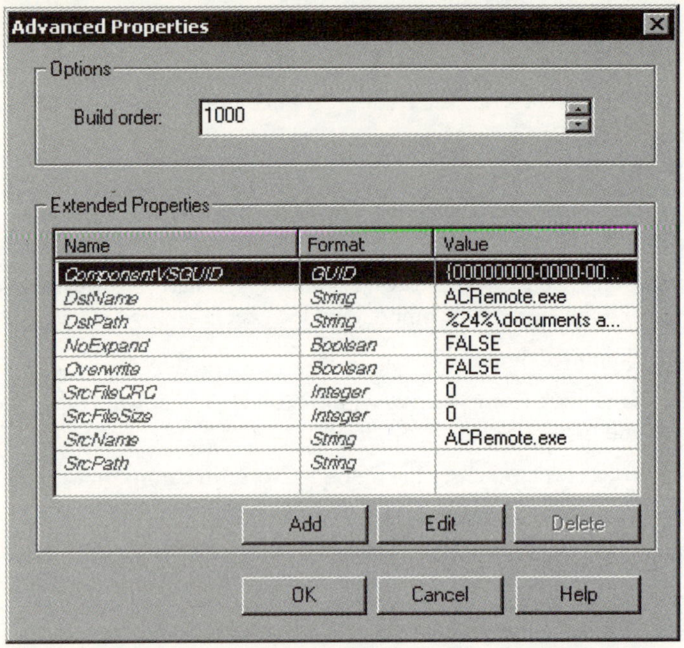

Figure 14-3: Use the Advanced Properties dialog box to add components.

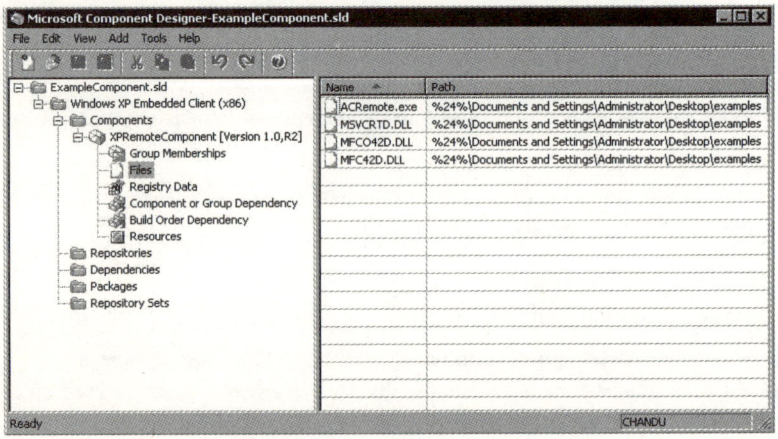

Figure 14-4: Component Designer

- Run the Target Designer (Start ⇨ Programs ⇨ Microsoft Windows Embedded Studio ⇨ Target Designer).
- Create a new configuration by selecting File ⇨ New from the menu bar and entering the configuration name **XPTarget**.
- Now import the `devices.pmq` file from the File menu and click Start.

- After completion of the import operation, add the following components from the Component Navigation pane:
  - FAT, which is under `\Software\System\Storage and File System\Infrastructure\File System`
  - English Language Support, which is under `\Software\System\International\Infrastructure`
  - Windows Logon, which is under `\Software\System\Security\Infrastructure`
  - NT Loader, which is under `\Software\System\System Services\Base`
  - FAT Format, which is under `\Software\System\Storage and File System\Applications`
  - Explorer Shell, which is under `\Software\System\User Interface\Shells`
- Now import your custom component (ExampleComponent) by selecting Tools ⇨ Component Database Manager on the menu bar.
- After importing the custom component, save and restart the Target Designer and open XPTarget to load the custom component.
- Right-click on the ACRemoteComponent in the Component Navigation pane and click Add.
- From the menu bar, select Configuration ⇨ Check Dependencies. If any error occurs, the list of components required will be displayed. Add these components, depending on the target system's configuration.
- After clearing all the errors, select Configuration ⇨ Build Target Image. In the Build Target Image window, select Release from the Build Type drop-down list, and enter **F:\ACSampleTarget** in the Destination field (assuming that ACSampleTarget is the directory in the F drive in which the target image is stored. (Instead of F:\, use the appropriate drive of your system.) Now click Build. At this stage, your screen should look like the one shown in Figure 14-5.
- After completing the build operation, the Target Designer appears as shown in Figure 14-6.
- Copy all the files from the `\ACSampleTarget` directory to the boot drive of the target system's hard disk and reboot the target system.

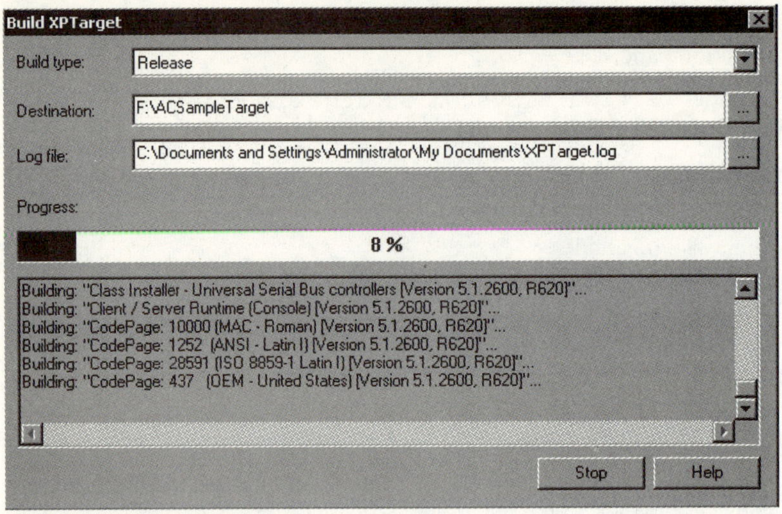

Figure 14-5: Building XPTarget

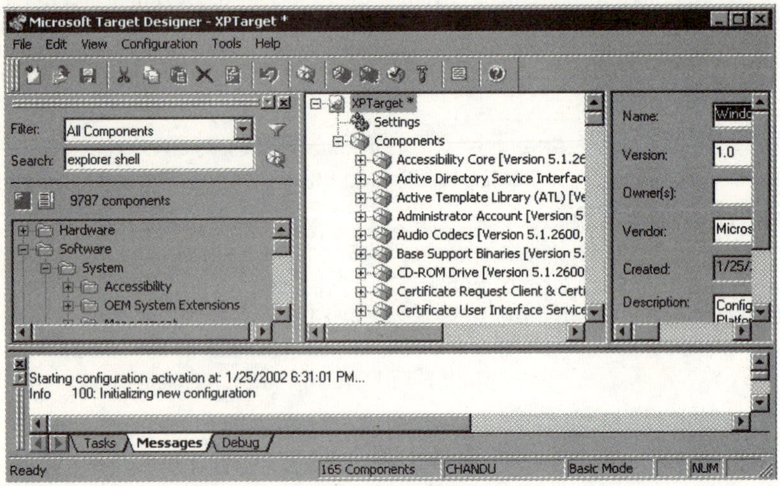

Figure 14-6: Target Designer window after the build operation

Note that you can build the target image in a number of ways. If you have the target hardware, you can transfer the image to the memory device. Otherwise, you can create a CD-ROM that contains the target image, and boot the embedded system using that CD.

> **TIP** Another alternative is to take an empty hard disk, transfer the image onto it, and then boot the embedded system using the hard disk. This is a good approach for testing in the laboratory. This was the approach followed in testing the applications presented here.

For each of the remaining projects, the same procedure is used to create the target image. You may want to refer to this section when creating the target image for the rest of the applications.

Project: Remote Control of an Audio Player

This project demonstrates how to control an audio player through an embedded system. The audio player will be running on a Windows 9*x* machine and the commands will be sent from the Embedded XP system. We will again use a serial communication link between the two systems to simulate a radio communication link such as Bluetooth.

Project overview

This project contains two applications that run on the two machines. MP3Remote runs on the Embedded XP machine and MP3Client runs on the Windows 9*x* machine.

The MP3Remote application contains four files:

- `Serial.h` is a header file containing the declaration of the `Cserial` class.
- `Serial.cpp` is a file containing the definition of the `Cserial` class and the methods to open and close the serial port, as well as methods to write data to the serial port.
- `MP3RemoteDlg.h` is a header file containing the declaration of the `CMP3RemoteDlg` class.
- `MP3RemoteDlg.cpp` is a file containing the definition of the `CMP3RemoteDlg` class and methods to send commands to play, stop, and auto-rewind.

The MP3Client application is explained in Listing 10-8, which describes how to control an audio player with RTLinux.

This application uses the files used in the previous application for serial communication. The source code for these two files, `Serial.h` and `Serial.cpp`, are provided in Listings 14-1 and 14-2.

Source code listing for MP3RemoteDlg.h

Listing 14-6 provides the source code for `MP3RemoteDlg.h`, a header file containing the declaration of the `CMP3RemoteDlg` class. The variables used in this file are explained in the code explanation given for `MP3RemoteDlg.cpp`.

Listing 14-6: Source code for MP3RemoteDlg.h

```
// MP3RemoteDlg.h : header file

 #if!defined(AFX_MP3REMOTEDLG_H_4F8B62E9_0E26_11D6_AC5C_0080C80496C8_INC
LUDED)
#define
AFX_MP3REMOTEDLG_H__4F8B62E9_0E26_11D6_AC5C_0080C80496C8__INCLUDED_
```

```
#if _MSC_VER > 1000
#pragma once
#endif // _MSC_VER > 1000
class CMP3RemoteDlg : public CDialog
{
// Construction
public:
CMP3RemoteDlg(CWnd* pParent = NULL); // standard constructor
// Dialog Data
//{{AFX_DATA(CMP3RemoteDlg)
enum { IDD = IDD_MP3REMOTE_DIALOG };
CButton m_rewind;
CButton m_stop;
CButton m_play;
//}}AFX_DATA
// ClassWizard generated virtual function overrides
//{{AFX_VIRTUAL(CMP3RemoteDlg)
protected:
virtual void DoDataExchange(CDataExchange* pDX);   // DDX/DDV support
//}}AFX_VIRTUAL
// Implementation
protected:
HICON m_hIcon;
// Generated message map functions
//{{AFX_MSG(CMP3RemoteDlg)
virtual BOOL OnInitDialog();
afx_msg void OnSysCommand(UINT nID, LPARAM lParam);
afx_msg void OnPaint();
afx_msg HCURSOR OnQueryDragIcon();
afx_msg void OnPlay();
afx_msg void OnStop();
afx_msg void OnRewind();
//}}AFX_MSG
DECLARE_MESSAGE_MAP()
};
//{{AFX_INSERT_LOCATION}}
#endif //
!defined(AFX_MP3REMOTEDLG_H__4F8B62E9_0E26_11D6_AC5C_0080C80496C8__INCLUDED_)
```

Source code listing for MP3RemoteDlg.cpp

The source code for `MP3RemoteDlg.cpp` is provided in Listing 14-7. This file contains the class definition and methods for sending commands to play, stop, and auto-rewind the audio player.

Listing 14-7: Source code for MP3RemoteDlg.cpp

```
#include "stdafx.h"
```

```
#include "MP3Remote.h"
#include "MP3RemoteDlg.h"
#include "Serial.h"
#ifdef _DEBUG
#define new DEBUG_NEW
#undef THIS_FILE
static char THIS_FILE[] = __FILE__;
#endif
CSerial serObj;
class CAboutDlg : public CDialog
{
public:
CAboutDlg();
// Dialog Data
//{{AFX_DATA(CAboutDlg)
enum { IDD = IDD_ABOUTBOX };
//}}AFX_DATA
// ClassWizard generated virtual function overrides
//{{AFX_VIRTUAL(CAboutDlg)
protected:
virtual void DoDataExchange(CDataExchange* pDX);    // DDX/DDV support
//}}AFX_VIRTUAL
// Implementation
protected:
//{{AFX_MSG(CAboutDlg)
//}}AFX_MSG
DECLARE_MESSAGE_MAP()
};
CAboutDlg::CAboutDlg() : CDialog(CAboutDlg::IDD)
{
//{{AFX_DATA_INIT(CAboutDlg)
//}}AFX_DATA_INIT
}
void CAboutDlg::DoDataExchange(CDataExchange* pDX)
{
CDialog::DoDataExchange(pDX);
//{{AFX_DATA_MAP(CAboutDlg)
//}}AFX_DATA_MAP
}
BEGIN_MESSAGE_MAP(CAboutDlg, CDialog)
//{{AFX_MSG_MAP(CAboutDlg)
// No message handlers
//}}AFX_MSG_MAP
END_MESSAGE_MAP()
CMP3RemoteDlg::CMP3RemoteDlg(CWnd* pParent /*=NULL*/): CDialog(CMP3RemoteDlg::IDD, pParent)
{
//{{AFX_DATA_INIT(CMP3RemoteDlg)
```

```
//}}AFX_DATA_INIT
// Note that LoadIcon does not require a subsequent DestroyIcon in Win32
m_hIcon = AfxGetApp()->LoadIcon(IDR_MAINFRAME);
}
void CMP3RemoteDlg::DoDataExchange(CDataExchange* pDX)
{
CDialog::DoDataExchange(pDX);
//{{AFX_DATA_MAP(CMP3RemoteDlg)
DDX_Control(pDX, IDC_REWIND, m_rewind);
DDX_Control(pDX, IDC_STOP, m_stop);
DDX_Control(pDX, IDC_PLAY, m_play);
//}}AFX_DATA_MAP
}
BEGIN_MESSAGE_MAP(CMP3RemoteDlg, CDialog)
//{{AFX_MSG_MAP(CMP3RemoteDlg)
ON_WM_SYSCOMMAND()
ON_WM_PAINT()
ON_WM_QUERYDRAGICON()
ON_BN_CLICKED(IDC_PLAY, OnPlay)
ON_BN_CLICKED(IDC_STOP, OnStop)
ON_BN_CLICKED(IDC_REWIND, OnRewind)
//}}AFX_MSG_MAP
END_MESSAGE_MAP()
BOOL CMP3RemoteDlg::OnInitDialog()
{
CDialog::OnInitDialog();
// Add "About..." menu item to system menu.
// IDM_ABOUTBOX must be in the system command range.
ASSERT((IDM_ABOUTBOX & 0xFFF0) == IDM_ABOUTBOX);
ASSERT(IDM_ABOUTBOX < 0xF000);
CMenu* pSysMenu = GetSystemMenu(FALSE);
if (pSysMenu != NULL)
{
CString strAboutMenu;
strAboutMenu.LoadString(IDS_ABOUTBOX);
if (!strAboutMenu.IsEmpty())
{
pSysMenu->AppendMenu(MF_SEPARATOR);
pSysMenu->AppendMenu(MF_STRING, IDM_ABOUTBOX, strAboutMenu);
}
}
// Set the icon for this dialog.  The framework does this automatically
//  when the application's main window is not a dialog
SetIcon(m_hIcon, TRUE);                        // Set big icon
SetIcon(m_hIcon, FALSE);               // Set small icon
// Add extra initialization here
if(!serObj.Open(2,9600,'n',8,1))
```

```
{
AfxMessageBox("failed to open Comm Port");
return FALSE;
}
return TRUE;  // return TRUE  unless you set the focus to a control
}
void CMP3RemoteDlg::OnSysCommand(UINT nID, LPARAM lParam)
{
if ((nID & 0xFFF0) == IDM_ABOUTBOX)
{
CAboutDlg dlgAbout;
dlgAbout.DoModal();
}
else
{
CDialog::OnSysCommand(nID, lParam);
}
}
void CMP3RemoteDlg::OnPaint()
{
if (IsIconic())
{
CPaintDC dc(this); // device context for painting
SendMessage(WM_ICONERASEBKGND, (WPARAM) dc.GetSafeHdc(), 0);
// Center icon in client rectangle
int cxIcon = GetSystemMetrics(SM_CXICON);
int cyIcon = GetSystemMetrics(SM_CYICON);
CRect rect;
GetClientRect(&rect);
int x = (rect.Width() - cxIcon + 1) / 2;
int y = (rect.Height() - cyIcon + 1) / 2;
// Draw the icon
dc.DrawIcon(x, y, m_hIcon);
}
else
{
CDialog::OnPaint();
}
}
HCURSOR CMP3RemoteDlg::OnQueryDragIcon()
{
return (HCURSOR) m_hIcon;
}
void CMP3RemoteDlg::OnPlay()
{
m_play.EnableWindow(FALSE);
m_rewind.EnableWindow(TRUE);
m_stop.EnableWindow(TRUE);
char buf[5];
```

```
145. buf[0] = 0x02;                  // STX
146. buf[1] = 0x05;                  // Length
147. buf[2] = 2;                     // Play
148. buf[3] = buf[1] ^ buf[2];       // CRC
149. buf[4] = 0x03;                  // ETX
150. serObj.SendData(buf,5);
151. }
152. void CMP3RemoteDlg::OnStop()
153. {
154. m_play.EnableWindow(TRUE);
155. m_rewind.EnableWindow(TRUE);
156. m_stop.EnableWindow(FALSE);
157. char buf[5];
158. buf[0] = 0x02;                  // STX
159. buf[1] = 0x05;                  // Length
160. buf[2] = 3;                     // Stop
161. buf[3] = buf[1] ^ buf[2];       // CRC
162. buf[4] = 0x03;                  // ETX
163. serObj.SendData(buf,5);
164. }
165. void CMP3RemoteDlg::OnRewind()
166. {
167. m_play.EnableWindow(FALSE);
168. m_rewind.EnableWindow(FALSE);
169. m_stop.EnableWindow(TRUE);
170. char buf[5];
171. buf[0] = 0x02;                  // STX
172. buf[1] = 0x05;                  // Length
173. buf[2] = 4;                     // Rewind
174. buf[3] = buf[1] ^ buf[2];       // CRC
175. buf[4] = 0x03;                  // ETX
176. serObj.SendData(buf,5);
177. }
```

Following is the line-by-line explanation of the source code:

- **Lines 1–4:** Includes the header files.
- **Lines 5-9:** Preprocessor declarations.
- **Line 10:** Declares an object of the `CSerial` class.
- **Lines 11–29:** Definition of the `CAboutDlg` class. This code is generated by the VC++ editor.
- **Lines 30–34:** Definition of the constructor for the `CAboutDlg` class, generated by the VC++ editor.
- **Lines 35–40:** Definition of the `DoDataExchange` method for `CAboutDlg` class, generated by the VC++ editor.

- **Lines 41–45:** Message map definition for handling events of the dialog box `CAboutDlg`, generated by the VC++ editor.
- **Lines 46–52:** Definition of the constructor for the `CMP3RemoteDlg` class, generated by the VC++ editor.
- **Lines 53–61:** Definition of the `DoDataExchange` method for `CMP3RemoteDlg` dialog, generated by the VC++ editor.
- **Lines 62–71:** Message map definition for handling events of the dialog box `CMP3RemoteDlg`, generated by the VC++ editor.
- **Lines 72–101:** Definition of the `OnInitDialog` method, generated by the VC++ editor.
    - **Lines 95–99:** Opens the serial communication port 2 with baud rate 9600, NONE parity, 8 data bits, and 1 stop bit.
- **Lines 102–113:** Definition of the `OnSysCommand` method, generated by the VC++ editor.
- **Lines 114–134:** Definition of the `OnPaint` method, generated by the VC++ editor.
- **Lines 135–138:** Definition of the `OnQueryDragIcon` method, generated by the VC++ editor.
- **Lines 139–151:** Definition of the method `OnPlay` to send a command to the MP3Client application to play the sound. The command structure is as follows:

STX	***Length***	***Data***	***CRC***	***ETX***
(1 byte)	(1 Byte)	(variable)	(1 byte)	(1 byte)

STX	0x02
Length	Length of the packet
Data	2 to play, 3 to stop, 4 to auto rewind.
CRC	CRC for length and data.
ETX	0x03

    - **Line 147:** Sets 2 to play.
    - **Line 148:** Calculates CRC.
    - **Line 150:** Sends data to the serial port.
- **Lines 152–164:** Definition of the method `OnStop` to send a command to the MP3Client application to stop the sound.
    - **Line 160:** Sets 3 to stop.
    - **Line 161:** Calculates CRC.

  - **Line 163:** Sends data to the serial port.
- **Lines 165–177:** Definition of the method `OnRewind` to send a command to the MP3Client application to auto-rewind the currently playing sound.
  - **Line 173:** Sets 4 to auto-rewind.
  - **Line 174:** Calculates CRC.
  - **Line 176:** Sends data to the serial port.

Executing the program

To test this project, connect two PCs (one Embedded XP and one Windows 9*x*) using a null modem cable. Port the MP3Remote application in Embedded XP and run it. Run the MP3Client application in the Windows 9*x* system. The MP3Remote application is shown in Figure 14-7.

Figure 14-7: MP3 remote control panel

Porting the software onto the Embedded XP platform

To port this application to the target system, follow the same steps as outlined for the ACRemote application except that instead of copying `ACRemote.exe`, you copy `MP3Remote.exe`.

Project: Typing Speed Indicator

This project consists of two modules: one tests a user's typing speed, and the other tests how fast a user can type a letter after identifying a letter "falling" on the screen. In the first module, the result displays the number of words typed per minute and the number of keystrokes typed per minute. Words are recognized based on the blank space between successive strings. In the second module, letters randomly fall from the top of the screen. Before the letter reaches the bottom of the screen, the user must identify it and press the key corresponding to that letter. (You may find this test simple on the desktop, but try it on a handheld!) The objective of this project is to determine the typist's proficiency in order to improve his or her typing skills. The project is developed in Visual Basic.

Source code listing for frmmain.frm

Listing 14-8 provides the source code for the file `frmmain.frm`.

Listing 14-8: Source code for frmmain.frm

```
1. Private Sub cmdExit_Click()
2.    Unload Me
3. End Sub
4. Private Sub cmdFallingletters_Click()
5.    frmfallingletters.Show
6. End Sub
7. Private Sub cmdTest_Click()
8.    frmtest.Show
9. End Sub
```

Following is the line-by-line explanation of the source code:

- **Lines 1–3:** Definition of the `cmdExit_Click()` event, to close the application.
  - **Line 2:** Unloads the form.
- **Lines 4–6:** Definition of the `cmdFallingLetters_Click()` event, to enter into the Falling Letters form.
  - **Line 5:** Loads the Falling Letters form.
- **Lines 7–9:** Definition of the `cmdTest_Click()` event, to enter into the Test form.
  - **Line 8:** Loads the Test form.

Source code listing for frmtest.frm

Listing 14-9 provides the source code for the file `frmtest.frm`.

Listing 14-9: Source code for frmtest.frm

```
Dim starting As Boolean, FIRST_OVER As Boolean
Dim examx As Integer
Dim examy As Integer
Dim time_count As Integer
Dim total_words As Integer, words_typed As Integer
Dim keystrokes As Integer
Dim typed_text1 As String, typed_text2 As String
Dim temp As String
Dim typedtime as Integer
Private Sub cmdExit_Click()
   Unload Me
   frmMain.Show
End Sub
'Thisevent is to start the timer when the start button is clicked
Private Sub cmdStart_Click()
  On Error Resume Next
  tipedtime = 0
  time_count = 300
  Text1.text = ""
```

```
  Text1.SetFocus
  cmdStop.Enabled = True
  If (starting = False) Then
     Timer1.Enabled = True
     starting = True
  End If
End Sub
 'This event is for stopping the timer when the stop button clicked
Private Sub cmdStop_Click()
  Timer1.Enabled = False
  Call display_result
  Text1.text = ""
  Label1.Caption = "5:00"
  starting = False
  keystrokes = 0
End Sub
 'this event is to load the form
Private Sub Form_Load()
  FIRST_OVER = False
  time_count = 300
  Text1.text = "    "
  Timer1.Interval = 1000
  Timer1.Enabled = False
  Text1.SelStart = 4
  starting = False
  cmdStop.Enabled = False
End Sub
 'This event is to close the form
Private Sub Form_Unload(Cancel As Integer)
  frmMain.Show
End Sub
Private Sub Text1_Change()
  keystrokes = keystrokes + 1
End Sub
Private Sub Timer1_Timer()
  If (time_count > 0) Then
    time_count = time_count - 1
    typedtime = typedtime + 1
    Label1.Caption = str(time_count \ 60) + " : " + str(time_count
Mod 60)
  Else
    Call cmdStop_Click
  End If
End Sub
 'This procedure is used to display the results such as words_per_min,
no_of_keystokes, Keys / minute
Sub display_result()
   Dim keys_per_min As Double
   Dim words_per_min As Double
```

```
62.    Dim minutes As Integer
63.    Dim time_ratio As Double
64.    temp = ""
65.    Timer1.Enabled = False
66.    time_ratio = (300 - time_count) / 60
67.    typed_text1 = Text1.text
68.    words_typed = words_count(typed_text1)
69.    If (typed_text1 = "") Then
70.       time_ratio = 1
71.    End If
72.     words_per_min = words_typed / time_ratio
73.     words_per_min = words_per_min \ 1
74.     keys_per_min = keystrokes / time_ratio
75.     keys_per_min = keys_per_min \ 1
76.     temp = temp + "Allowted Time   : 2 min" + vbNewLine
77.     temp = temp + "Typed Time      : " + str(typedtime) + ”sec” +
vbNewLine
78.     temp = temp + "Words typed     : " + str(words_typed) + vbNewLine
79.     temp = temp + "Words / minute  : " + str(words_per_min) +
vbNewLine
80.     temp = temp + "Key strokes     : " + str(keystrokes) + vbNewLine
81.     temp = temp + "Keys / minute   : " + str(keys_per_min) +
vbNewLine
82.     MsgBox temp
83.     Text1.text = ""
84.     cmdStop.Enabled = False
85. End Sub
  'this function is used to calculate the no of words
86. Function words_count(str As String) As Integer
87.     words_count = 0
88.     Dim space_pos As Integer
89.     Dim text As String
90.     text = str
91.     text = LTrim(text)
92.     text = RTrim(text)
93.     Do
94.        text = Mid(text, space_pos + 1, Len(text) - co)
95.        text = LTrim(text)
96.        space_pos = InStr(1, text, " ", vbTextCompare)
97.        words_count = words_count + 1
98.     Loop While (space_pos <> 0)
99.     If (Len(str) < 1) Then
100.        words_count = 0
101.     End If
102. End Function
```

Following is the line-by-line explanation of the source code:

- **Lines 1–9:** Variable declarations.

- **Lines 10–13:** Definition of the `cmdExit_Click()` event, to close the application.
  - **Line 11:** Unloads the Test form.
- **Lines 14–25:** Definition of the `cmdStart_Click()` event, to start the timer.
  - **Line 15:** Error handling.
  - **Lines 16–17:** Assigns the values of `typedtime` and `time_count`
  - **Line 19:** Sets the cursor position.
  - **Lines 21–24:** Checks whether the value of `starting` is true or false. If it is false, the timer is started.
- **Lines 26–33:** Definition of the `cmdStop_Click()` event, to stop the application.
  - **Line 27:** Stops the timer.
  - **Line 28:** Calls the `display_result` procedure.
- **Lines 34–43:** Definition of the `Form_Load()` event, to load the application.
  - **Lines 36–41:** Assigns the values to the variables `time_count`, `timer1.interval`, and `starting`.
- **Lines 44–46:** Definition of the `Form_Unload()` event, to stop the application.
- **Lines 47–49:** Definition of the `Text1_Change()` event, to count the number of keystrokes.
- **Lines 50–58:** Definition of the `Timer1_Timer()` event, to set the time.
- **Lines 59–85:** Definition of the `display_result()` procedure, to display the results, such as words per minute and keystrokes per minute.
  - **Lines 60–63:** Variables declaration.
  - **Lines 66–81:** Calculates the words typed, words per minute, keystrokes, and keystrokes per minute.
  - **Line 82:** Displays the words typed, words per minute, keystrokes, and keystrokes per minute in the message box.
- **Lines 86–102:** Definition of the `words_count()` function, to calculate the number of words.
- **Lines 91–92:** `LTrim` is a function to strip leading spaces, and `RTrim` is a function to strip trailing spaces from a string variable. It uses the `Trim` function to strip both types of spaces.
- **Line 96:** Returns the position of the first occurrence of one string within another.
- **Lines 99–101:** Checks whether the length of the string is more than one character.

Source code listing for frmfallingletters.frm

Listing 14-10 provides the source code for the file `frmfallingletters.frm`.

Listing 14-10: Source code for frmfallingletters.frm

```
Dim count1 As Integer, count2 As Integer, marks As Integer
Dim hits As Integer, i As Integer
Dim key_typed As String
Dim starting As Boolean
Dim char_count As Integer
Dim level_count(10) As Integer
Dim temp As String
Dim atempts As Integer
Function getchar() As String
   Dim i As Integer
   i = Int(25 * Rnd + 97)
   getchar = Chr(i)
End Function
Private Sub Command1_Click()
   Unload Me
End Sub
Private Sub Form_Load()
   atempts = 0
   char_count = 0
   ch1.Caption = "Press any Key to Start"
   ch1.Left = 100
   i = 0
   While (i < 10)
      level_count(i) = 0
      i = i + 1
   Wend
   starting = False
   Timer1.Enabled = False
   Timer1.Interval = 100
   ch1.Visible = True
End Sub
Private Sub Picture1_KeyPress(KeyAscii As Integer)
   If (KeyAscii = 27) Then
     Timer1.Enabled = False
     Unload Me
   End If
   If (starting = False) Then
      starting = True
      Timer1.Enabled = True
   Else
      key_typed = Chr(KeyAscii)
   End If
End Sub
Private Sub Timer1_Timer()
   If (char_count <= 50) Then
      If (key_typed <> ch1.Caption) Then
        ch1.Top = ch1.Top + 190
```

```
        Else
          atempts = atempts + 1
          hits = hits + 1
          If (ch1.Top <= Picture1.Top + Picture1.Height / 10) Then
            level_count(9) = level_count(9) + 1
          ElseIf (ch1.Top <= Picture1.Top + 2 * Picture1.Height / 10) Then
            level_count(8) = level_count(8) + 1
          ElseIf (ch1.Top <= Picture1.Top + 3 * Picture1.Height / 10) Then
            level_count(7) = level_count(7) + 1
          ElseIf (ch1.Top <= Picture1.Top + 4 * Picture1.Height / 10) Then
            level_count(6) = level_count(6) + 1
          ElseIf (ch1.Top <= Picture1.Top + 5 * Picture1.Height / 10) Then
            level_count(5) = level_count(5) + 1
          ElseIf (ch1.Top <= Picture1.Top + 6 * Picture1.Height / 10) Then
            level_count(4) = level_count(4) + 1
          ElseIf (ch1.Top <= Picture1.Top + 7 * Picture1.Height / 10) Then
            level_count(3) = level_count(3) + 1
          ElseIf (ch1.Top <= Picture1.Top + 8 * Picture1.Height / 10) Then
            level_count(2) = level_count(2) + 1
          ElseIf (ch1.Top <= Picture1.Top + 9 * Picture1.Height / 10) Then
            level_count(1) = level_count(1) + 1
          ElseIf (ch1.Top <= Picture1.Top + Picture1.Height) Then
            level_count(0) = level_count(0) + 1
          End If
          char_count = char_count + 1
          ch1.Caption = getchar
          Picture1.Cls
          ch1.Top = Picture1.Top
        End If
     Else
        Timer1.Enabled = False
        ch1.Visible = False
        temp = ""
        marks = 0
        For i = 9 To 0 Step -1
           temp = temp + "Hits at Row " + Str(i * 2 + 2) + " -> " +
           tr(level_count(i)) + vbNewLine
           marks = marks + level_count(i) * (i * 2 + 2)
        Next
        temp = temp + "Atempts        -> " + Str(atempts) + "/50" + vbNewLine
```

```
88.         temp = temp + "Total score     -> " + Str(marks) + "/1000" +
vbNewLine
89.         MsgBox temp
90.         Call Form_Load
91.      End If
92.      If (ch1.Top > (Picture1.Top + Picture1.Height - ch1.Height)) Then
93.      char_count = char_count + 1
94.      Picture1.Cls
95.      ch1.Caption = getchar
96.      ch1.Top = Picture1.Top
97.   End If
98. End Sub
```

Following is the line-by-line explanation of the source code:

- **Lines 1–8:** Variables declaration.
- **Lines 9–13:** Definition of the `getchar()` function; the characters are generated randomly.
  - **Line 11:** Produces random integers in a given range.
  - **Line 12:** The `Chr` function, to return the character associated with the specified character code.
- **Lines 14–16:** Definition of the `cmdExit_Click()` event, to close the application.
- **Lines 17–31:** Definition of the `Form_Load()` event, to load the application.
- **Lines 32–43:** Definition of the `Picture1_KeyPress()` event, to check whether the key pressed is Esc.
  - **Lines 33–36:** Checks whether the key pressed is Esc.
- **Lines 44–98:** Definition of the `Timer1_Timer()` event, to set the time.
  - **Lines 51–71:** Finds the postion, whenever the falling letter is struck.

Executing the program

The step-by-step procedure for executing the program is as follows:

1. Open Visual Basic 6.0. A window will open showing Existing Projects, New Projects, and Recent Projects tabs. In the New Projects tab, select StandardEXE and click the OK button. The default form will be displayed.
2. From the menu bar, selectProject ⇨ Project Properties and set the project name as Sample. Save the form as `main.frm` and save the project as `Sample.vbp`. Note that `.FRM` is the extension for Visual Basic Form. The extension for Visual Basic Project is `.VDP`.
3. Select the form and set the following form properties in the Properties window:
   - Name: **`frmmain`**

- Caption: **Sample**
- Height: **4380**
- Width: **3780**

4. Select the required controls from the Toolbox and set them as shown in Figure 14-8.

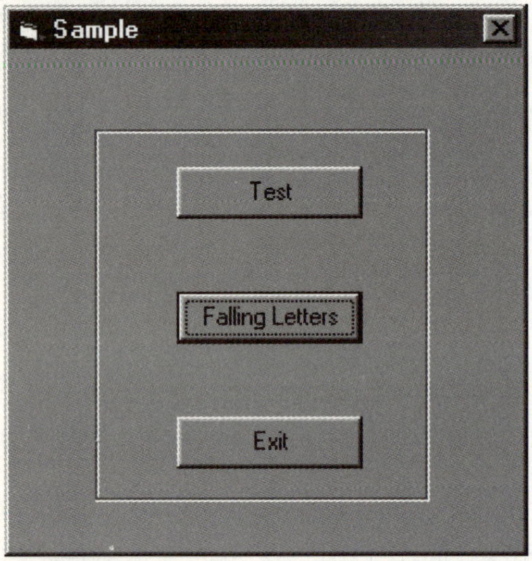

Figure 14-8: frmmain form with caption Sample to create the three command buttons

The `frmmain` form contains three command buttons. These button properties should be set as follows:

The Test command button is a Command Button control. Set the command button properties as follows:

- Name: **`cmdTest`**
- Caption: **Test**

Functionality: To display the `frmTest` form when this button is clicked.

- Font: Arial, Regular.

The Falling Letters command button is a Command Button control. Set the command button properties as follows:

- Name: **`cmdFallingLetters`**
- Caption: **Falling Letters**

Functionality: To display the `frmFallingLetters` form when this button is clicked.

The Exit command button is a Command Button control. Set the command button properties as follows:

- Name: **`cmdExit`**
- Caption: **Exit**

Functionality: To close the application when this button is clicked.

5. On the menu bar, select Project ⇨ Add Form. Set the form name as "frmtest," and save the form as `frmtest.frm`.
6. Select the `frmTest` form and set the following form properties in the Properties window:
   - Name: **`frmtest`**
   - Height: **4380**
   - Width: **3780**
7. Select the required controls from the Toolbox and set them as shown in Figure 14-9.

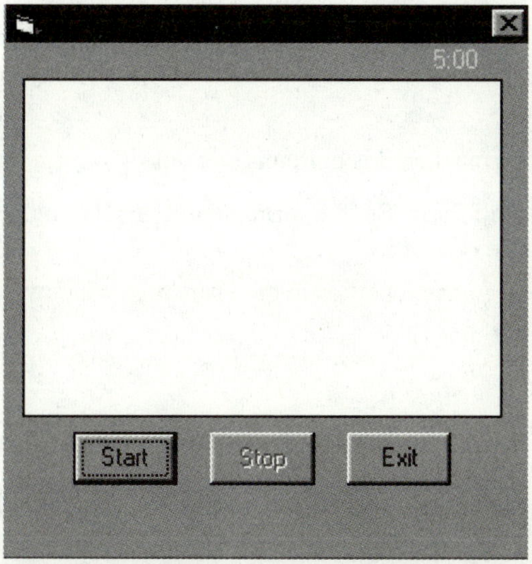

Figure 14-9: frmtest form to generate the three command buttons and a text box to enter text

The test form consists of three command buttons and a text box. These buttons and text box properties are to be set as follows:

The text box properties are:

Name: **Text1**

The Start command button is a Command Button control. Set the command button properties as follows:

- Name: **`cmdStart`**
- Caption: **Start**

Functionality: To start the timer and count the number of words typed when this button is clicked.

The Stop command button is a Command Button control. Set the command button properties as follows:

- Name: **`cmdStop`**
- Caption: **Stop**

Functionality: To stop the timer and display the number of words, the number of words per minute, the number of keystrokes, and the number of keystrokes per minute typed, when this button is clicked.

The Exit command button is a Command Button control. Set the command button properties as follows:

- Name: **`cmdExit`**
- Caption: **Exit**

Functionality: To close the frmtest form when this button is clicked.

8. On the menu bar, select Project ⇨ Add Form. Set the form name as frmfallingletters, and save the form as `frmfallingletters.frm`.
9. Select the form and set the following form properties in the Properties window.
   - Name: **frmfallingletters**
   - Capation: **Falling Letters**
   - Height: **4380**
   - Width: **3780**
10. Select the required controls from the Toolbox and set them as shown in Figure 14-10.

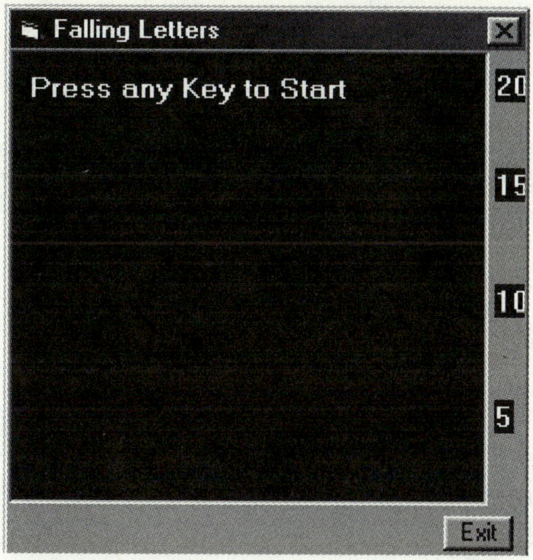

Figure 14-10: frmFallingLetters form with five labels, one picture box and one command button

The Falling Letters form consists of five labels, one picture box, and one command button. Set the properties of these controls as follows:

- Name: **`cmdExit`**
- Caption: **Exit**

Functionality: To close the frmFallingLetters form when this button is clicked.

The "Press any Key to Start" control shown is a Label control. The label properties are to be set as follows:

- Name: **`chl`**
- Caption: **Press any Key to Start**

The 20, 15, 10, and 5 shown are Label controls. Set the label properties as follows:

- Names: **`label1`**, **`label2`**, **`label3`**, and **`label4`**
- Captions: **20**, **15**, **10**, and **5**

The picture box properties are to be set as follows:

- Name: **`Picture1`**
- Height: **4000**
- Width: **3500**
- Picture: none
- Backcolor: blue

11. On the menu bar, select Run ⇨ Execute or click the Run button on the toolbar.

Output

Figure 14-11 shows the output screen for the typing speed indicator with a text box to enter the text and the command buttons. Figure 14-12 shows the output screen displaying the results of the typing speed indicator. The total words typed, words per minute, and keystrokes per minute are displayed. Figure 14-13 shows a screen displaying a falling letter. Figure 14-14 shows the results which indicate how fast the user could identify a falling letter and type it.

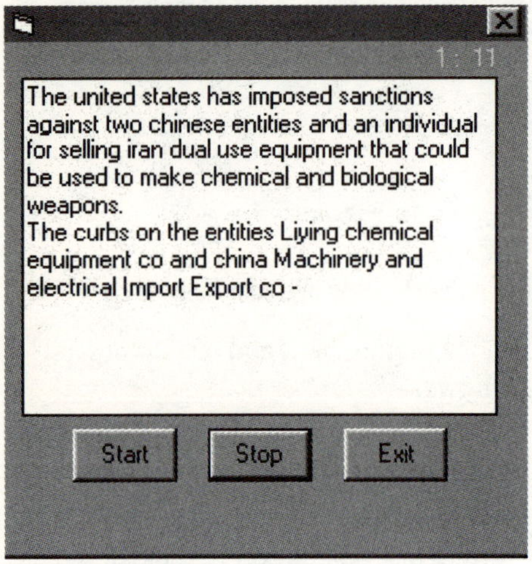

Figure 14-11: Ouptut screen for the test form while typing

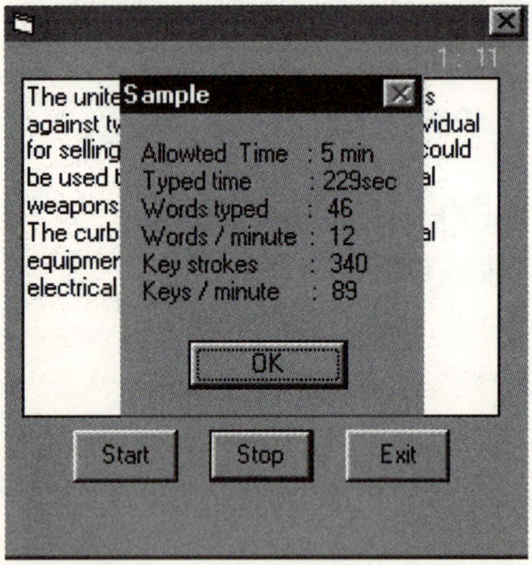

Figure 14-12: Ouptut screen for the test form when the Stop button is clicked

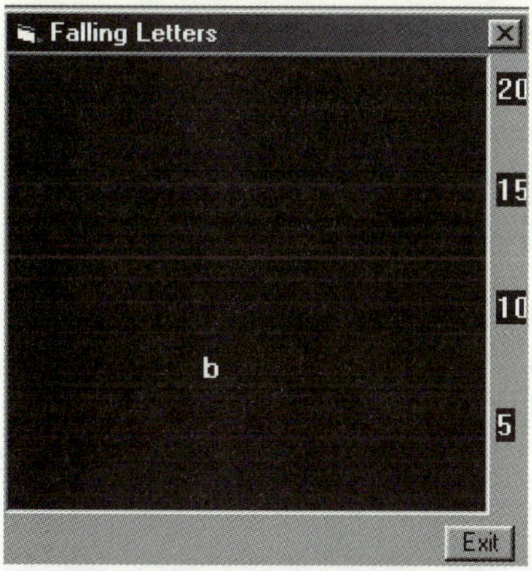

Figure 14-13: Ouptut screen for the falling letters form while letters are falling

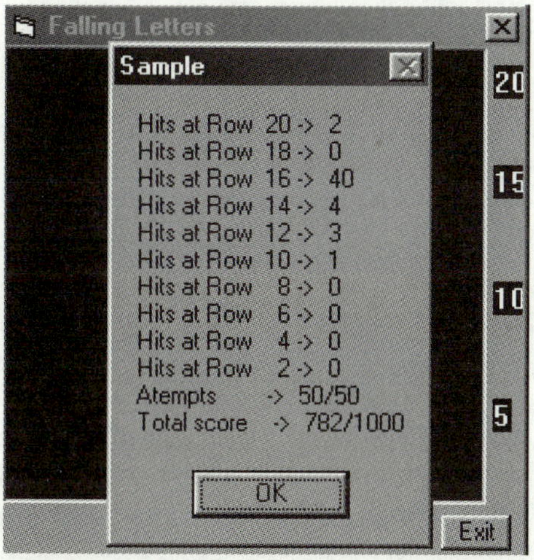

Figure 14-14: Ouptut screen for the fallingletters form while displaying results

Porting the software onto the Embedded XP platform

To port this application to the target system, follow the same steps as outlined for the ACRemote application. Instead of copying `ACRemote.EXE` and the three DLL files, copy the following files:

- `Sample.exe` (application file)
- `MSVBV60.DLL`

The DLL is required to run a Visual Basic application on the target platform.

Project: Embedded Database Application

This project develops a database application for field personnel to use in carrying out a productivity survey. The field personnel can obtain the following data from different organizations: type of organization, number of employees, and annual turnover. Based on this data, the productivity of the organization (i.e., turnover per employee) can be calculated for different types of organizations. This application is developed in VB and MS Access and then ported to the embedded XP environment.

Database definition

The database's name is `Productivity.mdb`, and it consists of the following table:

Field Name	*Field Type*	*Field Size*	*Required*	*Contraints*
ID	Autonumber	Long Integer	Yes	Primary Key, Indexed
OrganizationType	Text	25	Yes	—
AreaOfFocus	Text	25	Yes	—
AnnualTurnover	Currency		Yes	—
NoOfPeople	Number	Long Integer	Yes	—

Source code listing for Productivity.frm

Listing 14-11 provides the source code for the file `Productivity.frm`, which supplies all the functionality for the database operations.

Listing 14-11: Source code for Productivity.frm

```
' Form Global Declarations
Option Explicit
Dim CnProductivity As ADODB.Connection
Dim RSProductivity As ADODB.Recordset
Dim RSProductivityNew As ADODB.Recordset
Dim RSProductivityModify As ADODB.Recordset
Dim MyQuery As String
Dim MyQueryNew As String
Dim MyQueryModify As String
Dim MyButtonAction As String
Dim i As Integer
Dim OrganizationType As String
Dim AreaOfFocus As String
'This event is to select a value from the combobox
Private Sub cboAreaOfFocus_KeyPress(KeyAscii As Integer)
Select Case KeyAscii
  Case 8
  Case Else
    KeyAscii = 0
```

```
        MsgBox "Selection only"
    End Select
End Sub
  ' This event is to select a value from the combobox
Private Sub cboOrgType_KeyPress(KeyAscii As Integer)
    Case 8
    Case Else
        KeyAscii = 0
        MsgBox "Selection only"
    End Select
End Sub
  'This control event is to delete a record.
Private Sub cmdDelete_Click()
    Dim MyVar
    MyVar = MsgBox("Do You Want to Delete?", 65, "Productivity")
    If MyVar = 1 Then
        RSProductivity.Delete
        If RSProductivity.RecordCount > 0 Then
            RSProductivity.MoveNext
            If RSProductivity.EOF Then
                RSProductivity.MovePrevious
            End If
            EnableFields
            ClearAllFields
            Display
            DisableFields
        Else
            MsgBox "No records"
            ClearAllFields
        End If
    Else
        MsgBox "NO Record Deleted"
    End If
End Sub
  'This control event is to cancel the operation or close the
application.
Private Sub cmdExit_Click()
    If cmdExit.Caption = "E&xit" Then
        Unload Me
    Else
        EnablecmdButtons
        cmdExit.Caption = "E&xit"
        MyButtonAction = ""
        ClearAllFields
        Display
        DisableFields
    End If
End Sub
   ' This control event is to Display the first record
```

```
Private Sub cmdFirst_Click()
  cmdSave.Enabled = False
  RSProductivity.MoveFirst
  ClearAllFields
  Display
End Sub
 ' This control event is to Display the last record
Private Sub cmdLast_Click()
   cmdSave.Enabled = False
   RSProductivity.MoveLast
   ClearAllFields
   Display
End Sub
  ' This control event is to get the record to be modified
Private Sub cmdModify_Click()
  EnableFields
  MyQueryModify = "select * from Productivity where ID= " &
 CLng(txtID.Text)
  Set RSProductivityModify = New ADODB.Recordset
  RSProductivityModify.Open MyQueryModify, CnProductivity,
adOpenKeyset,
 adLockOptimistic
  If RSProductivityModify.RecordCount > 0 Then
     OrganizationType = RSProductivityModify(1)
     AreaOfFocus = RSProductivityModify(2)
     MyButtonAction = "Modify"
     cmdExit.Caption = "&Cancel"
     DisablecmdButtons
     cmdSave.Enabled = True
     cboOrgType.Clear
     OrganizationTypesToCboOrgType
     i = 0
     For i = 0 To 2
       If cboOrgType.List(i) = OrganizationType Then
          cboOrgType.Text = cboOrgType.List(i)
          Exit For
       End If
     Next
     cboAreaOfFocus.Clear
     AreaOfFocusTocboAreaOfFocus
     i = 0
     For i = 0 To 4
       If cboAreaOfFocus.List(i) = AreaOfFocus Then
         cboAreaOfFocus.Text = cboAreaOfFocus.List(i)
         Exit For
       End If
     Next
  Else
     MsgBox "NO Record"
```

```
  End If
  RSProductivityModify.Close
  Set RSProductivityModify = Nothing
  cboOrgType.SetFocus
End Sub
' This control event is to enter data for new record.
Private Sub cmdNew_Click()
   EnableFields
   ClearAllFields
   MyButtonAction = "New"
   cmdExit.Caption = "&Cancel"
   DisablecmdButtons
   cmdSave.Enabled = True
   MyQueryNew = "select max(ID) from Productivity"
   Set RSProductivityNew = New ADODB.Recordset
   RSProductivityNew.Open MyQueryNew, CnProductivity, adOpenKeyset,
 adLockOptimistic
   If RSProductivityNew.RecordCount > 0 Then
      If Not RSProductivityNew.Fields(0) Then
          txtID.Text = RSProductivityNew.Fields(0) + 1
      Else
          txtID.Text = "1"
      End If
   End If
   RSProductivityNew.Close
   Set RSProductivityNew = Nothing
   OrganizationTypesToCboOrgType
   cboOrgType.ListIndex = 0
   AreaOfFocusTocboAreaOfFocus
   cboAreaOfFocus.ListIndex = 0
End Sub
'This control event is to display the next record
Private Sub cmdNext_Click()
   cmdSave.Enabled = False
   ClearAllFields
   RSProductivity.MoveNext
   If RSProductivity.EOF Then
     MsgBox "Last Record"
     RSProductivity.MovePrevious
   End If
   Display
End Sub
'This control event is to display the previous record
Private Sub cmdPrevious_Click()
   cmdSave.Enabled = False
   ClearAllFields
   RSProductivity.MovePrevious
   If RSProductivity.BOF Then
       MsgBox "First Record"
```

```
        RSProductivity.MoveNext
    End If
    Display
End Sub
 'This control event is to display the data report
Private Sub cmdReport_Click()
    DataEnvironment1.Command1
    DataReport1.Show
End Sub
 'This control event is to add new record or update existing record
Private Sub cmdSave_Click()
    If MyButtonAction = "New" Then
        RSProductivity.AddNew
        RSProductivity.Fields("OrganizationType") =
Trim(cboOrgType.Text)
        RSProductivity.Fields("AreaOfFocus") =
Trim(cboAreaOfFocus.Text)
        RSProductivity.Fields("AnnualTurnover") =
Trim(txtAnnualTurnover.Text)
        RSProductivity.Fields("NoOfPeople") = Trim(txtNoOfPeople.Text)
        RSProductivity.Update
        EnablecmdButtons
        cmdExit.Caption = "E&xit"
        MyButtonAction = ""
        ClearAllFields
        Display
        DisableFields
    ElseIf MyButtonAction = "Modify" Then
        RSProductivity.Fields("OrganizationType") =
Trim(cboOrgType.Text)
        RSProductivity.Fields("AreaOfFocus") =
Trim(cboAreaOfFocus.Text)
        RSProductivity.Fields("AnnualTurnover") =
Trim(txtAnnualTurnover.Text)
        RSProductivity.Fields("NoOfPeople") = Trim(txtNoOfPeople.Text)
        RSProductivity.Update
        EnablecmdButtons
        cmdExit.Caption = "E&xit"
        MyButtonAction = ""
        ClearAllFields
        Display
        DisableFields
    End If
End Sub
 'This form event is to display first record data while the
application is
 loading.
Private Sub Form_Load()
    txtID.Enabled = False
```

```
  ClearAllFields
  EnablecmdButtons
  Set CnProductivity = New ADODB.Connection
  CnProductivity.Open "DSN=Productivity"
  MyQuery = "Select * From Productivity"
  Set RSProductivity = New ADODB.Recordset
  RSProductivity.Open MyQuery, CnProductivity, adOpenKeyset, adLockOptimistic
  If RSProductivity.RecordCount > 0 Then
    RSProductivity.MoveFirst
    Display
  Else
    MsgBox "No Records In the Database"
    cmdModify.Enabled = False
    cmdSave.Enabled = False
    cmdDelete.Enabled = False
    cmdFirst.Enabled = False
    cmdLast.Enabled = False
    cmdNext.Enabled = False
    cmdPrevious.Enabled = False
  End If
  DisableFields
End Sub
  'This control event is to close the record set, connection and application
Private Sub Form_Unload(Cancel As Integer)
  RSProductivity.Close
  Set RSProductivity = Nothing
  CnProductivity.Close
  Set CnProductivity = Nothing
  End
End Sub
  'This procedure is to clear all the text boxes
Private Sub ClearAllFields()
  txtID.Text = ""
  cboOrgType.Clear
  cboAreaOfFocus.Clear
  txtAnnualTurnover.Text = ""
  txtNoOfPeople.Text = ""
End Sub
   'This procedure is to assign database fields data to text fields
Private Sub Display()
  If (RSProductivity.BOF) Or (RSProductivity.EOF) Then
     Exit Sub
  End If
  txtID.Text = RSProductivity.Fields("ID")
  cboOrgType.Clear
  cboOrgType.AddItem RSProductivity.Fields("OrganizationType")
  cboOrgType.ListIndex = 0
```

```
    cboAreaOfFocus.Clear
    cboAreaOfFocus.AddItem RSProductivity.Fields("AreaOfFocus")
    cboAreaOfFocus.ListIndex = 0
    txtAnnualTurnover.Text = RSProductivity.Fields("AnnualTurnover")
    txtNoOfPeople.Text = RSProductivity.Fields("NoOfPeople")
End Sub
'This procedure is to add Organization types to combobox
Private Sub OrganizationTypesToCboOrgType()
    cboOrgType.AddItem ("Small Enterprises")
    cboOrgType.AddItem ("Medium Enterprises")
    cboOrgType.AddItem ("Multi National Company")
End Sub
'This procedure is to add Area Of Focus to combobox
Private Sub AreaOfFocusTocboAreaOfFocus()
    cboAreaOfFocus.AddItem ("Embedded Software")
    cboAreaOfFocus.AddItem ("Networking")
    cboAreaOfFocus.AddItem ("E -Commerce")
    cboAreaOfFocus.AddItem ("Telecom")
    cboAreaOfFocus.AddItem ("Business Applications")
End Sub
'This procedure is to enable all text fields
Private Sub EnableFields()
    cboOrgType.Enabled = True
    cboAreaOfFocus.Enabled = True
    txtAnnualTurnover.Enabled = True
    txtNoOfPeople.Enabled = True
End Sub
'This procedure is to disable all text fields
Private Sub DisableFields()
    cboOrgType.Enabled = False
    cboAreaOfFocus.Enabled = False
    txtAnnualTurnover.Enabled = False
    txtNoOfPeople.Enabled = False
End Sub
'This procedure is to enable the command buttons
Private Sub EnablecmdButtons()
    cmdSave.Enabled = False
    cmdNew.Enabled = True
    cmdModify.Enabled = True
    cmdDelete.Enabled = True
    cmdFirst.Enabled = True
    cmdLast.Enabled = True
    cmdNext.Enabled = True
    cmdPrevious.Enabled = True
End Sub
'This procedure is to disable the command buttons
Private Sub DisablecmdButtons()
    cmdSave.Enabled = True
    cmdNew.Enabled = False
```

```
276.   cmdModify.Enabled = False
277.   cmdDelete.Enabled = False
278.   cmdFirst.Enabled = False
279.   cmdLast.Enabled = False
280.   cmdNext.Enabled = False
281.   cmdPrevious.Enabled = False
282. End Sub
    ' This event is to validate for numeric values
283. Private Sub txtAnnualTurnover_KeyPress(KeyAscii As Integer)
284.   Select Case KeyAscii
285.     Case 8, 46, 48 To 57
286.     Case Else
287.       KeyAscii = 0
288.       MsgBox "Enter Numbers only"
289.   End Select
290. End Sub
    ' This event is to validate for numeric values
291. Private Sub txtNoOfPeople_KeyPress(KeyAscii As Integer)
292.   Select Case KeyAscii
293.      Case 8, 46, 48 To 57
294.      Case Else
295.         KeyAscii = 0
296.         MsgBox "Enter Numbers only"
297.   End Select
298. End Sub
    ' This event is to validate for null.
299. Private Sub txtAnnualTurnover_LostFocus()
300.     If txtAnnualTurnover.Text = "" Then
301.         MsgBox "This field is manditory"
302.         txtAnnualTurnover.SetFocus
303.     End If
304. End Sub
    ' This event is to validate for null.
305. Private Sub txtNoOfPeople_LostFocus()
306.     If txtNoOfPeople.Text = "" Then
307.         MsgBox "This field is mandatory"
308.         txtNoOfPeople.SetFocus
309.     End If
310. End Sub
```

Following is the line-by-line explanation of the source code:

- **Lines 1–12:** Variables declaration.
- **Lines 13–20:** Definition of the `cboAreaOfFocus_KeyPress()` event, to select a value from the combo box.
- **Lines 21–27:** Definition of the `cboOrgType_KeyPress()` event, to select a value from the combo box.

- **Lines 28–49:** Definition of the `cmdDelete_Click()` event, to delete a record.
  - **Line 30:** Takes the input from the message box and assigns the value to the variable, `MyVar`.
  - **Line 32:** Deletes a record from the database.
  - **Lines 33–45:** Displays the next record.
- **Lines 50–61:** Definition of the `cmdExit_Click()` event, to cancel the operation or close the application.
- **Lines 62–67:** Definition of the `cmdFirst_Click()` event, to display the first record.
- **Lines 68–73:** Definition of the `cmdLast_Click()` event, to display the last record.
- **Lines 74–110:** Definition of the `cmdModify_Click()` event, to retrieve the record to be modified.
  - **Lines 76–79:** Creates a recordset and finds the current record in the database.
  - **Lines 86–94:** Adds all organization types to the combo box.
- **Lines 111–134:** Definition of the `cmdNew_Click()` event, to enter data for a new record.
  - **Lines 121–126:** Displays the ID No. in the text field.
- **Lines 135–144:** Definition of the `cmdNext_Click()` event, to display the next record.
  - **Line 139:** Checks for the last record.
- **Lines 145–154:** Definition of the `cmdPrevious_Click()` event, to display the previous record.
  - **Line 149:** Checks for the first record.
- **Lines 155–158:** Definition of the `cmdReport_Click()` event, to display the data report.
- **Lines 159–186:** Definition of the `cmdSave_Click()` event, to add a new record or to update the existing record.
  - **Line 161:** Adds a new record to the database.
- **Lines 187–210:** Definition of the `Form_Load()` event, to display the first record of data while the application is loading.
- **Lines 211–217:** Definition of the `Form_Unload()` event, to close the recordset, connection, and application.
- **Lines 218–224:** Definition of the `ClearAllFields()` procedure, to clear the all text fields.
- **Lines 225–238:** Definition of the `Display()` procedure, to assign the database fields' data to text fields.

- **Lines 239–243:** Definition of the `OrganizationTypesToCboOrgType()` procedure, to add organization types to the combo box.
- **Lines 244–250:** Definition of the `AreaOfFocusTocboAreaOfFocus()` procedure, to add area of focus to the combo box.
- **Lines 251–256:** Definition of the `EnableFields()` procedure, to enable all text fields.
- **Lines 257–262:** Definition of the `DisableFields()` procedure, to disable all text fields.
- **Lines 263–272:** Definition of the `EnablecmdButtons()` procedure, to enable all command buttons.
- **Lines 273–282:** Definition of the `DisablecmdButtons()` procedure, to disable all command buttons.
- **Lines 283–290:** Definition of the `txtAnnualTurnover_KeyPress()` event, to validate numeric values.
- **Lines 291–298:** Definition of the `txtNoOfPeople_KeyPress()` event, to validate numeric values.
- **Lines 299–304:** Definition of the `txtAnnualTurnover_LostFocus()` event, to validate null values.
- **Lines 305–310:** Definition of the `txtNoOfPeople_LostFocus()` event, to validate null values.

Executing the program

The step-by-step procedure to execute the program is as follows:

1. Open Microsoft Visual Basic 6.0. A window will open showing Existing Projects, New Projects, and Recent Projects tabs. Select the New Projects tab, select Standard EXE, and click the Open button. The default form will be displayed.
2. On the menu bar, select Project ⇨ Project Properties and set the project name as **Productivity Survey**; save the form as **`ProductivitySurvey.frm`** and save the project as `ProductivitySurvey.vbp`.
3. Select the form and set the following form properties in the Properties window:
   - Name: **`frmProductivitySurvey`**
   - Caption: **ProductivitySurvey**
   - Height: **4005**
   - Width: **3780**
4. Select the required controls from the Toolbox and set them as shown in Figure 14-15.

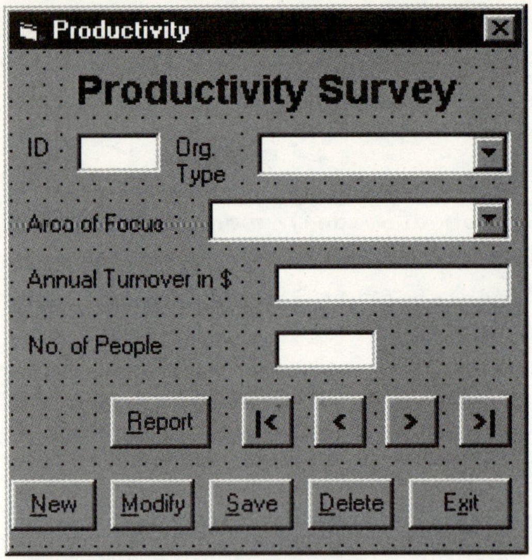

Figure 14-15: Productivity survey form to facilitate data entry

The "Productivity Survey" label shown in bold at the top of the form is a Label control. The label properties are to be set as follows:

- Name: `lblTitle`
- Caption: **Productivity Survey**
- Font: Arial, Bold.

The ID shown is a Label control. Set the label properties as follows:

- Name: `lblID`
- Caption: **ID**

The Org.Type shown is a Label control. The label properties are to be set as follows:

- Name: `lblTypeofOrg`
- Caption: **Org.Type**

The Area of Focus shown is a Label control. Set the label properties as follows:

- Name: `lblAreaofFocus`
- Caption: **Area of Focus**

The Annual Turnover in $ shown is a Label control. Set the label properties as follows:

- Name: `lblAnnualTurnover`
- Caption: **Annual Turnover in $**

The No. of People shown is a Label control. Set the label properties as follows:

- Name: `lblNoOfPeople`
- Caption: **No. of People**

The text box next to the ID label is a Text Box control. Set the text box properties as follows:

- Name: `txtID`

The combo box shown next to the Org. Type label is a Combo Box control. The combo box properties should be set as follows:

- Name: `cboOrgType`

This combo box contains organization types.

The combo box shown next to the Area of Focus label is a Combo Box control. Set the combo box properties as follows:

- Name: `cboAreaOfFocus`

This combo box contains area of focus.

The text box shown next to the Annual Turnover in $ label is a Text Box control. The text box properties should be set as follows:

- Name: `txtAnnualTurnover`
- MaxLength: **15**

The text box shown next to the No. of People label is a Text Box control. Set the text box properties as follows:

- Name: `txtNoOfPeople`
- MaxLength: **7**

The |< command button is a Command Button control. Set the command button properties as follows:

- Name: `cmdFirst`
- Caption: |<

Functionality: When clicked, this button displays the first record available in the database.

The < command button is a Command Button control. The command button properties should be set as follows:

- Name: `cmdPrevious`
- Caption: <

Functionality: When clicked, this button displays the previous record available in the database.

The > command button shown is a Command Button control. Set the command button properties as follows:

- Name: `cmdNext`
- Caption: >

Functionality: When clicked, this button displays the next record available in the database.

The >| command button is a Command Button control. Set the command button properties as follows:

- Name: `cmdLast`
- Caption: >|

Functionality: When clicked, this button displays the last record available in the database.

The New command button is a Command Button control. The command button properties should be set as follows:

- Name: `cmdNew`
- Caption: **&New**

Functionality: When clicked, this button clears all the text fields and enables the user to input data.

The Modify command button shown is a Command Button control. Set the command button properties as follows:

- Name: `cmdModify`
- Caption: **&Modify**

Functionality: When clicked, this button enables the user to modify the values of the currently displayed record.

The Save command button is a Command Button control. The command button properties should be set as follows:

- Name: `cmdSave`
- Caption: **&Save**

Functionality: When clicked, this button saves the existing record, which may be either a new record or a modified record.

The Delete command button is a Command Button control. Set the command button properties as follows:

- Name: `cmdDelete`
- Caption: **&Delete**

Functionality: When clicked, this button deletes the existing record after prompting for a confirmation.

The Exit command button is a Command Button control. Set the command button properties as follows:

- Name: `cmdExit`
- Caption: **E&xit**

Functionality: When clicked, this button unloads the application.

The Report command button is a Command Button control. The command button properties should be set as follows:

- Name: `cmdReport`
- Caption: **&Report**

Functionality: When clicked, this button displays the report.

5. On the menu bar, select Project ⇨ References ⇨ Microsoft ActiveX Data Object 2.0 Library. This reference is used for database connectivity.
6. On the menu bar, select Project ⇨ More ActiveX Designers ⇨ Data Environment. The screen shown in Figure 14-16 will appear.

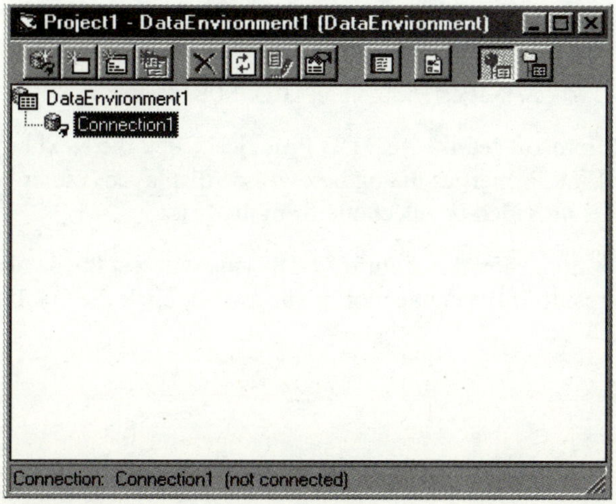

Figure 14-16: Data Envrionment screen

In the window, right-click on Connection1 and select the Properties option. The Data Link Properties window shown in Figure 14-17 will be displayed.

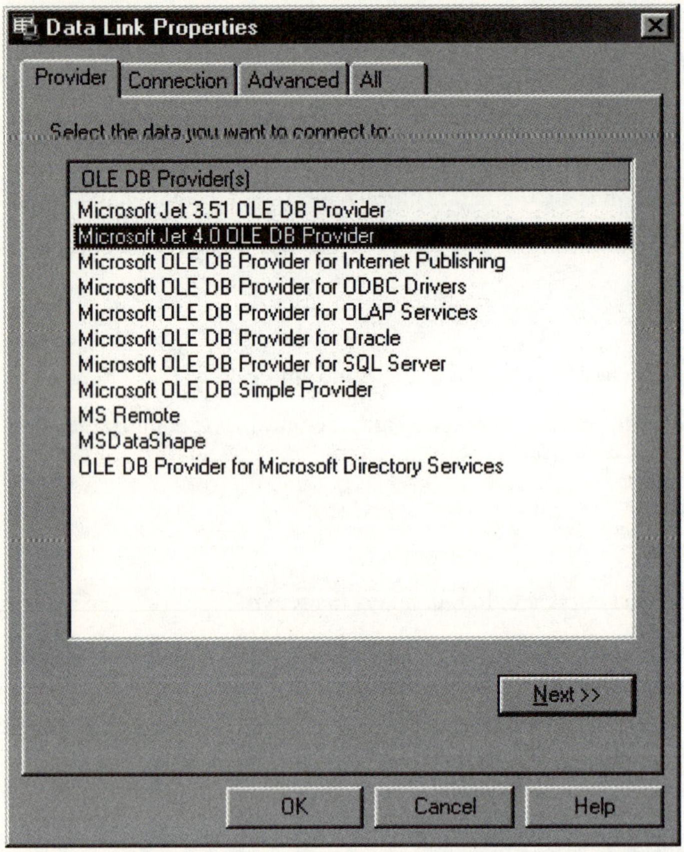

Figure 14-17: Data Link Properties window to select Microsoft Jet 4.0 OLE DB Provider

In the Provider tab, select Microsoft Jet 4.0 OLE DB Provider. Click the Next button. The Connection tab of the Data Link Properties dialog box will be displayed. Either enter the database name in the text box provided or select one from the list.

Click the Test Connection button, shown in Figure 14-18. This will test the database connectivity and return the result. If the connection is successful, click the OK button.

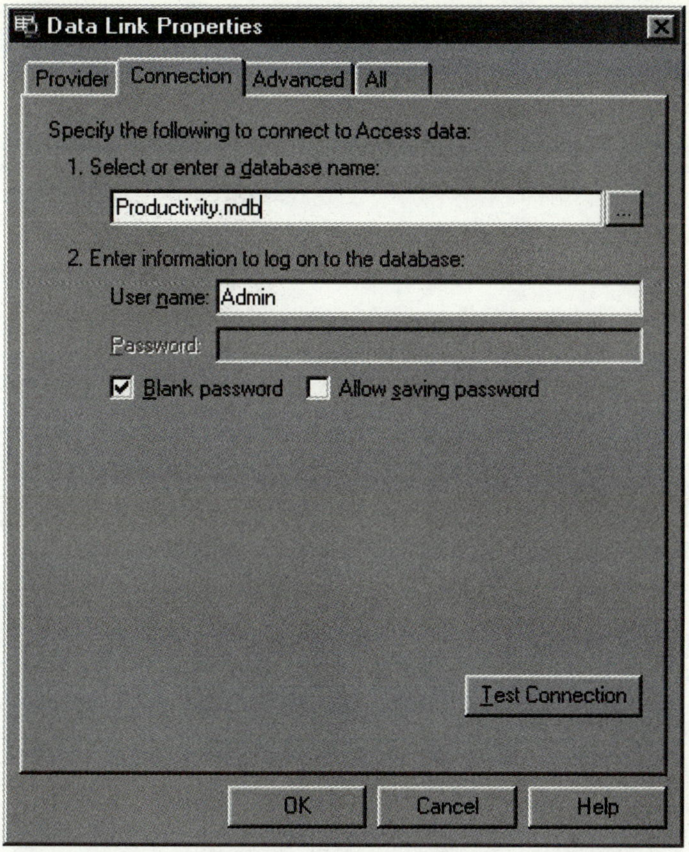

Figure 14-18: Data Link Properties window to select or enter the database name and the username to access the database

7. Right-click on Connection1 and select the Add Command option. The screen shown in Figure 14-19 will appear.

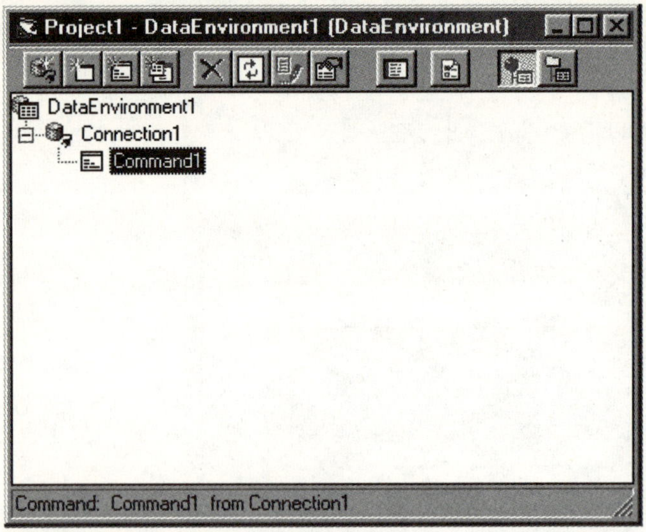

Figure 14-19: Data Environment window

Right-click on Command1 and select the Properties option. The dialog box shown in Figure 14-20 will appear.

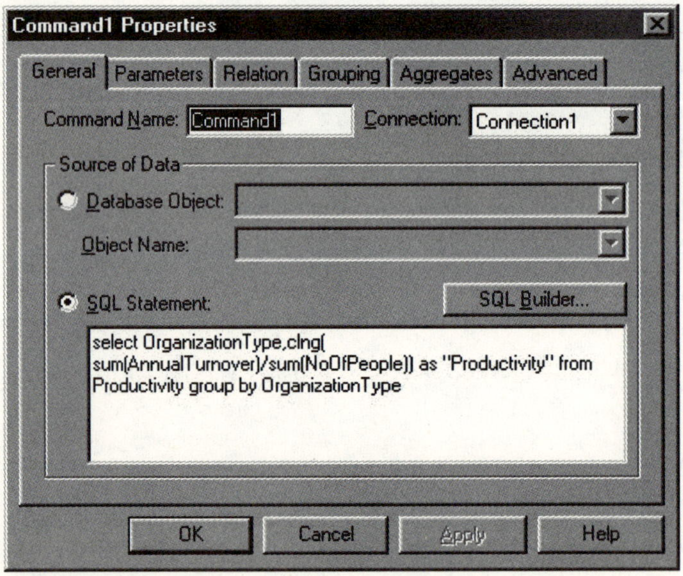

Figure 14-20: The General tab of the Command Properties dialog box

In the General tab, select the SQL Statement radio button and enter the following SQL statements in the text box provided:

```
select OrganizationType,clng( sum(AnnualTurnover)/sum(NoOfPeople))
as "Productivity" from Productivity group by OrganizationType
```

Click OK.

8. On the menu bar, select Project ⇨ Add Data Report. The data report will appear as shown in Figure 14-21.

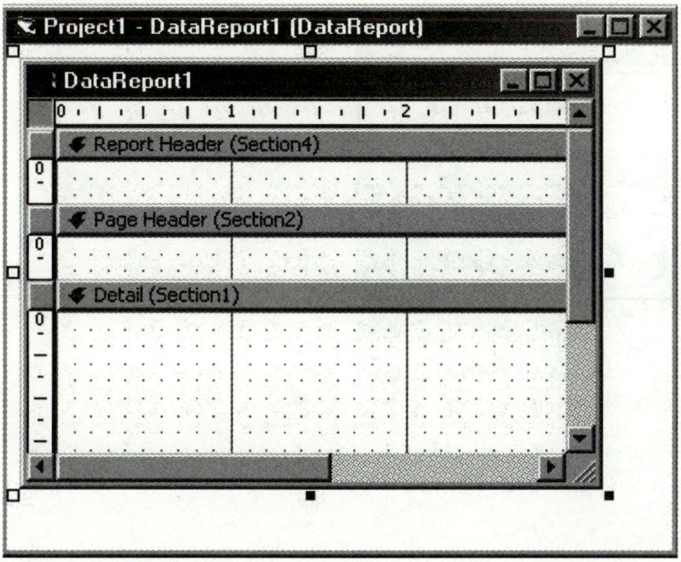

Figure 14-21: DataReport screen

Select the DataReport1 and set the following DataReport properties in the Properties window:

Name: **DataReport1**

Caption: **Productivity Report**

DataMember: **Command1**

DataSource: **DataEnvironment1**

RightMargin: **0**

LeftMargin: **0**

TopMargin: **0**

Height: **3975**

Width: **3765**

Select the required controls from the Toolbox and set them as shown in Figure 14-22.

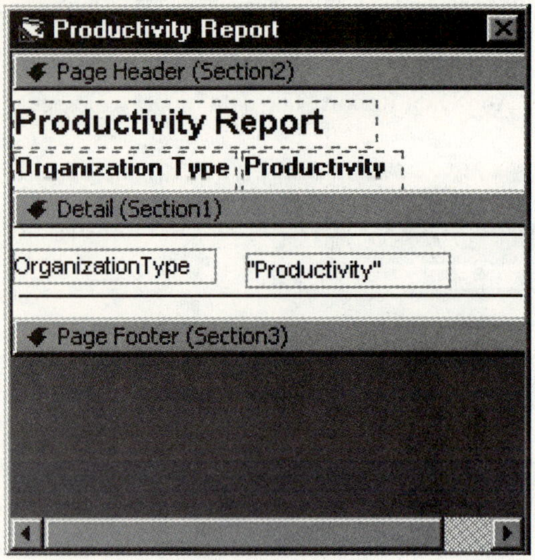

Figure 14-22: Productivity Report window

The "Productivity Report" shown in bold at the top of the report is a Label control. The label properties are to be set as follows:

- Name: `lblTitle`
- Caption: **Productivity Report**

The Organization Type shown is a Label control. Set the label properties as follows:

- Name: `lblOrganizationType`
- Caption: **Organization Type**

The Productivity label shown is a Label control. Set the label properties as follows:

- Name: `lblProductivity`
- Caption: **Productivity**

The text box shown below the Organization Type label is a Text Box control. Set the text box properties as follows:

- Name: `txtOrganizationType`
- DataField: **Organization Type**
- DataMember: **Command1**

The text box shown below the Productivity label is a Text Box control. Set the text box properties as follows:

- Name: `txtProductivity`
- DataField: **Productivity**
- DataMember: **Command1**

9. On the menu bar, select Run ⇨ Execute or click the Run button on the toolbar.

Output

The output screen displayed will look like the one shown in Figure 14-23. The report generated is shown in Figure 14-24.

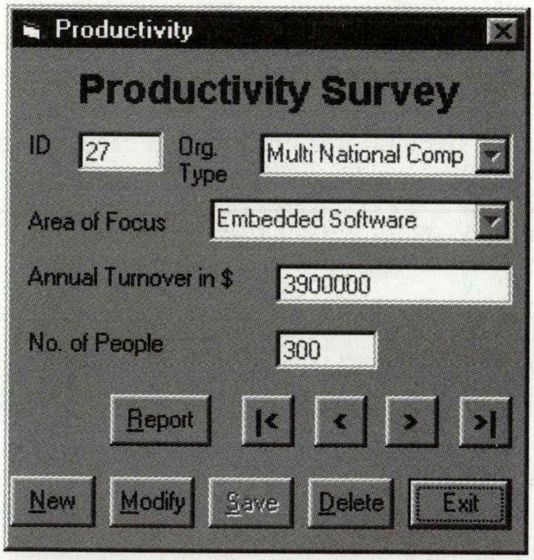

Figure 14-23: Output screen for the database application for data entry

Figure 14-24: Report for the database application

Setting up the database application

Before porting the application to Embedded XP environment, you need to create setup for the database application using the following steps:

1. On the Windows taskbar, select Start ⇨ Programs ⇨ Microsoft Visual Studio 6.0 ⇨ Microsoft Visual Studio 6.0 Tools. Open the Package & Deployment Wizard. A Window with the title Package and Deployment Wizard will be displayed.
2. A text box with Select Project as the caption will be shown at the top. Select the project to be packaged by clicking the Browse button.

   After selecting the project, click the Package button. The wizard automatically compiles the files needed, along with the dependencies. After compiling all the required files, a window with title Package and Deployment Wizard — Packing Script will be displayed.
3. In the window will be a Packing Script drop-down list with Standard Setup Package1 as the default option selected. Click the Next button.
4. A window with the title Package and Deployment Wizard — Package Type will be displayed. There will be a Package Type text box with Standard Setup Package as the default option selected. Click the Next button.
5. A window with the title Package and Deployment Wizard — Package Folder will be displayed. There will be a Package Folder text box with a default folder selected. Change the folder name if you want. Click the Next button.
6. A window with the title Package and Deployment Wizard — Include Files will be displayed. This window displays all the included files. If you want to add any more files or if some files are missing, you can add them by clicking the Add button. Click the Next button when you are finished.
7. A window with the title Package and Deployment Wizard — Cab Options will be displayed. Depending on your need, the file can be a single `.CAB` file or multiple `.CAB` files. Click the Next button.
8. A window with the title Package and Deployment Wizard — Installation Title will be displayed. This window includes an Installation text box with a default title selected. You can change the title if you like. When you are done, click the Next button.
9. A window with the title Package and Deployment Wizard — Start Menu Items will be displayed. A default group and items are shown. If you want to change the group and items, you can do so by clicking the relevant buttons. When you are done, click the Next button.
10. A window with the title Package and Deployment Wizard — Installation Locations will be displayed. A default location for each file that is being installed on the system is displayed. If you want to change an installation location, click on the relevant file and change the location. Click the Next button when you are finished.

11. A window with the title Package and Deployment Wizard — Shared Files will be displayed. A default list of files that will be installed as shared files is displayed. Click the Next button.
12. A window with the title Package and Deployment Wizard — Finished! will be displayed. In it will be a Script Name text box with a default name selected. You can change the name if you like. Click the Finish button when you are done.

The package is now ready for distribution. The `\Package` directory contains the following:

- `ProductivitySurvey.CAB`
- `setup.exe`
- `Setup.lst`
- `\Support` (directory)

Porting the software onto an Embedded XP platform

To port this application onto the target system, follow the same steps as outlined for the ACRemote application. You need to copy the following files:

- `ProductivitySurvey.CAB`
- `setup.exe`
- `Setup.lst`
- `\Support` (directory)

To copy the `\Support` directory, right-click on the Files option in the Navigation pane and select the Add Directory option. The remaining steps are exactly the same as those given in the application for the remote control of an air conditioner.

After booting the target system, install the application by executing the `step.exe` file and then run `productivity.exe`.

Project: Electronic Voting

Electronic voting is an active research area. It is certainly conceivable that voters could elect presidents and prime ministers over the Internet, assuming that the Internet infrastructure could support the sudden increase in traffic for a short duration. Of course, enough security would also have to be built in, and both voters and politicians would have to be confident that an Internet voting process was fair. In the meantime, a small-scale electronic voting system for local elections — such as on a campus, for professional bodies, etc. — could certainly be done through the Internet.

This example demonstrates a simple electronic voting system to elect the president, secretary, and treasurer of a local body. The electronic ballot form is presented to the user after he or she invokes the appropriate URL from a device running Embedded XP. The user can vote for the candidates in each of the categories and submit the ballot electronically. Without human intervention, the ballot form is sent to the database and the database is immediately updated to indicate the number of votes polled by each candidate. An administrator can also see the number of votes polled by each candidate through the URL (this module has been added only to test your application; in practice it should not be there). Because this is a Web-based application, you need to run Internet Information Server (IIS) or Personal Web Server (PWS) on one of the machines on which the ASP code is running. You can use the browser of the XP machine to test the code. You need to ensure that the Internet Explorer component is also in the target image.

Database details

The database stores the votes of different candidates and details about the voters. Two tables, Contest and Votes, are required as per the following description. Create these tables and enter the corresponding data related to the candidates and the voters.

Table: Contest

Field Name	***Field Type***	***Field Size***	***Description***
PersonName	Text	50	Name of the person
Votes	Number	Long Integer(4 bytes)	Number of votes
Post	Text	50	Name of the post

Table: Voters

Field Name	***Field Type***	***Field Size***	***Description***
ssn	Text	50	Social Security Number
pwd	Text	50	Password
status	Number	Byte (1 byte)	Status of the voter (voted, not voted)

Project files

There are five files for this project:

- `vote.asp`: To create the user interface, session and to accept the social security number and password of the voter.
- `insertvote.asp`: To validate the voter's social security number and password with the database values, update the database tables, and redirect to `thanks.html`. If the social security number and password are invalid, redirects to `checkvote.asp`.
- `checkvote.asp`: To display the form to the voter again to retrieve a valid social security number and password.
- `thanks.html`: To display a "Thanks" message to the voter.
- `display.asp`: To determine the results of polling. This page will update every minute.

Source code listing for vote.asp

Listing 14-12 gives the source code for `vote.asp`.

Listing 14-12: Source code for vote.asp

```
1. <%session("ssn")=""%>
2. <html>
3. <head>
4. <title>Electronic Voting</title>
5. <script language=JavaScript>
6. function message(form){
7. if( (document.f1.ssn.value.length <= 0) ||
   (document.f1.pwd.value.length <= 0)) {
8. alert("SSNumber and Passwod both are compulsory")
9. return false;
10. }else
11. return true;}
12. </script>
13. </head>
14. <body>
15. <center><h4>Electronic Voting</h4></center>
16. <form name="f1" method="post" action="insertvote.asp">
17. <pre>
18. President:
19. <input type=radio name=president value=”Stan Fleming”> Stan Fleming
20. <input type=radio name=president value=”Deborah Ross”> Deborah Ross
21. Secretary:
22. <input type=radio name=secretary value=”Elizabeth Kaplan”> Elizabeth
Kaplan
23. <input type=radio name=secretary value=”Michael Sweet”> Michael
Sweet
24. Treasurer:
25. <input type=radio name=treasurer value=”George Sunders”> George
Sunders
26. <input type=radio name=treasurer value=”Collatte Hallinan”> Collatte
Hallinan
27. Enter Social Security Number: <input type=text name=ssn size=10>
28. Enter Password:               <input type=password name=pwd size=10>
29. <input type=submit name=s1 value=Submit onClick="return
message(this.form)">
30. <input type=reset name=r1 value=Cancel>
31. </pre>
32. </form>
33. </body>
34. </html>
```

Following is the line-by-line explanation of the source code:

- **Line 1:** Creates a session variable `ssn`.

- **Line 2:** Starting element of HTML document root, `HTML`.
- **Line 3:** Starting element of HTML document head.
- **Line 4:** HTML document `TITLE` element with the title "Electronic Voting" will be displayed as the page header or window title.
- **Line 5:** Starting element of `SCRIPT` using JavaScript as the script language.
- **Lines 6–12:** This is a JavaScript function `message` for validating the text fields Social Security Number (ssn) and Password (pwd).
  - **Line 8:** Displays an alert message.
- **Line 13:** Ending element of HTML document head.
- **Line 14:** Starting element of HTML document body.
- **Line 15:** Displays heading with heading style `H4` and aligns it to the center of the document.
- **Line 16:** Starting element of HTML interactive form with the following: attribute as `f1`, method as `Post`, and action as `insertvote.asp`.
- **Line 17:** Starting element of preformatted text.
- **Lines 19–20:** This is a form control of type `radio buttons` with the name `president`, and the values Stan Fleming and Deborah Ross.
- **Lines 22–23:** This is a form control of type `radio buttons` with the name `secretary`, and the values Elizabeth Kaplan and Michael Sweet.
- **Lines 25–26:** This is a form control of type `radio buttons` with the name `treasurer`, and the values George Sunders and Collatte Hallinan.
- **Line 27:** This is a form control of type `text field` with the name `ssn` and the size 10.
- **Line 28:** This is a form control of type `password` with the name `pwd` and the size 10.
- **Line 29:** This is a form control of type `submit` with the name `s1`, which calls the function `message` when clicked and redirects to `insertvote.asp` when the function returns true.
- **Line 30:** This is a form control of type `reset` with the name `r1`, which resets all the controls to their initial values.
- **Line 31:** Ending element of preformatted text.
- **Line 32:** Ending element of HTML interactive form.
- **Line 33:** Ending element of HTML document body.
- **Line 34:** Ending element of HTML document root.

Source code listing for insertvote.asp

Listing 14-13 gives the source code for `insertvote.asp`.

Listing 14-13: Source code for insertvote.asp

```
<%
Dim flag,pname,sname,tname,m,n
pname=request.form("pre1")
sname=request.form("sec1")
tname=request.form("tre1")
m=request.form("ssn")
n=request.form("pwd")
session("ssn")=m
if(pname="") then
pname="none"
end if
if(sname="") then
sname="none"
end if
if(tname="") then
tname="none"
end if
set myconn=server.createobject("ADODB.Connection")
set myconn1=server.createobject("ADODB.Connection")
set myconn2=server.createobject("ADODB.Connection")
set cmd=server.createobject("ADODB.Command")
set cmd1=server.createobject("ADODB.Command")
set rs=server.createobject("ADODB.Recordset")
myconn.open "DSN=vote"
myconn1.open "DSN=vote"
myconn2.open "DSN=vote"
rs.open "select * from voters",myconn,adopendynamic
flag=0
stat=0
session("status")=0
session("status1")=1
do while not rs.eof
if(m=rs.fields(0)) then
if(n=rs.fields(1)) then
status=rs.fields(2)
flag=1
session("status")=1
else
%>
<b>Enter User name and Password Correctly <br></b>
<%
end if
end if
rs.movenext
loop
if(stat=status) then
session("status1")=0
```

```
48. end if
49. if(flag=1 and stat=status) then
50. cmd.ActiveConnection=myconn2
51. cmd1.ActiveConnection=myconn1
52. str1= "update Contest set votes=votes+1 where PersonName
in('"&pname&"','"&sname&"','"&tname&"')"
53. cmd.commandText=str1
54. tnames="none"
55. if(pname=tnames and sname=tnames and tname=tnames) then
56. str2= "update voters set status=status+2 where ssn='"&m&"'"
57. else
58. str2= "update voters set status=status+1 where ssn='"&m&"'"
59. end if
60. cmd1.commandText=str2
61. cmd.execute
62. cmd1.execute
63. %>
64. <!-- #include file="thanks.html" -->
65. <% else %>
66. <!-- #include file="checkvote.asp" -->
67. <%
68. end if
69. myconn.close
70. myconn1.close
71. myconn2.close
72. %>
```

Following is the line-by-line explanation of the source code:

- **Line 1:** Start of the ASP code.
- **Line 2:** Declares the variables.
- **Lines 3–7:** Retrieves the information (social security number and password) from the client and assigns these values to the variables.
- **Line 8:** Assigns the ssn value (`m`) to the session variable, `ssn`.
- **Lines 9–17:** Validates the variables `pname`, `sname`, and `tname`.
- **Lines 18–20:** Creates objects for `ADODBConnection`.
- **Lines 21–22:** Creates objects for `ADODB Command`.
- **Line 23:** Creates a `recordset` object.
- **Lines 24–26:** Opens the connection.
- **Line 27:** The recordset is opened by passing a SQL string and the name of the Connection object.
- **Lines 28–29:** Assigns the variables (`flag,stat`) to 0.
- **Line 30:** Assigns the session variable `status` to 0.

- **Line 31:** Assigns the session variable `status1` to 1.
- **Lines 32–45:** Checks the social security number and password within the `do while` ....loop until the end of the recordset.
  - **Line 33:** Checks the social security number.
  - **Line 34:** Checks the password.
  - **Line 35:** Sets the variable `status`.
  - **Lines 36–37:** Sets the variable `flag` to 1 and the seesion variable `status` to 1 if the user is valid.
  - **Line 44:** Moves to the next record.
- **Lines 46–48:** If the variables `stat` and `status` are equal, assigns `status` to 0.
- **Lines 49–68:** Checks the variable `status` and updates the database tables.
  - **Lines 50–51:** The commands `cmd` and `cmd1` are associated with open database connections (`myconn2` and `myconn1`, respectively) by using the `Command` object's `ActiveConnection` property.
  - **Line 52:** Assigns the `Update` statement to the string `str1`.
  - **Line 53:** Assigns the string, `str1`, to `commandText` of the Command object.
  - **Line 54:** Assigns `"none"` to `tnames`.
  - **Lines 55–59:** If the user doesn't check a radio button, assigns one update query to the string `str2`; otherwise, assigns another query to the string `str2`.
  - **Line 60:** Assigns the string `str2` to the `commandText` property of the `Command` object.
  - **Lines 61–62:** The method `execute` is called to update the database.
  - **Line 64:** Includes the file `thanks.html`.
  - **Line 66:** Includes the file `checkvote.asp`.
- **Lines 69–71:** Closes the `Connection` objects.

Source code listing for checkvote.asp

Listing 14-14 gives the source code for `checkvote.asp`.

Listing 14-14: Source code for checkvote.asp

```
<%session("msg")="Please Check your Information"%>
<%
if session("status")=0 then
%>
<html>
<head>
<title>Electronic Voting</title>
```

```
8. <script language=JavaScript>
9. function message(form){
10. if( (document.f1.ssn.value.length <= 0) ||
   (document.f1.pwd.value.length <= 0)) {
11. alert("SSNumber and Passwod both are compulsory")
12. return false;
13. }else
14. return true;
15. }
16. </script>
17. </head>
18. <body>
19. <center><h4>Electronic Voting</h4></center>
20. <font color=red size=3><%=session("msg")%></font>
21. <form name=f1 method=post action=insertvote.asp>
22. <pre>
23. President:
24. <input type=radio name=president value="Stan Fleming"> Stan Fleming
25. <input type=radio name=president value="Deborah Ross"> Deborah Ross
26. Secretary:
27. <input type=radio name=secretary value="Elizabeth Kaplan"> Elizabeth
Kaplan
28. <input type=radio name=secretary value="Michael Sweet"> Michael
Sweet
29. Treasurer:
30. <input type=radio name=treasurer value="George Sunders"> George
Sunders
31. <input type=radio name=treasurer value="Collatte Hallinan"> Collatte
Hallinan
32. Enter Social Security Number: <input type=text name=ssn size=10
value=<%=session("ssn")%> >
33. Enter Password:              <input type=password name=pwd size=10>
34. <input type=submit name=s1 value=Submit onClick="return
message(this.form)">
35. <input type=reset name=r1 value=Cancel>
36. </pre>
37. </form>
38. </body>
39. </html>
40. <%
41. else
42. response.write "<font color=red size=4>You are already voted</font>"
43. end if
44. %>
```

Following is the line-by-line explanation of the source code:

- **Line 1:** Creates a session variable `msg`.
- **Lines 3–4:** Checks the session variable's status.

- **Line 5:** Starting element of HTML document root, HTML.
- **Line 6:** Starting element of HTML document head.
- **Line 7:** HTML document TITLE element with the title "Electronic Voting".
- **Line 8:** Starting element of SCRIPT element for JavaScript.
- **Lines 9–15:** This is a JavaScript function `message` for validating the text fields for social security number (ssn) and password (pwd).
    - **Line 11:** Displays an alert message.
- **Line 17:** Ending element of the HTML document head.
- **Line 18:** Starting element of the HTML document body.
- **Line 19:** Displays the heading with level 4 heading style and aligns it at the center of the document.
- **Line 20:** Displays the session variable `msg` with font color red and size 3.
- **Line 21:** Starting element of HTML interactive form with the following: attribute as f1, method as Post, and action as `insertvote.asp`.
- **Line 22:** Starting element of preformatted text.
- **Lines 24–25:** This is a form control of type `radio buttons` with the name `president` and the values `Stan Fleming` and `Deborah Ross`.
- **Lines 27–28:** This is a form control of type `radio buttons` with the name `secretary` and the values `Elizabeth Kaplan` and `Michael Sweet`.
- **Lines 30–31:** This is a form control of type `radio buttons` with the name `treasurer` and the values `George Sunders` and `Collatte Hallinan`.
- **Line 32:** This is a form control of type `text field` with the name `ssn` and the size 10.
- **Line 33:** This is a form control of type `password` with the name `pwd` and the size 10.
- **Line 34:** This is a form control of type `submit` with the name `s1`; it calls the function `message` when clicked and redirects to `insertvote.asp` when the function returns true.
- **Line 35:** This is a form control of type reset with the name `r1`; it resets all the controls to their initial values.
- **Line 36:** Ending element of preformatted text.
- **Line 37:** Ending element of HTML interactive form.
- **Line 38:** Ending element of HTML document body.
- **Line 39:** Ending element of HTML document root.
- **Line 42:** Sends the text to the client.

Source code listing for thanks.html

Listing 14-15 gives the source code for `thanks.html`.

Listing 14-15: Source code for thanks.html

```
1. <html>
2. <head>
3. <title>Electronic Voting</title>
4. </head>
5. <body>
6. <h4>Thank you for participating in Electronic voting</h4>
7. </body>
8. </html>
```

Following is the line-by-line explanation of the source code:

- **Line 1:** Starting element of HTML document root, HTML.
- **Line 2:** Starting element of HTML document head.
- **Line 3:** HTML document TITLE element with the title “Electronic Voting”.
- **Line 4:** Ending element of HTML document head.
- **Line 5:** Starting element of HTML document body.
- **Line 6:** Displays the heading with the heading style H4.
- **Line 7:** Ending element of the HTML document body.
- **Line 8:** Ending element of the HTML document root.

Source code listing for display.asp

Listing 14-16 gives the source code for `display.asp`.

Listing 14-16: Source code for display.asp

```
<html>
<meta HTTP-EQUIV="REFRESH" CONTENT="60">
<head>
<title>Displaying Votes</title>
</head>
<body>
<%
set myconn=server.createobject("ADODB.Connection")
set myconn1=server.createobject("ADODB.Connection")
set rs=server.createobject("ADODB.Recordset")
set rs1=server.createobject("ADODB.Recordset")
myconn.open "DSN=vote"
myconn1.open "DSN=vote"
rs1.open "select count(*) from Votes where status=2",myconn1,adopendynamic
```

```
15. rs.open "select * from Contest order by post",myconn,adopendynamic
16. Dim post1,post2,post3,flag1,flag2,flag3
17. post1="President"
18. post2="Secretary"
19. post3="Treasurer"
20. flag1=0
21. flag2=0
22. flag3=0
23. do while not rs.eof
24. pname = rs.fields(0)
25. votes = rs.fields(1)
26. post = rs.fields(2)
27. response.write "<b>"
28. if((post = post1) and (flag1=0)) then
29. response.write "<br>"&post1
30. flag1=1
31. end if
32. if((post = post2) and (flag2=0)) then
33. response.write "<br>"&post2
34. flag2=1
35. end if
36. if((post = post3) and (flag3=0)) then
37. response.write "<br>"&post3
38. flag3=1
39. end if
40. response.write "</b><br>"
41. response.write "               
 "
42. response.write pname
43. response.write " got "
44. response.write votes
45. response.write " votes."
46. rs.movenext
47. loop
48. response.write "<br><br><b>Invalid Votes:   </b>"
49. response.write rs1.fields(0)
50. rs1.close
51. myconn1.close
52. rs.close
53. myconn.close
54. %>
55. </body>
56. </html>
```

Following is the line-by-line explanation of the source code:

- **Line 1:** Starting element of HTML document root HTML.
- **Line 2:** Refreshes the page every minute using the `meta` element.

- **Line 3:** Starting element of HTML document head.
- **Line 4:** HTML document TITLE element with the title "Displaying Votes" will be displayed as the page header or window title.
- **Line 5:** Ending element of the HTML document head.
- **Line 6:** Starting element of the HTML document body.
- **Line 7:** Starts the ASP code.
- **Lines 8–9:** Creates the `Connection` objects
- **Lines 10–11:** Creates a `recordset` object.
- **Lines 12–13:** Opens the connection.
- **Lines 14–15:** Opens recordsets by passing a SQL string and the name of the `Connection` object.
- **Line 16:** Declares the variables.
- **Lines 17–22:** Initializes the variables.
- **Lines 23–47:** Displays the candidates and their corresponding votes, dependending on Category (post).
- **Lines 48–49:** Displays the number of invalid votes.
- **Lines 50–51:** Closes the recordsets.
- **Lines 52–53:** Closes the connections.
- **Line 55:** Ending element of the HTML document body.
- **Line 56:** Ending element of the HTML document root.

Executing the program

Follow these steps to enable a voter to participate in the electronic voting (or polling):

1. Save all files (`vote.asp`, `insertvote.asp`, `checkvote.asp`, `thanks.html`, and `display.asp`) in the folder `\elecvote` under the `c:\inerpub\wwwroot`.
2. Create the database tables and DSN with the name `vote`.
3. Start the Personal Web Server or Internet Information Server.
4. Open Internet Explorer and enter the URL **http://<*hostname*>/elecvote/vote.asp** in the address bar. The screen shown in Figure 14-25 appears.

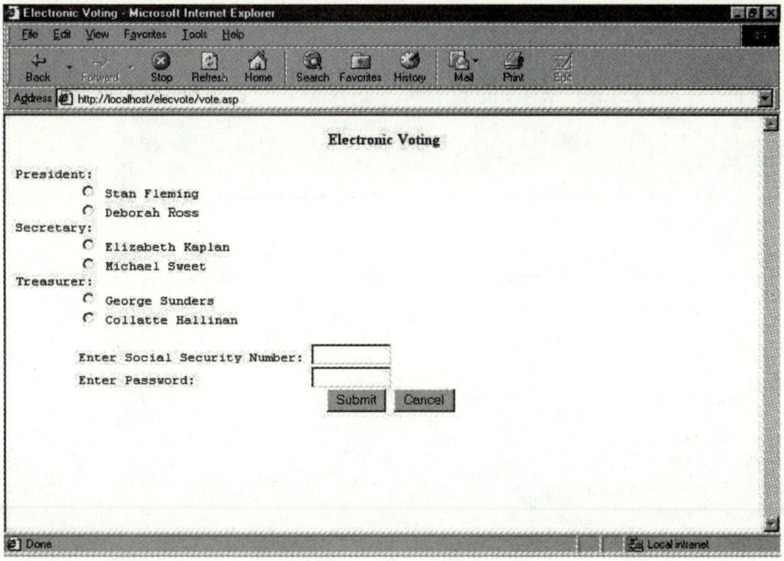

Figure 14-25: Electronic voting form

The user fills out the form and clicks the Submit button. The screen showing a "Thank you" message will be displayed.

If the user has already voted and tries to vote again, the screen shown in Figure 14-26 will be displayed.

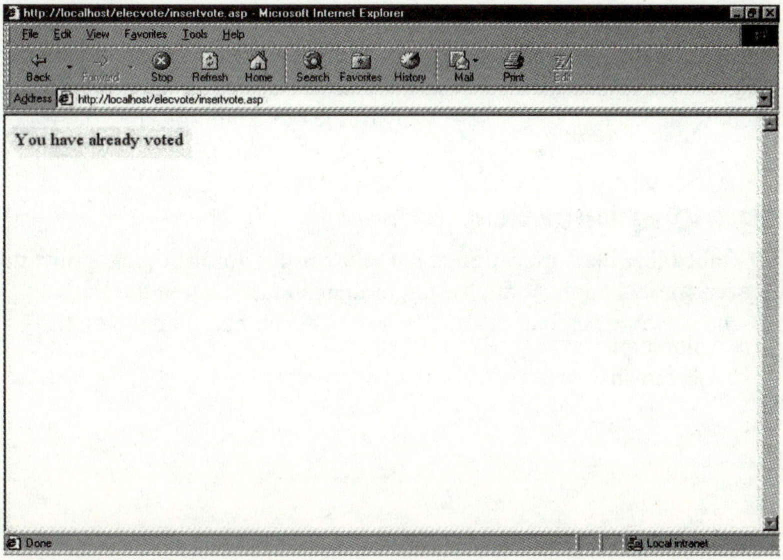

Figure 14-26: Message displayed if a voter tries to vote more than once

If the user enters an invalid social security number or password, the screen shown in Figure 14-27 will be displayed.

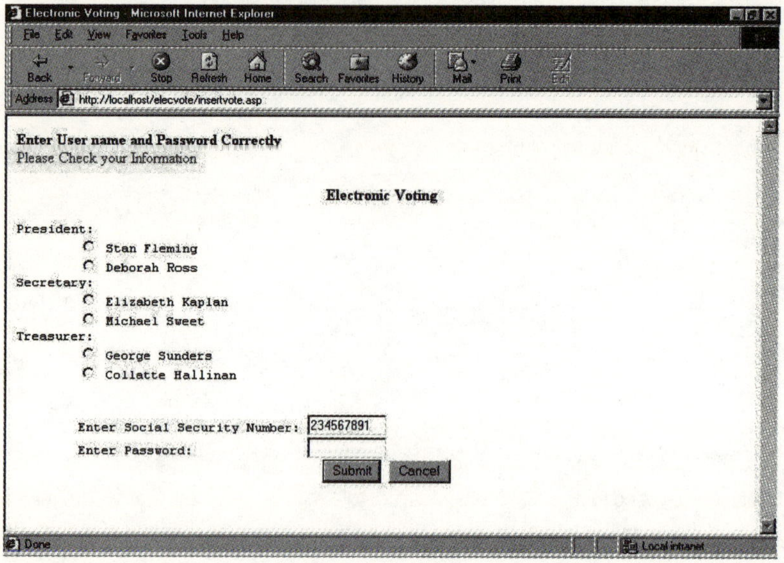

Figure 14-27: Message displayed when the social security number or password are entered incorrectly

In order for the administrator to determine the results, the following procedure is to be followed:

Open Internet Explorer and enter the URL http://*<hostname>*/elecvote/display.asp in the address bar. The screen shown in Figure 14-28 will appear. The votes obtained by each candidate as well as the number of invalid votes are displayed. In this application, if the voter does not select any of the radio buttons, the vote is considered as invalid.

Embedding the application

The procedure for embedding the application is the same as that for the other applications in this chapter. However, for this application, the target image must contain the Internet Explorer component and all the networking components, as this is a Web-based application.

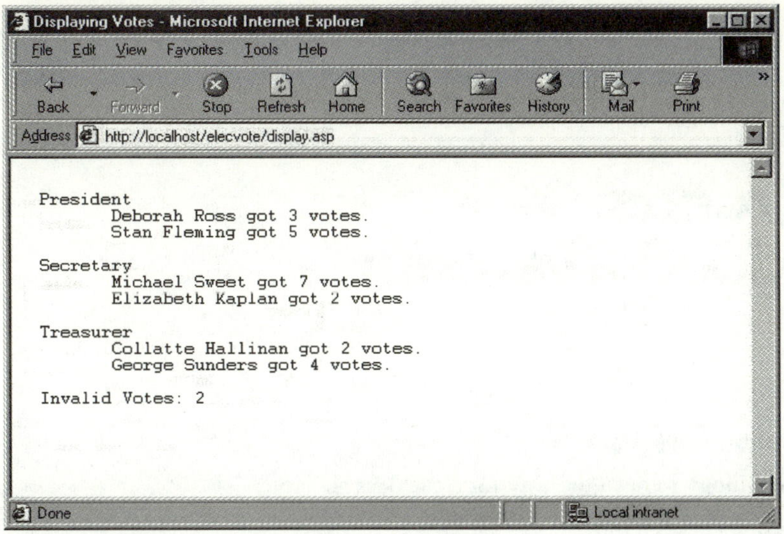

Figure 14-28: Results of the electronic voting application

Summary

In this chapter, you learned how to develop applications using Windows XP Embedded. These applications demonstrated how to control appliances such as an air conditioner and an audio player. You also learned how to create educational tools and embedded database applications, as well as how to develop Web-based applications in the Visual Studio and ASP environment and then port them onto the embedded XP platform. Microsoft's embedded operating systems enable you to easily port existing applications developed in the Visual Studio environment to embedded systems. Windows XP Embedded will play an important role in creating networked information appliances.

Chapter 15

Future Trends in Embedded Systems

In This Chapter

- The future of embedded systems
- Smart-card technology to pave the way for a cashless society
- Securing embedded systems

With advances in semiconductor electronics, processors are becoming more powerful and cheaper, and the advances in software tools are leading to faster and more reliable software development. Together, these advances are paving the way for exciting developments in embedded systems. In this chapter, you review the developments that will significantly affect your lives. This chapter also briefly discusses the smart-card technology that may finally lead to a cashless society. As embedded systems become network-enabled, their security is sure to become a major issue in future years, so you study security aspects in this chapter as well.

System on a Chip (SOC)

The fast-paced development in semiconductor electronics during the past 30 years has brought about a phenomenal change in the realm of computing. The power of so-called mainframes is now available on desktop machines. In the late 1980s, hard disks of 64MB capacity were considered "high-end" storage devices; today, a RAM chip is available with the same capacity. During the coming decade, memory chips of as much as 1GB capacity are sure to become common. As a result, you can expect the power of desktop systems to soon become available on handheld computers and to do what you do today on a desktop with a handheld computer.

Similarly, the communication capability of these devices is increasing tremendously. Today's wireless networks can handle data only at rather low rates. In the next decade, however, because of large-scale deployment of third-generation (3G) wireless networks, data rates up to 2 Mbps are certain to become common, leading to multimedia communication across mobile networks through palmtops. Expect to see these mobile, embedded systems driven by high-power software that can handle data, graphics, and voice and video applications, making "anywhere, anytime" communication a reality.

Very Large Scale Integration (*VLSI*) is even now resulting in reduced sizes and costs for embedded systems. Instead of using separate chips for the processor, memory, and associated digital circuitry, technicians can now build a single integrated circuit (IC) that contains the complete functionality of the embedded system. So you can simply build an entire system on a single chip. This "system on a chip" (SOC) concept isn't new, but only recently has the technology matured to a stage where you now can expect many consumer items, such as digital wristwatches, to use it, resulting in immense savings in cost, power, and size.

SOC technology is sure to make ubiquitous computing a reality — wherein each and every device or gadget that you encounter or use is, in effect, a computer, although it may not necessarily look like a "computer" as you know one today. Expect all the electronic gadgets at your homes and offices to become computers that can communicate with one another. You can network-enable these appliances and control them from a desktop across the Internet, or you can control them through any device of your choice, such as a mobile phone.

Advances in sensor technology are also leading to interesting developments, such as development of the electronic nose (e-nose), electronic eye (e-eye), and so on. You need very powerful software to drive these systems so that they can "smell" or "see." The field of robotics is certain to experience major developments in the coming years, thanks to sensors, SOC, and embedded software technologies.

Smart Cards and the Cashless Society

Technology developments haven't changed society much in the area of money matters. Only the credit card has changed the process of money transactions to any extent. Now, smart-card technology is bringing about revolutionary changes, and people are starting to use these smart cards because of the reliability of their embedded hardware and software. People are using smart cards — which are simply credit-card-sized electronic systems containing embedded processing elements and memory — for such applications as storing a patient's health record, security and authentication information, and so on. The smart card can also act as an electronic wallet. No longer do banks need to provide paper passbooks to record transactions; the smart card can act as a passbook for all transactions. This trend is likely to lead to a truly cashless society, where people accomplish all their monetary transactions through smart cards. At present, using these cards to handle small transactions — 10 cents or even $1 — is a problem, and you still need coins and bills. In the near future, however, expect smart-card technology to mature to such an extent that you can carry out even small cash transactions through smart cards — with every person using a smart card (the e-wallet) and every retail outlet maintaining a networked smart-card reader.

The smart card, of course, can act as more than just an e-wallet; you can Java-enable it to access Web objects, such as HTML pages and applets. Java Card Web Servlet (JCWS), the framework recently introduced by Sun Microsystems — enables smart cards to integrate with existing Web services. A doctor, for example, can access a patient's medical record through a conventional Web browser on a desktop if the patient stores that record on a smart card. The architecture of JCWS, as shown in Figure 15-1, makes available this type of service.

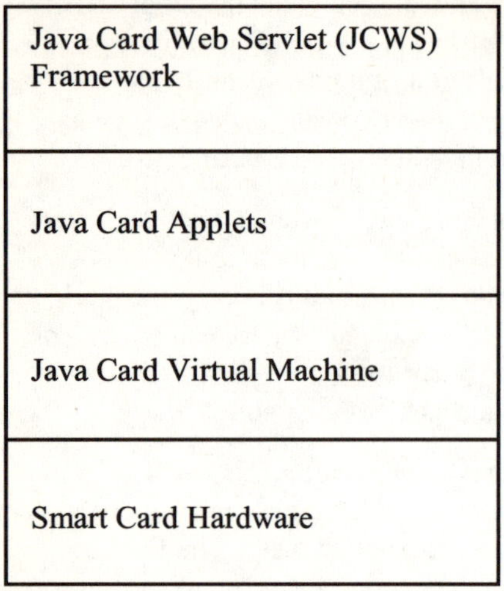

Figure 15-1: Architecture of Java-enabled smart card

A small-footprint virtual machine, Java Card Virtual Machine, which can interpret HTML pages or Java applets, runs over the smart-card hardware. JCWS permits the Web access. The *International Organization for Standardization* (ISO) standardized the protocols for communication between a smart card and the smart-card readers in the ISO 7816 specification. Sun Microsystems released the Java Card API specifications to develop smart-card-based applications that you can port onto any smart card, irrespective of the underlying hardware platform. Developers are sure to find major applications for smart cards in the banking, security, health-care, and transportation industries.

Security in Embedded Systems

Today's desktop computers are vulnerable to attack because of existing security holes in the Internet. If embedded systems remain network-enabled, the situation threatens them as well. Networked embedded systems that you can access via the Internet, whether at home, at the office, or in factories, hospitals and elsewhere, are likely targets for hackers. Today's embedded systems in particular have limited processing and memory resources and hence are more vulnerable to attack. Providing embedded security solutions is also a problem. Because of the various platforms and operating systems used in these embedded systems, their operating systems don't handle security-related issues as effectively as desktop operating systems do. Incorporating the necessary encryption for security concerns into these low-capacity embedded systems isn't an easy task. At present, developers of embedded systems are addressing this issue.

One solution to the security problem that's now finding acceptance is to use a gateway to secure the embedded systems. As shown in Figure 15-2, a desktop system can act as a gateway to a network's embedded systems. In this example, you can access all the embedded systems at home — TV, VCR, digital camera, networked door lock, air conditioner, and DVD player — only through your desktop, which acts as the gateway. The desktop system runs the protocol stack, as shown in Figure 15-3. The SSL/TLS (Secure Socket Layer/Transport Layer Security) runs above the TCP/IP stack to provide encryption and authentication services. In accessing the embedded system across the Internet, the gateway acts as a firewall so that you can password-protect the embedded systems and encrypt the data sent by the embedded system.

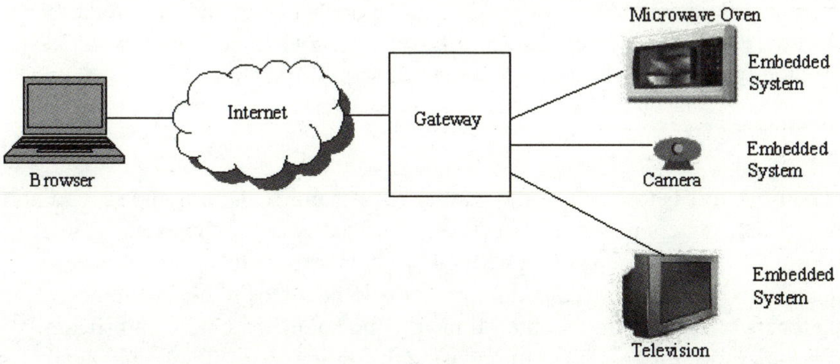

Figure 15-2: Securing embedded systems through a gateway

HTTP
Secure Socket Layer (SSL) Transport Layer Security (TLS)
Transmission Control Protocol (TCP)
Internet Protocol (IP)

Figure 15-3: TCP/IP with SSL/TLS

Another popular approach entails using the IPSec (IP Security) protocol. IPSec provides security at the network layer by encrypting TCP data. You can install the IPSec software in the gateway computer or run it on high-end embedded systems. IPSec operates in two modes, transport mode and tunnel mode, as the following list describes:

- In *transport mode*, IPSec leaves the IP header unchanged and encrypts only the TCP data. If the gateway runs the IPSec protocol, the embedded systems can decode the source and destination addresses in the IP header without any overhead.
- In *tunnel mode*, it encrypts the entire packet, including the IP header, and as a result, the embedded systems can't read the source and destination addresses directly. If a highly secure system is a requirement, the embedded systems need to run the IPSec.

While developing networked embedded systems, the developers need to address security aspects in detail. If the processor can run the security-related protocol stack, that's the best approach to take; otherwise, you're best off following the gateway approach.

Summary

Technology's main objective is to improve the quality of human life. During the second half of the twentieth century, computers improved our lives significantly. With the exciting developments taking place in the arena of embedded systems, expect to see even more revolutionary changes in the future — embedded systems in health care, e-governance, security, banking, energy, transportation, entertainment, and so on are sure to significantly affect our daily lives. You simply can't overemphasize the anticipated role of embedded systems in life-saving medical equipment, in artificial organs for the physically disabled, in deep-space probes searching for extra-terrestrial intelligence, and in similarly spectacular applications.

Appendix A
What's on the CD-ROM

This appendix provides you with information on the contents of the CD that accompanies this book. For the latest information, please refer to the `ReadMe` file located at the root of the CD. Here is what you will find:

- System Requirements
- Using the CD
- What's on the CD
- Troubleshooting

System Requirements

Make sure that your computer meets the minimum system requirements listed in this section. If your computer doesn't match up to most of these requirements, you may have a problem using the contents of the CD.

For Microsoft Windows 9*x* or Windows 2000:

- PC with a Pentium processor running at 120 Mhz or faster
- Minimum 128 MB of RAM
- Ethernet network interface card (NIC) or modem with a speed of at least 28,800 bps
- A CD-ROM drive — double-speed (2x) or faster

For Linux:

- PC with a Pentium processor running at 90 Mhz or faster
- Minimum 128 MB of RAM
- Ethernet network interface card (NIC) or modem with a speed of at least 28,800 bps
- A CD-ROM drive — double-speed (2x) or faster

You will also need Conexant GPS receiver, which is used in the project discussed in Chapter 7.

More information is available at `www.conexant.com/cnxt/index.html`.

Using the CD

This section provides instructions on accessing the CD's contents.

Using the CD with Microsoft Windows

To install the items from the CD to your hard drive, follow these steps:

1. Insert the CD into your computer's CD-ROM drive.
2. A window will appear with the following options: Install, Explore, Links, and Exit. If you do not have autorun enabled or if the autorun window does not appear, follow the steps below to access the CD.
   - Click Start ⇨ Run.
   - In the dialog box that appears, type ***d*:\setup.exe**, where *d* is the letter of your CD-ROM drive. This will bring up the autorun window described above.
3. Choose the Install, Explore, Links, or Exit option from the menu.
   - **Install:** Gives you the option to install the supplied software and/or the author-created samples on the CD-ROM.
   - **Explore:** Allows you to view the contents of the CD-ROM in its directory structure.
   - **Links:** Opens a hyperlinked page of Web sites.
   - **Exit:** Closes the autorun window.

Using the CD with Linux

To install the items from the CD to your hard drive, follow these steps:

1. Log in as root.
2. Insert the CD into your computer's CD-ROM drive.
3. If your computer has Auto-Mount enabled, wait for the CD to mount. Otherwise, follow these steps:
   - Command-line instructions: At the command prompt, type **mount /dev/cdrom /mnt/cdrom**. (This will mount the "cdrom" device to the mnt/cdrom directory. If your device has a different name, then exchange "cdrom" with that device name — for instance, "cdrom1.")
   - Graphical: Right-click on the CD-ROM icon on the desktop and choose "Mount CD-ROM" from the selections. This will mount your CD-ROM.
4. To remove the CD from your CD-ROM drive, follow these steps:
   - Command-line instructions: At the command prompt, type **umount /mnt/cdrom**.
   - Graphical: Right-click on the CD-ROM icon on the desktop and choose "UMount CD-ROM" from the selections. This will unmount your CD-ROM.

> **NOTE** The RTLinux programs in Chapter 10 will work only in the Linux environment. The RTLinux operating system software has to be installed on a machine running Linux.

What's on the CD

The following sections provide a summary of the software and other materials you'll find on the CD.

Author-created materials

All author-created material from the book, including code listings and samples, are on the CD in the folder named `\Embedded Programming Source Code`.

The source code folder is further categorized into subfolders corresponding to source code listing for the projects discussed in the book. A brief description about the contents of each folder is provided here as an aid to handling the CD-ROM effectively.

Folder Names	*Code Listings*	*Filenames*
Chapter 3	3-1	CRC32.cpp
Chapter 5	5-1	lcd.asm
Chapter 6	6-1	CserialCommDlg.h
	6-2	CserialCommDlg.cpp
	6-3	Serial.c
Chapter 7	7-1	Serial.h
	7-2	Serial.cpp
	7-3	GPSDlg.h
	7-4	GPSDlg.cpp
	Image	GPS.bmp
Chapter 8	8-1	Test.h
	8-2	Test.c
	8-3	GlobalVar.h
	8-4	Buffers.c
	8-5	PTFunction.c
	8-6	serverDlg.h
	8-7	serverDlg.cpp
	8-8	clientDlg.h

Folder Names	***Code Listings***	***Filenames***
	8-9	clientDlg.cpp
Chapter 9	9-1	sound.c
	9-2	idbusage.c
Chapter 10	10-1	hello.c
	10-2	blink.c
	10-3	SerialCommDlg.cpp
	10-4	Temperature.c
	10-5	play.c
	10-6	stop.c
	10-7	repeat.c
	10-8	AudioPlayerDlg.cpp
Chapter 11	11-1	SalarySurvey.ebf
	11-2	EnergyConsumption.ebf
Chapter 12	12-1	ICustomer.java
	12-2	CustomerImpl.java
	12-3	CustomerStub.java
	12-4	Customer.pkg
	12-5	ICSEngineer.java
	12-6	CSEngineerImpl.java
	12-7	CSEngineerStub.java
	12-8	CSEngineer.pkg
	12-9	Ilocation.java
	12-10	LocationImpl.java
	12-11	LocationStub.java
	12-12	Location.pkg
	12-13	TempMeasure.java
	12-14	Isecurity.java
	12-15	SecurityImpl.java
	12-16	SecurityStub.java
	12-17	Security.pkg

Folder Names	***Code Listings***	***Filenames***
Chapter 13	13-1	CityGuide.java
	13-2	Cities.jsp
	13-3	Categories.jsp
	13-4	CityDetails.jsp
	13-5	NameCategory.jsp
	13-6	ACRemoteServiceInterface.java
	13-7	ACRemoteService.java
	13-8	ACRemoteClient.java
	13-9	ClientGUI.java
Chapter 14	14-1	Serial.h
	14-2	Serial.cpp
	14-3	ACRemoteDlg.h
	14-4	ACRemoteDlg.cpp
	14-5	ACSimulator.cpp
	14-6	MP3RemoteDlg.h
	14-7	MP3RemoteDlg.cpp
	14-8	frmmain.frm
	14-9	Frmtest.frm
	14-10	frmfallingletters.frm
	14-11	Productivity.frm
	14-12	vote.asp
	14-13	insertvote.asp
	14-14	checkvote.asp
	14-15	Thanks.html
	14-16	Display.asp

Additional notes:

- The code listings can be viewed in Windows Notepad. In the case of `.ASP` and `.FRM` files, you may have to explicitly select Notepas for opening the files.
- `.EBF` files will open automatically in eMbedded Visual Tools if you have that installed on your system. Otherwise, you can view the files in Notepad.

- For compilation and execution of the programs, follow the steps given in the text.
- In the case of projects involving databases, you need to create the tables as per the descriptions given and then execute the programs.
- When you create a new project in VC++, some header files are created automatically by the class wizard. The listings of such header files are not included on the CD.

Software

This section discusses the software you need to have on your computer to be able to run the applications discussed in this book.

Shareware programs are fully functional, trial versions of copyrighted programs. If you like particular programs, register with their authors for a nominal fee and receive licenses, enhanced versions, and technical support. *Freeware programs* are copyrighted games, applications, and utilities that are free for personal use. Unlike shareware, these programs do not require a fee or provide technical support. *GNU software* is governed by its own license, which is included inside the folder of the GNU product. See the GNU license for more details.

Trial, demo, or evaluation versions are usually limited either by time or functionality (such as being unable to save projects). Some trial versions are very sensitive to system date changes. If you alter your computer's date, the programs will "time out" and will no longer be functional.

Forte for Java, release 3.0 Community Edition

Commercial product. The Forte for Java release 3.0 is an integrated development environment used for developing Java applications. A commercial product, it is available on the accompanying CD. This toolkit has been used in the projects developed in Chapter 13. You can learn more about it at `http://www.sun.com/forte/ffj`.

Java 2 Software Development Kit Standard Edition version 1.4, from Sun Microsystems

Trial version. This is a software development kit for developing standard Java applications. Applications discussed in Chapters 12 and 13 have been developed using this SDK. You will find the trial version of this SDK on the CD. You can learn more about it at `http://java.sun.com/j2se`.

Java 2 Platform Micro Edition, Wireless Toolkit 1.0.3 (J2ME), from Sun Microsystems

Commercial product. This is a software development kit for developing MIDP applications. It is a commercial product. This toolkit has been used in the projects developed in Chapter 13. It is available on the accompanying CD. You can learn more about it at `http://www.sun.com/products/j2metoolkit`.

RTLinux, from Finite State Machine Labs, Inc.

GNU Software. RTLinux is an embedded operating system that provides controlled hard real-time processing and convenient interaction with general-purpose OS and its applications. This embedded operating system is used in projects developed in Chapter 10. You will find its GNU version on the CD. For a detailed descriptions of RTLinux, go to `http://www.fsmlabs.com`.

Troubleshooting

If you have difficulty installing or using the CD-ROM programs, try the following solutions:

- **Turn off any anti-virus software that you may have running.** Installers sometimes mimic virus activity and can make your computer incorrectly believe that it is being infected by a virus. (Be sure to turn the anti-virus software back on later.)
- **Close all running programs.** The more programs you're running, the less memory is available to other programs. Installers also typically update files and programs; if you keep other programs running, installation may not work properly.
- **Reference the `ReadMe`:** Please refer to the `ReadMe` file located at the root of the CD-ROM for the latest product information at the time of publication.

If you still have trouble with the CD, please call the Wiley Customer Care phone number: (800) 762-2974. Outside the United States, call 1 (317) 572-3994. You can also contact Wiley Customer Service by e-mail at `techsupdum@wiley.com`. Wiley will provide technical support only for installation and other general quality-control items; for technical support on the applications themselves, consult the program's vendor or author.

Appendix B
Embedded Software Resources

The following URLs point to Web or FTP sites that provide information on and/or software for specific vendors and technologies involved with embedded systems and software:

- ActiveSync: `http://www.microsoft.com/mobile/pocketpc/downloads/activesync35.asp`
- Analog devices: `http://www.analog.com`
- BREW SDK: `http://www.qualcomm.com/Brew`
- Chip directory, embedded resources: `http://www.embeddedlinks.com/chipdir/`
- Conexant GPS receiver: `http://www.conexant.com/cnxt/index.html`
- Embedded Linux: `http://www.redhat.com/embedded/technologies/embLinux/howtobuy.html`
- Embedded NT: `http://www.microsoft.com/windows/embedded/xp/previous/default.asp`
- Embedded resources: `http://www.embedded.com`
- eMbedded Visual Tools: `http://www.microsoft.com/mobile/downloads/emvt30.asp`
- Hitachi: `http://www.hitachi.com/`
- HP Chai: `http://www.hp.com/go/embedded`
- Intel Processors architecture: `http://www.intel.com/design/intarch/`
- J2ME: `http://java.sun.com/products/j2mewtoolkit/download.html`
- Jini: `http://www.javasoft.com/products/jini/`
- Linux free downloads: `http://www.linux.org/dist/ftp.html`
- Lucent Technologies: `http://www.lucent.com/`
- Motorola Power PC: `http://www.motorola.com/PowerPC/`
- On-line education portal for embedded systems: `http://www.techonline.com`
- Palm OS: `http://www.palmos.com/`

- Pocket PC: `http://www.microsoft.com/mobile/pocketpc/downloads/default.asp`
- QNX operating system: `http://qdn.qnx.com/download/index.html`
- Red Hat Linux: `ftp.redhat.com/`
- RTLinux: `ftp.rtlinux.org`
- Symbian developer's kit: `http://www.symbian.com/developer/downloads/v5sdks.html`
- Texas Instruments: `http://www.ti.com/`
- Windows CE download: `http://www.microsoft.com/windows/embedded/ce/downloads/default.asp`
- Windows CE: `http://www.cetoolbox.com`
- Wireless resources: `http://bwrc.eecs.berkeley.edu/JS_Default.htm`

Index

GNU General Public License

Version 2, June 1991

Preamble

The licenses for most software are designed to take away your freedom to share and change it. By contrast, the GNU General Public License is intended to guarantee your freedom to share and change free software — to make sure the software is free for all its users. This General Public License applies to most of the Free Software Foundation's software and to any other program whose authors commit to using it. (Some other Free Software Foundation software is covered by the GNU Library General Public License instead.) You can apply it to your programs, too.

When we speak of free software, we are referring to freedom, not price. Our General Public Licenses are designed to make sure that you have the freedom to distribute copies of free software (and charge for this service if you wish), that you receive source code or can get it if you want it, that you can change the software or use pieces of it in new free programs; and that you know you can do these things.

To protect your rights, we need to make restrictions that forbid anyone to deny you these rights or to ask you to surrender the rights. These restrictions translate to certain responsibilities for you if you distribute copies of the software, or if you modify it.

For example, if you distribute copies of such a program, whether gratis or for a fee, you must give the recipients all the rights that you have. You must make sure that they, too, receive or can get the source code. And you must show them these terms so they know their rights.

We protect your rights with two steps: (1) copyright the software, and (2) offer you this license which gives you legal permission to copy, distribute and/or modify the software.

Also, for each author's protection and ours, we want to make certain that everyone understands that there is no warranty for this free software. If the software is modified by someone else and passed on, we want its recipients to know that what they have is not the original, so that any problems introduced by others will not reflect on the original authors' reputations.

Finally, any free program is threatened constantly by software patents. We wish to avoid the danger that redistributors of a free program will individually obtain patent licenses, in effect making the program proprietary. To prevent this, we have made it clear that any patent must be licensed for everyone's free use or not licensed at all.

The precise terms and conditions for copying, distribution and modification follow.

Terms and Conditions for Copying, Distribution, and Modification

1. This License applies to any program or other work which contains a notice placed by the copyright holder saying it may be distributed under the terms of this General Public License. The "Program", below, refers to any such program or work, and a "work based on the Program" means either the Program or any derivative work under copyright law: that is to say, a work containing the Program or a portion of it, either verbatim or with modifications and/or translated into another language. (Hereinafter, translation is included without limitation in the term "modification".) Each licensee is addressed as "you".

   Activities other than copying, distribution and modification are not covered by this License; they are outside its scope. The act of running the Program is not restricted, and the output from the Program is covered only if its contents constitute a work based on the Program (independent of having been made by running the Program). Whether that is true depends on what the Program does.

2. You may copy and distribute verbatim copies of the Program's source code as you receive it, in any medium, provided that you conspicuously and appropriately publish on each copy an appropriate copyright notice and disclaimer of warranty; keep intact all the notices that refer to this License and to the absence of any warranty; and give any other recipients of the Program a copy of this License along with the Program.

   You may charge a fee for the physical act of transferring a copy, and you may at your option offer warranty protection in exchange for a fee.

3. You may modify your copy or copies of the Program or any portion of it, thus forming a work based on the Program, and copy and distribute such modifications or work under the terms of Section 1 above, provided that you also meet all of these conditions:

   a) You must cause the modified files to carry prominent notices stating that you changed the files and the date of any change.

b) You must cause any work that you distribute or publish, that in whole or in part contains or is derived from the Program or any part thereof, to be licensed as a whole at no charge to all third parties under the terms of this License.

c) If the modified program normally reads commands interactively when run, you must cause it, when started running for such interactive use in the most ordinary way, to print or display an announcement including an appropriate copyright notice and a notice that there is no warranty (or else, saying that you provide a warranty) and that users may redistribute the program under these conditions, and telling the user how to view a copy of this License. (Exception: if the Program itself is interactive but does not normally print such an announcement, your work based on the Program is not required to print an announcement.)

These requirements apply to the modified work as a whole. If identifiable sections of that work are not derived from the Program, and can be reasonably considered independent and separate works in themselves, then this License, and its terms, do not apply to those sections when you distribute them as separate works. But when you distribute the same sections as part of a whole which is a work based on the Program, the distribution of the whole must be on the terms of this License, whose permissions for other licensees extend to the entire whole, and thus to each and every part regardless of who wrote it.

Thus, it is not the intent of this section to claim rights or contest your rights to work written entirely by you; rather, the intent is to exercise the right to control the distribution of derivative or collective works based on the Program.

In addition, mere aggregation of another work not based on the Program with the Program (or with a work based on the Program) on a volume of a storage or distribution medium does not bring the other work under the scope of this License.

4. You may copy and distribute the Program (or a work based on it, under Section 2) in object code or executable form under the terms of Sections 1 and 2 above provided that you also do one of the following:

a) Accompany it with the complete corresponding machine-readable source code, which must be distributed under the terms of Sections 1 and 2 above on a medium customarily used for software interchange; or,

b) Accompany it with a written offer, valid for at least three years, to give any third party, for a charge no more than your cost of physically performing source distribution, a complete machine-readable copy of the corresponding source code, to be distributed under the terms of Sections 1 and 2 above on a medium customarily used for software interchange; or,

c) Accompany it with the information you received as to the offer to distribute corresponding source code. (This alternative is allowed only for noncommercial distribution and only if you received the program in object code or executable form with such an offer, in accord with Subsection b above.)

The source code for a work means the preferred form of the work for making modifications to it. For an executable work, complete source code means all the source code for all modules it contains, plus any associated interface definition files, plus the scripts used to control compilation and installation of the executable. However, as a special exception, the source code distributed need not include anything that is normally distributed (in either source or binary form) with the major components (compiler, kernel, and so on) of the operating system on which the executable runs, unless that component itself accompanies the executable.

If distribution of executable or object code is made by offering access to copy from a designated place, then offering equivalent access to copy the source code from the same place counts as distribution of the source code, even though third parties are not compelled to copy the source along with the object code.

5. You may not copy, modify, sublicense, or distribute the Program except as expressly provided under this License. Any attempt otherwise to copy, modify, sublicense or distribute the Program is void, and will automatically terminate your rights under this License. However, parties who have received copies, or rights, from you under this License will not have their licenses terminated so long as such parties remain in full compliance.

6. You are not required to accept this License, since you have not signed it. However, nothing else grants you permission to modify or distribute the Program or its derivative works. These actions are prohibited by law if you do not accept this License. Therefore, by modifying or distributing the Program (or any work based on the Program), you indicate your acceptance of this License to do so, and all its terms and conditions for copying, distributing or modifying the Program or works based on it.

7. Each time you redistribute the Program (or any work based on the Program), the recipient automatically receives a license from the original licensor to copy, distribute or modify the Program subject to these terms and conditions. You may not impose any further restrictions on the recipients' exercise of the rights granted herein. You are not responsible for enforcing compliance by third parties to this License.

8. If, as a consequence of a court judgment or allegation of patent infringement or for any other reason (not limited to patent issues), conditions are imposed on you (whether by court order, agreement or otherwise) that contradict the conditions of this License, they do not excuse you from the conditions of this License. If you cannot distribute so as to satisfy simultaneously your obligations under this License and any other pertinent obligations, then as a consequence you may not distribute the Program at all. For example, if a patent license would not permit royalty-free redistribution of the Program by all those who receive copies directly or indirectly through you, then the only way you could satisfy both it and this License would be to refrain entirely from distribution of the Program.

If any portion of this section is held invalid or unenforceable under any particular circumstance, the balance of the section is intended to apply and the section as a whole is intended to apply in other circumstances.

It is not the purpose of this section to induce you to infringe any patents or other property right claims or to contest validity of any such claims; this section has the sole purpose of protecting the integrity of the free software distribution system, which is implemented by public license practices. Many people have made generous contributions to the wide range of software distributed through that system in reliance on consistent application of that system; it is up to the author/donor to decide if he or she is willing to distribute software through any other system and a licensee cannot impose that choice.

This section is intended to make thoroughly clear what is believed to be a consequence of the rest of this License.

9. If the distribution and/or use of the Program is restricted in certain countries either by patents or by copyrighted interfaces, the original copyright holder who places the Program under this License may add an explicit geographical distribution limitation excluding those countries, so that distribution is permitted only in or among countries not thus excluded. In such case, this License incorporates the limitation as if written in the body of this License.

10. The Free Software Foundation may publish revised and/or new versions of the General Public License from time to time. Such new versions will be similar in spirit to the present version, but may differ in detail to address new problems or concerns.

    Each version is given a distinguishing version number. If the Program specifies a version number of this License which applies to it and "any later version", you have the option of following the terms and conditions either of that version or of any later version published by the Free Software Foundation. If the Program does not specify a version number of this License, you may choose any version ever published by the Free Software Foundation.

11. If you wish to incorporate parts of the Program into other free programs whose distribution conditions are different, write to the author to ask for permission. For software which is copyrighted by the Free Software Foundation, write to the Free Software Foundation; we sometimes make exceptions for this. Our decision will be guided by the two goals of preserving the free status of all derivatives of our free software and of promoting the sharing and reuse of software generally.

No Warranty

12. BECAUSE THE PROGRAM IS LICENSED FREE OF CHARGE, THERE IS NO WARRANTY FOR THE PROGRAM, TO THE EXTENT PERMITTED BY

APPLICABLE LAW. EXCEPT WHEN OTHERWISE STATED IN WRITING THE COPYRIGHT HOLDERS AND/OR OTHER PARTIES PROVIDE THE PROGRAM "AS IS" WITHOUT WARRANTY OF ANY KIND, EITHER EXPRESSED OR IMPLIED, INCLUDING, BUT NOT LIMITED TO, THE IMPLIED WARRANTIES OF MERCHANTABILITY AND FITNESS FOR A PARTICULAR PURPOSE. THE ENTIRE RISK AS TO THE QUALITY AND PERFORMANCE OF THE PROGRAM IS WITH YOU. SHOULD THE PROGRAM PROVE DEFECTIVE, YOU ASSUME THE COST OF ALL NECESSARY SERVICING, REPAIR OR CORRECTION.

13. IN NO EVENT UNLESS REQUIRED BY APPLICABLE LAW OR AGREED TO IN WRITING WILL ANY COPYRIGHT HOLDER, OR ANY OTHER PARTY WHO MAY MODIFY AND/OR REDISTRIBUTE THE PROGRAM AS PERMITTED ABOVE, BE LIABLE TO YOU FOR DAMAGES, INCLUDING ANY GENERAL, SPECIAL, INCIDENTAL OR CONSEQUENTIAL DAMAGES ARISING OUT OF THE USE OR INABILITY TO USE THE PROGRAM (INCLUDING BUT NOT LIMITED TO LOSS OF DATA OR DATA BEING RENDERED INACCURATE OR LOSSES SUSTAINED BY YOU OR THIRD PARTIES OR A FAILURE OF THE PROGRAM TO OPERATE WITH ANY OTHER PROGRAMS), EVEN IF SUCH HOLDER OR OTHER PARTY HAS BEEN ADVISED OF THE POSSIBILITY OF SUCH DAMAGES.

End Of Terms And Conditions